METHUEN'S HISTORY OF THE GREEK AND ROMAN WORLD

III

A HISTORY OF THE GREEK WORLD FROM 323 TO 146 B.C.

METHUEN'S HISTORY OF THE GREEK AND ROMAN WORLD

I *A HISTORY OF THE GREEK WORLD FROM 776 TO 479 B.C.*

In preparation.

II *A HISTORY OF THE GREEK WORLD FROM 479 TO 323 B.C.*

by M. L. W. LAISTNER. With four maps.

III *A HISTORY OF THE GREEK WORLD FROM 323 TO 146 B.C.*

by M. CARY. With three maps.

IV *A HISTORY OF THE ROMAN WORLD FROM 753 TO 146 B.C.*

by H. H. SCULLARD. With four maps.

V *A HISTORY OF THE ROMAN WORLD FROM 146 TO 30 B.C.*

by F. B. MARSH. Revised by H. H. SCULLARD. With five maps.

VI *A HISTORY OF THE ROMAN WORLD FROM 30 B.C. TO A.D. 138*

by E. T. SALMON. With five maps.

VII *A HISTORY OF THE ROMAN WORLD FROM A.D. 138 TO 337*

by H. M. D. PARKER. Revised by B. H. WARMINGTON. With four maps.

A HISTORY OF THE GREEK WORLD

FROM 323 TO 146 B.C.

M. CARY, M.A., D.Litt.
Late Professor of Ancient History in
the University of London

With a new Select Bibliography
by V. EHRENBERG

METHUEN & CO LTD
11 New Fetter Lane, London E.C.4

First published 1932
Second edition, revised 1951
Reprinted 1959
Reprinted with a new bibliography 1963
Reprinted 1965
Reprinted 1968
Reprinted 1972
First published as a University Paperback 1972

Hardback SBN 416 43650 1
University Paperback SBN 416 70200 7

Printed and bound in Great Britain by
Butler & Tanner Ltd., Frome and London

Distributed in the U.S.A.
by Barnes & Noble Inc.

PREFACE

AFTER a long period of neglect, the Hellenistic age has in recent years become an object of intensive study, and by the combined labours of many scholars the main lines of its history have now been fixed with a considerable measure of certainty. In this volume I have made an attempt to provide for the English-speaking public an up-to-date account of the Hellenistic world, with special but not exclusive regard to its political history.

It is a pleasure to me to acknowledge my general indebtedness to the scholars whose fruitful research has made it possible for me to write this book. To the following authors my obligations are particularly great: to Beloch, Otto and Wilcken among the Germans; to Bouché-Leclercq and Holleaux among the French; to Cardinali and Corradi among the Italians; to Bevan, Ferguson, Rostovtseff and Tarn among the writers in English. Nearly every page of this book contains proof of my debt to Mr. Tarn, who has guided me both by his printed work and by correspondence and discussion. I also wish to express my thanks to Professor A. D. Nock, of Harvard College, for his kindness in reading and criticizing my chapter on Hellenistic Religion, and to Mr. Sidney Smith, of the British Museum, for his courtesy in giving me detailed information about the Babylonian Tablet relative to the First Syrian War.

M. C.

In revising the first edition of this book, I have endeavoured to consult all the literature on Hellenistic Greece since 1922, so far as recent world-conditions have made this possible. My chief new obligations are to Rostovtzeff's *Social and Economic History of the Hellenistic World,* and to Tarn's *The Greeks in Bactria and India*, whose influence on some aspects of Hellenistic studies has been nothing less than revolutionary.

I wish to thank Mr. R. H. Dundas for a number of corrections and addenda.

M. C.

January 1950

CONTENTS

PAGE

LIST OF ABBREVIATIONS xiii

INTRODUCTION xv

PART I

CHAPTER I

THE BREAK-UP OF ALEXANDER'S EMPIRE 1–20

§ 1. The conference at Babylon 1
§ 2. The Bactrian mutiny 3
§ 3. The Lamian War 4
§ 4. The failure of Perdiccas' regency 10
§ 5. Antipater's stop-gap regency 15
§ 6. The end of Alexander's dynasty 16

CHAPTER II

THE RISE AND FALL OF ANTIGONUS I 21–41

§ 1. The candidates for the succession 21
§ 2. The duel between Antigonus and Eumenes 22
§ 3. Antigonus' first throw for empire 25
§ 4. The years of uneasy truce 29
§ 5. Athens under Demetrius of Phalerum 32
§ 6. The foundation of the new monarchies 34
§ 7. The siege of Rhodes 36
§ 8. The battle of Ipsus 37

CHAPTER III

THE ESTABLISHMENT OF A BALANCE OF POWER 42–64

§ 1. Demetrius' fresh start 42
§ 2. Demetrius, king of Macedon 46
§ 3. The Anabasis of Demetrius 49
§ 4. The rise of Lysimachus 52
§ 5. The passing away of Alexander's marshals 54
§ 6. The Galatian invasion 58
§ 7. Retrospect 63

CHAPTER IV

THE FARTHER EAST 65–78

§ 1. Principles of division 65
§ 2. India to 250 B.C. 65
§ 3. The rise of the Bactrian and Parthian monarchies . . . 67
§ 4. Antiochus III, Restitutor Orbis 69
§ 5. India and Bactria after Antiochus III 73
§ 6. Parthia after Antiochus III 76
§ 7. Conclusion 78

CHAPTER V

PAGE
SYRIA AND THE ASIAN BORDER 79–94
§ 1. The Red Sea and Arabia 79
§ 2. The Problem of Syria 82
§ 3. The First and Second Syrian Wars 83
§ 4. The Third Syrian War 86
§ 5. The Fourth and Fifth Syrian Wars 90

CHAPTER VI

ASIA MINOR 95–114
§ 1. The limits of Greek penetration 95
§ 2. The northern kingdoms 95
§ 3. Galatia 99
§ 4. The southern border 100
§ 5. The west coast 103
§ 6. The rise of Pergamum 107
§ 7. The rebellion of Achæus 112

CHAPTER VII

RUSSIA AND THE BALKAN LANDS 115–124
§ 1. Russia 115
§ 2. Thrace 117
§ 3. The Dardanelles 120
§ 4. Macedonia and its hinterland 121
§ 5. Illyria 123

CHAPTER VIII

THE GREEK HOMELAND FROM 280 TO 239 B.C. 125–146
§ 1. The first revolt against Antigonus Gonatas 125
§ 2. Gonatas and Pyrrhus 127
§ 3. Gonatas' régime in Greece 131
§ 4. The Chremonidean War 132
§ 5. Cos and Cyrene 137
§ 6. Alexander, son of Craterus 139
§ 7. The rise of the Achæan League 141
§ 8. The expansion of the Ætolian League 145

CHAPTER IX

THE GREEK HOMELAND FROM 239 TO 217 B.C. 147–166
§ 1. The War of Demetrius 147
§ 2. The kingdom of Illyria 150
§ 3. Sparta : King Agis IV 152
§ 4. Sparta : King Cleomenes III 155
§ 5. Antigonus Doson 159
§ 6. The début of Philip V 164

CHAPTER X

PAGE
THE GREEKS OF THE WESTERN MEDITERRANEAN 167–181
§ 1. Agathocles of Syracuse 167
§ 2. Pyrrhus and Hiero 171
§ 3. The Greeks of South Italy 176
§ 4. Massilia 181

CHAPTER XI

THE GREEK HOMELAND FROM 217 TO 146 B.C. 182–205
§ 1. Earlier contacts with Rome 182
§ 2. The First Macedonian War 184
§ 3. Philip's raids in the Ægean 186
§ 4. The Second Macedonian War 189
§ 5. The Syrian War in Europe 194
§ 6. The years of uneasy peace 196
§ 7. The Third Macedonian War 200
§ 8. The end of Greek liberty 203

CHAPTER XII

ASIATIC GREECE AND EGYPT IN THE SECOND CENTURY B.C. . 206–230
§ 1. The antecedents of the Syrian War 206
§ 2. The Syrian War in Asia 209
§ 3. Asia Minor to 133 B.C. 213
§ 4. Antiochus IV and Egypt 216
§ 5. Civil war in Syria 220
§ 6. Civil war in Egypt 222
§ 7. The break-up of the Seleucid monarchy 225
§ 8. The kingdom of Judæa 227

PART II

CHAPTER XIII

HELLENISTIC WAR-CRAFT 231–243
§ 1. Numbers and recruitment of the armies 231
§ 2. Conditions of service 234
§ 3. Strategy and tactics 236
§ 4. Naval warfare 240
§ 5. The Hellenistic rules of war 241

CHAPTER XIV

THE HELLENISTIC MONARCHIES 244–267
§ 1. Greeks and Orientals 244
§ 2. The triumph of monarchism 247
§ 3. The Hellenistic courts 249
§ 4. Hellenistic administration 251
§ 5. Macedon 253
§ 6. Pergamum 255
§ 7. The Seleucid monarchy 256
§ 8. Egypt : General administration 259
§ 9. Egypt : Financial departments 262

CHAPTER XV

PAGE
THE HELLENISTIC CITIES 268–286
§ 1. Oriental self-government 268
§ 2. The Greek cities : General conditions 270
§ 3. The Greek cities : Local details 272
§ 4. The municipal governments 275
§ 5. Relations between the cities 278
§ 6. Federations : The Amphictionic and Ætolian Leagues . . 282
§ 7. Federations : The Achæan League 285

CHAPTER XVI

HELLENISTIC ECONOMIC LIFE 287–306
§ 1. General effect of Alexander's conquests 287
§ 2. Geographical exploration 288
§ 3. Agriculture 291
§ 4. Manufactures 294
§ 5. Transport 296
§ 6. Money-dealing 299
§ 7. The condition of the workers 302

CHAPTER XVII

HELLENISTIC ART 307–317
§ 1. Architecture 307
§ 2. Sculpture 311
§ 3. Painting and minor arts 313
§ 4. The influence of Greek art upon the East 315
§ 5. Hellenistic Music 317

CHAPTER XVIII

HELLENISTIC LANGUAGE AND LITERATURE 318–342
§ 1. Appreciation of literature 318
§ 2. The Hellenistic reading public 320
§ 3. Greek as a lingua franca 322
§ 4. Epic and dramatic poetry 327
§ 5. Oratory and history 332
§ 6. Philology and scholarship 338
§ 7. Conclusion 340

CHAPTER XIX

HELLENISTIC SCIENCE 343–353
§ 1. Geography 343
§ 2. Pure and applied mathematics 345
§ 3. The organic sciences 350
§ 4. Conclusion 352

CHAPTER XX

HELLENISTIC PHILOSOPHY 354–362
§ 1. The older schools 354
§ 2. Sceptics, Cynics, Epicureans 356
§ 3. The Stoic school 360

CHAPTER XXI

PAGE

Hellenistic Religion 363–374

§ 1. Greek religion on its trial 363
§ 2. King-worship 367
§ 3. Religious contacts between Greeks and Orientals . . 370

Conclusion 375–6

APPENDICES

1. Sources and Authorities for the Hellenistic Period . 377
2. The Naval Operations of the Lamian War 381
3. Seleucus and the Peace of 311 b.c. 384
4. The Strengths of the Fleets at Salamis 385
5. The First Syrian War 387
6. Ptolemy "the Son" 390
7. The Reign of Magas of Cyrene 393
8. The Third Syrian War 395
9. Antigoneia-on-the-Aous 400
10. Alexander, Son of Craterus 401
11. The Ptolemaic Thalassocracy in the Aegean . . . 403
12. Cleomenes III and Archidamus 404
13. The Numbers of the Ptolemaic Army at Raphia . . 405
14. The Antigonids and the Adriatic 406
15. Eratosthenes' Measurement of the Earth's Circumference 407

LISTS AND STEMMATA OF THE HELLENISTIC DYNASTIES

(A) Rulers of Macedon before the Foundation of the Antigonid Dynasty 410
(B) The Antigonids 410
(C) The House of Lysimachus 411
(D) The Æacids 411
(E) The Agid Kings of Sparta 411
(F) The Ptolemies 412
(G) The Seleucids 414
(H) The Attalids 416

Select Bibliography 417

Index 425

LIST OF MAPS

FACING PAGE

I. GREECE AND THE AEGEAN AREA 1

II. THE NEAR EAST *c.* 275 B.C. 21

III. THE EASTERN PROVINCES OF THE SELEUCID EMPIRE . . 66

From Drawings by Richard Cribb

LIST OF ABBREVIATIONS

Hicks = E. L. Hicks, *Greek Historical Inscriptions.*

Ditt. Syll. = W. Dittenberger, *Sylloge Inscriptionum Græcarum*, 3rd edition.

Ditt. O.G.I. = W. Dittenberger, *Orientis Græci Inscriptiones Selectæ.*

Michel = Ch. Michel, *Recueil d'Inscriptions grecques.*

S.E.G. = J. Hondius and others, *Supplementum Epigraphicum Græcum.*

Brit. Mus. Inscr. = E. L. Hicks and others, *The Collection of Ancient Greek Inscriptions in the British Museum.*

Magnesia = O. Kern, *Die Inschriften von Magnesia-am-Mäander.*

Milet = A. Rehm, *Das Delphinion in Milet* (vol. I, pt. 3 of Th. Wiegand, in *Milet, Ergebnisse der Ausgrabungen*).

Priene = Hiller von Gärtringen, *Inschriften von Priene.*

Archiv = *Archiv für Papyrusforschung* (ed. U. Wilcken).

P. Amherst = B. P. Grenfell and A. S. Hunt, *The Amherst Papyri.*

P. Elephantine = O. Rubensohn, *Die Elephantine Papyri.*

P. Halensis = F. Bechtel and others, *Dikaiomata, Auszüge aus alexandrinischen Gesetzen, herausgegeben von der Græca Halensis.*

P. Hibeh = B. P. Grenfell and A. S. Hunt, *The Hibeh Papyri.*

P. Lille = P. Jouguet, *Papyrus grecs.*

P. Oxyrh. = B. P. Grenfell and A. S. Hunt, *The Oxyrhynchus Papyri.*

P. Petrie = J. P. Mahaffy and J. G. Smyly, *The Flinders Petrie Papyri.*

P. Rylands = J. de M. Johnson, V. Martin and A. S. Hunt, *Catalogue of the Greek Papyri in the John Rylands Library, Manchester.*

P.S.I. = G. Vitelli, *Papiri Greci e Latini della Societa Italiana per la Ricerca dei Papiri Greci e Latini.*

P. Tebtunis = B. P. Grenfell, A. S. Hunt and J. G. Smyly, *The Tebtunis Papyri.*

P. Zeno Cairo = C. C. Edgar, *Zenon Papyri.* (Catalogue général des antiquités égyptiennes du Museé du Caire, vols. 79–81.)

U.P.Z. = U. Wilcken, *Urkunden der Ptolemaerzeit.*

INTRODUCTION

IT has been well said that the Greek city-state was a forcing-bed of political and cultural progress. Under the shelter of their city walls, and in comparative isolation from intrusive influences, the Greeks gradually established a distinct physical type, peculiar methods of government, and a particular civilization, which to this day is recognized as " classical " and exemplary.

But Greek culture could not thrive indefinitely in the nursery ; once it was well set, it required transplanting and propagating in a wider field. To some extent the necessity of expansion was met by the great movement of colonial emigration of early Greek history. But this outward growth was checked by the counter-thrust of the Persian and Carthaginian empires, which pressed back the Greek frontiers and threatened the Greek nation with loss of independence. In the Wars of Liberty of the early fifth century the Greeks won their most famous victories and ushered in the spacious days of Pericles. But if the age of Pericles marks the climax of Greek history from a literary and artistic point of view, from a political standpoint it was the beginning of a slow but long decline. Not only did the Greeks fail to follow up their successes in the field with a fresh colonial movement, but they proved unequal to the task of putting their own house in order. Unable to liberate their energies in outward expansion, they frittered them away in a never-ending round of wars between city and city, or of faction against faction within each town wall. Nay more, in the fourth century the consciousness of political failure was beginning to undermine that national self-confidence which had been the highest reward of Greek valour in the Persian Wars.

The fruit of Greek disunion and Greek disillusion was the conquest of the Greek Homeland by Philip II of Macedon. Yet captive Greece caught her Macedonian conqueror more effectually than ever she ensnared Rome; and the partnership of Greeks with Macedonians brought about the most astonishing of ancient feats of war, the Anabasis of Alexander. It is the strangest paradox of Greek history that the catastrophe of the Macedonian conquest raised the Greeks to the pinnacle of their power. At the death of Alexander they were the dominant people in each of the three continents, and had a unique opportunity of hellenizing the world. On the other hand, their statecraft was now confronted with immense new problems of imperial administration, and their culture was brought into competition with the deep-rooted civilizations of the Near East. In a word, the Greeks were called upon to play for higher stakes, and the Hellenistic age was their supreme testing-time.

Unfortunately, while the interest of Greek history remains unabated after the Macedonian conquest, its records become more scanty and broken. For the first twenty years after the death of Alexander we have a competent contemporary account by Hieronymus of Cardia, as excerpted by the first-century compiler, Diodorus. For the period 228–146 B.C., we possess considerable portions of the work of Polybius, whether in his own text or in the paraphrase of Livy. For various other episodes of Hellenistic history we obtain comparatively full information from a series of Plutarch's most readable Lives. Where these sources fail us, we must be content to piece together scraps of knowledge derived from stray allusions in a miscellany of Greek and Latin authors, and from the continuous but highly condensed epitome of Justin. But the gaps in our literary sources are being filled in an ever-increasing degree by inscriptions, of which far greater numbers survive from the Hellenistic than from the classical period, and by papyri, which throw a vivid light on several corners of Ptolemaic Egypt.[1] Though the deficiencies and ambiguities in our materials leave over many problems of detail on which specialists may break their teeth, they can no longer serve as an excuse for treating the Hellenistic period as a Dark Age.

[1] For a brief review of the principal sources of information for Hellenistic History, see Appendix 1.

A HISTORY OF THE GREEK WORLD FROM 323 TO 146 B.C.

PART I

CHAPTER I

THE BREAK-UP OF ALEXANDER'S EMPIRE

§ 1 THE CONFERENCE AT BABYLON

THE sudden death of Alexander in June 323 B.C. left his companions to deal with an emergency for which no provision had been made. Alexander had found no time to compose a political testament,[1] to train a cabinet of confidential ministers, or even to nominate a successor But by a fortunate accident the king's Grand Army still lay concentrated at his head-quarters in Babylon, where he had breathed his last. The chief officers of this force were mostly Macedonian nobles, men born and trained to command, who made the political history of the next forty years. These marshals of Alexander at once formed themselves into a council of state.

The first question debated at Babylon was the choice of a new king. This problem was seemingly simple, for in Alexander's family only one male relative survived,[2] a half-brother named Arridæus, the offspring of Philip and of a Thessalian mistress. But this youth, besides being illegitimate, was

[1] A document described as " Alexander's testament " is preserved in the " Alexander Romance " of pseudo-Callisthenes (Ch. III, § 33). But this is evidently a forgery. Presumably it was concocted c. 320 B.C. by a Rhodian in the service of the party opposed to Antipater. A. Ausfeld, *Rhein. Mus.*, 1895, p. 357 ff.; 1901, p. 517 ff.

[2] On " Heracles the son of Barsine," see p. 30.

mentally unfit to rule. The officers therefore resolved to defer action until August, at which season Alexander's queen Roxane was expected to give birth to a child. To this decision the younger Macedonian nobles who served in the Horse Guards gave their adherence. But the infantry, which claimed to represent the Macedonian nation in arms, and so to have acquired by Macedonian custom the right of approving the new ruler, had meanwhile made up their minds to proclaim Arridæus without delay. However unsuitable this appointment, the rank and file seemed to be in earnest about it: in the previous year they had openly mutinied against Alexander's policy of diluting the Macedonian army with Oriental soldiers, and now they appeared equally determined not to dilute the Macedonian dynasty with the blood of an Eastern queen. Both parties prepared to carry their point in battle; but before actual blows were exchanged the cooler heads in either camp improvised a rough-and-ready compromise which found general approval. It was agreed that Arridæus should at once assume the diadem and the royal name of Philip, but that he should be required to share the throne with Alexander's son, in the event of a boy being born. With the birth of a son to Roxane in August 323 a dual kingship was accordingly set up, so that Alexander III was jointly succeeded by Philip III, Arridæus and by Alexander IV. This partition of the royal power harboured many possibilities of future conflict;[1] but since neither king was ever to be more than a figure-head, it did not give rise to any serious practical inconvenience. In the meantime it averted a civil war between the Macedonian gentry and peasantry, in which Alexander's empire might have dissolved into chaos while he yet lay unburied.

The jealousies in the Grand Army which hindered the appointment of a sole king also precluded the nomination of a single regent. After protracted negotiations between the officers and the troops it was agreed to select three of Alexander's marshals for the posts of highest responsibility. In Europe Antipater was confirmed in his position as viceroy of Macedon, which carried with it the supervision of the Greek city-states. In the rest of the empire the supreme authority was shared out between two senior officers named Perdiccas

[1] In documents of the period 323-317 Philip is often cited as sole king.

and Craterus.[1] Of this pair Craterus bore the more distinguished record, but at the time of Alexander's death he was absent from Babylon on a special mission. Perdiccas, on the other hand, had been in close touch with Alexander during his last illness, and as the bearer of his signet he had taken the lead in the conference at Babylon. Craterus accordingly was made guardian of Philip Arridæus and keeper of the royal purse; Perdiccas was given chief executive authority and the general direction of the imperial armies. By this disposition Craterus received a general power of veto; but the initiative rested with Perdiccas, and this officer used his opportunities so well that in effect he acquired the authority of a regent, and his office came to be generally regarded as such.

One further resolution was passed at Babylon. Among Alexander's papers had been found some memoranda relating to various grandiose schemes of building and engineering, and perhaps also to new military expeditions.[2] The obvious needs of the situation demanded that for the time being nothing more should be attempted than to consolidate Alexander's gains. On submission to the Grand Army his plans were, therefore, cancelled by common consent. As a result of this decision the greater number of Alexander's marshals could hope for no immediate opportunities of further campaigning. For the present they contented themselves with the governorships of various provinces of the empire which were assigned to them by mutual agreement.[3]

§ 2. THE BACTRIAN MUTINY

The administration of Perdiccas was at first attended with a success which augured well for the future unity of the empire. The most serious danger which he had to guard against was

[1] There has been much dispute as to the precise legal definition of the respective attributes of Perdiccas and Craterus. For recent discussions, see W. Schwahn, *Klio*, 1930, p. 211 ff.; 1931, p. 306 ff; W. Schur, *Rheinisches Museum*, 1934, p. 129 ff.

[2] Diodorus, XVIII, 4. Many of the details here set forth may be dismissed as later embroideries. (See the damaging criticism by W. W. Tarn, *Journ. Hell. Stud.*, 1921, p. 1 ff.; 1939, p. 124 ff.)

The chief item in Diodorus' list was an expedition to Carthage and the western Mediterranean lands. According to Arrian (IV, 15, 6, V, 21, 2), Alexander contemplated the conquest of North Africa and the complete reduction of India. (C. A. Robinson, Jr., *Amer. Journ. Philol.*, 1940, p. 402 ff.)—But did he leave any *written* plans of campaign?

[3] Complete lists of these assignations have been preserved. But only two of the appointments, those of Lysimachus and Ptolemy, were of more than transitory importance.

an uprising by the conquered Orientals against the Macedonian yoke. But he was spared this trial of strength, for Alexander had done his work too thoroughly. Already he was becoming a hero of legend in the East, and from his tomb he still overawed his subjects. For a century to come the prestige of the European overlords protected them against overt rebellion: not even in Persia, with its long traditions of empire, was there any open unrest. Like Pizarro's officers in Peru, the Macedonian marshals could afford to wage internecine wars under the eyes of the impassive natives.

The only challenge to Macedonian rule came from the Greeks. In the " upper " or far eastern regions of the empire a fire which had been smouldering since 325 broke out into full blaze after Alexander's death. The rebels were drawn from the numerous detachments of Greek auxiliaries which Alexander had told off for permanent garrison service on the outskirts of his dominions. A large contingent of these homesick men collected their forces in Bactria and prepared to emulate the exploits of Xenophon's Ten Thousand by cutting their way back to Greece.[1] But Perdiccas forestalled their retreat by a counter-mobilization of all the loyal forces in the upper provinces under an officer named Peithon. With the assistance of the local Macedonian governors Peithon headed off the runaways and defeated them in battle. Contrary to Perdiccas' orders, he arranged a capitulation on easy terms; but he was in turn disobeyed by the Macedonian soldiery, who were led on by hopes of plunder to break the convention and massacre their prisoners. The Macedonians could ill afford this loss of European man-power in the Far East; but for the time being they completely restored their authority in those parts. (Autumn 323)

§ 3. THE LAMIAN WAR

A far more serious rising against Macedonian supremacy took place on the Greek mainland. Here king Philip II had established a comprehensive federal union, whose duty to

[1] Their force was estimated at 23,000 men. This total probably includes some Orientals whom the Greeks may have induced to rebel, in hopes of creating a diversion.

Macedonia consisted in the rendering of collective military support against Persia, and to Greece in the enforcement of a general *pax Hellenica.* Under this constitution the Greek city-states had enjoyed an era of unwonted tranquillity. Yet by 323 B.C. they had been thrown back into a state of ferment. The cause of this unrest lay partly in a demobilization crisis, which followed upon the return of great numbers of discharged Greek soldiers from the Persian War, partly in the continued presence of Macedonian garrisons at Corinth and other places, which made Philip's pact of alliance with the Greeks appear insincere. But the chief responsibility for Greek discontent rested with Alexander, who in his later years had quite openly treated his Greek allies as subjects, for instead of preferring requests to their federal parliament, he had issued proclamations which were in the nature of commands. In 324 he had demanded recognition of his divinity from all the Greek cities. This injunction, whose object may have been to place his usurpation of autocratic power on a quasi-legal basis,[1] was obeyed without serious demur, for in itself it did not gravely offend Greek sentiment (p. 367). But it was followed by an order to some Greek states to make territorial concessions to others, and to all of them to receive back their political exiles, to the number of 20,000. This last demand was impolitic as well as illegal, for the outlaws could have been more readily accommodated in the numerous new colonies of Alexander. Their return to Greece involved the cities in the usual endless disputes touching the restoration of confiscated property,[2] and it renewed that strife between political parties which the Macedonian conquest had in the first instance gone far to allay.

Thus, on the news of Alexander's death the Greek Homeland stood in readiness to revolt, and it now only needed a campaign fund and a lead from some important state to declare itself openly. The lead was given once again by Athens. This city, it is true, had been treated with marked favour by Alexander, and during his lifetime even the irreconcilable party of Demosthenes and Lycurgus had been content to

[1] So Ed. Meyer, *Kleine Schriften,* I, p. 267; but this is denied by U. Wilcken, *Alexander der Grosse,* p. 198.

[2] The complicated issues raised by a resettlement of *émigrés* in the Greek cities are well illustrated by texts from Mytilene (Hicks, *Greek Historical Inscriptions,* 164) and Tegea (Ditt., *Syll.,* 306).

prepare for some future day of delivery, without daring to hope that this day was near. But in 324 the proclamations of Alexander had raised a new war-spirit. In one of these the Athenians were bidden to surrender their hold on the island of Samos. Their title to Samos was disputable, but its evacuation touched them at a sore point, and Alexander's tone of command added insult to the imagined injury. The tidings from Babylon in 323 rallied the patriot or chauvinist elements round the orator Hyperides, who now carried the day against Phocion and Demades, the spokesmen of the wealthy minority that desired peace at all costs. The Ecclesia voted a full mobilization and issued a general manifesto for the liberation of Greece and the expulsion of the Macedonian garrisons. Thus Athens took the initiative in the Greek revolt, and she also supplied it with a war-fund. By a strange windfall the Athenians had acquired a potential war-fund from an absconding minister of Alexander named Harpalus; in the first instance they dutifully sequestrated this treasure, pending instructions from Alexander, but after the king's death they appropriated it as a gift from Fortune to the brave.

In autumn 323 the war began with a surprise move by an Athenian *condottiere* named Leosthenes, who had been secretly commissioned by Hyperides to enlist a corps of demobilized mercenaries at the market of Tænarum in Laconia. From Tænarum Leosthenes sailed to the Corinthian Gulf and joined hands with the Ætolians, who had also been threatened by Alexander with loss of territory. With Ætolian help he occupied Thermopylæ, where he was presently reinforced by the Athenian home-levy. On sea the Athenians mobilized a fleet of 240 vessels, a total not surpassed since the days of the Peloponnesian War. Against these forces the Macedonian commander, Antipater, could dispose of no more than 110 ships, and of a barely sufficient army on land, for in the course of Alexander's campaigns the military resources of Macedonia had been heavily depleted. He nevertheless offered battle to Leosthenes beyond Thermopylæ, but during the engagement he was deserted by his Thessalian contingent, and he saved his force only by throwing it into the city of Lamia. Here he was kept under blockade during the winter, and eventually reduced to offer terms. But Leosthenes would accept nothing short of complete surrender, and despite the subsequent death of the Athenian general in a sortie, the siege of Lamia was maintained.

After the first victories of the war the Greek league enrolled many new adherents. The Bœotians, who still bore gratitude to Alexander for the destruction of Thebes, took sides with Antipater; the Spartans and Arcadians, unable to sink their long-standing feud, stood fixedly on guard against each other; and Corinth remained in Macedonian hands. But the greater part of Peloponnesus and almost the whole of Central and Northern Greece joined the rebel coalition. Yet these accessions brought no corresponding gain to the Greek field forces. As in the war of old against Xerxes, the lesser Greek cities left the hard fighting to the leading states, and in 322 the brunt of the campaign was borne by the Athenians, together with their new allies from Thessaly.

Antipater, for his part, had at once called upon the Macedonian commanders in Asia Minor to relieve him, but during the first campaign he received no assistance from this quarter. In all probability the Athenians had detached part of their fleet to close the Dardanelles against Macedonian reinforcements. In spring 322, Leonnatus, the governor of Phrygia, anticipating the return of the Athenian squadron from winter quarters, stole across to Thrace and to Thessaly, where he disengaged Antipater from Lamia. But shortly after this success he perished in a skirmish with the Thessalian horse; and the superiority of the Thessalian cavalry so impressed Antipater, that he used his newly-won liberty to withdraw his army into Macedonia. Leonnatus's reinforcements had not sufficed to turn the tide of war. But in summer 322 a second Macedonian army under Craterus was mobilized in Asia Minor, and the arrival of a strong detachment from Alexander's main fleet in Levantine waters brought the Macedonian strength in the Ægean up to 240 vessels.[1] In reply to this concentration the Athenians prepared a battle-fleet of 170 ships, but finding themselves both outnumbered and outweighted, they lost two engagements to the enemy admiral, Clitus. The former of these actions was fought in the Dardanelles near Abydus, the latter took place off the island of Amorgos, towards which Clitus had apparently headed off

[1] For a discussion of the problems relating to the fleets of the Lamian War, see Appendix 2.

the defeated Athenian fleet. These naval battles gave Craterus a free passage into Macedonia, where he joined hands with Antipater. Their combined forces now re-occupied Thessaly and engaged the Athenians and Thessalians near Crannon. Despite superior numbers, they merely succeeded in pushing back the Greeks without crushing them. But this partial victory served their purpose, for after the battle of Amorgos and the consequent loss of the sea, the insurgents could afford nothing short of a decisive advantage over the Macedonian land forces. Their failure to achieve a compensating success so damped their spirits, that they opened negotiations with Antipater, and upon his refusal to treat with the rebels collectively they made separate capitulations. Only the Ætolians stood out and avoided subjugation;[1] but their escape was solely due to a new call upon the troops of the Macedonian generals, whose presence came to be urgently required in another field of war.

In the "Lamian" or, as it was miscalled at the time, the "Hellenic"[2] War, the Greeks fought with a genuine sense of grievance; man for man they proved a match for their opponents, and thus disposed of the legend of Macedonian invincibility. But with their old pride and courage they retained their former incapacity for co-operation: though the war was styled "Hellenic," its battles were mostly left to be fought by a few of the leading states. Even so, the Greeks might have achieved their independence, but for the intervention of Alexander's Grand Armada, whose admiral, Clitus, was the real winner of the war. Nay more, Clitus effected what Lysander could not accomplish: he disheartened the Athenians from any further attempt at thalassocracy; though Athenian vessels took part in sea-fights among Alexander's successors, Athenian naval history virtually terminates with the battle of Amorgos. For the next century the lordship of the Ægean generally remained in the hands of a navy recruited, like that of Clitus, from Asiatic Greeks or Levantines.

In the settlement that followed the Lamian War, Antipater

[1] The threatened attack by Antipater and Craterus induced the Ætolians to build themselves fortified places of refuge, instead of trusting to the natural difficulties which their country presented to invaders. Many of these Ætolian *enceintes* are excellently preserved. See W. H. Woodhouse, *Ætolia.*

[2] E.g. in Hicks, 134; Ditt., *Syll.*, 346.

broke with the principles of Philip and frankly converted the Greeks from allies into subjects. By the same policy of isolation as had broken up the recent war coalition he dissolved the Hellenic confederacy which Philip had founded and Alexander had never quite superseded. He extended his system of garrisons and defrayed their expenses by direct contributions upon the cities in their custody; and in some towns he remodelled the constitutions in favour of the wealthier and more pacific elements. Antipater's general policy is reflected in the terms which he dictated at Athens. Not content with the proscription of the war-leaders and the exaction of an indemnity, he established a garrison on the hill of Munychia overlooking the Piræus, and he imposed a new form of government which harked back to Solon and beyond. His basic reform was the restriction of citizen rights to some 9000 residents with a property qualification of 2000 drachmas.[1] Antipater also transferred higher criminal jurisdiction from the dicasteries to the Areopagus, and he probably abolished or curtailed payment for public service or attendance at festivals. Whether he also replaced sortition of Council and magistrates by election is not certain; but it may be assumed that the restriction of public pay carried with it the disappearance of many superfluous officials. Excessively reactionary though this constitution might appear, it was nevertheless the most durable of Antipater's political innovations in Greece. Athenian democracy was the offspring of Athenian thalassocracy; when this terminated, the proletariate lost its livelihood and its title to political power. It is probable that after 322 its numbers underwent a permanent reduction; in any case, it never again exercised more than a transient influence upon Athenian policy, and the administration henceforth remained essentially a plutocracy.

With the Athenian democracy died the last of the great Athenian demagogues, the orator Demosthenes. By a curious

[1] The number of disfranchised citizens was 12,000, according to Plutarch (*Phocian*, 29 § 6). On this reckoning, presumably, Antipater deprived the entire class of Thetes of its franchise. The statement of Diodorus (XVIII, 18, 5, ed. C. T. Fischer), that more than 22,000 of the disfranchised emigrated to Thrace, is utterly improbable.

and unexampled turn of domestic politics Demosthenes had been proved or assumed guilty of embezzlement from Harpalus' treasure and had gone into exile in **324**.[1] He took no hand in organizing the outbreak against Antipater, and although he was recalled to Athens in **323**, he does not appear to have recovered his former influence. None the less, he was placed by Antipater on the list of the proscribed. He attempted flight, but was run down by the head-hunters in the temple of Poseidon at Calauria (in Argolis), and to escape execution he took poison. To review his career and to appreciate his genius does not fall within the scope of the present story. But it must be noted here that the cause for which he fought and died perished soon after him. The Lamian War was the last national conflict between Greeks and Macedonians, and its result was in a sense irrelevant. The future relations between the two peoples had been irrevocably fixed by Alexander's Anabasis, which destined them to work together in close co-operation as joint rulers of the East, and eventually to be blended into one nation. Moreover, though Macedonian beat Greek in the Lamian War, in the larger task of consolidating Alexander's conquests and of reaping their fruit the Greeks had their revenge upon their victors. Though the Hellenistic dynasties were mostly Macedonian, their soldiers and administrators were largely Greek, and their traders and teachers were predominantly of Hellenic stock. If it can be said that the Italians by losing to Rome gained the Mediterranean, still more is it true that Alexander conquered for Greece rather than for Macedon. Hellenistic history is therefore essentially an extension of Greek history, and, except in cases where the term " Macedonian " is especially appropriate, we shall in future speak of the rulers of the East as Greeks.

§ 4. THE FAILURE OF PERDICCAS' REGENCY

While Antipater and Craterus were reducing the insurgent Greeks, Perdiccas was engaged in rounding off Alexander's conquests in the more remote and mountainous parts of Asia Minor, which the Macedonian king had for the time being left

[1] For a recent review of his trial, see G. Colin in *Rev. Ét. Grecques*, 1925, p. 306 ff.; 1926, p. 31 ff.

in the possession of the natives or of resident Persian dynasts. His main campaign was directed against a Persian nobleman named Ariarathes, who had formed the nucleus of a new kingdom in Cappadocia, and was thrusting towards Sinope and Trapezus along the Black Sea coast.[1] For the conduct of this war Perdiccas had chosen Antigonus and Leonnatus, the governors of Central and of Hellespontine Phrygia. But Leonnatus, as we have seen, answered the rival call of Antipater to Greece, and Antigonus made no move at all. Not to be denied, Perdiccas took the field in person with the remnant of Alexander's Grand Army and made short work of Ariarathes. He disfigured his victory by impaling his Persian captive. Similar instances of execution in Oriental fashion are not unknown in the history of the Hellenistic kings, but they never became a regular practice.

Perdiccas' most thorny problem, however, lay not with the Greeks and Orientals, but with the Macedonians. The Macedonian rank and file, it is true, gave him no further trouble after the settlement of the royal succession ; but he could not count in equal measure on the loyalty of the officers, some of whom were not disposed to take orders from anybody save Alexander. Rightly judging that he must make an immediate example of disobedience, Perdiccas took proceedings against the first offenders, and with the nominal concurrence of king Philip Arridæus, who was staying on at Babylon pending the return of Craterus from war-duty, he came off victorious in his earliest trials of strength. His first victim was Meleager, the commander and spokesman of the infantry in the original dispute over the succession, whom he executed after trial before the Grand Army. Antigonus, who was summoned to answer before the same court for his refusal to march against Ariarathes, sought safety in flight.

A more serious threat to Perdiccas' ascendancy lay in the attitude of the two senior marshals, Antipater and Craterus. At first, indeed, it seemed as if Perdiccas had little to fear from this quarter. Craterus had acquiesced in the settlement at Babylon, by which Perdiccas had in effect been promoted over

[1] Ariarathes probably made himself master of Sinope, for his name occurs on coins of that city. (Head, *Historia Numorum*, 2nd ed., p. 508.) Whether he also conquered Trapezus is uncertain.

his head; and in the campaign of Crannon he showed equal generosity, playing Outram to Antipater's Havelock. Antipater for his part had never turned his quasi-royal authority in Macedon to his own advantage; and in summer 322 he complied with Perdiccas' request for the hand of his daughter Nicæa. But this match was marred by the intervention of an inveterate mischief-maker, when Alexander's mother, Olympias, opened a new round in her war of intrigue against Antipater, whom she could never forgive for refusing to submit to her dictation in her son's absence. By way of taking the wind out of Antipater's sails she now offered her daughter Cleopatra, the full sister of Alexander, to Perdiccas. After some hesitation Perdiccas jilted Nicæa and wooed Cleopatra, only to discover that she was as good a wrecker as her mother, and preferred, like Queen Elizabeth, to have many lovers so that she might disappoint them all. But Olympias had at least succeeded in embroiling Perdiccas with Antipater. The breach between them, moreover, was widened by Antigonus, the exile from Phrygia, who had taken refuge with Antipater, and lost no opportunity of blackening Perdiccas in the eyes of his host. On hearing of the affair with Cleopatra, Antigonus put it about that Perdiccas was set on usurping the crown of Alexander for himself and transferring his seat of power to Macedonia. This rumour, it may safely be asserted, was false, for at this stage any such open attack on the existing dynasty would have been suicidal, in view of the strong attachment which the rank and file of the Macedonian armies still felt to Alexander's house. But Perdiccas' conduct certainly lay open to misconstruction, and Antipater and Craterus resolved to take no risk. At the end of 322 they withdrew their forces from Greece and prepared to forestall Perdiccas' expected attack by an advance into Asia Minor.

While Antipater and Craterus were drifting into war with Perdiccas, another of Alexander's marshals deliberately invited a trial of strength with him. By the settlement of Babylon the province of Egypt had been awarded to an officer named Ptolemy, who was the first to divine that a field-marshal's baton might serve as a royal sceptre, and had accordingly asked for Egypt as the safest seat for a new dynasty. In 322 Ptolemy took advantage of a domestic revolution at Cyrene to acquire control of that city and its neighbourhood.[1] But his chief acquisition was the corpse of Alexander, which he brought to Egypt by as profitable a feat of body-snatching as that by which the Venetians subsequently stole St. Mark out of that country. At the end of **322** Perdiccas had arranged to transfer the remains of Alexander to the burying-place of the royal house at Ægæ in Upper Macedonia, and had entrusted an officer named Arridæus (not to be confused with king Philip Arridæus) to take charge of the convoy. Ptolemy spread a report that Alexander had willed to be buried in the Oasis of Amon, and induced Arridæus to change his course in deference to the dead king's alleged request.[2] Accordingly, at Damascus the *cortège* swerved from its westward course and turned towards Egypt. But it never went further than Memphis, where Ptolemy detained the body pending the construction of a permanent tomb in his future capital at Alexandria. Thus Ptolemy won a precious relic, but his action was in such flat defiance of Perdiccas that the latter had no option but to prepare a punitive expedition against him. As a guarantee of mutual support against Perdiccas, Antipater now arranged three matrimonial alliances. To Craterus he gave his daughter Phila, and Eurydice to Ptolemy. Nicæa was bestowed upon Lysimachus, the governor of Thrace, who in return offered a benevolent neutrality. Thus Perdiccas was faced with a coalition on two fronts.

In the campaign of **321** Perdiccas' plan was to lead the remains of the Grand Army in person against Ptolemy, and to contain Antipater and Craterus with a lesser force, which he entrusted to an officer named Eumenes. Unlike the other chief actors in these events, Eumenes was a Greek (from the Hellespontine town of Cardia), and of bourgeois estate. During Alexander's reign he had held a civilian post as head of the imperial chancery. After Alexander's death he had transferred his services to Perdiccas, and had lent a helpful hand

[1] A new constitution (largely preserved in an inscription) which Ptolemy conferred upon Cyrene, belongs to this date (or possibly to 312).—See, Cary, *Journ. Hell. Stud.*, p. 222 ff.

[2] Diodorus (XVIII, 3, 5) relates that at the conference of Babylon it had been decided to convey Alexander to the Amon Oasis. Pausanias (I, 6, 3) states that he was to be buried at Ægæ. It is not unlikely that Alexander's own intention was to be buried in the Amon Oasis, but the feeling of the Macedonian officers and men alike would be in favour of his returning to Ægæ. Pausanias therefore here deserves preference over Diodorus.

in the negotiations at Babylon. In return, Perdiccas carried his appointment as governor of Cappadocia and installed him there after the campaign of 322. To place an untried Greek in command of Macedonian forces was a risky experiment. But Eumenes, by the very fact of his being a *novus homo*, was securely bound to the cause of his patron, and in the ensuing warfare he proved himself fully a match for the ablest of Alexander's marshals. In spring 321 Antipater and Craterus, having crossed the Dardanelles without opposition, divided their forces. Antipater moved off with a flying column to the aid of Ptolemy, while Craterus sought out Eumenes. The odds were all in favour of Craterus, for although Eumenes had equal numbers, his army contained few Macedonians, and he was exceedingly ill served by his officers, some of whom refused obedience to the Greekling or even colluded with the enemy. Nevertheless Eumenes accepted battle, and he carried the day with an improvised corps of Cappadocian horse whom he had trained up to the Macedonian standard.[1] Craterus' army made good its retreat and rejoined Antipater, but its commander was left on the field. In the events after Alexander's death Craterus took a strangely self-effacing part, so that it is difficult for us to estimate his real ability ; but his reputation in the Macedonian army was second to none, and his death was a severe blow to his party. Yet its effect was nullified by the decisive turn which the war had taken on the Egyptian front.

In the campaign between Perdiccas and Ptolemy, the first round was a war of words, in which Perdiccas sought to justify his expedition to his troops, but found himself out-argued by Ptolemy. Abandoning the diplomatic offensive, he advanced without opposition to the Egyptian frontier. Not that Ptolemy lacked men. On his arrival in Egypt he had appropriated a large treasure—the proceeds of some resolute and unscrupulous taxation by Alexander's agent, Cleomenes, in that province—and he had used it to enlist mercenaries from all quarters. But he put his chief trust in the Nile, and by so doing won an almost bloodless victory. After two vain attempts to force the river near Pelusium, Perdiccas slipped away to the apex of the delta and began to

[1] The site of this battle is uncertain. It is usually located near the Dardanelles.

throw his army across. But while he had chosen the season well (June 321)—for the Nile floods were not yet due—he had selected an unsuitable spot for his passage. Under the weight of his troops the river-bed shifted and carried the men with it. After this disaster the discontent in Perdiccas' army, which resented the harshness of his discipline, broke out into open mutiny. Three of his officers. Peithon (the victor of the eastern campaign in 323), Antigenes and Seleucus, sought him out in his tent and murdered him. Thus Alexander's empire, while keeping its two kings, was left without a government.

§ 5. ANTIPATER'S STOP-GAP REGENCY

The death of Perdiccas brought the operations in Egypt to a sudden close. The contending armies joined hands and constituted themselves into a Macedonian parliament. At this meeting Ptolemy was offered Perdiccas' place, but he showed no mind to stake his winnings on a greater hazard. In his stead he fobbed off two lesser officers, Peithon and Arridæus, upon the assembly, and had them voted into the dead man's shoes. Hereupon the remnants of the Grand Army withdrew into Syria.

In putting forward Peithon and Arridæus, Ptolemy no doubt had an ulterior purpose, for these two officers plainly lacked the prestige for carrying on Perdiccas' work. To say nothing of their fellow generals, they could not even control a female intriguer who was planning to gather the regency into her hands This aspirant to Perdiccas' place was a princess named Eurydice, a granddaughter of Philip by an illegitimate union, who had been promised in Alexander's lifetime to Philip Arridæus. After the proclamation of Philip Arridæus as king, Eurydice sought him out in disregard of Perdiccas' veto, and forced herself upon him. After Perdiccas' death she set herself to become her husband's guardian as well as his queen, and to this end she played successfully upon the personal loyalty of the troops to the royal house. Thus affairs were moving to another crisis in the Macedonian army, when Antipater arrived in Syria with his forces, and succeeded in patching up a new compromise. At Triparadisus on the upper Orontes the combined armies transferred authority from Peithon and Arridæus (who were duly grateful for their deposition) to Antipater. At the same time they satisfied outstanding claims among his adherents by a fresh distribution of provinces, and they outlawed the remainder of Perdiccas' officers who stood under arms in Asia Minor.

For a brief while Antipater pulled Alexander's empire together. He overawed Eurydice into submission, and he gained the effectual custody of both the kings, whom he brought back with him to Macedonia. For the conduct of the war in Asia Minor he made a wise choice in his friend Antigonus, who made a clean sweep of Perdiccas' party in one campaign. In spring 320 Antigonus first advanced upon Eumenes, who had retired into Cappadocia, and destroyed his army at one blow. Eumenes himself escaped to a hill-fort on the northern edge of Mt. Taurus, but was placed under close investment, so that his surrender seemed merely a question of time. This success Antigonus owed largely to the disloyalty of Eumenes' colleagues, who had stood aloof in the south of Asia Minor while their chief was falling back eastward, and to the discouragement of his troops, many of whom deserted him at the first contact. But in the second campaign of the year Antigonus proved himself a worthy successor of Alexander. Marching forty miles a day for a week on end, he pounced upon Perdiccas' remaining adherents in Pisidia and made short work of them. Antipater also achieved a somewhat unexpected success in a marriage alliance with Antigonus. By this match Phila, the widow of Craterus, was given in hand to Antigonus' young son, Demetrius. Despite Demetrius' scandalous infidelities, Phila nobly played the part of Octavia to his Antony, and she gave him a son who finally laid the fortunes of his house on secure foundations.

But Antipater's regency was of short duration. He belonged to the generation of Philip and had outlived most of his contemporaries. In 319 he succumbed to old age.

§ 6. THE END OF ALEXANDER'S DYNASTY

On his death-bed Antipater made over his authority to an officer named Polyperchon, who had accompanied Alexander to India, and had done good service in stamping out the last embers of the Lamian War. This choice was ratified by the troops in Macedonia, who now perhaps had the best claim to represent the Macedonian people in arms. But Polyperchon, however good his title, lacked the personal ascendancy of Antipater. We may ask whether Antipater would not have done better to select Antigonus, on the chance that his ambitions might be satisfied by a regency without a crown. But it is doubtful whether any regent could have coped with the after-effects of Ptolemy's successful rebellion, which now began to show through. Antipater was the last of Alexander's marshals whose loyalty was equal to his ability and personal prestige.

Polyperchon naturally failed to assert his authority over Ptolemy, who at once defied the new regent by making war upon Laomedon, the governor of Syria and Phœnicia, and by annexing this province to his dominions. By this invasion Ptolemy raised a " Syrian question " which vexed Hellenistic rulers for more than a century (ch. V). But its immediate effects were of little consequence. A more serious threat to Polyperchon arose in Asia Minor, where Antigonus now held the largest of the Macedonian armies. In 319 he attacked Arridæus and Clitus, who had been made governors of Hellespontine Phrygia and of Lydia by the settlement of Triparadisus, and expelled them from their provinces. Having thus obtained a sea-front to his territories he began to build a fleet. Furthermore, he arranged an easy capitulation with Eumenes, in the hope of securing his services, and he lent a force to Antipater's son Cassander, who was preparing to contest Polyperchon's authority in Macedonia. According to Antipater's dispositions Cassander had been destined to act as Polyperchon's second-in-command, and in view of the fact that he was a younger man and had not participated in Alexander's campaigns this appointment did him fair justice. But Cassander had expected to step straight into his father's place, and he expressed his disappointment by going over to seek Antigonus' help.

In the face of this new coalition Polyperchon showed unexpected vigour. He drew round himself a council of Macedonian magnates and cast about for allies. He successfully detached Eumenes from Antigonus, and provided him with a letter patent from king Philip Arridæus, giving him an overriding authority over all the Macedonian officials in Asia, and empowering him to take command of the Silver Shields, a veteran corps from Alexander's army, which was then stationed on light duty in Cilicia. With this commission Eumenes won the allegiance of the Silver Shields, and with the royal treasures which had been deposited in Cilicia he enlisted a new mercenary force. From Cilicia he passed over to Phœnicia, where he proposed to secure a fleet on Polyperchon's behalf. (319–8)

But Polyperchon's main hopes were based on the cities of the Greek mainland. With a view to enlisting their active support he issued a proclamation in which he cancelled Antipater's recent settlement and purported to restore the regulations of Philip and Alexander ; and he invited the cities to expel their garrisons and to receive back their exiles. The former of these two measures was a statesmanlike move, and coupled with a restoration of Philip's federal parliament it might have been the basis of an enduring friendship. But his order for the readmission of exiles, like Alexander's previous decree, met with strong opposition. By his proclamation he fired a train of revolution which brought numerous Greeks over to his side. But in Athens he gained no more than a half-success. He carried the city itself, where many of the poorer citizens whom Antipater had transplanted returned and effected a transient democratic restoration. But the commander of Antipater's garrison at Munychia declared for Cassander, and with the connivance of Phocion, who welcomed a Macedonian force as a bulwark against social revolution, he seized the town of Piræus into the bargain. It was but a poor satisfaction to the Athenian Ecclesia that it passed a tumultuary sentence upon Phocion and hurried him off to a traitor's death.[1]

But once again, as in the Lamian War, the fate of Greece was decided on the sea. In autumn 318 Clitus, who had taken refuge from Antigonus with Polyperchon and had received from him the command of a remnant of the imperial fleet, engaged the ships recruited by Antigonus in Asia Minor. He gained a victory at the entrance to the Bosporus, but on the next day let his vessels be caught at their moorings by the remainder of the enemy fleet, and by an army which Antigonus had slipped across to the European shore with the

[1] For a recent discussion of Phocion's policy see Cloché, *Revue Historique*, vol. 143, p. 161 ff. ; vol. 145, p. 1 ff.

connivance of the free and supposedly neutral city of Byzantium. Polyperchon's navy was completely destroyed, and since he never received the expected reinforcements from Phœnicia, he definitely lost the command of the Aegean Sea to Antigonus.

The fruits of the Bosporus campaign were not gathered by Antigonus in person, for he at once returned to Asia to meet the growing menace of Eumenes (ch. II), but were left by him to be reaped by Cassander. The first plum that fell into Cassander's lap was Athens, where the restored democrats, well knowing that Athens could not exist without the freedom of the sea, made overtures to him without delay. Cassander in return made a show of generosity. He evacuated Piræus and promised that Munychia should only be held "for the duration of the war against the kings"; and he fixed the property qualification for citizenship at a mere 1000 drachmas. But in general he reimposed Antipater's constitution,[1] and with it he appointed a liaison officer who in effect became the dictator of Athens. (Early 317) The man of his choice, Demetrius of Phalerum, was a distinguished Athenian citizen, a former friend of Aristotle, and himself a scholar of no small repute. Nominally he governed as an Athenian magistrate, with the office of strategus or archon; in actual fact he was the spokesman of Cassander, with the garrison of Munychia at his beck and call. Since Demetrius of Phalerum remained in power for ten years, and the garrison stayed on in Munychia long after him, the settlement imposed by Cassander outlasted the war-emergency for which it was ostensibly intended.

From Athens Cassander sailed to Macedonia, where the people, no longer knowing to whom their loyalty was due, accepted him as the stronger of the pretenders to Antipater's position. With Macedonia he won Eurydice, who had been chafing at the control exercised in turn by Antipater and by Polyperchon, and now induced king Philip Arridæus to depose Polyperchon and to nominate Cassander in his stead. With this new mark of legitimacy Cassander returned to Greece and carried the whole country except Ætolia and part of Peloponnesus. To complete his conquest he began a campaign of sieges in Peloponnesus.

[1] The details of Cassander's constitutional reforms are uncertain. But since Athens passed virtually under a tyranny they are of no great importance.

In the meantime Polyperchon had fled with Alexander's son and widow to Epirus, where Alexander's mother, Olympias, was still residing, and was pressing her to reconquer Macedonia for him. Olympias had previously refused to engage herself on Polyperchon's behalf, but she now realized that if Eurydice and Cassander had their way the crown of Macedon would be definitely lost to her grandson. With the remnant of Polyperchon's forces and an Epirote contingent under her cousin, king Æacidas, she marched upon Macedonia. Eurydice and Philip Arridæus met her at the frontier, but were deserted by their entire army on the mere appearance of Alexander's mother, and thus fell into their rival's hands. Philip Arridæus was promptly executed, and Eurydice received an invitation to commit suicide, which she did with a will. But Olympias, who was utterly lacking in political restraint, went on to perpetrate a wanton massacre among Cassander's adherents. In so doing she really played into Cassander's hands, for she at once forfeited the support of the Macedonians, who were not accustomed to vendettas on such a scale. (Summer 317)

At the news of Olympias' invasion Cassander had hastened back from Peloponnesus to Macedonia. He found the Ætolians in occupation of Thermopylæ, but he circumvented this position by slipping his men across the Malian Gulf on rafts and caught Olympias by surprise. Unable to raise further troops in Macedonia, the Epirote queen threw herself into the town of Pydna with a few retainers. Æacidas, who had returned to Epirus, made an attempt to disengage her, but could not induce his troops to fight ; and a similar experience befell Polyperchon, who came to the rescue from Thessaly. In spring 316 Olympias capitulated on a promise of her life. But Cassander, egged on by the clamour of those relatives she had murdered, invited his army to pass sentence on her, and procured some personal enemies of the queen to put her to death. By the fall of Pydna he also gained possession of Alexander and Roxane. For six further years he spared their lives, and he did not formally abrogate the young king's royalty. But he kept the pair under close arrest and treated them like persons of common rank. To all intents and purposes Alexander's dynasty came to an end in 316 B.C.

CHAPTER II

THE RISE AND FALL OF ANTIGONUS I

§ 1. THE CANDIDATES FOR THE SUCCESSION

WITH the death of Philip III, Arridæus, and the imprisonment of Alexander IV, the Macedonian royal house had virtually become extinct. But the fate of Alexander's empire still hung in the balance. Would it break up at once into an aggregate of independent sovereignties, or would one pasha climb over the others' heads into the sultan's seat ?

In general, the high officers of the Macedonian army lacked either the power or the will to achieve more than a local sovereignty. The governors of the eastern provinces could not procure an adequate supply of Macedonian or Greek soldiers, without whom none could hope to tread in Alexander's footsteps : indeed, it might be set down as an axiom that no succession-state could hope to become a first-class power unless it possessed a Mediterranean seaboard and easy access to the Aegean area.

Among the rulers thus situated there were three who might rank as possible candidates for empire. Ptolemy possessed from the outset an ample fund of money, and he drew a large revenue from Egypt, whose abundant natural resources he further developed by good stewardship. With these resources he could enlist as many European troops as he needed. Moreover, after his conquest of Phœnicia he had laid the foundations of a fleet which eventually grew to be the strongest in Greek waters. In spite of these advantages, Ptolemy never aspired to Alexander's throne. Lacking the gambler's temperament, he was loth to stake all his past gains on a big throw, and he set a definite limit to his risks and his objectives.

With all the military resources of Macedonia and Greece at his immediate disposal, Cassander appeared to possess the means for a repetition of Alexander's conquests. But under Alexander the drain upon the man-power of Macedonia had been so heavy that there was now a dearth of recruits. At the same time the gold mines of Philippi were ceasing to be as productive as in the " boom " period of king Philip, and Macedonia was becoming the poor relative among the Hellenistic monarchies. In Greece the supply of good soldiers was still ample, but it was not at the absolute disposal of Cassander, for even a masterful overlord of that country had to pay some regard to the Greek spirit of independence; and still more did he need to exercise moderation in drawing upon its slender store of money. Moreover, Cassander had inherited the European outlook of his father: far from desiring to emulate Alexander, he harked back to the traditions of Philip, whose daughter Thessalonica he had taken to wife. To recover the European portion of the Macedonian empire he had fought hard and without scruple; once in possession, he was satisfied to play for keeps.

There remained Antigonus. During Alexander's Grand Tour of the East this officer had stayed behind as governor of the unimportant province of Central Phrygia, with his headquarters at the small town of Celænæ. But since the king's death he had acquired the greater part of Asia Minor, an extensive seaboard, and a large portion of Alexander's army. As a leader of troops in the field he excelled all his Macedonian colleagues and had no match except Eumenes; as an organiser and financier Ptolemy alone was his equal. Above all, Antigonus recalled Alexander himself in his unflagging energy and in his breadth of vision. Of all the dead king's officers Antigonus was best qualified to reunite his empire. His attempt to achieve its reunion is the leading topic of Greek political history in the last years of the fourth century.

§ 2. THE DUEL BETWEEN ANTIGONUS AND EUMENES

While Cassander was cornering Polyperchon, Antigonus threw his whole weight against Eumenes, whom he rightly singled out as his most formidable opponent. After a hurried march across Asia Minor he arrived in Phœnicia too late to save Ptolemy, who had evacuated it at Eumenes' approach, but early enough to prevent Eumenes from mustering a fleet or making good the ground won by him. Unable to face the superior numbers of Antigonus, Eumenes in turn abandoned Phœnicia and retired into the interior of the Asian continent. His last hope now was to win over the forces of the governors in the upper provinces, over whom Polyperchon's warrant had given him formal authority. In Babylonia he had an ominous reception, for its governor, Seleucus, disregarding Polyperchon's writ, treated him as an outlaw and almost succeeded in destroying his force by flooding a disused arm of the Tigris. Eventually Eumenes struggled clear of the fenlands and proceeded towards Susa, where he found the eastern governors assembled with their combined field forces. (Spring 317) This concentration was the result of a local civil war in which all the other Macedonian governors had joined hands to crush the strongest of their number, Peithon, the satrap of Media or Central Persia. After his brief experience as regent of the empire, this officer had been no longer content to play a minor part, but had endeavoured to secure all the eastern provinces for himself. In this attempt he had been frustrated by the united action of his colleagues. On Eumenes' arrival the war against Peithon was ended, but the coalition troops had not yet been disbanded. At Susa it required all Eumenes' ingenuity to bring the Macedonian officers under his authority. He finally obtained a precarious allegiance from them by representing to them in a dramatic manner that their loyalty was due neither to him nor to themselves, but to Alexander and his house. He transferred their war-council to a tent furnished with royal trappings and a throne, and he bade the Macedonian governors imagine Alexander in the Chair while they debated on an equal footing under his posthumous orders.[1] With the reinforcements which he thus acquired from the eastern provinces Eumenes was roughly equal to Antigonus in other arms and far superior in the number of his elephants.

In summer 317 Antigonus caught up Eumenes and drove him back to the southern edge of the Persian plateau; but

[1] Plutarch (*Eumenes*, ch. 13) states that Eumenes first set up this tent, Diodorus (XIX, 15, 4) that the Macedonian officers had previously used it to sacrifice to the dead Alexander. But hero-worship was a Greek rather than a Macedonian custom. Besides, Diodorus stultifies himself by saying that the Macedonians had held war-councils in the tent *before* Eumenes' coming. At this point Plutarch is clearly preferable to Diodorus.

forced marches under an intense heat tried his men so highly that he found it necessary to give them a rest in the cooler regions of Central Persia. In so doing he left open the road to Babylon, and would have been cut off by Eumenes, had not the governors of the eastern provinces refused to join Eumenes in a manœuvre which would in turn have exposed their own lines of communication. Thus foiled, Eumenes staked his chances on a set battle. The action of Parætacene (near Isfahan) has been described for us in some detail,[1] and may serve as an example of Hellenistic warcraft at its best. Following the practice of Alexander, Eumenes threw his whole weight upon the right wing, where he had concentrated his best horsemen, while his left, with a protecting front line of elephants, stood on the defensive. His onset at first miscarried, because Antigonus parried it with an encircling movement, but by summoning a further brigade of cavalry from his weak left flank he finally succeeded in pushing home his attack. At the same time his centre, on which the Silver Shields were posted, drove back the opposite infantry. But Antigonus retrieved the battle by throwing a reserve force of horsemen into a gap which had formed between the advancing centre and right wing of Eumenes. With this drawn event the campaign of 317 drew to a close.

In midwinter Antigonus made an attempt in Alexander's best vein to surprise Eumenes' winter quarters, and would have succeeded, but for the severe cold, which compelled his men to light fires and so to give away their position. In spring 316 he again joined battle with Eumenes in the district of Gabiene (near Susa), and here he squared accounts with his rival. The cause of Eumenes' defeat lay chiefly in the treachery of the Macedonians under his command. At the outset of the action an officer named Peucestas, who had fought with distinction under Alexander in India and had subsequently been an efficient and popular governor in Persis (Southern Persia), sullied his record by a deliberate retreat out of the battle line. Eumenes, it is true, repaired this misfortune by a successful counter-attack with his reserves, and on balance he had the best of the exchanges. But a mishap, trifling in itself, sealed his doom. During the engagement his camp was surprised by a flying column of enemy horsemen,

[1] Diodorus, XIX, 27–31.

and the families and other property of the Silver Shields were captured. The action had hardly been broken off when the men of this corps, who were old soldiers in rapacity as well as in valour, bought back their baggage from Antigonus at the price of Eumenes' person. At the same time the rest of Eumenes' army came to terms with Antigonus. Still hoping to secure the services of Eumenes in his own cause, Antigonus seemed disposed to spare his life ; and his son Demetrius, who was winning his spurs on this campaign, interceded for him with boyish chivalry. But Antigonus was driven by the clamour of the other officers to execute him. Thus died the ablest and most loyal servant of Alexander's dynasty. But in the meantime the cause for which Eumenes had planned and struggled had also perished (p. 20). The real importance of Eumenes' fate is that it removed Antigonus' most dangerous enemy from his path and set him on the course for Alexander's vacant throne.

§ 3. ANTIGONUS' FIRST THROW FOR EMPIRE

Antigonus, having gathered in his hands the entire military strength of the upper provinces, at once made it clear that he intended to be master in those regions. While he retained the more docile of the governors, he removed all those who might contest his authority. Peucestas was deposed under some honourable pretext ; Peithon and others were arraigned before the army on whatever charge and put to death. Antigenes, the commander of the Silver Shields, was executed by being burnt alive, a useless piece of savagery that contrasted strangely with Antigonus' habitual policy of calculated moderation. The victor of Gabiene further showed his hand by appropriating a large imperial treasure which no Macedonian officer had yet dared to touch without a warrant from a regent. To remove all doubts as to his intentions, on his return to Babylon he treated Seleucus as his underling and called for his accounts. Seleucus, who understood this language, at once decamped to Egypt and sounded the alarm before Ptolemy, who in turn warned Cassander and the Thracian governor Lysimachus. Antigonus in return offered negotiations on the basis of the *status quo*. But his antagonists, realizing that under cover of the treaty he would play odd man out with them, replied with a joint ultimatum, demanding a redistribution of the imperial monies and a new allocation of territory which would have reduced Antigonus to the possession of little beside his original province of Central Phrygia. With this move they opened a war which they took fifteen years to bring to a decision. (Spring 315)

At the outset of this protracted struggle Antigonus possessed far greater resources than any one of his opponents. With a campaign fund of 25,000 talents and an estimated annual income of 11,000 talents, he could recruit and maintain in the field the largest armies of his day. Besides, he had that advantage of working on inner lines which was of such value to the Central Powers in the war of 1914–18. Antigonus' constant aim was to isolate his adversaries and to crush one at a time while keeping the others fixed. He began military operations with an attack upon Syria, with a view to securing the great naval resources of Phœnicia. But at the same time he launched a diplomatic offensive against Cassander, in the hope of fomenting rebellion in Macedonia and Greece. By way of impressing the Macedonians, he formally invited Cassander to stand trial for his behaviour to Alexander's mother and son. In order to seduce the Greeks he used the same device as Polyperchon, promising them self-government and freedom from garrisons, and he sent agent upon agent to raise local centres of resistance to Cassander. At the same time he stirred up trouble for Lysimachus among the Greek towns of his seaboard and the natives of the hinterland (p. 118).

Antigonus' campaign in Syria was no more than a half-success. Without difficulty he drove out Ptolemy, who had resumed possession since the departure of Eumenes, and occupied the country as far as Gaza. But he failed to secure the Phœnician fleet, which Ptolemy had removed betimes to Egypt. The island fortress of Tyre defied him for fourteen months, and he could not prevent Ptolemy from using his elusive navy to conquer Cyprus, which had previously lived in semi-detachment under its own kings. But once in control of Phœnicia Antigonus proceeded with characteristic vigour to build a large new fleet, which stood ready for action by autumn 314. As soon as his ships were ready, he transferred his main effort to his western front. He first acquired the

Cyclades group of islands, and in imitation of Alexander's methods formed them into a confederation which became his organ of control over them. By this conquest he also brought under his patronage the sanctuary of Apollo at Delos.[1]

In the ensuing year Antigonus intensified his propaganda on the Greek mainland and followed it up with troops and ships. At first his attack in this quarter achieved nothing more than local successes, for Cassander defended himself vigorously, and won goodwill by restoring the town of Thebes, thus undoing one of Alexander's worst mistakes. But in 313 Antigonus' generals carried the greater part of Peloponnesus. We may also trace back to Antigonus a rebellion in Cyrene, where Ptolemy's governor Ophellas established himself as an independent ruler in the same year. Yet these operations were mere diversions. Antigonus' main object was now to seek out Cassander in Macedonia, and for this critical attack he brought up his fleet and his strongest army to the Dardanelles. The mere threat of invasion induced Cassander to open negotiations, and the coalition against Antigonus would now have broken up, had not Cassander's allies stiffened him with fresh promises of support.

In failing to detach Cassander Antigonus lost his best chance of an early victory. On the resumption of hostilities his generals won for him the greater part of Central Greece and received a tentative offer of capitulation from Demetrius of Phalerum at Athens. But Antigonus himself never succeeded in crossing to Europe. On the Dardanelles he was foiled by Lysimachus, who brought up the reinforcements promised by him to Cassander, and he failed to repeat the turning movement which had given him victory over Polyperchon in 318, for on this occasion the Byzantines insisted upon complete neutrality and refused him facilities of transport. At the end of 313 the western front of the coalition had become ragged, but it remained unbroken at the vital points.

In 312 Antigonus was called away to his eastern sector. Here Ptolemy, having secured his hold on Cyprus, made a counter-move against Syria, where Antigonus had left his son Demetrius in command. He engaged Demetrius with superior forces and inflicted a heavy defeat upon him near Gaza. Demetrius, after a vain attempt to roll up one of Ptolemy's

[1] On Antigonus as a federalist, see A. Heuss, *Hermes*, 1938, p. 133 ff.

wings with his cavalry, ordered his elephants, in which arm he was superior, to break through the other flank. But Ptolemy, foreseeing this move, had planted a stout palisade, which checked the elephants and threw them into confusion.[1] A general rout ensued, which Demetrius could not arrest until he had lost all Syria. This reverse, it is true, was made good on the arrival of Antigonus, whom Ptolemy as usual declined to face in set battle. But before he fell back upon Egypt Ptolemy sent Seleucus forward with a small flying column to recover his province of Babylonia, and thus initiated a new movement which achieved results of lasting importance.

For a man who had held a high place in Alexander's retinue, Seleucus had since the king's death been relegated to strangely subordinate positions. In 323 he had been transferred to Perdiccas' staff, but remained in the background until he bore a part in the murder of the regent. For this deed—the only bad blot on his record—he was rewarded with the governorship of Babylon; but he was so ill provided with troops that he became little more than an onlooker in the great duel between Antigonus and Eumenes. In 312 he set out on what might appear a forlorn hope; but by the very audacity of his invasion he carried Babylon at slight cost, and thanks to his knowledge of the country, he was able to set a trap for Nicanor, Antigonus' generalissimo in the eastern provinces, and to capture most of his army. In 311 he momentarily lost Babylon to a raiding corps under Demetrius; but for some unknown reason Demetrius was recalled by his father before he could make good his gain. Seleucus therefore recovered Babylon, and confirmed his possession with a second victory over Nicanor.

While Seleucus was gaining solitary advantages in Babylonia, the other combatants confessed themselves at a deadlock, so that in 311 they came to an understanding. By this convention Lysimachus and Ptolemy were confirmed in their existing territories, and the Greek cities conserved their autonomy. Cassander was acknowledged as "general of Europe," with authority over Macedonia, Thessaly, most of Central Greece and part of Peloponnesus; but his title was

[1] A somewhat elliptic account of the battle of Gaza is given in Diodorus, XIX, 82–4.

to hold only until 305 B.C., the year in which Alexander IV would come of age. The ostensible purpose for which Antigonus agreed to this peace is expressed in an extant letter of his to the little Greek city of Scepsis in the Troad[1]: if he had thrown away a chance of crushing Ptolemy, and had given way to some hard bargaining on Cassander's part, the reason lay in his solicitude for the welfare and liberty of the Greek cities. These were not mere empty phrases, for Antigonus was far-sighted enough to realize that the Greeks were better allies than subjects, and he had forborne to secure with garrisons the cities from which he had ejected Cassander's forces. But his real purpose in coming to terms with the rest was in order to isolate Seleucus,[2] in whom he could discern his most dangerous adversary.

§ 4. THE YEARS OF UNEASY TRUCE

The pact of 311 was destined by its very nature to be a mere "Peace of Amiens," for the belligerents had not renounced their ambitions or abated their fears, but merely sought a breathing space to prepare for the next round. The history of the next four years moves tortuously in a maze of intrigues, recalling the truce in the Peloponnesian War after the Peace of Nicias.

One natural result of the peace was that Antigonus resumed hostilities against Seleucus. From 310 to 308 he fought a round of battles, of which no details have survived.[2] In any case, he failed to win any decisive advantage. Another logical consequence of the peace terms was that Cassander ended the imprisonment of Alexander IV and Roxane by putting them to death. The conditions of the treaty were a plain incitement to him not to await Alexander's coming of age. In 310 Alexander the Great's last male relative perished at the age of twelve.

In the same year a new train was fired by a nephew of Antigonus named Polemæus, who had served his uncle well during the previous campaigns on the Greek front, and had since received the province of Hellespontine Phrygia. Having

[1] For the text of this valuable inscription (which was discovered by Mr. J. A. R. Munro) see Ditt., *O.G.I.*, 5.

[2] See Appendix 3.

apparently expected a better award, Polemæus declared himself free from Antigonus and offered an alliance to Cassander, which the latter accepted. Antigonus, whose fleet was probably engaged in the Levant (see below), took no immediate steps against the deserter, and even allowed him to gain possession of the Cyclades ; but he resumed his diplomatic offensive against Cassander. For this purpose he enlisted Polyperchon, who had sunk from his regency to the level of a common *condottiere* and had recently campaigned in Peloponnesus under Antigonus' command. He was now provided by Antigonus with a fund to raise new troops, and with a lad of about seventeen years, Heracles by name, who was given out to be a son of Alexander and of the Persian princess Barsine.[1] Thus equipped, Polyperchon invaded Macedonia to set up a new king, and no doubt with the ulterior purpose of resuming his own regency. But the attempted checkmate of Cassander ended in the capture of Antigonus' knight. Cassander played upon Polyperchon's latent distrust of his employer, impressing upon him that Antigonus treated his colleagues as mere instruments, and offered him a safer post as his own representative in Peloponnesus. It sounds almost incredible that Polyperchon should have swallowed this bait ; yet he broke off the campaign against Cassander and finally stultified himself by murdering the pretender whom he had called to the throne. (309)

Having thus outwitted Antigonus, Cassander made no further move. But in the meantime Ptolemy had resumed active warfare against Antigonus. The immediate reason for Ptolemy's reappearance in the field may have been a belated desire to save Seleucus from the consequences of the recent peace, or a suspicion that Antigonus might be fomenting revolt against him in Cyprus ; but behind these motives we may detect Ptolemy's growing ambition to confirm and extend his thalassocracy. In 310 Ptolemy suppressed the last native king in Cyprus and definitely annexed the island to Egypt ; he seized new naval bases along the south coast of Asia Minor, and in the following year he occupied the island of Cos, thus acquiring a gateway into the Aegean Sea.

Once in Aegean waters, Ptolemy felt the lure of Greece.

[1] For proof that Heracles was supposititious see W. W. Tarn, *Journ. Hell. Stud.*, 1921, p. 18 ff.

Forgetting his habitual prudence, he thrust himself into the European war-zone. He answered an offer of alliance from Polemæus by inviting him to Cos and putting him to death on a pretended charge of treason. (309 or 308) From Cos he sailed to Delos, where he outbad Antigonus in his marks of attention to Apollo. But in addition to the lordship of the isles Ptolemy now aimed at hegemony in the Greek Homeland. This intrusion into the politics of Greece Proper was not altogether a new idea with him. In 314 he had replied to Antigonus' declaration of freedom for the Greeks with a counter-manifesto in which he made similar promises and sought to prove that Short, not Codlin, was the friend ; but this proclamation, not being backed up with a show of force, made no impression. He now made a landing at Corinth and assembled a congress of representatives from the Peloponnesian states, to whom he re-averred his intention of setting Greece free. But he coupled this promise with a request for aids in money and kind, and thus awakened doubts as to his real intentions. Moreover, he was but a casual visitor to Greece, and unlike Antigonus or Cassander he did not seem in a position to stay and enforce his demands. His Peloponnesian clients therefore voted him supplies but omitted to deliver them. Ptolemy met this rebuff by throwing garrisons into Corinth and Sicyon. But by this action he merely confirmed Greek suspicions of his good faith. Realizing that he had overreached himself, he presently cut his losses and vanished from the Aegean as suddenly as he had come, retaining nothing but the Isthmus towns, Cos, and a few positions in Caria. (308) His failure in Greece, however, was partly compensated by the recovery of Cyrene, which had been left without an overlord since the death of Ophellas in 309 (p. 170).

The political somersaults of Ptolemy in 309–8 may seem an irrelevant episode in our narrative. Yet in spite of their ill-success, they exerted a lasting influence on the foreign policy of his dynasty, and they had the immediate effect of re-arranging the Macedonian generals in their former alignment. By making his bid for power in Greece, Ptolemy had opened a frontal assault upon his former ally Cassander, for his proclamation of Greek liberty had no point, unless it was intended, like the previous manifestos of Antigonus, to incite the Greeks against Cassander's garrisons. Yet Cassander, who perhaps foresaw the futility of Ptolemy's gesture, took no overt action against his false friend. On the other hand, Ptolemy's plagiarism of Antigonus' political ideas was in the nature of a flank attack upon him. Moreover—and this no doubt was the decisive point—the growth of Ptolemy's naval power and ambitions was a direct menace to Antigonus, who understood no less clearly the importance of thalassocracy in Greek seas. In reply to Ptolemy's Aegean campaign Antigonus, who had held his hand in 309–8 because of his commitments on the Asiatic continent, suspended his warfare against Seleucus and prepared for a decisive encounter with the rival sea-king. At the same time he planned a new descent upon Greece, with a view to holding Cassander there.

§ 5. ATHENS UNDER DEMETRIUS OF PHALERUM

In 307 Antigonus' attack was opened by his son Demetrius, who now made his mark as the foremost successor of Alexander in his generation. From Ephesus Demetrius swooped across the Aegean with a rapidity recalling his father's tear-away expeditions in Asia Minor, entered the Piræus by surprise, and forced the garrison of Munychia into a speedy surrender. Having thus obtained virtual control of Athens, he offered the city an alliance on equal terms and as a pledge of his good faith dismantled the captured stronghold. With Cassander's garrison went his civil governor, Demetrius of Phalerum.

The ten years of this man's ascendancy in Athens provide our best example of practical administration by a Greek philosopher-king. True to his type, Demetrius of Phalerum was at pains to make Athens safe against democracy. With this end in view he added fresh constitutional safeguards to those which Antipater had imposed in 322.[1] He transferred to the Areopagus the punitive jurisdiction of the Board of Eleven; he instituted a board of seven Nomophylakes, whose "guardianship of the laws" carried with it a veto on legislation; to promote plain living he introduced a small corpus of

[1] The constitutional history of Athens in 322–317 is not altogether clear, and some uncertainty exists as to the apportionment of new legislation between Antipater and Demetrius. On the whole, the more fundamental reforms appear to have been due to Antipater.

sumptuary ordinances and appointed a body of Gynækonomoi to assist the Nomophylakes in enforcing these rules against the more determined offenders. On behalf of the wealthy and middle classes he abolished the system of "liturgies," by which the cost of particular public services was transferred from the treasury to individual taxpayers. As a pupil of Aristotle and friend of Theophrastus he brought order and system into the unwieldy mass of Athenian statutes by classifying them into a code, and he instituted a special bureau for the official registration of all land-transfers.[1] Under his régime Athens enjoyed a spell of material prosperity which recalled the happy days of Alexander's reign. In return for the boons which he conferred, Demetrius of Phalerum accepted statues and chaplets on a scale that could have brought blushes to the cheeks of Pericles.

Yet his popularity was not built on solid foundations. It was perhaps a minor matter that his laws on luxury were hardly needed in a community where popular opinion had long been an effective guardian of good taste, and that, good or bad, they were stultified by the un-Attic lavishness of his private life, and by his expenditure on public festivals, which outshone those of the democracy in its most extravagant days. It was but a negative criticism of his rule that the main source of Athenian welfare during his decennium lay not in him, but in the immunity from war which Athens enjoyed at the time. But this immunity was bought at the price of a foreign garrison. Nay more, Demetrius of Phalerum not merely acquiesced in this foreign occupation, which indeed he could not refuse, but by way of reaction from the occasional chauvinism of the democracy he prepared Athens for its future rôle as a neutral city, where academics and intellectually-minded *rentiers* might live in a Phæacian seclusion from political storms and stresses. To this rôle Athens took a long time to accommodate itself, for its traditions of hegemony still ran strong.

As soon, therefore, as Demetrius of Phalerum was gone, the Athenians restored their democracy, retaining only a few of his innovations, such as the land-registration and the abolition of liturgies. To the liberator Demetrius and to his father they

[1] Demetrius probably held a special office as νομοθέτης.—See S. H. Dow and A. H. Travis, *Hesperia*, 1943, p. 153 ff.

passed the most fulsome votes of thanks. They made father and son into eponymous heroes of two new tribes, Antigonis and Demetrias, a reform which obliged them to raise the numbers of their Council from 500 to 600 and to make other consequential changes. They accorded them various forms of divine worship, and they addressed them as "kings." For this excess of flattery the Athenians were afterwards severely criticized, and its chief instigator, Stratocles, thereby effectively condemned his own memory.[1] But their adulation, however extravagant in form, sprang in the first instance from a genuine sense of gratitude. Antigonus, moreover, at once turned his moral victory at Athens to practical account. He sent supplies of money and ship-timber, with which the Athenians partly repaired the wreck of their fleet, so that in the ensuing year they were able to contribute thirty vessels to Antigonus' navy. On the other hand, Antigonus, rightly judging that the material and moral damage accruing to Cassander from the loss of Athens would stay his arm for some time to come, withdrew Demetrius' force from Greece at the end of 307, and prepared to throw his whole weight upon Ptolemy.

§ 6. THE FOUNDATION OF THE NEW MONARCHIES

In the campaign of 306 Antigonus' main object was to cripple Ptolemy's fleet. With this end in view he sent Demetrius to attack Cyprus, which was the pivot of Ptolemy's naval power. Demetrius made an unopposed landing and invested Ptolemy's brother Menelaus in the city of Salamis. Ptolemy hereupon brought up his full force to disengage Menelaus, but suffered the completest defeat which one Greek fleet ever received at the hands of another on the high seas. At the battle of Salamis Demetrius with some 160 vessels had to face 200 or 210 enemy craft all told,[2] and his inferiority in numbers was but slightly offset by heavier tonnage. But, applying the tactics of Epaminondas and Alexander to naval warfare, he outweighted Ptolemy at the decisive point by taking the risk of a double defeat on less vital fronts. To keep

[1] On Demetrius' liberation of Athens and the refinements of adulation which the Athenians practised upon him see the lively account in Plutarch, *Demetrius*, chs. 8–13.

[2] On the numbers engaged at Salamis, see Appendix 4.

up the blockade of Menelaus in Salamis he detached a mere skeleton force of ten ships ; in the actual battle-line he allowed Ptolemy to overpower his inshore wing ; but by a great concentration of strength on the open-sea flank he made sure of victory there, and thus won the opportunity of rolling up the whole enemy line against the coast. At slight loss to himself he sank or captured all but twenty of Ptolemy's ships, and subsequently received the surrender of Menelaus' squadron.

This disaster cost Ptolemy all his overseas possessions and exposed him to a new attack in Egypt which had every prospect of meeting with better success than Perdiccas' invasion, for Demetrius' fleet was now at hand to turn the defences of the Nile. Antigonus, who at this time was busy transferring his capital from Celænæ to a new city named Antigoneia, on the lower Orontes (in northern Syria), now took the hint conveyed to him by the Athenians. He invited his army to confer the title of king upon himself and his son, thus formally claiming the succession to Alexander's sovereignty. By all the tokens Alexander's realm was about to be reunited under a stronger dynasty.

In autumn 306 Antigonus began his march upon Egypt. He had collected an army of 88,000 men—a larger muster than Alexander had ever put into the field—and had amassed abundant provisions and camel-transport for the passage of the Sinai desert. With Demetrius' fleet acting in concert, he seemed to be prepared for every contingency. But he had not reckoned with Boreas, the god of the north wind. In the Persian Wars this sudden ally had equalized chances for the Greeks by a surprise swoop upon Xerxes' navy ; in 306 he redressed the balance in Ptolemy's favour by sending a succession of gales which prevented Demetrius from landing in force upon the harbourless Egyptian coast. Thus Antigonus was left after all to carry the line of the Nile unaided. But the river was in flood, and could not be crossed without careful exploration. In the meantime the invaders' provisions had begun to run low, and colossal bribes by Ptolemy were luring the sorely tried troops to desertion. With Perdiccas' fate before his eyes, Antigonus retreated betimes into Syria.

Ptolemy's counter-offensive to Antigonus' expedition took the form of a political manifesto. In 305 he crossed Antigonus' claim to Alexander's undivided empire by taking the title of king for himself and inducing his allies, Cassander, Lysimachus and Seleucus, to follow suit.[1] This act had the same significance as Napoleon I's self-promotion to the rank of emperor, by which he killed the Holy Roman Empire. It formally proclaimed that Alexander's realm had perished with his dynasty, and it laid the foundations of a new international right, based on the coexistence of several lesser monarchies which recognized each other's legitimacy. As an outward sign of the new order, the kings presently issued personal coinages with their own names and portraits in place of Alexander's types.

§ 7. THE SIEGE OF RHODES

Despite his failure in Egypt, Antigonus still possessed the strategic initiative over his opponents, who had neglected to draw up any joint plan of campaign. But repeated disappointments in the hour of success and advancing age—for he was now close on eighty years—had abated his colossal energy. In 305, instead of resuming the offensive against one of his major antagonists, he sent Demetrius with his fleet and a supporting army against the city of Rhodes. With a burgess-roll of only 6000 men, this town might appear unworthy of Demetrius' undivided attention. But it possessed a flourishing trade (p. 299), a well-found fleet, and ample facilities for ship-building. In foreign politics the Rhodians endeavoured to preserve a friendly neutrality with all their neighbours. In 315–4 they had assisted Antigonus in his original Big Navy programme, but since the rise of the Ptolemaic thalassocracy they had held close intercourse with Egypt, and Antigonus now feared that they might help Ptolemy to repair his shattered fleet. For this reason he sent his son to overawe the republic into a formal alliance, and he would probably have gained his point without recourse to arms, had not Demetrius demanded hostages and insisted on the right to occupy the city-harbour. The Rhodians, who had jealously defended their liberties against the Athenian

[1] Since Ptolemy did not assume the diadem until November 305, a full year after Antigonus' retreat from Egypt, it may be assumed that he had previously conferred with his colleagues.

thalassocracy and had promptly ejected Alexander's garrison in 323, met Demetrius' summons with preparations for a siege.

Of all operations against Greek fortresses, the siege of Rhodes left the strongest impression upon Greek memory.[1] On both sides the fighting was hard and clean. In addition to the old-fashioned devices of ramming and undermining, Demetrius employed a formidable array of the most modern catapults and stone-hurling engines. His chief instrument of assault was the "Helepolis," a hundred-foot tower, which was armoured like a battleship and bristled with artillery. For the blockade of the port he utilized the whole of his war-fleet and further pressed into his service flotillas of pirates, who resented the interferences of the Rhodian patrol-squadrons with their freedom of the seas. But the Rhodians kept Demetrius' artillery out of effective range by resolute counter-battery work, or by setting fire to his engines; and their blockade-runners, reinforced by cornships from Ptolemy, Cassander and Lysimachus, kept up the town's supplies. Demetrius struggled on for a whole year and turned back successive embassies from Athens and other Greek states whose trade was being hurt by the siege. But he eventually accepted the good services of some Ætolian envoys, who brought him to terms with the Rhodians, on the understanding that they should support him against all enemies "except only Ptolemy." The siege thereupon ended in mutual compliments. (305–4) The title of "Besieger" which Demetrius derived from this investment does him both more and less than justice.

§ 8. THE BATTLE OF IPSUS

Demetrius' half-success at Rhodes made no difference to the war-situation, as measured by the map. But it wasted a year of Antigonus' time, and this at a juncture when the initiative was about to pass out of his hands. For the moment, indeed, no irreparable harm had been done to his cause. On Demetrius' departure from Greece Cassander had opened a "four years' war" against Athens, but he failed to recapture the

[1] A detailed account of the siege is preserved in Diodorus, XX, 81–88, 91–99.

city. With the material aids supplied by Antigonus and Demetrius, a new war-minister named Demochares, who inherited the administrative talents of his uncle Demosthenes, together with some of his gifts of speech, had restored the Athenian army to a respectable level of strength. In 305 a general named Olympiodorus had met an invasion of Attica by sailing round to Ætolia and raising a diversion in Cassander's rear, and having drawn his enemy into Phocis he had defeated him in battle at Elatea. Cassander was therefore unable to invest Athens before 304. But by the end of that year the city was being hard pressed, and at the same time Polyperchon, who was now fighting his last campaign under Cassander's flag, was recapturing for him the Peloponnesian towns which he had lost to Antigonus' generals since 314.

In autumn 304 Antigonus sent Demetrius back to Greece with forces for which Cassander was no match. In that year Demetrius relieved Athens and expelled Cassander from Central Greece ; in 303 he won over Corinth, which Ptolemy had in the meanwhile ceded to his ally, and carried most of northern and central Peloponnesus. After these sweeping successes he was able to bring into force a scheme which Antigonus had devised ten years before, of restoring the Hellenic Confederacy of Philip and Alexander. Unlike its prototype, the new league extended only as far as Thermopylæ, and it did not include Sparta or Messene ; but it probably comprised the confederation of the Cyclades. This restitution of the Hellenic League of 338 gave the crowning proof that Antigonus stood for a return from Antipater's and Cassander's policy of isolation and subjection to Philip's plan of an equal alliance between Macedon and a United States of Greece. The new federal constitution, it is true, conferred upon Demetrius special powers in time of war, as well as the right to garrison Corinth until the next peace, and he at once made unsparing use of his right of war-time conscription. But under conditions of peace it allowed the constituent states to choose their own chairmen and to draw up their own agenda paper. The federal parliament therefore was well fitted to become the school in which the Greeks might learn to "get together" and to outgrow the mutual jealousies which were the prime cause of their political failures. At the least, the league of 302 deserved a fuller trial than it got.[1]

Demetrius' conquests in Greece alarmed Cassander so much that he sued Antigonus for peace. But Antigonus, who evidently believed that he had fought the coalition to a standstill and could reduce Cassander at his leisure, would accept from him nothing short of complete surrender. Once more, as in 313, he lost his flood-tide. Cassander broke off the negotiations and made an urgent appeal to his allies. Despite difficulties of communication, all four members of the coalition came to an understanding; henceforth, instead of making isolated thrusts, they agreed to crush Antigonus by combined pressure.

The effects of their improved co-operation began to show in 302, when Demetrius resumed his offensive against Cassander. With the aid of his fleet he circumvented Thermopylæ and landed a force in Thessaly, where Cassander, having lent a division of his army to Lysimachus, was outnumbered by nearly two to one. But he failed to bring his adversary to battle, and ended by offering him an armistice. The reason for this tame ending to a critical campaign was that Demetrius had received a call from Antigonus to Asia Minor.

The sudden concentration of Antigonus' forces in Asia Minor was due to a surprise move by Lysimachus, who now made a belated but decisive entry into the field. Until the campaign of 302 Lysimachus had been little more than a sleeping partner in the coalition. His distinguished record of service on Alexander's staff had earned him the province of Thrace in 323; and this reward was no doubt the highest that a man of Thessalian origin (albeit an enfranchised Macedonian) could expect. But its resources lay as yet undeveloped, the natives of the hinterland remained restive, and the Greek cities of the seaboard were jealous of their independence. For twenty years Lysimachus was engaged in making himself master in his own house. But by 302 he had pacified the Thracians, had subdued most of the other Greek towns, while Byzantium preserved its friendly neutrality, and

[1] A large fragment of this constitution has been discovered by P. Cavvadias at the sanctuary of Epidaurus. For the text see *S. E. G.*, I, 75, and U. Wilcken, *Berichte Berliner Akademie*, 1927, p. 277 ff. Commentaries by M. Cary, *Class. Quart.*, 1923, p. 137 ff.; and J. A. O. Larsen, *Class. Philology*, 1925, p. 313 ff.; 1926, p. 52 ff.

by careful finance had amassed a considerable war-fund. With Cassander's help he was now able to launch a well-timed attack. Suddenly crossing the Dardanelles, he caught Antigonus' governors and the Greek maritime cities unawares, and overran western Asia Minor as far as Sardes and Ephesus. At the time of this unforeseen raid Antigonus was occupied with the inauguration of his new capital at Antigoneia. On receiving news of Lysimachus' advance he hurriedly paid off the artistes at the ceremony, sent a summons to his son, and hastened with his main force to Asia Minor. In summer 302 Lysimachus had to bear the brunt of a counter-attack delivered with superior numbers. After Demetrius' departure from Greece Cassander had sent him further reinforcements, but these had been mostly intercepted by Demetrius' fleet or shipwrecked in crossing the Black Sea.[1] He was therefore not in sufficient force to meet Antigonus in set battle ; yet for the rest of that season he held his adversary in a " Torres Vedras " campaign for which Greek History offers no parallel. Taking up his position in an entrenched camp at Dorylæum in Phrygia, he coolly allowed himself to be invested. When his supplies at last gave out he slipped away to another prepared position, and Antigonus' pursuit was checked by the autumn rains which were foundering the roads. By next year the odds had turned in favour of the coalition.

In 301 the allies had arranged to muster their full forces for a combined campaign. Early in the year Ptolemy advanced through Syria to join hands with Lysimachus. But he allowed himself to be flustered by a false rumour of a decisive victory by Antigonus over his colleagues and withdrew prematurely to Egypt. Yet his defection mattered little, for another partner of Lysimachus gave him better support. From 308, when Antigonus broke off his attack upon him, Seleucus almost disappears from history. For several years he fought a series of obscure wars against the governors of the upper provinces, all of whom he eventually brought under his authority, and against an Indian rajah named Chandragupta (p. 66). In fighting thus for his own hand Seleucus was in effect declaring himself free from the allies who had left him in the lurch in 311; but in 303 he rejoined the former coalition. Surrendering

[1] A naval action off Lampsacus, revealed in a new inscription, may be referred to this occasion. (Cary, *Journ. Hell. Stud.*, 1930, p. 253 f.)

his Indian lands to Chandragupta in return for a corps of elephants,[1] he set out on his westward march to disengage Lysimachus. In 302 Antigonus endeavoured to head him off with a flying column which temporarily broke into Babylon, but Seleucus no more allowed himself to be put off by this diversion than Frederick of Prussia by the Russian irruption into Berlin in 1760. In 301 he effected his junction with Lysimachus and brought Antigonus and Demetrius to battle at Ipsus in Central Phrygia. In this " battle of the nations," or rather, " of the dynasts," some 75,000 men took part on either side. Little is known of its course,[2] but it is fairly clear that the issue was decided by a blunder on Demetrius' part. After a successful charge with his mounted men Demetrius rode on and on, thus exposing the flank of his father's infantry, which was enfiladed by Seleucus' elephants and took to flight or surrendered. Hoping against hope for the return of his son, Antigonus remained on the field until he perished under a rain of missiles. With his death the second stage in the transition from Alexander's empire to the Hellenistic kingdoms comes to an end.

[1] The traditional number of 500 elephants is almost certainly exaggerated. Seleucus may have had 150 elephants with him.—(Tarn, *Journ. Hell. Stud.*, 1940, p. 84 ff.)

[2] The surviving portion of Diodorus' History breaks off on the eve of the battle of Ipsus.

CHAPTER III

THE ESTABLISHMENT OF A BALANCE OF POWER

§ 1. DEMETRIUS' FRESH START

AFTER the battle of Ipsus the reunion of Alexander's empire passed out of the sphere of practical politics, and the only task that appeared to remain for his successors was to consolidate the separate kingdoms which they had created out of its ruins. In recognition of this fact the victors of Ipsus agreed to partition his Asiatic dominions. Seleucus chose Syria for his share; Lysimachus obtained western and central Asia Minor. Cassander did not acquire any Asiatic territory for himself, but the southern coastlands of Asia Minor from Caria to Cilicia were carved off for his brother Pleistarchus into a buffer state resembling the Lotharingia of the Carolingians.

But, just as the mirage of Constantine's empire lured on Justinian, and the phantasm of Charlemagne's realm incited the Hohenstaufens, so the dream of Alexander's monarchy did not wholly fade from the minds of his successors; and in the division of territory after Ipsus there was material enough for fresh wars among the war-winners. A misunderstanding between Seleucus and Ptolemy arose immediately after the battle, when Seleucus entered into possession of Syria. He occupied the northern part of that country and transferred his capital from Babylon to a new foundation of his named Antioch, close by the abandoned site of Antigoneia. But he found that his claim to Phœnicia and southern Syria (also known as "Cœle-Syria"—see n. 2 to p. 82) had been jumped by Ptolemy. In view of his failure to appear at Ipsus Ptolemy's colleagues had refused to him all share in the spoils; but during the campaign of 301 he had reoccupied

Syria as far as the river Eleutherus. For the time being Seleucus did not press his claim, for he was loth to take up arms against his former protector. But in anticipation of future trouble Ptolemy sought insurance in matrimonial alliances with the other kings. To Lysimachus he gave Arsinoë, the daughter of his second queen, Berenice; upon Cassander's son Alexander he conferred Lysandra, a child of his previous consort, Eurydice.

Relations between the kings were further involved by the reappearance of Demetrius as their common rival. From Ipsus Demetrius had escaped with a mere fragment of his father's army. Returning to Greece, he found himself abandoned by all his allies, except where he had left a garrison. The first rebuff which he experienced came from the Athenians. The enthusiasm with which Demetrius had been received at Athens in 307 had since cooled down under the impression of his wanton habits, for Demetrius had taken his deification too seriously and during his winter sojourns in the city had rivalled Zeus in the number of his amours: in the words of a contemporary, "he had converted the house of the Virgin Goddess into a brothel."[1] Besides, the Athenians and his other Greek confederates had reason to fear that he might use the new Hellenic League to sanction further heavy drafts upon its man-power. Thus Demetrius found himself reduced to the possession of Corinth and a few lesser towns of Peloponnesus. On the other hand, he had kept his fleet intact, and with the help of this he retained his hold on the Cyclades and Cyprus, and on the chief cities of western Asia Minor and Phœnicia.

In 299 Demetrius was reintroduced into the circle of the Great Powers by Seleucus, who replied to Ptolemy's matrimonial deals by asking for the hand of Stratonice, the daughter of Demetrius and Phila. Thus assured of Seleucus' friendship, Demetrius turned upon Pleistarchus and recovered from him the southern coast of Asia Minor. (299 or 298) This was the end of Pleistarchus' short-lived realm; but a memorial of it survives in the fortifications of his capital at Heraclea-on-Latmus, which rival those of Messene as examples of Greek military architecture. Demetrius' attack upon

[1] These were the words of the comic poet Philippides, quoted by Plutarch *Demetrius*, ch. 26.

Pleistarchus was overlooked by Cassander, who was now probably verging upon his last illness, and by Ptolemy, with whom his patron Seleucus now came to a durable understanding.[1] But it had, strangely enough, the effect of embroiling him with Seleucus. Intent upon enlarging his sea-front, Seleucus claimed Tyre and Sidon from Demetrius as the price of his friendship, but was met with an angry refusal. For the moment, however, the quarrel was left unsettled, for in 296 Demetrius forgot Seleucus over a new adventure in Greece.

To the Greek Homeland the battle of Ipsus had brought a spell of almost unfettered liberty. In casting off Demetrius the Greek cities had not played themselves back into the hands of Cassander, for since Demetrius' departure from Greece in 302 Cassander had made no serious effort to recover lost ground, and in 299 he concluded a formal peace with Athens. But they lost the chance of taking the Hellenic League into their own hands and of establishing it as a permanent instrument for common action : no doubt the presence of Demetrius' garrison at Corinth and his command of the sea served them as a sufficient excuse for not making the attempt. But in allowing the United States of Greece to fall to pieces they gave away whatever chances they might have possessed of meeting Demetrius' impending attack. In 296 Demetrius, having attained a *modus vivendi* with the other kings, opened a new campaign in Greece with a descent upon Athens. This city was particularly ill prepared for defence. After the battle of Ipsus the Athenians had transferred their confidence from Demochares and Stratocles to a friend of Cassander named Lachares, who betrayed his trust in the following year by setting up a tyranny.[2] While maintaining the existing forms of the constitution and assuming no higher office than that of strategus or, more probably, strategus autocrator,

[1] Under date 296, Eusebius (*Chronicon*, II, 119) reports the capture by Demetrius of the town of Samaria. This is plainly a mistake, for in 296 Demetrius was fully employed elsewhere. But the error lies in the date rather than in the fact. The best solution is to transfer Demetrius' campaign in Palestine to 298. (Corradi, *Studi Ellenistici*, p. 40, n. 3.) But in any case, his expedition was a mere raid.

[2] Some new details of Lachares' career have recently come to light in a papyrus from Oxyrhynchus. For the fresh light which they throw upon Athenian history see W. S. Ferguson, *Classical Philology*, 1929, p. 1 ff.

he kept up a professional army of his own, and for fear of a counter-revolution he abolished the compulsory training of the citizens of hoplite census which Lycurgus had instituted after Chæroneia and even Demetrius of Phalerum had not wholly discouraged.[1] The Athenians therefore had to bear the brunt of Demetrius' assault without an efficient citizen-levy and without help from any other city; their only hope was in Ptolemy, who sent a fleet of 150 ships to their aid in 295, but failed to break the blockade of Demetrius' 300 men-of-war. Under such desperate conditions the Athenians nevertheless rallied round Lachares and fought with a tenacity recalling the last days of the Peloponnesian War. When funds ran short they allowed the despot to seize the temple treasures and even to melt down the gold from Pheidias' statue in the Parthenon; when supplies gave out they endured famine as doggedly as after Ægospotami. But in the end they were deserted by Lachares himself, who slipped through Demetrius' lines and left the city to arrange its own capitulation. Demetrius, having convoked the entire people to the theatre, staged his re-entry into Athens with a general pardon and prompt gifts of corn; but henceforth he treated it frankly as a subject community. Not content with reoccupying the castle of Munychia, he drafted a permanent garrison into the town of Piræus and built a new fortress on the Museum Hill overlooking Athens on the south side.

But in returning to Europe Demetrius had set his eyes on a greater prize than Athens and Greece. In 298 his old enemy Cassander had died prematurely of a wasting disease. He left behind him a bad reputation, for the Greeks remembered him as the ruler who held them down with garrisons, and the Macedonians as the murderer of Alexander's kin. Yet he had at least this great merit, that best of all his contemporaries he knew his own mind and how to limit his ambitions. He realized from the first that Philip's former dominion in Europe was large enough to absorb his energies, and eventually he acknowledged that Macedon alone required his whole attention. In his later years he gave Macedon a much needed

[1] Ferguson (*Hellenistic Athens*, p. 125 ff.) attributes the abolition of conscription to Lachares. Otto (*Göttingen Gelehrte Anzeigen*, 1914, p. 643 n.) tentatively assigns it to Demetrius of Phalerum. Ferguson's view seems virtually established by the phenomenal decline in the numbers of the ephebic corps, *c.* 300 B.C., which then sank from 800 to 30.

respite from war-demands; but his death threw the country back into the melting-pot.

§ 2. DEMETRIUS, KING OF MACEDON

After a brief reign by Cassander's eldest son, Philip IV, who had inherited his father's consumptiveness, the Macedonian realm was divided between his two other sons, Antipater and Alexander V, so that the elder brother received western Macedonia and Thessaly, the younger one the districts east of the river Axius. The blame for this blunder rested with Cassander's widow, Thessalonica, who set aside the Macedonian rule of primogeniture on behalf of her favourite child. She was herself the first victim of her intervention, and she left the Macedonians a legacy of civil war and foreign invasion. Her elder son asserted his rights by murdering her and making war upon his brother; the younger king defended his privilege by appealing in turn to Demetrius and to his neighbour, king Pyrrhus of Epirus. (295–4)

The monarchy of Epirus, which henceforth becomes an integral part of the Greek political system, was a state of recent creation. Until the close of the fourth century its constituent parts, the tribes of the Molossi (in the interior) and of the Chaones and Thesproti (on the northern and southern seaboards), had formed a loose confederacy under the precarious presidence of the Molossi. Compared with Macedon even a united Epirus was a power of the second class, for its folk, consisting of herdsmen rather than tillers, were neither as numerous nor as obedient to royal authority as their Macedonian neighbours. Yet under Pyrrhus Epirus for a while played a leading part in Hellenistic politics.

The stormy career of Pyrrhus began and ended in adventure. In early childhood he was driven out of Epirus in a revolution fomented by Cassander against his father Æacidas, in return for the assistance given by Æacidas to Cassander's enemy Olympias (p. 20). In 307 he was placed on his father's throne by another adversary of Cassander, Glaucias of Illyria (p. 124); but five years later he was again expelled in a rising of which Cassander no doubt was the prime instigator. For a time he took service under Demetrius, who gave him his baptism of fire at Ipsus and subsequently used him as his liaison officer with Ptolemy. But in 297 Ptolemy transferred him to his own staff and financed another coup in Epirus by which Pyrrhus definitely secured the royal power for himself and his house. At first, it is true, he had to share the throne with his cousin Neoptolemus, the nominee of Cassander and king in possession; but in 295 he got rid of an unwelcome and disloyal partner by murdering him at a banquet—a fitting prelude to the stratagem by which Demetrius acquired Macedon. By 294, when he received the call for aid from Alexander V of Macedon, Pyrrhus was firmly established in power. He went to Alexander's help and restored the balance of sovereignty between him and his elder brother. In return for his services he received back a strip of borderland which Philip of Macedon had taken from Epirus, together with the districts of Ambracia and Acarnania, which Cassander had recently acquired. Though Acarnania soon recovered its independence, Ambracia was retained as an Epirote possession to the end of Pyrrhus' dynasty, and the city of that name became his capital.

The call which Alexander had previously addressed to Demetrius was answered less promptly, for at the moment Demetrius was engaged in a campaign in Peloponnesus which gave him back most of the ground lost after Ipsus, and nearly put him into possession of Sparta. When at last he became free to proceed to Macedon the civil war there had been ended, and Alexander went to meet him in Thessaly and to thank him for nothing. Demetrius pretended to pocket his disappointment cheerfully, and prepared as if to return to Peloponnesus; but at a farewell banquet he suddenly gave orders for the murder of his guest.[1] Thereupon he took over Alexander's army, which readily accepted him as a stronger and hardly less legitimate ruler, and re-entering Macedonia with it he expelled Antipater from the western half of the kingdom. The exiled prince took refuge with Lysimachus, but for the moment received no active assistance from him. Thus Demetrius became seated on Cassander's throne. (294)

For his successes in Europe, it is true, Demetrius had to pay

[1] According to Plutarch (*Demetrius*, ch. 36), Demetrius anticipated a counter-plot by Alexander. This is likely enough. The circumstances of the banquet recall those described by Scott in *Quentin Durward*, when Louis XI entertained the Comte de Crèvecœur.

a price. Seleucus and Ptolemy, foreseeing a new danger to themselves in his reconquest of Greece, broke their treaty with him as soon as his back was turned, and made a pact with Lysimachus for the partition of his Asiatic possessions. Their desertion was well timed, for Demetrius, intent on the siege of Athens, had withdrawn his main fleet from Levantine waters and had left insufficient garrisons in the towns. At one blow Lysimachus won the western seaboard of Asia Minor, while Seleucus seized eastern Cilicia and Ptolemy helped himself to Cyprus and to the rest of the southern mainland coast. By these acquisitions East Cilicia was durably attached to the Seleucid realm, and Cyprus to that of the Ptolemies. For the time being Demetrius retained little else in Asia except Tyre and Sidon, and Ptolemy could now set about restoring the fleet which he had lost at Salamis. (296)

Even so, Demetrius retained the command of the sea, and Ptolemy's resurgent navy would not venture to engage him for the relief of Athens. Moreover, when he became king of Macedonia, he acquired the means of building up a greater land force than any of his rivals. In the next two years he extended his power by further conquests in Greece. In 293 he carried Thessaly (which made its last serious resistance to a Macedonian conqueror in the Lamian War) and Central Greece. He was now master of all the states of the Greek Homeland save Ætolia and Sparta. In Central Greece, to be sure, he had to contend against two successive risings of the Bœotians, who appeared to have recovered some of their old war-spirit under the restored leadership of Thebes.[1] In each of these campaigns Demetrius had to put Thebes under siege; but unlike Alexander in 335, he let off the rebels gently. (292 and 291)

In 289 Demetrius made an attempt to round off his European conquests with an attack upon Ætolia. With the consolidation of the Ætolian League, which had recently been converted from a loose concourse of tribes to a federation of cities (p. 283), its foreign policy was beginning to turn to systematic expansion. Its principal thrust was towards Thessaly and the Malian Gulf, so as to cut off Macedonian

[1] We still possess the epitaph of a Bœotian horseman who took part in eighteen charges in an action of the campaign of 292. (*Bull. Corresp. Hellénique*, 1900, p. 70.) A veritable Bœotian wild boar.

connection by land with central and southern Greece. About 300 the League had taken its first important stride by occupying Delphi.[1] In the same year and in 291 it gave support to the Bœotians and thus was drawn into conflict with Demetrius. In 289 it sustained an invasion by the Macedonian king, but was set free by Pyrrhus, who did not wish to be taken in flank by a westward extension of Demetrius' power. In a set battle on Ætolian territory Pyrrhus heavily defeated a general of Demetrius, thus establishing his own reputation as a tactician and releasing the Ætolians from all danger. But when he followed up this success with a raid into Macedonia, he was driven off with severe loss. Honours now being easy, Demetrius made peace with Pyrrhus and the Ætolians. The most durable result of Demetrius' recent conquests was the foundation of the fortress of Demetrias on the Gulf of Pagasæ, which became the starting-point of a new Macedonian line of communications to Chalcis and Corinth.

§ 3. THE ANABASIS OF DEMETRIUS

At the end of 289 B.C. Demetrius stood at the height of his power. His military establishment was comparable with that of Philip and Alexander before the Persian conquest; in naval strength he far surpassed them. But in order to raise his forces to this level he had to apply conscription in the most rigorous manner and to overstrain the resources of the countries governed by him. His military preparations, moreover, could not fail to awaken the apprehensions of his former antagonists. In 288 accordingly they agreed to forestall Demetrius' attack by a general offensive against him, and they invited Pyrrhus to join their coalition. Seleucus, indeed, could offer no active assistance against an opponent who lay out of his range; but Ptolemy undertook to stir up rebellion in Greece with his fleet, while Lysimachus and Pyrrhus jointly invaded Macedonia. In this scheme the part assigned to Lysimachus appeared the most hazardous: although a personal enemy as well as a political rival of Demetrius, Lysimachus had never ventured to cross swords with him on the Macedonian frontier. Yet the invaders

[1] For this date, see R. Flacelière, *Les Aitoliens à Delphes*, p. 50 ff.

actually gained their point without a struggle. When the Macedonians accepted Demetrius as their ruler, they had expected him to conform to the affable and unpretentious style of Macedonian kingship, and they had hoped that he would carry on the pacific policy of Cassander's latest years. By introducing among them the pomp and arrogance of Asiatic courts, and making fresh levies upon them in the style of Alexander, Demetrius forfeited their customary loyalty. At the outset of the campaign he established a front against Lysimachus, but an incipient mutiny warned him that at the first contact his army would melt away. He swung round to meet Pyrrhus, who meanwhile had advanced as far as Berœa. But even a foreigner like Pyrrhus now appealed to them more strongly than their king. A trickle of mutiny soon swelled into a stream, and to escape the fate of Eumenes Demetrius had to flee in disguise. The invaders partitioned Macedonia on the same lines as Antipater and Alexander V.

While Lysimachus and Pyrrhus were carrying Macedonia, Ptolemy's fleet entered the Aegean and gained an important albeit an isolated success. At Athens a peaceful revolution transferred power from Demetrius' new spokesman, Phædrus, and gave it back to Demochares and Olympiodorus. With a corruption fund provided by Ptolemy Demochares undermined the defences of the Museum Hill, and Olympiodorus easily effected its capture with an improvised citizen force. The Piræus, it is true, remained in Demetrius' hands; but in the absence of Demetrius' fleet Ptolemy's admiral revictualled Athens through other channels. (288)

Nevertheless, Demetrius recovered from this double blow. Apart from Athens he retained all his key positions in Greece, and he had nothing further to fear from Ptolemy's fleet, which quitted the Aegean as soon as Demetrius rallied his naval forces. In Thessaly and Central Greece he collected a new army, and he would without doubt have recaptured Athens, had not Pyrrhus hastened from Macedonia to its rescue[1]; and to compensate for the loss of Athens he obtained a treaty from Pyrrhus which guaranteed to him the remainder of his Greek possessions. At the end of 288 Demetrius' resources were still far greater than after the disaster at Ipsus. Besides,

[1] Presumably Pyrrhus circumvented Thermopylæ by marching through the territory of his Ætolian allies.

he could now afford to bide his time until the unstable coalition of the other kings should have fallen apart.

But Demetrius was not Antigonus. He had no patience to play the long game, and his heart was set on a new Anabasis. As soon as he had settled with Pyrrhus he swept together a force of 11,000 men, the utmost that he could spare at the moment from his Greek garrisons, and set sail for Asia Minor. In view of the dissensions which were already showing among his opponents, he had a reasonable hope that his army, backed by an invincible fleet, would at least restore to him the lost coastlands of Asia Minor. But he let himself be carried away by an initial success. After an unopposed landing at Miletus he gained several of the Ionian towns, whose allegiance to Lysimachus was reluctant, and captured Sardes, the gate of the continent. (287) In the next campaign Demetrius made his irretrievable mistake. He deliberately abandoned his communications with the Aegean seaboard and plunged into the hinterland of Asia Minor, with a vague intention of cutting through to Armenia and replenishing his forces, like a second Eumenes, from the eastern provinces. In making this move he threw away the command of the sea, which was his one solid asset, and staked all on the remote chance of fomenting rebellion in Seleucus' firmly established dominion.[1] Moreover, Demetrius failed to reckon with the uncertain temper of his men, who felt, like Cyrus' Ten Thousand, that they were being expatriated on false pretences, or with the strategic ability of Lysimachus' son, Agathocles, who had inherited his father's talent for running warfare and now displayed his skill by shadowing Demetrius and heading him off Armenia. With a disgruntled and half-famished army, he abandoned his march and drifted across Mt. Taurus into Cilicia. Here he gained some delusive successes against Seleucus, who feared to grasp his nettle and played with the idea of negotiations. But eventually Demetrius was beaten by his own men, who deserted in ever-increasing numbers to Seleucus. In spring 285, with a mere handful of troops remaining to him, he made his capitulation. Seleucus treated him well and spoke him fair. Had Demetrius lived longer,

[1] Demetrius' strategy in 286 recalls the irruption into Asia Minor by Sextus Pompeius after the battle of Naulochus. But in 35 B.C. Sextus had at least the excuse of being no longer a thalassocrat.

his captor might yet have released him for a further trial of strength against his doubtful ally, Lysimachus. But Demetrius, unable to bear a spell of enforced idleness, drank himself to death.

Among Alexander's successors Demetrius was the one who, on a superficial view, might seem most worthy to wear the great king's mantle. As a man, he possessed the same zest for life and the same personal charm. He displayed a like boldness of tactics and an equal resilience from misfortune. On the other hand, unlike Alexander, he was nothing but a general. Himself the son of the ablest organizer among Alexander's marshals, he could not endure the drudgery of administrative work, and therefore could not consolidate his conquests. If his relatively harmless love of pomp united him with Alexander, his scandalous licentiousness offered a most damaging contrast. Yet all these weaknesses might not have ruined his career, had he, like Alexander, been able to tie victory to his chariot-wheels. However, if Demetrius could strike hard, he lacked the equally important power of holding his hand. By his impetuosity he lost the battle of Ipsus and made a certain fiasco of his last campaign in Asia Minor. Demetrius could therefore not be considered seriously as the founder of a new imperial dynasty. In the politics of his day he was merely a disturbing factor, and the Greek world could never regain its equilibrium so long as he lurched out of one adventure into the next.

§ 4. THE RISE OF LYSIMACHUS

In the final partition of Demetrius' dominions his antagonists did not take any agreed measures, but helped themselves severally as occasion offered, and received very unequal shares. Seleucus, the captor of Demetrius, was for the time being content with this prize, and acquired no fresh territory. Ptolemy, who had sat still since 288, caught a big plum in his lap, when Demetrius' admiral, Philocles, surrendered to him the greater part of the captive king's fleet, and thus conferred upon him without a struggle the thalassocracy for which he had contended during the past thirty years. This windfall also carried with it the acquisition of Sidon (Philocles' native city) and Tyre, and of the Cyclades, where a change of rulers was highly welcome, in view of Demetrius' heavy exactions.[1] To this period we may also assign Ptolemy's establishment of a naval base at Itanus in eastern Crete, which was the most permanent possession of his dynasty in the Aegean area.

In the Greek Homeland Demetrius had left his son by Phila, Antigonus Gonatas, with a skeleton army and a few warships. With such slender resources Gonatas (as we shall henceforward call him) could not hold his own after his father's capture. Egged on by Lysimachus and Ptolemy, who sent gifts of corn and money, the Athenians made two successive attacks upon Gonatas' garrison in the Piræus. The first attempt was a disastrous failure, thanks to the loyalty of Gonatas' governor, who shammed traitor and opened the gates of the harbour, but only to close them behind the in-rushing Athenians and to slaughter all who had been caught in his trap. In the following year, however, Olympiodorus won his triple crown by taking Piræus in an open attack. (286–5) A worse loss befell Gonatas in Thessaly, where Pyrrhus made a surprise assault upon him in 286. His irruption was in direct contravention of the compact made by him with Demetrius in 288 (p. 50); but Lysimachus had convinced him that the treaty contracted by him earlier in that year with Demetrius' enemies was a prior charge upon his conscience. Gonatas rated his present chances against Pyrrhus so low, that he ceded to him the rest of Thessaly in return for the unmolested possession of Demetrias. In addition to this fortress, Gonatas retained of his father's heritage Bœotia, Eubœa, and the larger part of Peloponnesus. After his seizure of Thessaly Pyrrhus held a territory extending from the Adriatic to the river Axius and the Gulf of Pagasæ. For the moment he was the most powerful monarch in the European part of Alexander's empire. But his rule over this extended territory lasted barely a year. The complaisance which Lysimachus had shown to him since the two kings became neighbours in Macedonia was based on nothing but fear of Demetrius. He was but playing Pyrrhus for his own ultimate gain, and at the news of Demetrius' death he lost no time in throwing off the mask of friendship. In an

[1] The early popularity of Ptolemaic rule in the Cyclades is plainly illustrated by Ditt., *Syll.*, 390, which records the abatement of tribute under the new régime.

open fight Lysimachus might have found his rival more than a match for himself; but true to his bent for winning campaigns without battles, he attacked Pyrrhus by guerilla warfare and by diplomatic siege-work. Pyrrhus, who had the disadvantage of being not merely a usurper but a stranger in Macedon, found his army being charmed away from him as surely as he had seduced Demetrius' men in 288. He withdrew to Epirus, and for the next ten years lost interest in Greek affairs. Lysimachus thereupon gathered western Macedonia and Thessaly into his hands; at the same time he detached Acarnania from Pyrrhus and induced the Ætolians to transfer their friendship to him.

In 285 B.C. the political situation in the Greek world was simpler than for many years before or after. If exception be made of the attenuated dominions of Pyrrhus and Gonatas, and of a few territories of independent city-states, Alexander's empire was now cleanly divided between three of his former officers, Ptolemy, Seleucus and Lysimachus. Of these Ptolemy alone possessed a strong fleet; but on land Lysimachus had become the most powerful. In Europe, where his dominions extended from the Danube to Thermopylæ, he had a better recruiting field than any previous successor of Alexander. From Asia Minor, in which he possessed the centre and the valuable western coast, and from the Black Sea region, where he had acquired Heraclea and possibly Sinope in addition to the Balkan seaboard, he derived an ample revenue. Since Lysimachus never wasted a penny in peacetime, nor in war a soldier, he had accumulated a substantial capital in men and money. Yet between the three kingdoms there was an approximate parity of resources, pointing to the maintenance of a triangular balance of power among them.

§ 5. THE PASSING AWAY OF ALEXANDER'S MARSHALS

By 285 B.C. the surviving marshals of Alexander had outlived their king by a whole generation, and had passed their seventieth year. Yet only one of them had made definite arrangements for the succession. In 292 Seleucus had taken Antiochus, his son by Apama, into partnership, and had made over to him his own second consort, Stratonice. The old king did not marry again, and at his death Antiochus held an undisputed title to the throne. But neither Ptolemy nor Lysimachus adhered to a consistent dynastic policy. On his first arrival in Egypt Ptolemy had taken to wife a descendant of the last native Pharaoh, Nectanebo,[1] but in 321 he supplanted her by Antipater's daughter, Eurydice (p. 13), whose son, usually named Ptolemy Ceraunus, became heir apparent. In old age he succumbed to an intrigue by his mistress Berenice, who beguiled him into dismissing Eurydice and disappointing Ptolemy Ceraunus, so that she might become queen and a son whom she had previously borne out of wedlock, Ptolemy II or Philadelphus,[2] might be made Crown Prince. In the hope of placing the succession beyond dispute, Ptolemy formally appointed Philadelphus as joint-king in 285,[3] and he had the good fortune to see Ceraunus leave Egypt to try his fortunes at another court. In 283 he died quietly, and Philadelphus took over unchallenged.

But in Lysimachus' realm a similar dynastic history ended in catastrophe. In common with all the kings of the period, Lysimachus had begun by making marriages for purely political reasons, but like Ptolemy, he finally let policy be deflected by sentiment. His first match was with Antipater's daughter, Nicæa (p. 13); after Nicæa's death he had espoused a Persian lady named Amestris, the widow of a tyrant of Heraclea, in order to gain possession of this important city; after the battle of Ipsus he had sent Amestris away for the sake of a closer connexion with Ptolemy. His third wife, Arsinoë II, was the most remarkable of the earlier Hellenistic queens. To the masculine strength of will and ambition which she shared with other Macedonian princesses she added a peculiar diplomatic ability, the birth-gift of her mother, Berenice. Having given Lysimachus three sons, she determined that one of these should be his successor. But

[1] On this marriage see Tarn, *Class. Quart.*, 1929, p. 138.

[2] In this book the convenient modern system of attaching numerals to kings of like name will be followed. In Hellenistic times such kings were usually distinguished by surnames. They commonly received an official surname derived from their cults before or after death (the name of Philadelphus being conferred posthumously); but these titles were sometimes displaced in common usage by popular nicknames.

[3] It is sometimes stated that Ptolemy I actually retired in favour of the Crown Prince. But papyri of 284–3 still date by him as reigning king. (*P. Elephantine*, 3 and 4.)

the claims of the king's eldest son, Agathocles (by Nicæa), could not be lightly set aside : not only was he far older than Arsinoë's children, but he had proved his worth and was highly popular. Yet Arsinoë eventually carried her point. She contrived so to poison the mind of the ageing king that he put Agathocles to death on the suspicion of treason. (283) To the murmurs which Agathocles' execution evoked among his partisans the king replied with a reign of terror after the fashion of a Roman Cæsar, but in so doing he merely spread the unrest. Among the Greeks in his dominions Lysimachus had not achieved popularity. He had treated them as subjects, imposing garrisons upon them and intervening in their local affairs, and had taxed them severely. Under the added impression of his savage reprisals the Greek cities were growing ripe for rebellion.

In addition, Lysimachus had long been on strained terms with Seleucus. The partition after the battle of Ipsus had harboured the germs of future disputes, for by setting Lysimachus astride of Asia Minor from north to south it had shut off Seleucus from the western coastlands and had thus denied him an extension of his sea-front to the Mediterranean. Thenceforward Seleucus had shown an ill-concealed dislike of Lysimachus. Like his rival, he knew how to bide his time, and for many years he made no overt move. But in 282, at the instigation of refugees from Lysimachus' court and of discontented officers in his army, he advanced in force across Asia Minor. Governor after governor opened the gates to the invader, so that by 281 most of Asia Minor was in his hands. With his European levies Lysimachus endeavoured to retrieve his losses in a set battle, but on the field of Corupedium (near Magnesia-ad-Sipylum) he sustained a complete defeat. Like Antigonus at Ipsus, he died fighting.

The ease with which Seleucus had carried Asia Minor and the anarchy at Lysimachus' court led him on to claim the dead king's European dominions and the crown of Macedon.[1] No further army could bar his progress ; indeed, given time,

[1] The question whether Seleucus was actually proclaimed king of Macedon has been much discussed. Evidence for such a proclamation has been found in a Babylonian tablet of 269 B.C., in which he is described as "king of Macedon." But this Babylonian titulature hardly weighs against the complete silence of our literary authorities. For a recent review of the dispute see Corradi, *Studi Ellenistici*, p. 91-2.

he could now hope to win Greece into the bargain. Once more, for a moment, the reunion of Alexander's empire seemed to be emerging from dreamland. But at best Seleucus could not reckon on a term of life sufficient to round off his conquests. Besides, he was not the only candidate for the Macedonian throne.

When Ptolemy Ceraunus left Egypt, he first repaired to Seleucus' court and obtained from him a promise of reinstatement. But Seleucus was perhaps not in earnest, and certainly did not intend to precipitate a conflict with Egypt in the lifetime of Ptolemy I. Ceraunus therefore passed on to Lysimachus, but met with no better fortune there, for Lysimachus was equally determined to maintain good relations with Egypt and recognized Philadelphus' claims to the succession by giving him the hand of his daughter by Nicæa, Arsinoë I. Nevertheless, Ceraunus stayed on with Lysimachus. During the lifetime of his host he never had a prospect of succeeding him on the Macedonian throne, and there is no evidence of his having abetted Arsinoë II against Agathocles. But after the battle of Corupedium he set up a counter-claim against Seleucus, and he enforced it by methods of which he became the most finished exponent among Alexander's successors. Early in 280, when Seleucus crossed the Dardanelles on the way to Lysimachus' capital, Lysimachia, he stabbed him with his own hand as he stepped out of the boat.

Seleucus was the founder of the kingdom which bore most resemblance to Alexander's empire, and he may be accounted the most successful of his marshals. His good fortune rested not so much on his military ability, which does not appear to have been outstanding, as on his statesmanship. Despite the part which he took in the murder of Perdiccas, he was reckoned the "justest" of Alexander's successors.[1] Along with Antigonus he came closest to Alexander in political acumen, and in his government he applied two of Alexander's guiding principles, that the Macedonian conquests in Asia could only be preserved by conciliation of the natives and by the founding of Greek colonies in their midst. He was the last survivor among Alexander's high officers, and with his death we pass over to a new generation which knew not Alexander.

[1] Pausanias, I, 16, 3.

§ 6. THE GALATIAN INVASION

Once rid of Seleucus, Ceraunus had no difficulty in obtaining Macedonia and Thrace for himself. He incorporated Seleucus' field force, which had been left leaderless, and was acknowledged by Lysimachus' army, which had known him as an officer: his descent (by his mother Eurydice) from Antipater no doubt made him acceptable to the Macedonians. Outside of Macedonia, it is true, there were three kings who might establish a counter-claim: Seleucus' son, Antiochus, as heir to his father's policy; Gonatas, as son of king Demetrius; and Pyrrhus, on the ground of former possession. But Antiochus was fully absorbed in defending himself against attacks elsewhere (p. 83 ff.); and Pyrrhus, who was now giving his whole mind to his forthcoming expedition to Italy, waived his claims to Macedonia in return for a small auxiliary corps from Ceraunus (p. 179). Gonatas alone tried conclusions with the new king; but his fleet was not a match for the combined squadrons of Lysimachus and of the allied city of Heraclea, which Ceraunus had at his disposal, and one defeat sufficed to raise such trouble for him in the Greek Homeland (p. 127), that during Ceraunus' lifetime, at all events, he could not return to the charge. There remained Lysimachus' widow, Arsinoë II, Ceraunus' own half-sister, who had retired to Cassander's former capital, Cassandreia, taking her three sons with her. Ceraunus disarmed her suspicions by asking her in marriage and promising the succession to her eldest son. On these terms Ceraunus became Arsinoë's second husband; but shortly after his admission into Cassandreia he had the two younger boys murdered.[1] The eldest son, Ptolemy by name, was not present to share his brothers' fate, and Arsinoë made good her escape. We shall presently find her wearing a third crown, and forming fresh schemes on behalf of her surviving son (p. 84).

Ceraunus now appeared to be securely seated on Lysimachus' throne. Yet his reign lasted barely one year. In 279 he had to bear the brunt of an attack which marks the

[1] Various sensational details in the story of these murders, as given by Justin (bk. 24, ch. 3), have been omitted from the present narrative. Ceraunus' brutality evidently stimulated the fancy of the Romantic school of Hellenistic historians.

opening of a fresh chapter in Greek history. Ever since the Dorian Invasion the Greeks had been exempt from invasion by wandering European peoples: for many centuries they had looked to Asia as the only seat of danger. But now that Alexander had ended the Asian peril, the Greek world received its first warning that it must keep a sharp watch on its European front.

Ceraunus' novel enemies were an offshoot of the Celtic peoples, who had begun to drift about 400 B.C. from the Alpine borders towards the Middle and Lower Danube. Isolated Celtic detachments had come into contact with Alexander in Illyria, and with Cassander and Lysimachus on the frontiers of Macedonia. But the first attack in force was delivered in 279, when three separate war-bands broke into Macedonia and Thrace. In the objects and methods of their warfare the "Galatians," as the Greeks came to call these eastern Celts, bore a close resemblance to the Gauls of France and Italy.[1] Though they had set out originally in quest of new lands for settlement—for which purpose they brought their families with them—during their wanderings they developed habits of plunder and blackmail. With the exception of the chiefs, the Galatians were poorly armed; they had little military training; they could move only as fast as their families and their loot would allow them. But on first contact they overawed the Macedonians and Greeks in much the same way as the Gauls unnerved the Italians. With their giant limbs, their impetuous onslaught, and the terrifying swoop of their two-handed broadswords they won a sudden reputation for being irresistible in close battle. Though it is probable that none of their war-bands much exceeded 20,000 men, rumour swelled their numbers to 300,000.

Early in 279 a Galatian division under a chieftain named Bolgius entered Macedonia from the west or north-west and demanded a danegeld of Ceraunus. The Macedonian king hurried out to battle without even waiting to call up all his men from their winter-quarters. The result was a Greek "battle of the Allia." Ceraunus himself was captured and decapitated. His death rid the Greek world of the most unscrupulous adventurer of an unsettled age, but it exposed

[1] On the vexed topic of the relation of the Galatians to the other Celts, see J. M. de Navarro, *Cambr. Anc. Hist.*, VII, p. 56 ff.

Macedonia to anarchy. The remnants of his army rapidly made and unmade two new kings, a brother of Ceraunus named Meleager, and a nephew of Cassander named Antipater, and eventually rallied under a Macedonian noble named Sosthenes, who refused the diadem and ranked as a plain general. For the next two years Macedonia had no government save that which its individual cities were able to provide for themselves. Behind their walls the inhabitants of the towns stood safe, for the Galatians lacked patience and skill for siegecraft; but the open country lay continuously at their mercy. Bolgius' band indeed was not unsuccessfully harassed by Sosthenes, and presently retired with its loot to Illyria, where it finally settled down or dispersed. But meanwhile another detachment under a chief named Brennus entered Macedon by the Axius valley and drove Sosthenes out of the field.

Having thoroughly gutted Macedonia, Brennus pressed on into Greece. At the time of his invasion the Greek Homeland had all but recovered its independence. Returning from his defeat at the hands of Ceraunus (p. 58), Gonatas had been greeted with wholesale defection in Peloponnesus and Central Greece, so that by 279 he had been reduced to a tiny and scattered domain, of which Demetrias, Corinth and Piræus (recovered from Athens in 281) were the key points. As in the days of Xerxes' invasion, Greece consisted of a cluster of free cities and federations. Once again some of these states abstained and the rest co-operated ill, but the campaign was won by the valour of particular contingents. In Thessaly not even an attempt at common defence was made, and the landed aristocracies paid Brennus off or incited him to find richer plunder elsewhere. As in 480, the Greeks made their first stand at Thermopylæ, but with a force of far different composition. With the single exception of Patræ, the Peloponnesian cities kept their heads within their shells, trusting to the Isthmus lines, which the Galatians had no means of turning by sea. The Athenians contributed a generalissimo named Callippus, but only 1500 men. On the other hand, to say nothing of the lesser contingents from Central Greece, the Bœotians sent full ten thousand, and the Ætolians rather more. The total army of defence thus fell little short of 30,000—a force amply sufficient to hold the pass. But it was outmanœuvred by Brennus, who detached the Ætolians by sending a flying column up the Spercheius valley to raid their country, and also repeated the turning operation of Xerxes across the ridge of Mt. Callidromus ; and the garrison in the defile did not stay to emulate the exploits of Leonidas. With the roads on either side of Parnassus now open to him, the Galatian chief made for Delphi, which was no doubt the main objective of his invasion. Though Greek tradition is not clear on this point, it is probable that Brennus' force entered the sanctuary, but was promptly driven out again.[1] A small Greek detachment, consisting mostly of Phocians, hung on the invaders' heels, and a thunderstorm followed by driving snow—for the season was now midwinter—and reinforced by cascades of rocks from Mt. Parnassus, drove the Galatians back in panic. Their retreat was of course attributed by Delphic legend to divine intervention, and stories were told of local heroes and two armed maidens who cheered the defenders like angels of Mons. In the meantime the Galatian flying column had broken across Mt. Œta into the Ætolian village of Callium and butchered its inhabitants ; but they were presently caught up by the Ætolian troops, who sniped them unmercifully in the retreat. Eventually the Galatian inroad resolved itself into a headlong rout, in which Brennus took his own life. The remnant of the invaders passed on through Macedonia to Thrace.[2]

The third of the Galatian columns made straight for Thrace, which in 278 became a rallying-ground for the invaders. One section took up its abode here permanently (p. 118) ; the others moved on across the Dardanelles and Bosporus into Asia Minor, where the king of Bithynia hired their services in a domestic war (pp. 97–8). This contract ended, the Galatians

[1] Though several ancient authors imply that the Galatians did not reach the sanctuary, and a contemporary inscription from Cos (Ditt., *Syll.*, 398) speaks of it as having been " kept safe right through " (διαπεφυλάχθαι), other writers assert that it suffered pillage. It is safer to assume that the invaders got in, for an episode of this kind might be hushed up but would hardly be invented. On the other hand it is certain that they were not given time to plunder systematically. On a terra-cotta frieze at Bologna (A. W. Lawrence, *Later Greek Sculpture*, plate 94b) the Gauls are represented as dropping their loot under stress of a counter-attack by Apollo in person. For a full discussion see Th. Reinach and R. Herzog, *Comptes Rendus Acad. Inscrs.*, 1904, p. 158 ff.

[2] A detailed and generally trustworthy account of Brennus' invasion is preserved in Pausanias, X, 19–23.

resumed their marauding expeditions, covering all Asia Minor from the Bosporus to the Mæander, and making frequent descents upon the rich territories of the Greek coastlands. Though they failed, as usual, to carry the towns, they encountered no organized opposition, save from isolated levies of Greek cities, or from bands of Greek volunteers who did not give way to the general panic.[1] In 277 or 276 they revenged themselves upon Apollo for their defeat at Delphi by raiding his temple at Didyma near Miletus.[2] In the former of these years king Antiochus brought an army to Sardes, but in 276 he was called back to Syria by the outbreak of another war (pp. 83–4). In 275 he returned to Asia Minor and won the first set battle over the invaders (at an unknown site). He owed this success to a small corps of elephants, who threw the horses of the enemy scythe-chariots into confusion and turned them back upon their infantry. With this victory the Galatian peril was by no means ended; but the "elephant battle" marks the beginning of the process by which the invaders were gradually forced back on to the plateau of Phrygia, where they eventually settled down (p. 99).

For Macedonia the Galatian invasions had two permanent consequences. They deprived it of Thrace and cut it off from the Black Sea; on the other hand, they provided it with a new and enduring dynasty. The founder of this line of kings was Demetrius' son, Antigonus Gonatas. Despite his failure in 280 (p. 58), Gonatas had kept up his claim to his father's dominions. In 279 he took advantage of the anarchy in the Balkan lands to acquire a base of operations in the Gallipoli peninsula, but for two years he failed to get a foothold in Macedonia. In 277, however, he happened on a large detachment of Galatian marauders from Thrace and succeeded in destroying them in an ambuscade, while they were plundering a camp which he had relinquished as a bait. By this chance victory Gonatas suddenly leapt into fame, and on returning to Macedon he was acclaimed king by the remnants of Sosthenes' forces, who had recently lost their leader. With this

[1] The horror and loathing with which the Galatian bands were regarded among the Asiatic Greeks is reflected in a contemporary decree of Priene in honour of a citizen who had improvised a volunteer defence force and headed off the marauders. (*Priene*, 17.)

[2] W. Otto, *Beiträge zur Seleukidengeschichte*, p. 20. (On the evidence of an unpublished inscription.)

force and some Galatian stragglers whom he took into his pay, he drove out the ex-king Antipater (Cassander's nephew) and Ptolemy the son of Arsinoë II, recovered Thessaly and stormed Cassandreia, the only Macedonian town which stood out against him. (276–5) Thus Macedonia, which since the death of Cassander had been a prey to every adventurer, found a king who could keep his throne.

§ 7. RETROSPECT

The year 275 may be taken as marking the end of the long period during which the fragments of Alexander's empire were being heaved and tossed in the melting-pot. Looking back upon the half-century from his death, we may feel tempted to condemn it as the biggest and worst blot on Greek history. On first reading it leaves a paramount impression of endless and meaningless collisions between self-seeking adventurers, who had no aim but their own aggrandizement and recoiled from no crime in pursuit thereof; of wars that breed new wars, and of battles that decide nothing; of Greek cities deprived of their liberty, crushed by conscription and taxation, or dragooned by mercenary garrisons; of pirates combing the seas and barbarian marauders holding the lands to ransom.

On further study this impression will be confirmed at some points and modified at others. It cannot be denied that Alexander's successors generally fought for their own hand, that they were disloyal to his dynasty; that they stooped to intrigue and murder, and with rare exceptions were utterly cynical in their family relations. Against this may be set their extraordinary virility, their refusal to accept final defeat, and, in some instances, an organizing ability of no mean order. But the real test of the period lies not so much in its principal personalities as in its broad effect upon Alexander's empire. Beyond question its warfare entailed a severe strain upon the Macedonians and Greeks, from whom the contending armies were mainly recruited; and the general instability of the times no doubt acted as a brake on economic development and on mental activity. From these points of view the suddenness of Alexander's death and the lack of a competent successor in his family may be accounted a serious misfortune to his empire. Yet the horrors of the period may easily be overdrawn. Though its armaments were large and its wars incessant, its casualty lists were comparatively slight. The generals fought too scientifically to indulge in useless slaughter and the troops readily granted quarter; and when cities were captured no wholesale executions or enslavements followed (p. 242). Though many Greek towns were subjected to garrisons, in outward form at least their autonomy was usually respected and commands were often conveyed in the form of requests.[1] The costs of the campaigns, moreover, were not wholly met by taxation, but were in some measure defrayed from the accumulated war-treasures of Alexander.

Finally, it must be acknowledged that the break-up of Alexander's empire was in itself desirable. As a mere police-state it might possibly have held together, so as to constitute the Sixth Great Oriental Monarchy with a European annexe. But none save Alexander, probably not even Alexander, could have shouldered the immense task of developing its resources and fostering its culture from one centre of government. The partition of his dominions was therefore a requisite of future good administration; and the main lines of its division, out of which emerged one first-class power on each continent, were in general accord with geographic conditions. The year 275 B.C. was not too late for a fresh start under more hopeful auspices, and if Greek history nevertheless followed a wrong course, the blame for this must rest mainly on the successors of the successors.

[1] E.g. in the rescript of Antigonus to Lebedus and Teos, which he reconstituted into one community. (Ditt., *Syll.*, 344.) He repeatedly issues his injunctions under the saving formula 'οἰόμεθα δεῖν.'

Decrees in honour of garrison commanders who kept their forces under good discipline are not uncommon in this or in later periods. E.g. Ditt., *Syll.*, 331 (Ægosthena); *Priene*, 20–23; Hicks, 188–9 (Megara and Ægina).

CHAPTER IV

THE FARTHER EAST

§ 1. PRINCIPLES OF DIVISION

A HISTORY of Alexander's empire in the first half-century after his death must perforce treat of that empire as a whole. It will not bear subdivision into independent records of particular dynasties or countries, for not until 275 B.C. had the new political units crystallized out of the boiling mass. Even after that date it is not easy to follow out separately the fortunes of each succession-state, for it was only after the Roman conquest that Alexander's world became thoroughly hard-set. In the meantime, new principalities still decomposed out of those already established, and frontiers continued to undergo frequent and violent fluctuations. On the whole the most convenient and perspicuous method of carrying the narrative down to the Roman conquest is to group the facts in the form of regional surveys. In the following seven chapters the history of the Greek world down to about 200 B.C. will be reviewed district by district, in a series progressing from east to west.

§ 2. INDIA TO 250 B.C.

The frontier of Alexander's empire in the Far East was formed by the Indus and its tributary the Hyphasis (Beas). The district enclosed between these rivers and the high mountains that form their watershed stood in 323 B.C. under a Macedonian officer named Sibyrtius; the Kabul valley and the Hindu Kush passes were committed to the care of Oxyartes, an Iranian nobleman, whose daughter, Roxane, was Alexander's widow. In the Punjab the strip between the Indus and the Hydaspes (Jhelum) was placed under the joint rule of a Macedonian named Eudamus and of the native rajah, Taxilas; the region between the Hydaspes and the Hyphasis was left in the hands of its former ruler, king Porus. This partition of the conquered lands between Alexander's own officers and Oriental princes, some of whom had but recently made a hard fight for their independence, shows that Alexander could not spare many Macedonian or Greek troops for India, and that his Macedonian officers could not afford to estrange the native rulers or to weaken their own forces by internecine quarrels. Yet after Alexander's death his governors made both of these mistakes. The worst offender was Eudamus. This officer, who coveted the elephant corps of king Porus, obtained it by procuring the assassination of their owner; and he removed the elephants with the rest of his army from India in order to participate in the war against Peithon of Media (p. 23).

In Eudamus' absence the native reaction against Macedonian rule declared itself. The leader of this movement, Chandragupta (or Sandrakottos, as the Greeks called him), was a captain of adventure from the Ganges lands, who had been incited by Alexander's example to create an Indian empire for himself, and with the help of "Yavana" (Greek) mercenaries he had extended his authority over the Ganges basin. About 316 he invaded the Indus valley, where he apparently made short work of the remaining Macedonian garrisons. About 305, it is true, Seleucus, who had meanwhile established his authority over the other eastern provinces, visited India and carried on a war with Chandragupta in the Punjab. But at best it is doubtful whether Seleucus would have had any chance against a native ruler who could draw upon the resources of half India; and in actual fact he could only engage Chandragupta by neglecting his more important war-front against Antigonus in the west. Therefore in exchange for a corps of elephants (p. 41) he abandoned the eastern margin of Alexander's empire up to the watershed of the Hindu Kush. (304–3) This bargain, which certainly was profitable to Seleucus—for it was with Chandragupta's elephants that he won at Ipsus—appears to have pleased both parties, for Seleucus and his successor kept a permanent resident at Chandragupta's capital, Palibothra (Patna). To this envoy, Megasthenes, we owe most of our

MAP III

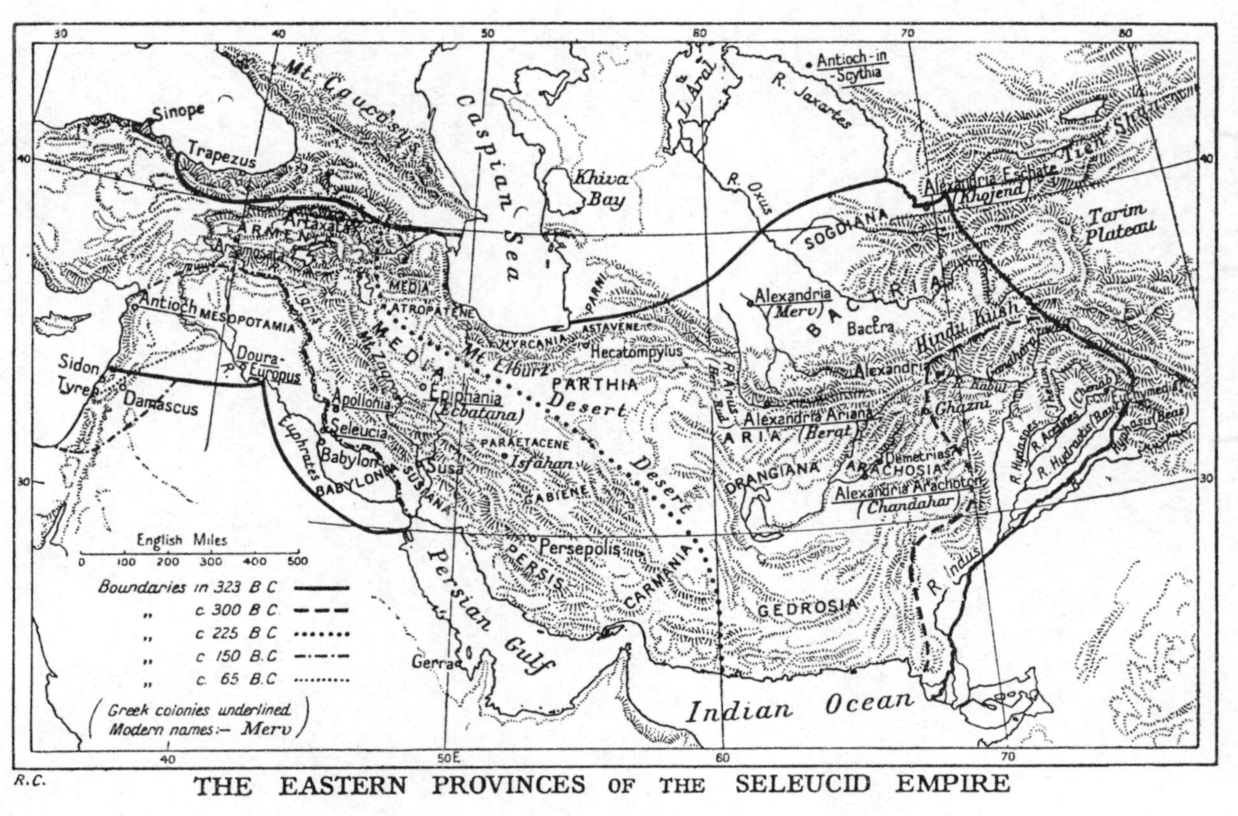

THE EASTERN PROVINCES OF THE SELEUCID EMPIRE

knowledge of Chandragupta's court.[1] From his description it appears that his monarchy was an essentially Hindu state, being based on the division by castes. His system of roads and his service of spies were probably copied from the Achæmenid realm rather than from Alexander's, if indeed it was borrowed from anywhere, and the only Greeks in his retinue seem to have been mercenaries and courtesans. The same friendly relations were kept up between the next king, Amitraghata (Greek: "Amitrochaites") and Antiochus I. The story that Amitraghata asked Antiochus for figs, wine, and a sophist, and that the Greek king sent him the *Delikatessen*, but not the sophist, because he had no stock of this commodity for export, may not be strictly true; but continued intercourse between the two monarchies is attested by the not infrequent finds of coins of the first two Seleucid rulers in north-west India.

The accession of Chandragupta's grandson Asoka (*c.* 275), who included the greater part of India under his empire, made no difference to the friendly relations between Hindu and Greek. About 260 Asoka, who was a devotee of Buddhism, sent missionaries to five Hellenistic kings, Antiochus I or II, Ptolemy II, Antigonus Gonatas, Alexander II of Epirus and Magas of Cyrene—the first invitation by an eastern prince to the western world. But Asoka's empire did not last long, and about 250 the Seleucid monarchy suffered defections in its upper provinces which put it out of touch with India.

§ 3. THE RISE OF THE BACTRIAN AND PARTHIAN MONARCHIES

From 250 B.C. the relations of the Greek world with India and Central Asia were largely determined by the rise of two new kingdoms on the Iranian plateau. In this region Alexander had originally appointed Oriental governors in preference to Macedonian or Greek, but shortly before his death he had in most cases replaced the natives by Europeans. Despite the reduction of the European population by their internecine wars at the end of the fourth century (pp. 4 and 23), an Oriental reaction did not set in so promptly in these

[1] Fragments of Megasthenes are preserved in extracts by Strabo (bk. 15, pp. 709–13), Arrian, *Indica*, and Diodorus (II, 35–42). On the general credibility of his descriptions, see B. C. J. Timmer, *Megasthenes en de Indische Maatschappij*.

lands as in India. During the reigns of the first two Seleucids nothing is heard of Iran, except that it was troubled with occasional incursions by nomads from the Central Asian grasslands. Seleucus sent a general named Demodamas to make a retaliatory raid across the Iaxartes (Syr-Daria), and founded a colony beyond this river, Antioch-in-Scythia, as an advanced outpost against the marauders. Similarly, Antiochus I ringed off the oasis of Merv with a group of military settlements.

But soon after 250 the greater part of the Iranian plateau was detached from the Seleucid dominions and constituted into two independent kingdoms. At this time the Seleucid monarchy was being severely shaken by dynastic disputes and by a war with Egypt, in which the Ptolemaic armies advanced into Babylonia and fomented rebellion in the upper provinces (p. 88). Under the impression of these disasters the governor of Bactria, Diodotus, made himself independent of Seleucid authority. It is probable that Diodotus had previously possessed in fact, if not in law, the power of a count palatine, and that he slipped out of control by a gradual usurpation of sovereignty. (245–230 *c.*) [1]

A parallel movement to the Bactrian secession took place in this same period on the northern edge of the Persian plateau. About 247 Arsaces, chief of a nomad tribe named the Parni, expelled the Seleucid governor, Andragoras, from Parthia (northern and north-eastern Persia) and permanently occupied the district of Astavene (Astrabad) in that province. This foray, insignificant in itself, led on to a more ambitious inroad under Arsaces' brother Tiridates, who took advantage of further dissension within the Seleucid dynasty about 235 B.C. (p. 109) to overrun the entire regions of Parthia and Hyrcania. This second incursion was too serious to be disregarded. About 230 king Seleucus II, having momentarily disengaged himself from other war-fronts, took the field in person against the invader. For a while Tiridates stood in danger of being caught between two fires, for Diodotus of Bactria showed signs of making common cause with Seleucus

[1] Diodotus' son and namesake acted as a wholly independent sovereign.—On the Greco-Bactrian rulers, see throughout Tarn, *The Greeks in Bactria and India*, pt. II.

in a war of Greeks against barbarians. But the timely death of the Bactrian ruler, and the changed attitude of his successor Diodotus II, who went so far as to enter into alliance with the nomad chief, rid him of danger from that quarter. Even so, Tiridates fled before Seleucus to the steppes, and he might have been permanently dispossessed of Parthia, had not his pursuer been called off by yet another domestic war (pp. 111–12). Thus Tiridates was able to recover his conquests and to consolidate them into the kingdom of Parthia.

On the north-western border of the Persian plateau the fertile district of Media Atropatene (Azerbaijan) had been left since 323 in the hands of a native dynasty. The relations of these princes to the Seleucids are not clear; it is probable that they acknowledged Seleucid suzerainty and sent occasional tribute, but enjoyed virtual independence. In the neighbouring province of Armenia a dynasty which was descended from the last Persian satrap had accepted conditions similar to those of Atropatene. But about 230 a vassal-prince named Arsames made himself independent and built himself a new capital at Arsamosata. Thus, while the Seleucid monarchy ceded nothing except the Punjab in the first fifty years after Alexander's death, in the disastrous period of civil wars which beset it between 250 and 225 it lost the entire northern edge of the Iranian tableland from the Hindu Kush to Asia Minor.

§ 4. ANTIOCHUS III, RESTITUTOR ORBIS

In 221 the crumbling of the Seleucid dominion was accelerated into a wholesale disruption, which threatened to reduce it to the Mediterranean borderlands, or to extinguish it altogether. Presuming on the chronic unrest in the western provinces of the kingdom (p. 118), and on the inexperience of a new and youthful ruler, Antiochus III, Molon, the governor of Media (Central Persia), broke into revolt and carried with him his brother, the governor of Persis (Southern Persia) and prince Artabazanes of Atropatene.[1] Advancing into Babylonia, the rebel leader was driven back across the Tigris by a large loyalist force under a general named Xenœtas; but in a sudden counter-attack he completely destroyed

[1] On the circumstances of Antiochus III's accession, see p. 112.

this force, which had spent the intervening night in premature carousals. By this stroke Molon won all the remainder of Persia, and Babylonia into the bargain. The Seleucid monarchy now seemed in the same plight as the Roman Empire after the Gothic invasions of the third century. But it was saved from dissolution by Antiochus III, the Greek Aurelian. With unsuspected energy Antiochus brought up heavy reinforcements in person, and by the advice of an experienced officer named Zeuxis he crossed the Tigris above Molon's position so as to threaten his communications with Media. By this movement Molon was cornered near Apollonia (to north of Seleucia) and brought to battle. Deserted at the first contact by half his army, he put an end to the rebellion by taking his own life. By way of warning to future insurgents, his body was impaled according to the old Persian custom. Antiochus followed up this success with a march across Mt. Zagrus into Atropatene, where Artabazanes at once made submission. (220)

In the next eight years Antiochus made an end to the internal dissensions which had vexed his dynasty and recovered much of the ground lost by his predecessors on other fronts (p. 113 ff.). Having thus secured his rear, he was able to apply his entire field force to a series of eastern campaigns which occupied him from 212 to 204. In 212 he penned up Xerxes the son of the rebel Arsames at Arsamosata, and forced him to make an early surrender. In accordance with a well-tried device of Seleucid statecraft he sought to bind the vassal dynasty to himself by giving Xerxes a daughter in marriage; but after the death of this prince (which was ascribed on doubtful evidence to Antiochus himself), he re-annexed the Armenian principality and placed it under two governors, Artaxias and Zariadris.

From 209 to 204 Antiochus was engaged on a Grand Tour of the eastern provinces, which was second only to Alexander's Anabasis in the annals of Greek conquest. He began his march from Ecbatana in Media, where he raised campaign-funds by despoiling a rich native temple—a bad example to himself and to his successors. His first objective was the Parthian capital, Hecatompylus (Sahrud), which lay beyond the Salt Desert of Central Persia. The Parthian king, Tiridates' successor, Priapatius, offered no armed opposition at this stage, but sent horsemen to destroy the cisterns, fed by conduits from Mt. Elburz, which former Persian rulers had constructed for the benefit of caravans. But Antiochus forestalled the Parthian horse with his own cavalry, and thus was able to cross the desert without mishap. From Hecatompylus his route lay across Mt. Elburz into Hyrcania (at the south-east edge of the Caspian), where the Parthian king had taken up a position. The march across this high ridge involved a climb of more than thirty miles up a deep and rugged gorge, the flanks of which were lined by enemy troops well provided with heavy missiles. Like Hannibal in his ascent of the Alps, Antiochus realized that the passage could not be forced unless the defenders were first dislodged from the cliffs above. He therefore waited for his light-armed men (mostly Cretans) to clamber up the sides of the mountains and drive off the enemy snipers. Under these conditions he took eight days to accomplish the ascent; but he carried the pass with slight loss. After the descent into Hyrcania he brought Priapatius to battle and forced him to sue for terms. In pursuance of his ordinary policy on the outskirts of his realm he did not expel the Parthian ruler, but kept him as a vassal.

After this settlement of the Parthian problem Antiochus passed on to Bactria. Here he had to deal with an upstart ruler, a Greek from Magnesia named Euthydemus, who had displaced Diodotus II.[1] At the frontier-river, the Arius (Heri-Rud), he found a strong detachment of enemy cavalry; but pouncing upon it with Alexandrian rapidity he routed it in a miniature Battle of the Granicus. The king took a personal part in this combat and had the satisfaction of losing a few teeth. (208) The movements of Antiochus during the next two years are lost; but it appears that he spent the greater part of this time in an attack upon Euthydemus' capital at Bactra (Balkh), the siege of which was compared by Polybius with the investment of Carthage in 147–6. The Bactrian war, however, ended in a compromise, for Euthydemus eventually persuaded Antiochus that a fight to a finish would be a betrayal of Hellenism, which could not afford to weaken in mutual warfare its outposts against the people of

[1] It is not known whether Euthydemus' native town was Magnesia-ad-Sipylum or Magnesia-ad-Mæandrum.

the steppes. Antiochus hereupon conceded the title of king to Euthydemus and guaranteed his rights by treaty; and to Euthydemus' son, Demetrius, he gave one of his daughters. (208–6)

The last stage of Antiochus' march lay across the "Caucasus" (Hindu Kush) to the Indus valley. The political condition of this country had reverted to that which Alexander had found there. The empire of Asoka had broken up, and princes of the rank of Taxilas and Porus had replaced him. With one such rajah, named Sophagasenus by the Greeks, but unknown to Hindu tradition, Antiochus made a convention of the usual kind, conceding to him virtual independence in return for the recognition of his overlordship, a sum of money and a corps of elephants. Unlike Alexander, he made but a short stay in India, and he had an uneventful homeward journey by way of Kandahar and Seistan to Seleucia-on-Tigris. (206–5) Herein again he differed from Alexander, that he made no attempt to open up communications to India by sea, still less to circumnavigate Arabia—for the benefit of Ptolemaic trade. But from Seleucia he sailed down the Tigris and along the Persian Gulf to the town of Gerra, on the east coast of Arabia, which played a part similar to that of its *vis-à-vis* Ormuz in the Middle Ages. His purpose in gaining this city was no doubt to have control of the trade in Arabian perfumes, which were forwarded thence to Babylonia or by the desert route to Petra and the Palestinian coast. But he allowed himself to be bought off with a lump payment in money and kind. (205 or 204)

At the end of Antiochus' eastern campaigns the Seleucid realm had in outward appearance attained the same dimensions as in the days of its founder. In its restored form, however, it showed this difference, that the frontier provinces were now all organized as palatinates, and that most of the quasi-independent rulers of these borderlands were Orientals. In this recourse to native rulers, and in the failure to follow up his military successes with intensive colonization such as Alexander had practised, we may see a confession of weakness on Antiochus' part. But compared with Alexander, Antiochus was under a double disadvantage. He had no means of drawing freely upon the population of Macedonia and of Greece, and the resources of his realm needed careful nursing after the havoc of the recent civil wars. On these grounds he had perforce to husband his man-power both in his campaigns and in his political settlements. The title of "Great King," which Antiochus assumed on his return from the East, was generally admitted by the Greeks to have been well earned: if Alexander was the greatest political builder in Greek history, Antiochus might claim to be the greatest restorer.

§ 5. INDIA AND BACTRIA AFTER ANTIOCHUS III

But the political system established by Antiochus in the upper provinces never received a proper trial. The catastrophic defeat which he suffered at the hands of the Romans in 190 (pp. 211–2), undid all that he had achieved on his tour of the East. Such was the blow to his prestige which this battle entailed that in Armenia, Parthia and Bactria alike the rulers ceased to send tribute or to acknowledge even the nominal authority of the Seleucids. After the return of Antiochus from his tour of the East, Euthydemus occupied himself with the consolidation of his Bactrian realm and with its extension "towards the Huns and the Seres" [1]—a phrase suggesting that he made contact across the Pamirs with the Chinese outposts in the Tarim basin. It may be doubted whether he established a regular traffic in Chinese silk,[2] but his mintage of coins in gold suggests that he drew supplies of that metal from the Altai mountains. After Euthydemus' death (*c.* 190) his son Demetrius first wrested from the Seleucids their remaining provinces in eastern Iran (modern Afghanistan and Seistan), and then undertook the third and most extensive Greek Anabasis into India (*c.* 185–175). Advancing in person down the Indus to its Delta, he left his brother Apollodotus to make further progress to the Gulf of Cambay and for some distance up the valley of the Nerbudda. In the meantime his general, Menander, took the route of the Delhi ridge to the Ganges valley and occupied Pataliputra (Patna), the point which marks the Farthest East of Greek penetration. The apparent facility of these conquests implies that Demetrius had native support: presumably the

[1] Strabo, bk. XI, p. 516.

[2] On this traffic, see A. Herrmann, *Die alten Seidenstrassen*, p. 1 ff. According to Chinese sources the silk trade began in 114 B.C.

Indians of the North-west looked to him to maintain Buddhist ascendancy against a Brahmin reaction.[1]

But Demetrius' deep thrust into India exposed him to a Seleucid counter-attack on his ill-guarded rear. In 169 Antiochus IV launched against him a general named Eucratides, who regained the recently lost Iranian provinces and in 167 wrested Bactria from Demetrius, who did not survive his defeat. Continuing his advance into India, Eucratides defeated Apollodotus, who died fighting like his brothers; but he was eventually held by Menander, who probably recovered the upper Indus region. (*c.* 162) Moreover, it was now the turn of Eucratides to be caught in the rear; though he had, like Diodotus II, revoked his allegiance to the Seleucids, this did not safeguard him against a preventive attack by Mithridates I of Parthia, who could hardly hope to extend or even to retain his conquests in Persia (p. 76), while he had a strong Greek power, Seleucid or otherwise, on either flank. In 159 Eucratides went down in battle against Mithridates, who then annexed Seistan, and all Afghanistan except the Kabul region, so that Eucratides' successor in Bactria, his son Heliocles, was virtually cut off from the Greek Near East. An attempt on his part to recover the ground lost to the Parthians, by alliance with the Seleucid king Demetrius II (p. 226), merely led to a second defeat at the hands of Mithridates. (141)

The Greek dynasties in Bactria appear to have succeeded in gaining the allegiance of the Iranian nobles, who continued to rule the countryside from their castles, and to the end of the third century at least they attracted sufficient new settlers from the West to found additional Greek or hellenized cities at the strategic points of their territory. But when Antiochus IV set Eucratides to undo the work of Demetrius —the most promising attempt to establish Greek ascendancy in the Farther East—, he prepared for the progressive weakening of Hellenism in these regions. Cut off from overland communications with the Greek world, and exposed to the growing power of Parthia, the Greek dynasts henceforth had but a precarious hold on their Indo-Bactrian dominions.

But the *momentum rerum* which led on to the extinction

[1] Tarn, *op. cit.*, pp. 172–7. Indian tradition made Menander into a Buddhist sage.

of Hellenism in the Farther East came from another quarter. In 128 a roving envoy from the court of China found Bactria overrun by a horde of nomads, the "Yueh-Chi"—or "Tochari", as the Greeks called them. Widespread unrest in the Central Asian steppes (where the "Hiung-nu" or Huns are reported to have been the prime disturbers), set the Yueh-Chi on their travels. Of their irruption into Bactria, all that can be said is that probably they encountered no prolonged resistance except from isolated Greek towns. Their advance was eventually halted by the Hindu-Kush.

Under the shelter of the Hindu-Kush the house of Heliocles retained a restricted dominion in the region of Kabul and in the extreme north-west of India. But *c.* 80–70 it lost the Indian remnant of its territory to an invader from an opposite quarter. While the Yueh-Chi were taking Bactria into their possession, another nomad horde, the Sacae, broke into the Parthian province of Seistan (*c.* 128). Driven out of Seistan by Mithridates II, they edged away towards India, which they entered *c.* 100 B.C. (probably by way of the Bolan pass), and on reaching the Indus they turned off both to north and to south. By their thrust up-stream they squeezed the Helioclid dynasty out of India. Its last scion, Hermæus, maintained himself in the Kabul region till *c.* 30 B.C. Apparently he obtained temporary support from the Chinese general commanding the western outposts of the Tarim plateau, who came to his assistance across Bactria. When this succour was withdrawn, Hermæus succumbed to the Sacæ.

The Greek retreat from India began *c.* 167, when Demetrius, compelled to face about against Eucratides' invasion from the west, abandoned the Ganges valley; but Menander held sway as far, perhaps, as Delhi in the east, and the Gulf of Cambay in the south. From the port of Barygaza (Broach) they maintained a sea-connexion with Egypt or Mesopotamia, and by treating the Indians as partners rather than subjects they insured themselves against native rebellions. After *c.* 100 B.C. they lost their seaboard to the Sacæ moving down the Indus valley and became restricted to the Punjab. With the help of his river-fleet the last ruler of Menander's dynasty, Hippostratus, made a stand against the Sacæ; but he was eventually overborne by them, at about the same time as

Hermæus fell to other Sacæ forces advancing up the Indus. (*c.* 30 B.C.).[1]

§ 6. PARTHIA AFTER ANTIOCHUS III

After the battle of Magnesia Artaxias and Zariadris, the governors installed by Antiochus III in Armenia, set themselves up as kings in their own right. Artaxias, the dynast of Armenia Major, became the founder of a royal line which endured to the time of Augustus. His new capital at Artaxata was laid out by the advice of Hannibal, who passed from the service of Antiochus III (p. 208) to that of the Armenian king.[2] Under the energetic rule of Antiochus IV Artaxias had for a while to submit again to Seleucid suzerainty (*c.* 175 B.C.), but he kept his crown, and in the dissensions that overtook the Seleucid realm after Antiochus IV's death Armenia definitely emancipated itself from Greek overlordship. (161 B.C.)

In Elymais (the south-western border of Persia) a local chieftain set himself up as an independent king, with his capital at Susa (a Seleucid colony). Though Antiochus regained possession of Susa, he was killed in a riot while attempting to extort a war-subsidy from a native temple. Antiochus IV retained Susa, but after his death all Elymais fell to Parthia (see below).

In Media the Seleucids retained possession through the first half of the second century, and in 165 its chief city, Ecbatana, was reconstituted as a Greek colony under the name of Epiphania. But about 160 B.C. the renewal of civil war in the Seleucid dominions (p. 220) gave an opportunity to the Parthian king, Mithridates I, to lay the foundations of the Parthian empire. He overran Media, apparently with little or no opposition, and gained Elymais shortly after.[3] By 141 he was in possession of Babylon. At this time the remaining Seleucid territories were divided between two rival kings, one of whom, a young man named Demetrius, held

[1] The Greek rulers of Bactria and India have left a splendid memorial of themselves in their copious and beautifully executed coinage, by means of which they established a money economy in those regions. Many of these pieces were struck by provincial viceroys, issuing money in their own names. (Tarn, *op. cit.*, pp. 90, 316–17.)

[2] Zariadris founded a lesser dynasty in Sophene (western Armenia).

[3] Susa remained an outpost of Hellenism under Parthian rule for at least two centuries.

The story that Antiochus IV also had designs on a native temple at Susa was probably due in part to a confusion with Antiochus III, and in part to point the moral of his premature death (by consumption).—See Tarn, *op. cit.*, Appendix 7.

the greater part of Syria, while his opponent was in occupation of Antioch (p. 226). Under these difficult conditions Demetrius set out to reconquer the lost provinces. His enterprise at first seemed justified, for he received assistance from the surviving dynasts in Bactria, and from the native ruler of Elymais, and he achieved several initial victories (at sites unknown). But eventually he let himself be taken by surprise. It is not clear whether he was captured in the field when his vigilance had been relaxed by a false offer of negotiations, or was kidnapped, like Crassus, during a parley. (140–39) He remained a prisoner for full ten years, and by 138/7 Babylon had fallen again into Parthian hands.

The last Seleucid counter-attack upon the Parthians was made in 130–29 by Antiochus VII. This ruler, a true descendant of Seleucus I and Antiochus III, had temporarily reunited Syria and northern Mesopotamia, the relics of the Seleucid empire, and from these he collected an army of considerable strength.[1] By a manœuvre like that which Antiochus III had used against Molon he forced the crossing of the Tigris near Mosul, after which he defeated the Parthian king, Phraates I, in three successive battles. Advancing into Media, where he received aid from several Parthian vassals, he thrust Phraates back upon Parthia Proper and drove him to sue for terms. Antiochus now considered himself strong enough to insist upon the same conditions as Antiochus III had imposed upon Priapatius, and to demand the extradition of the captive Demetrius, whom he feared as a possible adversary in a civil war fomented by Parthian diplomacy. But Phraates would not consent to these terms, and in the next campaign he sprang a double counter-attack upon Antiochus. He sent back Demetrius to Syria as a pretender to Antiochus' throne, and he organized local risings in Media against the invading forces, which had been dispersed too widely for the winter, and had not been kept under proper discipline. Thus Antiochus was caught in a position not unlike that of Cæsar in Gaul in the winter of 54/3 B.C. Collecting the troops nearest at hand, Antiochus threw himself upon Phraates north of Ecbatana. The Parthian forces, which seem to have been

[1] The story that Antiochus' force numbered 80,000 armed men and 200,000 camp-followers is on a par with the fable that the boots of his private soldiers were studded with gold. (Justin, 39, 10.) His numbers and equipment were evidently exaggerated in order to make his defeat appear the more impressive.

weaker on horseback and stronger on foot than was their wont, drew their opponent by a typical sham flight on to broken ground, where his cavalry was at a disadvantage. The defeat of the horse caused a general panic in Antiochus' army, ending in a disaster like Carrhæ. The greater part of his forces was taken prisoner; the king himself remained on the field.

Though Demetrius in the meantime had recovered his throne in Syria, he made no attempt to retrieve Antiochus' defeat. Phraates was therefore able to re-occupy Babylon unopposed. Here for the time being the Parthian advance was checked, for soon after this reconquest the Parthian Homeland fell a prey to nomad invasions. (125–115) Eventually king Mithridates II, having cleared Parthia of the tribes from the steppes, resumed the advance towards the Euphrates. Though no details of his campaigns survive, it is probable that by 100 B.C. he had occupied the whole of the Land of the Two Rivers.

§ 7. CONCLUSION

Within the space of two or three hundred years from Alexander's death his conquests in the interior of Asia had all been lost, and the Greeks were once more confined to the lands of the Mediterranean seaboard. In view of the paucity of the conquerors and of their continual internal dissensions, their eventual disappearance from Inner Asia was less remarkable than the length of the lease by which they held it. Another notable feature of their rule in these regions is that it was ended not so much by risings of the natives as by attacks from extraneous forces—the Parthians, the Tochari and the Sacæ. The extrusion of the Greeks from Bactria and Persia illustrates the secular rule that the chief danger to these countries has come from the nomadic tribes of the Central Asian grasslands.

But the loss of Inner Asia need not be regarded as a misfortune for the Greeks. It is even questionable whether in the long run the occupation of Babylonia was a net source of gain to them. It might be laid down as a condition for Greeks as for Romans, that they could not hope to maintain indefinitely an empire that extended far beyond the Mediterranean basin. The real test of the success of Alexander's conquests lay, not in the history of Inner Asia, but in that of the Mediterranean borderlands.

CHAPTER V

SYRIA AND THE ASIAN BORDER

§ 1. THE RED SEA AND ARABIA

ON the borderlands between Asia and Africa Alexander's successors not only maintained Greek ascendancy, but slightly increased its range. The extension of Greek influence in these regions was mainly due to the second Ptolemy. Unlike the men of the first generation after Alexander, Ptolemy Philadelphus was a stay-at-home monarch with an essentially civilian habit of mind. "Big Business," not war, was the sport of this king. But his very absorption in mercantile pursuits tempted him to adopt an energetic foreign policy. In support of Egyptian commerce, which was mostly overseas, he maintained the thalassocracy which his father had established, and he realized the advantages of sending the flag in front of trade. Moreover, Ptolemy II was in a more happy situation than any contemporary king: unlike the Seleucids and the Antigonids, he was not in constant anxiety about the loss of territory by rebellion, and he was free to seize opportunities of foreign expansion whenever they offered. Like other unwarlike rulers, Augustus or Louis the Fourteenth, Ptolemy II was a judicious enlarger of his dominions.

In Upper Egypt the first Ptolemy had accepted the old frontier line of Pharaohs and Persian kings at the First Cataract. In the early years of his reign (before 276) Ptolemy II sent a force to make a reconnaissance beyond this point. As there is no evidence of Ethiopian inroads into Egypt at this period, his expedition can hardly be explained as a counter-offensive or as a quest for a safer frontier. It appears more likely that he was feeling his way towards the gold mines of Nubia, or to the hunting-grounds of the Sudanese elephants, of which the Ptolemies were always at pains to keep up a supply for their army. This reconnaissance did not lead to any extensive annexations, but it established a regular intercourse between Egypt and the Ethiopian kingdom of Meroë (between Khartum and the Atbara). A well-known monument of Greek rule in Egypt, the temple of Philæ, survives to record a slight advance of Ptolemy II's boundary-line beyond the First Cataract.

Towards the end of the third century the formation of a Greater Ethiopia by a semi-hellenized prince named Ergamenes again turned the attention of the Ptolemies to the Upper Nile. Under the fourth Ptolemy friendly relations with Ethiopia appear to have been maintained; but Ptolemy V deemed it prudent to create an epistrategia or special military command for Upper Egypt at Thebes, and he probably was engaged in a brief war with Ethiopia in 185–4. This conflict did not result in any change of frontier; but about 165 the sixth Ptolemy, who suspected that the Ethiopians were lending support to a native Egyptian rebellion in the Thebais, occupied the Nile valley as far as the Second Cataract, so as to keep them at arm's length. Here the frontier remained fixed to the end of the Ptolemaic dynasty. The reason why the Ptolemies made no attempt to annex Nubia and the Sudan may be found in their discovery of an alternative route to Central Africa, which offered easier access to elephant-land, and was of greater commercial value. Under the first Ptolemy a Greek Red Sea fleet made a preliminary cruise as far as Zebirget Isle; but the effective opening up of this waterway was mainly the work of his successor. About 280 B.C. Ptolemy II repaired the old Pharaonic canal from the apex of the Nile delta to the southern end of the Gulf of Suez, in preparation for a regular Red Sea traffic. In 279 or 278 his admiral, Ariston, sailed the whole length of the Red Sea to Bab-el-Mandeb. From this point Ptolemy II made no attempt to occupy the Yemen coast of Arabia or to control the sea-route to India; but he sent an agent named Dionysius (presumably on a Hindu vessel) to visit the court of the emperor Asoka. On the other hand, both the second and the third Ptolemy systematically opened up the African seaboard as far as the "Cinnamon Country" (Somaliland), and they secured the ground thus won with a chain of forts extending from Arsinoë (Suez) and Berenice (near Ras Benas) to Ptolemais-of-the-Hunts (Suakim) and to a more southerly Arsinoë and Berenice in Somaliland. The Nile canal, which appears to have become quickly silted up, never carried much traffic; but its failure was of no great importance, for the Red Sea trade was successfully diverted to the northern Berenice, from which a desert route, well furnished with wells, was established for caravans which reached the Nile valley at Koptos. This overland track was patrolled by a special corps of "desert-guards," and the stations at Suakim and in Somaliland, which became the chief centres of elephant-supply, were converted into regular military bases. To the second Ptolemy we may no doubt attribute the patrol flotilla of the Red Sea which protected traffic against pirates. The later Ptolemies maintained an interest in the Red Sea trade, and kept up the patrol fleet until the first century B.C.[1]

In 278 and 277 Ptolemy II made reconnaissances in north-western Arabia, where the incense and spice routes across the desert converged upon the Gulf of Akaba and the isthmus city of Petra. This overland traffic had already excited the interest of Antigonus, who had sent a flying column in 311 to capture Petra by surprise. His expedition had met with disaster, for his troops had been overcome with fatigue after a forced march of three days, and had fallen an easy prey to the Nabatæan Arabs to whom the city belonged.[2] But Ptolemy II achieved Antigonus' purpose at slight cost by cultivating friendly relations with the Lihyanite tribes on the southern edge of the Nabatæan country, so as to divert part at least of the desert traffic to the head of the Gulf of Akaba. At this point he peopled a trading-post named Ampelone with Milesian castaways, and he provided a flotilla to protect the ferry-traffic across the Red Sea against Nabatæan raids from the head of the gulf. To tighten his hold on the desert trade he also advanced his Palestinian frontier into Ammonitis and Idumæa beyond the Dead Sea. In Ammonitis he subsequently founded a station named Philadelphia (Rabbath-Ammon), and left a detachment of troops at the service of the

[1] Ditt., *O.G.I.*, 132 (130 B.C.) and 186 (62 B.C.). On Ptolemaic enterprise in the Red Sea, see E. H. Warmington in Cary and Warmington, *The Ancient Explorers*, p. 67 ff.

[2] A detailed and graphic account of this campaign is preserved in Diodorus, XIX, 94–100.

native chief. By this extension he intercepted the overland traffic proceeding northward from Petra, and he made sure of a plentiful supply of bitumen from the Dead Sea for the mummifying of his native Egyptian subjects.[1] But the interest of the Egyptian kings in north-western Arabia does not appear to have outlasted for long the reign of the second Ptolemy; and the loss of Syria at the beginning of the second century (pp. 93–4) deprived them of their trans-Jordanian trade-stations.

§ 2. THE PROBLEM OF SYRIA

On the Asian border by far the most important frontier question concerned the boundary-line between Seleucis and Cœle-Syria,[2] i.e. between the Seleucid and the Ptolemaic portions of Syria. This problem arose out of the partition of Antigonus' dominions after the battle of Ipsus, when Syria as a whole was adjudicated to Seleucus, but Ptolemy held possession of all that country as far as the river Eleutherus, and refused to evacuate it (pp. 42–3). A further contention was raised between Ptolemy and Seleucus in 286, when Ptolemy seized the Phœnician cities to which Seleucus had previously lodged a claim with Demetrius (p. 44). The dispute about Syria was the main cause of the antagonism between the Ptolemaic and Seleucid dynasties, and it gave rise to a succession of hard-fought wars. The age-old competition of Pharaohs and Asiatic emperors for the Asiatic borderland was thus revived by the Hellenistic kings.

In essence, the object at issue was the Phœnician coast. Whichever king was lord of this would possess a plentiful supply of ship-timber, and would have the best shipwrights and navigators of the Mediterranean at his disposal; and by the ownership of Tyre and Sidon in particular he would control the terminal points of the two great trade-routes coming northward from Arabia and Petra, and westward from Babylonia and Damascus. A far-sighted statesmanship might have awarded all Syria to the Seleucids, as being the rulers who did most to foster Hellenism in the East. But on

[1] On Ptolemy II's Arabian enterprise, see Tarn, *Journ. Egypt. Archæol.*, 1929, p. 9 ff.

[2] Strictly speaking, Cœle-Syria included only the Palestinian seaboard as far as the Jordan to the east and Mt. Hermon to the north. (Corradi, *Studi Ellenistici*, p. 48 ff.) But the term may conveniently be extended to cover the whole of Ptolemaic Syria.

strictly legal grounds the opposing cases were evenly balanced: if the Seleucids could quote the partition pact of 301, the Ptolemies might retort that they had been unfairly excluded from that agreement. The most practical compromise probably would have been to draw the frontier at the river Leontes (Litany), so as to give Tyre to the Ptolemies and Sidon to the Seleucids. But in fact the boundary lines were drawn and re-drawn by the fortuitous event of war, and each delimitation provoked a further trial of arms.

So long as the founders of the two dynasties remained alive, the Syrian question was left in abeyance, for Seleucus temporarily waived his claims in consideration of past aid rendered to him by Ptolemy; and after the death of the latter he became too intent on his feud with Lysimachus to open a quarrel with Ptolemy II. But the new king of Egypt did not wait for Seleucus' successor to attack him. Taking advantage of the difficulties that beset Antiochus at the outset of his reign, he made the first move in the Syrian Wars by breaking into Seleucis.[1] Antiochus, who had lost his father's main army by desertion to Ptolemy Ceraunus (p. 58), and was weakened by some internal dissension near his capital (probably a military revolt fomented by Ptolemy at Apamea-on-the-Orontes, the "Aldershot" of the Seleucid War Office), was left defenceless while the invader occupied Damascus and the northern Phœnician coast as far as Aradus. But to save Seleucis, which he recognized as vital, he at once cut his losses in the west. By abandoning his claims on Macedonia to Antigonus Gonatas, with whom he now made a permanent peace, he was able to gather sufficient forces to restore order in Seleucis and to check Ptolemy's progress. (279) For the moment Ptolemy, who ever preferred to wait for walls to crumble rather than to batter them down, made a peace which left him in possession of Damascus and Aradus.

§ 3. THE FIRST AND SECOND SYRIAN WARS

For two years (278–7) Ptolemy busied himself with the affairs of Arabia (pp. 81–2). But he could not resist the opportunity which the Galatian inroads into Asia Minor gave him. As soon as Antiochus had removed his head-quarters to Sardes,

[1] On the problems of this war and the "First Syrian War," see Appendix 5.

he made a fresh encroachment upon Seleucis. (276) For a second time Antiochus decided to save his Syrian territories at all costs. Leaving Asia Minor for the moment to its own resources, he swung his army back into Syria and inflicted such a defeat upon the invader as to throw him back on the defensive on the Syrian front for the rest of the war. Thus freed from danger in Seleucis, Antiochus returned to Asia Minor and won his "elephant victory" over the Galatians. (275) In the meantime one of his generals recovered Damascus after a siege, and in 274 the king himself came back to prepare for an invasion of Cœle-Syria.

For the campaign of 274 Antiochus had acquired a new ally in Ptolemy's half-brother, Magas (a son of Berenice by a previous husband). For some thirty years Magas had occupied a post of special confidence as viceroy of Cyrenaica[1]; but he now broke his trust by accepting the hand of Antiochus' daughter, Apama, and agreeing to invade Egypt while Antiochus fell upon Cœle-Syria.

The defection of Magas may be connected with the reappearance of a comet that boded ill to princes, Arsinoë II. Having wrecked the home of her first husband and escaped murder at the hands of her second, this indomitable woman eventually found her way back to Egypt and determined to marry a third king. It was but a minor obstacle to her ambitions that Ptolemy II already had a queen, Arsinoë I (a daughter of Lysimachus), who had borne him three children. A more serious difficulty was that Ptolemy was her brother by the same father and mother. Among the Pharaohs marriages between a full brother and sister had been common enough, but they were not yet admitted by the dynastic law of the Macedonian houses, and they offended the sentiment of the Greeks, who regarded a union between offspring of the same mother as incestuous. Nevertheless, Arsinoë carried her point. In 275, or a little earlier, she persuaded the king to repudiate and banish Arsinoë I on a pretence of conspiracy, and to inaugurate the practice of sister-marriage at Hellenistic courts. Since Arsinoë was nearly forty years of age and had no political titles to offer to Ptolemy, save perhaps a shadowy claim on Macedonia by virtue of her marriage with Ceraunus, her success in winning his hand must be set

[1] For the chronology of Magas' governorship, see Appendix 7.

down entirely to her personality. With supreme tenacity of purpose she overbore her more malleable brother, and with a tact like the last Cleopatra's she won his sincere affection. But the fate of her stepson, Agathocles, at the court of Lysimachus was not calculated to reassure Ptolemy's relatives. We may therefore see in Magas' rebellion a consequence of her ominous ascendancy over the king.

In the campaign of 274 Magas made the opening move with a dash into Egypt which brought him within a few days' march of Alexandria. Ptolemy, who had perhaps been caught by surprise, and for a time had his hands tied by a revolt among some recently enlisted Galatian mercenaries, at first could offer no resistance. But once he had cornered and killed off the mutineers, he was able to hold Magas in check. After this abortive inroad Magas took no further part in the war; since he kept his post at Cyrene to the end of his life, it may be assumed that Ptolemy bought him off with a guarantee of continued possession. But Magas' raid had probably been intended as a mere diversion while Antiochus launched his main attack upon Cœle-Syria. The main operation, however, was brought up short by a counter-offensive on sea, in which Ptolemy brought all his superior forces to bear and even enlisted the co-operation of pirate flotillas.[1] By simultaneous descents upon all the vulnerable points of the Seleucid coastlands he threw Antiochus back upon the defensive in Syria, and he gained substantial advantages on another war-front (p. 104). In 272 Antiochus agreed to a peace by which he retained Damascus but left the entire Phœnician coast in Ptolemy's hands.

The success of Ptolemy's final counter-attack in the First Syrian War is probably to be attributed to the new vigour which Arsinoë instilled into his over-cautious disposition. It was no doubt in recognition of her services as a war-winner that the king instituted a state-cult in her honour—the first official worship of a living person in Hellenistic monarchies (p. 368)—and that after[2] her death in 270 he spared no pains to keep her memory green.

[1] The details of this naval campaign, which is known to us only from a brief allusion in Pausanias (I, 6, 3), have unfortunately not been preserved.

[2] Needless to say, Arsinoë continued to be worshipped after death as a "diva." Ptolemy II's efforts to perpetuate her memory are particularly evident in the large number of colonies to which he gave the name of Arsinoë.

In 260 the accession of a new Seleucid king, Antiochus II, brought on the Second Syrian War. In this instance Antiochus was the aggressor, and the main operations were conducted in Asia Minor (p. 105). But if Syria was not the scene of any heavy fighting, its frontiers were again shifted on the strength of gains and losses in other quarters. By the peace which was concluded in 255, Ptolemy agreed to retrocede all that part of the Phœnician coast which he had taken off Antiochus I, so that the boundary line was once again drawn a little north of Sidon.

§ 4. THE THIRD SYRIAN WAR

The losses sustained by Ptolemy II in the Second Syrian War were in a large measure due to the intervention of Antigonus Gonatas, who passed on his long-standing friendship with Antiochus I to his successor, and was seeking to pay back the king of Egypt for his interferences in the affairs of European Greece (p. 132 ff.). In order to obtain a free hand for a further round with Gonatas, Ptolemy carried out a master-stroke of diplomacy which seemed destined to lead to a durable understanding with his Seleucid neighbours. In return for a renunciation of Seleucid claims on Cœle-Syria he offered to Antiochus II the hand of his daughter, Berenice II (a child of his earlier wife, Arsinoë I), together with a fabulous dowry, which was probably nothing less than the restoration of the territories previously captured in southern Asia Minor to the Seleucid dominions.[1]

But the matrimonial alliance by which Ptolemy had schemed to confirm the peace with his Seleucid neighbours had the effect of wrecking it. Antiochus, indeed, accepted the hand of Berenice and gave her to believe that a son who was presently born of the marriage should be the next king. But, to say nothing of the fact that a middle-aged toper, such as he was, made an unattractive partner, Antiochus had been married for many years to his cousin Laodice I,[2] and had

[1] From a papyrus in Zeno's collection (*P. Zeno Cairo*, 59251) we learn that the bride was escorted to the Seleucid frontier by Ptolemy's minister Apollonius. (April, 252.)

[2] I here follow Beloch (*Griech. Gesch.*, IV, pt. 2, p. 200), who shows that in all probability Laodice was a cousin, not a half-sister of the king. The details of the grant of land to Laodice are partly preserved in a long and valuable inscription. (Ditt., *O.G.I.*, 225.)

four children by her. Though Antiochus endeavoured to console his divorced wife with a gift of a princely estate in Asia Minor, Laodice was not to be put off at this price. She worked hard for the recovery of her position at court, and in 246 induced Antiochus to visit her at Ephesus. During his stay in this city the king suddenly fell ill and died, but not before he had declared Seleucus II, his eldest son by Laodice, as his successor.

Antiochus' death-bed disposition was justified alike on grounds of law and of expediency. Seleucus was close on twenty years of age, whereas Berenice's son was still an infant; and the preference given to Laodice's son did not in itself involve the overthrow of the recent alliance with Egypt. But if Laodice could carry herself like a true Macedonian princess, Berenice was no whit inferior to her in resourcefulness and lack of scruples. Between the two queens a game of diamond-cut-diamond now began, in which Ptolemy's diplomacy was brought to nought. In the duel with Laodice Berenice had the advantage of position: while Laodice resided at Ephesus or Sardes, Berenice was at Antioch, and within easy reach of Egypt. In reply to Laodice's *coup d'état* she at once issued a proclamation in which she contested Seleucus' claim to the throne. According to Berenice's version of events Laodice had first removed Antiochus by poison, and had thereupon staged a scene in which a double of the dead king, previous to a fictitious death in the royal bed, nominated Laodice's son as his successor. With this manifesto she secured Antioch and the other towns of Syria to her cause; yet distrusting the effect of her propaganda she also sent a call for help to Alexandria.

Berenice's appeal reached Egypt shortly after the death of her father. The new king, Ptolemy III Euergetes, the eldest son of Arsinoë I,[1] exhibited in his reign the traditional cautiousness of his dynasty untempered by his father's peculiar enterprise. But on receiving the message of Berenice (who was his full sister),[2] he displayed an energy beyond his usual wont. He at once mobilized a fleet which was stationed at

[1] On the vexed question of the relation between Ptolemy and "Ptolemy the Son," see Appendix 6.

[2] Soon after his accession Ptolemy married another Berenice, the daughter of Magas of Cyrene, whom we may call Berenice III.

Cyprus or Phœnicia, and now proceeded at Berenice's suggestion to Soli in Cilicia. The Egyptian landing-parties surprised the Seleucid governor in the act of conveying a large treasure to Laodice, and seized the Taurus passes, so as temporarily to cut off Asia Minor from Syria. By these swift moves Berenice had apparently checkmated Laodice. But Asia Minor held firm for the elder queen, and in Antioch a counter-revolution was eventually effected by the household troops and by a corps of Galatian mercenaries, who contrived to kidnap Berenice's child and eventually to gain possession of Berenice herself, who capitulated to them on a promise of her life. They at once put the boy to death, and with equal readiness broke their covenant with Laodice. (Spring and summer 246)[1]

After the death of Berenice and the disappearance of her son the original purpose of Ptolemy's intervention had been completely frustrated. Nevertheless, the king in person now took the field and sailed to Antioch. On arriving at Seleucia-ad-Orontem, and at the capital itself, Ptolemy was received with all the honours of a distinguished visitor. The success of Laodice's party at Antioch had been short-lived, for Seleucid troops from districts friendly to Berenice had marched in upon the town and taken control. By some unexplained good fortune the death of Berenice and her child had not become generally known. Taking advantage of this state of ignorance, Ptolemy issued a proclamation purporting to come from Berenice, and pretending that both the queen and her son were still alive, so that the Egyptian king might appear, not as a foreign intruder, but as the champion of the legitimate dynasty against a usurper. On the strength of this manifesto he proceeded to make a progress through the heart of the Seleucid dominions as far as Seleucia-on-the-Tigris; and his bulletin at first found such ready credence that he met everywhere with a friendly or, at any rate, a peaceful reception. Nay more, while he lay at Seleucia, several if not all of the governors of the upper provinces offered him their obedience. (Summer 246) Having thus to all appearance subdued the whole Seleucid empire eastward of Mt. Taurus, Ptolemy returned to Egypt, leaving garrisons at Seleucia-on-the-Tigris, in Cilicia, and no doubt at Antioch.

[1] On this and other disputed details of the Third Syrian War, see Appendix 8.

It remains to ask what was his real object in overrunning the central Seleucid lands. Since it can hardly be supposed that he had any hope of retrieving Berenice's child, and was acting in good faith as the protector of his interests, it may be assumed that he had decided to profit by the confusion in the Seleucid realm to acquire the greater part of it for himself. If such was his resolve, it must have been the product of a sudden and ill-considered inspiration, for it ran contrary to the set policy of his dynasty, and it did violence to Ptolemy's personal disinclination to sustained military effort. Indeed, his conquests were abandoned as suddenly as they had been acquired. In 245 Seleucus II, having made sure of his position in Asia Minor, took the field for the recovery of his lost kingdom. Storming or turning the Taurus passes, he regained Babylonia in the course of the summer, and in the same or the ensuing year made himself master of Antioch. Once the legend that Berenice and her son were alive had been dispelled, the central and eastern provinces gave him prompt recognition, and the Greek cities in particular, having reason to prefer Seleucid rule to Ptolemaic (p. 259), readily rallied to him. At the same time Ptolemy became involved in a new war on his Aegean front, where Gonatas (acting, no doubt, in concert with Seleucus) had opened a flank attack upon the Ptolemaic possessions (p. 141). The unsupported Egyptian garrisons were therefore quickly expelled or disarmed, and the Asiatic empire of Ptolemy collapsed like a house of cards.

In 243 Seleucus prepared to recover the coastlands of Seleucis and Cilicia, and to invade Cœle-Syria. But this campaign ended in early and complete failure. The fleet which he had levied upon the towns of western Asia Minor was destroyed in a storm before it came into action, and the army which he directed against Cœle-Syria was heavily defeated in a pitched battle (on an unknown site). In 242 Seleucus was even in danger of losing Damascus, and he did not break its siege until 241, when a fresh levy from Asia Minor was brought to his aid by his brother, Antiochus Hierax. In this same year Seleucus accepted a peace-offer from Ptolemy on the basis of the existing war-map. The general effect of this treaty was to restore the frontiers of 255, but it gave to Ptolemy the entire Syrian coast as far as Seleucia-ad-Orontem, where he continued to maintain a strong garrison.

In addition to its disastrous effects on other fronts, some of which have already come under our notice (p. 68), the Third Syrian War left Seleucid Syria without a sea-front.

§ 5. THE FOURTH AND FIFTH SYRIAN WARS

After the peace of 241 the Syrian question was allowed to rest for twenty years. But during this interval Ptolemy III gave ground for complaint to Seleucus II by fomenting rebellion in Asia Minor (p. 112); at the same time he invited a counter-attack by permitting his army to fall into a sad state of deterioration. The opportunity for a new war was eagerly seized by the young king Antiochus III, who resumed hostilities against Egypt in 221, without even waiting to dispose of his various domestic enemies.[1] The moment appeared well chosen, for in that year Ptolemy III had died, and his son and successor, Ptolemy IV Philopator, carried the leisureliness of his family to the point of sheer indolence. Yet Antiochus would have done better to postpone his attack, for at that time he still had the rebellion of Molon (p. 69) on his hands, and was therefore unable to muster a sufficient force for the war against Egypt. In consequence, his offensive failed at the outset, for he could neither force nor turn the fortifications at the narrows of the Leontes valley (between Mts. Lebanon and Anti-Lebanon), which formed the main avenue into Cœle-Syria. But having no reason to fear a counter-attack on Ptolemy's part, Antiochus was left free to turn round upon Molon and to stamp out his rebellion (p. 70). This done, he swung back into Syria with his entire field force. In the meantime a palace crisis had been precipitated at Alexandria by the rivalries of Ptolemy's first minister, Sosibius, and of the king's relatives, chief among them his mother, Berenice III, who claimed a prior right to exercise rule over the king. Finally, Sosibius cleared the field for himself by murdering his antagonists one by one, and henceforth he governed with quasi-dictatorial powers, while Ptolemy admirably filled the part of *roi fainéant*. As an

[1] In 221 Antiochus was under the influence of a masterful minister named Hermias, who advocated vigorous measures against Egypt. But the King evidently sympathized with his policy, for having got rid of the minister by assassination (220) he pressed on with the Egyptian War.

administrator, Sosibius displayed a timely vigour and discernment; but his jealousy of all competitors extended even to the officers at the war-front, and he requited the services of Theodorus, the general who had baffled Antiochus in 221, by plotting against his life.

In 219 Antiochus opened his second campaign with an attack upon Seleucia-ad-Orontem. Despite the inconvenience and humiliation of leaving the port town of Antioch in alien hands, the Seleucids had for twenty years acquiesced in its loss. Unlike Alexander, they had no confidence in their siege-trains (p. 240); and indeed in his belated move to recover Seleucia Antiochus based his hopes on treachery within the walls rather than on his own artillery. His confidence in underhand methods was justified, for some disaffected officers of the garrison accepted his bribes and facilitated his entrance into the town. After the fall of Seleucia the king made a new attempt upon the Leontes valley, with no better results. But he eventually slipped through along the more difficult coast road and received from Theodorus, now turned traitor, the keys of Tyre and Ptolemais (Acre). With an open road through Palestine before him, he now contemplated a dash through the barrier of Pelusium into Egypt itself, but on second thoughts he contented himself with a war of sieges in Cœle-Syria, which filled up the season of 219. After a winter spent in vain peace-discussions, Antiochus began the next campaign with a victory over a new Ptolemaic force which had been shipped to Sidon to intercept his communications. With his rear secure, he advanced methodically through Galilee and Samaria with a front extending across the Jordan, and completed the year's work with the capture of Philadelphia in Ammonitis. (218)

In thus waging war according to the book, Antiochus was in reality missing his tide. Had he taken his chance of slipping past Pelusium in 219 or 218, he would have found the Egyptian defences unprepared. But in the meantime Sosibius, assisted by his lieutenant Agathocles, had worked hard for the creation of a better field force. To supplement the depleted regular establishments he had sent recruiting officers round Greece for mercenary contingents, and he had made the novel experiment of drafting native Egyptians, who had hitherto been restricted to the auxiliary services, into the fighting units (p. 233). Moreover, with rare good judgment, he had resolved to weld together the elements of his new army by systematic training before putting them into the field. Fortunately for his plans, Antiochus had wasted two summers by his leisurely conduct of operations, and the intervening winter by allowing himself to be entangled in illusory negotiations with the Egyptian ministers.

In 217 the remodelled Egyptian army, accompanied by the king and his sister and future wife, Arsinoë III, entered Palestine and engaged Antiochus' force in a pitched battle at Raphia (not far from the Egyptian frontier). Measured by the number of combatants, this was the most important action since Ipsus, for Antiochus brought up some 68,000 men and Ptolemy 55,000.[1] The battle opened with a combined onset by the Seleucid horse and elephants upon Ptolemy's left wing. This movement was completely successful, for Ptolemy's African elephants,[2] outweighted and perhaps not so well trained, gave way before Antiochus' Indians, and Ptolemy himself was carried away in the general rout. But Antiochus, like Demetrius at Ipsus, rode too far in pursuit, whereas Ptolemy, with unexpected presence of mind, disengaged himself and personally directed a counter-attack by the heavy infantry in his centre. This corps, secured on its right flank by a minor success of the Ptolemaic cavalry and on its left by Antiochus' failure to rein in, charged home and shattered the enemy phalanx.

The victory of Raphia was both the beginning and the end of troubles for Ptolemy. Within his dominions it gave rise to a " native problem," consequent upon the share which the native Egyptians had taken in the battle (p. 217); but it restored Cœle-Syria to him. Though Antiochus eventually rallied his forces he was so crestfallen by his defeat that he at once offered negotiations. Ptolemy for his part was satisfied with one day's strenuous work and did not press his advantage. By the peace of 217 Antiochus kept Seleucia-ad-Orontem, but surrendered all his other conquests.

[1] On the numbers engaged at Raphia, see Appendix 13.

[2] Polybius' conjecture, that African war-elephants were less powerful than Indian ones (V, 84, 5–6), has been confirmed by Sir William Gowers, who points out that African forest elephants are less tall and broad-shouldered than Indian ones; the bush elephants, which are taller than Indian ones, cannot be tamed.—See *African Affairs*, Jan. 1947, p. 42 ff.; 1948, p. 173 ff.

In the interval between the Fourth and the Fifth Syrian Wars Antiochus quelled a rebellion in Asia Minor (pp. 113–4) and restored his authority in the upper provinces (p. 70 ff.). Shortly after his return from the East Ptolemy IV died, leaving his kingdom to a young boy, Ptolemy V Epiphanes (probably in 204).[1] A struggle for the regency now ensued between his former ministers, Agathocles and Sosibius, and his widow, Arsinoë, which ended with Arsinoë's murder. But Sosibius died or left Egypt not long after, and Agathocles was lynched in a riot by the household troops and the populace of Alexandria, among whom Arsinoë had been a favourite. (202)[2] This revolution in the capital was followed by a native rising in the Delta—the first-fruits of Raphia—which reduced Egypt for the time being to a state of partial anarchy. (201–0) Meanwhile Antiochus, resuming the policy of alliance with the Antigonids, had agreed with Philip V of Macedon to take advantage of young Ptolemy's troubles by despoiling him of his foreign possessions.[3]

In 201 Antiochus opened the Fifth Syrian War with a new invasion of Cœle-Syria, in which he carried at one stride all the country as far as Gaza. In the following year he was momentarily dispossessed of Palestine by a worthy successor of Sosibius named Scopas. This capable if unscrupulous adventurer, who had formerly been a general of the Ætolian League, but had since transferred his services to Egypt, had combined with a resolute new regent named Aristomenes to restore order in Egypt, and in the campaign of 200 he evidently surprised Antiochus by his unexpectedly quick rally of the Egyptian field forces. But Antiochus presently turned the tables on Scopas by destroying his army in a set battle at Panium near the sources of the Jordan. (200)[4]

Though the victor of Panium was at once called away to

[1] The death of Ptolemy IV was probably concealed by his ministers until after the murder of Arsinoë in 203, which was promptly followed by Ptolemy V's coronation.—See F. W. Walbank, *Journal of Egyptian Archæology*, 1931, p. 20 ff.

[2] A detailed and graphic account of this *émeute* has been preserved in Polybius, bk. XV, chs. 26–33.

[3] Since Antiochus stood to gain far more than Philip by this compact, it can scarcely be doubted that he was its author.

[4] The chronology of the Fifth Syrian War is not quite certain. Some authorities date Panium one or two years later.

other fields of war (p. 103), Ptolemy V accepted a peace from him, by which he ceded Cœle-Syria, and as a pledge of future good relations with the Seleucid dynasty he undertook to marry Antiochus' daughter, Cleopatra I. (*c.* 195 B.C.) This treaty did not finally close the controversy between Ptolemies and Seleucids over Syria, but it settled the question of actual overlordship in favour of the Seleucids.

But Syria, albeit the chief, was not the only cause of dispute between the two dynasties. Their rivalry also extended to Asia Minor; and it was here rather than in Syria that the political destiny of Hellenism in the Near East was decided.

CHAPTER VI

ASIA MINOR

§ 1. THE LIMITS OF GREEK PENETRATION

IT is a paradox of Hellenistic history that while remoter regions of the East were effectively conquered by Alexander and kept in subjection by his successors, Asia Minor was never fully subdued and was the first country after India in which Oriental dynasts established independent states. The reason for this anomaly may be found in the fact that in Hellenistic times, as often in later days, Asia Minor was essentially a land of passage. To Alexander it served as the connecting link between Europe and the Asiatic continent, but was otherwise of little interest: hence he did not trouble to complete its conquest, and he did not colonize it. To the Seleucids it was of importance, in that it gave them outlets to the Levantine and Aegean seas. Therefore they fought hard for its western and southern seaboards, and they picketed their line of communications from Syria and Cilicia to the Aegean with colonies; but they gave comparatively small heed to the mountain lands which fringe its northern and southern shores. In this respect the history of Asia Minor in the Hellenistic age continued that of the Classical period, that its western seaboard was still its most important and coveted region.

§ 2. THE NORTHERN KINGDOMS

Of the districts of Asia Minor which Alexander left untouched, the most extensive was the plateau that stretches from the Taurus range to the northern seaboard and was then known by the collective name of Cappadocia. At the time of Alexander's death this tract remained under the rule of a dynast of Persian extraction named Ariarathes, who had his residence at Gaziura in the Iris valley and held the Black Sea coast from the neighbourhood of Sinope to that of Trapezus (p. 11). In 322 Ariarathes' principality was converted by the regent Perdiccas into a Macedonian province, which passed from the hands of Eumenes to those of Antigonus. After the battle of Ipsus the Black Sea border slipped out of Greek control (pp. 96–7), but the inland regions were annexed to Lysimachus' and subsequently to Seleucus' dominions. About 260 inland Cappadocia in turn reverted to Oriental rule. A second Ariarathes, presumably a descendant of Perdiccas' victim, at this time reoccupied it with Armenian help and beat off the Seleucid general, Amyntas.[1] The intruder was henceforth left in undisturbed possession by Antiochus II, presumably because of his preoccupation with the Second Syrian War (pp. 86, 105); in 245 his son Ariaramnes obtained recognition from Seleucus II, and the hand of his sister. His kingdom came to be known by the name of "Great Cappadocia," or "Cappadocia" *simpliciter*.

About 300 the coastal strip, "Cappadocia-ad-Pontum," was detached from inland Cappadocia and joined to the adjacent district of Paphlagonia, so as to form part of a new kingdom which eventually received the short title of "Pontus." The founder of this realm was a Persian named Mithridates, the nephew of a dynast of like name, who had attached himself to Eumenes and Antigonus, but had finally been put to death by the latter on a suspicion of treason.[2] The younger Mithridates escaped into the mountain fastnesses of inner Paphlagonia,[3] where he remained unmolested. About the time of the battle of Ipsus Mithridates crossed the river Halys and took possession of the coastlands as far as Trapezus, together with the Iris valley. His occupation of these districts was apparently not challenged by Lysimachus; but after the battle of Corupedium he was attacked by Seleucus, who at that time showed a serious intention of

[1] I follow Beloch (*Griech. Gesch.*, IV, pt. 2, pp. 217–8) in dating this event to 260 rather than to 300 B.C

[2] On the relation of Mithridates "the Founder" to his elder namesake, see Beloch, *op. cit.*, p. 214.

[3] The political status of Paphlagonia in the third century is uncertain. But it probably remained a dependency of Pontus until 179 B.C., when Eumenes II and other dynasts of Asia Minor wrested it from king Pharnaces and set it up as an independent buffer state (p. 214).

subduing the whole north coast of Asia Minor. But he defeated Seleucus' general Diodorus in a battle (of which the details are unknown), and in the early years of Antiochus I he effectually protected his domains by inciting the Galatian new-comers to harry the Seleucid possessions in western Asia Minor. Thus he established a dynasty which lasted to the days of his famous descendant, Mithridates Eupator. His grandson and namesake received recognition and another sister from Seleucus II. The relations of the Pontic kings to the Greek cities of the Black Sea coast are not altogether clear. The lesser towns were probably annexed early; but Sinope remained independent until 183, and Trapezus appears to have held out equally well.

The third native principality in northern Asia Minor was the kingdom of Bithynia. By reason of its proximity to the Bosporus and the Sangarius valley, this state lay on one of the natural highways from Europe into Asia, and it presented no serious difficulties to an invader. Yet throughout the period between the Persian and the Roman Empires it kept its freedom and its own line of rulers. Under Alexander, whose lines of communication lay farther west, the Bithynians were not called upon to defend their independence, save against a minor inroad by one of his governors. In 315 their dynast Zibœtes made an alliance with Antigonus on equal terms. After his ally's death he came into serious danger of subjugation by Lysimachus, who naturally coveted Bithynia as a link between his European and Asiatic territories. But Zibœtes beat off Lysimachus' attack, and by 297 he felt so secure that he ventured to assume the title of king. Sixteen years later he took sides with Seleucus against Lysimachus and sent a contingent to Corupedium.[1] But when Seleucus took over Lysimachus' policy with his crown and sent one of his generals to invade Bithynia, Zibœtes routed him in a local Battle of Killiecrankie. (280) His successor, Nicomedes, fought the Seleucids with equal effect, though with different weapons. It was this king who first brought the Galatians into Asia, for the purpose of assisting him in a

[1] See the epitaph of a Bithynian officer, who fell 'Φρυγίοιο παρὰ ῥόον,' in defence of his country. (*Bull. Corresp. Hellénique*, 1900, p. 380.) It has been shown by B. Keil (*Rev. de Philologie*, 1902, p. 257 ff.) that the Phrygius river was in Lydia, and that the battle site must be that of Corupedium.

domestic war against a brother. Having disposed of this pretender, Nicomedes (in concert with Mithridates of Pontus) diverted the Galatians into the Seleucid territory and kept king Antiochus on the defensive. Thus Bithynia alone of the states of Asia Minor preserved its independence without a break. But it remained a small principality, extending but a little way east of the Sangarius and no farther south than the great bend of that river. Moreover, its position on a natural highway of communications exposed it far more than Pontus and Cappadocia to pacific penetration by the Greeks; and its kings, being true natives and not of Persian ancestry, had no rival civilization to oppose to Hellenism. Hence from the reign of Nicomedes the Bithynian kings adopted Greek customs and founded cities of Greek type, chief among them the new capital of Nicomedia. From the middle of the third century Bithynia had almost qualified itself to be reckoned among the Greek kingdoms of Asia Minor.

In an enclave between Bithynia and Pontus the Greek city of Heraclea maintained an almost unbroken independence amid the surrounding monarchies.[1] Under Persian rule this state had been left in possession of virtual freedom, and of a considerable hinterland, which it cultivated by means of serfs. In 364 it came under a capable line of despots, who built up a small but well-appointed fleet. Under the tyrant Dionysius Heraclea entered into free alliance with Antigonus, and after his death it maintained a similar position in relation to Lysimachus. About 305 B.C. Lysimachus took Dionysius' widow, Amestris, to wife, but dismissed her shortly after in favour of Arsinoë II.[2] The divorced queen continued to rule over Heraclea as a free ally of Lysimachus until 289, when her adolescent sons, grown impatient of their mother's tutelage, drowned her in a collapsible boat—the same device which Nero subsequently tried upon Agrippina. Hereupon Lysimachus, under pretence of avenging Amestris, dispossessed them and incorporated the city in his kingdom. After the

[1] The record of Heraclea partly survives in the fragments of a writer named Memnon, who excerpted a contemporary history (c. 280 B.C.) by a Heracleote called Nymphis. (C. Müller, *Fragm. Hist. Græcorum*, III, p. 529 ff.)

[2] This was the second time that Amestris experienced this treatment at the hands of Alexander's marshals. She had previously been jilted by Craterus.

battle of Corupedium the Heracleotes, having reconstituted their government on a republican pattern, bought off Lysimachus' garrison and recovered their freedom. In the next years, distrusting the Seleucids as the heirs of Lysimachus' claims, they took an active share in keeping Antiochus I at arm's length. They made a temporary alliance with Ptolemy Ceraunus, assisting him to defeat Gonatas (p. 58), and they formed a more durable union, the so-called Northern League, with Byzantium, Chalcedon, and some minor Greek cities at the Black Sea entrance. By these precautions they preserved their independence through the Hellenistic age.

§ 3. GALATIA

Beside the Black Sea coastlands, Alexander's successors did not maintain their hold on the northern part of the central plateau, which eventually fell to invaders more recent than themselves. Shortly after their arrival in Asia the Galatians occupied the uplands of Phrygia and converted these into a spacious robber-castle and a base for their forays in the adjacent plains. After their defeat at the hands of Antiochus I they were held more or less securely at the western edge of the Asia Minor plateau, but pushed eastward across the Halys, so as to cut off a portion of Cappadocia. The district over which they were now spread, extending roughly from longitude 31° to 35°, and from the northern coastal range to the Central Steppe, became their permanent home and received from them the name of Galatia. The chiefs and their retainers took up their abodes in the old hill-forts, while the folk maintained a nomadic existence in the forests and grasslands. The few towns of the plateau were left to their former inhabitants, no doubt at the price of a regular danegeld; the natives on the countryside gave over one-third of their lands to their new masters, and for the rest they paid a rent in kind—a relation resembling that of the Italians to their Gothic overlords.[1]

[1] There is a legend of a Phrygian peasant, who was found excavating a pit and replied to an inquirer as to what he was digging for, "I am making search for Antigonus." (Plutarch, *Phocion*, ch. 29.) The point of this story no doubt is that the orderly reign of this king seemed a golden age to the natives of Phrygia in comparison with the wild days of the Galatian conquest.

Having arrived in several bands, the Galatians did not form themselves into a single state with a central administration. The three main tribes, each settled in a different district, maintained their separate identity; and for ordinary purposes of government split up into four "tetrads" or cantons apiece, each with its own petty judge and its special military leader. Once a year the tribes combined to send three hundred representatives to a lonely meeting-place like a Norse "Thingvalla," to try cases of homicide and to discuss matters of common interest. Living apart from their native subjects and from the hellenized elements in the towns, the Galatians maintained their Celtic tongue and customs through the Hellenistic into the Roman period.[1]

§ 4. THE SOUTHERN BORDER

The southern fringe of Asia Minor, despite the fact that its Alpine uplands are a more formidable barrier than the northern coastal range, engaged the attention of Alexander and his successors more continuously. The reason for this lay in its proximity to the trunk road from the Hermus and Mæander valleys to Cilicia and Syria, which in the third century was the chief link between the western seaboard and the Asiatic continent, and to the Levantine pocket of the Mediterranean, which had acquired a greater importance, political and commercial, than the Black Sea. Alexander fought a winter campaign in Lycia and Pamphylia; Perdiccas reduced the eastern, Antigonus the western Pisidians. Under the Seleucids the western end of the road was lined with colonies, among which Laodicea-ad-Lycum and Apamea Cibotus (near the site of Antigonus' former capital, Celænæ) attained considerable size. A little way off the high road isolated stations were established at the main entrances into the Carian and Pisidian highlands; of these Antioch-in-Pisidia continued to play an important part under Roman rule. The Seleucids left the government of the upland regions in the hands of the local dynasts; but they probably levied

[1] See the interesting description in Strabo, bk. 12, p. 567, and J. G. C. Anderson in *Journ. Hell. Stud.*, 1899, p. 312 ff. The political system of the Galatians might be compared with the tenth-century federation of the five Danish Boroughs in Mercia.

tribute upon these, and they nowhere allowed the native tribes to consolidate into kingdoms like those of northern Asia Minor.

On the southern seaboard of Asia Minor the chief political problem in Hellenistic times was the same as in Syria—the proper apportionment of territory between Ptolemies and Seleucids. For the Ptolemies it was a desirable acquisition because of the intermediate naval stations which it offered between Egypt and the Aegean area. In particular, the western part of the coast from Lycia to Caria, which immediately commanded the entrance into the Aegean, was valuable in their eyes. To the Seleucids, so long as they had an outlet to the Aegean on the western coast, the southern seaboard was of lesser importance; least of all were regions like western Cilicia and Lycia, shut off from the hinterland by the adjacent mountains, of interest to them. On the other hand, eastern Cilicia formed an essential part of their dominions, both because of its fertile inland plain, and because it received the Taurus passes through which lay the roads to the central plateau and the west coast.[1] Pamphylia and Caria, though of less consequence to them than East Cilicia, engaged their attention because of their comparatively easy connections with the interior.

The overlapping interests of the two dynasties determined the history of the southern seaboard during the third century. Although the main actions between Seleucid and Ptolemaic forces were fought in Syria, the outcome of the Syrian Wars was more than once reflected in changes of frontier along the south coast of Asia Minor. On this debatable ground the Ptolemies could at least claim that they were the first-comers, for in the course of his campaigns against Antigonus the founder of their dynasty had occupied a chain of positions from Cilicia to Caria. (310–09 B.C.) But by the division of territory after Ipsus he was deprived of these footholds (and apparently evacuated them without demur), for the entire southern coast was then made over to Pleistarchus (p. 42). By the disappearance of Pleistarchus' short-lived realm neither Ptolemy nor Seleucus was an immediate gainer, for in the first place southern Asia Minor passed into the hands

[1] From the Seleucid point of view Cilicia belonged to Syria rather than to Asia Minor or "the lands across Taurus," as Asia Minor was officially styled.

of Demetrius. But in 296–5, when Demetrius left his Asiatic territories to be scrambled for among the other kings, the southern seaboard was partitioned between them. At this time eastern Cilicia became, and almost uninterruptedly remained, a Seleucid possession ; and it is probable that western Cilicia now also fell into Seleucus' hands. The central coastlands, including Pamphylia and Lycia, went to Ptolemy ; and Lycia remained in Ptolemaic hands throughout the third century. For the time being southern Caria was retained by Demetrius ; but after his final overthrow all this face of it, together with the island of Cos, was added to the Ptolemaic dominions. (286)

Though no details are preserved of the Seleucid coastlands which the fleet of Ptolemy II occupied in the First Syrian War (p. 85), it may be assumed that a large portion of Cilicia was included in its captures. At any rate, by the peace of 272 Ptolemy was given possession of western Cilicia as far as the river Calycadnus. But it was not many years before he restored western Cilicia to the Seleucids, and gave them Pamphylia into the bargain. It is not certain whether he made these cessions as the price of peace at the end of the Second Syrian War, or as part of the dowry which his daughter Berenice brought to Antiochus II in 252. In the Third Syrian War the Ptolemaic fleet at once occupied eastern Cilicia with a view to cutting off Seleucus II in Asia Minor (p. 88) ; and it resumed possession of western Cilicia and Pamphylia. By the peace of 241 these districts certainly came back under Ptolemaic rule, and it is probable that Soli and Mallus on the coast of East Cilicia remained in the same hands. At this stage Ptolemy III held almost the whole of the Levantine coast.

In the Fourth Syrian War, so far as is known, Antiochus III made no attempt upon the southern seaboard of Asia Minor ; and by the peace of 217 he recovered nothing, except perhaps the lost portions of eastern Cilicia. But in his second attack upon Egypt Antiochus did not confine his action to the Syrian front. The conquest of Cœle-Syria in 200 plainly revealed the weakness of his adversary, and by putting Antiochus in possession of Phœnicia it provided him with the means of contesting the Ptolemaic thalassocracy. But he was not called upon to fight for the lordship of the seas, for the Ptolemaic navy, which had fallen into neglect towards the end of the third century, was no longer in a position to offer battle. In 197 Antiochus proceeded to a combined assault by land and sea upon the Ptolemaic possessions of the southern seaboard, and in the same year he all but completed their reduction. His campaign in fact was little more than a military promenade, for the unsupported Ptolemaic garrisons surrendered without much demur, and only at isolated places was any serious resistance attempted. On the Carian coast a few towns which had of their own accord expelled or bought off the Ptolemaic troops maintained their independence or passed under the rival authority of Rhodes. By the peace of 195 the Ptolemies lost all their possessions in the Levant save Cyprus, and a few rare posts on the mainland coast, while the Seleucids gained control of the seaboard from Pelusium to Halicarnassus in an almost unbroken stretch.

§ 5. THE WEST COAST

The importance of the western coast of Asia Minor to Alexander and his successors has already been emphasized. Without a seafront on the Aegean the Hellenistic rulers on the Asiatic continent were liable to be cut off from their most essential import, Greek soldiers and colonists. Furthermore, the western seaboard of Asia Minor was one of the districts which derived the greatest material gain from Alexander's conquests ; from its rising revenues it could well afford to pay the costs of wars waged for its possession.

The scramble for the possession of the western fringe began as early as 319, when Antigonus laid the foundations of his empire by a descent from the Central Plateau to the Aegean seaboard, and by 313 he had completed its conquest (pp. 17, 27). In 302 it was Lysimachus' thrust into the zone of the west coast that brought the conflict between him and Antigonus to a head (p. 40). After the battle of Ipsus the duel was carried on between Lysimachus and Demetrius. The latter maintained himself at first in some of the Ionian towns, but in 296–5, at the same time as he lost the southern coast to Ptolemy, he was deprived of the western seaboard by Lysimachus. In 287 he recaptured Miletus and used it as a base for his Anabasis, but after his departure into the interior

Lysimachus finally resumed possession. After the battle of Corupedium Seleucus lost no time in taking over the western coast as far south as Caria. But his son, Antiochus I, soon found himself at grips here with the same antagonist that crossed his path in Syria and in southern Asia Minor.

In 295 Ptolemy I followed up his successes on the southern coast with a second expedition into the Aegean, in the course of which he lent Lysimachus a hand in the recapture of Miletus, and although he left Lysimachus in possession, he kept up and bequeathed to his son a friendly interest in the city.[1] In 281 Ptolemy II was forestalled by Seleucus in the scramble for the western coast, and among Seleucus' prizes was Miletus, which he and Antiochus had previously courted with benefactions. But a year or two later he took advantage of the difficulties that beset Antiochus I on his accession to seize Miletus for himself—at the same time ingratiating himself with the citizens by an extension of their territory ; and it was probably at this time that he gained possession of Chios and Samos. Though little is heard of Chios in the third century, Samos now resumed a prominent place in Greek history as the head-quarters of Ptolemy's fleet in the Aegean. In 275 Antiochus followed up his " elephant victory " over the Galatians (which earned him the title of " Saviour " among the Ionian cities) with an investment of Miletus by land and sea. But in the next year the Samian squadron under an admiral named Callicrates broke the blockade, and by the peace of 272 Miletus was left in Ptolemy's hands.[2]

About 262 Ptolemy provoked a new conflict by inciting Eumenes of Pergamum to secede from Antiochus (p. 108). This struggle is usually called the " Second Syrian War," but the main seat of its operations, as well as its cause, was in western Asia Minor. While Eumenes successfully engaged Antiochus on land, Ptolemy's fleet acquired the city of Ephesus (which had been rebuilt by Lysimachus, and now possessed a flourishing harbour). He confided his prize to a stepson, the child of Arsinoë II, and of Lysimachus, who is usually known as " Ptolemy the Son."[3] This prince, the

[1] On Ptolemy's participation in this campaign, see Beloch, *Griech. Gesch.*, IV, pt. 2, p. 341.

[2] Our knowledge of the relations between Ptolemy and Miletus from 279 to 274 comes from an inscription (*Milet*, I, 3, 139), on which see Appendix 5.

[3] See Appendix 6.

sole survivor from the massacre of Arsinoë's family by Ptolemy Ceraunus (p. 58), had for some time led a roving life in the Balkans, but eventually he rejoined his mother in Egypt, and by her influence had been made heir apparent of Ptolemy II, overriding the prior claims of the king's first son by his earlier wife (the future Ptolemy III). Despite the favour shown to him by Ptolemy II, the Son broke faith with him in 260 : perhaps the death of his mother had made his position at court less secure, and had given him reason to fear that he might after all be passed over in favour of his half-brother. The rebel prince carried with him Timarchus the governor of Miletus, who also won Samos for himself by a sudden assault. Upon the death of the Son, who was killed by his own soldiers in 259, Timarchus established a personal despotism over the three towns which had been lost to Ptolemy II.

The eventual gainer by the defection of Timarchus and the Son was the new Seleucid king, Antiochus II. Though neither of the insurgents stood in formal league with him, in effect they played into his hands. In addition, Antiochus received active assistance from Antigonus Gonatas, who had been furnished by Ptolemy with excellent reasons for wishing to expel him from the Aegean (p. 132 ff.), and from the republic of Rhodes, which usually maintained an attitude of neutrality between Seleucids and Ptolemies, but now seemingly feared that an extension of the Ptolemaic dominion along the Aegean coasts might lead to restrictions upon its trade. In 259 the Rhodian admiral, Agathostratus, helped Antiochus to recover Ephesus, and subsequently beat off an Egyptian rescue squadron commanded by the Athenian exile, Chremonides (p. 133). In 258 Antiochus rid the Milesians of their tyrant Timarchus, and was greeted with divine honours by the grateful citizens. But the decisive event of the Second Syrian War was Gonatas' naval victory at Cos (p. 137), which gave to Antiochus secure possession of the Ionian coast and enabled him to round off his conquests with the capture of Samos. By the peace of 255 (which also increased his territories in Syria and in southern Asia Minor) his recent gains on the western seaboard were confirmed to him.

In the Third Syrian War, however, Ptolemy III took ample revenge for the losses of the Second War. At the outbreak of this conflict Seleucus II had the loyal assistance of the cities of western Asia Minor,[1] and in 245 his hands were strengthened by Gonatas' victory over the Egyptian fleet at Andros (p. 141). But he received no further aid from Rhodes, and the loss of Corinth in 243 (pp. 142–3) so weakened Gonatas as to neutralize his recent success. Furthermore, the destruction by storm of the fleet which Seleucus had raised in the same year among the Ionian cities for his Syrian offensive (p. 89) gave Ptolemy unhindered access to the Aegean coast. Of the details of his counter-attack on this seaboard nothing is known, save that Ephesus was handed to him by a treacherous Seleucid governor named Sophron. But in one or two campaigns he retrieved all the past losses and won new outposts at Abydus on the Dardanelles and on the coast of Thrace (pp. 120–1). He did not seek new acquisitions on the west coast to north of Ephesus or Erythræ, but left the greater part of this strip in the allied hands of Eumenes of Pergamum. The peace of 241 is the high-water mark of Ptolemaic ascendancy in the Aegean no less than in the Levantine Sea.

For half a century after the Third Syrian War the conflict between Seleucids and Ptolemies was suspended on the western coast. During the Fourth Syrian War Antiochus III made no attempt to recover lost ground in this quarter; he had as yet no fleet, and for the time being the hinterland of the Ionian seaboard had passed out of his possession (p. 113). The only challenge to the Ptolemaic ascendancy in this period came from Antigonus Doson of Macedonia, who made a landing in Caria in 227 (p. 160). But this descent was more in the nature of a raid than of a systematic conquest, and it is doubtful whether he retained any part of Caria after the peace of 223.

But in the Fifth Syrian War Antiochus carried all before him on the western coast, no less than on the southern. It is true that by the pact which he now made with Philip of Macedon (p. 93), he left the Aegean seaboard to his ally. But the defeat of Philip by the Romans in the Second Macedonian War (p. 191 ff.) gave Antiochus a free hand in regard to his

[1] A long inscription from Smyrna (Hicks, 176; Ditt., *O.G.I.*, 229) records the gratitude of this city to Seleucus II for various privileges, and its endeavour to requite the king by rallying the neighbouring cities and colonies in his favour.

former partner. In 197 he followed up his quick successes on the southern coast with an equally rapid series of conquests on the Aegean seaboard. He did not resume possession of Samos and Miletus, which Philip had rid of their Egyptian garrisons but had not kept for himself. But he regained Ephesus and extended his authority over the greater part of Caria and Ionia. By this war the Ptolemies were definitely expelled from the western as from the southern coast of Asia Minor. But their losses were not Antiochus' gain for long. The campaign of 197, which excluded the Ptolemies from the Asiatic mainland, introduced the Romans there (p. 207 ff.).

§ 6. THE RISE OF PERGAMUM

We have left to the end of this survey the north-western corner of Asia Minor. In earlier Greek history this district played a less brilliant part than Ionia, and indeed would hardly have been heard of but for the distinguished record of the adjacent island of Lesbos. In the Hellenistic period Lesbos, like its neighbour Chios, sank into relative obscurity; but the mainland city of Pergamum now sprang into prominence as the capital of a kingdom whose growth is the strangest and the most important event in the third-century history of Asia Minor. Originally a mere market village under the castle of a petty local dynast, Pergamum had become by 350 B.C. a city with a considerable Greek element in its population. But its first rise to fame was due to the pure accident that Lysimachus had selected it as a repository for a treasure of nine thousand talents accumulated by him, and had placed this hoard in charge of a warden named Philetærus, who found means to make political capital out of it.

Born in the small Greek city of Tios on the Paphlagonian coast, Philetærus first comes into notice as a dependant of one of Antigonus' officers, from whose service he passed into that of Lysimachus. Having been rendered physically impotent by an accident in his childhood, he was not a likely person to aspire to a crown, and it was perhaps for this reason that Lysimachus entrusted him with his funds. He remained faithful to Lysimachus until the execution of the Crown Prince Agathocles, whose cause he had supported, drove him to declare for Seleucus. By his timely desertion he contributed materially to Seleucus' victory at Corupedium, and after the murder of Seleucus he won favour with Antiochus by ransoming the dead king's body from Ceraunus and sending it to Antioch for burial. The new king rewarded his just steward by a matrimonial alliance,[1] and by asking for no accounts. In recognition of this mark of confidence Philetærus made no overt movement towards independence. But the Treasurer drew upon the royal fund for personal displays of munificence to Greek cities, for the minting of his own coins, and for the recruitment of a private corps of mercenaries. It is true that the money bore the effigy of Seleucus, and that the troops were not used in action, save for the legitimate purpose of defending Pergamum against the Galatians. Yet at his death in 263 Philetærus was virtually a ruler in his own right.

The political status of Pergamum was put to the test as soon as Philetærus' nephew and adoptive son, Eumenes, took over his ill-defined authority. The new warden at once showed his hand by substituting the head of Philetærus for that of Seleucus on his coins, and by using his soldiers to detach neighbouring towns from Antiochus. By this open challenge to the king's sovereignty Eumenes brought a punitive expedition upon himself, but for this contingency he was well prepared. In all probability his own considerable resources had been supplemented with subsidies or military aids from Ptolemy II, who certainly was not slow to see the advantage of playing Eumenes off against his overlord. In 262 Eumenes sprang a surprise upon Antiochus by carrying the war close up to Sardes and inflicting a severe defeat upon him under its walls. This single battle sufficed to establish Eumenes' independence. Antiochus I died soon after, and his successor, Antiochus II, was too intent upon a reckoning with Ptolemy (which he obtained in the Second Syrian War), to pursue the war against the rebel dynast. The liberty which Eumenes thus acquired was used by him to extend his authority along the coast of Æolis from Adramyttium to Cyme or Phocæa, and inland to the head waters of the river Caicus. At this point his career was nearly cut short. Having perhaps been deprived of financial support from Egypt when

[1] Probably a match between Philetærus' nephew Attalus (father of the future king Attalus) and of Antiochus' niece Antiochis.

peace was made between Ptolemy II and Antiochus II, he had recourse to sharp practice with his mercenaries, and thus became involved in a dangerous mutiny. (*c.* 255 B.C.)[1] After this experience Eumenes settled down to consolidate his gains. Whether or no he came to terms with the Seleucid kings, he made no move to embarrass Seleucus II in the Third Syrian War.

At the end of the Third Syrian War Seleucus II had lost the southern half of the western seaboard to Ptolemy III, and part of the north-western coast to Eumenes. But he still held Smyrna and the cities of the Troad, and so long as he remained master of the hinterland the lord of Pergamum, left without Egyptian support, could hardly venture to make further inroads upon Seleucid territory. But it was the crowning misfortune of Seleucus II that he never quite fought down the internal feuds that arose from the rivalry between Laodice I and Berenice II. In 245, when he moved out of Asia Minor for the reconquest of the central and eastern provinces, he had left at Sardes a younger brother named Antiochus Hierax. Despite Hierax' lack of experience—for he was still a minor—his mother, Laodice, showed a perverse preference for him,[2] and encouraged his ambition to become an independent ruler. Therefore when Seleucus applied to him for reinforcements at the end of the Third Syrian War (p. 89), he only obtained them on condition of recognizing Hierax as joint king, with a virtually unfettered authority in Asia Minor.

In making this concession, Seleucus practically cut himself off from the Aegean and reduced himself to the position of an inland Asiatic king. Naturally he sought to go back upon his forced bargain, and a war between the two brothers ensued. In 237 Seleucus invaded Asia Minor and won two encounters over Hierax in Lydia ; but he failed to carry Sardes and so gave his adversary a breathing-space. This respite was used by Hierax to contract alliances with the Galatians and with Mithridates II of Pontus, who was more allured by the

[1] On Eumenes' settlement with the mercenaries, see Ditt., *O.G.I.*, 266 ; A. J. Reinach, *Revue Archéologique*, vols. XII–XIV ; G. T. Griffith, *Mercenaries of the Hellenistic World*, p. 282 ff.

[2] Laodice's disastrous interference with the law of primogeniture recalls the partition of Macedon between Cassander's sons at the instigation of Thessalonice (p. 46).

prospect of disruption in the Seleucid realm than restrained by his marriage tie with Seleucus. In the next campaign Seleucus carried the war into Galatia, apparently with the intention of preventing a union between the enemy contingents. But the result of his invasion was to bring down the Galatians upon himself in force. In a battle near Ancyra his army was virtually destroyed by the Galatian onset, and the king himself had to flee in disguise. This disaster, and the consequent invasion of Media by the Parthians (p. 68), put Seleucus out of action and compelled him to make a peace by which he definitely ceded Asia Minor to his brother. (236)

But Hierax won his kingdom at a price which was ruinous to himself and to Asia Minor. In hiring the Galatians to win his battles for him he had caught a veritable Tartar, and in effect became the bondsman of his auxiliaries. Not only had he to pay them a danegeld on behalf of his own territory, but he had to grant them licence to plunder all other parts of Asia Minor. Under these conditions the Galatians, well blooded by their runaway success at Ancyra, renewed their depredations on a scale which recalled the worst days of their coming into Asia. Indeed, Asia Minor was now threatened with general political chaos, for Hierax lost authority within his own dominions and was in effect reduced to the status of a local dynast round Sardes, while other petty principalities grew up out of the remnants of his realm under various captains of adventure.

At this crisis a new ruler at Pergamum, Attalus, the adoptive son and cousin of Eumenes,[1] achieved for Asia Minor what Antiochus "the Saviour" had done in 275. Threatened with an invasion by the Galatian tribe of the Tolistoagii in 230, he refused to buy off his assailants, and stood up to them in an action at the head of the Caicus valley, which resulted in their defeat.[2] The real trial of strength, however, came later in the year, when the Tolistoagii, reinforced by the cognate tribe of

[1] Some confusion has been brought into the Attalid pedigree by Strabo (bk. XII, p. 543), whose stemma does not square with the data of inscriptions. For two recent reconstructions (which are agreed upon the essential points), see M. Holleaux, *Revue Études Anciennes*, 1918, p. 9 ff.; Ernst Meyer, *Klio*, 1925, p. 462 ff.

[2] For the chronology of Attalus' wars with the Galatians and Hierax, see G. Cardinali, *Il regno di Pergamo*, p. 399 ff.; A. Ferrabino, *Atti Accademia Torino*, vol. 48, p. 707 ff.

the Tectosages and by Hierax, whom the Galatians were probably offering to set up in Attalus' place—for a consideration—marched in upon Pergamum and forced a second battle "near the temple of Aphrodite." In this decisive encounter Attalus won such a victory as to check the Galatian reign of terror for his lifetime. Indeed, this triumph not only gave Attalus immunity from the Galatians, but it conferred upon him a reputation as a champion of Hellenism and legitimized his dynasty in the eyes of the Greek world. Its Panhellenic character was indicated by the memorials which he set up at Pergamum and also at Athens, the arbiter of fame in Hellenedom. Attalus could now think of achieving more than a local sovereignty, nay of supplanting Seleucid authority in Asia Minor. He therefore assumed the title of king and set himself to dispossess Hierax altogether. Deserted by the Galatians and discredited in the eyes of the Greeks, Hierax suffered three successive defeats and was driven from province to province. First he was expelled from Hellespontine Phrygia (on the northern borders of Pergamum); in two further battles he lost Lydia and Caria. (229–8) From Lampsacus on the Dardanelles to Teos on the boundary of the Ptolemaic territory, the cities of the coast deserted to Attalus: even Smyrna gave up the Seleucid cause. Apart from those regions which had passed under the rule of local dynasts, Attalus was now master of all Seleucid Asia Minor.

But the loss of Asia Minor was not the full measure of the harm which Hierax did to his house. After his expulsion from Sardes he took refuge with Arsames of Armenia Minor (p. 69), and enlisted him for a new domestic war with Seleucus II. The moment for this campaign was seemingly well chosen, for Seleucus was away on campaign against the Parthians, and a diversion was promised at Antioch by an aunt of the king named Stratonice, who had been disappointed in the hope of becoming his queen, and took her rebuff like a true Macedonian princess.[1] But Hierax was checked in Mesopotamia by Seleucus' reserve army under Andromachus,[2] the king's father-in-law, and Andromachus' son, Achæus;

[1] Stratonice had previously been wedded to Demetrius II of Macedon, but had been dismissed by him on political grounds (p. 147).

[2] Andromachus is usually considered a grandson of Seleucus I. This is denied by Corradi, *Atene e Roma*, 1927, p. 218 ff., who holds that Andromachus was connected with the Seleucids by marriage only.

and the king himself, hastening back from Parthia at a sacrifice of a decisive success on that front (p. 69), drove Hierax back into Asia Minor. After this fiasco Hierax found himself landless and friendless. He fled to Thrace and there met his fate, appropriately enough, at the hands of some Galatian soldiery. (227 or 226) In the meantime Seleucus recovered possession of Antioch, and with or without the help of Ptolemy's officers procured the murder of Stratonice, who had taken refuge at Seleucia-ad-Orontem. For the moment the Seleucid monarchy was free of civil war ; but thanks to the dissensions which had beset it for the last twenty years it was now shorn of its eastern and western provinces and of the greater part of its seaboard.

§ 7. THE REBELLION OF ACHÆUS

Seleucus II, who had at least saved his kingdom from disintegration, did not live to recover his lost territories ; and the short reign of his son and successor Seleucus III once again brought the realm within sight of final collapse. In 225 or 224 the new king sent an advance force to recover Asia Minor from Attalus, but his generals met with repeated reverses, and his kinsman, Andromachus, was taken prisoner. The fact that Attalus lodged his captive with Ptolemy III suggests that, like Eumenes, he was receiving support from that quarter. In 223 Seleucus set out with his main force to retrieve these defeats, but before he could achieve anything he was murdered by two of his officers. His nickname, "Ceraunus," suggests that he may have had a bad habit of fulminating against his staff.

The death of Seleucus III left his kingdom in a highly critical position. His successor, a brother named Antiochus, had not yet come of age, and at the moment he was absent in Babylonia. Thus everything depended on the attitude of Andromachus' son, Achæus, into whose hands the government had fallen by default. Fortunately at this stage Achæus had no thought of disloyalty ; nay more, when Antiochus put him in charge of the war in Asia Minor he conducted it with such success as to pen up Attalus in Pergamum and to recover all the ground lost since the Third Syrian War except a few towns in the Troad. (222–1)

But Achæus had hardly completed these conquests than he stultified himself by an ill-considered *volte-face*. He had of late been incited by Molon, the rebel governor of Babylonia (pp. 69–70), and by Ptolemy III, who held his father, Andromachus, in custody, to try his own fortune ; and he seems to have assumed that Antiochus would have his hands full for some time to come with his campaigns in Babylonia and Syria. Without waiting to starve out Attalus or to test the temper of his own troops, Achæus proclaimed himself king and made a dash for Antioch. (220) But his Anabasis ended in Pisidia, for after the first few marches his army declared that it would not follow him against its legitimate king. To save his face and to appease his men, Achæus plunged into the highlands of southern Asia Minor and plundered or blackmailed the natives. But in so doing he gave time to Attalus to repair his fortunes, and the Pergamene king with a new force of Galatian hirelings from Thrace regained most of the Greek cities which had recently passed into Achæus' hands. (220–18) Attalus, it is true, was brought up short in his turn, for his Galatians proved unruly and had to be dismissed ; but he had recovered sufficiently to keep Achæus henceforth in play.

After the suppression of Molon's rebellion in 220 Antiochus had his hands free to deal with Achæus. But coolly judging that Achæus was held in chancery by Attalus and by his own troops, and would therefore be unable to resume his Anabasis, he left the rebel at large while he prosecuted his war against Ptolemy IV (pp. 90–2). His calculation was justified by the event, for although Antiochus sustained defeat in the Fourth Syrian War Achæus was unable to make use of his reprieve.

In 215 or 214 Antiochus at last appeared in Asia Minor, and having procured the neutrality or assistance of Attalus, he bundled Achæus into Sardes. With a chance of succour from Egypt, Achæus prepared for a long siege. But some Cretan Alpinists in Antiochus' service found an unguarded way up the rock on which Sardes is built—perhaps the same stealthy ascent by which Cyrus' Caucasian cragsmen outwitted Crœsus—and Achæus himself was caught in an attempt to escape in disguise from the citadel. (213) Unlike Molon, who had taken no chances by committing suicide,

Achæus was mutilated before death.[1] With these un-Hellenic reprisals Antiochus seemed to be rehearsing his future part as "Great King."

In disposing of Achæus Antiochus stamped out civil war from his dominions for half a century. But for the present he did not recover all the ground that his house had recently lost in Asia Minor, for he was bound by his treaty with Attalus to leave the Caicus valley, the Troad, and the west coast from Lampsacus to Teos in Pergamene hands. In 212 he turned away to the reconquest of his eastern provinces, leaving the final settlement of Asia Minor for some future date. In 197—the year in which our present survey ends—the political situation in Asia Minor had been simplified, in so far as the Ptolemies had been expelled from it, and all its southern half had been gathered in the hands of Antiochus III. But its northern regions were apportioned among several minor states, mostly under "barbarian" kings. It is true that Antiochus was prepared to tolerate Cappadocia, Pontus, Bithynia and even Galatia. But in the long run the independent existence of the Pergamene kingdom, which shut him out from a considerable part of the Aegean seaboard, was calculated to provide fresh materials for war. In the event, the "Balkanization" of Asia Minor proved a factor of vital importance when the Romans were first drawn into Asiatic politics.

[1] A long account of the attempted escape and eventual capture of Achæus is preserved in Polybius, bk. VIII, chs. 15–21.

CHAPTER VII

RUSSIA AND THE BALKAN LANDS

§ 1. RUSSIA

THE European seaboard of the Black Sea engaged the attention of both Alexander and Lysimachus, but in the third century it passed out of the sphere of interest of the Hellenistic monarchs, and it became almost lost to history.

The interest which Alexander displayed in the trans-Danubian region sprang from the faulty geographic notions of his contemporaries, who knew less of Russia and the Eurasian steppelands than the Greeks of the sixth or fifth century. The prevalent idea among them was that Europe and Asia here crinkled as it were into a circumpolar region of narrow compass, and that the Oxus (Amu-Daria) flowed into the Black Sea under the more familiar name of Tanais (Don). In 325 Alexander ordered Zopyrion, the governor of Thrace, to emulate the Persian king Darius in a new Scythian Expedition, whose object no doubt was to annex to his empire the Tanais-Oxus stage of the supposed trans-continental route to India. Given Alexander's misconceptions about the northern arc across the Eurasian continent, his orders to Zopyrion were no more chimerical than his plans for the circumnavigation of Arabia. But Zopyrion penetrated no further than the Borysthenes (Dnieper). After a vain attempt to capture the Greek city of Olbia he turned against the Scythians, who killed him and destroyed his army, estimated at 30,000 men.

Alexander's policy of conquests in Russia was resumed by Lysimachus, albeit in a modified form. With the Thracian and part of the Asiatic coast of the Black Sea in his possession, and the fleet of Heraclea at his disposal (pp. 98–9), this vigorous ruler no doubt planned to complete the circuit by a reduction of its remaining seaboards. In 292 he crossed the Danube in an endeavour to run down king Dromichætes of the Getæ (in Bessarabia). But he could not bring his quarry to a stand, and less circumspect or fortunate than king Darius, he lost his line of retreat to the Danube and was starved into capitulation. Dromichætes, who perhaps foresaw the coming Galatian invasion and realized the need of a good understanding with Lysimachus, released his captive on a simple promise not to do it again. This lesson sufficed for Lysimachus, and no later Hellenistic king was in a position to try his fortune in Russia.

The failures of Alexander and Lysimachus to incorporate southern Russia in a larger empire left the Greek cities of that region to find other protectors against invasion from the hinterland. The most fortunate in this respect were Panticapæum and the adjacent colonies in the Crimea. Not only were these towns comparatively sheltered by their position, but they had their battles fought for them by a remarkable dynasty of local chieftains, the Spartocids. This family, which apparently was of Thracian stock, had since the fifth century held the territory on either side of the Tauric Bosporus (Straits of Kertch). In the Greek cities they were officially known as "archons of the Bosporus," and they exercised their authority according to republican forms. But in return for the protection which they gave to the Greeks against the mainland tribes, they levied taxes, and as owners of the Crimean soil they controlled the Greek corn trade in those parts.[1] In the last days of the fourth century (309–3) a dynast named Eumelus cast himself for a bigger rôle. Having risen to power by the murder of his brothers, he endeavoured to justify his usurpation by exalting Panticapæum into the capital of a small Black Sea empire. To this end he equipped a fleet for the patrolling of the coasts against Caucasian pirates, he cultivated friendly relations with Byzantium, and he supported the Greek cities of the Thracian seaboard against Lysimachus' rival attempt at dominion (pp. 117–8). To match this increase of power he assumed the title of king. But his premature death cut short his ambitious schemes. In the course of the third century the Spartocids were thrust back on the defensive by increasing pressure from the hinter-

[1] As chief exporters of Russian corn the Spartocids had long stood in close relations with the Athenians, who cultivated their friendship assiduously. (An Athenian vote of thanks to Spartocus III in 289/8 : Hicks, 159.)

land, where the incipient immigration of Sarmatian peoples from across the Don had the effect of squeezing the intermediate Scythian tribes more closely upon the coastlands. Yet they safeguarded the Greeks against invasion until at the end of the second century Mithridates the Great revived the dream of a Black Sea empire, and established a Pontic protectorate in southern Russia.

Further west the Greeks of Olbia stood in a more difficult position. In earlier times they had enjoyed the protection of enlightened Scythian rulers, who grew corn for export and appreciated Greek wine or works of art. But in the third century the Scythians of this region were thrust back by Getic tribes from the Danubian lands, themselves in retreat from the Galatian inroads. The Scythians and their pursuers alike took to plundering or blackmailing the Olbians, who lived henceforth in a permanent state of siege. Despite loss of trade and growing financial embarrassment, the citizens improved their fortifications and imposed conscription or hired mercenaries in their defence. They owed much to a public-spirited burgess named Protogenes, who appears to have monopolized the local commerce after the fashion of the Spartocids, and evidently enjoyed great personal wealth : his repeated gifts or loans enabled the city to strengthen its defences or to pay the required danegelds.[1]

§ 2. THRACE

In the eastern Balkans Macedonian authority had been extended by Alexander as far as the Danube. But the disaster which befel Zopyrion in 325 caused a general rebellion, and when Lysimachus was allotted the province of Thrace, he could take immediate possession of little else except the Greek cities of its southern coast. Of his warfare in the Thracian hinterland in the next ten years nothing is known ; but by 313 he had conquered and thrown garrisons into the Greek cities on the Black Sea shore. Since he could not have carried these towns by the help of his fleet alone, which as yet was quite diminutive, it is plain that he attacked them from the land side after establishing his authority over the

[1] See the long inscription in his honour in Ditt., *Syll.*, 494. The date of this decree is disputed. But it may be assigned on the high authority of M. Rostovtzeff (*Iranians and Greeks in South Russia*, ch. 4) to the early part of the third century. On the history of Olbia in general, see Rostovtzeff, pp. 116–120.

natives between either sea. In 313 Lysimachus had to face a widespread insurrection fomented against him by Antigonus (p. 26), but he stifled it by prompt measures of repression. Flinging his troops across to the Black Sea, he at once recovered the important town of Istria (at the Danube estuary) and Odessus (Varna), and put Callatis (Mangalia) under siege. For a moment he had his retreat cut off by a contingent from Antigonus which had been landed at the northern point of the Bosporus, and by the belated revolt of the Odrysian king Seuthes (in modern Rumelia), who occupied the passes of the main Balkan range against his homecoming. But Lysimachus hurried back before Seuthes and Antigonus' officer could join hands, and so overcame their forces in detail. Despite its isolation, Callatis held out for several years, and *c.* 308 it received assistance from Eumelus of Panticapæum ; but a year or two after it was brought to terms. The only town of the Thracian seaboard that stood permanently outside of Lysimachus' jurisdiction was Byzantium. Situated like Rhodes at the controlling point of a great commercial highway, this city pursued the same policy of friendly neutrality all round, and generally contrived to stand outside the conflicts of Alexander's successors.

During the remainder of Lysimachus' reign Thrace lived quietly under his rule. But in the confusion that followed his death it suffered worst of all Balkan countries. In the Galatian inroad of 279–7 it was at once abandoned by the Macedonian leaders, and having no walled strongholds in the interior it was the more completely swamped under the tidal wave. In addition to the Galatian detachments which entered it at the outset, it received all the remnants of the bands which gradually filtered back from Greece and Macedonia. The greater number of the invaders, it is true, ended by drawing off to Asia Minor, and others were rounded up by Antigonus Gonatas ; but a considerable body of them took up their permanent abode on either side of the main Balkan range and converted eastern Thrace into a kind of European Galatia. The " kingdom of Tylis," as this Galatian robber-state came to be called, held the native Thracians in bondage and blackmailed the Greek cities of the coast to the end of the third century, when at last the Thracian natives turned upon it and made an end of it.

The dissolution of Lysimachus' realm was a doubtful blessing for the Greek cities of the Black Sea coast, which regained their liberty but were hard put to it, until the reign of Augustus, to ward off attacks by native Thracians or Getæ, or by incoming Galatians and Sarmatians. But the towns which lay nearest the Danube, and especially the colony of Istria, succeeded in maintaining or even extending their up-river trade, which had received an impetus under Alexander and Lysimachus. One of the strangest survivals of Greek city-life in barbarian lands is exhibited by the trading station of Axiopolis on the lower Danube (near the Bucharest-Constanza railway). This settlement, which dates back to the reign of Lysimachus and may be one of his foundations, remained a Greek oasis until the period of the Roman occupation. On the other hand, the Greeks of Istria and Callatis were foiled in an attempt to gather the whole of the Danubian commerce into their hands. About 260 the Byzantines fought a successful war against them in the interests of free trade for all Greek cities.

But the pride of Byzantium was humbled, and its championship of free trade was forsaken, under the stress of the Galatian invasions. Though the walls of the city preserved it from capture by passing bands on the way to Asia Minor—as they subsequently protected Constantinople from the First Crusade—the Byzantines succumbed to the steady pressure of the kings of Tylis, and consented to a danegeld, which was raised by degrees to an annual level of eighty talents, or more than twice the highest contribution at which the Athenians had ever assessed them. So ruinous was this imposition, that in 220 they issued a general appeal to the Greek states, or at all events to the Greek trading communities, to rid them of this incubus, and when this suit failed they retaliated upon Greek shipping in the Bosporus by levying a toll upon it. By this breach of a tacit international convention they involved themselves in a short war with the Rhodians, whose trading interests in the Hellenistic period extended to the Black Sea. Eventually they restored the freedom of the Bosporus; presumably they also continued their payments to the Galatians so long as there remained kings of Tylis to enforce them.

§ 3. THE DARDANELLES

Unlike the hinterland of Thrace and its Black Sea coast, which usually lived in a political backwater, the southern Thracian seafront and the Dardanelles were of more general interest to the Greek states. This interest arose partly out of the concern of the Greek mercantile communities for the freedom of the Straits, and partly from the attempt of Seleucus to extend his empire to European soil. The victor of Corupedium was on the point of occupying the Thracian Chersonese (the Gallipoli Peninsula) when Ptolemy Ceraunus murdered him, and though he had no more than set foot on it he created a claim which his successors were loth to abandon. In 279 the fleet of Antiochus I (which his admiral Patrocles had brought up from Ionia or Cilicia) occupied the Straits and disputed their possession with Antigonus Gonatas. In this campaign the advantage presumably rested with Gonatas, for in 277 he had a footing on the Chersonese near Lysimachia (the scene of his victory over the Galatians, p. 62). But in 278 neither he nor Antiochus can have had any considerable force in its neighbourhood, for between them they offered hardly any opposition to the crossing of the Galatians into Asia. On the other hand, the coming of the Galatians had the effect of suspending the war between the two kings, for Gonatas now became preoccupied with the acquisition of Macedonia, and Antiochus with the defence of Asia Minor. At some later stage, probably after Antiochus' "elephant victory" (p. 62), a permanent treaty was made, by which Antiochus surrendered all claims to Macedonia and Gonatas abandoned the Thracian Chersonese.[1] By this compact Antiochus took over a strip of Thracian coast which perhaps extended from Perinthus to Abdera or the river Nestus.

But in Europe as in Asia the Seleucids had to reckon with the Ptolemies, who extended their competition in coast-snatching to a second continent. The Ptolemies' opportunity came in the Third Syrian War, after the shipwreck of Seleucus II's fleet. In 243 or 242 Ptolemy III, having occupied the Ionian coast, went on to seize the Seleucid territory in Europe,

[1] This convention was sealed by the marriage of Gonatas with Antiochus' half-sister Phila II. This match stood out among the matrimonial alliances of the Hellenistic courts by reason of its longevity, for Gonatas never had another queen.

inclusive of the Thracian Chersonese. Thus the entire eastern half of the Aegean seaboard, with the exception of the Pergamene king's sea-front, passed under Ptolemaic control.

Until the end of the third century the Ptolemies retained their winnings in Thrace. Indeed, the Seleucids would appear to have abandoned hope of recovering this area, for in 203 Antiochus III transferred his claim upon it to Philip V of Macedon. But in the event Philip played the part of catspaw to Antiochus. In two rapid campaigns (202 and 200) he carried the Ptolemaic posts, which were as ill-provided as any of the overseas possessions of the Ptolemies at that time (p. 103). But during the Second Macedonian War against the Romans he withdrew his forces from Thrace, and by the peace of 196 he formally renounced his conquests. By this evacuation he invited and in a sense justified a reoccupation of Thrace on the part of Antiochus, for the Greek cities of the coast, upon whom the Romans were pressing the questionable boon of liberty, now stood practically defenceless, and Lysimachus' former capital of Lysimachia was actually destroyed in a raid bysome hinterland Thracians. In 196 Antiochus, having recovered all else that his house had lost to the Ptolemies, reasserted his claim to Thrace and took possession of the Chersonese; in 194 he occupied Ænus and Maronea. Had the question rested solely between the three kings, this acquisition might have remained unopposed, for Antiochus was now the strongest of them in military power, and his title was as good as any. But by the peace of 196 the Romans had also obtained a *locus standi* here. The problem of Thrace thus became a matter of international importance.

§ 4. MACEDONIA AND ITS HINTERLAND

When Antigonus Gonatas was proclaimed king of Macedon by the national army, his authority was at once accepted by all the cities of that land except Cassander's former capital of Cassandreia. Here a demagogue named Apollodorus had set up a dictatorship of the proletariate, and with funds confiscated (with or without torture) from the well-to-do, he maintained a considerable force of mercenaries for use against all comers. Gonatas was held up for ten months outside the town, but eventually captured it from its sea-front with the aid of a pirate flotilla which he enlisted for that purpose. (276)

From this time until its forcible partition by the Romans, Macedonia remained a united kingdom. From the warfare of the previous half-century it had received at least this benefit, that its turbulent nobility had been scattered over three continents, so that under the Antigonids the country was no longer vexed by those internal feuds which had distracted it under the old Argead dynasty.

In this chapter we shall not consider the relations of the Antigonids to the other Hellenistic kings and to the cities of the Greek Homeland: we shall confine ourselves to their dealings with the surrounding Balkan states. In view of the part which Macedon played in the Aegean lands and in Asia, it is easy to forget that the first duty of its kings was not to make conquests overseas, but to defend their country on its continental frontiers. As a lowland surrounded by a horse-shoe of mountains, it was peculiarly exposed to depredations by its highland neighbours. Furthermore, it lay at the end of a natural track for invaders from the Danube lands, the avenue up the Morava and down the Axius (Vardar) valley.

The problem of Macedonian security had been temporarily solved by Philip and Alexander, who had subdued the Thracians and Epirotes, and had chastened their other neighbours. After Alexander's death the country had little further to suffer from Thracian marauders until Roman times. During the reign of Lysimachus the natives of Thrace were well kept in hand, and after the Galatian invasions the new kingdom of Tylis fortunately looked for its victims in other directions. On its northern border the point of salient importance for Macedon was the "Iron Gate" gorge in the middle valley of the Axius, where incomers from the Danube lands could most easily be checked. This pass was in the hands of a small people called the Pæonians, who had been subjects of Philip and Alexander, but had since become independent under a king named Audoleon. During the reign of Cassander Audoleon was on friendly terms with Macedon: about 310 B.C. he co-operated with the Macedonian ruler in a preventive attack upon a Serbian tribe named the Autariatæ. He was subsequently in league with Lysimachus, whose example he followed in sending corn to Athens after its revolt from Demetrius in 288 (p. 50).[1] But his son, Aristo,

[1] Hicks, 157.

was expelled by Lysimachus, who annexed Pæonia in 284. In this king's strong hands the Iron Gates proved an effective barrier against the main column of the Galatians, which came down the Axius valley before it was deflected to the more westerly passes ; but in the confusion that followed his death the invaders had disengaged from the Pæonian defile before Ptolemy Ceraunus could meet them. After the dispersal of the Galatians Pæonia for a short time recovered its independence, but it was re-annexed by Gonatas (at a date unknown) and received a Macedonian military colony named Antigoneia, close by the Iron Gates. During Gonatas' lifetime the northern barrier held good, though it may have required his personal attention in various unrecorded campaigns. About 230 B.C., however, it was carried by the Dardanians, a tribe from the upper Axius valley, who inflicted a heavy defeat upon Demetrius II and overran Pæonia. The next king, Antigonus Doson, cleared the invaders out of the lower Axius valley, but was unable to recapture the Iron Gate, and it was left to Philip V to recover this position, which he accomplished in 217. Even so, Philip was repeatedly called back to his northern frontier,[1] and while the Macedonian king was engaged with the Romans Pæonia again was in Dardanian hands. For this last inroad the blame partly rested with the Romans, who were not too proud to enlist a barbarian auxiliary against their Greek antagonist. But the Roman general Flamininus subsequently made amends for this discreditable alliance. In recognition of the common service to Greece which Macedon had rendered in standing guard against raiders from the Balkans, he left its home territory intact.[2] An eloquent commentary on Flamininus' speech was furnished by the increasing insecurity of Macedon in the early days of Roman rule. Not till the days of Augustus did the Romans improve upon the frontier protection given by the Antigonid kings.

§ 5. ILLYRIA

The Dardanians were an offshoot of the Illyrian race, which also included the people of Epirus. Since the Epirotes by the third century had become sufficiently hellenized to be counted

[1] In 212, 209 and 204 B.C.

[2] Polybius, XVIII, 37, 8–9.

in with the Greek world,[1] their history may best be treated in connection with that of the Greek Homeland. On the other hand, Illyria Proper (modern Albania) remained an essentially barbarian country, and its relations to Greece and Macedon require separate discussion.

Illyria is separated from Macedonia by one of the most difficult mountain clusters in the Pindus range. Its main outlet is on the Adriatic Sea, and it is here rather than on the Balkan mainland that its history lies (p. 151 ff.). The contacts between Illyria and Macedonia were accordingly comparatively few. Though not included in Alexander's empire, the Illyrians had felt the weight of his arm sufficiently to keep them quiet during his reign and for some years after. In 314, however, a chieftain of southern Illyria named Glaucias was suspected by Cassander of having been incited against him by Antigonus. Without waiting to be attacked, Cassander invaded Illyria and brought him to terms. Furthermore, to cut Glaucias off from Epirus he resolved to extend Macedon to the Adriatic Sea. He annexed the Greek coast towns of Apollonia and Epidamnus, and of the district of Atintania (the valley of the Apsus), in which he planted the colony of Antipatreia. But he could not spare enough troops to hold these conquests. In 312 Glaucias dispossessed him of the Greek seaboard towns, and his ally Pyrrhus subsequently recovered Atintania for himself. At some later date, 261 or 239, Atintania was re-annexed to Macedon, but by 230 it was again in Epirote hands.

The formation of a united kingdom of Illyria *c.* 230 B.C. (p. 151) proved a serious menace to its seaboard neighbours, but was of less concern to Macedonia. In 222 an isolated raid by the Illyrians into Macedonian territory was beaten off by Antigonus Doson (p. 164), and in 217 a second incursion was heavily punished by Philip V, who counter-marched into Illyria and annexed a considerable stretch of land near Lake Lychnis (Ochrida). This expedition marks the end of the raids and counter-raids between Macedon and Illyria. But it was also the beginning of a new policy of westward expansion by Philip, and thus formed a link in the chain that led to the conquest of Macedon by Rome (p. 183 ff.).

[1] We may compare the difference (which endures to this day) between the semi-hellenised Tosks of southern Albania and the Ghegs of the north.

CHAPTER VIII

THE GREEK HOMELAND FROM 280 TO 239 B.C.

§ 1. THE FIRST REVOLT AGAINST ANTIGONUS GONATAS

THE struggle between Ptolemies and Seleucids for the possession of the Aegean coastlands, which we have followed out in the preceding chapters, affords abundant proof that in the opinion of these rival dynasties the Aegean area, as the cradle of Greek man-power, remained the most vital part of the Greek world. Indeed, despite Alexander's conquests, the history of Greece Proper right through the third century was of greater political importance than that of Asia and Egypt.

At this period the chief problem in the politics of the Greek Homeland continued to be that of its relations to Macedon. After the battle of Ipsus the system of alliance between Macedon and the confederated Greek republics (p. 38) was lost out of sight for many years. The alternative policy, which Antipater and Cassander had applied, of isolating the Greek states and controlling them severally by garrisons, was adopted by Demetrius in his later days, and was inherited from him by Antigonus Gonatas. The best that can be said for this method is that it gave internal stability to the subject states, for each Macedonian overlord saw to it that his supporters should be permanently in power, and treated any attempt to supplant them as a revolution or an attack upon the "ancestral constitution."[1] In many cities accordingly the wealthier classes favoured Gonatas' system of control, as affording a guarantee against the social upheavals which of all things they most dreaded. But, to say nothing of the fact that Macedonian garrisons were a direct and obvious affront to the deep-rooted Greek passion for autonomy, the rule of

[1] The venerable catchword of the 'πάτριος πολιτεία' was used impartially by advocates and opponents of Macedonian intervention.

Macedonian kings had come to mean conscription and taxation for wars which merely subserved their personal ambitions, and could bring the Greek cities no equivalent gain. The flame of rebellion, which had blazed up in the Lamian War, therefore went on smouldering for years to come. The proclamations of liberty made by Polyperchon and Antigonus I's various agents never failed to find a response in the Greek Homeland; and even without such baits Athens and Thebes had repeatedly set the example of revolt against Demetrius. Hence in 280 B.C.—the point from which the present survey begins—the political condition of Greece was as unstable as ever, and its history during the third century was even more troubled than that of the neighbouring monarchies.

About 280 B.C. Greece appeared to be in a peculiarly favourable position for recovering its complete liberty. Thessaly had escaped in turn from the yoke of Lysimachus and of Ptolemy Ceraunus, and from the Galatian invaders; and Pyrrhus was preoccupied with plans of conquest in another country (p. 179). In Peloponnesus Gonatas possessed everything except Sparta, Messene, and a few Arcadian towns; in Central Greece he held Bœotia and Eubœa, and controlled Athens through the Piræus; and in Thessaly he retained Demetrias, his father's last capital. But the levies imposed by him for his attack upon Ceraunus, and the disastrous result of that venture, gave rise to a rebellion such as Greece had not seen since the Lamian War. The lead in this movement was taken by Sparta, which, after many years of quiescence, made a new bid for Greek hegemony. This re-awakening of a dormant but undying ambition was largely due to a young king named Areus, who disdained both the frugal habits and the narrow Peloponnesian outlook of the orthodox Spartan, and broke one of Lycurgus' most sacred rules by introducing coinage into his city. This emission of coins suggests that he was drawing a subsidy from Ptolemy II, the future paymaster-in-chief of Gonatas' enemies, or (as seems more likely at the present stage) from Antiochus I, the competitor of Gonatas for Macedonia (p. 120). Areus' appeal to arms met with a wide response. Elis and most of the Arcadian towns, and Patræ with a few other Achæan cities joined in with Sparta, thus reconstituting for a moment the old Peloponnesian League. Argos and Megalopolis, as usual, held aloof from Sparta, but expelled Gonatas' garrisons on their own account. At the same time the Bœotians, and probably the Eubœans,[1] asserted their independence. Had Athens now taken part, or had the Bœotians combined with Areus for a siege of Corinth, the complete extrusion of Gonatas from Greece might have been accomplished in 280. But Athens was overawed by the garrison in the Piræus,[2] and so long as Gonatas had the remnants of his fleet, while his opponents lacked a navy, co-operation between the Peloponnesians and Central Greeks was hardly attainable. In autumn 280 Areus made a plundering expedition against the Ætolians, who were suspected of complicity with Gonatas, but he incurred such losses from their guerilla bands that his Peloponnesian allies refused to follow him any further. Thus the new Peloponnesian League incontinently fell into pieces. Even so, Gonatas was now reduced to the lordship of Demetrias, the Piræus, Corinth, Sicyon, and a few places in Argolis and Achæa. In the following years, moreover, he was so much taken up with his struggle for the possession of Macedonia that he put up with further defections among his remaining Greek subjects. It is probable that by 275 Gonatas had lost all his possessions in Peloponnesus except Corinth. For the moment he combined a still precarious kingship in Macedon with a petty despotism in some scattered Greek towns.

§ 2. GONATAS AND PYRRHUS

In the critical years between 280 and 275 Gonatas had at least this good fortune, that Pyrrhus was absent on foreign adventures, and therefore could not profit by his neighbour's difficulties. But in 275 the king of Epirus came home, bringing with him a grievance against the Macedonian monarch. On his departure overseas Gonatas had lent him transport,

[1] Eubœa probably followed the lead of Bœotia, as on other occasions. Its cities were certainly independent by 275.

[2] About this time Demosthenes' nephew Demochares induced the Athenians to set up a public statue of the orator. This manifesto, however, was not accompanied by acts of defiance against Gonatas. The decree of Demochares (quoted by ps.-Plutarch, *Lives of the Ten Orators*, 850F) recalls Demosthenes' services *seriatim*, but it does so in studiously moderate and unprovocative terms.

and by way of encouraging him to commit himself more deeply in distant adventures had apparently promised him further aids, which, however, were never sent. Pyrrhus accordingly came back with the intention of holding a reckoning with Gonatas. It is true that he had lost the flower of his army on foreign service, but he had not long to wait before he was equipped with a new force. Twenty years before, Ptolemy I had subsidized him against Demetrius (p. 47 ff.); now Ptolemy II gave him assistance against Demetrius' son. For reasons which we shall presently examine (p. 132), it had become part of Ptolemy's policy to set Gonatas' neighbours against him, and Pyrrhus was his first choice for this object. In 274 accordingly Pyrrhus was able to make his third entry into Macedonia, and he repeated the triumphs of his previous invasion. In 288 the Macedonians had grown tired of Demetrius; in 274 they were not yet confirmed in loyalty to Gonatas, and they probably had a poor opinion of his chances against a warrior with such a formidable reputation as Pyrrhus. Unwilling to venture his uncertain troops in a pitched battle, Gonatas fell back from the borderland towards the Macedonian plain; but on the retreat he was closely pressed, and when driven into a tight corner at one of the mountain passes,[1] he was deserted by all save his Galatian mercenaries. For a second time Pyrrhus had acquired western Macedonia and most of Thessaly. Though Gonatas clung to the title of king of Macedon, he now possessed little more than its eastern half, together with the Greek towns of Demetrias, Piræus and Corinth. To all appearances he was doomed to become a king without a realm.

But Pyrrhus, as usual, neglected to consolidate his successes. Though he could win battles, he lacked patience for a campaign of sieges. Instead of pressing on against Gonatas' remaining positions, he made a halt for his troops to collect plunder; and in giving licence to his Galatian mercenaries to rifle the tombs of the older royal dynasty at Aegæ he threw away whatever popularity he might have acquired in Mace-

[1] Either on the retreat from the Macedonian borderland, or, as Beloch plausibly suggests, on a further retirement from Macedonia into Thessaly. (*Griech. Gesch.*, IV, pt. 1, p. 573 n.) The scene of Gonatas' catastrophe can hardly be laid at the gorge of the river Aous, in Atintania. (Tarn, *Antigonos Gonatas*, p. 264 n.) Previous to this event Pyrrhus had already captured several towns in Macedonia. (Plutarch, *Pyrrhus*, ch. 26.)

donia. In 273 a rally by Gonatas gave him back city after city, and at the end of the year Pyrrhus cheerfully abandoned his remaining conquests.

The reason for Pyrrhus' unconcern about his losses in Macedonia was that in the meantime he had started another hare which promised him a more exciting race. On his Macedonian campaign he had been joined by a Spartan pretender named Cleonymus, who had been passed over for the kingship in favour of his nephew Areus. In deference to Cleonymus' promptings Pyrrhus deserted the northern field of war for a coup against Sparta. (Spring 272) Having recently recalled the last remnants of his forces from overseas, he had a good-sized army at his disposal, and as so often in his campaigns, the luck at first ran in his favour. From the Ætolians, who had a grudge to repay against Areus, he obtained facilities for putting across the Corinthian Gulf. In Peloponnesus he was welcomed as a double safeguard against attempts at reconquest by Gonatas and against a revival of Spartan imperialism. He met with a friendly reception, and probably gathered reinforcements, alike from Sparta's inveterate foes, Megalopolis and Messene, and from her recent allies, in Elis and Achæa. By giving out that he had come to secure the freedom of Peloponnesus against Antigonus he lulled the Spartans into a false sense of safety, and in his unimpeded progress he came within an inch of carrying their city by surprise. But at the end of the last day's march he disregarded Cleonymus' advice to press on, and waited for the morning. In the intervening night the Spartans, who still possessed no ring wall, or at all events not a complete one, improvised a field defence of trenches and a double row of waggons embedded up to the axles in the upcast soil. This barrier was the work of the Spartan women, who spurned the suggestion that they should be smuggled out of Sparta under cover of dark, and took the entrenching tools from the hands of the men, so that these might rest themselves before the next day's battle. Even so, the defenders were in a desperate position, for Areus with a portion of the Spartan army was absent on a mercenary adventure in Crete, and mere boys had to be pressed into service. On the first day of the siege the assailants would have broken in, had not Areus' young son, Acrotatus, hurried with a flying column to repair a broken sector. On the second day sheer exhaustion might have compelled the Spartans to surrender, had not a detachment of mercenaries sent forward from Corinth by Gonatas slipped through the lines into the city. With this reinforcement the defenders held out until Areus' return from Crete. Once the crisis over, the Spartan women, who had incessantly fed the fighting-line with ammunition and supplies, went home quietly, as if their exposure to fire had merely been part of the day's work. Indeed, they had no further need to perform men's jobs, for after one more unavailing assault Pyrrhus abandoned the siege.[1] In 370 B.C., when Epaminondas appeared before Sparta in overwhelming force, a resolute defence under the veteran Agesilaus saved the city for a hundred years. In 272 an effort no less heroic gave Sparta a further respite of fifty years from capture.

In the meantime Gonatas, who promptly seized his opportunity to retaliate upon Pyrrhus, had shipped a force to Corinth. On his approach the party that had detached Argos from him sent to Pyrrhus for help. The Epirote king answered the call, but found Gonatas lying in wait for him outside the city, and with Areus pressing on his heels he fell in danger of being caught between two fires. A seeming escape from this false position was offered him when his partisans in Argos laid a plan to open a gate for him by night. With their assistance Pyrrhus actually stole into the town, but some elephants which he had unwisely brought with him got stuck in the gateway and gave the alarm. With Gonatas, Areus and some of the Argive citizens rushing in upon him, Pyrrhus was caught in a trap beyond hope of escape. Of the various stories of his death the best attested, which is also the most picturesque, relates that he was stunned with a tile hurled from a roof by an elderly woman, and was decapitated by one of Gonatas' soldiers.

The best compliment that can be paid to Pyrrhus is that he stood in the line of succession from Alexander through Demetrius, and was the last of the knights-errant in Greek history. In personal *bravura* he equalled Demetrius, as a tactician he was perhaps his superior. On the other hand, he

[1] A graphic account of the siege of Sparta is given by Plutarch, *Pyrrhus*, chs. 27–30.

displayed no more capacity than Demetrius to consolidate his military successes by wise administration, and he showed less persistence in following up his victories in the field with siege operations. Nay more, Pyrrhus was born out of his time. He belonged to a generation that was growing war-weary of big adventures. The fiasco of his last campaign, and the almost comic manner of his death, were a fitting end to a futile career.

§ 3. GONATAS' RÉGIME IN GREECE

After the death of its leader the Epirote army surrendered to Gonatas, who now found himself for the first time with the ball at his feet. In addition to Macedon and Thessaly, which he could count on recovering at his leisure, he virtually held the fate of Peloponnesus in his hands, for not even Sparta could have held out for long against the forces now under his command. Indeed, had he cared to do so, Gonatas could probably have recovered for himself the same position in Greece as his father had held before Ipsus. But the Macedonian king threw away his opportunity. Like Augustus and other founders of dynasties, he had gambled recklessly to win a crown, but was rendered cautious by success ; like Cassander, he realized that after a period of heavy strain Macedon required an interval of rest. He therefore sent the captured Epirote army home, and he left Pyrrhus' son and successor, Alexander II, in possession of most or all his father's territory on the western side of the Pindus range. In Peloponnesus Gonatas resumed control of Argos and Megalopolis, so as to act as a check upon the reviving imperialism of Sparta ; but instead of restoring Macedonian garrisons, he left them in the hands of individual supporters, whom he furnished with funds or mercenaries. In Central Greece he reconquered Eubœa and reinstated a garrison in Chalcis, as a link between Demetrias and Corinth. But he made no attempt to recover Bœotia, and he broke with the traditional Macedonian policy of hostility to the Ætolian League. The most striking proof of his moderation is that he left the Ætolians in undisputed control of Thermopylæ and Delphi, and that by abstaining from the use of the Thessalian votes in the Amphictionic League, which stood at his disposal, he conceded to the Ætolians a working majority on the Amphictionic Council.[1]

It may be asked why Gonatas maintained a straggle of garrisons as far as the Isthmus of Corinth, and beyond that a sphere of influence in Peloponnesus. His motives were perhaps partly sentimental, for Corinth at any rate had always remained his, and had more than once stood between him and complete political destruction. But the mainspring of his policy is probably to be found in his apprehensions of aggression by other powers, against whom he deemed it necessary to retain a number of strategic positions in Greece. On the one hand, he could not trust Areus, whose ultimate ambition no doubt was to reconstitute the old Peloponnesian League, with Corinth as a member; on the other—and here apparently he saw the greatest source of danger—he kept a watchful eye upon the king of Egypt. From 274 B.C., when Ptolemy II gave support to Pyrrhus' invasion of Macedonia, Gonatas again and again found the Egyptian ruler across his path. The antagonism between the Ptolemies and the Antigonids, like the rivalry between Ptolemies and Seleucids, runs like a red thread through the political history of the third century. This antagonism, it is true, was not founded on any direct clash of interests, for the Ptolemies had no such designs on Macedon and Greece as on Asia Minor. Indeed, it is not easy to find an adequate reason for Ptolemy II's unfriendliness to Gonatas. The most likely explanation is that he saw in Gonatas the heir of Demetrius' imperialistic policy and a menace to the Egyptian thalassocracy, and that his attacks were in the last resort preventive. The hostility between Egypt and Macedon may be traced to a mistaken yet not unnatural suspicion, which gave rise to acts of precaution, which in turn engendered more suspicions—a vicious coil not unknown to the political history of modern Europe.

§ 4. THE CHREMONIDEAN WAR

When Ptolemy II first launched Pyrrhus against Gonatas he was unable to give him more than financial assistance, for at that time he had his hands full with the First Syrian War. In 272 he had recovered his freedom of action, but had

[1] Tarn, *Antigonos Gonatas*, pp. 212–4.

lost his ally. Failing Pyrrhus, he cast about for new instruments of attack, and in 267 he brought about another Greek league of liberty, with Athens and Sparta for its protagonists. Not for two hundred years had these two states stood forth as joint champions of Greek freedom. In the campaign of Chæroneia and in the Lamian War Athens had captained the Greek cause without Sparta's help ; in 331 Sparta had moved against Antipater, and in 280 against Gonatas, while Athens kept aloof. But Ptolemy II brought Cimon's " yoke-fellows " together again. In Sparta the king of Egypt could play upon the ever-fresh hope of a restored hegemony in Peloponnesus, and upon the personal love of glory and appetite for money of king Areus. In Athens he had a more difficult task. Since 281 Gonatas had been at peace with Athens and had sought to conciliate her by making the occupation of Piræus as invisible as possible. Besides, invisible or not, the occupation was effective, and gave Gonatas control of the city's food-supply. In 272, when the fortunes of Gonatas were at their ebb, the Athenians had gone so far as to appoint representatives to the Amphictionic Council—a mild gesture of independence—and to send envoys to Pyrrhus in Peloponnesus. Yet they did not commit themselves overtly against Gonatas, and in 270, while the Macedonian king was recovering Eubœa, they came to terms with him and withdrew their representatives from Delphi. Nevertheless, the diplomacy of Ptolemy II induced the Athenians to open rebellion. It may be assumed that Ptolemy promised not to replace the Macedonian garrison in Piræus by an Egyptian one, and to use his thalassocracy to ensure the provisionment of the city.

In the late summer of 267 the first overt move against Gonatas was made by the Athenians on the motion of one Chremonides, who gave his name to the " Chremonidean War." His resolution, inviting Greek patriots to form a general league of liberation against the Macedonian oppressor, was the last manifestation of the spirit of Demosthenes at Athens.[1] But as a general call to arms it achieved but a limited success ; in particular, the Bœotians remained too well

[1] Hicks, 169 ; Ditt., *Syll.*, 434–5. A passing reference is made by Chremonides to queen Arsinoë II as a champion of Greek liberty. This, however, is not enough to prove that she was the prime instigator of the attack upon Gonatas.

satisfied with their existing independence to renew the fellowship of Chæroneia on behalf of the other Greeks. But the Athenians had entered into a definite covenant with the Spartans, and these brought to their side the Achæans, the Eleians and most of the Arcadians, though Megalopolis, as usual, held aloof. This alliance followed in general the former alignment of parties in Peloponnesus, but it was partly inspired by a fresh current of anti-Macedonian feeling, the result of Gonatas' collusion with several city-tyrants. The Eleians in particular had a vivid memory of a recently deposed despot named Aristotimus : though it is not certain whether this ruffian was one of Gonatas' creatures, the Macedonian not unnaturally was held responsible for his misdeeds.

In setting the Greeks at war with Gonatas, Ptolemy II took upon himself a clear moral responsibility to give them efficient military aid. This assistance was all the more essential, as communication by land between Athens and Sparta was barred by Gonatas' garrisons at Corinth and Megara. The Egyptian fleet therefore became the vital connecting link of the coalition, and upon it devolved the further task of keeping Athens provisioned. But Ptolemy was by nature a man of business, and a soldier only by circumstance. He was prone to misapply to warfare the sound commercial principle of limited liability, and never with worse results than in the Chremonidean War. Acting no doubt on the king's orders, the Egyptian admiral, Patroclus, never more than half-engaged his fleet, and the initiative from start to finish remained with Gonatas.

In 266 Gonatas opened the campaign by invading Attica and cutting off Athenian supplies. Patroclus, who had advanced bases on the island of Ceos and at Methana in Argolis (which for some time remained a Ptolemaic possession, and was renamed Arsinoë), replied by occupying Sunium and organizing a blockade-running service, which appears to have been tolerably successful. But he failed in his most important task, which was to help Areus' Peloponnesian force to turn Corinth and bring Gonatas to battle in Attica. However well Gonatas might have picketed the Attic coast, it is hard to believe that Patroclus could not have forced a landing, had he made a serious attempt. But all that he would undertake was to harass Gonatas, who carried on the blockade without being brought to battle. In 265 Areus, who realized better his duty to Athens, resolved to take the risk of a frontal attack upon Gonatas' lines across the Isthmus. In endeavouring to force this prepared position he was venturing on an almost impossible task; he was defeated and paid for the attempt with his life. After this failure the Spartans made no further move to relieve Athens; indeed, after Areus' death the Peloponnesian coalition fell to pieces. Thus reduced to its own resources, Sparta for a time sank back to the rank of a second-class power. In a fresh attack upon Megalopolis, which Areus' son, Acrotatus, made *c.* 260 B.C., the Spartan army was heavily beaten by the unaided forces of the Megalopolitans, led by a general named Aristodamus.

In 264 assistance came to Athens from another quarter. To make up for the loss of Sparta, Ptolemy once more brought Epirus into the ring. With Egyptian subsidies in his pocket, king Alexander II repudiated his recent treaty with Gonatas and invaded Macedon. He succeeded in drawing Gonatas away from Attica, but was not able to detain him for long, for the Macedonian king presently returned to Athens, leaving his home front under the command of his son Demetrius, a youth of some thirteen years. In making light of the Epirote inroad Gonatas showed sound judgment, for in 263 Alexander let himself be defeated by the boy-general in Macedonia. The fiasco in which his expedition had ended so discredited the Epirote king that he was dethroned by his own subjects. After a brief exile Alexander was restored to power with the help of the Acarnanians; but he now made a lasting peace with Macedon. (*c.* 261 B.C.) As a guarantee against further invasion Gonatas required Alexander to cede to him the district of Atintania and established a fortress named Antigoneia at the entrance to the defiles of the river Aous, the natural avenue out of Epirus into Macedon.[1]

During Gonatas' absence in Macedon the Athenians had obtained a brief respite, which Patroclus no doubt utilized to revictual the city. After Gonatas' return they held out against him with the same tenacity as they had once exhibited in defying his father (p. 45). But from 263 onward Gonatas was able to maintain a continuous blockade, and in winter 262/1 he brought the besieged to terms. After the disruption

[1] See Appendix 9.

of the Spartan coalition, Gonatas could, without any doubt, have proceeded to make some easy conquests in Peloponnesus. But he was content to maintain the limited ascendancy which he had acquired here after the death of Pyrrhus. For the time being, too, he was not ready to challenge the Egyptian thalassocracy. After the fall of Athens, therefore, he made peace with Ptolemy and his allies. (261) [1]

Apart from the light which it casts upon the foreign policies of the Hellenistic kings, the Chremonidean War is of interest in that it marks an epoch in Attic history. After the capitulation of Athens Gonatas was in no mood for generosity. He not only tightened his ring of forts round Attica, but he reverted to his father's policy of stationing a garrison on the Museum Hill overlooking the city. He dismissed all the magistrates of the current year and for the future imposed a Macedonian governor to control the administration. In 255, it is true, he withdrew his mercenaries from the Museum Hill; at the same time he restored full autonomy to the city, and henceforth he always selected an Athenian to command his garrison in Piræus. From this time to the close of the Hellenistic period the Athenian constitution underwent little further change. Though payment for public services was definitely abandoned, sortition of magistrates (perhaps with a property qualification attached) and of the Council of Six Hundred was retained; and the council, together with the Ecclesia, remained the supreme governing body: it is not till Roman times that the Areopagus resumes its pristine position as the chief organ of government. Nay more, Athens continued for long to be the teacher and the showpiece of the Greek world. But after 261 B.C. the city voluntarily adopted those habits of political quietism which Demetrius of Phalerum had vainly endeavoured to induce upon it half a century before. Though the Athenians were occasionally drawn into fresh wars not of their own making, they now abandoned all hope of political leadership in Greece.[2]

[1] The outbreak of the Chremonidean War has been dated back to 270 by W. B. Dinsmoor (*The Athenian Archons*, p. 81); but the ordinary dating has been effectually defended by Tarn (*Journ. Hell. Stud.*, 1928, p. 28 ff.).

[2] It is significant that after 261 the Long Walls between Athens and Piræus were left to fall into ruins.

§ 5. COS AND CYRENE

The peace signed by Gonatas and Ptolemy II in 261 was not observed by them for long. By 258 a new war between them had broken out. In this instance the aggressor was probably Gonatas. For the time being Ptolemy kept his hands off Greece, where no lever was left for him to work. About 260, it is true, Gonatas put the Athenian antiquarian Philochorus to death on the ground of treasonable correspondence with Egypt, but in this case it was probably Philochorus who had sent the first call to Ptolemy. In any case, Gonatas had a reason for breaking another lance with Ptolemy, and soon after 260 the right opportunity came to him. The Chremonidean War had plainly shown the advantages of thalassocracy in Aegean lands : if Ptolemy, despite his command of the sea, had lost the war, that was due to his weak naval policy rather than to the inherent limitations of a navy. Gonatas therefore determined to wrest the trident of the Aegean from Ptolemy. With his slender resources for shipbuilding he could not hope to raise a fleet of equal size with his rival's, but about 260 the outbreak of the Second Syrian War gave him a chance of attacking while Ptolemy, so to speak, had one arm tied behind him. In the Syrian War a Rhodian fleet had defeated an Egyptian squadron, and Antiochus II was menacing the Ptolemaic naval base at Samos (p. 105). Once informed of these facts, Gonatas hardly needed to be told, if indeed he was apprised, that in 260 the Romans had challenged an old-established thalassocracy in the western Mediterranean. With such ships as he had ready, he put out to Samos and engaged the rest of the Egyptian fleet near the isle of Cos. (258 or 256) [1] Even after its recent losses, the Ptolemaic squadron outnumbered or outweighted the Macedonian, yet Gonatas won a victory which was accounted as one of his most memorable exploits, for in the peace of 255 Ptolemy surrendered the Cyclades. Gonatas

[1] The battle of Cos has recently been dated back to *c.* 262 by E. Bikerman (*Rev. Ét. Anc.*, 1938, p. 369 ff.). It is assigned by A. Fellmann, (*Antigonos Gonatas, König der Makedonen*, p. 63 ff.) to 246 or later. For the evidence in favour of 258 or 256, see Tarn, *Cambr. Anc. Hist.*, VII, p. 862, and W. Peremans, *L'Antiquité Classique*, 1939, p. 401 ff.

now felt so secure that he relaxed his recent precautions against the Athenians (p. 136), and dedicated his flagship to Apollo of Delos. We may probably recognize another memorial of Cos in the famous statue of Victory from Samothrace.[1]

Gonatas' second counter-offensive was a diplomatic intervention in the affairs of Cyrene. Here Magas had ended his long viceroyalty in 258 or soon after.[2] He had betrothed his daughter, Berenice III, to the future Ptolemy III, so that on the death of Ptolemy II Cyrene and Egypt should be held in personal union. But this scheme found little favour with a party in Cyrene which desired Home Rule, and would sooner snap than tighten the bond with Egypt, and it was opposed by the queen-mother, Apama, whose sympathies had always remained with the Seleucid house. Gonatas therefore sent his half-brother, Demetrius, surnamed the Fair (the son of Demetrius the Besieger and of a stepdaughter of Ptolemy I), to forestall Ptolemy II's son in Cyrene. Demetrius proved acceptable to the Cyrenæans, and so commended himself to Apama as to win her hand. But Berenice, fearing that if this marriage were to come about she would find herself elbowed out of Cyrene, had Demetrius murdered,[3] and took the government into her own hands. (*c.* 255) Thus Cyrene was again lost to Macedon. The Home Rule party, it is true, did not submit to Berenice. After a period of indecisive wrangling it temporarily succeeded in dispossessing her, and called in two staunch republicans from Megalopolis, Ecdemus and Demophanes, who had gained a reputation as tyrant-killers (p. 139). These two stalwarts reconstituted the towns of Cyrenaica into a federal state owning no allegiance to Egypt. (*c.* 250) But this experiment in federalism was interrupted by Ptolemy's son, who recovered possession of Cyrene (shortly before or after his accession to the throne of Egypt), and effected the personal union which his father had designed.

[1] A suggestion by F. Studniczka, adopted by W.W. Tarn (*Cambr. Anc. Hist.*, VII, p. 714, n. 2) and B. Ashmole (*ibid.*, VIII, p. 676). A. W. Lawrence (*Journ. Hell. Stud.*, 1926, p. 213) connects the statue with the Lamian War.

[2] On the chronology of Magas' reign, see Appendix 7.

[3] The story of the murder has been embroidered with melodramatic detail by Justin, XXVI, ch. 3.

§ 6. ALEXANDER, SON OF CRATERUS

With the death of Demetrius the Fair at Cyrene the counter-offensive of Gonatas was broken off. The next blow was dealt by Ptolemy, and it caught Gonatas in a sensitive spot. Ever since he had assumed the crown of Macedon he had committed Corinth to the care of his half-brother Craterus (a son of Craterus the marshal of Alexander and of Gonatas' mother, Phila); and he had subsequently given him a general control over his garrison commandants in Attica and Eubœa. In this trust he was never deceived, for Craterus displayed the loyalty of a true Antigonid. But after his death (*c.* 255) his son Alexander aspired to a larger province and a more independent title, and *c.* 252 he was induced by Ptolemy to declare himself king in his own right.[1] At the time, it is true, Ptolemy would not risk the remnants of his navy in an Aegean war, but he enlisted a pirate flotilla which apparently frequented one of the remaining Egyptian bases in Crete. With the help of this squadron Alexander confirmed himself in the possession of Corinth and also acquired Chalcis. He failed to secure the Piræus, whose governor, an Athenian named Heraclitus, stood firm for Gonatas, and the most that he could achieve was to compel the Athenians to sign a treaty of peace with him. Even so, Alexander's defection temporarily paralysed Gonatas. It cut him off from his partisans in Peloponnesus, and it robbed him of a large part of his fleet and shipbuilding material, which lay concentrated at Corinth and Chalcis.

In Peloponnesus Alexander established a partisan named Nicocles as tyrant of Sicyon, and by isolating Gonatas' agents at Argos and Megalopolis he invited attacks upon them. At Argos the tyrant Aristomachus, an exceptionally good ruler of his kind, held his ground. But at Megalopolis Aristodamus, the victor over Acrotatus (p. 135), who had since made himself despot with Gonatas' support, was poniarded by two opponents, Ecdemus and Demophanes. These assassins, it is true, were no followers of Alexander; as their subsequent action at Cyrene (p. 138) was further to prove, they were champions of republicanism against monarchy in all its forms. But the loss of Megalopolis to Gonatas was none the less real.

[1] On the chronology of Alexander's reign, see Appendix 10.

Gonatas also experienced a second disappointment at Sicyon, where Alexander's agent, Nicocles, did not maintain himself for long. In 251 the tyrant was expelled in a singularly well-planned night attack, in which his guard was overpowered without a single drop of blood being spilt.[1] To the ringleader of this escapade, a native of Sicyon named Aratus, Gonatas at once made overtures, no doubt expecting that he would take Nicocles' place as despot. But Aratus, who had lost his father and his home at the hands of a previous tyrant named Abantidas, was, if possible, an even more fanatic republican than his friends, Ecdemus and Demophanes. He accepted Gonatas' money, but spent it on objects of civic welfare at Sicyon, and instead of affiliating the city to Macedon he annexed it to Achæa.

By 250 Gonatas retained nothing in Central Greece except Attica, and nothing in Peloponnesus save Argos. About the same time he lost his thalassocracy in the Aegean and his lordship of the Cyclades, which Ptolemy recovered without effort.[2] Yet he made no attempt to retrieve these misfortunes. Perhaps he was preoccupied with some unrecorded war in the Balkans ; perhaps he believed, in the light of his past experience, that his luck must soon turn. Alexander remained king of his small but commanding realm until his death in 247 or 246.

In the event, Gonatas suffered little by waiting, for in a few years' time he recovered most of his lost ground. In 246 he regained Corinth, where Alexander's lone widow, Nicæa, remained in charge. Playing upon her desire for a new partner Gonatas offered her his son, Demetrius, and arranged to celebrate the wedding at Corinth with great pomp. But hardly had his *cortège* been admitted into the town than he swerved off with a small band of retainers to the citadel and bluffed the guards into surrender. Neither he nor Demetrius gave a further thought to Nicæa, of whose ultimate fate nothing is known. Having thus jilted his way into Corinth, as once upon a time the Greeks had lied the Horse into Troy, he reaped the fruits of his sharp practice in every direction. Eubœa returned to its former allegiance, and the alliance

[1] A lively account of this coup is preserved in Plutarch, *Aratus*, chs. 4–9.

[2] In 249 Ptolemy instituted a festival named the Ptolemaieia at Delos, which presupposes his recovery of that island.

with Megalopolis was probably now renewed. This city had been the object of yet another Spartan attack *c.* 249, but by the influence of Ecdemus and Demophanes it received reinforcements from Achæa, and with their aid beat off the assailants with heavy loss. About 245 a citizen named Lydiadas, who had been chiefly responsible for the recent victory, made himself tyrant and, so we may assume, entered into friendly relations with Gonatas. Furthermore, the Macedonian king recovered his navy, and lost no time in putting out to sea with it. (246) The moment was well chosen, for Seleucus II was then making his rally in the Third Syrian War, and was preparing to meet Ptolemy III in a naval campaign (p. 89). He encountered the Egyptian admiral, Sophron, with such ships as Ptolemy could spare for Aegean service, near the island of Andros, and here gained his second naval victory.[1] This success, it is true, was counter-balanced by the destruction of Seleucus' fleet and Ptolemy's consequent conquests in the eastern Aegean (p. 106). Gonatas therefore did not press his victory, but contented himself with the recapture of the Cyclades, leaving Thera, Crete and the seaboard of western Asia Minor in Ptolemy's hands. But Delos and the neighbouring isles now passed definitely out of Egyptian control, and Ptolemaic interference in the affairs of the Greek Homeland was henceforth confined to financial aids.

§ 7. THE RISE OF THE ACHÆAN LEAGUE

After the recovery of Corinth and the victory of Andros, Gonatas' policy in Greece appeared to have definitely justified itself. Egypt and Epirus had been fought to a standstill, Sparta was held at arm's length, and the Ætolian League remained on friendly terms. But a new antagonist was being raised up against him in the Achæan League. This confederacy as yet comprised nothing but eleven small towns of Achæa Proper, together with Sicyon. But by the incorporation of Sicyon the Achæans had broken the bounds which

[1] For the date of the battle, see Tarn, *Antigonos Gonatas*, pp. 464–5, and E. Pozzi, *Memorie Accademia Torino*, 1913, p. 319 ff. The main argument in favour of 246 B.C. is supplied by the foundations of festivals by the Antigonids at Delos. (On which see also Appendix 2 of this volume.)

confined their league to their own petty nationality, and had prepared the way for an indefinite expansion like that on which the Ætolians had recently entered (p. 145). Moreover, with Sicyon they had annexed a new citizen whose views extended far beyond Achæa. Aratus was the natural leader of all those Greeks in whom the deep-rooted hatred of tyrants was a consuming passion. His sphere of interests therefore included all towns where there remained tyrants to be deposed, and he used all his influence with the League to free the Peloponnesian cities and protect them against reprisals by annexation. From 245 onward he held the office of strategus in the League with almost unfailing regularity in every second year, and during the statutory interval between his turns of office (p. 285) he was sure of a seat on the federal council. For thirty years he remained almost continuously the director of Achæan policy.

Aratus' first acquisition for the League was made during his second strategia in 243, when he seized Corinth by a surprise attack similar to that by which he had captured Sicyon. It is true that in 243 the League was at peace with Gonatas, and that at Corinth there was a double line of walls to be carried, for in addition to the fortifications of the town there were the defences of the citadel, which towered full thousand feet above the city. But Aratus counted Gonatas, the patron of tyrants, as the greatest of them all, and therefore beyond the pale of public law. Besides, the previous good relations between Gonatas and the Achæans gave him the chance which he needed of taking the king's troops by surprise. In addition to a select corps of Achæan soldiers he enlisted at great expense some unfaithful members of the garrison who offered to serve him as guides. On the day of the venture he found an unexpected ally in the moon, which alternately lighted up his path or hid him from view, as occasion might require. He carried the city gate without difficulty, but on the ascent to the Acropolis his followers scattered. The vanguard, led by Aratus in person, now stood in danger of being nipped between the defenders of the citadel and the town garrison hastening to the rescue. But by a sudden inspiration Aratus' stragglers rounded upon the rescue party as it defiled past them, and put it to rout. Eventually the Achæan forces reassembled and by a combined effort broke into Acrocorinth.[1] The Corinthians, who had never been free from a Macedonian garrison since the battle of Chæroneia, gladly joined the League and accepted a strong guard of Achæan troops.

The renewed loss of Corinth was a blow from which Gonatas never recovered. He again held Chalcis, and his fleet remained strong enough to maintain communications with Peloponnesus, and perhaps to put Corinth under blockade. But he was now past the age of seventy-five, and he evidently felt that it was too late for him to make a fresh start. He went so far as to enter into a compact with the Ætolians for the partition of the entire Achæan territory. But he left it to his allies to carry the treaty into effect. In 240 he confessed his inability to recover Corinth by making peace with the Achæans and leaving the prize in their hands.

The capture of Corinth eventually entailed the expulsion of all the despots and the rise of the Achæan League to predominance in Peloponnesus. But the despots, though doomed, died hard, and their disappearance left the Achæans face to face with more dangerous enemies. On the first impression made by the fall of Corinth Aratus won the adherence of Megara and of several minor towns of Argolis, and he secured alliances with two of Gonatas' habitual enemies, Egypt and Sparta.[2] On the other hand, he met with no better success than Alexander in detaching Athens from Gonatas, and an invasion of Attica which he undertook in 242 remained abortive. Similarly at Argos an attempt to procure the assassination of the tyrant Aristomachus met with such success as it deserved. Indeed, in 241 Aratus was thrown back upon the defensive. In that year the alliance between Gonatas and the Ætolians took effect, and though Gonatas remained passive the Ætolians prepared for their part to make their first invasion of Peloponnesus. On the other hand, Ptolemy III, though appointed generalissimo of the Achæan League and its allies, proved an even less trustworthy

[1] The story of the capture of Corinth is excellently told in Plutarch, *Aratus*, chs. 18–22.

[2] Aratus had previously visited Ptolemy II (*c.* 250) and had obtained from him a subsidy for the settlement of internal disputes in Sicyon. Though this deal did not involve the League directly, it was an earnest of help in future. On Aratus' adventures in a storm on the way to Egypt, see Plutarch, *Aratus*, ch. 12.

associate than his father had been in the Chremonidean War, Despite the fact that Gonatas had lost part of his navy in Corinth, the Egyptian king does not appear to have made any attempt to recover the thalassocracy of the Aegean[1]; and for the military assistance which Aratus was expecting he compounded with a meagre annual subvention of six talents. Furthermore, Aratus played false to a more trustworthy ally, king Agis of Sparta, who brought up a substantial contingent to help in holding the Isthmus lines against the projected Ætolian attack. Whether he was seized with a perverse mistrust of Agis or with one of his occasional losses of nerve, he withdrew at the first coming of the Ætolians, thus sacrificing the gate of Peloponnesus and the Spartan alliance. Fortunately for Peloponnesus, the Ætolians only stayed to plunder Pellene, the nearest Achæan town, and in the next year they joined Gonatas in making peace with the Achæans.

In 240 Aratus was left free to seek new acquisitions for the League. Despite the fact that Athens was a signatory of the recent peace with Gonatas, he planned a surprise attack upon Piræus. But the attempt miscarried, and Aratus aggravated his failure by pretending, yet not persuading anybody, that the attack had been made by a subordinate on his own responsibility. He further damaged his reputation in a second abortive assault upon Argos. In this city his old enemy, Aristomachus, had, after all, fallen to the dagger, but his murder had been a purely personal act of revenge, and its effect was merely to make room for the dead man's son, Aristippus. Against the new tyrant Aratus attempted a *coup de main* with a handful of volunteers, but again met with failure. His credit with the Achæans now sank so low that when Aristippus sent in a remonstrance against Aratus' breach of the peace, the League agreed to submit the case to a jury of Arcadians from Mantinea, who proceeded to sentence the culprit to a heavy fine. But Aratus had by now become indispensable to the League. He presently recovered his ascendancy and reaped the reward of his persistence.

In 239 Antigonus Gonatas brought his long reign to an end. In Greece he left a sinister reputation because of the tyrants whom he had set up or supported in the towns of Pelopon-

[1] See Appendix 11.

nesus, and indeed his system of control was at best a mere makeshift. But his failure to endow Greece with a lasting form of government must be judged in the light of two facts. He was being continually baulked by Ptolemy II, and he had another and more pressing task on his hands. His first duty was to Macedon, which he had found in a state of exhaustion and anarchy. In setting the Macedonian monarchy once more upon a secure basis he accomplished a task comparable to that of Philip II, and incidentally he rendered Greece a great service, for in view of the increasing pressure of peoples from the Balkans it is highly doubtful whether the Greek Homeland could have kept itself free from barbarian invasions if Gonatas had not set up Macedon as a strong shield over it.

§ 8. THE EXPANSION OF THE ÆTOLIAN LEAGUE

While the alternate growth and decline in the power of the Antigonid dynasty is the chief event of Greek political history in mid-third century, the extension of the Ætolian League constitutes an important side issue. The expansion of the Ætolian League began about 290, when it took possession of the sanctuary of Delphi. Aided by the reputation which it acquired by its services in repelling the Galatians (pp. 60–1), it proceeded to incorporate one by one the various small communities round Mt. Œta and the Spercheius valley.[1] In 254 the Confederacy also absorbed Phocis, and in 243 it instituted a new pan-Hellenic festival, the Soteria, at Delphi, in commemoration of the repulse of the Galatians in 279.[2] In 245 the Ætolians defeated the Bœotians in a war which these latter, fearing forcible incorporation in the League, had declared upon them. Though they forebore to annex Bœotia, they reduced it to the rank of a subordinate ally. About 260 B.C. they were induced to join with Acarnania in a defensive treaty against Alexander II of Epirus; but before long they let themselves be bought over by Alexander, who

[1] The dates of these annexations are not quite certain, but they mostly fall within the period of 278–260. They are deduced from the progressive appropriation by the Ætolians of the votes on the Amphictionic Council. See R. Flacelière, *Les Aitoliens à Delphes*, chs. 4–8.

[2] This panegyris replaced an earlier local festival. Its date, which Flacelière (p. 138 ff.) put on general grounds after 246, has been fixed by a new inscription. (B. D. Meritt, *Hesperia*, 1938, p. 121, no. 24.)

proposed to them a partitioning of Acarnanian territory, and appropriated its southern half.[1] By 245, therefore, they controlled all Central Greece outside of Attica. From this point they went on to establish their ascendancy in other parts of Greece. About 243 they accepted a call for help from the Eleians, who were then intent on one of their interminable border wars with the Arcadians, and they acquired not only Elis but several Arcadian places, including the cities of Mantinea and Tegea, as their clients. About the same time the Messenians safeguarded themselves against reprisals from Sparta by accepting an Ætolian protectorate. Thus by 240 the Ætolians had become the paramount power in western Peloponnesus. To this same period we may also date the first Ætolian incursions into the Aegean and Ionian Seas. Though the Ætolians never possessed a federal fleet, they encouraged privateering by individual captains, and under pressure from these several island states, including Cephallenia in the Ionian Sea, and Chios and Ceos in the Aegean, bought future immunity at the price of Ætolian overlordship.[2] At the death of Antigonus Gonatas the Ætolian League had become the second strongest power in Greece. But with increasing strength it learnt nothing of wiser statecraft. Though credit is due to the Ætolians for their ingenious and flexible federal constitution, and for a certain soberness in their control of the Amphictionic League at Delphi, their record as a whole is that of a robber-state, and their influence on Greek politics was mainly disruptive. The following chapters will show that the Ætolian League went a long way to play Greece into the hands of the Romans.

[1] For the terms of the treaty see Ditt., *Syll.*, 421; for the date (which is much disputed), see esp. G. Klaffenbach, *Klio*, 1930, p. 223 ff. In any case the Ætolians promptly went back on their word.

[2] For examples of such treaties of immunity, see Hicks, 178 (Ceos), Michel, 25 (Mytilene).

CHAPTER IX

THE GREEK HOMELAND FROM 239 TO 217 B.C.

§ 1. THE WAR OF DEMETRIUS

ANTIGONUS GONATAS was succeeded by his son, Demetrius II, who had made his mark as a mere boy in the war against Alexander of Epirus (p. 135). Apart from Aratus' further successes in Peloponnesus, his reign is chiefly notable because of the rupture of good relations between Macedon and Ætolia, which henceforth became habitual enemies.

The ultimate cause of this antagonism lay in the growing recklessness of the Ætolian League, whose appetite for annexations or plunder was becoming indiscriminate. Its immediate occasion was the disavowal of the treaty made between the Ætolians and Alexander of Epirus *c.* 260 (pp. 145–6). On the death of Alexander and the accession of a boy-king of Epirus (Pyrrhus II), the Ætolians demanded for themselves the northern half of Acarnania, which by the previous compact had been assigned to Epirus. In anticipation of an Ætolian attack the regent of Epirus, Alexander's widow, Olympias, appealed to Demetrius, and she reinforced her suit by offering him the hand of her daughter, Phthia. Demetrius, who had previously married and dismissed a Seleucid princess, Stratonice II (whose subsequent adventures have been related on pp. 111–2), accepted Phthia and prepared to assist Olympias. In return, the Ætolians contracted an alliance with Macedon's former enemy, the Achæan League. (239) By these negotiations a new alignment of states was created which cut right across the groupings of Gonatas' reign.

The operations of the so-called "War of Demetrius" (238–29) fall into two sections. On the northern front Demetrius fought the Ætolians to a standstill. Not only did he prevent their attack upon Epirus, but he landed a force from Demetrias in Bœotia and detached this country and Phocis from the Ætolian League. (236) On the southern front his Achæan opponents suffered defeats yet gained new ground. With the object of forcing Athens into the Achæan League Aratus again and again invaded Attic territory and ravaged the crops. But although these Archidamian tactics reduced the Athenians to sore straits—for they now depended in large measure on their home-grown corn—they achieved no greater success than in the Peloponnesian War. Under the direction of a wealthy citizen named Eurycleides they raised funds[1] and organized a defence corps by which the Achæans were eventually beaten off. In 235 Aratus concluded a checkered campaign in Peloponnesus with a notable gain. Renewing his attacks upon Argos, he at first fumbled away a victory over the tyrant Aristippus by a characteristic failure of nerve in battle; but later in the year he made amends by killing Aristippus and routing his army in an ambush near Cleonæ. For the moment the dead man's brother, Aristomachus II, staved off revolution in Argos; but while this city still eluded Aratus' grasp he won the no less important town of Megalopolis. The ruler of this city, Lydiadas, took the battle of Cleonæ so much to heart that he decided to come to terms with Aratus gracefully before he was forced to capitulate. He abdicated his tyranny and incorporated Megalopolis in the Achæan League, in which he henceforth held successive strategiæ, turn and turn about with Aratus. In 233 Demetrius made an attempt to repair this loss by shipping an army to Peloponnesus. His general Bithys invaded Arcadia from Argolis and won a pitched battle at Phylacia near Tegea.[2] But before he could achieve any lasting result he was recalled from Peloponnesus.

The withdrawal of Bithys was due to the outbreak of a new war in the Balkans, which henceforth engaged all of Demetrius' attention. About 233 the Dardanians broke into Macedon from the north and inflicted a severe defeat upon Demetrius (p. 123). For the rest of his reign the Macedonian king was wholly taken up with repairing this disaster, and the last campaigns of "Demetrius' War" were fought without his presence. His remaining ally in Peloponnesus, the Argive

[1] The record of a voluntary subscription for this purpose is preserved in Michel, 608; a decree of the Ecclesia in honour of Eurycleides in Ditt., *Syll.*, 497.

[2] For the locality of this battle, see Beloch, *op. cit.*, IV, pt. 2, p. 529–30.

tyrant, Aristomachus, now felt his isolation so keenly that he followed Lydiadas' example in abdicating and annexing his city to the Achæan League. (229) After this acquisition the League embraced all Argolis except the Egyptian station of Arsinoë-Methana, and all Arcadia save the Ætolian client-states, Mantinea and Tegea.

In 229 the long connection between Athens and Macedonia was dissolved. In the War of Demetrius the Athenians had discovered that if the Macedonian garrison in Piræus did not oppress them, neither did it protect them, for during the recent Achæan invasions they had been left to fend for themselves. After the death of Demetrius they resolved to sever a tie which gave them no support and called upon Diogenes, the commandant of Piræus, to evacuate his post. Diogenes, being himself an Athenian, agreed to disband his mercenaries, provided that 150 talents were found to pay them off. At a time when the Athenian treasury possessed no reserve funds, this was an almost prohibitive sum. Yet Athenian patriotism responded to the call, and with the assistance of loans from Thebes and Thespiæ,[1] and a free gift from Aratus, the requisite total was made up. Diogenes accordingly dismissed his troops, and Athens for the first time since 294 was free from the shadow of a foreign occupation. After their liberation the Athenians received a new appeal, backed up with a further offer of money, to join the Achæan League; yet Aratus' purse availed no more than his sword to win them over. Disillusionment by the bitter lessons of past centuries, and the self-contained system of agrarian economy to which the country was reverting, had fostered a narrow outlook among Athenian politicians. To the squires who now controlled the Ecclesia membership of the Achæan League merely signified an unnecessary entanglement; therefore they rejected Aratus' advances and pursued a policy of friendly neutrality all round. The Athenians have been blamed for their selfishness in thus standing aloof.[2] Yet in view of the League's actual history it is hard to believe that they could have raised that body to pan-Hellenic importance, or could have saved it from disaster in Peloponnesus. From their own point of view their policy

[1] Thespiæ had a long-standing tradition of friendship with Athens; Thebes had received Athenian aid at its restoration in 316.

[2] A severe judgment is passed upon them in Polybius, V, 106, 6–8.

of isolation proved remarkably successful. While they continued to stand in good relations with Egypt,[1] the Athenians came to a friendly understanding with Macedonia, and Aratus presently ceased to pester them. In the later years of the third century Athens was, so to speak, the calm centre of a whirlpool.

§ 2. THE KINGDOM OF ILLYRIA

In northern Greece, as in Peloponnesus, the Dardanian catastrophe produced far-reaching results. In Epirus it led to the abolition of the monarchy. In this country Pyrrhus I had by virtue of his personal prestige converted a limited monarchy into an autocracy, but his endless exactions and conscriptions had endangered the stability of his dynasty. A long period of minority reigns, in which the crown passed in turn to Alexander's two sons, Pyrrhus II and Ptolemy, and the withdrawal of Macedonian support in the last troubled days of Demetrius II, brought the royal house to fall. About 231 a revolution broke out, in which king Ptolemy was assassinated and his niece Deidamia was lynched by the mob of Ambracia. As the regent Olympias also died about this time, the royal line of Epirus now became extinct. The monarchy was succeeded by a federal republic, in which the constituent tribes of the Chaones and Thesproti enjoyed equal power with the royal tribe of the Molossi, and the seat of government was removed to Phœnice in Chaonia (near the straits of Corcyra).

The republic of Epirus reversed the foreign policy of the royal house by coming to terms with Ætolia and renouncing its claim on the northern half of Acarnania. Whether this peace treaty stipulated that the Ætolians should *pari passu* restore independence to the other part of Acarnania is not known. At all events the Acarnanians, with or without the leave of their neighbours, reconstituted themselves into a united and independent state. But in so doing they drew upon themselves an invasion by the Ætolians, who either had not countenanced the liberation of Acarnania or had promptly repented of their own generosity. In this emergency the Acarnanians, on the strength of their traditional friendship with Macedonia, applied to Demetrius for help. Unable

[1] About 224 B.C. the Athenians instituted a thirteenth tribe, Ptolemais, in recognition of a gift of a gymnasium by Ptolemy III.

to protect them personally, the Macedonian king took the novel step of referring them to his neighbour, Agron, the king of Illyria. In so doing he gave the Illyrians the first pretext for their short-lived experiment in imperialism.

We have hitherto made no more than passing mention of the Illyrians. For many centuries this people had enjoyed an evil reputation for piracy. From the tall-grown timber of their rainy coastlands they built handy little skiffs—the disreputable ancestors of the peaceful and dignified argosies of Ragusa; and from behind their curtain of islands, which foiled the ancient police-squadrons, as it baffled the submarine-hunters in the First World War, they raided Adriatic commerce. In earlier days their depredations had been kept within limits by the fleets of Athens[1] and Corinth, or of Syracuse and Tarentum. Moreover, until the third century the Illyrian nation remained split up into small tribes which showed no more capacity for common action than their Albanian descendants until recently. But by 250 the navies of Corinth and Athens had been laid up, and the Greek sea-lords of the western Mediterranean had been absorbed in the republic of Rome, which was slow to awaken to the duties imposed upon it by its newly won thalassocracy. Furthermore, at this time the chieftain Agron, whose residence lay near Cattaro, united all Illyria into a state which was strong enough to turn from raids to conquests.

At the invitation of Demetrius of Macedon, Agron mobilized a force sufficient to inflict a heavy defeat upon the Ætolian invaders of Acarnania and to relieve the town of Medeon, which the invaders had put under siege. But by revealing to them their collective strength this defensive campaign converted the Illyrians into systematic aggressors. In 230 Agron's widow, the queen-regent Teuta, sent out a fleet under a chief named Scerdilaidas with a roving commission, and Scerdilaidas put such a liberal interpretation on his orders as to make a pounce on the Epirote capital, Phœnice. Such was the terror caused by this invasion, that although the Illyrian raiders were presently called home by domestic disturbances, the Epirotes accepted a treaty by which they ceded Atintania (the lower Aous valley) to the Illyrians and

[1] In 324 the Athenians occupied a patrol station (probably on one of the off-shore islands) to protect Adriatic commerce. (Ditt., *Syll.*, 305.)

became their dependents. Lest worse should befall them, the Acarnanians also made submission. Thus the Illyrian sphere of power extended to the Corinthian Gulf. In 229 the Illyrian attack was directed against the island of Corcyra. Having long ago dismantled their navy, the Corcyræans called upon the Ætolians and Achæans. But the Ætolian captains were too busy privateering on their own account to heed the summons, and the Achæan fleet, despite the capture of some of Gonatas' ships at Corinth, was too weak or too ill-trained to be of service. The Illyrians made short work of the Achæan relief-squadron and forced Corcyra to surrender. By this acquisition they put themselves astride of one of the main lines of communication between the eastern and western Mediterranean.

At this point the imperial career of the Illyrians came to an end. Side by side with their military expeditions they had carried on an intensified campaign of piracy which endangered Italians no less than Greeks, and thus brought the Romans down upon them. Shortly after their capture of Corcyra a Roman fleet made a drive against them and confined them for the time being to the waters north of Lissus (Alessio). Though Illyrian corsairs reappeared in Greek seas, no further Illyrian conquests were attempted at the expense of the Greeks. But the Greeks only obtained exemption from one invader by the intervention of another alien ; and where this second alien went, he usually stayed. (229)

One further consequence of the Dardanian invasion of Macedonia requires our notice. Soon after the death of Demetrius the Ætolians gained compensation for the loss of Bœotia by overrunning Achæa Phthiotis and Thessaly, thus extending their territory to the Gulf of Pagasæ and occupying lands which had almost become an integral part of Macedon. For the moment, Macedonian authority in Greece was restricted to eastern Thessaly, Eubœa and the Cyclades ; and with Macedon itself under invasion it seemed as if this kingdom might disappear from Greek, and might never enter into Roman politics.

§ 3. SPARTA : KING AGIS IV

While the eclipse of Macedonian power gave the Achæan League free scope for expansion in Peloponnesus, it also removed a check upon the ambitions of Sparta. In this city, moreover, a domestic revolution now struck at those economic abuses which had been the fundamental cause of Sparta's military weakness since the days of Leuctra. Though Spartan institutions had resisted every attempt at political change, they could not hold out against the slow erosion of economic causes. Since the time of Epaminondas, and more particularly since the age of Alexander, Spartans had gone abroad in large numbers on mercenary service. Unable to enjoy the produce of their estates, these absentees had alienated them by sale or bequest, thus facilitating a concentration of land in the hands of the wealthier citizens.[1] Furthermore, the influx of gold and silver, which had begun after the Peloponnesian War, increased in volume after Alexander's campaigns, and a money economy had begun to supersede the pristine communism or barter of Laconia. In the third century unequal division of land and a debt question, which the free use of money soon raised up, at last carried Sparta to the stage which so many Greek states had attained in the seventh and sixth centuries, of being ripe for tyranny.

The first impulse to revolution at Sparta came from a young king, Agis IV, who had probably made acquaintance with the communistic theories then in vogue among some schools of philosophy, and as hereditary commander of the Spartan army was concerned with the steady diminution of the citizen levy, now reduced to seven hundred hoplites. With a view to social justice, and to the replenishment of the Spartan battalions, he advocated a redistribution of lands. But as a gift of land had but a small or a negative value if encumbered with a mortgage, Agis tacked on to his measure an ordinance for the abolition of debts. His programme, which he, of course, dressed up as a return to the disregarded institutions of Lycurgus, found support among the poorer citizens, who looked to receiving more land, and among some of the wealthy personages, who wished to bilk their debts[2]. In 243 his friend Lysander obtained the ephorate and framed Agis' proposals in the form of bills. With the help of the Popular

[1] Cary, *Class. Quart.*, 1926, pp. 186–7.

[2] It may be doubted whether there existed at Sparta any considerable number of poor debtors. In ancient Greece poor debtors were usually found in the peasant class; but the Spartan citizen-body did not include any peasantry.

Assembly he overcame the hesitations of the Council of Elders, and on a flimsy pretext he procured the dethronement of Agis' royal colleague, Leonidas, who headed the opposition to the reforms. Thus Agis' measures were carried into law. All debts were rescinded; the rich lands in the Eurotas valley were earmarked for 4500 poor citizens, Periœci and approved aliens, and these grants were to convey Spartan franchise to those who did not yet possess it; finally, the less fertile territories in outer Laconia were to be apportioned among 15,000 Periœci qualified for military service.

In 242 the execution of this scheme was delayed for a while by the hostility of the incoming ephors. But Agis at Lysander's instance used the royal authority to call his supporters to arms, and forcibly replaced the recalcitrant ephors by a more amenable board, among whom his uncle Agesilaus held chief place. By this coup, in which not a drop of blood was shed, Agis secured a free hand. But the redistribution of land was a measure which inevitably required much time. On this pretext Agesilaus induced the king to begin with the collection of all debt certificates, and to make a bonfire of these in the market place. Having thus lost the mortgages on his own land, Agesilaus cast about for means to preserve the land itself, and the chance of war played into his hands. In 241 Agis left Sparta for the campaign against the Ætolians (p. 144). In the meantime Agesilaus held up the land-assignation *sine die*. On his return Agis found that a reaction, due to Agesilaus' bad faith, had set in, and that Leonidas had carried out a counter-revolution, by which he recovered his kingship and carried his candidates for the ephorate of 241/0. Though his army appears to have remained loyal to him, Agis was too disheartened to make a fresh beginning; he disbanded his men and himself took sanctuary. The new ephors decoyed him away from the consecrated ground, and after a farcical trial before the Council of Elders put him to death.[1] With him, and in the same spirit of calm resignation, died his mother and his grandmother. As usual in a Spartan crisis, the women had freely entered the lists, and those on the losing side paid their forfeit without demur. Thus Agis was sacrificed to the

[1] The story of Agis is related by Plutarch in one of the shortest, and also one of the best, of his biographies.

cunning of friend and foe. Yet his career was more than a dramatic episode in Spartan history. Like his counterpart, Tiberius Gracchus, whose objects and methods recall those of the Spartan king even down to details, he lit a torch which was raised aloft again by a more resolute hand after it had been knocked out of his grasp.

The reprisals of the Spartan conservatives upon Agis' party involved them in a short war with the Ætolians, among whom some of the exiles had taken refuge. On the pretext of restoring these the Ætolians invaded Laconia; but since their real object was plunder, they did not press home their attack, but contented themselves with a huge haul of slaves among the Periœci or Helots. (240) But shortly after this foray the outbreak of the "War of Demetrius" drew away the attention of the Ætolians from Peloponnesus, and for some twenty years they left a free field here for the Spartans and the Achæans.

§ 4. SPARTA: KING CLEOMENES III

When Aratus first aggrandized the Achæan League at the expense of Antigonus Gonatas, he indirectly conferred a benefit upon Sparta, the habitual enemy of Macedon; and it was a natural corollary of his policy that in 241 he and king Agis fought a common campaign against Gonatas. But the bad support which he gave to Agis on that occasion revealed his latent distrust of Sparta. Though he probably had as yet no fixed plan for the annexation of all Peloponnesus to the Achæan League, he certainly did not intend that Sparta should pocket Gonatas' losses and recover its former hegemony. This nascent antagonism was intensified when the Achæan League incorporated Sparta's old enemies, Argos and Megalopolis, for the capable ex-tyrants of these towns, Aristomachus and Lydiadas, soon acquired an influence in the League second only to that of Aratus, and began to press for open war with Sparta.

But Sparta did not wait to be attacked. In 235 a new king, Cleomenes III, had succeeded his father, Leonidas. Like Caius Gracchus, Cleomenes deliberately held himself back until with growing years he should have gained more experience. But in 228, after the accession of Megalopolis to the

Achæan League, he entered on a career of conquest which was intended to make him the arbiter of Peloponnesus, if not of all Greece. In reply to Lydiadas' propaganda he invaded the territory of Megalopolis and so forced a war upon the Achæans. His aggression might easily have cost him his life, for he had fewer than 5000 men to oppose to the Achæan army, which met him at Pallantium (near Megalopolis) with a strength of 20,000. The Achæan commander, Aristomachus, was eager for battle, but he threw away his chance in deference to Aratus, who did not desire Achæan victories save in his term of office. Thus the campaign of that year remained undecided.

In 227 Aratus, having resumed office, overcame his scruples and engaged Cleomenes. But he had lost his tide. In the meantime Ptolemy III, who had promptly taken measure of Cleomenes, found him of fuller stature than Aratus, and transferred to him the subsidy which he had previously paid to the Achæans. As the event showed, he had rightly divined that Sparta would be a more suitable instrument for use against Macedon than Achæa. Henceforth Cleomenes was in a position to eke out his citizen levies with mercenaries, and in 227 his augmented army routed Aratus in two battles, at Mt. Lycæus and at Ladoceia (in Arcadia). In the second action the Achæan defeat was mainly due to Lydiadas, the commander of the cavalry, who nullified an initial advantage by a rash pursuit which cost him his life and gave Cleomenes the chance of a decisive counter-attack. But the impression current among the Achæans was that Aratus, who was notoriously on bad terms with Lydiadas, had deliberately sacrificed his subordinate by refusing him legitimate support.

With Aratus outfought and discredited, Cleomenes broke off the campaign to wage a civil war of five minutes' duration at Sparta. Despite his father, Leonidas, he was in domestic affairs the heir of Agis' policy. Having been given in marriage by his father to the widow of Agis, he did not convert his wife but was perverted by her; and the economic heresies which she taught him were driven in further by a Stoic philosopher named Sphærus, who expounded theoretic communism to him. But Cleomenes was first and foremost a soldier; what attracted him most in Agis' reforms was the promise which they gave of a bigger and better Spartan army, and in his choice of means he was wholly free from Agis' scruples. Though, needless to say, he quoted Lycurgus and the Good Old Days in his support, he grasped the lesson of Agis' failure, that Sparta could not be made safe for revolution without a tyrant to see the revolution through.

For his civil war Cleomenes decided to employ none but mercenary troops, for he would not trust the citizen levies in action against the ephors, and indeed he did not require their help. Having left his burgess contingent on the Arcadian front, he doubled back to Sparta and took the city by surprise. At a trifling cost of life—for he met with scarcely any resistance—he abolished the ephorate and replaced it by a board of patronomi, who were charged with the ephors' routine duties but were excluded from high affairs of state. At the same time he filled the seat of his fellow king, Archidamus (a brother of Agis, who had recently been murdered by Agis' former enemies[1]), with his own brother, who served as a sleeping partner. In destroying the ephorate and the kingship of the twin houses, he removed the two effective checks upon autocracy at Sparta and set up a virtual tyranny.

Cleomenes at once justified his usurpation by enforcing a second cancellation of debts, and by carrying into effect the main if not the whole of Agis' scheme of land-distribution. Since he enfranchised no less than four thousand Periœci, his reassignations of land were clearly on a large scale.

Having thus raised the numbers and the morale of the citizen army, Cleomenes exercised it with the old-time rigour, and re-armed it in the Macedonian style. In 226 he put his military reforms to the test by invading Achæa and forcing a battle at Hecatombœum (near Dyme). So complete was the defeat which he inflicted upon the Achæans as to make them sue for peace. The Spartan king offered them easy terms, with a guarantee of complete autonomy, provided that they would put their military forces at his disposal, as in the old Peloponnesian League. The Achæans accepted his conditions, and thus virtually conceded to him the hegemony of Peloponnesus.

But Cleomenes' hopes were dashed at the last moment by a pure accident. On the date appointed for ratification he was

[1] See Appendix 12.

prevented by a sudden hæmorrhage from attendance, and the ceremony was postponed from autumn 226 to spring 225. In the meantime, however, Aratus regained his ascendancy in the Achæan councils, which no succession of disasters seemed able to impair for long. At the spring meeting he deliberately chicaned Cleomenes into breaking off the negotiations. To say nothing of mere pique—of which he certainly was susceptible—Aratus as a man of means probably had an instinctive (though unnecessary) fear that Cleomenes might become a missionary of communism among the Achæans, despite his assurances of autonomy to them. Yet in wrecking the settlement with Sparta Aratus was playing into Cleomenes' hands. The prospect of bankruptcy and land-distribution at the point of Cleomenes' sword might alarm Aratus and the wealthier Achæans, but it was correspondingly welcome to the debtor class in the cities of Peloponnesus ; and those who did not share the hopes of an economic revolution had in large measure lost confidence in the League's war-craft. In the campaign of 225 Aratus, though still supreme in the federal parliament, found that he could neither muster a field force nor uphold the League's authority in the constituent towns, which Cleomenes proceeded to capture in rapid succession. Argos was delivered to him by its former tyrant, Aristomachus ; Corinth seceded under Aratus' very eyes, and the Achæan garrison on the citadel was put under siege. At the end of the year there remained nothing of the League save Achæa Proper, Sicyon, Megalopolis and a few of its neighbours.

There now seemed nothing left to Aratus but to capitulate ; and Cleomenes, far from seeking vengeance upon him for his recent breach of faith, made the path of surrender easy for him. He proposed that the Achæans should not evacuate Acrocorinth, but should share its occupation with a Spartan force, and he offered to sugar the Achæan leader's pill with a heavy personal bribe. But Aratus realized that Acrocorinth could not accommodate two masters, and as money meant nothing to him save as a means to power, he merely resented the proffered *douceur*. Moreover, he had a card up his sleeve, which for some time past he had surreptitiously fingered, and now resolved to play out—an alliance with Antigonus Doson, the new king of Macedon. By the mediation of Megalopolis, the traditional ally of Macedon, Aratus had sounded Doson as early as 227 or 226, yet at the end of 225 he had not completed his bargain. His hesitation to produce the hidden ace was but natural, for the greater part of his career had been a crusade against the kings of Macedon, whom he had treated not only as antagonists but as outlaws. In seeking alliance with his arch-enemy he appeared to be stultifying his whole political faith, and indeed critics ancient and modern have accused him of a pact with the Devil.[1] Moreover, Doson was less disposed to save Aratus' face than Cleomenes: on the question of Acrocorinth he intimated quite plainly that this fortress must be restored to him without compromise. For these reasons Aratus could not readily persuade himself to close with the Macedonian. On the other hand, since the death of Gonatas and the usurpation of Cleomenes, Peloponnesian politics had been standing upside down. The root cause of Aratus' aversion to Macedon had been the support given by Gonatas to Peloponnesian tyrants. But there were now no tyrants left for Macedon to support; on the other hand, Cleomenes was, in fact, if not in name, a despot. Furthermore, though Doson stood firm on the question of Acrocorinth, he offered solid guarantees against encroachments on Achæan autonomy (p. 163), and he could be trusted not to foment communism. Lastly, at the end of 225 Cleomenes was pressing the siege of Acrocorinth and seemed likely to carry it at any moment. If Achæa must needs lose it, why not hand it to Doson—for a consideration? In the winter of 225–4 Aratus accordingly signed Doson's bond.

§ 5. ANTIGONUS DOSON

After the death of Demetrius II the crown of Macedon passed by natural right to his son Philip by the Epirote princess, Phthia.[2] But as Philip was only nine years old the government devolved upon a cousin of the late king called Antigonus, and nicknamed Doson. With Macedon overrun

[1] See the severe reflection upon him in Plutarch, *Cleomenes*, ch. 16 (which is derived from the contemporary historian Phylarchus).

[2] Philip is sometimes styled " son of Demetrius and Chryseis ". Chryseis may be a later wife of Demetrius and adoptive mother of Philip. Or (more likely) she may have been Phthia under a pet name (" Goldilocks ").—See J. V. A. Fine, *Class. Quart.*, 1934, p. 99 ff.; Tarn, *ibid.*, 1924, p. 17 ff., and in *Athenian Studies presented to W. S. Ferguson*, p. 483 ff.

by northern barbarians, the situation which Doson had to face was not unlike that which had confronted the regent Philip in 359 B.C. Like his predecessor, Doson temporarily cleared Macedon of its invaders (p. 123), and then followed suit by assuming the crown for himself. In setting aside his ward he created a risk of civil war; but in effect he postponed rather than abrogated Philip's claim to the crown, for he guaranteed the next succession to the displaced prince. Moreover, Doson equally justified his usurpation: he found Macedon in peril of breaking up, he left it as hegemon of more than half of Greece.

Realizing that Macedon required a period of recuperation, Doson began by accepting his predecessor's losses in the Greek Homeland. But although his primary aim, like Gonatas', was to consolidate rather than to extend Macedonian power, he was never away for long from the field of war, and he ended by re-establishing Macedonian supremacy in Greece.

The first foreign expedition of Doson was a mysterious raid on Caria, by which he brought the seaboard towns, and especially Miletus, under Macedonian control. (227 or 226)[1] The reasons for this foray can only be conjectured. Possibly he made a preventive attack upon Ptolemy III in anticipation of a fresh attempt on his part to extend the Egyptian dominion in the Aegean. If Ptolemy ever had such a plan, he soon abandoned it, and he took no other measures of insurance against Macedonia except to pay subsidies to Aratus or Cleomenes. Neither did Doson persevere in his precautions against Egypt: he presently evacuated his posts in Caria, and he allowed the Macedonian fleet to fall into decay. The reason why he lost interest in Aegean affairs was no doubt the offer of alliance from Aratus, and the prospect of regaining Corinth. In spring 224 he put across from his base at Chalcis, renewed Demetrius' alliance with Bœotia, and brought up a force of 20,000 men against the Isthmus lines, which Cleomenes had refortified against his coming.

The mere arrival of Doson caused the tide to roll back upon

[1] The only direct evidence for this expedition is a partly corrupt passage in Pompeius Trogus, *Prologue*, 28: Thessaliam Moesiam (?) Cariam subiecit. Whatever may be wrong here, no attempt to amend away "Cariam" has been successful. (W. Kolbe, in *Göttingen Gelehrte Anzeigen*, 1916, p. 461, reads "Thessaliam et Dardaniam." But Doson did not subdue Dardania.) See W. Bettingen, *König Antigonos Doson*, p. 21 ff.

Cleomenes. The hopes of revolution which he had everywhere raised had been proved delusive : in Sparta social upheaval had been the indispensable first step in his career, in the rest of Peloponnesus his ulterior aim of restoring Spartan hegemony imposed upon him respect for local autonomy and abstention from communistic interference. But in rejecting the support of the Peloponnesian proletariates he did not recover that of the possessing classes, who gravitated back to the Achæan League as soon as Doson's arrival tilted the balance of military power. While Cleomenes was repelling Doson's attack upon Corinth, his line of communications was cut by the defection of Argos. He abandoned Corinth to recover Argos, but in the event lost both towns, and the rest of Argolis to follow. This succession of blows put Cleomenes out of action for some time to come. In 223 Doson was able to carry one by one the towns of Arcadia which had stood in with Sparta. Among these was Mantinea, which had broken its connection with Ætolia, and had ended a period of vacillation between Sparta and Achæa by revolting from the latter and murdering the Achæan garrison. (226) Aratus now exercised reprisals by razing Mantinea and selling its inhabitants into slavery. The destruction of Mantinea raised a general outcry among the Greeks ; unfortunately, as the history of the ensuing years was to show, the example set by Aratus was more potent than the reproofs showered upon him. In the meantime Cleomenes had replenished his army by enrolling liberated Helots and recruiting mercenaries. Taking advantage of the fact that Doson had sent home his forces at the end of the campaigning season, he carried Megalopolis by a surprise assault ; the inhabitants contrived to escape him, but the town suffered the fate of Mantinea. Cleomenes was the first Spartan to capture Megalopolis, but he did not hold his prize for long.

In 222[1] Doson called out his full field strength, and with the Achæan contingent he mustered a force of 28,000. Cleomenes swept together some 20,000 men, but he had difficulties in paying them, for Ptolemy III had withdrawn his subsidies as soon as Cleomenes' cause ceased to be the winning one. The Spartan king therefore staked all his chances on a pitched battle. For this purpose he selected a position at Sellasia,

[1] On the chronology, see the addendum to this chapter.

some eight miles north of Sparta. Here the valley of the Œnus, down which Doson was advancing, is dominated by two hills, of which Olympus, on the east bank, has a gentle declivity, while Euas, on the western edge, falls more steeply.[1] Cleomenes occupied both hills and intervening plain, and fortified his entire front with field-works. His plan probably was to let Doson wear out his army with fruitless attacks, and then to roll it down the slope of Olympus with the Spartan phalanx. But Doson disappointed these hopes, for instead of jeopardizing his Macedonians in a frontal charge, he utilized his superior numbers, and the high mobility of his light-armed mercenaries from Acarnania and Illyria, to work round Cleomenes' left flank. This enfilading movement nearly came to grief at the outset, for a gap soon opened between two of the attacking divisions ; but a young Achæan captain named Philopœmen covered the re-dressing of the line with a timely cavalry charge. Even so, Mt. Euas should have resisted capture. But Cleomenes' brother, Eucleidas, who was in command here, waited passively for the assailants to creep up to him and round him, thus throwing away the advantage of higher ground.[2] The fall of his post before a final rush by the escalading party virtually decided the whole battle. Cleomenes endeavoured to pull the fight round by a hoplite charge on his right flank. But, like Napoleon at Waterloo, he had not many minutes in which to drive home his decisive attack, and Doson's phalanx was still fresh. The Spartan column bent but could not break the enemy line, and a final counter-offensive by the Macedonians swept the Spartans off their feet. With its retreat cut off by the capture of Mt. Euas, Cleomenes' force was completely destroyed, and Sparta now lay at Doson's mercy.

Among the survivors of Sellasia was Cleomenes, who continued his flight to Egypt, in the hope that he would here find a rallying-ground. Ptolemy III, and after him Ptolemy IV, spoke their distinguished visitor fair, and made promises in plenty, but neither king ever meant these seriously. An impatient remark which Cleomenes dropped about Ptolemy

[1] On the topography of Sellasia I follow Kromayer (*Bull. Corresp. Hell.*, 1910, p. 508 ff.) and Kahrstedt (*Hermes*, 1913, p. 283 ff.) against Soteriades (*Bull. Corresp. Hell.*, 1911, p. 87 ff.).

[2] The Illyrians carried Mt. Euas in much the same way as the Boers captured Majuba Hill.

IV's loose manner of life was reported at court by a personal enemy, and furnished a pretext for interning him and his companions in Alexandria. After a while his party broke bounds and summoned the townsfolk to rise "on behalf of their liberties." But the Alexandrians, not understanding such language, went on their business. Cleomenes and his companions did not wait for Ptolemy's guards to corner them, but dispatched themselves in a quiet street. (219)

Doson entered Sparta without opposition, and carried out a bloodless reaction to the "ancient constitution," which he interpreted as government by ephors without kings—the exact contrary of Cleomenes' scheme. Whether he also rescinded the recent land-distributions is not certain: the mere slaughter of new Spartan landholders at Sellasia had probably accomplished this already.

In defeating Cleomenes and rehabilitating the Achæan League, Doson had merely put back the hands of the clock. But his expedition to Peloponnesus was accompanied by a constructive reform which marked him out as the greatest statesman in Greek politics since Philip II, the constitution of a new Hellenic federation. In autumn 224 he appended to the ordinary Achæan congress at Aegium a special convention, at which he laid his plan before delegates from Acarnania, Achæa, Bœotia, Epirus, Eubœa, Phocis and Thessaly. Together with Macedon, these formed the units of the new national league, and it was technically as their captain-general that Doson conducted the later stages of the war against Sparta. His Hellenic federation was less comprehensive than that of Philip and Alexander. Though Sparta was compulsorily enrolled after Sellasia, Elis and Messene remained outside, and neither Athens nor the Ætolian League joined in. It was also less rigid than previous leagues in the demands which it made upon its constituents, for decisions of the federal parliament were not to have force until confirmed by the local assemblies of the participant states [1]; nay more, individual states, if they so desired, were left free to contract out of federal wars. But for the fact that the new league was composed of a few ethnic groups, not of numerous

[1] A similar proviso was included in the original constitution of the United Netherlands, and probably also in the Bœotian League of the fifth and early fourth centuries B.C.

individual cities, Doson's scheme no doubt would have been unworkable. Yet its very looseness was an advantage among states which were intensely jealous of their local autonomy, and it was well calculated to remove the suspicion that Doson's constitution might merely be another scheme for exploiting Greece on Macedon's behalf. At any rate, Doson paved the way for a reunion of Greece and willing co-operation between Greece and Macedon, and this at a time when the need for common action was about to become more urgent than at any moment since the Persian Wars.[1]

§ 6. THE DÉBUT OF PHILIP V

Doson had scarcely settled the affairs of Sparta than he hurried home to Macedon, where the Illyrians had broken in (p. 124). He beat off the invaders, but in the strain of battle he burst a blood-vessel. Being consumptive by heredity, he never recovered from this injury, but died in the following year. (221) His usurpation had not really run contrary to the traditional family loyalty of the Antigonids : he had kept the crown for his ward in the safest place—on his own head—and Philip had only to wait till the age of seventeen before he assumed it.

The young king was put to the test forthwith, for hardly had Doson died than his settlement of Greece was challenged. In anticipation of Cleomenes' return from Egypt, some of his surviving partisans prepared a new revolution at Sparta, and although the wind was taken out of their sails by Cleomenes' death in 219, they persisted in their plan and set up two new kings in addition to a board of anti-Macedonian ephors. But the chief disturber of the peace was Ætolia. During the reign of Doson the Ætolians had taken advantage of their new sea outlet on the Gulf of Pagasæ, and of Macedon's growing naval weakness, to engage in vigorous piracy in Aegean waters, but they had respected his power on land. After Doson's death they threw off all restraint and plundered their neighbours with impartial thoroughness. As a typical specimen of their methods we may cite the raids which two of their captains of adventure, Scopas and Dorimachus, made upon

[1] For a more gloomy view of the new league's prospects, see P. Treves, *Athenæum*, 1935, p. 36 ff.

Achæa and Messenia in 220. Though technically waging a private war, they had the tacit sanction of their government. The ubiquitousness of the Ætolian raiders called for something more than local defensives, and a message was sent to Philip by Aratus, who had endeavoured to suppress the nuisance both by military and by diplomatic methods, but had been fooled by the Ætolians to the top of his bent.

The good relations between Aratus and Doson had been by no means to the liking of some Macedonian generals, who would have preferred Doson to revert to the methods of Cassander and treat the Greeks as subjects. These men tried by fair means and foul to discredit Aratus in Philip's eyes, but the veteran Achæan's diplomacy outwitted them. Philip fell under Aratus' influence, and when the disgruntled Macedonians attempted mutiny he executed them all. Thus at the outset of his reign Philip became a dutiful heir to Doson's policy and a loyal servant of the Hellenic federation. In autumn 219 he convened a congress at Corinth, enrolled Messene in the Hellenic League, and carried an ultimatum against Ætolia. In addition to compensation for past damage, the Federation unwisely required Ætolia to surrender her essentially harmless control over Delphi, a demand which could only stiffen Ætolian backs. But in their existing mood the Ætolians would probably have declined any conditions.

In the campaign of 219 the Hellenic Federation, despite its superior numbers, was reduced to a comically helpless defensive. Ætolia found allies in Sparta and Elis (which the longstanding feud with the Arcadians averted from Achæa and its allies); the lesser members of the Federation simply waited on Philip; and the Macedonian king was too preoccupied with a threatened Dardanian raid, and with a new Roman action in the Adriatic (p. 183), to pursue the war in Greece with energy. While the Spartans, who had in the meantime restored their dual monarchy, harried Argolis and southern Arcadia, the Ætolians descended upon Achæa, invaded Epirus, and even broke by the pass of Tempe into Lower Macedonia. Not content with ordinary booty, the raiders sacked the Epirote sanctuary of Dodona and the temples of the Macedonian town of Dium.

But once Philip felt secure on his northern and western fronts, he descended into Greece and conducted a series of tear-away campaigns. In midwinter he crossed the breadth of Peloponnesus and made an enormous haul of plunder in the fat and unsuspecting plains of Elis. Returning to Corinth, he improvised a fleet of transports for a surprise landing in the Ambracian Gulf and an irruption into Ætolia by the back-door. After some further hard marching, he captured and devastated the Ætolian place of assembly and sanctuary at Thermum—hitherto a virgin site—and made good his retreat to the sea. Without a pause he recrossed Peloponnesus and gutted the valley of the Eurotas. (219–8) As a measure of retaliation these counter-raids were brilliantly successful, but instead of paralysing they merely irritated his enemies. Philip, however, took another lesson from Alexander, for in the next winter he prepared a siege-train. In 217 he tested his artillery on the frontier-fort of Bylazora in the Axius narrows, which he now recaptured from the Dardanians (p. 123); next he applied it to the Ætolian stronghold of Phthiotic Thebes (near the Gulf of Pagasæ), which he reduced by a methodical attack. The Ætolians now agreed to take part in a national settlement. (217)

For the moment the prospects of Greek political union appeared brighter than at any time since Alexander's death. Not only was a nucleus of the United States of Greece now in being, but the will to peace among the Greeks was running strong. Philip had won golden opinions by his energy and loyalty; the worst boy of the Greek family, Ætolia, had been chastised; and not only Philip but the more far-sighted of his antagonists realized that the Greeks must close their ranks against the (as yet uncertain) winner of that conflict of giants, the Second Punic War.[1]

[1] For a warning about "a cloud in the West", see the speech of the Ætolian diplomat, Agelaus of Naupactus. (Polybius, V, 24.)

Addendum.—The choice of date for the battle of Sellasia has now been narrowed down to 223 or 222. 221 is ruled out by the fact that Ptolemy III, at whose court Cleomenes resided for some time after his flight from Sparta, is now known to have died early in 221. (H. Frank, *Archiv. für Papyrusforschung*, 1933, p. 37.) The counter-revolution at Sparta in spring 219 befell "nearly three years" after Sellasia. (Polybius V, 14, 8.) This points to 222.—See also W. H. Porter, *The Life of Aratus of Sicyon*, Introduction; F. W. Walbank, *Aratos of Sicyon*, p. 195 ff.

CHAPTER X

THE GREEKS OF THE WESTERN MEDITERRANEAN

§ 1. AGATHOCLES OF SYRACUSE

AT the end of last chapter we observed that by 217 B.C. the Greeks of the Homeland foresaw the danger of invasion from the western Mediterranean. Before we proceed to consider how this premonition came true, we must review the history of the Greeks of the West, and consider how they acquitted themselves of their duty as outposts of Hellenism in that quarter.

Among the western Greeks the Siceliotes claim most of our attention. Commanding the gateways of the western Mediterranean, they held a key position in trust for Hellenedom, and if they displayed scanty political wisdom, at all events they were not wholly devoid of self-help. In 323 B.C. the Sicilian Greeks were apparently on the eve of a settled era of prosperity. Some twenty years before this date Timoleon had beaten off one of the periodical attacks by Carthage, had re-peopled the cities with fresh settlers from Greece, while ridding them of their tyrants, and had imposed a general alliance upon the towns. Unfortunately he had not devised a federal system, under which the Siceliotes could have been schooled in regular habits of co-operation, and he had not found means, if such existed, of reducing party rivalry within each city wall to reasonable limits. About 323 a movement began in Syracuse, which at first appeared to be no more than a scramble for high position among a few adventurers, but ended in fresh civil war and tyranny. The issue at first lay between two oligarchs named Heracleides and Sosistratus, who probably aimed at the exclusion of the recently imported settlers from political privilege, and an upstart named Agathocles, who had immigrated from Thermæ (in northern Sicily) with no visible assets but a determination to make a career for himself at all costs. To this end Agathocles at first adopted the military profession, but when promotion lingered he doubled the part of soldier with that of demagogue, and thus became the leading opponent of Sosistratus and Heracleides. For a time this rivalry resulted in little more than a see-saw in which now the demagogue and now his twin antagonists took their turn to leave Syracuse. (323–17) But in 317 Agathocles, who had recently been readmitted under a political armistice, yet did not trust the oligarchs to keep their hands off him, decided to safeguard himself, and to satisfy his ambitions, by establishing a new tyranny. His usurpation followed the usual plan: with an army of personal followers he made a sudden sweep of the streets of Syracuse, slaughtered the oligarchs and confiscated their estates, which were divided among the poorer citizens. Like Dionysius, he paid outward respect to constitutional forms, contenting himself with the title of General Plenipotentiary; but in reality his rule was based on a continuous and unsparing use of force, and he made citizen blood flow even more freely than the elder tyrant.

The civil war in Syracuse, as before, fanned the latent jealousies of the Sicilian towns to open conflict. Sosistratus and other exiled oligarchs enlisted the aid of Acragas, Gela and Messana, all of which no doubt feared that Agathocles might continue in the tradition of Syracusan tyrants by making himself "Ruler of Sicily." Agathocles for his part did not wait to be attacked, but opened hostilities in 315, and in 312 he carried Messana. But his successes brought another and more formidable enemy into the field. True to the approved practice of Siceliot Greeks, his adversaries called in Carthage to redress the balance of their internecine war. Strangely enough the governor of Carthaginian Sicily, to whom the first appeal was made, offered no more than his services as a mediator, thus fondly hoping to stabilize conditions in Sicily. But in 312 the Punic home government took sides openly on behalf of Acragas and Gela. Their immediate intention was probably no more than to keep on knocking the heads of the Greeks together; but in 311 Hamilcar, son of Gisgo, who commanded the Carthaginian expeditionary force, won such a complete victory over Agathocles, that he was able to proceed to the siege of Syracuse.

Thanks to the care with which Dionysius had fortified this

city, the Carthaginians had little hope of taking it by storm. But Agathocles was worse off than his predecessor in this respect, that he as yet possessed no strong fleet, and that the former flow of mercenaries from the Greek Homeland to Sicily had since the time of Alexander turned into other channels. In summer 310 it appeared as if Syracuse, with the other Siceliote towns to follow, would at last fall into Carthaginian hands. But Agathocles had the advantage over Dionysius of having witnessed the career of Alexander. With a touch of the Macedonian's audacious genius he resolved to defend Syracuse by attacking Carthage. His original design was probably no more than to draw the Carthaginians off Syracuse, as Hannibal subsequently tried to coax the Roman siege-army away from Capua by a feint upon Rome. But such a plan was capable of expansion into permanent Greek conquests in North Africa.

In August 310[1] Agathocles slipped out of Syracuse with a small and lightly equipped army and an improvised fleet. Landing unopposed at a point a few days' march from Carthage, he burnt his boats—for he counted on his invasion to pay its own way—and pressed forward toward the Punic capital. Despite the paucity of his force, he accepted battle against a *levée en masse* of the Carthaginian burgesses, and drove them back into their town with heavy loss. Though he lacked the means of putting Carthage under strict siege, he effected a partial blockade of the town by cutting it off from the hinterland, where the native Libyans at first welcomed him as a deliverer. The Carthaginians, it is true, neutralized his gains by recalling their seasoned troops from Sicily ; and the Libyans, on discovering that their rescuer's war-requisitions were as onerous as their oppressor's regular imposts, drifted back to the Carthaginian side. But Agathocles overtrumped his opponents by enlisting the Ptolemaic governor of Cyrene, a Macedonian named Ophellas. This officer, who held his responsibilities to Ptolemy very lightly, agreed to take the field against Carthage, on the understanding that he should retain any African territory which they might jointly conquer, while Agathocles contented himself with the mobile booty. But Ophellas had hardly arrived in

[1] Agathocles' expedition is dated by a solar eclipse which took place on August 15th, 310, the day after his departure from Syracuse.

Agathocles' camp than a quarrel—probably due to the newcomer claiming the supreme command for himself—broke out between the two chieftains. Agathocles settled the dispute by murdering Ophellas in alleged self-defence and bluffing the Cyrenaic contingent into accepting his orders. (309)

After this increment to his forces Agathocles opened a more systematic attack upon Carthage. In preparation for a maritime blockade he besieged and captured Utica and other Punic towns to serve as naval bases. (308) In the following year the food supplies in the capital were running low, and a surrender appeared in sight. But the Carthaginians resolved to try their chances in one further field campaign. At the time of their sortie Agathocles happened to be absent in Sicily, leaving his son Archagathus in command. This inexperienced general scattered his troops too far, thus exposing them to defeat in detail. On his return Agathocles found his army so far reduced in numbers and morale as to resemble the Athenians before Syracuse in 413 B.C. Unwilling to play the part of Nicias, or to serve as scapegoat for his own mutinous troops, he made another of his quick resolves and stole away home by himself, leaving his soldiers to make what terms they might with the Carthaginians. Such was the inglorious ending of the only Greek Anabasis into Africa. Yet it came so near to success that it had an unmistakable influence upon Roman strategy in the Punic Wars, and it was no mere accident that Scipio Africanus the Elder was a frank admirer of Agathocles as a soldier. Moreover, his raid upon Africa, despite its failure, so impressed the Carthaginians, that in 306 they consented to a peace, by which they agreed to restore the former frontiers in Sicily, keeping only the western portion of the island as far as the river Halycus for themselves, and to pay a small war indemnity.

In Sicily the chance upon which Agathocles had staked his big throw, that the Carthaginians would recall part of their siege force from Syracuse, was presently fulfilled, and the blockade was partly lifted. The city was finally freed from danger by a victory which Agathocles' brother, Antander, gained over Hamilcar in 309. With reinforcements supplied by his Greek allies, Hamilcar was preparing to resume the siege, but his ill-compacted army was surprised and routed on the march, and the general himself was captured. After this disaster the Punic forces took no further part in the Sicilian campaigns. In spite of this desertion Agathocles' Greek opponents carried on the war under a new leader from Acragas named Xenodicus, and after his defeat they reformed under Deinocrates, an *émigré* from Syracuse. Though they never brought Syracuse under any real danger, their unexpected rally caused Agathocles to hasten back to Sicily, where he fought an indecisive campaign, while his African expedition was being irretrievably ruined by his absence. But after his failure in Africa Agathocles achieved a complete success in Sicily. While he kept Deinocrates in play with fictitious negotiations, he used the Carthaginian war indemnity to recruit a new army and to corrupt Deinocrates' forces. In 305 he quickly disposed of Deinocrates, whose army melted away from him, and made himself master of all Greek Sicily in one campaign. By this series of successes, and by a ruthless policy of wholesale executions among his opponents in the conquered Greek cities, he definitely established his authority in Sicily. In 304 he assumed the title of king, and received recognition as a peer by the recently crowned Macedonian monarchs in the eastern Mediterranean. The fifteen years of his reign (304–289) scarcely call for notice. Like Dionysius, he made spasmodic attempts to acquire a sphere of influence in the extreme south of Italy, and to control the entrance of the Adriatic. But his Italian forays were even less political and more piratical than those of the elder despot, and in his warfare with the Bruttians (in the toe of the peninsula) he got more than he gave. On the other hand, he scored a notable success *c.* 300 B.C., when he came into temporary possession of Corcyra, and inflicted a naval defeat upon Cassander, who had at that time acquired an Adriatic sea-front and coveted Corcyra for himself. The fleet which gained this victory was the nucleus of a larger navy which Agathocles was building up for a second and more methodical invasion of Africa. But he did not live to try conclusions again with Carthage.

§ 2. PYRRHUS AND HIERO

Agathocles played a final surprise upon the Sicilian Greeks in restoring to them their liberty by testament. After the death of Archagathus and of two other sons who accompanied him to Africa and were lynched by the soldiery after their father's flight, he had devised his crown to a son by a second wife; but the son of Archagathus traversed this plan by murdering the heir apparent. Agathocles, rather than allow his hand to be forced, put an end to his own dynasty. After the king's death Archagathus' son planned a new military coup, but was removed betimes by the dagger, and a general settlement of Sicilian affairs was now arranged with the help of a Carthaginian mediator. In accordance with this scheme the Syracusans agreed to receive back the surviving outlaws from Agathocles' régime, to enfranchise his mercenaries, and to restore independence to the other cities. In effect, and perhaps in intention, this compromise prepared the ground for a fresh Carthaginian offensive. In Syracuse the enfranchisement of the mercenaries, many of whom were Italians from Campania, led to the usual recriminations with the native burgesses. The soldiery were eventually paid to go home to Italy; but on the way they treacherously seized the town of Messana and made it into the capital of a veritable robber-state. (*c.* 288) Like the Galatians in Asia Minor, the "Mamertines," as this Grand Catalan Company called itself, systematically plundered or blackmailed the adjacent territories. Their forays extended to the Carthaginian province, but naturally the Greeks suffered most at their hands.

In the meantime the Greek towns lost their newly-won liberty to a new crop of despots, who lacked Agathocles' ability or ruthlessness, and could neither maintain order in their own city nor keep the peace between state and state. In Syracuse a new tyrant named Hicetas was emboldened by a victory over Phintias of Acragas to break a fresh lance with the Carthaginians. But the second Agathocles suffered a defeat which cost him his position. The leader who supplanted him, Thœnon, fared little better, for the Syracusan people rose against him and called in Sosistratus, the successor of Phintias at Acragas (and perhaps a grandson of Agathocles' antagonist). While Sosistratus was besieging Thœnon in the island-citadel of Syracuse, the Carthaginians followed up their victory over Hicetas by blockading Thœnon with their fleet and Sosistratus with their army. The situation in Syracuse now resembled that of 310, except that the city, instead of being controlled by one firm hand, was distracted between two pretenders. (278) But Sosistratus in a moment of insight realized that Syracuse and Sicily could only be saved by a renunciation of power on the part of all the local despots and the restoration of a general dictatorship like that of Agathocles. Fortunately, too, the necessary *deus ex machina* had not far to drop. King Pyrrhus of Epirus had recently landed in South Italy with a strong army, but the war in which he had there engaged had resulted in a stalemate, and a call to a more open field of war in Sicily could only be welcome to him (p. 180).

In autumn 278 Pyrrhus landed in Sicily with 10,000 well-trained men. He was received with a general enthusiasm which recalled the days of Timoleon, and an improvised parliament of deputies from the Greek cities formally voted him king of the Siceliotes. With his army swelled by contingents from his new adherents, Pyrrhus not only beat back the Carthaginians into the western corner of the island, but carried their strongholds in quick succession. At the almost inexpugnable mountain citadel of Eryx, which so long defied the Romans in the First Punic War, he was first over the wall. At the end of 277 he had the Carthaginians penned up in their only remaining fortress of Lilybæum, and ready to negotiate. Rightly judging that the Carthaginians must not be allowed to retain a single base in Sicily, if the Greeks were to be secure, he demanded the complete evacuation of the island; and on refusal of these terms he prepared to dictate others, as Agathocles had hoped to do, in or near Carthage. With larger forces and a stronger fleet than Agathocles had possessed in 310, the king of Epirus and Sicily had good reason to believe that he would settle the Carthaginian question once for all. But his Siceliote subjects, who had held his hand firm while he negotiated, now refused the additional effort which an expedition to Africa required. Hereupon Pyrrhus made an example of mutiny by putting Thœnon to death. But when this admonition failed of its object he threw up the whole enterprise and left the Siceliotes to fend for themselves. (275) Had Pyrrhus persisted in his first attitude of severity, he would have had reason as well as authority on his side; of all the chances which the Epirote king threw away by his habitual inconstancy, the opportunity of final victory over Carthage was of the best augury for Greece.

The departure of Pyrrhus deprived the Siceliotes not only of 10,000 Epirotes, but of the Syracusan navy. Until his return to Italy the king kept this fleet in his hands ; but in the act of crossing the Straits he was attacked by a Carthaginian squadron. The Syracusan seamen, who no doubt felt little interest in convoying Pyrrhus' runaways, let themselves be completely beaten : of their 110 vessels, 70 were sunk or captured.[1] His campaign in Sicily achieved this much, that after his return to Italy the Carthaginians did not resume the siege of Syracuse, but consented to a peace. But besides recovering all their losses they now acquired possession of Acragas and the other Greek cities of central Sicily, which they reduced to the position of dependent allies. In 275 Syracuse had lost its local thalassocracy for good, and its influence was now confined to the north-eastern corner of the island. In this district the depredations of the Mamertines called for a strong hand to repress them. During an armistice in his Sicilian campaign Pyrrhus had turned upon these raiders and had driven them out of the field, but had not been given time to exterminate them. After his departure the Syracusans made war upon the Mamertines under a new leader named Hiero, who was first elected general in the reconstituted republic, but soon afterwards raised himself to the tyranny by a bloodless military revolution. (269) He justified his usurpation by inflicting a crushing defeat upon the Mamertines, on the strength of which he assumed the title of king. (265/4)[2] After his victory he penned up the Mamertines in Messana and apparently had them at his mercy.

At this stage the history of the Sicilian Greeks merges into that of Rome. The Roman intervention on behalf of the Mamertines at first had the result of driving Hiero and the Carthaginians into each other's reluctant arms ; but this *mésalliance* was soon replaced by an enduring union between the Syracusan king and the Roman Republic. The treaty

[1] According to Justin (23.3.9), Pyrrhus won a parting victory over the Carthaginians by land. He may have beaten off an incautious pursuit ; but he was no longer in a position to inflict a serious defeat upon them.

[2] For the chronology, see Beloch, *op. cit.*, IV, pt. 2, p. 278 ff.

with Rome, though outwardly on equal terms, in effect degraded Syracuse into a dependant, and in the course of the first two Punic Wars all the Greek cities of Sicily sank to the level of municipia in a Roman province. Furthermore, under Roman rule the process by which Sicily ceased to be a Greek and definitely became an Italian island was completed. Not that the Romans worked of set purpose to extirpate Hellenism: it was rather the Greeks who ensured their own disappearance. Encamped as settlers on the coast of an island whose core contained a population of Italian stock, and confronted with the ever-present menace of a Carthaginian invasion, the Siceliotes had wasted most of their spare energy in quarrels between their rival factions and cities. By these internecine struggles they had not only reduced their own numbers, but had prepared for fresh settlements of Italians, whom they engaged to fight their battles for them. For this replacement of Greek by Italians a heavy responsibility rests with Agathocles, who bled his own countrymen profusely by the severity of his political repressions, and introduced the most destructive of the Italian settlers, the Mamertines. Yet Agathocles had at least given the Siceliotes some fifteen years of unity and mutual peace. The chief blame falls rather upon the republican governments which failed to stabilize the internal politics of their cities and were too proud to devise a federation or durable alliance among themselves. In the West as in the East the monarchies with all their faults probably delayed rather than hastened the decline of Hellenedom.

But the influence of Syracuse, while it remained an ally of Rome under its own king, was a factor of considerable importance in Roman politics. In the First Punic War the active co-operation of Hiero with the Romans contributed materially to the Roman victory: in all probability it was at his prompting that the Romans enlarged their war-object and instead of acquiring a mere bridge-head for themselves annexed the whole of Sicily. Moreover, when the Romans finally incorporated the kingdom of Hiero, they left untouched the financial system under which he had collected his tithes and quotas from the dependent cities in his realm. These "Leges Hieronicæ," which were still in force in the days of Cicero, were one of the most notable models of imperial administration presented by the Greeks to the Romans.[1]

§ 3. THE GREEKS OF SOUTH ITALY

From the fourth century B.C. the political history of the Italian Greeks tends to merge into that of the single city of Tarentum; while the influence of the other towns becomes restricted to their own narrow territories. The reduction of the Italiotes to this purely parochial rôle at first sight appears strange, for until the advent of the Romans they had no such highly organized enemy to deal with as the Siceliotes found in Carthage. But whereas the Carthaginians were hampered at all times by a deficiency of man-power which compelled them to husband their resources and to space out their offensives, the native Italics suffered from an excess of population which resulted in a steady pressure upon the Greek coastlands. Besides, though the Italian Greeks had in the fourth century formed a league of mutual defence, they never acquired the habit of willing co-operation, and they never produced a line of strong men like the Sicilian despots to coerce them willy-nilly into momentary efficiency.

Of the lesser Italiote towns it suffices to say that they were continually exposed to attacks from the neighbouring hinterland tribes, the Bruttians and Lucanians; that they received occasional help from Syracuse, which maintained its long-standing interest in the borderland of the Straits of Messina, but were liable to predatory assaults from the same quarter. About 323 B.C. Agathocles' antagonists, Heracleides and Sosistratus, sent one force to assist Croton against the Bruttians, another to make a raid upon Rhegium, which completely miscarried. About 300 Agathocles reversed this policy, giving aid to Rhegium and capturing Croton by an unprovoked attack. In the third century the smaller Greek cities began to turn away from Syracuse to Rome, which had made a lasting alliance with Neapolis in 327, and was coming to be known as a guardian that did not need to be guarded against. In 282 the Romans sent a consular army to assist Thurii against the Lucanians, and not long after they assumed a protectorate over Rhegium and Locri.

[1] On this subject see M. Rostowzew, *Geschichte der Staatspacht in der römischen Kaiserzeit*, pp. 350–6, and especially J. Carcopino, *La Loi de Hiéron et les Romains*.

The sending of the Roman expedition to Thurii was the occasion for the outbreak of a war between Rome and Tarentum. It is this conflict which redeems the history of the Italiotes from insignificance. Among the Italiote towns Tarentum stood out both in population and in man-power. Unlike Syracuse, where democracy and oligarchy alike were but the prelude to tyranny, Tarentum had an efficient democratic constitution and enjoyed an internal stability unusual in Greek towns. Though its civic muster of 33,000 men was largely a parade force—its field-army never appears to have exceeded 15,000,—it possessed abundant means for recruiting mercenaries, and it made a practice of inviting the most distinguished professional soldiers, preferably kings of Epirus or members of the Spartan royal houses, to conduct its wars. Tarentum therefore reckoned to achieve more than to avoid capture by its Lucanian or Messapian neighbours. It exercised a miniature thalassocracy in the Gulf of Otranto, and it aimed at an extension of territory in the Apulian downlands, where the best summer pastures were to be found for its famous flocks of sheep.

The interest of Tarentum in the Apulian hinterland was the original cause of its contacts with Rome. In 334–0 the Greek city temporarily obtained control of this region as far as Mt. Garganus, and it endeavoured to consolidate this gain by a treaty with Rome, which had as yet few commitments and exercised little power in the southern part of the peninsula. This compact contained a clause which excluded Roman warships from sailing beyond the Lacinian promontory (near Croton); presumably it also included a safeguard against Roman trespasses in Apulia. But the conquests on which this agreement was based had been made under an alien commander, Alexander I of Epirus. As a half-brother of Alexander the Great, this king had visions of balancing the Macedonian conquests in the East with the establishment of an Epirote dominion in Italy. He was therefore not content to remain an officer in Tarentine employ, and presently fell out with his paymasters. This quarrel, which was soon followed by Alexander's death, put a check for the time being upon Tarentine ambitions.

Relations between Rome and Tarentum were strained in the Second Samnite War, when the Roman armies, bent on exploring the back-door entrances to Samnium, entered Apulia and established a post at Luceria. About 320 the Tarentines endeavoured to prevent further encroachments by arranging a peace with the Samnites. But they merely irritated the Romans by their interposition, and they ended by withdrawing their claims on northern Apulia.[1] In 303–2, the Tarentines engaged a Spartan prince named Cleonymus (whose later attempt to become king at Sparta we have already noticed—p. 129) to defend them against Lucanian inroads. Like Alexander of Epirus, Cleonymus tried to use his commission as a stepping-stone to a personal dominion and was therefore dismissed from Tarentine service. He seized the island of Corcyra as a starting-point for piratical descents in the Adriatic, which he carried to Patavium at the head of that sea, but presently lost his base[2] and withdrew to Greece. There is no good evidence that he ever crossed swords with Roman troops or that he sowed misunderstanding between Rome and Tarentum.[3] But we need not doubt that the final subjugation of the Samnites and the foundation of a colony at Venusia in central Apulia (*c.* 290) made a profound impression upon the Tarentines. Lastly, the intervention of the Romans at Thurii, which lay this side of the Lacinian cape (from the Tarentine standpoint) could plausibly be interpreted as contrary to the treaty of Alexander's time; and the appearance of a Roman flotilla (for reasons unexplained) outside the harbour of Tarentum was, beyond any doubt, a breach of that instrument. The sudden destruction of the Roman fleet by the Tarentines, and their call for assistance to king Pyrrhus, will be familiar to most readers from their knowledge of Roman history. It will suffice here to review the war between Rome and Tarentum from the standpoint of Pyrrhus.

[1] Though the story of this negotiation in Livy (IX, 14) is plainly embroidered with patriotic Roman legend, it need not be rejected altogether (as was done by me in *Journ. Philol.*, vol. 70, p. 167 ff.). Presumably the river Aufidus was the new boundary between the Roman and Tarentine spheres of influence.

[2] In 300–280 Corcyra passed from Cleonymus to Demetrius, to Cassander, to Agathocles (p. 171), to Pyrrhus, to Demetrius again!

[3] Livy (X, 2) mentions a Roman victory over Cleonymus in the Sallentine territory (south of Brundisium). But how came a Roman army in 302 to be so far south? In the detailed account of Cleonymus' campaigns by Diodorus (XX, 104–5) the Romans do not figure at all.

The invitation from Tarentum reached Pyrrhus at a moment when his prospects of conquest in Greek lands appeared remote. (281) Four years previously he had been expelled from Macedon by Lysimachus, and his chance of recovering that country after Lysimachus' death had been forestalled by Ptolemy Ceraunus (p. 58). The king therefore readily accepted the offer from Italy, and he was eagerly ushered out of Greece by the various other pretenders to the crown of Macedon. Antigonus Gonatas lent him transport; Antiochus I furnished him with money; Ceraunus, who had most reason for keeping him at arm's length, made him a gift of a troop of elephants captured from Seleucus.

In 280 Pyrrhus landed at Tarentum with a seasoned army of 25,000 men. By resolute drilling he created an efficient field-force out of the Tarentine levies, and his aggregate numbers in battle were but slightly inferior to those of the Romans. The battles of Heraclea (280) and Asculum (279), which afforded the first trial of strength between the legions and a first-rate Hellenistic army, can unfortunately not be reconstructed in full from the incoherent accounts that survive.[1] But in each case it appears that Pyrrhus carried the day by tactics essentially similar to those of Alexander. Using the phalanx to wear down rather than to crush the enemy infantry, he reserved his elephants and horsemen for his main action. When the Roman line became ragged, he widened the breach with a charge of elephants and sent in the horse to complete the rout. At Heraclea he half-destroyed the Roman army, and at Asculum he would have done as much, but for the proximity of the Roman camp. After each battle the defeated party seriously entered into negotiations, and peace would have been made in 280 or 279 had not the Senate been stiffened on the former occasion by the censor Appius, and on the latter by a Carthaginian offer of help. But the readiness of the Romans to treat was no more remarkable than the moderation of Pyrrhus' demands. After Heraclea he stipulated for the freedom of the Greek cities and the surrender of recent Roman conquests in the south of Italy; after Asculum he merely sought to secure immunity for Tarentum.[2] Plainly

[1] On these two battles, see in general Beloch, *op. cit.*, IV, pt. 2, pp. 465–76.

[2] On the terms offered by Pyrrhus, see W. Judeich, *Klio*, 1926, pp. 1–18, and T. Frank, *Cambr. Anc. Hist.*, VII, p. 646 ff. The story of the negotiations has been obfuscated in our ancient sources by edifying anecdotes.

the visions of empire which Pyrrhus, like his kinsman, Alexander, had brought to Italy, had soon been dissipated. In addition to the tough resistance of the Romans the Epirote king had to reckon with the ill-will of the Tarentines. On his first arrival he had shown his hand by occupying the citadel and policing the town ; henceforth he was virtually fighting on two fronts. In 278 he was considering a return to Macedon, left vacant by the death of Ceraunus, when the call for aid from Syracuse offered him a seemingly better diversion. Had he won the war of the Siceliotes against Carthage, or had he at least kept the powerful Syracusan fleet intact, he could have resumed the conflict with Rome under favourable conditions. In the event, he returned from Sicily with barely a third of his original force, and his last Italian campaign was in the nature of a rearguard action. Under these conditions Pyrrhus planned his operations in a manner worthy of his pupil Hannibal. Anticipating the junction of two Roman consular armies in Lucania,[1] he crept in upon the nearer Roman division for a surprise attack. But the movement was faultily executed, and the resulting open battle ended in a repulse for Pyrrhus. (275) After this reverse the king finally quitted Italy. He left a garrison in Tarentum, and he gave out that he was coming back with a new army. But if he ever had such an intention, he soon lost it out of sight, and in 272 he withdrew his remaining forces from Tarentum. He had a good case for transferring himself to Sicily in 278, where his presence was more urgently needed ; but his second departure from Italy was in the nature of a desertion.

In 272 Tarentum capitulated to the Romans and received unexpectedly favourable terms, which included the retention of its full local autonomy. But its territory was cut down not long afterwards to that of an ordinary city-state ; moreover, unlike Syracuse, Tarentum exercised no political influence upon Rome. Indeed, the political history of the Italian Greeks may be said to come to an end in 272.

[1] The traditional site of Pyrrhus' last battle is at Beneventum. Beloch (*op. cit.*, IV, pt. 2, p. 475 ff.) gives reasons for transferring it to the neighbourhood of Pæstum.

§ 4. MASSILIA

In contrast with the general political failure of the western Greeks and their eventual subjugation by Rome, one isolated outpost of Hellenedom, the city of Massilia, shows a record of resolute and successful self-help. Under the government of a model oligarchy Massilia maintained a navy comparable with the fleet of Rhodes in eastern waters. By its unaided efforts it beat off all attempts by the Carthaginians to enter the Gulf of Lions, and it secured its hold on the Spanish coast as far as C. Palos, in whose neighbourhood it founded the colony of Acra Leuce (Alicante). But the most remarkable feature in Massilian history is the prescience with which from early times it cultivated good relations with Rome, and the extent of its influence on Roman policy. It cannot be doubted that the Romans were acting under Massiliote direction in making the compact of 348 with the Carthaginians,[1] which secured freedom of navigation along the Spanish coast as far as Cartagena, and in the treaty of 226, which forbad Carthaginian conquests north of the Ebro.[2] The tardiness of the Romans in annexing southern France also reveals Massiliote influence; and after the formation of the province of Gallia Narbonensis in 120 Massilia retained its status as an equal ally of the Roman Republic.[3] The history of Massilia, in common with that of Rhodes, shows that a well-conducted city-state could still wield considerable power and play an honourable political part in the Hellenistic age.

[1] Polybius, III, 24.
[2] T. Frank, *Roman Imperialism*, pp. 121–2.
[3] Strabo, bk. III, p. 181.

CHAPTER XI

THE GREEK HOMELAND FROM 217 TO 146 B.C.

§ 1. EARLIER CONTACTS WITH ROME

WE have now reached that stage of Greek History in which the destinies of the Greek nation pass into foreign hands. The cloud which observant Greeks had descried on the western horizon in 217 (p. 166) presently broke over the whole of their land. Yet at the time of Alexander's death it was no bigger than a man's hand. Could the Greeks of that day have evaporated the mists with a puff of east wind? According to a common tradition it had been Alexander's intention to balance his Asiatic Anabasis with an expedition to the western Mediterranean, in which Carthage was to be his first victim, with Italy to follow. Despite Livy's stout assertion that Alexander would have met the fate of Hannibal in Italy,[1] there can be little doubt that the Italians, distracted by the closely balanced struggle between Romans and Samnites, would—for the time being—have succumbed to him. But these alleged plans of the Invincible are mere speculation;[2] and the belated attempt of Pyrrhus to break the Roman confederacy showed that the Greeks had definitely missed their tide. After the departure of Pyrrhus the idea of a Greek attack upon Italy was lost out of sight, and the Romans achieved their conquest of the Italian and Sicilian Greeks without exciting any thought of interference on the part of the Greek Homeland. Among the Hellenistic states Egypt alone entered into any official relations with the Roman Republic, and the object of the alliance which Ptolemy II offered and obtained in 273 was

[1] Livy, IX, 17–19.
[2] On the state papers reputedly left over by Alexander, see p. 3, n. 2.

merely intended to open Italy to Alexandrian trade, and maybe to Egyptian recruiting sergeants.[1]

Similarly the Romans as yet had no thought of entangling themselves in Greek politics.[2] It was only in response to repeated calls from the Italian trading communities that they protested to Teuta, the widow of king Agron, against Illyrian piracy, and made their drive against the corsairs in 229. After this expedition they constituted a Roman protectorate at Corcyra and on a stretch of the Illyrian coast opposite the heel of Italy; but this Roman zone was intended only as a *point d'appui* for future Roman police operations against Illyria, should such be required.[3] Again, the embassy which the Romans sent to the Isthmian Games at Corinth in 228 merely served to announce the liberation of the Adriatic Sea, and it did not give rise to any engagements, formal or informal, between Rome and the Greek cities. Neither did a renewed Illyrian raid under Teuta's successor, Scerdilaidas, and his Greek vassal, Demetrius of Pharos, cause the Romans to alter their Adriatic policy. With the Second Punic War impending, they contented themselves with smoking out the principal pirate nests and extending their protectorate a little further north. (219)

Yet indirectly the second Roman expedition had far-reaching consequences. The pirate chieftain Demetrius took refuge with Philip V of Macedon, and presently became his chief adviser. With a view to his own reinstatement he diverted Philip's interest to the Adriatic and no doubt also suggested to him schemes of conquest in Italy.[4] Though Cassander had toyed with the idea of an Adriatic front for Macedon, the Antigonids had hitherto shown little disposition to revive this policy.[5] But Philip followed the vicissitudes of the Second

[1] On this treaty see esp. M. Holleaux, *Rome et la Grèce et les monarchies hellénistiques*, p. 60 ff. On the alleged but certainly fictitious treaty of 306 between Rome and Rhodes see the same author, p. 29 ff. A few Romans or Italians took service in the Ptolemaic army; but naturally most Italian soldiers of adventure preferred employment under the Roman colours.

[2] On this subject see Holleaux, *op. cit.*, and *Revue de Philologie*, 1926, whom I follow against T. Walek, *Rev. Phil.*, 1925, and Beloch, *op. cit.*, IV, pt. 1, p. 634, n. 3.

[3] For further details see Holleaux, *Cambr. Anc. Hist.*, VII, p. 831 ff.

[4] On Demetrius as the serpent in the Macedonian Eden, see Polybius, V, 12; VII, 13, etc.

[5] On this point see Appendix 14.

Punic War with eager interest, and as soon as the settlement of 217 in Greece (p. 166) gave him a free hand he embarked on an Adriatic adventure which could hardly fail to embroil him with Rome. In 216 he entered the Ionian Sea with a fleet of light cutters of Illyrian type, which he had built in the previous winter, and sailed as far as the Aous estuary. His ultimate intentions on this campaign were not revealed, for at the mere news of the approach of a Roman fleet from Sicily he hastily abandoned his enterprise. But his object could hardly have been less than to restore Demetrius; and it may be assumed that he aimed at obtaining an Adriatic outlet for Macedon at the expense of Scerdilaidas (who had since made his peace with Rome). This intrusion upon a Roman sphere of influence might have been overlooked by the Senate in the crisis of the Second Punic War. But in 215 Philip challenged the Romans in a way that could not be disregarded, by offering an alliance to Hannibal. This move was made too late to bring him any chance of substantial gain out of the Second Punic War, for the victor of Cannæ was not disposed to cede Italian territory to an ally who came (as it then seemed) after the decision, and would only admit his claim to the Roman zone in Illyria and Corcyra.[1] Yet for this small advantage Philip drew Macedon, and Greece to follow, into the sphere of Roman politics.

§ 2. THE FIRST MACEDONIAN WAR

Rome's First Macedonian War had little influence upon the issue of the Second Punic War. Though Philip gained fresh territory at the expense of Scerdilaidas and acquired an Adriatic sea-front near Lissus, he was hopelessly outmatched by the fleet which the Roman admiral, Valerius Lævinus, brought up from Sicily, and he was disappointed of the naval reinforcements from Carthage which he had expected. (211–08) Thus he could not join Hannibal in Italy, and he failed to dislodge Lævinus from the Roman zone in Illyria.

On the other hand, the First Macedonian War was the

[1] The text of this treaty is preserved in Polybius VII, 9. I agree with Holleaux (*Rome et la Grèce*, p. 181 ff.) against Groag (*Hannibal als Politiker*, pp. 87–90) that in all essentials the terms of the treaty were Hannibal's. On Philip's motives, see Walbank, *Philip V of Macedon*, pp. 76–7.

means of enmeshing Rome in the politics of the Greek Homeland. In 212 Lævinus supplemented his naval action with a diplomatic offensive against Philip. Finding the Ætolians still smarting under their recent defeat and spoliation (p. 166), he came to terms with them on the understanding that they should keep any territory taken off Philip, while the Romans carried off the portable booty. Soon afterwards this ill-assorted league was joined by king Attalus of Pergamum, who was seeking compensation for his losses in Asia Minor (p. 112) by acquisitions in the Aegean area. In 210 Elis and Messenia, as the habitual allies of Ætolia, and Sparta, the hereditary foe of Macedon, swelled the coalition. On the other hand, Philip called for assistance from the Hellenic Confederacy. But his principal partner in this union, the Achæan League, displayed no zeal in his service. Its veteran leader, Aratus, mortified by his loss of influence and the growing ascendancy of Demetrius over Philip,[1] would not engage the Achæans on his behalf, and after his death in 213 his son and namesake held them to a policy of neutrality. Besides, the attention of the Achæans was being diverted to a new threat from Sparta, where the army shattered at Sellasia had been reconstructed by a boy-king's regent named Machanidas. Thus Antigonus Doson's new League of Greeks went out of operation at the second call upon its services.

Although Philip was left to face his enemies almost single-handed, he had the better of the exchanges. Hurrying from one front to another, he drove back the Ætolians in Thessaly (210), and ignominiously bundled Attalus out of Central Greece, when this monarch made his first and last attempt at conquest in the Greek Homeland. (208) In the latter year the Achæans redeemed their military reputation by a crushing victory over Machanidas near Mantinea. For this triumph they were indebted to Philopœmen, the hero of Sellasia (p. 162), who had induced the League to re-model its army on the Macedonian pattern. Meanwhile the Romans were leaving their allies to bear the brunt of the fighting, and in 207–6 they virtually abandoned the Greek theatre of war.

[1] Early in 214 Aratus restrained Philip from a *coup de main* upon Messene, where he had been called in as an arbitrator. Later in the same year Demetrius was authorized by Philip to make an unprovoked assault upon the town. He lost his life in this attempt, and Messene presently joined Philip's enemies.

Under these conditions the Greek belligerents accepted the far-sighted advice of the Rhodians, who had been pressing for the termination of a war that was giving the "barbarians" a foothold on Greek soil, and in 206 they made peace in advance of the Romans. By this settlement Philip recovered the Thessalian territory lost to Macedon in the War of Demetrius (p. 152). In 205 the Romans, after a vain attempt to make the Ætolians go back upon their bargain, followed their example by negotiating with Philip. In the "Peace of Phœnice" Philip again was the gainer, for the Romans ceded to him the Adriatic seaboard between the rivers Aous and Apsus. Yet Philip had particular reason to regret the First Macedonian War. His territorial acquisitions were more than offset by the loss of Macedonian hegemony which Antigonus Doson had recovered and consolidated in his new Hellenic League. But this loss was not yet beyond repair, and a Greek reunion in the face of the western peril should not have been more difficult of achievement in 205 than in 217. Philip's worst mistakes were yet to come.

§ 3. PHILIP'S RAIDS IN THE AEGEAN

After the peace of Phœnice Philip supplemented his squadrons of light cutters with a battle-fleet of some fifty larger craft. This might seem a reasonable precaution against king Attalus, who had begun to build up a rival navy. But hardly had Philip's fleet been completed than he sent it out on piratical expeditions such as the Greek seas had not witnessed since the days of Polycrates.

In the winter of 203–2 Philip made a compact with Antiochus III for the partition of the foreign possessions of Ptolemy V (p. 93).[1] By this agreement the Macedonian king was to acquire the remaining Ptolemaic stations in the Aegean (consisting of some towns on the Thracian coast, Samos,

[1] The lack of proper military co-operation between Philip and Antiochus has suggested to D. M. Magie (*Journ. Rom. Stud.*, 1929, p. 32 ff.), that the alleged pact was an invention of Rhodian propagandists, bent on raising a scare at Rome. But disloyalty between war-allies is nothing unusual; and it is unlikely that the Roman Senate (and Polybius to boot) should have fallen into so clumsy a trap.

Thera, and a few minor posts), and probably also Cyrene. His portion was far inferior to that of Antiochus, and indeed it is not easy to understand why he should have embroiled himself with Egypt, which of late had cultivated good relations with Macedon, for so slender a booty. But the ensuing campaign was to show that Philip had lost count of friend or foe. In 202, instead of seeking out the Egyptian positions, he made surprise descents upon a group of cities on the Black Sea route, Lysimachia, Cius and Chalcedon. Of these towns the first alone appears to have belonged at any time to any Ptolemy, and of recent years all three had attached themselves by a curious predilection to the Ætolian League. Philip also captured the free island of Thasos, and directed his admiral, Dicæarchus, to plunder indiscriminately the cities of the Aegean seaboard. At Cius and Thasos he violated the established customs of war by selling the entire population into slavery. Was Philip aiming at a general thalassocracy over the Aegean ? If so, his policy at least was intelligible ; but his methods of realizing it were suicidal. If Aratus' isolated reprisals upon Mantinea had raised an outcry in Greece (p. 161), much more so the wholly wanton atrocities which Philip committed again and again. At one blow he forfeited whatever title he might have retained to the hegemony of Greece, and he drew upon himself more enemies than he had bargained for.

For the time being Philip escaped a new war with the Ætolians. These old antagonists, no longer daring to engage him single-handed, endeavoured to summon back the Romans to Greece. But the Senate saw no reason for renewing an alliance which previously had yielded such meagre results, and the unsupported Ætolians made no move. On the other hand, he brought upon himself the hostility of the Rhodians. Though the Macedonian king had made no direct attack upon their territory, his descents upon the Aegean islands and his campaigns on the Black Sea route seriously injured their trade, and though not definitely convicted, he was more than suspected of having planned a scheme to set the Rhodian war-fleet on fire. At the end of 202 the Rhodians declared war upon Philip and set about forming a new coalition against him. In 201 Philip made the Rhodians a gift of a valuable ally, king Attalus of Pergamum. Though the Macedonian king had begun the operations of that year by a successful and legitimate attack upon the Egyptian station of Samos, he went on to set siege to various free towns among the Aegean islands. Consequently Attalus resolved to forestall a suspected attack upon himself by allying with the Rhodians against Philip. In autumn 201 the combined fleets of Pergamum and Rhodes brought the enemy to battle off Chios, and the superior seamanship of the Rhodians, who eluded all attempts by the Macedonians to board them, gave the allies the victory. But while Attalus withdrew to refit, Philip made a characteristic raid across Caria into the Rhodian Peræa (mainland territory), and although he was trapped in the harbour of Bargylia on the reappearance of the Pergamene fleet, he broke the blockade in the ensuing spring. In summer 200 he prepared for an onset in force upon Pergamum by laying siege to Abydus, whose inhabitants, sooner than cast themselves upon Philip's scant mercy, killed each other off. For the moment Philip had fought his enemies to a standstill; yet before the end of 200 he had fallen back on the defensive, fighting against heavy odds.

In autumn 201 the Rhodians and Pergamenes, loth to admit that their recent failures were due to faulty co-operation rather than to lack of resources, had sent envoys to Rome to solicit the help of the Republic. This step, the most momentous in the history of Rome's conquest of Greece, was also one of the most unexpected. Though Attalus had allied with Rome in the First Macedonian War, and no doubt ranked as an "amicus," he had no legal claim upon them as a "socius."[1] The Rhodians had not only remained neutral in the First Macedonian War, but had been foremost in denouncing "barbarian" intervention in Greek politics. If they were now foremost in calling in the barbarian, the reason lies in the extraordinary embitterment caused by Philip's recent methods of warfare: against such a domestic enemy even a barbarian might legitimately be invoked.

Despite their urgent need of rest after their colossal effort in the Second Punic War, despite the heavy aftermath of that war in Cisalpine Gaul and Spain, the Romans again entered the lists against Philip. They no longer had any direct cause

[1] See the rejoinder by J. A. O. Larsen (*Class. Philol.*, 1937, p. 15 ff.) to E. Beckermann (*Revue de Philologie*, 1935, pp. 59 ff., 101 ff.).

of complaint against him,[1] yet it can hardly be doubted that their decision was mainly based on fear of him. After the campaigns of the two previous years it must have been an easy matter for the Greek envoys to show up Philip as a man whose ambitions knew no bounds, and to represent his pact with Antiochus as being aimed at other powers besides Egypt. Moreover, the Senate had a long memory: despite its readiness to make peace in 205, it had no more lost Philip out of mind than it had forgotten Hannibal. The Second Macedonian War may be described as a preventive attack by Rome upon Macedon.

§ 4. THE SECOND MACEDONIAN WAR

In spring 200 messengers from the Senate brought to Philip the double demand that he should indemnify Attalus for recent damage, and that he should in future abstain from war against any Greek state. These terms, if accepted, would in effect have converted Macedon into a Roman dependency, and they came from a power whose *locus standi* in the case was extremely uncertain. In spite of Philip's inevitable refusal the issue hung in the balance for a while, for the Comitia at Rome were slower than the Senate to see just cause for war. But they voted for war at the second time of asking, on the assurance that Philip had "attacked Rome's allies."

Though the Romans entered the war at the request of two Greek states, to the Greeks in general they appeared as intruders rather than protectors. In Greece the memory of Doson's Hellenic League and of Philip's early years had not wholly faded. On the other hand, the Romans during the First Macedonian War had impressed the Greeks more by their rapacity than by their efficiency. The only allies whom the Romans acquired at the outset in Greece Proper were the Athenians. In retaliation for the unjust execution of some visitors from Acarnania (a state allied with Macedon), Philip had recently sent troops to plunder their territory, thus driving them into alliance with Attalus and Rhodes, and

[1] The statement which Livy reproduces from one of the later Roman annalists (XXX, 33, 6) that a Macedonian corps fought with Hannibal at Zama is manifest fiction. Polybius does not mention a Macedonian contingent in his description of the battle. Besides, how could Philip have transported this force to Africa?

eventually with Rome[1]. But the adherence of Athens gave no more than a slight moral advantage to the Romans. Yet while the Greeks held aloof from Rome, they did not rally round Philip. Such popularity as Philip enjoyed in Greece was mostly among the poorer or the debtor classes, to whom, contrary to the usual custom of Macedonian kings, he promised better conditions. But in toying with the idea of social revolution Philip annoyed the wealthier citizens, in whose hands the effective control of most Greek cities now rested; and he further offended them by an increasing disregard for the local liberties of the cities in his dominions. Lastly, in autumn 200 he gave fresh displays of savagery in two further forays upon Attica which recalled the systematic devastations of Xerxes. Outside of Thessaly, which was now again in close union with Macedon, Philip obtained no appreciable assistance from the Greeks, though Bœotia, Acarnania and Epirus formally declared for him.

Despite the Roman intervention, Philip prosecuted the war with unabated energy. In 199 he parried successive attempts by a Roman expeditionary force to debouch from the Illyrian mountains into the Macedonian plain; he repelled the Ætolians, who had mobilized on a delusive report of an unimportant Roman victory; he hurled back the Dardanians, with whom the Romans had made an ill-considered alliance. On the other hand, the Romans and their allies co-operated as badly as in the First War, and a powerful Roman fleet in the Aegean accomplished nothing of consequence.

In 198 the Roman, Rhodian and Pergamene fleets combined to force the Achæan League to join in the war under threat of blockade. But the citadel of Corinth was retained in Macedonian hands, and the forces of the League were tied down to home service by the menace of further attacks from Sparta. A more substantial gain was achieved by a Roman general named Quinctius Flamininus, who had the good fortune to be shown a way round Philip's position in the Aous defile by an Epirote renegade. After this success Flamininus was free to overrun Thessaly and Central Greece, but he made little headway against the towns held by Macedonian

[1] This alliance was a mere afterthought. It played no part in bringing on the Second Macedonian War. See Holleaux, *Cambr. Anc. Hist.*, VIII, p. 161, n. 2.

garrisons, and he failed to pin down Philip's army on its retreat.

But Philip, with his army reduced to some 25,000 men, and increasing odds against him, had no option left but to take the risks of a quick decision. In 197 he re-entered Thessaly and forced a battle on the field of Cynoscephalæ. In this encounter the Macedonian heavy infantry proved that in a solid front-to-front charge not even the Roman legions could hold it, but that, once thrown out of order or taken in flank, it became helpless. While one Macedonian phalanx charged right home, another broke itself up by its own impetus and became an easy prey to the enemy; and the victorious division, without cavalry support on the flanks, was enfiladed and cut to pieces by the successful Roman wing wheeling in upon it. This was the first decisive victory of Romans over Greeks in a set battle on a large scale; but it sufficed definitely to establish Roman ascendancy in Greece.

Anticipating eventual defeat in a war of attrition, Philip had early in 198 offered to Flamininus to restore all recent conquests and to submit the question of indemnities to arbitration. But Flamininus, going beyond the terms of the Senate's ultimatum, had demanded not only security but complete liberty for the Greeks, and had required Philip to retire beyond the old fourth-century frontier of Mt. Olympus. In the ensuing winter the king had met delegates from all the enemy states at Nicæa (near Thermopylæ), and had undertaken to evacuate part of Thessaly. But his insistence on retaining Demetrias, Chalcis and the citadel of Corinth had disclosed that from these bases he was hoping to recover his ascendancy in Greece, as Gonatas had formerly done. He received leave from Flamininus to lay his terms before the Senate, but that assembly merely reiterated Flamininus' previous demands. After Cynoscephalæ Flamininus was in a position to dictate without negotiating. His Ætolian allies urged him to invade Macedon and dethrone the king. But the Roman general granted Philip's request for an armistice and referred his envoys to Rome. The Senate, following the best traditions of the Scipionic school, did not materially heighten its previous terms after the battle. But it limited Philip to Macedonia Proper, confiscated most of his fleet, and imposed a moderate indemnity upon him. (196) In return for his submission, it recognized him henceforth as an "amicus." The execution of these conditions was entrusted according to Roman custom to the victorious general, assisted by ten commissioners from the Senate.

Flamininus at once took from Philip the keys of Demetrias, Chalcis and Corinth, and garrisoned them provisionally with Roman troops. But he had to use force in carrying out the peaçe-terms in Peloponnesus, where a new dispute had arisen between the Achæans and Sparta. In 198 the town of Argos had taken the alliance of Achæa with Rome as a pretext for quitting the League and offering itself to Philip. The king, unable to protect Argos against reprisals, had made it over to Sparta. In this city Machanidas' successor, Nabis, had usurped the kingship and had accomplished a new social revolution in which Helots as well as Periœci received allotments from confiscated estates. (*c.* 205) With Cleomenes' programme of domestic reform Nabis also revived his dreams of conquest. He gave Sparta its first ring of walls ; he built a fleet which exercised itself in acts of piracy ; and in 198 he accepted Argos as a first instalment of Peloponnesus. But unlike Cleomenes Nabis did not restrict his social programme to Sparta : at Argos he established a reign of terror which gave him a bad name all over Greece.[1] In 195 Flamininus convened delegates from the Greek cities to Corinth and obtained without demur a general mobilization against the "tyrant." With a mixed army of Romans, Greeks and even Macedonians, he penned his enemy up in Sparta and forced him to capitulate. He left Nabis in possession of Sparta, but made him surrender Argos and the maritime towns of Laconia to the Achæans. The other main task of Flamininus was to dispose of those territories in Northern and Central Greece which Philip had evacuated. His chief difficulty here lay with the Ætolians, who claimed back all their past conquests. He conceded to them Phocis and the western half of Thessaly. The rest of Thessaly and the surrounding mountain regions he carved up into four tiny federal states, and he grouped the towns of Eubœa into a separate league. In the constituent cities of these states he remodelled the governments so as to

[1] Nabis was probably a member of the Eurypontid royal family. But his rapacity and cruelty earned him the name of "tyrant."

restrict the magistracies, and probably also the seats on Council, to the wealthier classes. In 194 he took the last step towards the liberation of Greece by withdrawing the Roman garrisons from the "three fetters of Greece."

In forcing the Second Macedonian War upon Philip the Romans intervened in a dispute which strictly did not concern them. But the terms imposed by them upon Philip are sufficient evidence that they had fought for no other end than security for themselves and the Greeks; and the withdrawal of their troops in 194 is proof conclusive that they had not taken Greece from Philip in order to keep it for themselves.[1] In expelling Philip from Greece the Senate unquestionably took a right step. It may fairly be contended that the original conquest of Greece by Macedon had been a blessing in disguise, and that the renewed ascendancy of Antigonus Doson was, at that time, the most promising approach to a "pax Hellenica." But, to say nothing of the difficulties involved in the eccentric situation of Macedon, of its monarchic constitution and its dangerous preponderance in man-power—for with good will all of these might have been surmounted—Philip's recent conduct had shattered hopes of a willing partnership between him and the Greeks, and a Macedonian hegemony had ceased to be within the range of practical politics. When Flamininus proclaimed Rome's gift of freedom to the Greeks at the Isthmian festival of 196, he evoked such enthusiasm as no Greek *panegyris* had ever witnessed. This outburst of feeling was not due to mere abstract love of liberty, but to joy at the riddance from Macedonian overlordship.

In the details of his settlement Flamininus made a fair compromise between the claims of Achæans and Spartans, of Ætolians and Thessalians. But he missed the opportunity of instituting a new and comprehensive Greek federation to replace Doson's Hellenic League or, failing this, a court of arbitration for the compulsory settlement of all inter-city disputes. If, on the other hand, the Romans considered that a United States of Greece constituted a danger to themselves, and that liberty in Greece must go, as of old, with particularism, they would have done better to encroach upon that liberty to the extent of maintaining a permanent staff of

[1] For a full discussion of Roman policy in Greece from 200 to 194 B.C. see L. Homo, *Revue Historique*, vol. 121, p. 241 ff.; vol. 122, p. 1 ff.

liaison officers to act as informal peace-makers and to keep the Senate advised about Greek affairs. As events fell out, the Greeks celebrated their liberty by falling out with each other, and with their liberator.

§ 5. THE SYRIAN WAR IN EUROPE

The peace of 196 aroused immediate discontent among the Ætolians, who were disappointed both in its terms and in the cavalier manner in which Flamininus had treated them during the negotiations. Beyond doubt they also chafed at the prospective loss, under the Roman ægis, of their federal industry of plunder. In 193 they sounded Philip and Nabis, and communicated with Antiochus, whose relations with Rome were then becoming strained (p. 208). From Philip, who had not forgotten how they had demanded and Flamininus had averted his dethronement, the Ætolians met with a rebuff. At Sparta they found too ready a response, for Nabis rushed to arms and opened a premature attack upon the liberated towns of the Laconian coast. The Romans promptly sent a flotilla to protect these, and Philopœmen with the Achæan levy trounced the Spartans in battle and put them under siege. Nabis was fortunate in securing a truce from the Roman admiral which left him in control of Sparta.

From Antiochus the Ætolian emissaries brought back promises of support, and on the strength of these the League broke with Rome. In spring 192 they formally invited Antiochus to " liberate Greece."

To facilitate Antiochus' landing, Ætolian flying columns were sent to occupy Demetrias and Chalcis, and another force was told off to seize Sparta, so as to keep the Achæans in check. At Sparta the Ætolians were amicably received by Nabis, whose hospitality they requited by assassinating him and plundering the town. But the citizens rallied against the pillagers and massacred them in a surprise attack. By their bad faith the Ætolians played into the hands of their Achæan rivals, for Philopœmen now induced the leaderless Spartans to join the Achæan League, and a year or two later he incorporated Ætolia's allies, Messene and Elis, under threat of war. Thus the Achæan League came to embrace all Peloponnesus, which henceforth remained free from Ætolian interference. At Chalcis the Ætolian *coup de main* was beaten off, but Demetrias (whose citizens were alarmed by a rumour that the Romans intended to restore them to Philip) was carried without effort.

In capturing Demetrias the Ætolians provided Antiochus with an excellent base ; yet the king did not take possession until autumn 192, and he brought with him a mere vanguard of 10,000 men. The meagreness of this contingent took the Greeks all the more by surprise, because the Ætolians had spread exaggerated reports about his strength, and his fame as second Greek conqueror of the East gave colour to these rumours. The envoys whom he sent round to negotiate alliances were everywhere received with politely evasive answers, and the Achæans formally declared war upon him. Worse still, the Ætolians were chilled by the king's half-heartedness and stayed at home to sulk while he went on campaign. Fortunately for Antiochus his landing in Greece, however belated, had taken the Romans by surprise. He made good use of this respite by sending out expeditions which gave him possession of Eubœa and Thessaly as far as Larissa.

But in spring 191 Antiochus lost these gains more quickly than he had acquired them. While he vainly waited for his reinforcements from Asia, a Roman army under the consul Acilius Glabrio had joined hands in Thessaly with king Philip. Despite the ties of common race and the pact which they had made in 203, the two kings were now not unnaturally ranged on opposite sides. The pact, dishonoured in turn by both parties, was dead. By allying with Ætolia and assuming the part of *hegemon* in Greece, Antiochus had offended Philip. On the other hand, the Romans had promised him that he might keep any Thessalian cities which he might recapture off the Ætolians (provided that in the first instance these towns should have made common cause with Ætolia *of their own free will*). With the Romans in pursuit, Antiochus fell back upon Thermopylæ, which he had carefully fortified. He successfully held up Acilius in the main pass ; but the inadequate contingent which the Ætolians had sent to his assistance made a present of the flanking route to the Romans. The ex-consul Cato (who served on this campaign under Acilius' orders) set out with a flying column to repeat the exploits of the Persian,

Hydarnes, and once again found the defenders of the Callidromus path ill-prepared. His descent behind Antiochus' position caused a general rout, in which the king himself avoided Leonidas' fate but lost his entire army. Thus the only Seleucid Anabasis into Greece came to a sudden end.

By their disloyalty towards Antiochus the Ætolians dealt themselves a worse blow than befel their ally, for after his flight they remained utterly isolated. They made a good stand at Heracleia, the key to the more westerly routes from Thessaly, but after its fall they sued for peace. Unable to secure from Acilius or from the Senate better terms than unconditional surrender, they prepared to stand at bay in their fortified places. In 190 they were fortunate enough to obtain an armistice from the consul L. Scipio, who needed Acilius' forces for his Asiatic front ; but the arrival of a new Roman army in 189 under the consul, Fulvius Nobilior, again brought them to their knees. From Fulvius they eventually obtained more merciful conditions ; but they were deprived of Delphi, and of all their gains except East and West Locris and a few other unimportant territories. In addition, they became subject-allies of Rome, and lost the power of making war on their own account.[1] The Romans thus settled in three years the Ætolian problem, which Macedon had never succeeded in solving. Henceforward Ætolia virtually disappears out of Greek history.

§ 6. THE YEARS OF UNEASY PEACE

After the war with Ætolia the Roman troops again evacuated Greece, but the Roman Senate found that it could no longer disentangle itself from Greek affairs. In the absence of a Greek federal government or court of arbitration new disputes between state and state were continually referred to Rome ; and the Roman decisions, being given by the Senate upon a summary hearing of the envoys, or by Roman

[1] It is related in Livy (XXXV, 33, 10) that an Ætolian general replied to Flamininus, who visited the Ætolian congress in 192 and asked for a copy of its message to Antiochus, that the Ætolian army would deliver it on the banks of the Tiber. This anecdote probably comes from Polybius (whose account of these events is lost) ; and it is quite in keeping with the pride that went before the Ætolian fall.

commissioners after a rapid tour of inspection, created more unrest than they allayed.[1]

The first signs of a breakdown in the Roman settlement came from Peloponnesus within a few months of the departure of the Roman troops. In this region the general peace seemed to be assured by the Achæan League, under which the whole of Peloponnesus was united for the first time in Greek history. Unfortunately the policy of the League was now committed to the wrong hands. It was the League's misfortune that Aratus was a statesman but no soldier, and that Philopœmen understood war-craft but not state-craft. In 189 his heavy hand descended upon Sparta, a city which in view of its proud past required particularly careful treatment. In anticipation of an attack by the victims of the recent social revolution, the Spartan government had sent a force against their rallying-places in the liberated towns of the Laconian seaboard. At the same time it had sought to justify its action to the consul Fulvius, who referred the matter to the Senate. But this body, perplexed by the intricacies of the case, gave a ruling which in effect left the whole question open. Hereupon Philopœmen, without consulting Fulvius, led a punitive expedition against Sparta and captured the town without resistance. On his own authority he instituted a Bloody Assize among Nabis' former partisans, demolished the new fortifications and dispossessed the Helots ; lastly, he abolished the time-honoured " institutions of Lycurgus," and forced upon the Spartans an ephebic training of Achæan type. This high-handed action brought upon the League a remonstrance from the Senate ; but Philopœmen, far from making excuses, stood upon the legal right of the Achæans to misuse their independence. (188)

A further misunderstanding with Rome was caused in 183 by the revolt of Messene. Undaunted by a characteristic half-measure of the Senate, which gave leave to Italian blockade-runners to assist the insurgents, yet did not forbid an Achæan mobilization, the League invested the revolted city and reduced it to submission, whereupon the Senate explained away its previous resolution with a belated proclamation of benevolent neutrality. Fortunately the conduct

[1] On the difference between Greek and Roman methods of arbitration see Miss L. Matthaei, *Classical Quarterly*, 1908, p. 241 ff.

of Achæan affairs was at this stage taken out of the hands of Philopœmen. The "last of the Greeks," as he has been miscalled, was captured by the Messenian insurgents in an abortive *coup de main* upon the city and put to death. The leadership of the League hereupon fell to a man named Callicrates, who was determined to keep on good terms with Rome at all costs. Callicrates overshot the mark with officious advice to the Senate to treat the League more firmly; but he did good service to the Achæans in persuading them to let the Spartans reconstruct their walls and resume Lycurgus' rules of life. (181) Though these concessions did not make an end of the "Spartan question," they kept Peloponnesus free from war for thirty years, and for the time they reduced tension between the League and Rome.

In Northern Greece the Syrian War laid the seeds of fresh controversies which ended by re-engaging the Roman armies. In recognition of the war-services rendered by Philip, who had helped to reduce the towns held by Antiochus or the Ætolians in Thessaly, and had provided excellently for the Roman troops on the way through Macedon to Asia Minor, the Senate had remitted the rest of his indemnity and had allowed him to retain Demetrias and other cities captured by him. After the war Philip busied himself with the replenishment of his army and treasury, levying fresh taxes, opening new mines, and introducing settlers into Macedon from Thrace. In ten years' time he had raised the man-power and wealth of the country to a higher level than it had attained since the death of Alexander. For his replenished army he found employment on his northern boundaries, where he planned a new line of fortresses and depopulated a frontier zone in order to hold off the Dardanians. With these projects on his hands, he might well have avoided further clashes with Rome, had he not been drawn into new contentions arising out of the settlement of 189.

In the wake of the homeward-bound Roman armies envoys from various Thessalian cities came to Rome complaining that Philip had not withdrawn his garrisons, as required by the peace-terms. The issue turned on a point of fact, whether the cities, prior to recapture by Philip, had made a voluntary or a forced surrender to the Ætolians (p. 195). To investigate this dispute the Senate sent commissioners to Thessaly, and on their report it ordered the appellant towns to be evacuated by Philip and annexed to the Thessalian League. This decision reduced Philip's possessions in Thessaly to Demetrias and the east border; whether justified or not—a question which we have no means of answering—it gave the king a sense of grievance against Rome. His disappointment was turned into rage when the Senate, confronted by king Eumenes II of Pergamum with an untenable claim to the Thracian towns of Ænus and Maroneia, which Philip had occupied after their evacuation by Antiochus (p. 121), compromised the case by giving these cities their freedom. A massacre perpetrated by an agent of Philip in Maroneia was generally, and no doubt rightly, believed to have been the king's answer to the Senate's award. (186–5)

The Senate's decisions encouraged Philip's Greek neighbours to send in a fresh batch of complaints to Rome. These new accusations, however, were parried by Philip with one well-judged move. Remembering the good impression which his younger son Demetrius had made as a hostage after the Second Macedonian War, the king sent him back to Rome to represent his interests. Such was the effect of Demetrius' diplomacy that the Senate silenced the Greek hue and cry with a comprehensive verdict in Philip's favour. (184) By this emphatic gesture the tension between Macedon and Rome was so far reduced, that during the rest of Philip's reign the risk of war passed out of sight. But the favour shown at Rome to Demetrius overstrained the robust family loyalty of the Antigonids and gave rise to a catastrophe recalling the last days of Lysimachus. On his return to Macedon Demetrius was accused by his elder brother Perseus of having intrigued to displace him as Philip's successor. The old king executed Demetrius without full inquiry; then, suspecting Perseus after the event, he prepared to disinherit his elder son, when death overtook him. (179) [1]

Among the later Hellenistic rulers Philip V most nearly recalled the giants of Alexander's generation, or his great-grandfather Demetrius. He was endowed with the same iron

[1] See C. F. Edson, *Harvard Studies in Classical Philology*, 1925, p. 191 ff., and Walbank, *op. cit.*, pp. 246–7, 251 ff. The story of Livy (XL, 24, 3), that a forged letter was used to incriminate Demetrius, is improbable.

constitution, which no amount of profligacy in his manner of life seemed able to undermine; he displayed the same exuberant energy and the same resilience after defeat. But he also reproduced the autocratic arrogance and the unbridled ambition of his ancestor, and with these he wrought more irremediable harm than Demetrius ever inflicted. At a time when Greece above all needed to present a united front to the Romans and to offer them no needless provocation, he made enemies of Greeks and Romans alike, and in effect set up the Romans as arbiters of Greek disputes. Upon him more than upon any other individual falls the blame for placing Greece at the mercy of a foreign people.

§ 7. THE THIRD MACEDONIAN WAR

Philip's successor Perseus inherited the cautious temperament of the true Antigonid breed, but was trained in the self-assertive traditions of his father. His early policy was an unsteady compromise between these conflicting tendencies. At the outset of his reign he conciliated the Senate by applying for a renewal of his father's treaty, and to the Greek cities in his dominions he was more considerate than Philip. But he placed himself in a false position by his ostentatious promises to bankrupts and political outlaws from the towns of the Greek Homeland. These appeals to the political and economic underworld brought him no solid support, while to the Romans they appeared as an attempt to overthrow their settlement of Greek affairs. Renewed visits by senatorial commissions, before whom Perseus failed to clear himself, gave rise in turn to fresh accusations from the king's malevolent neighbours. In 172 king Eumenes of Pergamum made a journey to Rome to present a crime-sheet against Perseus. Returning home by way of Delphi, he was all but killed by a falling rock from Parnassus, and he used this incident—which may quite well have been due to natural causes—to pillory the Macedonian king as an assassin. Hereupon the Senate resolved its doubts by sending an order to disarm as an ultimatum to Perseus, and thus virtually forced on the Third Macedonian War. (171) Like the Third Punic War, this conflict was the outcome of ill-defined suspicions rather than of clearly proved guilt.

The Third Macedonian War was a plain trial of strength between Macedon and Rome. Perseus received no Greek support save from a few minor towns of Bœotia. The Epirotes declared themselves sufficiently to draw Roman vengeance upon their country (p. 203), but gave Perseus no effectual aid. The abstention of the Greeks was partly due to Perseus' parsimony, which deterred him from spending the accumulated funds of the Macedonian treasury in a timely diplomatic offensive. But it is highly unlikely that he could have bought many Greek states for a war against Rome. Apart from the Greek exiles and debtors, he had on his side some political leaders who chafed at the inevitable restrictions entailed with Rome's gift of freedom to the Greeks. But the governing classes in general acquiesced in a Roman suzerainty which greatly added to their security, and they had not forgotten Cynoscephalæ. Under these conditions a general Greek rally to Macedon was out of the question. On the other hand Perseus had scrupulously avoided those blunders of policy which had brought the Greeks into the field against Philip. The Romans therefore received no Greek assistance except from the Achæan League, which supplied a small contingent, and from Pergamum and Rhodes, which furnished a few warships and transports. Their total field force, numbering some 35,000, hardly exceeded that of Perseus.

The Romans and Perseus, having fumbled into war, spent three years in trying to fumble out of it. Though the Roman generals had a fleet at their disposal, they derived scarcely any benefit from it. For two years they made vain endeavours to force the Olympus range between Thessaly and Macedonia. In 169 the consul Marcius Philippus carried the barrier, but more by luck than by management. On the other hand Perseus' congenital cautiousness recovered possession of him on the field of battle. A victory gained by him in a cavalry action near Larissa in 171 frightened him into making two successive attempts at negotiation, and in 169 he abandoned the Olympus position before the Romans had extricated their columns from the mountain defiles. It was not until 168 that the Roman army and fleet, brought into effective co-operation by the consul Æmilius Paullus, were able to acquire a definite foothold in Macedonia.

In 168, however, the war was decided in the course of a few

minutes. The battle of Pydna, in which Perseus' army was virtually annihilated, was in essentials a replica of Cynoscephalæ. Developing by chance from an affair of outposts, it began with a mass attack by the Macedonian phalanx, which Paullus, a seasoned veteran, declared to have been the most terrifying sight in his ample experience. The Roman legions, which never proved their elasticity and manœuvring power more brilliantly than on this field, fell back in good order upon higher ground, and as the momentum of the charging phalanx dislocated its ranks, they thrust themselves, company by company, into its gaps or round its flanks. The Macedonian infantry, unable to reform its line, and left unprotected by its mounted flank guards, was quickly killed off in a veritable battue.

During the Third Macedonian War anti-Roman feeling among the Greeks had been strengthened by the failure of the earlier Roman commanders to protect the civilian population against marauding troops and by their own excessive requisitions. But Greek resentment was allayed by the exemplary discipline enforced by Paullus upon his soldiery. Besides, the massacre of Pydna relieved the Romans of all further reason for fearing the Greeks. Nevertheless the generosity or insouciance with which the Senate had hitherto treated Greek affairs now gave way to anxious suspicion. Though for the third time they left the Greeks free and withdrew their troops, they took precautions, wise and unwise, against future misuse of their liberty. In Macedonia they dethroned the Antigonid dynasty and set up four federal republics extending in a line from the Illyrian frontier to the river Nestus. The new federations were in themselves a justifiable experiment, for the growth of town life in Macedon had made the people ripe for a measure of self-government. Moreover, in fixing the yearly rate of war-indemnity at a mere half of the former royal land-tax, they left Macedon in a better financial position than under the Antigonids. But in prohibiting all intercourse, political or economic, between the four succession-states, they violated the legitimate sense of nationhood among the Macedonians ; and in deporting to Italy not only Perseus but all the royal officials they left the republics without political leadership. (167)

In Greece the Romans made no alterations in the governments and but few changes in the frontiers. But they took strong measures to purge the cities of declared or suspected sympathizers with Macedon. In Ætolia they furnished troops to their principal supporters, who executed five hundred antagonists after a farcical trial. In Achæa, where a party led by Lycortas and his son Polybius (the future historian) had unsuccessfully advocated neutrality, they first demanded a judicial massacre on the Ætolian pattern; on discovering that they could not carry this point they deported one thousand suspects (whose names were supplied by Callicrates) under pretence of arranging for their trial in Italy. In Epirus the ex-consul Paullus was bidden to punish the ineffective sympathies of the people for Perseus with a systematic dragonade in which he carried off 150,000 souls to the Roman slave-market. (167) This utterly inexcusable brutality, which left Epirus half-desolate, was never requited upon the Romans. Their more venial mistakes in Macedon and Achæa brought their revenge with them.

§ 8. THE END OF GREEK LIBERTY

In Macedon the new federations so far proved their capacity to govern, that in 158 the Senate removed some of the previous commercial embargoes. But the restriction of intercourse between the four republics prevented their taking adequate measures for common defence. By a fortunate chance the Dardanians, having recently been engaged in a murderous war in the Balkan hinterland, were slow to seize their opportunity. But in 150 an adventurer named Andriscus, who claimed to be a son of Perseus, won enough adherents to gain successive battles against the cantonal levies on either side of the river Strymon. From a reunited Macedon the pretender mustered sufficient troops to defeat a small Roman force which the Senate hastily sent against him. (149) But his improvised levies were easily disposed of by an augmented Roman army under Cæcilius Metellus (148), and Macedon made its final surrender to Rome. After the Fourth Macedonian War the Senate did not repeat the mistake of partitioning Macedon, yet it dared not entrust the entire country to a native administration. It therefore broke with its long-standing policy of leaving Greek lands ungarrisoned and converted Macedon into a Roman province. By this act it virtually closed the book of Macedonian history.

In Peloponnesus the deportations of the Achæan suspects, far from cowing the League, drove it to open hostility against Rome. For sixteen years the Senate turned a deaf ear to the League's protests against the detention of its citizens ; in 151 it released without trial the surviving remnant of the prisoners. But this act of grace came too late to appease Achæan resentment. Since the Third Macedonian War the revolutionary element, whose chief strength lay in the proletariate of Corinth, had gained steadily upon the friends of Rome and of domestic peace. Moreover in 149 the death of Callicrates, whom Achæan patriots dubbed a traitor yet dared not disregard, removed the last effective check upon their rising temper. In the same year the stalwarts of the League fixed a fresh quarrel upon Sparta over the thorny question of its special privileges, and thus provoked a direct conflict with the Senate, to which the Spartans as usual carried their complaints. The extremist leader Diæus prepared a military execution upon Sparta without awaiting the Senate's decision, which was delayed through its preoccupation with the Macedonian and the Punic Wars. The Senate eventually answered his contumacy with an order to the Achæans to restore full independence to Sparta, which desired it, and to Corinth and Argos, who had no wish to secede. (148) With this sentence of mutilation it finally threw the League into the hands of the extremists, and the Senate's envoys barely escaped death at the hands of the Corinthian mob. In 147 the Senate endeavoured to re-open negotiations by tacitly rescinding its previous instructions, while Metellus sent a conciliatory message from Macedon. But the new Achæan general Critolaus, mistaking the Senate's overture for a confession of weakness, played off its commissioner with impudent chicanery, and the mob of Corinth hooted Metellus' envoys off the platform. To cut off the League's retreat, Critolaus had himself proclaimed dictator by tumultuary procedure. With his usurped powers he compelled the wealthier citizens to contribute heavy taxes and to set free a quota of slaves for military service ; and in 146 he directed an expedition against Heracleia-ad-Œtam, which had under unknown circumstances been annexed to the League, but had profited by the Senate's recent pronouncement to re-assert its independence. He was joined on the way by contingents from Thebes and other Central Greek towns, where the party of social revolution was in the ascendant. But while he lay before Heracleia he was taken unawares by Metellus, who put the Achæan forces to headlong rout and flung them right back upon Corinth. Meanwhile Diæus had collected a second forced levy of freemen and slaves, amounting to some 15,000 men. With this scratch force he offered a desperate resistance to Metellus' successor Mummius, who had brought up large Roman reinforcements. In a battle on the Isthmus the raw Achæan levies proved once more—if proof were needed—that Greeks under firm leadership could fight without flinching; but in the face of hopeless odds they met with irretrievable defeat. (146)

In Greece, as in Macedon, the Senate decided to take no further chances. By way of upholding the sanctity of ambassadors, it ordered the inhabitants of Corinth to be sold into slavery, and the town to be levelled to the ground. It dissolved the Achæan League and annexed its component states to the province of Macedonia. These states henceforth paid tribute to Rome and in some cases had their constitutions remodelled. Athens retained its full freedom; the small local leagues in which the states of Central Greece and Thessaly had been grouped by previous Roman action retained their autonomy under the supervision of the governor of Macedonia.[1] Under this settlement the Greek ideal of local autonomy was in large measure realized, and for the first time in its history the country enjoyed an enduring peace. But the ideal of a United States of Greece was finally shattered, and the era of liberty and of fertile political experiment in Greek lands gave way to two thousand years of forced inertia.

[1] See J. A. O. Larsen, in T. Frank, *Economic Survey of Rome*, IV, p. 301 ff.; S. Accarne, *Il dominio romano in Grecia dalla guerra acaica ad Augusto* (containing a full discussion of the settlement).

CHAPTER XII

ASIATIC GREECE AND EGYPT IN THE SECOND CENTURY B.C.

§ 1. THE ANTECEDENTS OF THE SYRIAN WAR

ALTHOUGH the intervention of the Romans in the Second Macedonian War was due to the solicitations of two Asiatic states, Pergamum and Rhodes, yet in the actual conduct of the war and in its conclusion these states played a very subordinate part. Their alliance with Rome would probably have been no more than temporary, but for the intrusion of another Asiatic power into Aegean politics.

The conquests of Antiochus III, which we have described in preceding chapters, at no point involved a direct clash of interests with Rome. Moreover the Seleucid king was habitually as prudent in his diplomacy as Philip V was reckless. With a view to keeping his principal enemy, the king of Egypt, in political isolation, he was at pains to cultivate good relations with his other Greek neighbours. In 203 he outwitted the Ptolemaic regent Sosibius, who had been approaching Philip for a league against the Seleucid monarchy, by concluding the " partition pact " with Macedon. In 197 he bought off the Rhodians, who were showing alarm at his conquests on the south coast of Asia Minor (p. 103), by leaving to them the Carian towns recently lost by Egypt. At the conclusion of the war with Egypt he insured himself against a revanche by a matrimonial alliance with Ptolemy V. Yet he failed to allay the suspicions of the new king of Pergamum, Eumenes II, who had succeeded Attalus I in 197. Though Antiochus did not pass the boundaries which he had guaranteed to Attalus in 215–4 (p. 113), his conquests on the west coast of Asia Minor in 196 threatened to hem in Pergamum on the north and south sides, and a couple of expeditions which Antiochus undertook in the Gallipoli peninsula in 196–5 appeared to Eumenes as an attempt to jump his rival claims in that region. Moreover, if Antiochus in his dealings with Rome did not light the fire, he played with it until he was caught in the blaze.

Diplomatic intercourse between Antiochus and Rome was opened in 200 B.C.,[1] when Roman envoys visited the king in Syria, ostensibly to arrange a peace between him and Ptolemy, but in reality to prevent co-operation between Antiochus and Philip, his nominal ally, during the Second Macedonian War. Since Antiochus withheld all assistance from Philip, the Romans had every reason to be satisfied with his attitude.

But a more dangerous discussion was started in 197 by emissaries from the cities of Smyrna and Lampsacus, which had refused very favourable terms of submission from Antiochus and applied to Rome to protect their independence.[2] These two towns had even fewer claims on Rome's intervention than Pergamum and Rhodes in 201; but the Senate could hardly have failed to detect behind their appeal the directing hand of Eumenes. In view of Eumenes' tie of friendship with Rome, the Senate went so far as to commend the Greek envoys to Flamininus on their home-journey. To counteract the effect of their visit, Antiochus sent a conciliatory message to Flamininus in 196. But the victor of Cynoscephalæ merely raised fresh objects of dispute. He warned the king to keep his hands, not only off Smyrna and Lampsacus, but off all autonomous Greek cities; he required him not to set foot upon Europe; he even bade him evacuate the towns recently acquired from Ptolemy. Furthermore, lest this admonition should not reach the king's ears, he sent a deputation to Lysimachia, where Antiochus was then stationed, to drive home his meaning. These terms were no less exorbitant than the Senate's demands on Philip in 201.

[1] The alleged treaty of friendship between Rome and "Seleucus," i.e. Seleucus III (226–3), on condition of Seleucus granting immunity from taxation to Rome's mother-city Ilium (Suetonius, *Claudius*, 25, 3), should probably be rejected as a fiction by some later Roman annalist. (Holleaux, *Rome et la Grèce*, p. 46 ff.)

[2] A complimentary decree of Lampsacus to one of its successful envoys is preserved in Ditt., *Syll.*, 591.

But Antiochus, being of a different temper from the Macedonian king, replied to the envoys point for point and completely out-argued them. Politely but firmly he questioned Flamininus' title to speak for all the Greek cities; his own title to his conquests in Asia Minor and Thrace he made good on the score of previous possession; and he produced the terms of his impending settlement with Ptolemy, which completely cut the ground from under Flamininus' feet. In 195 Antiochus sent a second embassy to Flamininus to re-open conversations *ab integro*. Again the Roman general refused to listen; but by his withdrawal of all Roman troops from Greece in 194 he proved that he saw no need to back up his strong words with deeds. Meanwhile the Senate had received with alarm the news that Hannibal had been welcomed at Antiochus' court and was prompting him to attempt an invasion of Italy. (Late 195) But Antiochus soon made it clear that he would not let the great Carthaginian stampede him, and by his firm attitude he diminished, if he did not dissipate, the Senate's apprehensions.

In 194 Antiochus made a fresh offer of negotiations to the Senate. Though his envoys had once again to deal with Flamininus (as spokesman of the Senate), they found him less obdurate, for in effect he now undertook to give the king a free hand in Asia, provided that he evacuated Thrace and recognized Rome's right to dispose of Europe. But Antiochus' agents stood on his full rights, and thus threw away his best chance of an amicable settlement. Had they agreed to Flamininus' proposals, they would have given away nothing worth retaining, for Antiochus' claims to Thrace were shadowy, and this European annexe, separated by water from his remaining possessions, made his empire still more unwieldy and vulnerable. In return for this slight sacrifice they would in all probability have obtained a secure peace, for the Senate had no antecedent grounds (as in the case of Philip) for keeping open the quarrel with Antiochus, and it could hardly pretend that a purely Asiatic empire could be a menace to Rome. Nay more, the Senate proved its good will by sending a new embassy to Antiochus to mend the broken threads of the discussion. But Antiochus left most of the resumed negotiations in the hands of a somewhat untactful minister, and the Roman envoys let their case be taken out of their hands by delegates from Smyrna, Lampsacus and other Greek cities, whom Eumenes had carefully coached in obstructive tactics. (193) The conference of Ephesus, therefore, merely raised tempers, and it impelled Antiochus to commit his irretrievable mistake. Soon after the breakdown of negotiations he received and accepted the Ætolian invitation to "liberate Greece." In complying with this offer Antiochus probably had no intention of making permanent conquests in the Greek Homeland, and his military expedition was no more than an incidental move in his diplomatic game. On this ground we may excuse his failure to discount Ætolian promises and the inadequacy of his own mobilization; but it was a fatal blunder on his part to disturb the political status of European Greece. Such action could only appear to the Senate as a deliberate attempt to overthrow their recent settlement of that country, and it constituted a better *casus belli* than any supplied by king Philip before the Second Macedonian War.

§ 2. THE SYRIAN WAR IN ASIA

The tardiness of his mobilization and the treachery of his Ætolian allies prevented Antiochus from fighting out the "Syrian" War in Europe. After his expulsion from Greece (pp. 195–6), the king made hasty preparations to dispute a Roman landing in Asia Minor. Despite his recent acquisitions on the coasts of Asia, he had hitherto done little to increase his navy. On the other hand the Romans had sent a strong squadron to Aegean waters, and not only king Eumenes but also the Rhodian Republic (acting on the sound commercial principle of backing the winner) had contributed a naval contingent. Nevertheless the maritime campaigns of 191–0 witnessed the hardest fighting of the whole war. In 191 Antiochus' admiral Polyxenidas (a renegade from the Rhodian service) forced a battle off C. Corycus (between Ephesus and Chios) against the combined Roman and Pergamene fleets, previous to the arrival of the Rhodian contingent. But he lost more than one-third of his capital ships to the Romans, who made excellent use of their approved grappling and boarding tactics.

Owing to the lateness of the season the victors of Corycus

were unable to follow up their advantage, and Polyxenidas' casualties were replaced by a vigorous programme of fresh construction which Antiochus at last put in hand. In 190 the Seleucid navy attained its highest strength. The main fleet under Polyxenidas was brought up to ninety battle-ships, and a second squadron of some fifty sail was collected in the Phœnician ports under the command of Hannibal, who now took up his first and last commission in Seleucid service.[1] Polyxenidas opened the second naval campaign with an isolated success over a Rhodian squadron which he destroyed by stratagem near Samos. But the Rhodians amply avenged their defeat under a new admiral named Eudamus. This able commander went out to intercept Hannibal's reinforcements at Side in Pamphylia, and despite the enemy's advantage in numbers and weight he out-manœuvred and virtually destroyed the Phœnician fleet. Returning to the Aegean front, he joined forces with the Romans and played a leading part in the decisive battle of Myonnesus (near Teos). In this engagement Polyxenidas executed an enveloping movement against the Roman fleet, which had gone into action without the Pergamene contingent and was, therefore, inferior in numbers. But his manœuvre was countered by Eudamus, who put out on his own initiative out of the reserve line and held Polyxenidas' wing while the Romans broke his centre. With the battle of Myonnesus the command of the sea passed definitely to the allies, and Antiochus could no longer contest the passage of the Roman armies into Asia.

Meanwhile the Roman legions, under the nominal command of Lucius Cornelius Scipio, but effectively led by his more famous brother, Scipio Africanus, were advancing to the Dardanelles. They were escorted through Macedon by Philip, and their crossing into Asia was unopposed, for after Myonnesus Antiochus had evacuated Thrace. But the Roman general, even after the accession of a contingent from Eumenes, had only 30,000 men, whereas Antiochus' mobiliza-

[1] Hannibal, who knew only too well that the Romans could not be defeated by half-measures, had previously advised Antiochus to form a war-coalition with Philip V, with Prusias of Bithynia and Carthage, and to lend him an expeditionary force for a second invasion of Italy. In theory, Hannibal was quite right; but his plan was a counsel of perfection, and it probably confirmed Antiochus' suspicions that Hannibal wanted to borrow his army for a Punic war of revenge.

tion, now complete, gave him some 75,000 troops, the largest Hellenistic levy since Ipsus. The first Roman Anabasis into Asia, therefore, might seem a venture comparable with Alexander's; yet Antiochus, with a true premonition of a more than counter-balancing advantage on the Roman side, was overawed into negotiations. To Scipio he now offered to withdraw all claims on Thrace and on such Asiatic towns as had sought Roman protection, and to pay one-half of Rome's war-costs. After refusal of these terms he still hesitated to try his chances in battle. But in autumn 190[1] he engaged the Romans near Magnesia-ad-Sipylum, on open ground which gave him full room to deploy his troops.

The weakness in Antiochus' army which made him hesitate to fight lay not so much in the poor quality of its ingredients —though the majority of his troops were oriental, they were drawn from Iranians and other good fighting stocks—as in the extreme variety of their equipment and in their lack of common training, which made cohesion between the several units difficult to maintain. In recognition of this defect Antiochus relegated the greater part of his force to a defensive part, and staked everything on a massed charge by his Iranian horsemen, whose movements he directed in person. With this division he routed the Roman left; but in the hour of victory he repeated the mistake which had cost him the battle of Raphia: instead of turning in upon the Roman centre, he carried on the pursuit of the broken Roman wing, and when at last he reined in he found that the rest of his army had left the field. The rout of the Seleucid centre and left wing was mainly due to king Eumenes, who had only put a small contingent into battle, yet had the general command of the allied right wing.[2] Having dispersed the opening attack of the Seleucid scythe-chariots with the missiles of his archers and slingers, the Pergamene king took advantage of the resulting confusion to charge the armoured horsemen who formed Antiochus' left flank-guard. By this quick thrust—which Lucullus imitated at Tigranocerta with like effect—Eumenes sent the "cataphracts" hurtling into the

[1] For the date of the battle see esp. Beloch, *Klio*, vol. 15, pp. 387–92.

[2] At Magnesia the Roman high command was effectively in the hands of a divisional general named Cn. Domitius Ahenobarbus. Scipio Africanus was absent from the battle on account of illness.

adjacent infantry and so threw the whole enemy wing into confusion. Yet Antiochus might have retrieved this disaster, had he brought timely help from his right wing. The phalanx in his centre, though hotly assailed in front and flank, made a stand that was worthy of the best Macedonian traditions. But the heavy infantry was left unsupported, and it eventually fell a victim to a new tactical disposition by which Antiochus had endeavoured to make it more flexible; for instead of massing it into a single corps, the king had arranged it in separate columns, with elephants to close the gaps. Under the Roman bombardment the elephants proved less steady than the men, and began a stampede which broke their ranks.[1] As in the Macedonian wars, the Roman infantry made short work of the disjointed phalanx, and it went on to destroy the rest of Antiochus' army in a slaughter unequalled since Cannæ.

After the battle Antiochus accepted without demur the Roman peace conditions, which were identical with those offered before their victory. But these terms were such as only a well-beaten enemy could have acknowledged. In addition to paying an indemnity of 15,000 talents—the highest known to Ancient History—the king was required to evacuate all Asia Minor this side of Mt. Taurus; and for fear of his challenging this settlement at a later date he was ordered to surrender all his elephants and most of his fleet, and forbidden to recruit troops from the Roman sphere of influence, i.e. from Greece and the Aegean area. The territories ceded by Antiochus were divided between the Rhodians and Eumenes, with the river Mæander as the boundary between their portions.[2] On the future status of the Greek cities of the western seaboard a dispute arose among Rome's allies, for whereas the Rhodians (whose interests were mainly commercial) urged the Romans to give these the full freedom of which they had professed themselves the champions, Eumenes claimed sovereignty over all the coast towns from the Mæander to the Troad. The Romans ended by assigning

[1] This critical incident is omitted in the narrative of Livy (XXXVI, 41–43), but is recorded by Appian (*Syriaca*, ch. 35), who makes it clear that the phalanx at first maintained an unbroken front. Polybius' account of the battle has been lost.

[2] On the details of the frontier demarcation, see Holleaux, *Cambr. Anc. Hist.*, VII, p. 229 and n.

as tributaries to Eumenes all those places which Antiochus had captured off king Attalus, and giving independence to the remainder. Soon after the signature of the "Peace of Apamea" the Romans withdrew their troops from Asia without annexing any of its territory. (188) But all the states of the Near East, both Hellenic and "barbarian," henceforth acknowledged that their fate ultimately depended on Rome's good will.

§ 3. ASIA MINOR TO 133 B.C.

While the Syrian War mutilated the Seleucid monarchy and virtually extinguished the Ætolian League, it raised two Greek states of Asia Minor to the height of their power. The Rhodians reaped the due reward of their naval victories in an undisputed thalassocracy in Aegean and Levantine waters; and they made worthy use of their supremacy by making the first resolute attempt, since the Athenian thalassocracy, to clear the eastern Mediterranean of pirates.

On the other hand the kingdom of Pergamum, whose very existence had hitherto been precarious, had now become the paramount power in Asia Minor. The aggrandizement of Eumenes did not fail to expose him to the ill-will of jealous neighbours. But his most formidable antagonists, the Galatians, had been thoroughly cowed in 189 by the Roman consul Manlius Vulso, who utilized the interval before the settlement of Apamea to conduct a systematic razzia on the Phrygian plateau and carried off the accumulated spoils of a century.[1] This robbery of a robber held the Galatians in check for the time being, and a chain of military colonies planted by Eumenes on his borderlands established a permanent barrier against them. In 186 king Prusias I of Bithynia, who had abandoned an earlier plan of an alliance with Antiochus at a mere word from the Romans, took Hannibal into his service and made war upon Pergamum. Another warning from the Senate eventually sufficed to disarm him, and Hannibal only escaped extradition to the Romans by taking his own life. (183)

[1] The story of this razzia is given at length in Polybius, XII, 16–19, and Livy, XXXVIII, 13–27. In addition to chastising the Gauls, Vulso led blackmailing expeditions against the Greek towns in Lycia and Pamphylia which had been subject to Antiochus III.

The readiness with which Prusias accepted peace may partly have been due to an attack from another quarter, which threatened him and Eumenes alike. In 183 king Pharnaces of Pontus took the first step towards the foundation of the Pontic empire by capturing the city of Sinope, which he presently made into his capital. From Sinope he began to extend his conquests westward along the Black Sea coast; but he was checked by a coalition of Bithynia with Pergamum, in which the free Greek cities of Cyzicus and Heracleia took part. After four years' fighting Pharnaces agreed to keep his hands off the Paphlagonian borderland. (179) In this war the Romans also intervened on Eumenes' behalf, but finding Pharnaces obdurate they let events take their course. In eastern Asia Minor Eumenes had acquired the constant friendship of Ariarathes IV of Cappadocia. Unlike Prusias, this monarch had actually contributed to Antiochus' army. But Eumenes used his influence with the Romans to have his indemnity reduced to a quite moderate sum. In return, Ariarathes supported the king of Pergamum against Pharnaces in the Four Years' War.

In the Third Macedonian War both Eumenes and the Rhodians compromised their friendship with Rome by untimely attempts at negotiation. The Rhodians, who had refused a request from Perseus for intercession at an earlier stage of the war, made a spontaneous offer of mediation to the Senate in 168. Their message was so timed that it did not reach Rome until after the battle of Pydna, and it made the worst possible impression upon the Senate, which hastily assumed that the Rhodians were bent on snatching Perseus' cause out of the fire. At the peace settlement it punished this apparent double-dealing by giving independence to the Carian cities assigned to Rhodes in 188, and by creating artificial competition with Rhodian commerce at Delos, which was handed back to the Athenians on condition that they should impose no harbour dues. The Rhodians succeeded in disarming Roman resentment by putting to death the authors of their ill-starred offer of negotiation and by asking for a formal alliance with Rome, which the Senate conceded after a suitable pause. (165) But the loss of revenue from their mainland possessions and from their diminishing trade so cramped their finances that they reduced their navy and gave up their pretensions to political leadership in the Greek world. The result of Rome's blind reprisals upon the Rhodians is seen in the Pirate Wars of the first century B.C.

The Rhodian offer of intercession sprang in large measure from a misplaced jealousy of Eumenes, who had helped to make the Third Macedonian War and appeared likely to be the chief gainer by it. Yet at the time when the Rhodians sent their message Eumenes had forestalled them in incurring the Senate's displeasure. Though he did not actually send a peace embassy to Rome, he fell under suspicion of having contemplated the very move which the Rhodians subsequently made, and it was asserted that he would have taken action sooner, but that the price which he quoted to Perseus for his good offices—rumour supplied the exact figure—was too high. This story may be dismissed as a mere character-sketch to illustrate the acquisitiveness of Eumenes and the tenaciousness of Perseus. Nevertheless, it nearly cost Eumenes his throne. In 167 the Senate gave a broad hint to Eumenes' brother, Attalus, whom the king had sent to Rome to clear his name, that he might have the crown of Pergamum for the asking, and when Eumenes announced his intention of pleading his cause in person, it virtually forbade him to set foot on Italy. Fortunately the family loyalty of the Attalids proved as strong as that of the Antigonids ; and a visit which Eumenes' neighbour, Prusias II, paid to Rome to play the good boy at Eumenes' expense caused a reaction in his favour. In 159 the king of Pergamum died, leaving a doubtful reputation as Rome's sycophant-in-chief. Indeed, it may be asked whether on a wider view it would not have been more politic, as well as more patriotic on his part, to stand in with Antiochus against the "barbarians." But if Eumenes was no national hero, he was the shrewdest of Hellenistic politicians ; and his practice of ringing the bell of the Senate-house, far from being peculiar to him, was becoming a common bad habit of the Greek politicians.

The uneventful reign of Eumenes' brother and successor, Attalus II, was marked by only one war of importance. Soon after his accession Prusias II made an ill-judged attack upon him ; but the new king brought about a general rally of the other states of Asia Minor against the aggressor, and the Romans intervened to force an unfavourable peace upon the

Bithynian king. A few years later Attalus avenged himself upon Prusias by instigating his own son, Nicomedes, to dethrone him. On this occasion the Senate made a half-hearted attempt to save Prusias, but took no further steps when Attalus presented it with an accomplished fact.

In 133 B.C. the inexplicable caprice of the next Pergamene ruler, Attalus III, in bequeathing his crown to Rome, made a sudden end of the Attalid monarchy.[1] The most successful of the Hellenistic states in the second century vanished like a ship that is scuttled by its own captain.

§ 4. ANTIOCHUS IV AND EGYPT

For the Seleucid monarchy the Peace of Apamea was to all appearances the beginning of the end. Deprived of its Aegean sea-front and of its recruitment areas in Greece, it seemed like the giant Antæus in mid-air. Moreover, the giant was now shedding limb after limb. Hardly had the Romans detached Asia Minor, than the kings and governors of the northern and eastern borderlands began to lop off other territories (pp. 73, 76). Nevertheless, the Seleucid realm recovered from its losses and for a while resumed a commanding position in the Near East. In the remaining provinces of Syria and Cilicia, Babylonia and Media, the colonizing activities of the dynasty had so far achieved their work, that a native revolt against Greek rule was now out of the question; and under a capable administration these districts could furnish resources sufficient to reconstitute the monarchy as a first-class power. Amputation had made the state more self-contained and had given it greater organic vitality. Under Antiochus III's nephew it displayed its renewed strength. Among Hellenistic kings, Antiochus IV stood out as the Bohemian on the throne. Having lived in Rome as a hostage, he played at Roman Republic in Antioch by instituting a toy ædileship and soliciting the votes of the burgesses in a snow-white toga; he played at Greek democracy by hobnobbing with the towns-

[1] There is no evidence that Attalus needed to buy Roman help against dynastic rivals, foreign enemies, or the smouldering discontent of serf cultivators on the royal domains; and it is reading Roman History backward to assume that at this stage the Romans coveted possession of his territory.

folk in the public baths. From these harmless antics, and from his ruinous showmanship, which eventually reduced him to serious financial straits, he derived the semblance of a Greek Nero. But with these frivolous traits he combined a true Seleucid capacity for hard work, and he clearly realized the importance of strengthening the Hellenic element in his dominions by other means than immigration from Greece. Under his rule many towns of mixed population which had become ripe for full self-government received new charters of a Hellenic type[1]; and the Seleucid army was reconstituted on a more Greek pattern than that of Antiochus III.

In 171 Antiochus IV had the opportunity of testing his strength upon the Ptolemies, who at this time reopened the question of Cœle-Syria and prepared for its reconquest. In Egypt the semi-anarchy of the opening years of Ptolemy V had been succeeded by a period of good administration under the regent Aristomenes (*c.* 201–195); and Ptolemy himself on coming of age proved a far more vigorous ruler than his father. Since 200 B.C. the country had been distracted with native revolts which flared up again from time to time for some fifteen years. In 187 the rebellion in Upper Egypt was ended by the recapture of Thebes; in 183 the insurgents in the Delta were finally suppressed. In those campaigns Ptolemy V laid the seeds of future trouble by acts of perfidy and savage reprisals; but he tempered severe military repression with wise political concessions,[2] and he obtained, at any rate, a respite from native unrest. He did not live to take up again the problem of Cœle-Syria, and after his death (181) his widow, Cleopatra, who assumed the regency on behalf of their eldest son, Ptolemy VI, maintained friendly relations with Antioch, as befitted a princess of Seleucid birth. But after the death of the queen-regent (*c.* 173) the ministers, Eulæus and Lenæus, prepared for a new invasion of Cœle-Syria in 170.

[1] A considerable number of Seleucid towns celebrated Antiochus' gift of autonomy by assuming the name of Antiocheia or Epiphaneia, and by issuing municipal coinages in bronze.

[2] The famous Rosetta Stone in the British Museum contains a vote of thanks by the synod of Egyptian priests to Ptolemy V for stamping out the rebellions and for various acts of liberality to the native clergy and laity (196 B.C.). *Brit. Mus. Inscr.*, 1065; Ditt., *O.G.I.*, 90; English Translation in E. R. Bevan, *Egypt under the Ptolemaic Dynasty*, p. 263 ff.

The Egyptian advance into Cœle-Syria was forestalled by Antiochus, who surprised the Ptolemaic frontier forces and marched straight on to Memphis, and Ptolemy himself fell into the invader's hands. (169) The Seleucid monarch now had himself proclaimed king of Egypt by his own troops, and was crowned at Memphis as a Pharaoh. But a popular revolution at Alexandria replaced the captive king by his younger brother, Ptolemy VII, and Eulæus and Lenæus by a more competent board of ministers. This new government so improved the defences of the capital that Antiochus left Ptolemy VI to carry on the war against his usurping brother and himself withdrew from Egypt, retaining only the frontier-fortress of Pelusium in his hands. A temporary reconciliation between the two Ptolemies, who agreed to set up a joint kingship at Alexandria, disappointed Antiochus' hope of the two brothers keeping each other in play.[1] But in 168 he suddenly re-entered Egypt, and at the same time occupied Cyprus with the help of a disloyal Ptolemaic governor. In this campaign the Seleucid invader reached Alexandria without a serious check, and prepared to put it under siege.

But Antiochus was baulked of his prey by foreign intervention. During his first campaign mediation had been offered by several Greek cities and, subsequently, by a deputation from Rhodes. The king out-argued the former mission and snubbed the latter; but on his second expedition he was made, so to speak, to put up his hands to an agent from Rome. Though Eulæus and Lenæus had obtained a centenary renewal of the treaty between Egypt and Rome, the Third Macedonian War and an embassy from Antiochus (who was sane enough to value good relations with the Republic) had prevented the Senate from assisting either of the Ptolemies. But it was the set policy of the Senate to check the growth of a new Seleucid empire. Therefore as soon as the battle of Pydna had freed its hands it sent an order to Antiochus to evacuate both Egypt and Cyprus. The Roman envoy, Popilius Lænas, handed to him the Senate's dispatch without comment, and when the king asked for time to consider his answer, drew a ring round him with his staff and bade him say "yes" or

[1] For fuller details of a long game of cross-purposes, see W. Otto, *Zur Geschicte des sechsten Ptolemäers*, ch. II; P. Jouguet, *Rev. Phil.*, 1937, p. 193 ff.

" no " before he stepped out of the circle. Antiochus pocketed the affront, abandoned his recent gains, and on his return to Syria took his revenge by celebrating at Daphne a pageant which far outdid the splendid triumph of Æmilius Paullus after Pydna.

By the masterful intervention of Popilius Egypt was freed once for all from the danger of Seleucid invasion. But hardly had Antiochus evacuated Egypt than the two kings fell out. In 165 the elder brother obtained evidence that his partner was plotting against him, but with a family loyalty unusual in his dynasty he gave the culprit a free pardon. In the next year the pardoned sinner repaid this generosity by expelling Ptolemy VI with the help of the Alexandrian mob, which at this time took sides with the younger king as being of its own choice. The exile repaired to Rome and presented himself to the Senate, like a fallen hero in a Euripidean tragedy, with all the trappings of misery. The Senate's decision, that Ptolemy VI should recover Egypt and Cyprus, while his brother received Cyrenaica, was forestalled by the Alexandrians, who had become incensed at their nominee's harsh rule, and sent him too on his travels. (163) From Cyrene Ptolemy VII in his turn repaired to Rome (in 162, and again in 154).[1] The Senate twice over awarded him Cyprus in addition to Cyrenaica, but gave him no military aid ; and a final attempt on his part to acquire Cyprus by self-help ended in his capture by Ptolemy VI. The elder brother, with a prudent resolve not to affront Rome too openly, restored his prisoner to Cyrene, and henceforth reigned unmolested in Egypt and Cyprus. Thus freed from domestic war, Ptolemy VI was able to requite the invasion of Antiochus by fomenting dissension in the Seleucid dominions.

[1] A so-styled " will " of Ptolemy VII, of date 155 B.C., has been brought to light in an inscription at Cyrene. (For text and commentary, see M. N. Tod, *Greece and Rome*, II, p. 47 ff. ; Otto, *op. cit.*, p. 97 ff.). In this document Ptolemy invokes Roman aid against aggressors and plotters against his life, and records that he has bequeathed his dominion to Rome, failing other successors. The purpose of the document was presumably to represent Ptolemy VII as an injured innocent, and to warn his brother's partisans that they might bring a Roman intervention and permanent occupation upon themselves.

Behind this and other moves in the game between the two brothers we need not look for the hand of the Roman Senate, which at this time appears to have had no settled policy in regard to the Ptolemies.

But by their quarrels the rival Ptolemies had in effect played themselves into the hands of Rome, though the Senate as yet hesitated to assume authority.

§ 5. CIVIL WAR IN SYRIA

In the Seleucid monarchy a new era of disputed successions had begun with the death of Seleucus IV in 175. This ruler had been murdered by his minister, Heliodorus, probably with the intention of exercising rule in the name of an infant son of the dead king (Antiochus by name).[1] But the legal succession was set aside by Seleucus' brother, Antiochus IV, who at that time was in favour with Rome and with Pergamum. With troops borrowed from king Eumenes he disposed of Heliodorus and his puppet, and saved the country from a minority reign with an unscrupulous regent. In 163 Antiochus IV died prematurely of disease, leaving a boy, Antiochus V, to succeed him, and a regent named Lysias. But for a second time a minority reign was averted by an intruder from abroad. When Antiochus IV became king, his place at Rome as a hostage was taken by his nephew, Demetrius, the eldest son of Seleucus IV. Until 162 the Senate detained Demetrius, despite the fact that he was the rightful heir to the throne of Seleucus IV; but in that year he escaped to Syria[2] and at once won over army and people. Having removed Lysias and his ward without difficulty, Demetrius prepared a campaign against the governor of Babylonia, Timarchus, who had set himself up as a rival king. But Timarchus' subjects went over to the legitimate ruler on his first appearance, and the pretender was promptly executed. The new king had greater difficulty in obtaining recognition from the Senate. In addition to the personal offence of his flight from Rome, he had to atone for the murder of a Roman commissioner, Cn. Octavius, who had been sent to Antioch in 162 to enforce some half-forgotten disarmament clauses of the Peace of Apamea and had been lynched by the folk of the capital, enraged at the sight of

[1] On Antiochus the son of Seleucus IV see E. R. Bevan, *Cambr. Anc. Hist.*, VIII, p. 713–4.

[2] The flight of Demetrius from Rome is narrated at length by Polybius (XXXIII, chs. 19 ff.), who had a hand in smuggling the prince away.

burning ships and of hamstrung elephants. Fortunately Demetrius had an opportunity of stating his case to an influential Roman named Tiberius Gracchus (father of the land-reformer), who was his personal friend. On Gracchus' recommendation the Senate made its peace with Demetrius.

But Demetrius had hardly come to terms with Rome than he began to make enemies elsewhere. He annoyed the townsfolk of Antioch with a haughty demeanour suggesting that Domitian had come to reign in place of Nero. He offended king Attalus by supporting a rival candidate for the throne of Cappadocia. He embroiled himself with Ptolemy VI by attempting to annex Cyprus in collusion with a traitorous governor. In revenge, Attalus and Ptolemy suborned a fresh pretender, a youth named Balas, who was passed off as a son of Antiochus IV. With Pergamene and Egyptian troops Alexander Balas (as he now styled himself) easily overpowered Demetrius, who was deserted by his own troops and fell in battle. (152–0) The new king, who had secured recognition from Rome in advance, at first also won the favour of the Antiochenes; but he proved himself utterly incompetent as a ruler. His incapacity invited a counter-attack from a son and namesake of Demetrius, who landed in Cilicia with a corps of Cretan mercenaries, although he was as yet a mere boy. (147) At the same time Ptolemy VI advanced with an army into Syria, ostensibly in aid of Balas. But he quarrelled with Balas—presumably about the price of his assistance—and transferred his support to the young Demetrius. Pressing on in pursuit of Balas, he entered Antioch and was offered the Seleucid crown by the townsfolk, who had not turned against Balas in order to make Demetrius king. After an interval of a hundred years a king of Egypt again was arbiter of the Seleucid dominions; but Ptolemy VI, who realized that by accepting the crown he might be drawn into fresh conflict with Rome and with his brother at Cyrene, persuaded the Antiochenes to accept Demetrius and kept nothing for himself except Cœle-Syria. By this arrangement the old frontiers between the two kingdoms were momentarily restored. But the compromise between Ptolemy and Demetrius was challenged by Balas, who made a rally in Cilicia and attempted a new dash upon Antioch. The evicted king was heavily defeated and lost his life in the rout; but Ptolemy also died from the effects of a fall during the battle, and his army fell into such confusion that Demetrius captured it and recovered Cœle-Syria at one blow. (145) With this campaign the long struggle between Ptolemies and Seleucids was brought to a close.

§ 6. CIVIL WAR IN EGYPT

In Egypt the sudden death of Ptolemy VI threatened to create a minority reign for the third time in succession. But the rightful heir to the crown was at once set aside by Ptolemy VII, who hastened from Cyrene to Alexandria, put his brother's child to death, and reunited the Ptolemaic dominions. In addition to his brother's throne, the new king also won his widow, Cleopatra II,[1] despite the fact that he had just killed her son, and he presently gave her a new son, Ptolemy Memphites. But in 142 he renewed civil war in taking Cleopatra's daughter by her first husband, Cleopatra III, to be his second wife. The elder Cleopatra, however willing to stifle natural sentiment in order to remain a queen, was not prepared to share her crown with a young girl. She therefore stirred up a fronde against the king among the Alexandrines. The king repeatedly set his troops on to the townsfolk; but in 131/0 he was cornered in the street-fighting and fled to Cyprus, taking Ptolemy Memphites with him. To punish his ungrateful wife he reproduced in actual life the story of Medea by carving up the boy Memphites and sending the severed limbs in a hamper as a birthday present to Cleopatra. In 129 he recovered Alexandria; Cleopatra II fled to Antioch, but in 124 came to final terms with her husband. Meanwhile the government of Egypt had fallen into confusion, and the people had to put up with much oppression from the officials. In 118 Ptolemy VII issued a comprehensive act of amnesty and strict and detailed warnings against future acts of maladministration.[2] With this belated example of statesmanship

[1] Cleopatra II was the sister of both the kings. Such sister-marriages no longer excited comment at Alexandria. On the family history of the later Ptolemies in general, see W. Otto and H. Bengtsoro, *Zur Geschichte des Niederganges des Ptolemäerreiches.*

[2] *P. Tebtunis*, I, 5.

the king restored order in his sorely tried realm. In the course of the civil wars the Alexandrines had appealed to the Senate against their monarch, and no less a personage than Scipio Æmilianus came to Alexandria on a tour of inspection. The destroyer of Carthage treated Ptolemy with little more courtesy than Popilius had shown to Antiochus IV; but on his recommendation the Senate took no action against the king.

At his death in 116 Ptolemy VII sprang one more surprise upon his house by leaving Cyrene to an illegitimate son named Apion. This arrangement apparently went uncontested, and henceforward Cyrene remained detached from Egypt. But its new dynasty did not survive its founder, for Apion, dying childless in 96, transferred his rights to the Roman Republic, which after some hesitation took up the legacy and converted his dominion into a Roman province. (74)

In Egypt the feud between Ptolemy VI and VII was repeated between the latter's two sons by Cleopatra III. The elder brother, Ptolemy VIII, at first had the support of the Alexandrines, and the younger, Ptolemy IX, had to be content with the appanage of Cyprus. But Cleopatra, who was a third claimant for power and hoped that her younger son would make a more convenient puppet, turned the passions of the city-mob against the elder by pretending that he had plotted her murder. (107) The two Ptolemies now played Box and Cox, for while the younger brother returned to Alexandria the reigning king escaped to Cyprus and established himself there. The further moves in this game of cross purposes need not be followed out here. Ptolemy IX got rid of his domineering mother by murder (*c.* 101), but thereby he forfeited the obedience of the Alexandrians. In 89 he was expelled but fought his way back; in 88 he was again driven out and lost his life in a second attempt to force his return. Hereupon Ptolemy VIII was received back in Alexandria and for a while reunited Egypt and Cyprus.

The outstanding feature of the closing epoch of Ptolemaic history is that the remaining kings were little more than the puppets of the Alexandrian mob or of Roman politicians, but that the last of the queens, Cleopatra VII, played for the highest stakes of all rulers of Egypt. In 80 B.C. the

Alexandrians, taking sides in a family dispute between Ptolemy X (the son of Ptolemy IX and successor of Ptolemy VIII) and his first cousin, stepmother and wife Berenice IV, lynched the king on the nineteenth day of his reign. Having thus extinguished the legitimate male line of the dynasty, they set up a bastard son of Ptolemy VIII, Ptolemy XI Auletes. After twenty-one years of suspense, in which the Roman Senate would neither avow nor repudiate him, Ptolemy XI paid a colossal bribe to the triumvirs Cæsar and Pompey to confirm his title by an act of the Comitia. (59) In the following year, it is true, he was expelled by the folk of his capital, who resented his humiliating and expensive subserviency to a foreign power, but in 55 (after a troubled interregnum by his eldest daughter, Berenice V, and a relay of improvised husbands) he was reinstated by a Roman force under Pompey's handy-man A. Gabinius. In 51 Ptolemy XI died peacefully, but in leaving his throne to be shared between an adolescent daughter, Cleopatra VII, and a boy, Ptolemy XII, he brought on a new spell of domestic discord and of mob-rule. The Alexandrians helped Ptolemy XII to expel Cleopatra, and when Cæsar, fresh from his victory at Pharsalus, made a descent upon Egypt with a flying column and forced the king to receive back his sister, they joined with Ptolemy's household troops in a surprise attack upon the Roman forces and kept them under close siege in the palace quarter. (48–7) With the help of a relief army from Syria Cæsar eventually routed his assailants and reinstated Cleopatra; in place of Ptolemy XII, who had disappeared in the rout, he associated with her a younger brother, Ptolemy XIII.

The "Bellum Alexandrinum" marks the end of mob-rule in Ptolemaic Egypt, and the beginning of the Ptolemaic dynasty's counter-attack upon the Romans. Quick to discover the weakest point in Cæsar's armour, Cleopatra had paid court to him, and she later gave out that a child of hers, "Cæsarion," was a son of the dictator. However this may be, it is unlikely that Cæsar intended to make her his consort in the new Roman monarchy. For the time being she merely took advantage of Cæsar's death to make away with Ptolemy XIII and set herself up as sole ruler.[1] Moreover,

[1] On Cæsar's intrigues with Cleopatra, see J. Carcopino, *Annales de l'école des hautes études de Gand*, 1937, p. 1 ff.

in 41 B.C. a progress by the triumvir Mark Antony through the Levant gave Cleopatra a second opportunity of assailing Rome through a Roman imperator. Though Antony for several years remained undecided between his passion for her and his loyalty to his colleague Octavian and to Rome, he eventually committed himself to an overt marriage with the Egyptian queen, and was induced by her to reconstitute a greater Egypt out of Roman territory by ceding to her a portion of Syria, Cilicia and Cyprus. (36) At Rome the report was put about that she was urging Antony to make her a Roman empress. We need not believe this ; but in any case, if Cleopatra had rightly gauged the pliant temper of Antony, she fatally miscalculated the stubborn pride of Octavian and his capacity for rallying Roman sentiment in the face of an attack by a foreign power. After the *débâcle* of Actium and the death of Antony, she resolutely took her own life.[1]

§ 7. THE BREAK-UP OF THE SELEUCID MONARCHY

The history of the Seleucid dynasty after 145 was no less stormy than that of the Ptolemies, and the consequences of its chronic feuds were more immediately suicidal, for their dominions fell a prey to watchful neighbours who made good use of their opportunities.

The misgivings with which the Antiochenes had accepted the boy-king Demetrius II were fully justified by the event. His Cretan mercenaries, led by a captain named Lasthenes, set up an undisguised military despotism, beating down successive risings by the townsfolk with indiscriminate savagery. In the worst of these riots the soldatesca deliberately fired a whole quarter of the town and systematically fusilladed the crowds from the housetops. But the native troops in the depôt at Apamea, whose sympathies lay with the civilians against the foreign Janissaries, rallied round an officer named Diodotus, who raised up an infant son of Balas in opposition to Demetrius and drove the

[1] The tale that Cleopatra betrayed Antony and offered herself to Octavian may be dismissed as posthumous Roman propaganda.

Cretans out of Antioch. Once in possession of the capital Diodotus made away with Balas' son and assumed the crown under the name of Tryphon. (142) But his authority did not extend beyond the Orontes valley, for Demetrius retained the coast-towns and Babylonia. Thus the partitioning of the Seleucid dominions between rival rulers, which had nearly destroyed the kingdom in the later years of the third century, was resumed; and it was repeated henceforth until there were no dominions left to divide.

For the moment, indeed, civil war was suspended owing to a surprise move by Demetrius, who had now come of age and had taken the government into his own hands. Ignoring Tryphon, and apparently not troubling to make a truce with him, he collected his forces for a counter-attack upon Mithridates I of Parthia, who had profited by the recent disorders to invade Babylonia (p. 76). Had Demetrius won his Parthian campaign, no doubt his reputation would have grown in such measure as to give him an easy victory in the final reckoning with Tryphon. By his defeat and capture he left a free field to Tryphon. But this king's authority rested on little else than the resentment of the Antiochenes against the tyranny of Demetrius, and with the disappearnace of the latter the basis of the usurper's power was withdrawn. Moreover, the intrusion on the Seleucid throne of a man who had not a drop of Seleucid blood in his veins was bound to be challenged by the remaining members of the royal family. In 139 a brother of Demetrius II named Antiochus Sidetes made a descent upon Syria and easily expelled Tryphon. Under Antiochus VII Syria, Palestine and Cilicia, the surviving remnants of the Seleucid empire, were reunited under a ruler of high ability. By 130 these territories had so far recovered from previous misrule, that they could provide the king with a strong army for his expedition against the Parthians.

The disaster which befell this expedition in 129 (pp. 77–8) was a blow from which the Seleucid kingdom never recovered. Its man-power was fatally reduced, and its last capable ruler perished in the rout. The vacant throne was in the first instance re-occupied by Demetrius II, whom the Parthian king had released in the earlier stages of the war in order to foment trouble in Antiochus' rear. But with the stigma of ten years' bondage added to his previous unpopularity, he was swept away in a new rebellion. (125) Henceforth Seleucid history resolves itself into a struggle between the two branches of the royal house, the descendants of Demetrius II and of Antiochus VII, who engaged in a never-ending round of robber raids upon each other and lost the ordinary duties of government out of sight. The preoccupation of the Parthian kings with nomad invasions on their northern and eastern frontiers saved the Seleucid lands from complete absorption in an Oriental empire. But its remaining territories were nibbled away by other neighbours. The Jews creep up to Mt. Carmel (p. 230); the Nabatæans advance from Petra to Damascus; in 83 king Tigranes of Armenia carries all Syria save a few coastland towns. In annexing Syria and Cilicia (65–3 B.C.) Pompey ended the Seleucid anarchy; the monarchy had virtually perished with Antiochus VII.

§ 8. THE KINGDOM OF JUDÆA

The establishment of an independent kingdom of Judæa was the combined result of mistakes by the Seleucid kings in their treatment of that country, and of their incessant domestic feuds.

When Palestine was transferred from Ptolemies to Seleucids as the result of the Fifth Syrian War (pp. 93–4), the native populations were at first little affected by the change of rulers. In Judæa internal administration remained in the hands of the priestly caste, subject to the payment of the usual taxes and approval of new High Priests by the king at Antioch. The first conflict between Jews and Seleucids arose out of the financial embarrassments of the monarchy after the peace of Apamea, which made them cast envious eyes on the temple treasures at Jerusalem. About 175 Heliodorus, the minister of Seleucus IV, attempted a raid upon this fund, but was deterred, presumably by fear of a popular riot. In 169 Antiochus IV, returning from Egypt, actually carried off part of the sacred moneys.

But the chief cause of Jewish rebellion was an ill-judged endeavour of Antiochus IV to force Hellenic customs upon the people. The policy of Hellenization, which Antiochus embraced as a means of making his subject-population more homogeneous and more actively loyal, was not without adherents in Judæa. Early in his reign the High Priest "Jason" (i.e. Jesus) founded a gymnasium and a corps of ephebi, and had Jerusalem reconstituted as a Greek city under the name of Antioch. These innovations naturally raised opposition among strict followers of the Law; and indeed it seems clear that Jason—who had bought his office from Antiochus with a promise of higher tribute, only to be deposed later on in favour of a still higher bidder named Menelaus—was a mere adventurer with no enlightened ideals of reform. Yet so long as Antiochus merely approved the actions of the native Hellenizers, and so long as these did not offend the cardinal tenets of the Jewish faith, the risk of revolt against the Seleucids remained remote. But in 167 the king issued a double challenge to the Jewish people. On the pretext of some slight disturbances during his Egyptian campaigns, he entered Jerusalem, let his troops loose upon the townsfolk and established a fortress for a permanent garrison. Furthermore, he transferred the Temple to the service of Zeus Olympius and attempted to enforce Zeus-worship both in Jerusalem and in the country.[1]

In abandoning the tolerant attitude of all Hellenistic rulers since Alexander towards the Jewish religion, Antiochus discredited the Hellenizing party in Palestine and mobilized the upholders of the strict faith. About 166 a priest named Mattathias took up arms against the agents of proselytization at Modein (N.W. of Jerusalem), and after his death his son Judas collected an insurgent band which defeated in guerrilla two expeditionary forces, the second under the minister Lysias. (165–4) Unable to procure reinforcements from Antiochus, who was engaged at this time in Armenia, Lysias bought peace with concessions. He restored the Temple to Jehovah and granted an amnesty to the rebels, on condition that they should not molest the Hellenizers. Thus after three years' trial the policy of persecution was abandoned, and it was never resumed. But the victims of the persecution were no longer in the mood for reciprocal toleration. On the outskirts Judas made reprisals on gentile populations which had attacked their Jewish residents, and in Jerusalem

[1] At Samaria a worship of Zeus Xenius was instituted with seeming success.

they set siege to the Hellenizers and the Seleucid garrison. In 162 Lysias, as regent of Antiochus V, returned to Palestine with a strong army and overpowered Judas in a battle south of Jerusalem, but owing to the insecurity of his position at Antioch he did not press the pursuit. He therefore renewed the previous treaty with Judas and replaced the High Priest Menelaus, whose extortions had made him odious, by a person named "Alcimus" (Eliakim).

This compromise fared no better than that of 164. Judas could not agree with Alcimus, whose orthodoxy was more than suspect; and in 161 he entered into negotiations with the Roman Senate, which accorded him a treaty.[1] Though this compact never became operative, it held the menace of Roman intervention over the Seleucid kings, and it implicitly repudiated their authority. In 161–0 the new king, Demetrius I, sent three successive expeditions to Palestine, the third of which, under a general named Bacchides, resulted in the defeat and death of Judas. For ten years Jerusalem lay quiet, and Palestine was held by a network of fortified posts. Near the desert border two of Judas' brothers, Jonathan and Simon, kept up a guerrilla; but it is probable that Seleucid rule would have been permanently restored in Judæa, had not new dynastic quarrels undone Bacchides' work. In 150 two disputants for the Seleucid throne held an auction for the support of Jonathan. Demetrius undertook to withdraw Bacchides' garrisons from Palestine, and to confer upon him the title of "ally"; Balas offered him the High Priesthood. Jonathan accepted all these gifts in turn, and under pretence of assisting one Seleucid against another he extended his authority beyond Judæa. In 147, as an ally of Balas, he captured Joppa and gave his dominion a sea-front; in 145 he supported Demetrius II with a corps which outdid the Cretans at the great massacre of Antioch (p. 225). From Tryphon Jonathan subsequently received the title of "kinsman," and Simon the governorship of Cœle-Syria; and the brothers used their new authority to capture Gaza and to

[1] The genuineness of this compact has often been impugned, but without adequate reason. For a recent discussion see Ed. Meyer, *Ursprung und Anfänge des Christentums*, II, p. 246, n. 4; M. S. Ginsburg, *Rome et la Judée*, ch. 3; Täubler, *Imperium Romanum*, p. 239 ff. But the last-named author has shown that the treaty was granted by the Senate alone and not ratified by the Comitia.

renew the siege of the garrison at Jerusalem. It is true that, once established, Tryphon turned against the Jewish leaders and got rid of Jonathan by kidnapping. But Simon maintained the siege of the citadel, which surrendered in 141. With the fall of this fortress the process of eradicating Hellenic influence from Jerusalem was completed. Meanwhile Tryphon's rival, Demetrius II, had offered to remit all future tribute from Judæa on payment of a lump sum. The virtual independence of Palestine now seemed assured. But in 134 Antiochus VII, as king of a reunited realm, required submission of Simon, and tribute for Joppa and other Jewish conquests outside of Judæa. Upon Simon refusing these terms he invested Jerusalem and starved it into surrender. (134–2) Though some of his staff advised him to settle the Jewish question by exterminating the Jewish people, he merely enforced acceptance of his previous conditions and made the Jews liable to military aids. In 131–29 John Hyrcanus, the son of Simon (who had been murdered in 134 in a family quarrel), accompanied Antiochus VII on his Parthian expedition, but survived the rout and lived on for another twenty-five years in complete emancipation from Seleucid authority. Not content with independence, he profited by the now chronic confusion in Syria to extend his power in all directions. Under his successors, Aristobulus (104–3) and Alexander Jannæus (103–78), the growth of Greater Judæa continued. In Transjordania expansion was checked by the parallel advance of the Nabatæans from Petra towards Damascus; but southward the new Jewish state extended to the Egyptian frontier, and in a northern direction to Mt. Carmel. In some of the conquered regions the Jews secured their ascendancy by forcible conversions such as Antiochus had vainly attempted at their expense. Their proselytizings were attended with more lasting results, and in Galilee (which was incorporated by Aristobulus) the introduction of the Jewish Law had results as far-reaching as any conquest of Hellenism under Alexander's successors.

PART II

CHAPTER XIII

HELLENISTIC WAR-CRAFT

§ 1. NUMBERS AND RECRUITMENT OF THE ARMIES

IN no respect did the Macedonian conquests make a cleaner cut between classical and Hellenistic history than in military matters.

The forces of the Hellenistic states generally comprised a lesser percentage of their total population than those of the earlier city-states ; yet in absolute numbers they were so much larger as to introduce new problems of organization and tactics. A city-state could seldom put into the field a force of more than 10,000, a coalition rarely exceeded 20 to 25,000. In the Hellenistic period these maxima were habitually surpassed. It is true that the strength of 40,000 assigned to the army of the Achæan League was only a paper estimate ; but Philip V actually mustered 30,000, Perseus 35 to 40,000 Macedonians against the Romans. 80,000 soldiers are alleged to have defiled through Alexandria in a pageant of Ptolemy II, and this figure is in keeping with the field-strength of the Egyptian army at Raphia, which amounted to not less than 55,000.[1] Antiochus III put 68,000 into line at Raphia, and 72,000 at Magnesia. In 306 Antigonus I collected a force of 88,000 for the invasion of Egypt—a greater multitude than Alexander ever led on a single expedition. The numbers engaged at Ipsus and at Magnesia are the highest authenticated totals of Greek history.

With the increase of size in the Hellenistic armies went a greater variety in their racial composition. This diversity of personnel was an inheritance from Alexander, in whose forces Greeks and Balkan barbarians fought side by side with Macedonians, and Persians eventually found admittance. Naturally the Macedonians continued to enjoy the highest

[1] See Appendix 13.

prestige,[1] and supplied the recruits for the *corps d'élite:* at Alexandria and Antioch "Macedonian" and "Guardsman" became almost synonymous terms. But if the demand for Macedonians was unlimited, their supply quickly ran short. As soon as Macedon again became a separate kingdom the flow of recruits to other countries was stopped, for Cassander and the Antigonids could spare none for service abroad. In the third century the "Macedonians" in the Seleucid and Ptolemaic forces were mostly the descendants of Macedonian settlers; by 200 the term had come to include Greeks, and possibly even Asiatics, admitted to the household troops. Outside Macedonia the part played by Macedonians was therefore a declining one, like that of the Italians in the army of the Roman empire.

When Macedonians became scarce, their place was taken in the first instance by Greeks. Already in the fourth century there had been a steady outward flow of Greek soldiers of adventure. In Alexander's army the Greek element eventually became the strongest in numbers, and in the third century the Greeks everywhere outside of Macedonia Proper furnished the largest European contingents. The Greek recruits were not drawn uniformly from all parts of the Greek lands. The cities of the Aegean seaboard continued to supply sailors rather than soldiers, and with Leosthenes the line of famous Athenian *condottieri* came to an end. On the other hand, Crete and the Peloponnesus remained as prolific as ever, and in Central Greece Ætolia became an important new source of supply. In 201 a Ptolemaic agent met with such alarming success in enlisting the youth of Ætolia that the government of that country had to put an embargo upon his activities. In point of quality the Greeks were approximately equal to the Macedonians, and where uniformity of drill and equipment was considered desirable they could readily adapt themselves to Macedonian methods. But towards the end of the third century the stream of Greek recruits began in turn to fail. In the second century Crete alone kept up its former quotas; outside of Europe the Greek element in the Hellenistic armies was henceforth supplied from the colonies in Asia and Egypt.

[1] A remarkable tribute to the Macedonian troops of his own day was paid by Polybius (V, 2, 5), who declared that they were both the best fighters and the most patient at enduring fatigue work.

Though Alexander had freely admitted barbarians into his army, his immediate successors, intent on maintaining Greco-Macedonian ascendancy, made more sparing use of these alien elements, mostly relegating them to the auxiliary services. Yet it was not long before barbarian troops reappeared in the fighting-line. The governors of the upper provinces probably had recourse to Iranian troops from the first; the Seleucids certainly made plentiful use of them. In Asia Minor Eumenes defeated Macedonian troops with his Cappadocian horsemen (p. 14); the Seleucids drew freely upon the mountaineers of the southern highlands who subsequently served the Byzantine emperors so well, and the Attalids similarly enrolled the Mysians and the hill-folk of the north. The Ptolemies probably employed auxiliary corps of Jews in Egypt, as the Persians had done before them; and Ptolemy IV won the battle of Raphia by drafting Egyptians into his phalanx (pp. 91–2). In Europe Lysimachus imitated Alexander in the use of Thracian troops; at Sellasia Doson's Illyrian contingent played a winning part (p. 162). Galatians were first enlisted by Gonatas; but Seleucids and Attalids and even Ptolemies followed suit. At Raphia Antiochus III's army counted three Macedonians or Greeks to every four Asiatics; at Magnesia it contained only one soldier of European stock to every two Asiatics. But however much reduced in numbers, the Greco-Macedonian element always formed the nucleus of the Hellenistic fighting forces. The barbarian troops were sometimes equipped and drilled in Macedonian fashion, and their commanders were frequently (though not invariably) drawn from the ruling race. At the least the Hellenistic armies were as Greek as Wellington's force at Waterloo was British, and more so than the army of the Roman Empire was Roman in the strict sense of that term. In the third century the various nationalities were usually grouped in separate corps, but in the second ethnic distinctions were often relaxed. Just as "Macedonian" had come to mean "guardsman," so "Persian," "Mysian," etc., stood for a certain drill or accoutrement.[1]

[1] Compare the ethnic names of the Roman auxilia. Papyri of the second century often mention a class of people known as Πέρσαι τῆς Ἐπιγονῆς. The exact meaning of this term remains uncertain, but it cannot mean real Iranians.

§ 2. CONDITIONS OF SERVICE

The army of Alexander was mainly composed of regular soldiers who remained continuously with the colours. His immediate successors maintained their forces on a similar basis. Being engaged in almost incessant warfare, they required to keep their troops on a permanent war footing, and they could raise the funds for their upkeep by drawing upon the unspent treasures of Alexander, or by resolute taxation. But in the third century, when longer spells of peace intervened, and pay-lists had to be cut down for lack of unlimited funds, the regular establishments were reduced to skeleton cadres consisting of the royal guards, the garrisons, and a few special units such as the elephant corps.

Of the devices for supplementing the standing forces, conscription was familiar alike to Macedonians, Greeks and Orientals, and was applied to all three. In Macedon and the Greek Homeland, where the troops were seldom required to fight far from home, the greater part of the field forces was usually raised in this fashion. In Egypt conscription was certainly employed for the fleet,[1] and it may be assumed that both here and in the Asiatic monarchies the natives were liable to be impressed into the army. But in practice there were strict limits to this method of recruitment. In the Hellenistic period the aversion to military service which had begun to show in the Greek cities before the time of Alexander had more and more to be reckoned with ; in particular, the Achæan League had great difficulty in obtaining its conscript recruits, many of whom joined up too late or not at all. In Macedon the Antigonids found it advisable to restrict the levy of large conscript quotas to the major campaigns.[2] In Asia and Egypt there is no sure instance of conscription among the Greek elements of population.[3]

[1] One of the benefactions for which the Egyptian priests thanked Ptolemy V in the Rosetta decree (l. 17) was the exemption of the temple staffs from naval conscription.

[2] At Sellasia two-thirds of Doson's army were Macedonians. (Polybius, II, 65.)

[3] The Pergamene and probably also the Seleucid kings encouraged the institution of ephebeia in the cities of Asia Minor. But these corps were probably on a voluntary basis. They might be compared to our Officers' Training Corps.

As a substitute for conscription the Greek cities in the fourth century had made occasional experiments in the use of mercenaries. But so long as the Persian empire stood, they had to compete with a power which could easily outbid them. After the fall of that empire the Hellenistic succession-states took over Persia's markets and became the chief employers of soldiers of adventure. Already in the days of Alexander the buying and selling of professionals had become an organized business with a technique of its own. Special markets for these transactions were established at Cape Tænarum in Laconia, at Aspendus in southern Asia Minor, and at various towns of Crete, where soldiers in search of employment formed themselves into companies of fixed strength under captains of their own choice. At these centres expert " xenologi " or " enlisters for the Foreign Legion " made collective bargains with the men's leaders. The traffic in mercenaries was based on recognized rates of pay (usually one to two drachmas per day).[1] The wealthier monarchs sometimes added a premium to the standard wage. The Ptolemies were notoriously liberal in their offers, and Ptolemy IV once paid the fabulous sum of one thousand drachmas a day to a distinguished Ætolian officer. On the other hand, the Antigonids could scarcely afford the minimum rates of pay. The reason why Gonatas introduced the custom of hiring Galatians was that they were cheaper.

But the most characteristic device of the Hellenistic rulers for the provision of additional troops in war-time was the creation of a militia among the small-holders whom they attracted to their kingdoms as colonists. Though this expedient was also employed by the Attalids, and probably by the Seleucids and Antigonids, it may best be studied in Egypt, where the conditions of service are illustrated by numerous papyri.[2] While this system of settlement also subserved political and economic purposes, its primary object was to provide a military reserve. The original nuclei of these colonies were probably formed by pensioning mercenaries with plots of land ; their subsequent recruitment was largely

[1] On conditions of pay and provisionment, see G. T. Griffith, *Mercenaries of the Hellenistic World*, ch. X.

[2] On the Egyptian militia, see esp. J. Lesquier, *Les institutions militaires de l'Égypte sous les Lagides*.

from the progeny of the foundation members.[1] The militiamen were predominantly of Greek origin ; but the Ptolemies probably also formed some Jewish soldier-colonies, and after the battle of Raphia they provided land, albeit in smaller quantities, to Egyptian reservists, thus reviving the military tenancies of the later Pharaohs.[2] The reservists were usually grouped together on adjacent plots, and in peace as well as in war were enrolled in tactical units with a full complement of officers. Though not obliged to cultivate their land in person, they were required to remain in residence on it. Where separate houses were not available for the colonists, the natives of the nearest villages were bound to provide them with half of their own house-space.[3] In theory the settlers always remained tenants-at-will, and liable to forfeit possession if they did not obey the conditions of service. But from the end of the third century, when immigration from Greece was slackening off and vacancies in the militia became more difficult to fill, life tenure became almost universal, and a quasi-right of bequest grew up.

§ 3. STRATEGY AND TACTICS

The strategy and tactics of the Hellenistic armies, as was but natural, were based on those of Alexander, and his early successors worthily maintained and at some points even improved upon his standards. The later Hellenistic captains forgot or misapplied the lessons of Alexander's campaigns, and the defeats sustained by the later Greek armies at the hands of the Romans were due in greater measure to defects of leadership than to a decline in the quality of the troops. But in the period of the Roman conquests it was a divided Greece that fought a united Italy ; the Romans never waged

[1] Much discussion has been devoted to the meaning of the terms *οἱ ἐπίγονοι* and *οἱ τῆς ἐπιγονῆς*. Probably *οἱ ἐπίγονοι* were a limited class of younger men enrolled in cadet corps and entitled to the reversion of their fathers' land ; *οἱ τῆς ἐπιγονῆς* were the settlers' progeny in general, and formed a juristic rather than a military category.

[2] Henceforth the term *κληροῦχος* was restricted to native militiamen, *κάτοικος* to Greeks.

[3] Disputes, sometimes ending in blows, often arose out of this billeting rule. (*P. Petrie*, II, XII, c ; III, 20 ; *Tebtunis*, 45–50 ; *Lille*, vol. 2, *passim*.) For an edict of Ptolemy II, protecting the natives from abuses, see *P. Halensis*, 5.

a war against Greek enemies without Greek allies, and in one of the three decisive land-battles, at Magnesia, the chief credit for the Roman victory belonged to a Greek auxiliary, king Eumenes (pp. 211–2).

A superficial feature of resemblance between Alexander's armies and the Hellenistic forces is that these latter were frequently led in the field by the king in person. Some of the Hellenistic monarchs imitated Alexander so closely as to take a personal part in the fighting. By such personal displays of valour Pyrrhus won a useful reputation as a *beau sabreur ;* on the other hand, Demetrius jeopardized his cause at Ipsus, and Antiochus at Raphia and Magnesia, by doubling the functions of a general with those of a company commander. As a rule, the Hellenistic kings stayed behind the fighting line, but accompanied their armies on major campaigns and directed operations in person. In qualities of leadership the Antigonids surpassed all the other dynasties ; but the record of the Seleucids and Attalids was not far inferior. The Ptolemies took the field more rarely ; but even a voluptuary like Ptolemy IV could on occasion march out with his troops and take charge of a battle.

Alexander's influence upon the Hellenistic captains is clearly seen in the extreme rapidity of motion which some of these attained. Cassander's forced march from Peloponnesus to Pydna in 317, Antigonus' drive against Perdiccas' adherents in Asia Minor in 319, and his winter campaign against Eumenes on the Persian plateau in 316, compare well with Alexander's greatest feats of mobility. The later Hellenistic armies, being less highly drilled than Alexander's veterans, could not maintain the pace which these had set ; and the presence of a Galatian contingent might slow them down considerably, for these warriors sometimes insisted on bringing their families along in ox-waggons. Yet the tear-away expedition of Philip in 219–8, in which three widely separated enemies were in turn taken by surprise, and Antiochus' Grand Tour of the East in 210–205, show that a hundred years later Hellenistic soldiers were still capable of sustained efforts of hard marching. Naturally enough, those kings who had trained their men to a high turn of speed favoured Alexander's policy of vigorous attack. But in one instance a successor of Alexander gave a display of dilatoriness which deserved an

Ennius to celebrate it. The cunning and coolness with which Lysimachus kept Antigonus in play during the campaign of 302, while Seleucus was closing in from behind, ranks high as a specimen of containing strategy. The Hellenistic generals did not always combine Alexander's boldness of attack with his circumspection in reconnoitring. When they adventured themselves into unexplored hill-fastnesses, as in Bithynia and Judæa, they commonly ended their progress in an ambush. Yet Alexander's example was nowhere more fruitful than in strategy. The interest of Hellenistic warfare lies largely in the quick movements of its armies over long distances. Herein it differs widely from the city-state campaigns, with their leisurely pace and circumscribed zone of operations.

The introduction of scientific tactics into Greek battles was the work of Epaminondas, who was the first to realize clearly, and to stake his fortunes on his discovery, that a greater result could be achieved at lesser cost by dislocating the enemy line at a vital spot than by making a dead heave at its entire length. But it was left to Alexander to reap the full fruit of this invention by combining foot and horse in his attack and transferring the decisive part to the cavalry. Among Alexander's successors this principle of economy of effort was well understood, for their battle-line was habitually divided into a containing and a striking wing. They carried the practice of combined tactics one step further than Alexander by the use of elephants. But whether they were unwilling to engage too closely a corps which could not easily be replaced, or whether they realized that elephants were only formidable so long as they were strange, they did not often employ them as substitutes for heavy cavalry ; indeed, the only sure instance of their delivering the main shock was at Gaza, and here their attack proved a complete fiasco (p. 28). More commonly the elephants were posted in front of the defensive wing, or as a flank guard. In the early battles of the period the chief part was still assigned to the cavalry, which was directed to penetrate or to enfilade the enemy line at the key-point.

In the application of Alexander's tactics his immediate successors were hardly inferior to their master. The battles of Alexander's marshals have a particular interest, in that they were fought out among equals, and offer examples of scientific thrust and counter-thrust such as are not found in the more one-sided battles of Alexander, except possibly at Arbela. From this point of view the actions of Paraetacene and Gabiene (pp. 24–5), in which the two best generals of the age were pitted against each other, are almost unique in ancient warfare: even Roman history has no real parallel to offer save the duel between Hannibal and Scipio at Zama. The high standard of Alexander's marshals, it is true, was not maintained in subsequent battles. The heterogeneous character of the later Hellenistic armies, and the low proportion of regular troops among them, impeded the accurate application of combined tactics by their leaders. The lack of cohesion in the later battle-lines is clearly illustrated by the actions of Raphia and Magnesia, where Antiochus played Prince Rupert to Alexander's Cromwell and completely lost touch with his defensive wing.

In Europe the Hellenistic forces, being mainly composed of Greek or Macedonian infantry, were of more uniform structure; their capacity to carry out a concerted manœuvre is well displayed by the manner in which Antigonus Doson rolled up Cleomenes' wing at Sellasia. But Macedonian and Greek infantry was burdened by a long-standing tradition which sacrificed its mobility in order to increase its weight. Despite the mountainous character of the Greek landscape, and the successes which light-armed divisions won on it from time to time—as when Ætolian skirmishers repelled the Galatians from Greece, and Illyrian Alpinists stormed the heights above Sellasia,—the main body of Greek infantry always remained saddled with a ponderous equipment. The Macedonian foot even had its dead-weight increased in the third century, for the length of its spears was increased from some thirteen to eighteen feet.[1] A Macedonian phalanx thus armed offered an impenetrable defence and was well fitted to wear down an enemy line by slow pounding. But in the hands of a commander who used it as a substitute for heavy horsemen it was a double-edged weapon. Unlike the cavalry, it could not keep its ranks closed while moving

[1] In the time of Polybius the Macedonian sarissa had grown from twelve to fourteen and even sixteen cubits (XVIII, 29). (I here follow Tarn, *Hellenistic Military Developments*, p 16, in assuming a short Macedonian cubit of c. 13 inches.)

rapidly, still less could it swerve or reverse. Such an unwieldy mass was unfairly matched with Roman legionaries in lighter armour and more elastic formation.

The branch of operations in which Hellenistic armies fell away soonest from Alexander's standard was siegecraft. Among his successors Demetrius alone acquired a reputation as a taker of cities, and his principal siege, the investment of Rhodes in 305–4, was a failure. Of the later Hellenistic kings Philip alone displayed any proficiency in this branch of war, and his captures were all places of minor importance. In the third century, when a town changes hands, the result is usually due to treason (Seleucia-ad-Orontem, 219), to stratagem (Corinth, 246 and 243), or to famine (Athens, 295 and 262). The general lack of success in siegecraft may be explained by the more than equivalent strengthening of the defence-works. The chief new weapons of assault in the time of Alexander were the catapult and the stone-thrower. The latter of these was seldom powerful enough to batter down walls built throughout their thickness of dressed stone, the former could not easily reach a garrison posted behind high battlements. On the other hand artillery mounted on city walls could do effective counter-battery work against siege-engines in the field.[1]

§ 4. NAVAL WARFARE

The Hellenistic fleets were actually inferior in the number of their fighting craft to the largest of the city-state navies. The Egyptian fleet under Ptolemy II rose to 336 battleships —a lesser total than that of the Athenian navy at its strongest; the Macedonian fleet under Gonatas did not count more than about one hundred ships of the line, the Rhodians had scarcely more than fifty.[2] It is true that the 410 galleys engaged at Abydus (pp. 381–2) constitute the highest aggregate in an encounter between two Greek admirals; but the combined totals at Salamis and Cos, where some 300 vessels

[1] The effective range of catapults is estimated by Schramm (in Kromayer-Veith, *Heerwesen und Kriegführung der Griechen und Römer*, p. 212) at less than 400 metres; by Tarn (*op. cit.*, p. 115) at a mere 200 yards.

The remaining fortifications of Heraclea-ad-Latmum are visible proof of the strength of Hellenistic town walls. (See F. Krischen in *Milet*, vol. III, pt. 2.) Illustrations of many lesser Hellenistic fortifications will be found in W. J. Woodhouse, *Ætolia*.

[2] Tarn, *Antigonos Gonatas*, p. 456–7.

were put into line, were less than in some actions of the Peloponnesian War.

But in the size of the individual fighting unit the Hellenistic navies definitely outgrew those of the city-state period. In place of the trireme the quinquereme became the standard ship-of-the-line, and each fleet usually contained a few "super-Dreadnoughts" of even higher displacement. Demetrius used vessels of the order of thirteen and even of sixteen oars, and Gonatas' flagship at Cos was of the eighteen-oar type. These larger craft were indeed not so monstrous as their names might suggest. A quinquereme did not contain five banks of oars, but one bank with five men to each oar; a sixteen-oar type was furnished with two banks in which eight men pulled at each oar.[1] Yet the tonnage of the larger ratings was substantially higher than that of the trireme, and the increase in the crews was considerable. The greater size of the Hellenistic men-of-war was not, however, a sign of any notable advance in Greek naval tactics. The object of building larger vessels was not, as in modern times, to provide space for artillery: the ancient man-of-war, of whatever size, had not sufficient stability to serve as a gun-platform. Neither were the quinqueremes superior in speed or manœuvring power to the triremes; their advantage lay rather in their stouter build, which rendered them less vulnerable to ramming. Their increased tonnage rather implies a reversion from the open tactics of the period of Athenian thalassocracy to the earlier method of close-in combat. This retrogression may be explained by the need in which Hellenistic rulers often found themselves, of manning improvised fleets with crews which lacked the high training and the long naval traditions of Athens or Carthage. Moreover, the victories of the Roman over the Punic fleets seemingly justified the return to shock tactics; and we may no doubt attribute the successes of the Antigonid over the Ptolemaic navies to similar robust methods.

§ 5. THE HELLENISTIC RULES OF WAR

The change in the personnel of the Hellenistic armies brought with it new problems of discipline which the

[1] Tarn, *Hellenistic Military and Naval Developments*, pp. 124–41.

officers did not always succeed in solving. In the warfare of Alexander's marshals entire divisions repeatedly deserted to enemy commanders who enjoyed higher prestige or offered better terms of pay. In the third century all the dynasties in turn had to cope with mutinies by Greek or Galatian mercenaries, and in the civil wars of the later Ptolemaic and Seleucid monarchies the troops changed their loyalties with the same readiness as the armies of the later Roman Empire. The civilian populations at times suffered severely from the depredations of unruly soldieries. Galatian troops were ever prone to relapse into habits of looting, and the Ætolians reduced plundering to a system and a discipline. The votes of thanks which Greek cities passed on behalf of garrison-commandants for keeping a tight hand on their men are a reminder of the risks to which the burgesses of the occupied towns were exposed.[1] Worst of all was the intensified danger from piracy to the seaboard populations. Between the Athenian thalassocracy of the fourth century, and the Rhodian thalassocracy of the second, none of the Hellenistic powers took adequate steps to police the seas—indeed more than one Hellenistic king was in collusion with the corsairs; and the ranks of the sea-rovers were constantly being recruited from the discharged mercenary companies.[2]

Yet the improved standard of strategy and tactics in the Hellenistic age is evidence that field-discipline in general had been tightened rather than relaxed. Moreover there is abundant testimony to an increasing humanity in the code of war of the later Greeks. The Hellenistic soldiers for the most part were not under the influence of strong national or municipal hatreds, and were therefore in general free from blood-lust. Instead of making a carnage among beaten enemies they usually accepted their surrender on easy terms, and they commonly entered into conventions for the ransom of prisoners.[3] A general embargo was placed upon the slaughter or enslavement of the inhabitants of captured towns, and an increasing number of individual cities received guarantees of immunity from plunder by right of war or

[1] Examples in Ditt., *Syll.*, 331 (Megara); *Inschriften von Priene*, 20–23.

[2] H. A. Ormerod, *Piracy in the Ancient World*, chs. 4 and 5.

[3] E.g. the conventions between Rhodes and Demetrius (Diodorus, XX, 84, 6); between Miletus and various cities of Crete (*Milet*, I, 3, no. 140).

commercial reprisal (ἀσφάλεια and ἀσυλία).[1] Though the new military code was of course broken from time to time, the indignation with which such infractions were received (as when Aratus sold off all the inhabitants of Mantinea, after a century's cessation from this kind of barbarism) shows that these were the exceptions which set off the rule.[2] On balance, Hellenistic warfare was both more scientific and more humane than that of the preceding ages.[3]

[1] See esp. Tarn, *Antigonos Gonatas*, p. 209–10 and n.

[2] The general rule is clearly expressed in Polybius, XVIII, 3.

[3] The opposite view of M. Rostovtzeff (*Social and Economic History of the Hellenistic World*, I, pp. 201–2) appears to be based on particular cases rather than on a wider survey.

Addendum.—New light has been thrown on the Hellenistic armies by an inscription containing regulations for camp and outpost discipline in the forces of Philip V. The leniency of the penalty for sleeping on guard—deduction of pay—contrasts oddly with the mercilessness of the Roman *fustigatio* (which duly impressed Polybius—VII, 37). But, except at Sparta, Greek military codes of any age probably did not err on the side of severity.—See M. Feyel, *Revue Archéologique*, 1935, p. 29 ff.

CHAPTER XIV

THE HELLENISTIC MONARCHIES

§ 1. GREEKS AND ORIENTALS

OF the new political questions with which Alexander's conquests confronted Greek statecraft the most fundamental was that of the relations between the Greek rulers and their Oriental subjects. Were the conquered populations to remain in a state of political nonage, or were they to be admitted as partners in a commonwealth of nations?

To the Hellenistic rulers this problem was of far more immediate concern than to their Persian predecessors. Under the Achæmenid régime there had been no extensive colonization in the subject countries, and the governing race had kept itself in every way distinct. On the other hand, the Greek conquests in the East were followed by a displacement of population which probably equalled any other such movement in ancient history, if regard be had to the number of new settlements, and was certainly the most extensive in range of territory occupied. From the time of Alexander Greek colonization, which had previously dispersed itself in several directions, was canalized into a continuous eastward current. The Hellenistic rulers, realizing no less clearly than Alexander himself that a settled Greek population was indispensable as a source of supply for their armies, as a recruiting-ground for their civilian administration, and as an instrument for the economic development of their territories, were at one in giving a ready welcome to Greek settlers. For the greater part of a century the stream of immigration flowed on. After 250, it is true, the river gradually ran dry, but in the meantime it had irrigated every province of Alexander's empire and had even overflowed its boundaries. The names of some 275 Hellenistic colonies have been preserved.[1] Some of these

[1] V. Tscherikower, *Die hellenistischen Städtegründungen.* (*Philologus* Supplement XIX, vol. 1.)

were second foundations under a new name; on the other hand our surviving list of settlements is certainly not complete: the full catalogue would no doubt comprise well over 300 names. The colonies, naturally enough, clustered most thickly in the borderlands of the Mediterranean. Some eighty were established in Asia Minor, and a like number in Syria and Palestine. But they also formed a chain along the middle and lower Euphrates, and a horseshoe round the Persian plateau. In Bactria and the adjacent regions nineteen Greek settlements are known by name, a further twenty-seven in India, and eleven on the African coast as far as Somaliland.

But if Alexander's conquests produced an extensive interspersion of Greeks among the Orientals, they also caused a partial fusion between the two elements. In the Hellenistic world the natural tendency of colonial movements to send forth more male than female emigrants was reinforced by the Greek custom of exposing unwanted girl babies. As this practice was particularly common in the Hellenistic period,[1] the excess of men among the Greek colonists must have been unusually high. But in the absence of any strong race prejudice, from which the Greeks in general were free, the inevitable result of this disproportion in the sexes was a progressive blending of Greeks and Orientals by intermarriage.[2] If we seek a parallel to the Hellenistic conquests in the history of modern imperialism, we shall find a closer analogy in the settlement of Central and South America by the Spaniards than in the dominion exercised over Asiatics and Africans by transitory Nordic residents.

Under conditions which tended to blur the ethnic contrast between conquerors and subjects it might seem but natural that the political distinctions between them should have been abolished. Indeed this was the political goal which Alexander himself appears to have held in view, and he had taken a step towards its attainment by accepting Persians in his administrative service. But herein he ran counter to the general

[1] Tarn, *Hellenistic Civilisation*, pp. 91–4.

[2] At Naucratis intermarriage between Greeks and natives was illegal. But this city was an older settlement of the seventh century. It is unsafe to assume that a similar ban was in force at Alexandria or in other Hellenistic foundations; indeed a general prohibition of this sort would be extremely unlikely.

opinion of Macedonians and Greeks. However little the Greeks were affected by physical prejudices, they had an unassailable belief in the superiority of their culture and of their political abilities. Accordingly in all the new Greek monarchies of the Near East the status of Greeks and Orientals was kept distinct. The Oriental stood under a different law from the Greek. While the Greek enjoyed full personal liberty, the Oriental was in large measure tied down to the soil and made liable to compulsory labour. He paid "native" taxes and in certain cases appeared before separate courts of law. In the civilian administration he could only aspire to the lower posts. All government business was transacted in Greek; and in Egypt, where the natives had from time immemorial used a scientific solar calendar, official dates were expressed until about 150 according to the Macedonian system, which followed the clumsy Greek method of reckoning now twelve now thirteen lunar months to the year.[1]

It is true that, in view of the increasing dearth of fresh immigrants and the progressive mixture of races, it eventually became impossible to uphold the privileges of the Greeks in full. From the middle of the third century Asiatics occasionally appear as governors of Seleucid provinces; in the second century Egyptians hold similar positions under the Ptolemies, and in the first century we find a native governor-general of Upper Egypt. Yet even if allowance is made for the fact that some of the officials who appear in Greek guise may be Orientals under assumed names, it is probable that the Greeks or half-Greeks succeeded to the end in keeping most of the important official posts and of the high places at court to themselves. In the Seleucid service Iranian names occur in the third century, but no Babylonian or Asianic ones; and in the second century, as the empire grew less in extent, it again became more Hellenic in its governing personnel. Finally, it may be taken as an axiom that every Oriental aspirant to high office was required to be conversant with Greek and to have adopted the outward style of Hellenism. Indeed, if we follow Isocrates in taking the name "Hellene" to stand for a certain culture rather than for a particular race, we may say that the governing classes

[1] See the calculations of B. P. Grenfell in *P. Hibeh*, Appendix, p. 332 ff.

in the succession-states of Alexander's empire always remained Hellenic.

§ 2. THE TRIUMPH OF MONARCHISM

Another problem of far-reaching importance which Alexander's conquests forced upon the Greeks concerned their systems of government. Previous to these conquests the choice between monarchy and republic might appear to have been made by the Greeks beyond recall: monarchy might be suitable to barbarians, but Greeks could only be republicans. This hard-set tradition, it is true, had been somewhat undermined by the criticisms of philosophers and by the stern lessons of practical experience, which taught that a republican constitution was no sure guarantee against foreign invasion or domestic disturbance. In the fourth century there had been sporadic revivals of tyranny; in Sicily this method of government so far commended itself that by the time of Agathocles it was playing over into legitimate kingship; and at Heraclea-ad-Pontum a regular dynasty reigned from 364 to 287. Yet on the whole renewed experience of despotism tended to confirm the Greeks in their aversion to it, and even in such flexible politicians as Aratus and Polybius the hatred of tyrants degenerated into positive fanaticism. Hence in the Greek Homeland at least monarchy remained ruled out as a regular form of government.[1] Except at Sparta, where the kingship was in fact a mere military office, the cities always reverted to republican rule, or never departed from it. In recognition of this fact Cassander and the Antigonids did not incorporate Thessaly into Macedonia, but secured it by a bond of personal union, whereby its republican constitutions were in appearance left intact. In Peloponnesus Antigonus Gonatas went so far as to give support to local despots, but the failure of this expedient induced Doson to fall back upon Philip II's system of simple alliance with a Greek confederation, with an *ultima ratio* of Macedonian garrisons at a few key points.

[1] Cf. the lines of the Attic comedian Diphilus (fr. 97, ed. Kock):

αὐλὰς θεραπεύειν δ' ἐστίν, ὡς ἐμοὶ δοκεῖ,
ἢ φυγαδὸς ἢ πεινῶντος ἢ μαστιγίου.

Outside the Greek Homeland the republican tradition lived on wherever Greeks had made their abodes, and it was transplanted to the new settlements in eastern lands. But it survived only on condition of confining itself to municipal affairs. In Macedonia and the Persian empire monarchical forms of government were as firmly rooted as republican constitutions in Greece; and in the succession-states carved out of the latter the wide extent of their territory and the mixed character of their population practically excluded parliamentary government and imposed one-man rule. In Macedon, Asia and Egypt accordingly the Greeks came to terms with monarchy. They retained republican forms of government in their local administration and sought to conserve the greatest possible measure of local autonomy; but they acknowledged the overriding authority of the Crown. Though individual kings might give displeasure and lose their throne, such change was merely from Amurath to Amurath; the principle of monarchy was generally accepted.

The Hellenistic kings moreover were free from the restraining influence of powerful hereditary nobilities. In Egypt the ancient feudal aristocracy had been disarmed by the Pharaohs a full thousand years before Alexander's time; in the Ptolemaic era scarcely a trace of it survived. In Asia Minor and Babylonia the native grandees had been crushed by the Persians, and Alexander's successors completed the process by breaking up the large estates which had been the economic basis of their power. On the other hand the vigorous Iranian nobility, whose will the Achæmenid kings had never been able to disregard, had paid the price of a gallant resistance to Alexander and remained weak for loss of blood. Lastly, the unruly barons of Macedon, who had been a veritable thorn in the side of the older Argead dynasty, had been mostly expatriated by the conquests of Alexander, in whose footsteps they had traversed the length and the breadth of the Persian empire and had found crowns or graves there. It is true that at the Hellenistic capitals, and more especially at Alexandria and Antioch, a new court aristocracy grew up and was eventually graded into a hierarchy of "Kinsmen," "Friends," "Body-Guards," etc.[1] But this nobility did not

[1] On these court charges in general see Corradi, *Studi Ellenistici*, p. 268 ff.

become hereditary; in fact as well as in theory it remained wholly dependent on the king's pleasure.

§ 3. THE HELLENISTIC COURTS

In a description of the Hellenistic monarchies it will be convenient to begin with a general survey and to conclude with a separate notice of each particular kingdom.

Hellenistic kings had one striking feature in common with the Roman Cæsars, in that they combined autocratic power with a comparative simplicity of outward style. Just as the establishment of the Cæsars reflected their republican origin, so the courts of the Hellenistic rulers were modelled on that of the old Argead dynasty of Macedon, to whose pattern Alexander's successors reverted by a deliberate reaction from the orientalizing habits of their chief. The retinue of the courts was organized in Macedonian fashion, with the traditional heads of departments (Lord Chamberlain, High Steward, Chief Huntsman, etc.), and the corps of pages, in which many of the aspirants to high position at court served their apprenticeship. The royal insignia consisted of a sceptre or long staff, which the Argead dynasty had inherited from Homeric royalty; a cape and broad-brimmed hat of purple colour, which reproduced the field uniform of the old Macedonian rulers; and a diadem or jewelled headband. In one personal detail the Hellenistic rulers commonly followed a new fashion set by Alexander, by going clean-shaven, and thus fixed the beardless type in the Greek and Roman world for several centuries.[1] On the other hand they did not imitate Alexander in adopting the Oriental custom of "proskynesis" or prostration before the king's person, a practice which had given grave offence to his Macedonian staff. Neither did they require to be addressed in terms of Byzantine servility: a plain 'ὦ βασιλεῦ' was considered a sufficient mark of respect; and the language of their proclamations was almost as unpretentious as that of city-state officials.[2]

[1] In the second century Philip and Perseus of Macedon and the Seleucid Demetrius II broke this rule. But Demetrius lost favour with his subjects on this ground.

[2] The chief point of difference lies in the use of the plural form ἡμεῖς. In Egypt petitions by subjects were addressed quite briefly βασιλεῖ Πτολεμαίῳ.

The family history of the Hellenistic monarchs presents on first impression greater affinities to Oriental sultans than to European kings. Not a few of them had two or three wives in succession; Demetrius I, Pyrrhus and Ptolemy VII kept two consorts at the same time. The practice of marriage with a full sister, which became a fairly common custom of the Ptolemies, suggests direct borrowing from Persian practice. But on closer inspection the analogies with Oriental usage prove to be delusive. It is significant that at Alexander's death all his high officers except Seleucus dismissed the Oriental wives whom they had taken at the king's bidding. Seleucus, whose consort Apama was of the Persian blood-royal,[1] retained her until 299; and subsequent members of his dynasty not infrequently intermarried with the Iranian royal houses of Cappadocia and Pontus. But in the other Hellenistic dynasties all the queens were of Macedonian, Greek or Epirote race. Polygamy in the Oriental sense was not practised among the Hellenistic kings, save perhaps by Ptolemy VII, for neither Demetrius nor Pyrrhus had both his wives simultaneously at court. The frequency of divorces in the royal families was not so much due to personal fancies as to considerations of political advantage. If Achæmenid sister-marriages had been the model for similar unions at Hellenistic courts, one would have expected them to be most frequent along the Seleucids; yet in this dynasty there is no certain case of such a practice.[2] In Egypt the first such match, between Ptolemy II and Arsinoë II, was almost certainly made at Arsinoë's instance to gratify her political ambitions; the later sister-marriages of the dynasty were probably a means of reducing the number of collateral branches to the royal house, so as to diminish the risk of pretenders.[3] The turbulence of the Ptolemaic and Seleucid families was clearly an inheritance from the old Argead dynasty. The example of precautionary murders had been given by none less than Alexander, and the pugnacity of the Arsinoës and Cleopatras

[1] Tarn, *Class. Quart.*, 1929, p. 139.

[2] It is possible that the Laodice who married Antiochus IV was his sister. The queens of Antiochus II and Seleucus II, also named Laodice, were probably cousins of their husbands. The other sister-marriages adduced by Kornemann (*Mitteilungen der schlesischen Gesellschaft für Volkskunde*, 1923, p. 17 ff.) are highly problematic.

[3] So J. Kaerst, *Gesch. des Hellenismus* (2nd ed.), II, p. 344.

had its counterpart in the irruptions of Olympias and Eurydice into the warfare of Alexander's marshals. Indeed at no point is the difference between Oriental and Hellenistic courts more marked than in the liberty and power enjoyed by the queens.

In view of the influence of the Hellenistic queens it may appear strange that the law of succession in all the dynasties was strictly agnatic, and that women did not acquire or transmit a right to the crown except where male heirs failed. Yet herein again the Hellenistic courts followed the ordinary Greek and Macedonian usage. Greco-Macedonian custom was equally observed in the law of primogeniture, which gave preference to eldest sons over those born in the purple.[1]

§ 4. HELLENISTIC ADMINISTRATION

The essentially autocratic character of the Hellenistic monarchs is somewhat obscured by the survival of quasi-constitutional forms in the act by which sovereignty was conferred upon them, and in occasional trials of subjects for high treason. Under the Argead dynasty the Macedonian military levy, as representing the folk, had exercised the right of confirming the appointment of a new king, and of pronouncing sentence in cases of treason. After Alexander's death his Grand Army, so long as it held together, secured the reversion of this right to itself and played an active part in settling the succession (pp. 2, 15). After the dispersion of this force the semblance of co-operation between king and folk was kept up by Antigonus, who submitted sentences of outlawry to his soldiers and invited them to sanction his assumption of the royal title. At Alexandria and at Antioch new rulers were presented for approval to the "Macedonians," in whom we should probably recognize the household troops, of whatever race. But at best this was a mere ceremony, like the swearing in of Roman troops to a new emperor; at worst it was a cloak under which the royal guards or the mobs of the capital cities effected a violent transfer of the crown. The Hellenistic rulers also conceded the right to petition to their subjects. In Egypt a common form of instituting a lawsuit was by way of complaint to

[1] M. Strack, *Die Dynastie der Ptolemäer*; E. Breccia, *Il diritto dinastico nelle monarchie dei successori d'Alessandro Magno.*

"king Ptolemy." The greater number of these pleas of course did not reach the king's ears; yet at Alexandria a special "petition wicket" was built into the palace,[1] and on occasion even a humble subject of Ptolemy might obtain redress by personal application to him during a royal progress.[2] But in effect the populations of the Hellenistic monarchies had no intermediate resource between petition and revolution.

The administrative practice of the Hellenistic kings was that of an undisguised despotism. They were subject to no antecedent body of law, for the law was of their own making: like the "Constitutions" of the Roman emperors, it was no more than a parcel of royal edicts, instructions and rescripts. Neither were they obliged to report to any consultative assembly, for the only deliberative body in a Hellenistic monarchy was the Privy Council, consisting solely of the king's nominees, whom he could summon or dismiss at will. The kings appointed all executive officials and all judicial magistrates at their own pleasure, and they exercised a general overriding control over local administration. In sum, the doctrine that "the king's will is right," which was formulated by the courtiers of Demetrius and reaffirmed by the advisers of Seleucus, substantially described the true position of affairs in the Hellenistic monarchies.

The absolute character of Hellenistic monarchy is further expressed in one typical institution of later Greek religion, the deification of rulers in lifetime. This practice will be discussed from the standpoint of Greek religion in ch. 21. For the present it is enough to point out that king-worship was plainly incompatible with a contractual relation between ruler and subject, and it obviously involved the admission that the king was a law unto himself.

Last but not least, Hellenistic monarchy signified personal government. If exception be made of the numerous minority reigns, the only known examples of *rois fainéants* in the Hellenistic dynasties are those of Ptolemy IV, of Alexander Balas, and perhaps of Antiochus II. In general, the monarchs presided in person over their Privy Council; they read and wrote replies to a vast number of reports from officials and

[1] Polybius, XV, 31.

[2] Wilcken, *U.P.Z.*, I, no. 42, ls. 4–5. In *P.S I.*, VI, 551, an allotment-holder καταβοᾷ τῷ βασιλεῖ on a progress up Nile.

petitions from subjects;[1] they went on tours of inspection through their dominions; they frequently took personal command of their armies. Whatever the faults of Hellenistic kings, they showed themselves by their personal vigour to be true descendants of Alexander.

§ 5. MACEDON

Of the individual Hellenistic monarchies Macedon, as was natural, preserved most faithfully the characteristics of the old Argead kingdom, and it is here that we find the nearest approach to constitutional kingship. Under Antigonus Gonatas the traditions which had been set aside by Alexander and Demetrius were deliberately revived. It is true that the conquests of Philip and Alexander had entailed some permanent changes in the country. A new element was introduced into Macedonian politics when Philip annexed Amphipolis and other Greek cities of the seaboard and Cassander created two new towns of considerable size, Cassandreia and Thessalonice, of which the former stood close by the site of ancient Olynthus, while the latter replaced a mere village on a hitherto strangely neglected spot. On the other hand the old Macedonian nobility had been disseminated over the newly conquered lands of the East, and the remnant who stayed at home or came back appear to have been virtually exterminated in the Galatian invasions. None the less the Antigonids might be regarded as the lineal successors of the Argeads. Their founder Gonatas had a natural simplicity of taste which stood in sharp contrast with his father's sumptuousness, and he was a life-long pupil in the Stoic school of philosophy, which reinforced his inborn dislike of pomp. His court at the old Macedonian capital at Pella made no vain display: it was the place of business of one engaged in a " noble servitude "—for so he defined his position. In keeping with this simplicity of style, the Antigonids led a comparatively pure family

[1] Witness the *mot* of Seleucus, that nobody who knew his burden of correspondence would want to pick up his crown, if it were dropped at his feet. (Plutarch, *An Seni sit gerenda Res publica*, ch. 11, p. 790 A.) In consequence of the personal activity of the kings the office of the vizier (ὁ ἐπὶ τῶν πραγμάτων) never became a regular one at the Hellenistic courts. (Corradi, *Studi Ellenistici*, p. 256 ff.)

life, and in general kept free from those family quarrels which wrought havoc in the Ptolemaic and Seleucid dynasties.

A more essential link between the Argeads and the Antigonids lay in the partnership between king and folk which the latter kept up in theory. Gonatas and Doson submitted their title for confirmation by the Macedonian nation-in-arms, and Doson dedicated his trophies from Sellasia in the name of himself " and the Macedonians," who thus appeared as allies rather than as subjects. Philip V in the early years of his reign kept alive the Argead custom of handing persons convicted of treason to be sentenced by the army. In this respect too the Antigonids were Macedonians of the old stock, that they never instituted a state cult of themselves. Though some members of the dynasty received worship here and there in the Greek cities of their realm, they were never deified by the Macedonians proper, before or after death. Similarly before the time of Philip V they rarely struck coins with their own portraits.

Of Macedonian administration under the Antigonids very little is known. So much however is clear, that it retained some of the old-time simplicity: compared with the system of the Ptolemies it would have appeared primitive. The small size and compactness of the territory rendered superfluous any complicated division into counties and districts, though it is not unlikely that the Roman partition of the kingdom into four republics followed a previous administrative demarcation. The finances of the kingdom did not require any elaborate machinery. Except when mercenaries were needed for a major land campaign, or ships and sailors for a naval effort, the expenditure of the government was on a lesser scale than in the days of Philip II. The upkeep of the conscript militia which constituted the core of the Macedonian army cost little or nothing; the pay list for officials was short. The sources of revenue were correspondingly exiguous. The gold mines of Pangæum, upon which Philip II had drawn so freely, had ceased to be productive; the land-tax yielded a mere two hundred talents,[1] and in view of the peasants' burden of military service it would not bear increase; the harbour dues brought in little, for the volume of trade was small; and the royal domains do not appear to have

[1] Plutarch, *Æmilius Paullus*, ch. 28.

been extensive. Finally, the Antigonids gave all that personal attention to government which was expected of Hellenistic rulers, for none of the dynasties produced a more consistently vigorous line of rulers.

§ 6. PERGAMUM

Of the other monarchies, Pergamum offers the most points of resemblance with Macedon. Not that the Attalids could in any sense claim to be affiliated to the old Argead dynasty, for they were the parvenus among Hellenistic kings, Greek middle-class intruders into the circle of the Macedonian nobility. But they belied their upstart origin by a studied simplicity of outward style. Their palace—the only one of which the ground-plan survives—was an ordinary Greek residence with added ante-room space, and less commodious than some of the larger houses at Pompeii. Though they sometimes intermarried with the Seleucids or other Asiatic dynasties, the first wearer of a crown in their house, Attalus I, did not disdain to wed the daughter of a plain citizen of Cyzicus ; and this lady, Apollonis, was an embodiment of all the *bourgeois* virtues which graced their family life. Though the Attalids received worship in several of their Greek subject cities, and a state cult after death, they were not officially deified during their reigns.

But in their methods of government the Attalids copied their Ptolemaic friends or their Seleucid rivals rather than the kings of Macedon. Under Eumenes II they took over the Seleucid system of administration in the territories acquired from that dynasty in Asia Minor. The spirit in which they ruled was closest akin to that of the Ptolemies, whom they followed in viewing statecraft as a branch of money-making. By resolute taxation and by direct state-enterprise in economic production (p. 296) they replenished or even enlarged the treasure inherited from their founder. On the side of expenditure they exhibited the same nicely calculated generosity as the Ptolemies in courting the public opinion of the Greek world. While they economized strictly upon themselves, they spent lavishly to make Pergamum a show-place and a centre of learning (pp. 307 ff., 318 ff.) ; and no other line of kings was more ostentatiously generous in its donations to cities and temples in the Greek Homeland.

§ 7. THE SELEUCID MONARCHY

In regard to the extent of its territory and the diversity of its populations the Seleucid kingdom might be considered the successor of the Persian empire. Had the political situation preceding the battle of Ipsus become stabilized, so as to confine Seleucus permanently to the regions east of the Euphrates, his kingdom would almost inevitably have ended by becoming purely Oriental. But the battle of Ipsus gave him a Mediterranean sea-front and made him the political heir of Antigonus I, who realized most clearly among Alexander's marshals the value of the Greek element in his dominions and had the greatest respect for the autonomy of the Greek cities. Seleucus therefore retained the Persian framework of administration, but built into it a Hellenic type of state.

The Seleucids took over from the Achæmenids their policy of decentralization in administrative matters, which was indeed best suited to a realm so unwieldy and so little homogeneous in its population. In territories of difficult access and in lands where national feeling ran strong they permitted native dynasts to retain their full local autonomy in return for occasional military assistance and a none too regular payment of tribute. From the time of Antiochus III most of the Iranian plateau was allowed to pass into the hands of dependent kings, Greek or Oriental, and the successors of Antiochus IV were content to recognize the local independence of the new Maccabæan dynasty. These timely concessions to Home Rule were one of the chief devices by which the Seleucids postponed the secession of their outlying dominions. For the administration of the regions under their direct rule the Seleucids followed in general the Persian scheme of division into some twenty large provinces, which were officially designated as "strategiæ," but in common usage preserved the old Persian name of "satrapies." For the supervision of their satraps they maintained the "royal roads" and the staffs of couriers which had been the most efficient instrument of control in the Achæmenid realm and had since been kept in use by Alexander and Antigonus I.

On the other hand the Seleucids introduced a new method of subdivision by which each province was split into three or four "eparchies" (to the total number of 72), and each eparchy fell into several "hyparchies."[1] They also departed from Achæmenid practice in grouping all the satrapies east of the Euphrates into a United Province with a sub-capital at Seleucia-on-Tigris, whose governor-general was not infrequently the heir apparent. They further refined upon the Persian system in withdrawing financial functions from the satraps and other local officials and entrusting them to a separate fiscal staff. The Seleucids indeed had need to improve upon the easy-going financial methods of the Achæmenids, for they had far heavier costs of administration. It is not unlikely that their expenditure even exceeded that of the Ptolemies, for if they had fewer officials on their pay-lists and were less free-handed towards artists and scholars, the defence of their far-flung frontiers and the plague of domestic wars which became almost endemic among them compelled them to keep their military forces continuously on a war-footing. To meet this increased outlay they did not multiply imposts like their neighbours in Egypt. They drew their income from three main sources, from a tithe or quota upon King's Land (whether tilled by serfs or military tenants),[2] from royalities of mines (which must have been prolific in Asia Minor and the Taurus lands), and from fixed contributions paid by the cities. For the collection of this revenue they did not create a complicated bureaucracy like that of the Ptolemies, but they maintained a lesser hierarchy of functionaries rising from the ἐπὶ τῶν προσόδων of the hyparchy to the "œconomus" of the satrapy.[3]

The Seleucids introduced other changes more important than these details of administration. The Achæmenid kings had carried religious tolerance to the point of allowing priestly corporations to set up regular states within states. The almost complete autonomy enjoyed by the "theocracy," or better, "hierocracy" at Jerusalem is a well-known case in point; but many other temple-authorities in Syria and

[1] On this scheme see Tarn, *Seleucid-Parthian Studies* (Procs. British Academy, vol. 16), p. 24 ff.

[2] I follow Rostovtseff (*Cambr. Anc. Hist.*, VII, p. 171) and Tarn (*Hellenistic Civilisation*, p. 117) against Örtel (Pauly-Wissowa, *Real-encyclopädie*, s.v. Katoikoi) in assuming that normally the military settlers paid a rent, as in Egypt.

[3] On the administration and finance of the Seleucids, see E. Bikerman, *Institutions des Séleucides*, chs. 4 and 5.

Asia Minor possessed similar powers of levying revenue and conveying justice. In true Greek fashion the Seleucids endeavoured to carry out the principle of the State's sovereignty over the Church. While they allowed liberty of conscience (a rule to which the persecution of the Jews under Antiochus IV was a single and short-lived exception), and even provided funds to restore ancient temples, as at Babylon (where the Persians, contrary to their usual practice, had destroyed the great sanctuary of Esagila), they curtailed the wealth and the independence of the priesthoods. In some instances they confiscated the territory over and above that which the temples required for their necessary revenue and redistributed it among new colonists; in others they placed the sanctuary under the authority of the nearest town, which thereupon took over the priests' jurisdiction.

But the most distinctive of Seleucid innovations was the increased importance of the municipalities within their dominions. Under Achæmenid rule old-established city-states, as in Phœnicia and on the Greek fringe of Asia Minor, had been left in possession of their local autonomy, but in general town life had not been encouraged, and municipal government had remained in a rudimentary condition. But from the days of Alexander the Seleucid territory became the main field for Greek colonization, and in the process of town-making the Seleucids themselves assumed the leading part. The founder of the dynasty created a cluster of settlements in northern Syria and along the middle Euphrates, where new towns with old Macedonian names (Edessa, Chalcis, etc.) privided homes for his veterans. Antiochus I resumed Alexander's colonizing activities in the eastern provinces by creating a horseshoe of Greek towns on the fertile fringes of the Persian plateau and establishing Greek outposts in the oasis of Merv. Antiochus II tightened his control over the lines of communication in Asia Minor with chains of colonies, and Antiochus IV reconstituted many of the older foundations in Syria and Babylonia.[1] But the Seleucids were not

[1] Many Seleucid foundations were semi-autonomous military settlements before they became full πόλσς.

It is probable that serf populations on territories transferred to Greek cities received personal freedom (but not municipal franchise).—Rostovtzeff, *op. cit.*, I, pp. 509–12.

merely the greatest town-builders among Greek kings; they were also the most liberal in their grants of municipal autonomy. In pursuing this generous policy towards the cities in their territory they often but made a virtue of necessity, for in times of stress they found it politically advisable or financially profitable to make concessions to them. Yet it may be claimed on their behalf that they anticipated the Roman Cæsars in recognizing administrative devolution to cities as the most efficient means of decentralization in a large monarchy.

In their outward style the Seleucids were far more sumptuous than the Antigonids or Attalids. Antiochus III was seemingly the first to create an elaborate hierarchy of court officials, and Antiochus IV was unquestionably the greatest showman of Greek kings. Yet in all essentials the court at Antioch followed Macedonian rather than Persian usage.

§ 8. EGYPT: GENERAL ADMINISTRATION

The internal history of Ptolemaic Egypt stands apart by reason of the wealth of information which is preserved for its study. For the history of the other monarchies we have to make shift with stray allusions in authors and rare inscriptions; from Egypt a mass of papyri has been recovered, mostly official or semi-official documents. These papyri, it is true, do not illustrate uniformly all parts of the Egyptian administration. They mostly date from the second and third Ptolemy or from the second century; on the earliest years of the dynasty they throw hardly any light. Moreover, being chiefly derived from up-country towns (especially from the Fayum region), they illustrate the dealings of the petty officials rather than the acts of the high functionaries. But they include a number of important royal ordinances, and in the aggregate they afford such knowledge about the daily work of the administration as we do not possess from any other Greek state.

In Egypt the Ptolemies had a far simpler task than the Seleucids in Asia. To make the king's writ run along an open valley amid a homogeneous and unwarlike population was not a difficult problem, and it had been fully solved by the

Pharaohs of old. But the native administration had fallen into disrepair under the Persian kings, who appear to have adopted a studiously neglectful attitude in regard to their Egyptian satrapy. Under Alexander a tentative reorganization was effected, and the principle of keeping the officials under control by increasing their numbers and dividing their functions was introduced. But the complete system as it appears in the papyri was essentially the work of the Ptolemies, and it was probably Ptolemy II rather than the founder of the dynasty who thought out its details.

Though Ptolemy I was a man of homely habits, his successor was fond of display, and being the wealthiest of Hellenistic rulers he outstripped all his contemporaries in the splendour of his appointments. The pageant held by him at Alexandria to inaugurate the cult of his deified father (280/79) was not rivalled in Greek history, save by Antiochus IV's procession in 167 (p. 219). A tradition of pomp thus attached to the court of Alexandria, which in this respect was closely akin to that of Antioch. Furthermore, from the time of the fifth king a similar hierarchy of titles (" King's Friends," etc.) appears at Alexandria as at Antioch. But the Ptolemies never adopted any of the old Egyptian ceremonial. The style of the Alexandrian court was essentially Macedonian; the kings did not intermarry with any Oriental house;[1] and the last of the dynasty, queen Cleopatra VII, was almost purely Macedonian in breed.[2]

For general administration the Ptolemies retained the old Pharaonic division of Egypt into " nomes," whose number, though variable, usually stood near forty. At the head of each nome was a strategus, whose primary duty was to maintain order. For this purpose he had at his disposal a corps of policemen, including special divisions for patrolling the Nile and the desert trade-routes; no doubt he could also draw in emergencies upon the military settlers in his district. He was probably chief judge in criminal matters. In regard to civil pleas he received petitions and sent cases on to an arbitrator or, when an amicable settlement had failed, to the

[1] In 323 the first Ptolemy seemingly married a descendant of one of the fourth-century native rebel Pharaohs. (Tarn, *Class. Quart.*, 1929, pp. 138–9.) But this union was short-lived and had no male issue.

[2] Bevan, *Egypt under the Ptolemies*, p. 120, n. 1.

appropriate court.[1] By the second century he had also usurped the right of pronouncing by informal procedure on suits which in strict law should have been tried in court. But he had no jurisdiction in fiscal matters, which were entirely detached from the cognition of the ordinary tribunals (p. 265). The staff of the strategus included an *ἐπιστάτης*, who was a deputy-judge, an *ἐπιστάτης τῶν φυλάκων* or chief of police, and a registrar who preserved the Pharaonic title of *βασιλικὸς γραμματεύς*. Each nome fell into a number of *τόποι* under *τόπαρχαι*, and within the *τόπος* each village had its *κωμάρχης*, its secretariate and its police.[2] In the early part of the second century the governor or "epistrategus" of the Theban nome was charged with the general supervision of the counties of Upper Egypt and the direction of military operations in that region.

The civil jurisdiction of the nome, so far as it could not be settled by arbitration, was reserved for two special courts, the "laocritæ" and the "chrematistæ." The laocritæ were an old Pharaonic court, drawn from the priestly class, who took cognisance of disputes between natives. The chrematistæ were travelling justices, in numbers from three upwards, who went in circuit from nome to nome and heard suits between the Greek or Hellenized inhabitants; being laymen, they no doubt required a good deal of prompting from their *εἰσαγωγεύς* or registrar. Their chief duty was to pronounce on questions of fact in accordance with instructions from the strategus, so that their position resembled that of the "iudices" or "recuperatores" of the prætors' courts at Rome. In the third century cases in which suitors were of different nationality went before a mixed commission. Subsequently the forum was determined by the language in which the plaintiff had drawn up his petition, i.e. the plaintiff chose the court.[3] It may be taken for granted that appeals were

[1] In the third century the strategus was authorized to deal at discretion with petitions addressed to Ptolemy but handed in at his office. In the second he lost this right. P. Collomp, *Recherches sur la chancellerie et la diplomatique des Lagides*, p. 141 ff.

[2] The village constabulary was native. The officers and mounted police troops were largely Greeks from the military reserve.

[3] The Pharaonic usage of entering all pleas in writing was imposed on both these courts. The Ptolemies also preserved the Pharaonic record offices (*χρεωφυλάκια*), in which private contracts could be lodged for reference. Each nome had its own archives.

allowed to higher courts, but nothing is known of the constitution of these; nor yet can we say on what principles the king delegated cases submitted to him.

In Egypt a Nile Conservancy Board has always been an indispensable branch of the administration. Under the early Ptolemies an " architecton " was appointed to overhaul and improve the entire system of irrigation. His orders were executed by officials of like name in each nome, who were empowered to requisition, with the help of the strategus, the necessary amount of forced labour.[1]

§ 9. EGYPT: FINANCIAL DEPARTMENTS

By far the most elaborate department of the Ptolemaic administration was the Treasury. Under Persian rule the revenues drawn from Egypt were remarkably small. But the rebel native chiefs who wore Pharaoh's crown in mid-fourth century cast about resolutely for new sources of income, and Alexander's financial officer Cleomenes achieved notoriety by his wealth of resource and lack of scruples in collecting funds. Yet Cleomenes was a mere fumbler compared with the second Ptolemy. It has been disputed whether this king, the greatest of ancient " Big Business " men, increased his revenue to subserve his policy or, as seems far more likely, enlarged his frontiers in order to swell out his revenue. In any case, he viewed the internal administration of Egypt from a purely fiscal standpoint, and he displayed a perfectly devilish ingenuity in diverting every surplus grain of wheat and scruple of money into his treasury.

Among the chief objects of expenditure in the Ptolemaic budget the army was probably less costly than that of the Seleucids, for it was less continually on active service. On the other hand their fleet, being by far the largest in Hellenistic times, and the most regularly in commission, must have constituted an exceptionally heavy charge. The outlay on public works was another large item, for the labour on improvements (though not on routine conservancy work) was paid at fair rates. The cost of the administrative staff, though somewhat reduced by part-payments in land-grants,

[1] The functions of the " architecton " are well illustrated in the second volume of the Petrie Papyri.

was probably well in excess of that in any contemporary state, for its numbers were disproportionately great. Finally, no dynasty was more liberal in support of art and literature, or spent more on diplomatic propaganda in Greece and the Aegean lands.

But Ptolemy II aimed at something more than to make ends meet, and he succeeded in accumulating a treasure which even in the first century, after long years of misrule, was large enough to make the mouths of Roman politicians water.[1] He imposed a variety of taxes which no ancient state and few modern ones could equal. From Egyptian papyri and ostraca pot-sherds (on which tax-receipts were inscribed) a list with two hundred and eighteen headings has been compiled.[2] A few of the titles in this catalogue may be synonymous, some others are of Roman date; yet if allowance is made for other items which have not come to our notice, the total number of Ptolemaic imposts may be reckoned at a full two hundred.

The largest source of revenue was the land. By right of sole ownership of the "spear-won" soil of Egypt the Ptolemies took toll upon the cultivators in the shape of a rent. While they allowed a permanent rebate to military tenants and a few other favoured persons, and temporary remissions all round in seasons of a low Nile,[3] their ordinary practice was to exact a fixed quantity of grain from each acre of arable land, a quota of all garden and vineyard produce, and a fee for grazing rights. Again, licences were payable for the right of exercising a large number of industries and trades.[4] Customs were levied at the frontiers of Egypt and of each nome;[5] transit and market dues were exacted, and even such trivial services as sifting the wheat paid by way

[1] We have no reliable figure of this treasure's absolute amount.

[2] U. Wilcken, *Griechische Ostraka aus Ägypten*, vol. I, ch. 4; Rostovtzeff, *op. cit.*, I p. 267 ff.; Claire Préaux, *L'économie royale des Lagides*, *passim*.

[3] Thanks to Ptolemy III for such a remission are expressed by the Egyptian priests in the well-known "Canopus Decree." (Hicks, 179; Ditt., *O.G.I.*, 56, l. 17.)

[4] In one papyrus a purveyor of cooked lentils declares that he cannot pay his licence because competitors have spoilt his trade. (*P.S.I.*, IV, 402.)

[5] Some customs dues and octrois stood at no higher rate than one or two per cent. But protective tariffs on some imports were fixed at a rate of 25 or even of 50 per cent. (*P. Zeno Cairo*, 59015.) On customs in general, see A. Andréadès, in *Mélanges Glotz*, I, p. 7.

of taxation and providing the baskets for its transport were not offered gratis. The priests and the Greek population paid an exemption-tax in consideration of their freedom from forced labour;[1] and the wealthier Alexandrines probably carried the burden of equipping the warships. To these regular imposts were added requisitions of food and transport for the progress of the king and other important personages, and special contributions on the accession of a new sovereign. To the revenue derived from Egypt must be added the proceeds of the multifarious taxation imposed upon the foreign possessions of the Ptolemies.[2] The estimate that Ptolemy II had a revenue of 14,800 talents in money alone, though unofficial, was probably not wide of the mark.

The collection and disposal of the Ptolemaic revenue gave employment to a large staff of fiscal officials. The statistical information required for poll and property taxes, and more especially for the land rents, was prepared by the *βασιλικὸς γραμματεύς* in each nome.[3] The levying of the imposts was to some extent facilitated by recourse to private tax-farmers, according to a common Greek usage. But charges bringing a fixed revenue, such as the rents of arable lands, were collected directly; and the private contractors who collected the more fluctuating taxes were bound down by elaborate regulations entailing continuous supervision by the officials.[4] The whole process of collection in each nome stood under the control of two *οἰκονόμοι* (one for taxes paid in kind, the other for money imposts), and either of these *οἰκονόμοι* was shadowed by an *ἀντιγραφεύς*, whose counter-signature he required at every turn. Another dual set of officials was responsible for the storage of the revenue, for while the *σιτολόγος* took charge of all the natural produce, the

[1] This privilege is amusingly illustrated by a claim for exemption from harvesting duty by some αἰλουροβοσκόι, who maintain that they have a right not to be called away from their cats. (*P.S.I.*, IV, 440.)

[2] Ditt., *O.G.I.*, 55, supplies a long list of imposts levied upon the Lycian town of Telmessus; *O.G.I.*, 41, mentions the transfer of court fees from Samos to the Egyptian fiscus. *P. Zeno Cairo*, 59035, appears to prove that the citizens of Halicarnassus were liable to trierarchy.

[3] For a good example of a fiscal land survey see *P. Tebtunis*, p. 538 ff.

[4] *Rev. Law.*, cols. 3–22. The essential function of the tax-farmers was to underwrite the revenue from taxes of uncertain yield, in return for a percentage commission on the intake.

βασιλικὸς τραπεζίτης received the payments in money. The work of all these functionaries was further supervised by inspectors (ἐπιμεληταί) and accountants (ἐκλογισταί). At the head of the whole financial machine stood the Diœcetes. In addition to the duties usually incumbent on such a minister, the Diœcetes was charged with the drafting of the numerous regulations by which the whole process of economic production in Egypt was controlled (pp. 292–6); and he was the chief judge in all revenue suits, which included not merely disputes about taxes, but all matters in which those "involved in the revenue department" became engaged, i.e. the official collectors, the tax-farmers, the cultivators of the king's land, and the workers in monopolized industries. The importance of the Diœcetes' office is illustrated by the almost regal style of life of Ptolemy II's minister Apollonius, and the enormous influence which he wielded in administrative matters.[1]

Apart from the Diœcetes, little is known about the Heads of Departments and the Secretariate at Alexandria. Communication between the capital and the chief towns of the nomes was kept up by a system of couriers. An express horse-post conveyed the urgent dispatches, a slower camel-post forwarded the more voluminous ordinary correspondence.[2]

The scheme of government in the foreign possessions of the Ptolemies was naturally less uniform. Under Ptolemy II a sheikh named Tubias was left in charge of the borderland of Ammonitis near the Arabian desert, and held authority over a detachment of Egyptian militiamen settled in his country. Cyrene was alternately a province under a "Libyarch" and a semi-independent principality under a kinsman of the Egyptian sovereign. The Confederation of the Islands (Cyclades) was supervised by a "Nesiarch" whose functions, in theory at least, were those of a resident and adviser rather than of a military governor.[3]

Two opposite impressions of the Ptolemaic administration may be derived from the surviving documents. On the one

[1] The wide activities of Apollonius have been abundantly illustrated by the Zeno Papyri. He was the author of part, if not of the whole, of Ptolemy II's Revenue Law.

[2] See the remains of a Ptolemaic post-book in *P. Hibeh*, 110, and the commentary by F. Preisigke (*Klio*, 1907, p. 241 ff.); also *P. Oxyrhynchus*, IV, 710.

[3] Tarn, *Journ. Hell. Stud.*, 1911, p. 241 ff.

hand they present a picture of a bureaucracy out of hand, like that of the later Roman Empire.[1] The tyranny of the officials is revealed in the unfair imposition of forced labour, in fiscal extortions occasionally accompanied by "forcible persuasion,"[2] in detentions of untried prisoners which sometimes extended into a second year. The cumbrousness of the machine is illustrated by numerous complaints of officials in arrears of pay; by the circumlocution involved in simple acts of routine—an application by a young Greek to the militia required thirty-five separate administrative acts before it was finally disposed of;[3] in the lack of co-ordination between courts of law, which allowed cases to be bandied about and for sentences to remain unexecuted. In one notorious suit an ex-officer named Hermias carried on a veritable "Jarndyce *v.* Jarndyce" dispute about a piece of land for nine years.[4] In another such case two girl-attendants at an Egyptian temple gallantly carried a complaint about defraudation of rations to the king and queen, and thus obtained a payment long overdue.[5] It is not unlikely that the inertia into which the second and the third Ptolemy fell towards the ends of their reigns was the result of sheer overwork in a vain attempt to keep abreast of current business. The unnecessary complexity of administration is also shown up by the expedient of cumulating more than one office in the hands of one man, which was adopted not infrequently in the second century. Finally, there is the evidence of the native revolts which lasted intermittently through the second century, and of still more frequent "strikes," when overburdened peasants took sanctuary and refused to resume cultivation until their grievances had been redressed.[6]

[1] According to *P. Halensis*, IV, royal officials enjoyed a general immunity from accusation and arrest. The Zeno papyri give the impression that Apollonius and his agents could take the law into their own hands with impunity.

[2] 'πειθανάγκη' (*P. Amherst*, II, 31). An ordinance of Ptolemy forbad claimants in fiscal cases to have recourse to an advocate. (*P. Amherst*, II, 33.) Probably a not uncommon cause of extortion was the (de facto) necessity for officials to "pay their footing" on receiving an appointment.

[3] See the documents in Wilcken, *U.P.Z.*, I, pp. 150–177, and the summary in Bevan, *Egypt under the Ptolemies*, pp. 137–9.

[4] Bouché-Leclercq, *Histoire des Lagides*, vol. IV, pp. 218–33.

[5] Wilcken, *U.P.Z.*, I, pp. 177–296.

[6] Instances in *P.S.I.*, V, 502; *P. Zeno Cairo*, 59245 (where the nomarch receives instructions to "rouse" the strikers); *P. Tebtunis*, 41 and 72.

The better side of the Ptolemaic government is best revealed in the so-called "Revenue Law of Ptolemy Philadelphus," a lengthy document which regulates the levying of taxes on oil and wine and displays the utmost care and ingenuity in safeguarding alike the interests of the Crown, of the tax-farmers and the tax-payers; [1] in royal ordinances of 167 and 118 B.C., reprobating in strong terms the abuses then current, and making wholesale remissions of accumulated debts to the Treasury; [2] and in a code of instructions (also *c.* 118 B.C.), which emphasizes the need of fair dealing and of keeping the subjects in good humour.[3] Such orders did not always remain dead letters: instances of fines on delinquent officials are on record, and even the highest functionaries were not immune from punishment.[4] Ptolemy II dismissed his chief engineer Cleon, and his successor took the same step in regard to the great Apollonius. It also appears that the legal remuneration of officials was on an adequate scale. Under the later Ptolemies voluntary candidates for office sometimes failed, and recourse was had to civilian conscription; but as a rule there seems to have been no lack of applicants, whether Greek or native.

In all probability the standard of government varied widely, according as the king and his chief ministers maintained an effective supervision of the machine, or let it run at will. Under *rois fainéants* like Ptolemy IV, and during the frequent spells of civil war in the second century, the subjects suffered considerably; under vigorous rulers like Ptolemy II it is probable that Egypt was more prosperous than under any previous régime. The worst failures of the Ptolemies, as of most Hellenistic dynasties, are to be found in their foreign policy rather than in their internal administration.

[1] Ed. Grenfell and Mahaffy. The general conclusion from the wide survey by Melle Préaux (*op. cit.*), is that the Ptolemies did not lack common sense, and that their system was more flexible than a casual inspection might suggest.

[2] Wilcken, *U.P.Z.*, I, no. 106.

[3] *P. Tebtunis*, I, 5; III, 703. Cf. also the ordinance of Ptolemy II against unfair billeting. (*P. Halensis*, V.)

[4] *P. Tebtunis*, 27, contains a severe reprimand by a Diœcetes of an intermediate official for choosing bad subordinates. In *P. Petr.*, II, 38b, and Wilcken-Mitteis, *Chrestomathie der Papyruskunde*, no. 301, government action is taken against traders retailing oil at a higher price than the official one.

CHAPTER XV

THE HELLENISTIC CITIES

§ 1. ORIENTAL SELF-GOVERNMENT

AMONG the native populations of the Near East the general mass of the peasantry, living scattered in small villages, had never had much opportunity of common action, and their Hellenistic rulers did not deem it part of their duties to educate them to greater political activity. In Egypt the Ptolemies left it to the " komarchs " or village chiefs to supervise field-work, to collect rents, and in conjunction with the village elders to select each year's quota for forced labour ; and it may be assumed that in the Asiatic monarchies the local sheikhs were entrusted with similar duties. This, however, merely amounts to saying that the headmen were conduits for the conveyance of the government's orders.

A greater measure of self-administration was granted in Egypt to immigrant Orientals in the towns. At Alexandria the Jews were organized into a " politeuma " or corporation with a Council of Elders and an Ethnarch who exercised jurisdiction within his own community ;[1] presumably the Phœnicians domiciled at Memphis and in other towns of the Delta enjoyed similar privileges. In the Phœnician homeland Ptolemies and Seleucids in turn gave to Tyre and Sidon, Byblus and Aradus, the same self-governing rights as to Greek cities. In Asia Minor Sardes ranked as a Greek town ; but

[1] The documents which attest these privileges are of the Roman period ; yet it may be taken for granted that in this, as in so many other matters, the Romans merely confirmed the arrangements of the Hellenistic rulers.

No doubt the Jewish colonies at Memphis and in the Seleucid and Attalid towns had similar communal organizations. But it is unlikely that the Jews received the full franchise of any Greek city. Their own law would preclude them from exercising many civic functions that involved acts of heathen worship.

there is no evidence of autonomy on the Greek pattern being conceded to the native towns of Babylonia. It may be assumed that a grant of municipal autonomy was everywhere dependent on a high degree of hellenization.

The attitude of the Seleucids towards the powerful priestly corporations which under Achæmenid rule had formed veritable states within the state has been described in the previous chapter (p. 258). In Egypt, where the native dynasts of the fourth century had already introduced a secularizing policy, the Ptolemies curtailed the privileges of the clergy no less drastically than the Seleucids, though they left them more of the appearance of self-administration.[1] They did not confiscate the temple lands, but they diverted part of their rents and transferred the management of the estates to the royal treasury; they appropriated a special tax on garden and vineyard produce which had previously been paid to the temple authorities;[2] and they restricted the industrial and commercial activities from which the priests had drawn a considerable income. They further mulcted the clergy by making them pay a licence for their right to co-opt new members and to ply a few reserved manufactures and trades. By way of compensation, the kings made grants out of state funds for the upkeep of temples and the payment of stipends, and they made donations for new buildings and special festivals. They left the general ordering of the ritual at the discretion of the Deans and Chapters; but they assumed the right to prescribe new ceremonies; they severely limited the right of asylum, by which malefactors contrived to evade the secular arm; and to ensure obedience they imposed on each temple an "epistates" or overseer. The Ptolemies admitted the native priesthoods to a share in the secular administration by selecting the "laocritæ" or native judges from them; and they summoned occasional synods of the clergy to Alexandria, which were no doubt the chief means of putting them in touch with native opinion. Yet it is probable that these congresses met by royal order only, and that they

[1] On this subject in general see W. Otto, *Priester und Tempel im hellenistischen Ägypten*.

[2] See the regulations in *Rev. Law*, col. 38 ff. The proceeds of the tax were devoted in the first instance to the cult of the deified Arsinoë; but it may be taken for granted that part of the money was paid back in the form of a subsidy to the native temples.

spent most of their time in mere manifestations of loyalty.[1] In the policy of conciliating yet disarming the Egyptian priesthoods the Ptolemies were but partially successful. We may suspect that the priests of Amon at Thebes, with their long traditions of quasi-independence, had a hand in the revolts of Upper Egypt in the second century. On the other hand, Memphis, the religious capital of Lower Egypt, appears to have been consistently loyal to the Ptolemaic dynasty.

§ 2. THE GREEK CITIES: GENERAL CONDITIONS

Within the Hellenistic monarchies the status of the Greek cities varied as greatly as that of the municipia in the Roman Empire, and was similarly made the subject of continuous experiments. Among Alexander's marshals Antipater and Cassander frankly aimed at curtailing the liberties of the Greeks; the others held out offers of freedom and of reduced taxation in order to detach them from their rivals, but at times forgot their promise when it had served its purpose. Even Antigonus, the most genuine phil-Hellene among them, occasionally transplanted or amalgamated Greek cities and interfered drastically in their internal affairs.[2] Lysimachus and (in his later days) Demetrius were notorious for the high-handed way in which they imposed conscription or taxation. But in general the harsh measures of Alexander's marshals flowed not so much from a deliberate intention to keep the Greeks in subjugation as from the exigencies of their mutual warfare.

In the third century many cities of the Greek Homeland retained or recovered their freedom and were at liberty to enter into alliances on equal terms with the neighbouring kings, or to combine in federal leagues. Elsewhere the Greek towns were for the most part reduced to the position of dependents, who owed such political rights as they might exercise to a royal grant and were liable to forfeit them at the

[1] The Canopus and Rosetta decrees contain fulsome votes of thanks to Ptolemy III and V for sundry benefits. The Rosetta decree, however, has an undertone of independence.

[2] See the rescript to Lebedus and Teos relating to the "synœcism" of these towns. (Ditt., *Syll.*, 344.) Several new foundations of this period, e.g. Cassandreia and Thessalonice, and Antigoneia in the Troad, were created by forcible transplantation. Ephesus was moved to a new (and more suitable) site by orders of Lysimachus.

king's pleasure. Save in rare instances where a king gave a charter of immunity, they were liable to conscription and taxation. The right of coinage was generally withheld from the new foundations and withdrawn from the older ones. The internal affairs of the cities were subject to interference by royal "diagrammata" or ordinances. Some kings appointed resident "epistatæ" to enforce their authority, or maintained control by nominating the chief magistrates.

On the other hand, the right of conscription was seldom exercised, save in the Macedonian dominions and in the towns of the Aegean seaboard (p. 234). Except in the Ptolemaic territories, taxation was usually in the form of a lump sum, which the cities were allowed to collect through their own officials, and in view of the military protection afforded by the king a contribution to his exchequer might be no more than a fair return for service rendered.[1] The substitution of a royal coinage, which was accepted everywhere, for municipal mintages with a restricted currency, was manifestly of advantage to Greek trade. Lastly, there is no evidence of frequent and undue interference by kings in the local affairs of Greek cities; and where such interference took place, the epistates often submitted the royal message in the form of a resolution to the municipal Ecclesia, so as to preserve at least the appearance of spontaneous legislation on its part.[2]

Perhaps the chief reproach against the Hellenistic kings in regard to their treatment of the Greek cities is that outside the Aegean area they nowhere made provision for parliaments (like the provincial concilia of the Roman Empire), in which municipal deputies might meet the monarch or his ministers in regular conference. For lack of such an assembly communications from the Crown had to be sent separately to each town in a special diagramma, and messages from the cities had to be conveyed by the epistates, by an embassy appointed for the purpose, or in a more informal manner by residents at court who had the king's ear. At the least, parliaments of municipal deputies might have assisted the Crown in distributing the royal imposts equitably; at best,

[1] In western Asia Minor the Seleucids levied a tax called Γαλατικά, which was plainly earmarked for defence against Galatian inroads. (Ditt., *O.G.I.*, 223.)

[2] See also the addendum on p. 286.

they might have formed a valuable supplement to the Privy Councils in shaping royal policy; in any case, they must have contributed to keep up the political aptitude of the Greeks in the new monarchies.

§ 3. THE GREEK CITIES: LOCAL DETAILS

In Peloponnesus and Central Greece the Antigonids made it a general rule to treat the cities as allies rather than as subjects. In individual towns they kept garrisons and governors or (as in the case of Gonatas) they maintained local tyrants in power. In Athens, if we may judge by the paucity of silver coins of mid-third century, they curtailed the right of mintage;[1] but at Corinth they allowed a free issue of silver as well as of bronze. In Macedonia the cities, with the exception of Cassandreia, were frankly treated as subjects. They were supervised by governors, and they lacked the right to issue coins. In Thessaly, despite the fact that the Antigonids here ruled as federal magistrates, and not as kings, the cities stood on substantially the same footing as in Macedon.[2]

The old-established cities on the west coast of Asia Minor reflected in their domestic history the fact that they lay in one of the principal war-zones of the third century. Their situation was a diplomatic asset to them, in that it enabled them from time to time to strike good bargains with kings desirous of winning them over or of retaining their allegiance. On the other hand, it exposed them to stricter supervision by military governors and to war-time requisitions. Among the more favoured cities Smyrna and Ilium enjoyed complete internal autonomy and freedom from tribute under Antiochus II, and they succeeded in retaining these privileges when they were transferred from Seleucid to Attalid suzerainty; Cyzicus remained from first to last an ally rather than a subject of the Attalids. But in general the cities paid tribute in turn to Seleucids, Ptolemies and Attalids; in some towns (e.g.

[1] The theory that Gonatas set up a royal mint at Athens rests on insufficient evidence. (W. Kolbe, *Göttingische Gelehrte Anzeigen*, 1916, pp. 447–8.)

[2] But the Antigonids followed the usual custom of conveying their orders in the form of advice or, if necessary, of expostulation. See the two letters of Philip V to Larissa, in which he urges but does not command it to enrol new citizens. (Ditt., *Syll.*, 513.)

Ephesus under the Seleucids) royal governors exercised control, in others, as at Pergamum, the board of strategi was nominated by the Crown.[1] The more important places retained possession of their mints, and from about 200 B.C. a large silver piece called the "cistophorus" was issued at Ephesus and Pergamum and attained a widespread currency alongside the royal Attalid money.[2]

The new foundations in the Seleucid and Attalid dominions included not only cities but smaller communities known as *κατοικίαι*, which were usually composed of reservists or veterans. These minor settlements possessed an organized assembly, a communal revenue, and executive officials (sometimes called "brabeutæ"), who probably exercised an informal jurisdiction; but for purposes of taxation and higher jurisdiction they were either placed under royal officials or were attributed, like Roman "vici," to the nearest municipality.

The full-fledged towns usually possessed the complete apparatus of Greek municipal government: from the capital city Antioch,[3] and from the distant colony of Antioch-in-Persis, we still possess decrees passed by Council and Assembly in the best style of a free Greek city.[4] In the third century municipal mints were not operative in the Seleucid realm, but from the reign of Antiochus IV numerous towns of Syria began to strike coins. But the most distinctive feature of the Seleucid cities was the large amount of territory which they might possess. By gift or sale from the king, or by transfer of confiscated temple domains,[5] the more favoured of the towns acquired an estate such as Athens and Sparta alone in the Greek Homeland possessed; they controlled whole groups of native villages and exercised administrative functions comparable with those of the most powerful municipia in the Roman empire.

[1] On Pergamum and the Attalid towns, see G. Cardinali, *Il regno di Pergamo*, p. 233 ff.; Esther V. Hansen, *The Attalids of Pergamon*, p. 172 ff.

[2] Head, *Historia Numorum* (2nd ed.), p. 534.

[3] Ditt., *O.G.I.*, 248 (under Antiochus IV).

[4] *Ibid.*, 233. A large measure of autonomy is also known to have been enjoyed by Dura-Europus, Seleucia-ad-Orontem and Susa among the more easterly cities. Seleucia-on-the-Tigris (which had a large non-Greek population) possessed at least a municipal council.

[5] The Seleucids also required recipients of *δωρεαί*, i.e. large estates carved out of royal or temple domains, to attach these to the jurisdiction of some neighbouring city. (Ditt., *O.G.I.*, 221.)

In Egypt on the other hand the Greek communities played but a slight part in the administration. The density of the native population in this country left little room for new Greek settlements of greater size than villages. The typical Greek colony in Egypt was a group of military reservists resembling the Seleucid or Attalid *κατοικίαι*. Though these groups were called "politeumata," their political functions were quite rudimentary, and the privileges of the inhabitants were individual rather than collective. The same probably applies to the Greeks domiciled at Memphis, who lived in a separate quarter and no doubt formed a special politeuma. Of the three Greek settlements large enough to rank as cities, Naucratis was an older foundation which had enjoyed self-administration under the later Pharaohs. Under the Ptolemies its former rights were no doubt preserved, but for fiscal purposes it stood under the control of a royal official.[1] At Alexandria, where a Greek population exceeding that of any other Hellenistic colony had its residence, it was enrolled in tribes and demes and had law-courts and a municipal code of its own.[2] But it lacked a popular assembly, and if it possessed a Council—a point on which the opinion of scholars is divided—this merely served as a means of consultation between the king and his subjects; and the chief municipal official, the "exegetes," was probably little more than the spokesman of the Greek community.[3] In a word, the Greeks of Alexandria were substantially on the same footing as the Jewish colony. The administration of the city as a whole, and the supervision of the large native element in the population, lay entirely in the hands of the royal officials.[4] The only real instance of municipal autonomy in Egypt is offered by a

[1] An *οἰκονόμος τῶν κατὰ Νάυκρατιν* is mentioned in Ditt., *O.G.I.*, 89. His title proves that he was not a municipal but a district officer, and therefore held his post from the Crown.

[2] Extracts from this code survive in *P. Lille*, I, 29, and esp. in *P. Halensis*, II. Alexandrian law contained a large Attic element, but also drew upon other earlier city codes. It illustrates the evolution of a Greek "ius gentium" in Hellenistic times.

[3] We have no direct evidence bearing on this problem. The lack of references to an Alexandrian *βουλή* in Polybius' detailed account of the revolution in 201 B.C. (XV, 26–33) indicates that the Council—if such there was—had no executive officers at its disposal.

[4] These included an *ἀρχιδικάστης* and a *νυκτερινὸς στρατηγός*, who survived under Roman rule as municipal officials (Strabo, XVII, p. 797), and a *εὐθηνίαρχος* or "Minister of Cheapness."

colony of Ptolemy I in Upper Egypt, which was named Ptolemais after him. This settlement received a Greek population of several thousands, and in view of the difficulty of attracting immigrants to so remote a place it was endowed with special privileges. It possessed a Council, a popular assembly and courts of law, and its municipal politics were at times lively and even riotous. Yet in the second century at least its ἀρχιπρύτανις or Chairman of Council was *ex officio* the Governor-General of Upper Egypt.[1]

§ 4. THE MUNICIPAL GOVERNMENTS

Among the Hellenistic cities the majority of those situated in the Greek Homeland, and a few others in the Aegean and Black Sea area, such as Rhodes, Cyzicus, Byzantium and Heraclea, retained the right of making their own foreign policy (whether individually or as members of a confederacy), and were therefore under obligation to maintain their own army or navy. These towns still had their war ministries and ephebic corps,[2] and sent out their head magistrates in command of the field forces, as in the classical age. In the subject cities the war offices naturally lost much of their former importance, but in the older cities of Asia Minor at least the ephebi still received military instruction.

The question of food supply, which had already become urgent in classical times among the towns of the Aegean basin, eventually became one of the first charges upon the attention of municipal governments. In Athens the decrease of population during the third century rendered the problem of provisionment less pressing than formerly, save in times of siege ; but the people of the Aegean islands and of the west coast of Asia Minor, which were specializing more and more in the cultivation of vine and olive, became increasingly dependent on imported wheat. It therefore became the custom of many Aegean towns to regulate the trade in grain

[1] In Roman, and no doubt also in Hellenistic times, it had a citizen body of 6475 persons. See G. Plaumann, *Ptolemais in Oberägypten*, and *Archiv*, vol. VI, p. 176 ff.

[2] Numerous lists of ephebic year-classes from the towns of Bœotia have been preserved. See Michel, 618–39. On military training at Rhodes see Rostovtseff in *Cambr. Anc. Hist.*, VIII, p. 636 ff.

by law and to provide a board of "sitophylakes" or corn-wardens; and in times of emergency they set up special commissions to relieve the crisis. On such occasions the officials often tided over the difficulty by appealing to the generosity of the corn-dealers, who sometimes agreed to sell at less than the market price, or by raising subscriptions for a special purchase fund; others made up the difference between cost and sale price out of their own pockets. By the second century some towns had established a permanent fund (provided in the first instance by a call upon the wealthier citizens) for the importation of corn and its sale at easy rates.[1] In a few cities (e.g. Delos and Samos) provision was even made for free distributions at fixed intervals. Thus the Greek cities led the way in acknowledging the burgesses' right to subsist at the public expense. But whatever dangers these experiments in municipal socialism might have involved, they illustrate the vigour with which the Hellenistic cities could face their administrative problems, and the readiness for self-sacrifice in the common interest which its citizens could display.

If free corn was an innovation of Hellenistic times, free amusements were an old-established institution in Greek cities. But in the third and second centuries the rivalry between cities in providing public games and festivals was intensified, and new officials (ἀγωνοθέται, ἱεροποιοί) frequently appear as marshals of ceremonies. A notable addition to the duties of Greek cities in Hellenistic times was the superintendence of education (other than preparation for war). Herein the Hellenistic towns definitely surpassed those of the classical period, which had left literary and scientific training to private enterprise.

The finances of Hellenistic cities were eased by the somewhat lessened demands for war expenditure and by the curtailment of pay for public service. On the other hand, the costs of social services mounted up, and new taxes had to be paid into the royal treasuries in the monarchical states. The sources of regular income underwent little change. In

[1] See H. Francotte, *Le pain à bon marché et le pain gratuit dans les cités grecques.* (Mélanges Nicole, p. 135 ff.) At Samos a special corn purchase fund had been instituted by 246 (*Suppl. Epigr. Græcum*, I, p. 366) and was reorganized about 200 B.C. (Ditt., *Syll.*, 976.)

the Seleucid dominions towns with a large territory would derive a substantial rent from the native cultivators ; but the prejudice against a permanent property tax upon citizen landowners ran as strong as ever. Harbour towns like Rhodes which lay on important trade routes might collect an ample customs revenue ; but the resentment caused by the Byzantines in levying a transit toll at the Bosporus (p. 119) shows that there were strict limits to the yield of indirect taxation.

In financial administration it remained the custom to appropriate certain revenues to particular objects of expenditure. The disposal of sums not thus earmarked, and the levy of additional income, usually necessitated a special vote of Council or Assembly. At Athens a small committee of experts had been instituted about 350 B.C. to advise the Council and Assembly on financial policy. Under Demetrius of Phalerum the duties of this board were transferred to a single minister (ὁ ἐπὶ τῇ διοικήσει) ; but in the third century they were repeatedly put back into commission after a temporary return to individual management. The gathering of the revenue was usually left to private contractors ; but since these were mostly citizens, and in any case were kept under close supervision, they could not practise extortion on the scale of the Roman "publicani." The weakest point of the municipal finances lay in the lack of a budget and the absence of provision for accumulating reserves. Cities like Delos, which had a wealthy temple at beck and call, followed the example of fifth-century Athens in making loans from the sacred treasures ;[1] others borrowed from individual capitalists.[2] But the most typical device for covering a deficit was to make a call upon the more opulent burgesses, and this expedient often met with remarkable success. In Hellenistic cities there seems to have been no lack of public-spirited men, whether in office or in private life, who were equally ready to relieve a corn famine, to equip a flotilla, to repair the

[1] See the accounts of the Delian temple treasurers (e.g. Michel, 594, ll. 25 ff.).

[2] Examples from Miletus (*Milet,* I, 3, 138) ; Arcesine (Ditt., *Syll.*, 955) ; Orchomenus (*Brit. Mus. Inscrs.*, 158 ; Michel, 1362) ; another loan, from a wealthy woman, in Dareste-Haussoullier-Reinach, *Recueil des Inscriptions Juridiques grecques,* I, 14. These inscriptions show that private lenders often had trouble in securing punctual repayment.

town walls, or to ransom prisoners out of their own pockets.[1]

The constitution of most Hellenistic cities was democratic in outward form. The election of magistrates and the final decision on matters of policy rested with an Ecclesia comprising the whole citizen body and entitled by statute to be convened at regular intervals ; the principal lawsuits (subject to the restriction mentioned on p. 281) were submitted to dicasteries of common jurors ; the Council, whether elective or recruited by lot, was too large to become the preserve of a governing class. But in actual practice affairs usually fell into the hands of a few wealthy men who commended themselves by acts of generosity and on these terms secured the highest offices. In many towns the chief magistrates formed a *συναρχία* or cabinet whose corporate decisions were almost certain to be ratified by Council or Assembly. The government of the Hellenistic cities might therefore be described as plutocratic, and the methods by which rich men acquired political power were not far removed from collective bribery. Moreover, in the days of Polybius (*c.* 150 B.C.) an abuse had crept in, by which municipal officials recouped themselves for their outlay in buying public favour by embezzling the public funds. But this malpractice was probably a recent innovation, due to the impoverishment and demoralization of Greece consequent upon the Roman conquest. We need not doubt that in the third century at least wealthy donors expected no return save in power and popularity. Their administration resembled that of the municipia of the early Roman Principate rather than that of Rome under the late Republic.

§ 5. RELATIONS BETWEEN THE CITIES

The most pleasing feature in the history of the Hellenistic cities was their readiness to cultivate more friendly mutual relations. It is true that where Greek towns retained full liberty of action, they went on gratifying their indulgence in hereditary feuds. The tenacity of the traditions of mutual enmity is copiously illustrated by the numerous wars in the Greek Homeland, and especially by the never-ending conflict

[1] See esp. the " Protogenes " inscription from Olbia (Ditt., *Syll.*, 494), and the " Bulagoras " inscription from Samos (*S.E.G.*, I, 366).

between Sparta and Megalopolis. In Asia Minor neighbourly feuds were revived when the cities regained a free hand. Early in the second century Miletus celebrated its liberation under Roman auspices by engaging in wars with Magnesia-on-Mæander and Heraclea-on-Latmus.[1] In Crete active enmities between city and city survived to the end of the second century. About 220 B.C. the citizens of Drerus took oath that "they would do all manner of harm to those of Lyttus."[2] Yet in the Hellenistic period the tendencies which in classical times had acted as a curb on Greek animosities were heavily reinforced. In the realm of thought the cosmopolitan trend of the later Greek philosophers (ch. XX) acted as a solvent on traditional particularism. In practice, increased commercial intercourse broke down sentimental barriers between city and city. Above all, the decongestion of over-peopled districts by emigration, and the quickened consciousness of a common Hellenic nationality amid the subject Oriental populations, drew the sting out of many an ancient feud.

The growing solidarity of the Greek world was reflected in an increased exchange of courtesies between cities. Delegates from other towns were invited to the city festivals. In 206 Magnesia-on-Mæander summoned representatives from all Hellenedom to a new local holiday and received favourable replies from states as far apart as Epirus and Antioch-in-Persis.[3] The institution of a liaison service between towns by means of "proxeniæ" or consulships attained a development far exceeding that of the classical period, so that the proxeniæ came to cover the Greek world in a network which caught cities both great and small.[4] The very frequency of these covenants, it is true, shows that many of them must have been without practical effect; yet the mere conclusion of a proxenia pact helped to create an atmosphere of good will. Similarly the pacts of "asylia" by which contracting states bound their citizens not to enforce claims on each other by acts of reprisals must often have remained inoperative; but

[1] *Milet*, I, 3, 148, 150.

[2] Ditt., *Syll.*, 527; Michel, 23.

[3] *Magnesia*, nos. 18–64.

[4] Twenty-six proxenia pacts are preserved from Miletus (*Milet*, I, 3, 94–119), ten from the tiny city of Oropus (Michel, 207–216). A Delphic list of proxeniæ from 197 to 164 contains 133 names. (Ditt., *Syll.*, 585.)

they were a straw to show which way the wind was blowing.[1] A highly practical form of mutual aid consisted in the financial help rendered by one state to another. Kings and cities vied with each other to assist in the rebuilding of Thebes after 316 B.C.,[2] and an even greater competition in benevolence took place after the demolition of Rhodes by an earthquake (*c.* 225).[3]

Hellenistic cities guarded their franchise with less jealous care than the towns of the classical age. Too much stress perhaps should not be laid on the not infrequent cases in which whole batches of new citizens (usually ex-mercenaries) were created by a single act: such collective grants were sometimes conditional upon the payment of an entrance-fee, and in general they arose out of some special need to replenish the burgess-roll.[4] But a significant innovation was the practice by which one community conferred "isopoliteia" or rights of naturalization upon the citizens of another town. Though some of these grants were unilateral (as when Athens in 200 B.C. conferred potential franchise upon all Rhodians), more frequently the benefits were made reciprocal.[5] The most notable of the isopolity pacts was that which all the cities of Bœotia made with each other: in view of the past animosities of these towns, their all-round grant of franchise to each other marks an unusually rapid healing of an old feud.

A notable feature of Hellenistic politics is the increased recourse to arbitration for the composure of disputes between cities. This method of settling claims was naturally made compulsory upon towns enrolled in confederacies and upon the subjects of monarchies. But it also came into extended use among unattached cities, and even such unruly peoples as those of Crete made resort to it. Hence the number of recorded cases of arbitration in the third and second centuries

[1] Eighteen such treaties, all of the second century, are preserved from the small town of Teos. (Michel, 51–68.)

[2] Ditt., *Syll.*, 337.

[3] Polybius, V, 88–90.

[4] In 228–2 Miletus enfranchised over 1000 Cretans. (*Milet*, I, 3, 33–8.) Dyme sold its citizenship for one talent, payable in two instalments. (Ditt., *Syll.*, 531.)

[5] Two good examples survive in treaties made *c.* 323 B.C. by Miletus with her colonies Olbia and Cyzicus. (*Milet*, I, 3, 136–7.) Cf. also Ditt., *Syll.*, 443 (Chios and the Ætolian League); *ibid.*, 472 (Messene and Phigaleia); Ditt., *O.G.I.*, 265 (Pergamum and Temnos).

far exceeds those of the classical period.[1] In a few instances dissatisfied parties endeavoured to get round the arbitral award and ended by taking the matter to the Senate, which sometimes had much trouble in imposing a final settlement. In other cases the issues, though successfully closed, were trivial in themselves, such as small frontier adjustments. But the importance of the arbitral judgments lay not so much in the stakes as in the method of procedure, which was tantamount to a repudiation of war as a means of settling inter-city disputes. The Hellenistic Greeks were beginning to shake themselves free from the tyranny of communal vendettas.

Though cases of arbitration were sometimes referred to a king,[2] more often they went to a third city (ἔκκλητος πόλις), which appointed a special jury with full powers to make an award. A similar procedure for resolving deadlocks between private litigants within the same city came into common use in the Hellenistic world. The number of instances in which ξενόδικαι or visiting justices were called in, and the rapidity with which they worked off arrears of litigation, offer one of the most pleasant surprises of Hellenistic history. At Calymna in Caria a board of five judges from Iasus disposed of over 250 suits.[3] In the third and second centuries Priene sent out at least thirteen such tribunals[4] and Delphi received not less than ten between 156 and 131.[5] At Magnesia-on-Mæander arrangements were made for regular assizes by foreign arbitrators at six months' interval.[6] In spite of the full dockets of the itinerant justices, it need not be assumed that there was any general breakdown of the municipal tribunals. The suits reserved for their hearing probably consisted in the main of disputes about property which remained over as a legacy from former faction-fights, for such cases would be peculiarly difficult for a domestic court to settle to the general

[1] Of the cases recorded in inscriptions, three are previous to 338, twenty-two belong to the third century, twenty-four fall between 200 and 146. (Tod, *International Arbitration among the Greeks.*) Raeder (*L'arbitrage international chez les Hellènes*) mentions twelve instances prior to 338 and thirty-two from 338 to 100. On the whole subject see esp. Tod, *op. cit.*

[2] King Lysimachus pronounced in person upon a dispute between Samos and Priene. (*Brit. Mus. Inscrs.*, 403.)

[3] Hicks, 130 ; Michel, 417.

[4] Priene, *passim.*

[5] H. Pomtow, *Klio*, vol. 18, p. 259 ff.

[6] *Magnesia*, 99.

satisfaction. An incidental but hardly less useful result of the visits of the itinerant justices was that they gave an impetus to the standardization of municipal codes. Though in particular instances they were required to apply the statutes of some specified city, more usually they followed the general rules of equity and thus helped to lay the foundations of a Greek "ius gentium." The incipient unification of Greek civil law in Hellenistic times is illustrated by the fact that the mercantile code of Rhodes came into general use in Greek courts for the trial of maritime actions.

A further sign of a change of heart in the Hellenistic cities was the readiness with which they tendered their good offices in the negotiation of peace treaties. During the siege of Rhodes in 305–4 Demetrius was himself besieged by successive delegations from Greek cities, and he finally capitulated to the Ætolians. In 218–7, and again in 209–6, it was the turn of the Rhodians to interpose between the Ætolians and the kings of Macedon (pp. 166, 186). In the second century, despite the fact that the Roman Senate was now becoming the general arbiter in Greek disputes, Greek cities again and again offered their services as peacemakers. Though the Hellenistic world moved too late and too slowly towards a national union, it made progress in that direction.

§ 6. FEDERATIONS: THE AMPHICTIONIC AND ÆTOLIAN LEAGUES

In the Greek Homeland the main problem of inter-city relations now turned upon the institution of some durable league in which the towns might salvage as much as possible of their municipal autonomy and yet acquire habits of regular co-operation. Beyond any doubt the solution lay in a permanent union of the cities in a federal state. In 338–7 B.C. Philip II of Macedon had created a confederacy which had the merit of being practically all-inclusive; but after the death of Alexander this league broke into fragments, and the work of integration had to be done over again.

Of the older district-federations, the Bœotian League lived on, and thanks to the decline of Thebes (which never recovered its old preponderance) it finally overcame the mutual jealousy between that town and the lesser cities which had formerly endangered federal stability. But if the Bœotians finally set their house in order, they never threw it wide open to their neighbours. Their League remained essentially sectional, and in the Hellenistic age it did not attain more than local importance.

Another old institution, the Amphictionic League of Delphi, formed a better nucleus for a more general confederacy. It drew its membership from the greater part of Northern and Central Greece, and as the custodian of the Delphic sanctuary it could make its voice heard all over Greece. But its occasional incursions into the politics of Greece had not added to its prestige. It is significant that Philip II of Macedon won his footing in Greece as the champion of the Delphic sanctuary, yet rejected the League as a foundation-stone for his general Greek confederation. Similarly in the third century the Ætolians became protectors-in-chief of Delphi and obtained complete control of the Amphictionic Council (pp. 131–2), yet made but sparing use of it.[1]

A new impetus was given to the formation of Greek leagues after the death of Alexander. Between 320 and 314 the Ætolians, having replaced their villages by fortified towns, made these into the constituent units of a new confederacy which supplanted their previous tribal union. In answer to this move their Acarnanian neighbours also built walled towns and modernized their cantonal association. In 314 the "League of the Islanders" (the Cyclades) came into being. These organizations, it is true, were of a very diverse order of importance. The Island League was *octroyé* upon the islanders by Antigonus I, and passed successively under the tutelage of the Ptolemies, the Antigonids and of Rhodes. Like the maritime leagues of Athens, it was at the mercy of the predominant naval power of the day, and it did not even possess the semblance of free initiative. It lacked an Ecclesia, and its council was convened by the representative of the suzerain power, such as the Ptolemaic or Rhodian "nesiarch," who chiefly used it to sanction his demands for financial or naval aids. The Acarnanian League, though self-created and independent, never extended beyond its original boundaries.

[1] The Ætolians placed their treaties of "asylia" under the sanction of the Amphictiones. But this was little more than a gesture.

The Ætolian League, on the other hand, broke its tribal barriers and since 278 incorporated the other states of Central Greece, until its territory extended from the western to the eastern sea. The government of the Ætolian League was solely concerned with military and foreign policy, and it left the local liberties of its constituent states virtually intact. It established a federal monopoly of coinage, but since none of its members had much commerce this restriction could not have borne hard upon them. The federal parliament met but twice a year; the autumn congress took place regularly at the sanctuary of Thermum in Ætolia, the spring conference moved from town to town. In accordance with the usual Greek federal practice, Parliament contained an Ecclesia to which all citizens of the participating states were admitted, and a Council of deputies from the constituent units, which sent members in proportion to the strength of their military contingents. The Ecclesia elected the federal officers and gave the final decision on questions of high policy; it is not known whether the voting was by individuals or (as seems more probable) by cities. The Council both exercised the usual deliberative functions of such a body, and was the court of criminal jurisdiction for offenders against the federal statutes. But as its membership was increased with the accession of new states until it exceeded one thousand, it became too unwieldy for debate. For this reason, and because of the infrequency of its meetings, it delegated its authority to an executive committee named the "apocleti" (seemingly about a hundred in number), which remained in constant touch with the federal officials. In contrast with the Council, the executive was reduced to the smallest possible proportions, so as to comprise nothing but a secretariate and a few military officers under a single strategus.[1] The danger of this sole general making himself into a dictator was parried by the provision that he might not hold office in successive years. So far as is known, the League exercised no general judicial functions and possessed no special courts of law.

Under this form of government the Ætolian League avoided the two chief dangers besetting a Greek federation,

[1] In the Hellenistic age the advantages of a single generalissimo over a board came to be generally recognized. At Athens the στρατηγὸς ἐπὶ τὰ ὅπλα became *ex officio* the field commander.

the excessive restriction of local self-government among its members, and the exploitation of the lesser states in favour of one preponderant city or group. The limitation of the federal congresses to two annual sessions made it practically impossible for parliament to go beyond its primary and legitimate functions. The risk of a single city turning tyrant over the others was never serious in the Ætolian League, because it possessed no urban centres of any importance. The real peril lay in the chance that the original Ætolian members of the League should endeavour to treat the later comers as subjects rather than partners, or should be suspected of such intentions. But the federal constitution removed this risk by ensuring adequate representation to all states of the Council—to the detriment of the Council's efficiency as a debating body—and by throwing open its general assembly and its executive posts to all its citizens.

The general bad record of the Ætolian League is no proof of weakness in its consitution. Given the predatory habits of the Ætolians themselves and of others of its members, no conceivable scheme of government could have ensured that the League should be put to honest uses. The Ætolian constitution was a well-built engine in the hands of a reckless driver.

§ 7. FEDERATIONS: THE ACHÆAN LEAGUE

In 251 B.C. the Achæans followed the example of the Ætolians in throwing open their league to all applicants; by 191 they had extended it over the whole of Peloponnesus. Their federal constitution bore a general resemblance to that of the Ætolians, but contained variations of detail. It provided for spring and autumn sessions of a parliament consisting of a primary assembly and a council of Deputies (contributed by the constituent cities in proportion to their military strength), whose functions were substantially the same as those of their Ætolian counterparts. The high military command, which until 255 had been vested in two strategi, was from that year conferred upon a single general, who was re-eligible every second year only. The Achæan League placed somewhat heavier restrictions upon the governments of its constituent cities. Instead of closing the local mints, it merely required them to conform to a certain type and standard of weight. But it obliged the cities to remodel their executives on the pattern of the towns of Achæa Proper, where the head magistrates always consisted of a board of "damiurgi." In addition to these local magistrates, it provided for the election of a board of ten federal damiurgi, who came to form an inner advisory committee like the Ætolian apocleti. It further allowed the summoning of parliament at extraordinary sessions on any sudden emergency. At these additional meetings the Council was invariably in attendance; in a serious crisis the Ecclesia would also be convoked. But membership of the Ecclesia was seemingly limited to men above thirty.[1]

The Achæan constitution earned the highest measure of praise from the historian Polybius, who saw in it a truly democratic system of government and an ideal combination of liberty, equality and fraternity. In view of the League's actual record this glowing tribute may appear to us as the product of a somewhat naïve patriotism. Yet the Achæan Confederacy had at least the merit that, in common with the Ætolian League, it held together a considerable group of Greek cities in such a way as to keep the peace among them without undue curtailment of their local autonomy, and without giving to any of its constituents an opportunity of tyrannizing over the rest. Its worst failure was that it could not wholly achieve the most important ideal in the republican trinity, fraternity. Yet it eventually won the full allegiance of all Peloponnesian cities save Sparta, the most intractable of all Greek states. In the main, it acted as a stabilizing force in Peloponnesus, and it may be regretted that it did not get into its full stride before the destiny of Greece passed into the hands of Rome.

[1] The above description differs in some respects from that given by A. Aymard, *Les assemblées de la confédération achéenne.*

Addendum.—For recent work on the relations between kings and cities, see esp. A. Heuss, *Stadt und Herrscher des Hellenismus*; A. H. M. Jones, *The Greek City*, pt. II, ch. 6; Tarn, *The Greeks in Bactria and India*, ch. 2.—The present general tendency is to maintain that the cities (in theory at least) possessed a large measure of autonomy.

CHAPTER XVI

HELLENISTIC ECONOMIC LIFE

§ 1. GENERAL EFFECT OF ALEXANDER'S CONQUESTS

PREVIOUS to the conquests of Alexander, the Greek world had been living in a state of economic stagnation, or even of slight recession.[1] But Alexander's campaigns gave the Greeks access to an abundance of fresh land and unexplored markets, and brought them an almost embarrassing profusion of gold and silver. Alexander's haul of Persian treasure, which is estimated to have amounted, in specie alone, to 170- or 180,000 talents, furnished all the capital required by the Greeks to develop the estate into which they were entering, and quite relieved them of that besetting difficulty of settlers in new lands, lack of ready money. Indeed, the first effect of putting the Persian hoards into circulation was an unpleasantly sharp rise in prices. But this upward movement was compensated by a steady fall which lasted through the first half of the third century, during which the surplus funds were gradually absorbed into capital.[2]

The substitution of a few large monarchies or federal states for a multiplicity of city-states, and the increasing tendency to friendly co-operation among the individual cities, removed many political obstacles to trade. A further lowering of economic barriers was effected by the reduction in the number of mints and of the variety of coin-standards. A great impetus to the unification of coin-weights had been given when Alexander issued a new imperial money on the Attic standard, and this norm was subsequently adopted by the

[1] For evidence of a shrinkage in oversea markets during the fourth century, see Rostovtzeff, *op. cit.*, I, p. 90 ff.

[2] On the price-curves of the third century, see Tarn in Bury, *The Hellenistic Age*, ch. 4; F. M. Heichelheim, *Wirtschaftsgeschichte des Altertums*, vol. I, ch. 7.

Antigonid, the Attalid and the Seleucid monarchies. The Ptolemies abandoned Alexander's standard for that of the Phœnicians, which was firmly established on the Levantine coasts, and the Peloponnesians held fast to the old Æginetan norm. Under these conditions the money-changer could not yet be wholly dispensed with, but he was no longer needed at every turn.

Lastly, aristocratic contempt for economic enterprise, which had lingered on in many Greek states before the Macedonian conquest, was thoroughly dispelled in the Hellenistic age. In a few corners of Greece such as Thessaly or Elis sedentary squires might carry on the tradition of the self-contained estate; but such habits of mind could only survive where people remained rooted to the soil, and in the general upheaval which followed Alexander's conquests the spirit of commercial adventure carried everything before it. This change of attitude is well illustrated in Ptolemy II, the grandson of a Macedonian baron, who would have agreed with Vespasian that money, from whatever source, smells delicious. If Ptolemy II ever had a rival in the race for profits, it was in his own financial minister Apollonius, who doubled or rather blended the part of a high official with that of an entrepreneur on a royal scale. In the numerous surviving papyri which illustrate his activities Apollonius appears as an improving landlord on several large estates in Egypt and Syria, as the owner of a textile factory at Memphis and of two distinct fleets for the conveyance of his merchandise along the Nile or between Egypt and Syria.[1]

§ 2. GEOGRAPHICAL EXPLORATION

The quest for wealth in Hellenistic times gave an impetus to fresh exploration beyond the limits attained by Alexander. In the course of his travels the Macedonian king had picked up clues to further discoveries which he was planning to follow up at the time of his death. His schemes included a search for a more commodious route between India and the Black Sea lands so as to avoid the laborious climb across the Iranian plateau. The hope of finding such a route was

[1] *P. Zeno Cairo* and *P.S.I.*, IV–VII, *passim*. Cf. also *P Cornell*, I (ed. W. L. Westermann and C. J. Kraemer), which contains an extract from Apollonius' private accounts.

fostered by the belief that the Oxus (Amu-Daria) or Iaxartes (Syr-Daria) and the Tanais (Don) formed a continuous waterway between Turkestan and the Black Sea. By order of Seleucus I this theory was tested by two officers named Demodamas and Patrocles, of whom the former was told to work his way down the Iaxartes, while Patrocles sailed northward up the Caspian Sea. From the silence enshrouding the results of Demodamas' expedition it may be gathered that he reported unfavourably on the chances of through travel to Europe. Patrocles, on the other hand, announced that the Caspian Sea received both the great rivers from Turkestan.[1] Seleucus was thus encouraged to plan a canal from Black Sea to Caspian, so as to complete the suppose water-route to India. But the loss of northern Asia Minor after his death caused his successors to lose interest in the northern trade routes. Alexander's plans for the circumnavigation of Arabia, which his admiral Nearchus was about to carry into effect at the time of his death, were lost out of sight after 323. The Ptolemies eventually opened up the whole of the Red Sea (pp. 80–1); but the Seleucids showed little interest in the navigation of the Persian Gulf, and the belated exploration of these waters by an admiral of Antiochus IV named Numenius was rendered abortive by the subsequent expulsion of the Seleucids from Babylonia.

A promising beginning of discovery in the Indian Ocean was made *c.* 120 B.C., when Ptolemy VII found a Hindu sailor at Alexandria who knew the law of the monsoons and was willing to reveal the secrets of the open-sea route to India to the Greeks. Under the Hindu's guidance a captain named Eudoxus[2] made the trip to India, and a few years later he repeated the journey, apparently without his Hindu pilot, at the instance of Cleopatra III. But a quarrel with the queen about his share in the proceeds of the venture induced Eudoxus to abandon the Ptolemaic service, and his subse-

[1] Patrocles was probably deceived by an arm of Khiva Bay, which in his time may have reached to the neighbourhood of the Aral Sea. (Tarn, *The Greeks in Bactria and India*, pp. 488–90.)

On Oriental exploration in general during the Hellenistic period, see E. H. Warmington in Cary and Warmington, *The Ancient Explorers*, chs. 4 and 7.

[2] On Eudoxus' Indian ventures, see J. H. Thiel, *Eudoxus van Cyzicus*; Otto-Bengtson, *op. cit.*, p. 194 ff.

quent disappearance in an attempt to circumnavigate Africa from the Straits of Gibraltar (pp. 290–1) robbed the Greeks of the fruits of his discoveries in eastern waters. Whether Eudoxus' Indian cruises were followed up in Ptolemaic times remains a matter for discussion.[1]

The discoveries of Alexander in the East had their counterpart at the other extreme of the Greek world. Towards the end of the fourth century (probably *c.* 310–6 B.C.) the merchants of Massilia organized an expedition to the lands of the North Atlantic, the main object of which was to open up the trade route to the sources of Atlantic tin. The leader of the venture, a Massilian citizen named Pytheas, slipped past the Carthaginian guardships at the Straits of Gibraltar, felt his way along the Spanish and French coasts as far as Brittany, and put across from that point to Cornwall, where he observed the natives at work in the stannaries.[2] From Cornwall he set sail round Britain, making occasional excursions inland and taking note of the country's resources. Finally, he followed the continental coast as far as Heligoland, where he found the former depôt of the forgotten trade in Jutish amber. In the extent of his explorations Pytheas takes rank with Alexander, yet his Grand Tour was as barren of results as Alexander's was momentous. The very wealth of information which he brought back raised doubts as to his veracity, and no opportunity was given to the Massiliotes to test his report by a second expedition, for the Carthaginians let no other interloper through. The only tangible result of his journey was an increase in the overland traffic in Cornish tin and a more intensive penetration of France by Massiliote prospectors, who opened up the various river routes across the continent in the third and second centuries.[3]

At the end of the second century the traders of Massilia combined with those of Puteoli (a Roman colony with a Greek trading population) and of Gades (now no longer a Carthaginian gate-house) to equip Eudoxus for his projected voyage round Africa. Out of their funds the ancient Vasco da Gama fitted out two ships with the elaborate care of a modern polar

[1] See addendum on p. 306.

[2] A brief description of British tin-mining, evidently derived from Pytheas, survives in Diodorus, V, 22. On Pytheas in general, see G. E. Broche, *Pythéas le Massaliote.*

[3] Cary, *Journ. Hell. Stud.*, 1924, p. 166 ff.

explorer, and started out with seemingly adequate provision for a journey of several years. But his venture was dogged with misfortune from the outset. After several false starts he sailed out into the unknown and was held there: his ultimate fate is uncertain.[1]

§ 3. AGRICULTURE

Hellenistic agriculture derived a considerable stimulus from the great increase in the knowledge of plants and herbs that followed upon Alexander's conquests. This new information was reproduced in systematic form in the botanical works of Theophrastus, which in turn gave rise to an extensive literature of practical manuals. The kings of Pergamum were the chief patrons of the technical authors on husbandry, but the principal field of practical experiment was in Egypt, where the first two Ptolemies proved themselves the greatest land-improvers in Greek history.[2] In addition to the maintenance of existing dykes and canals the Ptolemies carried out extensive reclamations in districts which had fallen into neglect under Persian rule. Their greatest undertaking was the construction of a canal and sluice, by which Nile water could be conveyed across a low intervening ridge to the Fayum, the basin of a dried-out lake near Memphis.[3] By this engineering exploit they reclaimed a large expanse of irrigable land, which became the principal area of settlement for Greek husbandmen: of the hundred villages which sprang up in it, more than half bore Greek names. On this land, and wherever else wastes were reclaimed, the cultivators received rights of hereditary tenancy and paid reduced taxes during the first years of their lease. Their subsequent taxation was so adjusted as to encourage irrigation by

[1] The doubts expressed by Strabo (bk. II, pp. 99–102) as to the credibility of this story have been set aside by Warmington (*op. cit.*, pp. 99–102) and Thiel (*op. cit.*, p. 30 ff.).

[2] See M. Schnebel, *Die Landwirtschaft im hellenistischen Ägypten*; F. M. Heichelheim, *op. cit.*, I, pp. 576–622.

[3] The history of the Fayum has been reconstructed in the light of a geological investigation. See Miss G. Caton Thompson and Miss E. W. Gardner, *The Desert Fayum*.

Frequent mention is made in the Zeno papyri of reclamation by ξυλοκοπία and ἐκπυρισμός (*P.S.* 1. III, 338–9; IV, 499–500).

trenching or, if necessary, by water-hoisting.[1] Within the Fayum district Apollonius undertook to develop a Bonanza farm of 4000 acres, which he provided with some fifty miles of irrigation-canal.[2]

The Ptolemies allowed the native fellahin, or *βασιλικοὶ γεωργοί*, to retain their holdings, and did not interfere with their traditional system of cultivation. The Egyptian method of tillage, which was based on a simple rotation of wheat (on the prepared land) and vegetables (on the fallow), was well suited to the conditions of the country, and had enabled it to export grain before the Greek conquest. But the Greek government kept the peasantry under strict supervision. It prescribed the acreage to be tilled for each kind of crop ; it stocked the arable farms and supplied seed from pedigree plants,[3] exacting an oath from the cultivators that they would use none other ; and it required them to remain on their land from sowing to harvest. Those who disobeyed these rules were liable to summary eviction, for the natives were not given a fixed lease, but held their plots by a precarious tenancy. In addition to this superintendence of routine cultivation the Ptolemies made experiments with improved seeds on selected plots. On Apollonius' estate an attempt was made, apparently at Ptolemy II's initiative, to raise a main crop of barley and a catch-crop of " three-month wheat " between January and June.[4]

Before the Macedonian conquest the pastoral industry of Egypt had been of small importance, despite the abundance of suitable grazing land and the mild winter climate, which rendered stall-feeding quite unnecessary. Under the Ptolemies, who had special need of mounts for their cavalry and of wool for their textile factories, pasturage underwent great extension and improvement. In the Fayum wide tracts of irrigation land were turned into ranches and sown with artificial grasses. The herds, which were provided by the king

[1] On irrigation in Ptolemaic Egypt see W. L. Westermann, *Classical Philology*, 1920, 1922–3.

[2] For a plan of this estate, with estimate of costs of new works, see *P. Lille*, I, 1.

[3] For examples of seed distribution cf. *P. Lille*, I, 5 ; *P. Rylands*, II, 72.

[4] *P. Zeno Cairo*, 59155. The three-month wheat may have been Indian (so Schnebel), or more probably from Syria. (H. A. Thompson, *Archiv für Papyrologie*, IX, p. 207 ff.)

and remained royal property, were kept up to a high standard by the importation of Milesian rams and other pedigree animals;[1] the herdsmen too were largely drawn from Greek lands.

But the Ptolemies, in true Greek fashion, gave special attention to plantation husbandry. In order to encourage the formation of vineyards and olive groves, they granted heritable leases and reduced taxation to settlers who would undertake to convert reclamation-land into orchards. They imposed a frankly protectionist tariff—an unusual instrument of finance in ancient times—on luxury oils and wines from Greece, and prohibited importation of such brands as Egypt itself might produce. Greek colonists accordingly introduced the vine into every part of Egypt, and acclimatized the olive more particularly in the Fayum. Among the most zealous planters was Apollonius, who laid out a large nursery at Memphis and stocked his other estates with its produce. Besides transplanting many varieties of garden fruit and at least eleven species of vine, he made an attempt to establish standings of fir-timber for the benefit of the Alexandrian shipyards.[2]

In the Seleucid and Attalid monarchies the cultivation of the arable lands was left in the hands of the natives, who might be peasant proprietors or (as commonly in Asia Minor) serf tenants. But wherever Greek colonists went they took the vine with them, so that viticulture became a flourishing industry as far east as Persia.[3] The cultivation of vine and olive also prospered in the older centres of the Aegean area: indeed, the vintages of Thasos, of Cnidus, of Cos and of Rhodes, and the oil of the west coast of Asia Minor, never enjoyed a greater reputation.[4] The finest brands overtopped the tariff wall of Egypt; eventually they found their way to the courts of Indian rajahs. The rougher sorts of wine had a ready sale in the Balkan lands, where the Greek merchant of strong drink became a familiar figure.

[1] *Ibid.*, 59195, 59430.

[2] See esp. *P. Zeno Cairo*, 59156–62. In no. 59221 Zeno receives an order to plant 20,000 saplings.

[3] For Greek vine-planting in Babylonia and Susiana see Strabo, XV, pp. 731–2.

[4] Rhodian wine-amphoræ in considerable numbers have been found in Sicily, on the Black Sea coasts, and in Susiana.

§ 4. MANUFACTURES

Among the various forms of production manufacturing probably underwent the fewest alterations in the Hellenistic period.[1] Despite the influx of Persian money into Greek lands, social fashions passed through no profound change, and the scientific discoveries of the age had little effect on technical processes. The only notable inventions were by-products of the genius of Archimedes, the "Archimedean screw," which served to raise water from mines, and the compound pulley. The staple of Greek craft production was still its fine ceramic ware (with moulded instead of painted decorations), though this was partly displaced by glass ware and silver plate. Besides silver ware, fashion also created a greater demand for textiles of the finer sort. Though wool remained the standard dress material, silk came into favour, and a new clothing industry was established at Cos, where thread was spun from the wild silk-worm of Asia Minor. The spread of education and of the habit of reading caused a great increase in the production of papyrus and of books. Among the heavy industries quarrying and building received an impetus wherever Greek colonies were founded or Oriental cities were reconstructed in Greek style,

While the articles of manufacture underwent little change. there was a considerable displacement in the seats of industry. In the Greek Homeland Athens remained the chief centre of the ceramic industry until *c.* 250 ; but little is heard in Hellenistic times of Corinthian bronze ware. Among the Italian Greeks the Tarentines held their own as producers of fine textiles, and they introduced the new style of moulded and ribbed pottery into the western world. Among the Italian Greeks the Tarentines held their own as producers of fine textile wares and carried on the manufacture of fine pottery which had gone out of fashion in other parts of the Greek world. Among the older towns of Asia Minor Miletus benefited by the demand for good cloths and retained her industrial ascendancy ; but new textile centres were established at Pergamum, whose kings took a personal interest in the weaving industry, and at Laodicea-ad-Lycum, which lay close to the Phrygian downs, the chief source of the weavers'

[1] On Hellenistic industry, see Rostovtzeff, *op. cit., passim* ; Heichelheim, *op. cit.*, I, pp. 576–89.

raw materials. The busiest of all the manufacturing towns was Alexandria, where a regular fever of work laid hold of the population. In addition to the paper-making industry, of which it held a natural monopoly, it developed the old Egyptian crafts of casting and cutting glass, and of ornamentation with coloured metal glazes ; it became the chief centre of toreutic art in silver, while its bric-à-brac permeated the villages of Egypt and was exported as far as the Black Sea. Glass and silver crafts had another important centre in Syria. Thus the prevailing tendency in the Hellenistic period was for industry to spread from Greece Proper to the Levantine capitals.

The effect of the Macedonian conquest upon native eastern industries may best be studied in Egypt. Here a system of village manufactures with highly specialized craftsmen and firmly organized gilds was in existence. In addition, a variety of manufactures, notably that of linen-weaving, was carried on under the direction of the priests. The Greek immigration made little difference to the native methods of production. It is noteworthy that the native workers, who were either small masters or free wage-earners, were not displaced to any extent by slave labour under Greek direction. Apollonius, it is true, operated a textile factory at Memphis with unfree workers imported from Syria ; but in the Fayum the same employer gave out wool-work to free Egyptians at piece rates, and we may doubt whether his experiment with slave labour was long-lived.[1] But if native industries were not much disturbed by competition from Greek capitalists, they were brought under a strict government control. A large number of Egyptian industries were converted into monopolies, under which all manufacturers had to pay a special licence, while some (e.g. the wool-workers) were required to concede a right of pre-emption to the State. The production of oil was wholly forbidden save in the government's own factories, where the workers were tied down to their task like serfs and kept under the most rigid supervision.[2] A

[1] I here follow Westermann (*Upon Slavery in Ancient Egypt*) and Wilcken (*Griechische Ostraka*, I, p. 681 ff.) against Rostovtseff (*Cambr. Anc. Hist.*, VII, p. 135). Since slaves could only be imported into Egypt by special licence (*P. Zeno Cairo*, 59093), it may be assumed that the Ptolemies discouraged their use.

[2] See *Rev. Law*, col. 38 ff.

similar system was applied in quarries and mines, where the labourers were indentured to remain at their posts for stated periods. In the gold mines of Nubia men and women of all ages were chained together and kept to their work under the lash till they thankfully dropped dead.[1] But no general conclusions can be drawn from this nightmare, for the workers were prisoners of war and convicts, like the "damnati in metalla" of the Roman mines.

The Ptolemaic experiment of operating factories with government capital was imitated at Pergamum, where the Attalids manufactured fine textiles by the labour of state slaves. Probably, too, the parchment industry which they set up to break the Egyptian monopoly of papyrus was an instance of direct state enterprise. The Hellenistic world also offers several examples of municipal socialism. The city of Miletus—perhaps in anticipation of the kings of Pergamum—owned its textile workshops and their slave-weavers. Rhodes and Cnidus produced in municipal factories the jars which their merchants required for their extensive export trade in wine. Even Sparta engaged in municipal industry, for the tiles used by the tyrant Nabis for the strengthening of the city walls were baked at a public kiln.

§ 5. TRANSPORT

The economic progress made in the Hellenistic period is seen most clearly in the history of its commerce. The age was one of intensified traffic, for not only were the political obstacles lessened, but its natural difficulties were reduced by technical improvements. It is true that communications by land were not much developed by the Hellenistic governments. In Greece metalled roads remained as rare as ever. In Asia the Seleucids and Attalids maintained and at points extended the fine trunk roads of the Persian empire. In Egypt the Ptolemies furnished the desert tracks between Nile and Red Sea with dak-bungalows, water-points and police pickets; they organized a special corps of teamsters for the caravans, and they made experiments with camel-transport.[2]

[1] See the gruesome description in Diodorus, III, 12.

[2] A camel-post is mentioned in *P. Oxyrh.*, IV, 710 (111 B.C.). The introduction of camels into Egypt was probably due to Ptolemy II. (*P. Zeno Cairo*, 59143, 59207.)

But the road-work of Hellenistic kings is not to be compared with that of Roman emperors.

On the other hand, Hellenistic governments expended considerable care on their harbours. At Alexandria a bleak roadstead was converted into a safe and commodious meeting-point for Mediterranean and Nile traffic. On the inland side a fresh-water lake fed by an arm of the Nile was connected by a new cut with the Mediterranean; on the sea-front a mole was built to the off-shore island of Pharos, so as to provide a sheltered basin on either side. On the island Ptolemy I's architect Sostratus erected the famous lighthouse, a huge tower from whose summit a flare of pine-wood, projected seaward by lenses, marked the site of the harbour at a distance, it is said, of over thirty miles.[1] Though the sea-walls of Alexandria found no rival in the ancient Mediterranean, save at Ostia under the Roman emperors, they were copied on a smaller scale at numerous other Greek ports.[2] Towns situated at a natural sea-inlet ran out breakwaters from either side of the bay and extended the city-walls on to these, so as to make the harbours proof against weather and pirates. The improved accommodation thus provided made it practicable for Hellenistic shipwrights to increase the displacement of their craft, so that vessels capable of carrying 10,000 talents (250 tons) became normal for cargo-transport. A further aid to navigation was provided by Timosthenes, an admiral of Ptolemy II, who wrote a practical manual "On Harbours," as a predecessor to our "Mediterranean Pilots."[3] Despite better conditions of seafaring, the Greeks continued to lay up their ships for the winter; but in the summer they ventured out more freely than before on open seas and unfamiliar routes.

By their conquest of Egypt and Mesopotamia the Greeks came into possession of two natural centres of river-traffic.

[1] Josephus, *Bell. Jud.*, IV, 10, 5. It has been suggested by Wilamowitz-Moellendorff (*Hellenistische Dichtung*, p. 154, n. 2) that Sostratus did not design the Pharos but paid for it as a special "liturgy." But could any private person of Hellenistic times have defrayed its cost of 800 talents out of his private pocket?

[2] See Lehmann-Hartleben, *Antike Hafenanlagen*.

[3] Part of Timosthenes' work is probably preserved in the *Stadiasmus Maris Magni* (C. Müller, *Geographici Græci Minores*, I, p. 427 ff.), a competent survey of the Mediterranean coasts, probably dating from the third century A.D.

On the Euphrates the Seleucids did not proceed with Alexander's grandiose scheme of harbour works at Babylon; but they founded a busy river-port at Seleucia-on-Tigris, to which even Indiamen had access. In Egypt the Ptolemies found a ready-made system of inland navigation, and under their rule much of the traffic remained in native hands. But the Nile now became much more than a vehicle for local commerce. It carried the surplus produce of Egypt, and the merchandise brought by caravans from the Red Sea, to Alexandria for consumption or re-export. The fleets required for this augmented river-traffic were partly provided by the kings themselves, who hired out their shipping to private skippers (like the Venetian Republic in the later Middle Ages),[1] partly by private capitalists like Apollonius.

In the West the Carthaginians kept their general monopoly of sea-borne trade; and after 200 B.C. the semi-Italian town of Puteoli displaced Tarentum and Syracuse as the chief mart for eastern trade with Italy. Delos displaced Athens as the principal clearing centre of the Aegean area, and became an important entrepôt for the trade in grain. Greek commerce with the Black Sea remained brisk in the third century,[2] for despite competition from Egypt Russian grain still found good markets in the Aegean lands, but it eventually fell off when the cultivation of the corn-lands was endangered by invasions from the hinterland (pp. 116–17). The chief gainers by the new economic order were the stations on the trade routes to the East. At the entrance to the Aegean Ephesus acquired a new importance as the main terminus of the overland roads from the Asiatic continent, and Rhodes became a focus of sea-borne trade from the Levant to the Aegean, the Black Sea, and Sicily.[3] Alexandria made one fortune by exporting the overplus of Egypt, another as the entrepôt between the Mediterranean and eastern waters. On the Syrian coast Tyre and Sidon, though overshadowed by Alexandria, retained a share of

[1] According to *P. Petrie*, III, 107, the king took three-quarters, the skipper one-quarter of the fares and freights.

[2] The coins of Panticapæum found between the Altai and the Tien-Shan ranges (Rostovtseff, *Cambr. Anc. Hist.*, VIII, p. 653) may indicate Hellenistic trade with China; but they may be mere loot.

[3] Evidence of this trade survives in copious and widely scattered finds of wine jars with official Rhodian stamps.

the Arabian and Indian trades travelling overland. The commercial development of Antioch was stifled in the third century by the loss of its port of Seleucia to the Ptolemies; but in the second it assumed its natural function as the terminal point of traffic from Mesopotamia and opened a brisk trade with the Aegean area. Seleucia-on-Tigris supplanted Babylon as a distributing centre for water-borne traffic from the Persian Gulf; under the Roman empire it became an important station on the trans-continental routes to India and China, but it is probable that these were not systematically opened in the Hellenistic period.[1] The destruction of Corinth in 146 removed one of the oldest of Greek commercial centres, but its trade was diverted rather than suppressed. In the later second century the Piræus enjoyed a Martinmas summer of prosperity; Delos became a rendezvous for merchants from Palestine and even from Arabia, and the collecting-point for the slave traffic to Italy.

A rough index of the relative volumes of Hellenistic and of classical Greek commerce is furnished by the fact that the customs revenue of Rhodes *c.* 170 B.C. was five-fold that of Athens in 400 (the rate of duty in either case being probably 2 per cent). Athenian trade, it is true, was then in a "slump"; even so, this figure proves that Hellenistic trade was on a different scale from that of the preceding period.[2]

§ 6. MONEY-DEALING

In Hellenistic times the increase in the circulation of money more than kept pace with the growth of commerce.[3] Before the conquests of Alexander the Near East had but a slight acquaintance with coined money. Even at Tyre and at Sidon a mint was not set up until the fourth century; and the Persian darics which were not pocketed by Greek mercenaries mostly remained stacked in the treasure-houses. After Alexander's campaigns vast masses of gold and silver from the Persian hoards were coined or recoined in Greek mints. The consequent introduction of a money economy into the

[1] Syrian stuffs have been found in Mongolia (Rostovtseff, *Cambr. Anc. Hist.*, VII, p. 174); but these cannot be proved of Seleucid date. On the Chinese trade, see p. 73.

[2] Beloch, *Griech. Gesch.*, IV, pt. 1, p. 299–300.

[3] On Hellenistic money-dealing, see Heichelheim, *op. cit.*, pp. 550–69.

conquered countries can be clearly traced in Egypt. Under the Ptolemies the rents of the peasants and a few other imposts were still delivered *in natura*, and part payment of salaries to officials and of wages to workmen was made in land or produce. But as the stock of coins increased the government proceeded to pay and to collect most of its debts in money.

With this diffusion of money economy went a growth in the importance of money-dealers. In the fourth century Greek banking had hardly passed the rudimentary stage of money-changing and petty usury: only at Athens and a few great temples was money borrowed and lent on any considerable scale. The extent to which banks multiplied in the Hellenistic age is somewhat obscured by the ambiguity in the word "trapeza," which signifies both bank and treasury.[1] Yet it is significant that Thespiæ, a Bœotian market town, possessed its bank; in Egypt banks were set up even in the villages.

Among the functions of the Hellenistic banks money-changing had lost much of its former importance, but the receipt of money on deposit played a far larger part. With the general increase of travel the convenience of confiding cash reserves to a money-dealer would become almost a necessity: it is significant that in the plays of Plautus (who on this point undoubtedly reflects Hellenistic usage) ordinary soldiers of adventure figure as depositors in banks. At the same time it became a common practice for city-treasurers to deposit money, usually on short term, for the sake of the accruing interest.[2] The uses to which Hellenistic bankers could put their augmented loan funds were not much more various than in the classical period. Industry, being still manufacture in the strict sense of that word, required little capital; and if we may judge by the surviving loan-deeds from Egypt, cultivators in need of funds for improvements had recourse to each other or to petty usurers. But with the increased volume of trade the amount of money advanced in mercantile loans must have risen in proportion, for it remained the custom of mer-

[1] It is a moot point whether the *βασιλικαὶ τραπεζαί* in Egypt were state treasuries or private banks under state control. On Egyptian banking in general, see Rostovtzeff, *op. cit.*, I, pp. 404–6, II, pp. 1282–8; Préaux, *L'économie royale des Lagides*, pp. 280–97.

[2] In a long financial inscription from Tauromenium dating to *c.* 100 B.C. (Ditt., *Syll.*, 954) recurrent entries refer to sums placed "on deposit" and "on current account" with local bankers.

chants, as in the days of Demosthenes, to borrow their trading capital. Rhodian bankers lent their funds to Aegean corn-dealers, and Alexandrians to venturers in the Red Sea. We still possess a loan-deed signed by five traders (including a Carthaginian and a man from Massilia with a Celtic name), who were about to set sail to the Spice Coasts in Arabia or Somaliland.[1]

To the Hellenistic banks we may probably attribute a considerable advance in the technique of payment by book entry in place of cash transfers.[2] The Hellenistic Greeks did not, it is true, use the Bill of Exchange, and there is no clear evidence of their acquaintance with cheques. But they issued bankers' orders for the payment of debts on the spot and at a distance.[3]

A form of money-lending for which the Hellenistic age offered increased opportunities was that of tax-farming. In Egypt the farming system was only applied to those imposts whose yield was speculative, and the contractors were controlled by an extremely ingenious system of supervision.[4] But in addition to the prospective profits of their speculation they were allowed five per cent commission on their intake (raised in the second century to ten per cent). The capital required for the purchase of a tax was subscribed by several partners, who underwrote the offer of the head contractor. By this device it was made possible for men of slender means to take part in the tax-auctions : probably the majority of the tax-farmers were military tenants and other small landholders. The right to bid stood open to others than Greeks, and occasionally taxes were knocked down to Jewish speculators. But tax-farming, like every other branch of finance, remained essentially a Greek business.[5]

[1] E. Ziebarth, *Beiträge zur Geschichte des Seeraubes und Seehandels im alten Griechenland*, p. 54.

[2] Most of the evidence is of Roman date ; but the names of the bankers are Greek. In *P. Zeno Cairo*, 59297, the words *ἀριθμεῖν* and *διαγράφειν* appear to be used in their later technical sense of paying in cash and by book entry respectively.

[3] The technique of Hellenistic banking (as still practised in Roman times) is excellently described by F. Preisigke, *Girowesen im griechischen Ägypten*.

[4] See esp. *Rev. Law*, parts A and B ; Wilcken, *Ostraka*, I, p. 513 ff.

[5] Josephus (*Jewish Antiquities*, XII, 4) retails an excellent anecdote of a Hellenistic " Jew Süss," who secured important contracts at Alexandria over the heads of the Greek bidders (late third century). Though the story shows traces of embroidery, it may be accepted as substantially historical.

Though partnerships were regularly formed by Hellenistic entrepreneurs for collecting taxes, for setting up a bank, for undertaking a maritime venture, there is no evidence that they ever organized themselves into permanent joint-stock companies, like the societies of the Roman publicani. Hellenistic craftsmen and traders followed the prevalent ancient habit of association in gilds. In Egypt it is probable that membership of a gild carried with it special economic rights and duties and was made compulsory by the government. But like most of the Greek clubs, the Hellenistic gilds appear to have had a predominantly social purpose.

The widened range of Hellenistic commerce, and the increased facilities for the circulation of money, are reflected in the general tendency of prices to conform to a uniform level.[1] The Hellenistic age marks a distinct stage in the progress from district economy to world economy.

§ 7. THE CONDITION OF THE WORKERS

A general balance sheet for the Hellenistic world would reveal a remarkable increase in the aggregate assets of the Greek nation. To say nothing of the treasures amassed by the royal dynasties of Egypt and Pergamum, personal fortunes beyond the dreams of city-state avarice were acquired by some of the chief functionaries of the new monarchies. The several large estates, the factories and the merchant fleets of Ptolemy II's minister, Apollonius, have repeatedly come to our notice. Antigonus I and the Seleucids rewarded their officers with the same liberal hand. A captain of Antigonus I named Mnesimachus became the proprietor of a "latifundium" embracing entire native villages and settlements of Greek colonists in addition to the home farm;[2] and Hermias the minister of Antiochus III was able, like the triumvir Crassus, to pay off an army out of his private purse.[3] Compared with Hermias, his wealthiest contemporary in the Greek Homeland, an Ætolian named Alexander, was no doubt poor; yet his fortune was estimated at two hundred

[1] Heichelheim, *Wirtschaftliche Schwankungen der Zeit von Alexander bis Augustus*, pp. 70–1.

[2] See W. H. Buckler and D. M. Robinson in *American Journ. Archæol.*, 1912, p. 11 ff.

[3] Polybius, V, 50.

talents, equal to that of Callias, the richest Athenian of the Periclean age.

But a better index of Hellenistic prosperity is furnished by the general opulence of the *bourgeoisie*. Tried by its expenditure on luxuries like silver plate and costly textiles, or by the sums which it contributed to dowries and trust-funds, the Hellenistic middle-class was evidently in affluent circumstances.[1]

On the other side of the account stands the bad distribution of the newly acquired riches. Though it achieved considerable progress in methods of transport and of money circulation, the Hellenistic age was not prolific in technical inventions. Its economic changes therefore fell short of constituting an economic revolution; prices of manufactured articles remained relatively high, and apart from the grain trade, which stood in a special category, commerce was still in the main confined to articles of luxury. Furthermore, if the Hellenistic world gave handsome rewards to commercial enterprise, it did little or nothing to raise the status of labour. In the Near East it created a greater demand for labour and offered the natives somewhat better wages (as measured in real values);[2] but it maintained or even intensified the restraints on their personal liberty, and thus effectually cut them off from the hope of any substantial rise in the economic scale. In Greece and the Aegean area it held fast to the institution of slavery, and was held fast by it. Because the Hellenistic world was full of slaves, it was empty of machines;[3] for the same reason it inevitably kept the free labourer near the level of subsistence, or sometimes below it.

The effect of slavery upon the scale of life of the free wage-earner is forcibly illustrated by surviving records from the temple accounts of Apollo at Delos.[4] The real wages of the free workers in the high-price period of the early third century left them worse off than before the Macedonian conquest: even with regular distributions of free corn, which the city of

[1] For details see Tarn, in Bury, *The Hellenistic Age*, ch. 4.

[2] Heichelheim, *Wirtschaftliche Schwankungen*, pp. 101–3.

[3] Tarn, *Hellenistic Civilisation*, p. 4. W. L. Westermann, Pauly-Wissowa-Kroll, supplement VI, cols. 927–44.

[4] These statistics were first collected and put to use by G. Glotz in *Journal des Savants*, 1912–13. Further details in Tarn (Bury, *The Hellenistic Age*, ch. 4), and Heichelheim, *op. cit.*

Delos had introduced by 300 B.C., it is difficult to understand how any but the highly skilled artisans could have reared a family. Possibly the wage-levels at Delos, which was a slave-trading centre, were somewhat lower than elsewhere; yet the statistics from that town are sufficient to prove that the free workers in the Greek world can nowhere have attained an improvement of wages commensurate with the general rise of the wage-fund.

In Egypt, where slavery never assumed large proportions, economic development was at first stimulated but eventually arrested by the policy of the Ptolemies, which has been aptly compared with that of Colbert and the "Mercantilist" rulers of the seventeenth and eighteenth centuries.[1] The pervasive but in itself not ill-considered system of regulations which Ptolemy II imposed upon business in Egypt was calculated to keep everything up to a minimum standard of efficiency; under a government of great driving power it might yield quick results, but without such a stimulus it would tend to level production down rather than up. Hence the chronic condition of semi-anarchy, resulting from the dynastic feuds and civil wars of the second and first centuries, fatally led to an economic recession. The gravest symptom of this decline was the falling productivity of the Egyptian land, due simply to under-cultivation, which could not be remedied by spasmodic official attempts at reform.

For the mitigation of the hardships entailed by the ill-distribution of wealth, the Greek governments anticipated the system of "panis et circenses" which proved so effective at Rome, and individual men of substance subscribed generously to the same object (p. 276). Where these palliatives did not suffice, they occasionally applied that panacea of Greek social reformers, abolition of debts and redistribution of land. Debt crises were tided over by moratoria of short duration, as at Ephesus in 297,[2] or extending over several years, as in Bœotia in the early second century.[3] At Sparta the cancellation of debts was followed by drastic reallotments of land (p. 157). But these devices offered no permanent solution of the economic problems. In some instances, as the record of the Spartan prince Agesilaus shows, bankruptcy laws played

[1] Wilcken in *Schmoller's Jahrbuch*, 1921, p. 349 ff.
[2] Ditt., *Syll.*, 364.
[3] Polybius, XX, 6, 1.

into the hands of fraudulent debtors;[1] in others these reforms, and still more the changes in the ownership of land, inflicted excessive hardships upon the dispossessed. In general, the result of this kind of social legislation was to create two contending groups which took it in turn to be rentiers and proletarians. In any case, it did not touch the root of the evil, which lay not so much in the condition of the landed proprietors as in the plight of the labourers, slave and free.

Among the Hellenistic workers symptoms of active resentment against their lot were neither many nor effective. In the second century a series of abortive revolts was attempted by the Egyptian peasantry (p. 217). About 133 a wave of unrest spread through the Greek world, causing a revolt of agrarian slaves in Sicily, an insurrection of industrial slaves at the silver mines of Laurium, and a mixed rising of rustic serfs and urban slave workers in the Pergamene territory. But the Athenian militia repressed the outbreak at Laurium, and the Roman legions the more serious commotions in Sicily and Asia Minor; and in the eastern Mediterranean at any rate the revolts were not repeated.

On the other hand, passive resistance was often and successfully applied. In Egypt the peasantry occasionally obtained redress of grievances by a collective strike (p. 266); and in the second century many of them disappeared, one by one, from their holdings, so that much of the land which the first Ptolemies had raised to full productiveness fell back into a state of under-cultivation (p. 304). In the Greek Homeland the rise of competitive industries in the Near East (pp. 294–5), and consequent loss of export markets, brought about the same condition of stagnation or decline as in the fourth century (p. 287 and n. 1) and, from 200 B.C. at least, an appreciable decline of population.

But the most rapid cause of impoverishment in the Hellenistic world lay in the Roman Republic, which paid itself for its interventions in Greek affairs by appropriating much of its wealth in the form of indemnities and plunder. The first cost of the Roman protectorate may be measured by the fact that by 150 B.C. all Hellenistic states had ceased to strike gold coins, and a considerable number of them had been driven to

[1] A deservedly unsuccessful attempt at debt-relief in Ætolia (c. 200 B.C.) is mentioned by Polybius (XIII, 1).

depreciate their silver. Though it took another century of peculation by provincial governors and publicani to bleed the Greeks white, the Roman armies in the second century had already rendered them anæmic. If the Hellenistic world began in affluence and ended in embarrassment, the cause of this decline was not wholly in the inherent flaws of its economic system; in a large measure it sprang from the political errors which led up to the Roman domination.

Addendum.—The discovery of the "law of the monsoons," by which navigation in the Indian Ocean was eventually reduced to a routine, was credited to a captain named Hippalus (*Periplus Maris Erythraei*, § 57). Both Thiel (*op. cit*, pp. 20–1) and Otto-Bengtson (p. 201 ff.) recognize in Hippalus a ship-mate of Eudoxus who resumed the latter's Indian cruises, and therefore date him *c.* 100 B.C. On the other hand it is clear from Strabo (bk. II, p. 118), and from the coin-finds in India, that the Indian Ocean routes did not become frequented before the early Roman Empire. Warmington would therefore date Hippalus *c.* A.D. 15–20 (*op. cit.*, p. 75).

CHAPTER XVII

HELLENISTIC ART

§ 1. ARCHITECTURE

THE conquests of Alexander not only changed the course of Greek political and economic life, but opened new chapters in the history of Greek art, thought and religion.

To the artists of Greece the Hellenistic world offered opportunities recalling the spacious days of Pericles. The Hellenistic rulers and the opulent bourgeoisies disposed of a patronage fund far exceeding the resources of cities and individuals in the classical age, and they were willing donors. The natural appreciation of art which was the common heritage of the Greeks was being reinforced by a trained dilettantism among the more well-to-do. Visits to show-sites like Athens, Delphi or Olympia were coming to form part of a polite education, and a special literature of guide-books was being formed for the benefit of sightseers.[1] Connoisseurship of art extended even to the Hellenistic courts. One of the baits by which Aratus secured financial support from Ptolemy II was a promised gift of paintings from the famous Sicyonian school of the fourth century. Attalus II sent to Delphi to copy old masters, and it is said that he offered a hundred talents to the Roman captors of Corinth for a celebrated picture from that city. The Hellenistic world, it is true, lacked that untroubled belief in the traditional religion of Greece which had inspired much of the best work in the classical period: its art, like that of modern times, was essentially secular. For this reason it was less bound by rule and more liable to lapse into occasional extravagance. Yet it followed tradition more

[1] The chief writers in this genre were Diodorus the Periegete (late third century), and especially Polemo of Ilium (early second century). Part of their work no doubt is embodied in Pausanias' *Descriptio Græciæ.*

closely than might have been expected, perhaps more than was desirable.

Among the various branches of Greek art architecture was naturally the first to benefit by the special conditions of the Hellenistic age. In the Greek Homeland, it is true, building on an extensive scale was confined to a few of the show places. The share of the older Greek cities in the wealth of the Hellenistic period was relatively small, and most of them had to be content to wear a "provincial" air.[1] But Hellenistic kings who found it in their interest to earn the good opinion of the Homeland Greeks left many visible memorials of their favour. At the religious centres of Olympia, Delphi and Delos the political competition between the dynasties expressed itself in rival dedications of commemorative statues. At Delos the Antigonids marked their successive spells of ascendancy by the erection of porticos. Athens was endowed with a new library and gymnasium by Ptolemy III and with two colonnades by Eumenes II and Attalus II of Pergamum; and construction on Peisistratus' gigantic temple of Zeus was resumed, though not completed, by Antiochus IV.

In the newer portions of the Greek world, where cities sprang up on virgin soil, and on the west coast of Asia Minor, where several of the old towns were rebuilt for greater security or commercial convenience on adjacent sites, the municipal architect was given free scope for his talent. Since only a few Hellenistic cities have been systematically explored, the work of their builders cannot yet be appraised with certainty.[2] But it is clear that the construction of towns on a preconceived plan, which had been introduced experimentally into classical Greece, now became the general rule. The ordinary practice of Hellenistic architects was to lay out sites on a rectangular pattern, preferably on the southern slope of a ridge extending from west to east, but with due

[1] The modest architecture and crooked streets of Athens are commented in a guide-book written c. 250 B.C. by Heracleides Criticus. (See W. H. Duke's text in *Essays and Studies presented to William Ridgeway*, p. 228.)

[2] The general architectural appearance of Hellenistic cities is best illustrated by the results of excavations at Delos, Pergamum, Priene, and Magnesia-on-Mæander. Our knowledge of Alexandria, and of Antioch (where recent American excavations have revealed few Hellenistic remains), rests solely on literary descriptions. On Pergamum, see E. V. Hansen, *The Attalids of Pergamon*, ch. VII; on the whole subject, see A. v. Gerkan, *Griechische Städteanlagen.*

regard to the natural conformation of the ground, and without any pedantic preference for an exact check-board shape. Alexandria, which extended on a level but narrow site between the sea and a lake, was laid out as a regular oblong; Priene approximated to the square plan. On the other hand, Smyrna formed a curve round the head of its gulf; Seleucia-ad-Orontem rose in tiers along the face of a steep promontory. The upper part of Pergamum was set out in terraces along the windings of a concave hill-side, and its ruins still offer a fine example of an irregular but harmonious grouping of edifices.

Hellenistic cities were usually provided with a few wide avenues for wheeled traffic or processions. At Alexandria the two main streets intersecting at the centre of the town measured ninety feet. But most of the streets were made only large enough for the use of pedestrians and pack animals.

On steep gradients stone flags were laid at intervals for a better foothold, but paving had not yet come into general use. To judge by a surviving municipal law from Pergamum, the cleansing of the streets was rigorously enforced upon the occupiers of the adjacent houses.[1] Closed drains were provided in the main streets of some larger towns (Alexandria, Pergamum, Athens, Syracuse), but were far from universal. On the other hand, Hellenistic town-builders were at pains to supply good drinking water. Alexandria was fed by underground pipes from an arm of the Nile; the citadel of Pergamum drew its water from a pressure aqueduct—a device which the Romans seldom imitated except in Asia Minor. At Pergamum and at Priene the water was purified in filter-beds before passing into the street pipes. But the practice of laying on water in private houses was not common before Roman times.

In the choice of their materials Hellenistic builders made no important innovation. For public buildings and the more ambitious private houses they used dressed stone; for the less costly houses, sun-dried brick on stone foundations. In Mesopotamia they became acquainted with burnt brick, and they constructed part of Seleucia-on-Tigris with brickwork from the materials of dismantled buildings in Babylon. Babylonian influence may perhaps be discerned in an

[1] Ditt., *O.G.I.*, 483. The lettering of this inscription is of Trajanic date, but its contents clearly go back to the Attalid period.

increased use of arches for gateways and in the occasional construction of entire arcades, as in the portico of Eumenes at Athens; but vaults were used in substructures only. Where Hellenistic architects had to span large spaces, they still relied on stone beams and supporting columns.

In accordance with the predominantly secular character of Hellenistic art, temples occupied a less important place in the architectural scheme than in classical times. Though some of the temples whose plans can be recovered were of more than ordinary magnitude (e.g. at Didyma and at Magnesia-on-Mæander), they were usually not conspicuous by their size or the costliness of their materials. In details of construction they differed but little from the usage of the classical period, and although pillars with Corinthian capitals were used experimentally, the temple colonnades were generally of the Doric or (most commonly) of the Ionic order. Of secular buildings the palaces have mostly disappeared without a trace; but to judge by the surviving plan of the modest domicile of the Pergamene kings, the royal residences were not "palatial" in magnitude, however costly their appointments might have been. Gymnasia and theatres were built on a generous scale: at Ephesus the theatre could accommodate some 23,000 spectators (as compared with 17–18,000 at Athens). The main market-square was often enclosed on three sides with continuous porticos. On the other hand, the practice of constructing continuous colonnades along the fronts of streets (as in modern Bologna) was Roman rather than Hellenistic; and we must also ascribe to the Roman period the basilicas or covered halls and the elaborate Turkish baths which have sometimes been considered typical of Hellenistic towns. In the construction of ring-walls the later Greek architects were far ahead of those of classical days (p. 240). Following the example of Dionysius at Syracuse and of Epaminondas at Messene, they were careful to carry the fortifications along the strongest strategic line and, if necessary, to take them along or near the crest of an adjacent ridge.[1]

From the few remains of Hellenistic private houses it may be gathered that the courtyard residence of one storey, with the main apartments at the top end of the court, continued to

[1] As at Heracleia-on-Latmus and Priene.

be the prevailing type.[1] In the more ornate dwellings the court was sometimes colonnaded in the fashion which afterwards became common at Pompeii, and additional house space was gained here and there by joining up two quadrangles into one residence—another Hellenistic feature that was freely imitated at Pompeii.

Hellenistic cities were built up closely, like those of the classical period, and did not provide for many open spaces within the ring-wall. But at Alexandria the entire royal quarter was designed in the form of a park interspersed with buildings. Within easy reach of the city the suburb of Canopus was laid out with pleasure gardens; and below Antioch the banks of the Orontes were lined with the groves and villas of the garden-suburb Daphne, which has been well compared with the Prater of Vienna.

Hellenistic architecture in general was sober and practical. It did not imitate the colossal manner of the Egyptians and Babylonians, and it did not anticipate the florid decorative style of the Romans. But neither did it show the resourcefulness in the use of new materials and methods of construction that distinguished Roman builders. In the main it adhered to the classical traditions. But it improved upon these in various details, and it took a big step forward by introducing systematic planning into town-construction.

§ 2. SCULPTURE

As an essential adjunct to architecture, sculpture benefited by the intensified building activity of the Hellenistic age. It also derived advantage from the habit of setting up memorial statues, which was never stronger than in Hellenistic times. At the Ætolian sanctuary of Thermum, a site which only began to attain importance with the formation of the Ætolian League, two thousand statues had been crowded together during the first century of the League's existence; at Athens three hundred and sixty images of Demetrius of Phalerum were placed on view in the ten years of his administration.

[1] The best-preserved houses are at Priene and Delos. Residences of the courtyard type have been found at Doura-Europus on the middle Euphrates. (F. Cumont, *Fouilles de Doura-Europos*, p. 241 ff.) At Philadelphia in the Fayum the dwellings faced the street, as in modern houses. (P. Viereck, *Philadelpheia*.)

The output of Hellenistic sculpture was therefore immense, and a comparatively large number of specimens is preserved.

In point of craftmanship the finest work of the period stood on a level with the masterpieces of the fifth and fourth centuries. The Nike of Samothrace, the Aphrodite of Melos, the so-called "Dying Gladiator," the "Wrestlers" (really pancratiasts) of the Uffizi Gallery at Florence—to mention but the most famous of later Greek statues—show the same command over material as the best classical pieces. Moreover the technical proficiency of Greek sculptors endured to the very end of the Hellenistic period: the Laocoön is now generally regarded as a work of the first century. But the later Greek artists were handicapped by the fact that several fields of sculpture had been all but worked out by their predecessors, and they were not wholly successful in their quest for original effects. In the rendering of familiar subjects they had recourse to all manner of expedients in order to preserve the appearance of novelty. They applied the pictorial device of foreshortening to carving in relief; they arranged drapery in new and ostentatious fashions; they combined the special features of different classical schools into eclectic types; more frequently they stressed the characteristics of a particular school to the point of exaggeration. Their sprinters are lighter, their boxers more lumpy than their classical prototypes; the boy Cupids become fat babies; in scenes of combat effort is heightened into strain. The Hellenistic tendency to over-emphasize is best exemplified in the frieze of Eumenes II's great altar at Pergamum.[1] Here the hackneyed theme of a battle between gods and giants is furbished up by methods bordering on caricature. The field is crowded with figures to the point of confusion; the tension and the lack of poise of the combatant groups produce an effect of restlessness and almost of distortion. But the ambition which misled the Hellenistic sculptors into "going one better" than their classical predecessors was in itself a sign of health: whatever their defects of method, they possessed enterprise and were not afraid of making new experiments.

The field of work in which the later Greek sculptors were on

[1] It is uncertain what event this altar was intended to commemorate. Hardly the battle of Magnesia, which brought Eumenes much profit but little honour; more probably some later encounter with the Galatians.

the whole least successful was the rendering of deities. The Demeter of Damophon at Messene and some figures of bearded gods (Zeus, Asclepius, Sarapis), which recall the dignity of classical statues, are but stray exceptions to the rule that they did not take religious subjects with sufficient seriousness. Their best achievement was in portraiture, which formed a suitable pendant to the biographical literature of the period (p. 334), and revealed in equal measure the enhanced interest which the Greeks since Alexander's time took in outstanding personalities. Like the men of letters, the portraitists commemorated leaders of thought no less than men of action. The increased acquaintance of the Hellenistic Greeks with foreign peoples is reflected in the faithfulness with which the sculptors rendered strange racial types. Excellent specimens of their realism are preserved in the figures of captive or wounded Galatians from Pergamum, commemorating the victories of Attalus I. But strangely enough the Hellenistic sculptors hardly tried their hand in a genre which would have afforded full scope to their talents in portraiture, the historical relief. A solitary example of this class survives in the so-called " Alexander Sarcophagus," on which a king of Sidon and former ally of the Macedonian king caused scenes of battle and of hunting from Alexander's life to be carved. Unfortunately the later Greek artists were held fast at this particular point in the classical tradition, which required that historical events should be rendered indirectly and symbolically in battles of gods and giants and other mythological episodes.

§ 3. PAINTING AND MINOR ARTS

Of Hellenistic painting it is difficult to speak with confidence, because of the disappearance of all original works of acknowledged merit. Despite occasional fresh discoveries, as at Delos and Doura-Europus, our knowledge of Hellenistic pictures is still mainly derived from the house-decorations at Pompeii, which at best are workmanlike copies of Greek masters. The range of subjects represented at Pompeii suggests that Hellenistic painters paid the same regard to tradition as the sculptors. A few family portraits and scenes from still life are preserved, but most of the surviving frescos depict episodes from classical legend. The growing interest in landscape which is noticeable in Hellenistic literature is not reflected in painting: like the masters of the Renaissance, the Hellenistic artists thought of scenery merely as a background to human action. In regard to technique the Pompeian pieces make it clear that the arts of shading and perspective, which were inventions of the fourth century, had come to be well understood in Hellenistic times. Though precise inferences cannot be drawn from the colour schemes of the Pompeian copies, it may be gathered that the later Greek masters used their palette with discretion and did not sacrifice outline and design to chromatic effect.

Unlike fresco and easel painting, which were in great demand for the decoration of house-interiors, vase-painting lost its former importance. In the fourth and third centuries Greek fashion set in favour of metal-ware for table services, and at the same time the decline and impoverishment of the Etruscan nobility deprived the Greek ceramic industry of its best foreign customer. The principal finds of Hellenistic painted pottery come from South Russia, Cyrene and especially from South Italy, where the products of local schools of clay-workers replaced the imported Attic ware of previous centuries. The Italian potters, whose chief centres were at Tarentum and Canusium, at Pæstum and Cumæ, followed the Attic red-figure technique, but seldom attained the Attic proficiency in firing the vessel or designing the pictures. They overcrowded their field with figures, and they spoilt the simple contrast of black and red by using additional pigments. In the later third century painted pottery was partly replaced by a new type of ceramic ware (usually of red clay with black glaze), on which the decorations, consisting of scroll work, or of the customary figures of classical legend, were applied in relief. Though this type of vase was the predecessor of the stamped pottery which became the prevalent ware of the early Roman Empire, it has not been found in any large quantities, and it is a matter of conjecture whether its place of manufacture was in Bœotia or Megara, where most of the surviving pieces have been discovered. Another form of ceramic art, the production of terra-cotta figurines, experienced a revival in Hellenistic times, when two centres of manufacture were established at Tanagra in

Bœotia and at Myrina on Lemnos.[1] These figurines were mere toys, but the best of their kind were in imitation of good statuary work, and in colouring and design they surpass all other ancient terra-cottas.

Among the minor branches of art jewellery and work in the precious metals derived a considerable impetus from Alexander's hauls of gold and silver and from the opening up of new sources of precious stones in the East. Except in South Russia, where the tombs of the Scythian chiefs and of the wealthy Greek merchants have yielded large treasures in jewellery, remains of Hellenistic work in these costly materials are rare. The Russian gold and silver (mostly consisting of embossed ornaments and inlay) exhibits the usual Greek qualities of good design and careful finish, together with a capacity, not always found in Greek art, of adapting its subjects to the tastes of its customers.[2] A characteristic excellence of Hellenistic art, the rendering of individual likenesses, is displayed in the gems of the period and in the coins of Alexander and his successors. Among ancient specimens of coin-portraiture there is nothing to surpass the idealized head of Alexander on the pieces of Lysimachus or the realistic effigies of the Greco-Bactrian kings.[3]

§ 4. THE INFLUENCE OF GREEK ART UPON THE EAST

Oriental influence upon Hellenistic art is scarcely discernible, except in a new tendency to polychromy in cameos and metal inlays. In Babylonia and Persia the Greek conquest did not lead to a revival of native or to the imitation of Hellenic art. In Egypt the native ceremonial sculpture was resuscitated by the Ptolemies, who caused effigies of themselves, with explanatory hieroglyphs, to be set up on temple walls. But these command performances were negligently executed and brought about no genuine renascence of Pharaonic art.[4] In Phœnicia, where Greek models had been

[1] Copious finds of terra-cottas by Greek craftsmen or native imitators have been made in Egypt (W. Weber, *Die œgyptisch-griechischen Terrakotten*), but these were of less artistic merit.

[2] See Rostovtzeff, *Iranians and Greeks in Southern Russia*, ch. 5. The best Greek metal-work from Russia is of the fourth and third centuries.

[3] B. V. Head, *Guide to the Coins of the Ancients*, pl. 31, no. 20, 34, nos. 24–5.

[4] See Miss M. A. Murray, *Egyptian Sculpture*, ch. 8.

copied even before the time of Alexander, Hellenistic influence is plainly apparent in the cult-statues and in the anthropoid lids of sarcophagi. But the most notable field of conquest of the Hellenistic artists was in India. It is true that Hindu art did not originate from the Macedonian conquest; its first borrowings, as in the palace of Chandragupta, were from Persian models. But Greek influence shows through in regard to drapery, pose and facial expression, in the earliest statues of Buddha. Most of these, significantly enough, have been found in N.W. India near the Afghan border, and should, therefore, be dated to the century of the Greco-Bactrian invasions rather than to the period of the Roman Empire, when Greek merchants, and perhaps Greek artists, visited the Indian coastlands, but did not penetrate far into the interior.[1] From India the influence of Greek art can be traced in one direction to Malacca and Java, in another through Tibet to China, Korea and Japan. This diffusion was a very slow process, extending through several centuries of the Christian era, and Greek art forms only reached the farthest East at many removes from the original types. But the lines of transmission through Central India and through the Tarim plateau are clear enough. On the Tarim plateau the Buddhist frescos at Miran, with their chiaroscuro shading, betray Greek inspiration at the first glance.[2] Another significant discovery on this plateau is a Chinese clay seal on which appear Greek types, the Macedonian Athena Alcis and a head, seemingly, of the Bactrian king Diodotus I.[3] The documents to which these seals were affixed belonged to the third century A.D.; but the signet-rings may have been in use long before, and the types are sufficient proof that Greek influences were reaching Chinese territory before the close of the Hellenistic period.

In the western Mediterranean the influence of Greek art upon the Etruscans is less apparent in the Hellenistic than in the preceding periods. On the other hand, the later sculptures and architectural remains from Carthage (notably

[1] The chief finds have been made at Gandhara, near Peshawar. See esp. A. Foucher, *L'art gréco-bouddhique du Gandhara*, vol. II, p. 741 ff. On Greece and India in general, see Goblet d'Alviella, *Ce que l'Inde doit à la Grèce*; Sir John Marshall, Cambridge History of India, I, ch. 26; Tarn, *The Greeks in Bactria and India*, pp. 393–408.

[2] See the illustrations in Stein's *Serindia*.

[3] Tarn, *Journ. Hell. Stud.*, 1902, p. 268.

the tombs) show distinct traces of copying from Greek models,[1] and several of the Carthaginian coin-types of the fourth and third centuries are plainly borrowed from those of Syracuse.[2] At Rome the wholesale importation of Greek works of art (chiefly in the form of loot) began with the capture of Syracuse and Tarentum in the Second Punic War. In the last century before Christ connoisseurship of Greek art became a not uncommon accomplishment among the wealthier Romans, and Greek stonemasons opened a regular business of copying old masters for the Italian market. In the age of Augustus the study of Greek models at last created a native school of sculpture, which in true Roman fashion was not content with mere imitation. Of the two genres in which ancient Italian sculptors excelled, historical relief and portraiture, the former was essentially indigenous ; but the latter plainly reveals the debt of Rome to Hellenistic Greece.

§ 5. HELLENISTIC MUSIC

Of Hellenistic music the few surviving scores do not give us any adequate idea. The best preserved pieces are two hymns written for the service of the Delphic Apollo towards the end of the second century B.C.[3] To modern ears these compositions sound stiff and ungainly ; but they were no doubt written in a deliberately archaizing style. Whatever the merits of the Hellenistic composers may have been, appreciation of music was never keener among the Greeks than in the Hellenistic period. At the public festivals musical events were gaining in popularity upon athletic performances, and at Alexandria in particular musical displays were given on a scale hitherto unknown. The esteem in which virtuosos now were held is illustrated by a Delphic decree of 90 B.C., in which a musician receives a public vote of thanks for a performance on a water-organ.[4]

[1] S. Gsell, *Histoire ancienne de l'Afrique du Nord*, vol. IV, pp. 200–205.

[2] Compare the coins of Agathocles (*Guide to the Greek and Roman Coins in the British Museum*, pl. 35, nos. 28–9) with the contemporary Carthaginian pieces (*ib.*, nos. 37–8).

[3] For a recent modern transnotation see Th. Reinach, *La Musique grecque*, pp. 177–192.

[4] Ditt., *Syll.*, 737.

CHAPTER XVIII

HELLENISTIC LANGUAGE AND LITERATURE

§ 1. APPRECIATION OF LITERATURE

THE general conditions of the Hellenistic age were in many ways favourable to the production of a good and even of a great literature. At no other period in ancient history was literary talent held in wider esteem or furnished with ampler opportunities.

In the city-states of classical Greece men of letters had occasionally enjoyed the patronage of tyrants, but these had been a rare and uncertain source of benefits. In the Hellenistic age permanent monarchies with resources far exceeding those of the city-despots endowed literature on a scale unprecedented. Among the kings not a few had genuine literary tastes; others followed tradition or acted in a spirit of emulation; at all the courts patronage of authors was accepted as a definite duty. Of the Hellenistic rulers those who had least leisure to cultivate the Muses were the kings of Macedon and the Seleucids. Yet Cassander was reputed to know Homer by heart; Antigonus Gonatas was a devotee of the Stoic philosophy; and not a few men of letters, albeit not the most distinguished, were attracted to the courts of Antioch or Pella. Under king Eumenes II Pergamum became an important centre of literary studies.

But none of the Hellenistic dynasties exercised patronage as lavishly as the Ptolemies. Whatever we may think of the methods by which these rulers made their fortune, they set such an example in the spending of it as few other royal lines have cared to follow. In 294 Ptolemy I invited Demetrius of Phalerum to Egypt and instructed him to establish the greatest of ancient academies of learning, the Museum of Alexandria.[1] This institution, which reproduced on a much

[1] After his flight from Athens (p. 32) Demetrius of Phalerum had lived in Macedonia; but after the death of his patron Cassander he had been obliged to resume his travels.

enlarged scale the colleges of the philosophical schools at Athens (p. 355), provided a meeting-place, and no doubt also studies and lecture-rooms, for a select company of scholars whom the king chose in person and endowed with a regular stipend from his treasury.[1] In creating the Museum Ptolemy I made Alexandria into a rival of Athens for the intellectual primacy of the Greek world.

In the classical period one of the chief incentives to literary production had been the recitations and dramatic contests at public festivals. In Hellenistic times the number of such festivals was multiplied.[2] In Greece Proper the Athenian holidays continued to be celebrated with much of their former splendour; at Delphi the Pythian games were supplemented with a new "panegyris" named the Soteria (p. 145). At Delos Attalids, Antigonids and Ptolemies vied with each other in founding a whole cycle of celebrations.[3] At Alexandria a national holiday named the Ptolemaieia was inaugurated by Ptolemy II in memory of his father. In the country places of Egypt the Greek settlers instituted local festivals for which the wealthier members of the colony usually found the money: the small town of Oxyrynchus in the Fayum gave employment to "Homerists" and "biologists" (actors); Ptolemais, in Upper Egypt, possessed a complete dramatic company. Two pan-Hellenic holidays were instituted at Pergamum, another at Magnesia-on-Mæander. In these festivals, old and new, the predominant events were usually athletic or musical, but manifold opportunities were also given for displays of literary prowess in epic or dramatic contests.[4]

The popularity of the drama in Hellenistic times is further proved by the erection of theatres wherever Greeks took up their abode, and by the formation of regular troupes of professional actors and choristers (*τεχνῖται περὶ τὸν Διόνυσον*). The earliest of these troupes was constituted at Athens *c.* 300

[1] According to Strabo (XVII, p. 793), the Museum contained grounds and a large residence with the Fellows' dining-hall. We may assume that it also contained places for study or research and lecture rooms.

[2] See the records of Greek festivals in Michel, nos. 879–960, or Ditt., *Syll.*, 1055–94. Most of these were Hellenistic.

[3] Four Ptolemaic and six Antigonid festivals were founded between 280 and 217.

[4] J. U. Powell, *New Chapters in Greek Literature*, pp. 35–8.

B.C.; but the primacy of Athens was disputed by Corinth, where a well organized "Isthmian" society, with affiliated bodies in other towns of Central Greece and Peloponnesus, set up its head-quarters,[1] and by Teos (the reputed birth-place of Dionysus), whose company stood under the protection of the Attalids. The Dionysiac artists enjoyed safe-conducts and "asylia" in their travellings; their leading companies communicated with monarchs and cities in the manner of sovereign states; their "stars" were honoured with proxeniæ. On some of the theatrical staffs a composer of plays was a regular member.[2]

§ 2. THE HELLENISTIC READING PUBLIC

In the Hellenistic period a reading public grew up such as had hardly existed in the classical age. Before the Macedonian conquest the Greek cities had not established any regular system of school education, and the only notable private foundation of pre-Hellenistic times was the Academy of Plato at Athens. But about 315 B.C. Aristotle's pupil Theophrastus set up a second Athenian college, the Lyceum, on the model of the Academy,[3] and the Stoics and Epicureans followed suit shortly afterwards with institutions of their own. Though philosophy formed the chief subject of study in all these colleges, the Lyceum also provided instruction in literature. Concurrently with the establishment of these private places of study the Athenian state, having abolished compulsory military service (p. 45), remodelled the ephebeia into a High School in which philosophy and literature displaced the art of war as the main subjects of instruction. In other Greek towns school education was placed under the control of a public official (usually named the "pædonomus"), the popular assembly elected the teachers, and the scholars *ex officio* attended the chief city festivals. It can hardly be

[1] See Ditt., *Syll.*, 704–5, for a record of a dispute between the Corinthian and the Athenian troupes which lasted from 128 to 112 and engaged the Amphictionic Council and the Senate.

[2] A ποιητής is enumerated in the troupe of Ptolemais in Upper Egypt. (Michel, 1018.)

[3] Since Theophrastus was not an Athenian citizen, he required a special licence to found a school. This permit was procured for him by Demetrius of Phalerum.

doubted that the municipalities which made these arrangements also provided buildings and found salaries for the teachers. But schools also received benefactions from wealthy citizens,[1] sometimes even from foreign potentates: not only Pergamum, but Rhodes and Delphi received donations for educational objects from Eumenes II and Attalus II. Under these conditions it may be taken for granted that the percentage of literates in Greek cities rose above that of the classical period.

The Hellenistic author's public was increased by the gradual intellectual awakening of Greek women, which was a natural result of their incipient emancipation after the Macedonian conquest.[2] For the improvement in their position Greek women had chiefly to thank the Macedonian princesses, whose unrivalled vigour and resourcefulness must have given a rude shock to classical Greek preconceptions about the general ineptitude of the female sex. Though the increased consideration given to Hellenistic women was not reflected in Greek private law, which still refused to recognize women as grown-up persons and required a *κύριος* to represent them in court, their social status rose, and greater liberty of movement was conceded to them. Provision was made for the education of girls in the endowed schools;[3] a few women proceeded to advanced studies at the philosophical colleges; others took to their pens and occasionally achieved local celebrity by their compositions. In Hellenistic Greece literary appreciation was no longer confined to one sex, and men of letters had to take their women readers into consideration.

The wider diffusion of education in Hellenistic times created an increased demand for books, which was more than met by enlarged production. Collections of books were formed at Pella and Pergamum, at Antioch and Alexandria. The most extensive of these, which was attached to the Museum at Alexandria, eventually comprised 700,000 volumes, and *c.* 250 B.C. it already contained 4– or 500,000

[1] E.g. at Miletus and Teos, *c.* 200 B.C. (Ditt., *Syll.*, 577–8.) On the whole subject see E. Ziebarth, *Aus dem griechischen Schulwesen*.

[2] The abortive attempt by Demetrius at Phalerum to put Athenian women in their place by means of *γυναικονόμοι* was the last recorded protest against their emancipation.

[3] E.g. at Teos. (Ditt., *Syll.*, 578.)

rolls.[1] The value of the Museum Library was enhanced by the labours of a succession of scholars who established authoritative texts of the earlier Greek classics—a necessary precaution in the days of MS. reproduction—and provided them with linguistic and historical annotations for the guidance of the general reader. A further aid to the use of the library was furnished by the scholar-poet Callimachus (*c.* 250 B.C.), who compiled a catalogue of authors in 120 volumes, together with full schedules of each author's compositions and brief biographical details.[2] The lead thus given by the Ptolemies was followed with notable success by Attalus I and Eumenes II of Pergamum, whose library eventually rose to 200,000 volumes. In addition to the royal collections, libraries were also formed at Athens and in other cities. Lastly, the business of commercial publication underwent a great expansion in Hellenistic times. The centre of this trade was Alexandria, where the two chief requisites, authentic texts of writers and cheap papyrus, were ready at hand.[3] Under these conditions Hellenistic men of letters had unprecedented opportunities of finding readers and of being immortalized.

§ 3. GREEK AS A LINGUA FRANCA

Greek literature also benefited by the emergence of a universal Greek language, the *κοινὴ διάλεκτος*, which gradually supplanted the local dialects and spread even beyond the bounds of Hellenedom. The standardization of the Greek tongue was a necessary consequence of the general displacement of population and the increased travel and intercourse that followed upon Alexander's conquests. The process of fusion was facilitated by the ascendancy which the parlance of Attica had already acquired during the fourth century: indeed the " common dialect " was a modification of Attic,

[1] The figures are variously given by ancient authors. (The labour cost of a papyrus roll would far exceed that of a printed book.)

[2] It is not stated on any good authority that Callimachus held the post of chief librarian, yet it seems fairly certain that he did so. See Beloch, *Griech. Geschichte*, IV, pt. 2, pp. 595, 599.

[3] The collection of books that was destroyed during the siege of Alexandria in 47–6 B.C. was in all probability not the Museum Library, but a quay-side dump awaiting export. See T. Rice Holmes, *The Roman Republic*, III, pp. 487–9.

with a few Ionian forms thrown in, rather than a new tongue. The rate at which it absorbed the local patois was by no means uniform. In Thessaly and Bœotia Æolic forms of speech lingered on until after the Roman conquest; the "north-western" dialect was retained by Delphi and the Ætolian League, and Doric showed similar vitality in Peloponnesus, Rhodes and Sicily. On the other hand, the Macedonians and the Ionian Greeks soon forgot their separate modes of speech, and the standard tongue naturally enough was used in all official acts of the Hellenistic monarchies. Of the technical writers, Archimedes was the only person of pan-Hellenic importance who clung to Doric Greek. Among the composers of pure literature Theocritus mostly wrote in Doric, Herondas in Ionic, and various poets occasionally tried their pen in some obsolescent medium. But these were merely devices for producing local colour, like the Scots dialect of Burns and Scott, or for displaying linguistic versatility. Broadly speaking, all Hellenistic literature was composed in the *κοινή*, and thus was able to reach a pan-Hellenic public.

Another inevitable consequence of Alexander's conquests was that Greek became the lingua franca of the Near East. In the interior of Asia Minor the native languages generally held their own; in Palestine the Jews continued to speak Aramaic; in Babylonia, Iran and India the use of Greek did not extend far beyond the radius of the colonies. But in every part of the Near East the educated classes and many of the townsfolk learnt as much Greek as they needed for political or commercial purposes. In Egypt the native priesthoods commonly kept their records in Greek. In Alexandria and other Levantine cities the Jews of the Diaspora became so habituated to Greek as to lose the use of their own tongue. In Lydia and Phrygia, if we may judge by the complete disappearance of dialect inscriptions, Greek became the sole medium of writing.

The learning of the Greek language did not lead on to any serious study of Greek literature among Orientals. If in the first century B.C. Greek plays were staged at the courts of the Armenian and Parthian kings,[1] this was a mere tribute to fashion; and there is no sufficient evidence for the claim that Indian playwrights ever consulted Greek models. Yet

[1] Plutarch, *Crassus*, ch. 33.

despite this neglect of Greek literature, not a few Oriental writers adopted Greek as their vehicle of expression. An Egyptian priest named Manetho and the Babylonian scholar Berossus, compiled histories of their countries from the native documents for the benefit of Greek readers ; but these works, being dedicated respectively to Ptolemy II and Antiochus I, were probably " command performances." More significance attaches to the considerable literature composed in Greek by Jewish writers resident in Alexandria or Cyrene. In the course of the third and second centuries Alexandrian Jews composed the Septuagint version of the Old Testament on behalf of compatriots who had lost the knowledge of Hebrew.[1] Alexandria also became a centre of propaganda in which semi-Hellenized Jews sought to disarm their Greek critics by proving the fundamental similarity between Jewish and Greek civilization.[2] Most remarkable of all was the achievement of Zeno, a native of the Phœnician town of Citium in Cyprus, who founded an essentially Greek school of philosophy at Athens (p. 360), and taught and wrote in Greek, however halting, for a cultivated Greek public. Among the Iranians the only Greek author was the Armenian king, Artavasdes (*c.* 50 B.C.), who composed tragedies in the Attic style. But these may be dismissed as mere dilettantism.

In the western Mediterranean Greek also bade fair to become a language of international intercourse after the death of Alexander. In Carthage it may be assumed that the merchant classes possessed a practical knowledge of Greek. It is also noteworthy that histories of the First and Second Punic Wars respectively were composed under Carthaginian patronage by Greek writers named Philinus and Silenus. Though these works were probably written for the special benefit of the Greeks, they must have found plenty of readers among the educated Carthaginians. In Gaul the penetration of the hinterland by the Massiliotes after 300 B.C. (p. 290) led to the adoption of Greek by the Druids for their written records. But the fate of Greek in the West rested with the Romans. The infiltration of the Greek language into Rome

[1] The tradition that the Septuagint was composed by a committee of seventy scholars at the bidding of Ptolemy II is now generally discredited.

[2] On Jewish literature in the Greek tongue see O. Stählin, in Christ-Schmid, *Geschichte der griechischen Literatur* (6th ed.), II, 1, pp. 535–656.

began during the Punic Wars; in the second century the visits of Roman expeditionary forces to the East and the influx into Italy of Greek prisoners of war accelerated the process of Hellenization. About 200 B.C. two Roman authors, Fabius Pictor and Cincius Alimentus, wrote histories of their city in Greek; but these, like the works of Philinus and Silenus, may have been primarily intended for a Greek public. In any case, Roman national consciousness was too strong to allow the displacement of Latin by a foreign tongue, and the successes achieved in Latin by the epic poet Ennius, the playwright Plautus, and the antiquarian Cato, definitely established Latin as a literary language. But by the end of the second century Greek had become the second tongue of all educated Romans, and Greek men of letters found an appreciative public in Italy.

If Orientals did not acquire more Greek than they needed for the purposes of daily intercourse, the Greeks ignored the eastern tongues altogether.[1] Of the Hellenistic rulers the only one known to have been conversant with a native language was the last Cleopatra, and her linguistic accomplishment was regarded by her compatriots as something prodigious. Nay more, the interest of the Greeks in the eastern civilizations with which they now came into daily contact remained strangely dormant. Under Ptolemy I a writer named Hecatæus of Abdera compiled a history of Egypt whose purpose was to displace Herodotus.[2] But it showed no closer acquaintance with Egyptian documents than the work of the older writer, and being conceived in a panegyric vein like the Cyropædia it was actually less trustworthy. Hecatæus also wrote an excursus on Jewish history which had at least the merit of coming from an authentic source—no doubt a Jew of Alexandria—and was not the mere travesty which became common form among later Gentile writers; but he did not penetrate beyond the externals of Jewish life. The court of Chandragupta and the main outlines of Hindu social organization were described in a work by Seleucus' envoy, Megasthenes. The excerpts of this book in later

[1] A papyrus of the second century (*Brit. Mus. Papyri*, I, 148) introduces us to a young Greek studying Egyptian. But he was driven to do this in order to earn his living as a house tutor in an Egyptian family.

[2] This writer was the source of Diodorus in his résumé of Egyptian history (bk. I).

Greek writers[1] prove it to have been tolerably accurate, but it rested on nothing but observation or hearsay. With the writings of Megasthenes may be compared those of a second-century traveller named Simonides, who described Ethiopia after a five years' stay at Meroë. But this book, like the Phœnician histories of Menander of Ephesus, is a mere name to us.

In one respect at least the later Greeks left their predecessors far behind, in the sheer quantity of their literary output. The names of some 1100 Hellenistic writers are still on record, and the list includes some authors whose individual catalogue of works would fill many pages. No general conclusions, it is true, can be drawn from the activities of a first-century scholar named Didymus, who is credited with 3500 papyrus volumes (say 350 good-sized books of the present day), for this man was a portent to his own generation and earned the name of "Brazen Guts." But authors with an output of 100 volumes were nothing unusual. Among the poets of the New Comedy Menander, Diphilus and Philemon each composed about that number of plays; the Peripatetic savant Aristoxenus had 453 separate works to his name, the Stoic Chrysippus 700, and the poet-scholar Callimachus 800. This increased productivity was partly due to a new fashion of versatility which lured on writers to try their pen in several genres.

But the surviving remains of Hellenistic literature are small out of all proportion to its bulk. In the first centuries of the Christian era the Greek reading public reached that stage of senility in which texts are labelled canonical or apocryphal, and while it saved the classical authors on pedantic grounds of form and vocabulary rather than on their intrinsic merits, it condemned the later writers more or less indiscriminately. Our list of Hellenistic works, extant wholly or in part, is being slowly increased by finds of papyri, which include some hundreds of lines of Menander and the works of a previously unknown poet named Herondas. Yet the sum-total of our remnants is so slight that it does not even constitute a representative selection. To arrive at a true

[1] Especially in Strabo, Diodorus and Arrian. The general accuracy of Megasthenes has been recently proved by Miss B. C. Timmer, *Megasthenes en de indische Maatschappij*.

valuation of Hellenistic literature is all the more difficult, because several of its leading writers are known to us by nothing but isolated scraps, or by second-hand excerpts and descriptions.

§ 4. EPIC AND DRAMATIC POETRY

It might be thought that in the Hellenistic age the epic branch of poetry had reached a stage at which a successful revival was no longer possible. Not that the ancient legends on which Greek epic was based were wholly dead. Each city-state kept alive the tale of its own foundation, and scholars found it worth while to compile " mythographies " for the general reading public. But the old full-blooded pride in the *κλέα ἀνδρῶν,* the Glory of Heroes, had died out with the gradual disappearance of the aristocracies who could trace back their line to those heroes. Besides, every later epic poet had to compete against the Iliad and Odyssey, which remained firmly fixed in popular favour, and for centuries to come remained the " best sellers " in the Greek book trade. Nevertheless, a resuscitation of epic poetry took place in the society of the Alexandrian scholars. Addressing themselves to the Ptolemaic court and to the literary connoisseurs rather than to the masses, the younger Homeridæ cultivated a perfection of form and metre which far surpassed that of the Master ; on the other hand, they discreetly avoided direct comparison with him in the choice of their material and their method of treatment.

The nearest approach in point of scale to the Homeric poems was the *Argonautica* of Apollonius,[1] and this was only half as long as the Odyssey. In the selection of his subject Apollonius showed good judgment, for the legend of Jason, with its alternate episodes of prowess and of travel-adventure, combined the attractions of Iliad and Odyssey, yet no previous poet of any consequence had unfolded its full tale. The *Argonautica* achieved a notable success, for it was read continuously in antiquity, and its entire text has therefore been preserved for us. To modern readers its main attraction

[1] Apollonius was a native of Alexandria, who emigrated to Rhodes and came to be known as "the Rhodian." It is probable that he returned to Alexandria and became Chief Librarian in succession to Callimachus. (Beloch, *op. cit.*, IV, pt. 2, p. 592 ff.)

lies in one significant novelty. Apollonius was not content to represent Medea as the conventional sorceress and virago, but portrayed her as Jason's lover, and rendered her feelings with an insight and sympathy such as no male writer among the classical Greeks would have cared to show. On the other hand, he displayed little of that zest for adventure, and frank admiration of gallant deeds, which is the essence of epic poetry. He imparted to Jason neither Odysseus' heroic will to win, nor Æneas' heroic sense of duty. The good ship Argo meant little to Apollonius : therefore his poem does not carry us along.

In Apollonius' own day the chief complaint against him was based on quite different grounds. He had failed to provide the *Argonautica* with a proper unity of plot, so that his epic gave an impression of unwieldiness and offended the Hellenistic litterateurs' highly developed sense of form. His severest critic, and his most influential rival, was his own master Callimachus. To the Hellenistic Greeks Callimachus was the most accomplished poet of the day, and to us he appears as the most typical. A most prolific and versatile writer, he nevertheless aimed at high finish in his work, and he devoted great care, not only to metre and vocabulary, but to neatness of arrangement. His epic style may be appreciated in his *Hymns* (of which six survive), in his *Ætia* and *Hecale*, of which several fragments are preserved. Callimachus' *Hymns* followed the example of the so-called Homeric Hymns in narrating episodes out of the deities' legendary history. The *Ætia* were elegiac in metre, but epic in matter : like Ovid's *Fasti*, they related legends of the past under pretence of explaining surviving rites and customs of his day. The *Hecale* recounted a homely and insignificant episode out of Theseus' cycle of legend. In all these works Callimachus displayed a mastery of form such as no other Greek poet surpassed ; he boldly adapted the old legends so as to produce piquant or arresting situations ; and he tickled his readers' palates with a judicious admixture of learned allusion. With his inexhaustible store of small surprises Callimachus achieved his ambition of being original, despite the hackneyed character of most of his materials. But if he surpassed Apollonius in sheer literary dexterity, he was even more incapable of enthusiasm. For him the gods and heroes of old were as unreal as they are to us; the manipulation of their legends was a literary sport and it was nothing else. His only passion was pride of craftsmanship, yet this commended him sufficiently to his contemporaries. Hence Callimachus found both readers and imitators, indeed he created a new genre of poetry, the ἐπύλλιον or miniature epic. Surviving specimens of this school, such as the *Heracliscus* of Theocritus and the *Europa* of Moschus (probably of the late third century), reproduce the master's neatness of style and originality of detail; they keep the reader alert but never engross him.

At the beginning of the Hellenistic period Greek tragedy was in a somewhat similar condition to epic poetry. The cycle of ancient legends which had served as a quarry for its plots was giving out, and the continued popularity of the old masters, especially of Euripides, was smothering the efforts of younger poets. At Athens no play worth preserving was produced after Alexander's death; but in the early third century tragedy enjoyed a brief spell of new life at Alexandria, where dramatic contests formed part of the Ptolemaieia. The best of the Alexandrian dramas achieved a short-lived success, and their poets survived for a time under the name of the "Pleiad." The playwrights were presumably free to select their subjects more freely than at Athens, and had opportunities of dramatizing incidents from actual Greek history. One play at least, the *Men of Cassandreia*, by Lycophron of Rhegium, drew its plot from a real event, the sufferings of that town under the tyrant Apollodorus (p. 121). But we cannot tell whether Lycophron rose to his theme, for Alexandrian tragedy has been totally lost. After a period of splendour the Pleiad set in early autumn, and its works ceased to be staged or read.

In this connexion we may mention an extant poem which formed a single episode in a dramatic setting, the *Alexandra* by Lycophron of Chalcis (*c.* 200 B.C.).[1] In this scene the Trojan prophetess Cassandra (here called by her alternative name Alexandra) forecasts the world's history from the

[1] This Lycophron should be held distinct from the tragedian, Lycophron of Rhegium. The confusion between them was due partly to the identity of their names, partly to the similarity of their themes (Κασσανδρεῖς and Cassandra). See Beloch, *op. cit.*, IV, pt. 2, p. 566 ff.

burning of Troy to the emergence of the Roman world-dominion, and she uses to the utmost the seer's privilege of speaking in riddles. The tendency to recondite allusions was prevalent in Alexandrian poetry, but other writers merely used them as seasoning. In the *Alexandra* learned references were not the spice but the meal and marrow : the whole poem in fact was a running enigma. As a challenge to the acumen of literary coteries it achieved an enduring success—hence its survival to the present day. But it was a *jeu d'esprit* in verse rather than poetry.

Greek comedy had shown more vitality in the fourth century than tragedy. At Athens it had adapted itself to altered conditions by transferring its attention from politics to life and manners. No subject could have suited Hellenistic conditions better than this, for the new age, like any period of rapid transitions, must have produced many amusing incongruities. But Hellenistic comedy did not make bold use of its opportunities. Its only important representative, the Attic New Comedy, enjoyed a vogue at Athens *c.* 300 B.C., under the influence of three playwrights named Menander, Diphilus and Philemon (of whom the first and most famous was an Athenian); attempts to transplant comedy to Alexandria met with little success. But Athens in Hellenistic times was becoming the prisoner of past tradition. The surviving fragments of Menander (who is for us the sole representative of the New Comedy), show that he was content to reproduce, with slight modifications, stock types from the old city-state life,[1] and to re-fashion familiar stories of Euripidean pattern. His plays frequently turned on an irregular love affair with a happy ending, and were peopled with recurrent figures such as the Heavy Father, the Confidential Slave, the Not-really-so-bad Courtesan. By careful plot-construction and by refinements of shading in his characters, Menander produced a continuous illusion of freshness ; and the touch of Euripidean compassion with which he softened his humour was well adapted to Hellenistic audiences, whose maturer civilization could no longer enjoy the brutal fun of the Old Comedy. His mirror distorted less grotesquely than that of Aristophanes ; but his scenes

[1] For a recent more sympathetic study of Menander, see A. W. Gomme, *Essays in Greek History and Literature*, pp. 249–95.

lacked the animation and the abandon of its ancestor; in reading Menander we admire his craftsmanship and his good feeling, but we may forget to laugh.

Beside the complete five-act drama the Greeks of the classical age had invented brief character-sketch scenes known as mimes, which ordinarily were recited or sung instead of being acted. From these eventually developed the purely dramatic mimes that swept the Roman stage, a medley of loosely strung scenes as in a modern revue. But it is not certain whether this branch of entertainment had come into existence before the first century. The recitative mime on the other hand acquired literary form in the third century, and attained a position in relation to the older drama like that which Callimachus gave to the epyllia by the side of the Homeric epic. Among the surviving specimens of this new genre the comic sketches of half-educated townsfolk and of underworld characters by Herondas may be taken as typical of their kind.[1] The figures of Herondas are real persons and do credit to their author's power of observation; but his scenes are trivial or unsavoury. Such reputation as the mime has acquired in the world's literature is mainly due to Theocritus, a native of Syracuse who was attracted to the court of Ptolemy II and adopted the accomplished technique of the Alexandrian poets, yet remained at heart a Sicilian. Though his sketches included incidents from town life, his favourite subjects were pastoral scenes, in which Sicilian herdsmen make love to dairymaids or compete in singing-matches. Like a true mime-poet, Theocritus was a realist, whose shepherds called a crook a crook; yet his persons carry less conviction than their setting. Theocritus' peculiar genius lay in his descriptions of the sights and sounds of the Mediterranean summer-fields. But his landscapes were of the tame and serene type. Hellenistic travellers might bring home tales of the Alps and Himalayas, but no Hellenistic poet was fired in his imagination by these wilder and grander works of nature.

The merits and defects of Hellenistic poetry are summed up in its most characteristic product, the epigram. This

[1] The six extant mimes of Herondas were recovered in 1891 in a papyrus. It is uncertain whether the author was from Cos or from Miletus, and whether he lived at the time of the second or the third Ptolemy.

branch of composition had a long history, but it became particularly fashionable in the Hellenistic age. Even the great Callimachus practised it, and its popularity endured so long that collections of the best specimens came to be formed: hence of all forms of Hellenistic poetry it is best represented in its survivals.[1] The Hellenistic epigram not only served its original purpose of accompanying a dedication, but it took the place of the older lyric poetry by condensing the author's reflections in a few lines. No other form of poem could show off better the *esprit* with which Hellenistic writers knew how to give a novel and arresting turn to a familiar theme, or their gift of neat and terse expression. But many of their efforts were half wasted on the trite trinity of Wine, Woman, Song: not many probed the deeper problems of life or betrayed serious searchings of heart. In general the Hellenistic epigrams reveal the poet's wit but conceal his personality.

§ 5. ORATORY AND HISTORY

The prose literature of the Hellenistic age largely consisted of works on philosophy or science which will be discussed in the following chapters. Of Hellenistic oratory there is little to be said, because none of it is preserved. Not that the art of fine speaking fell wholly into discredit. Greek eloquence had behind it a tradition extending to Nestor and Odysseus, and it possessed a recent master in Demosthenes, whose best speeches at once became classics and were studied in Greek schools. After the Macedonian conquest occasions for public oratory were still to be found. To say nothing of epideictic displays at the numerous festivals, there remained some scope for a well-turned speech in the municipal assemblies and courts, and especially on embassies which went to solicit a monarch's good-will or to offer peace between belligerents. Furthermore, the study of oratory was now pursued as part of a higher education, being even admitted, though with misgivings, into the curriculum of the philosophical colleges. Formal treatises on rhetoric were published by Aristotle and

[1] The earliest known anthology was by Meleager of Gadara (a writer of the first century B.C.), whose specimens were mostly from the third century. Our chief collection, the *Anthologia Palatina*, was not compiled until the tenth century A.D.

Theophrastus, and henceforward specialists in this branch of teaching established themselves in all the busier towns (especially at Rhodes and in western Asia Minor). Yet in practical politics oratory hardly repaid the trouble of such intensive study. In the monarchical administrations of course it went for nothing, and in the city-governments the conversion of nominal democracies into actual plutocracies (p. 278) created an atmosphere that was less receptive to eloquence. At Athens Demosthenes' nephew Demochares acquired some influence as a speaker (p. 38), but the temperature of the Ecclesia eventually fell to a point at which speech lost the free use of its wings. The prevailing style of Hellenistic oratory was that of the "Asianic" school, founded *c.* 275 B.C. by Hegesias of Magnesia-on-Sipylus. Hegesias led a deliberate reaction against Attic oratory as exemplified by Isocrates. For the Athenian's rotund periods he substituted brief staccato sentences; in place of his predecessor's sober and precise diction he cultivated a strained and turgid style. The less the occasion, the greater the passion.

It is hardly less difficult to pass a confident judgment upon the historians of the Hellenistic period, for most of them are only preserved in fragments or at second hand. Yet the Hellenistic output of historiography far surpassed that of classical times, and much of this work was undoubtedly of more than momentary interest. The fecundity of the Hellenistic historians was partly due to the stimulus which Aristotle and his school gave to historical research, partly to the obvious historical interest of the Macedonian conquests. Increased production also carried with it higher specialization.

Among the works of narrow scope the most numerous were histories of particular Greek cities or districts, a type coeval with Herodotus, which Aristotle had brought back into favour. Scarcely any of the older parts of the Greek world failed to find its chronicler: even Laconia produced its own antiquarian (Sosibius, a writer of early third century). The most notable of the municipal histories was the Atthis of the Athenian Philochorus (*c.* 275), which filled seventeen volumes and became a standard work. It would be rash to assume that all these local chronicles were based on serious research; but the best of the Hellenistic historians fully appreciated the value of documentary evidence. A collection of acts and treaties from the archives of Athens, and perhaps of other cities, was published by Antigonus Gonatas' brother-in-law Craterus; and a whole series of local histories was written by the antiquarian Polemo of Ilium (*c.* 175), in which extensive use was made of the epigraphic evidence collected by him on the spot.

In addition to monographs on particular cities Hellenistic historians composed a copious biographic literature. It is not surprising that with the career of Alexander before their eyes these writers should have appreciated the importance of the individual in history; but far from confining their interest to men of action they equally studied the philosophers, artists and men of letters. Philosophers were immortalized in a series of Lives by Aristotle's pupil Aristoxenus, and artists by Antigonus of Carystus. (*c.* 240) About 200 B.C. standard collections of biographies were compiled by two scholars named Satyrus and Hermippus; though these authors were not rigidly critical and lent too much ear to mere gossip, they were at any rate comprehensive in their picture galleries.[1] To the Hellenistic period also belongs the only notable specimen of autobiography by a Greek writer, the Memoirs of Aratus of Sicyon. Though this work has been lost, it is clear that, like most of the Roman books of that type, it was, in effect, an Apology.[2]

The general histories produced in the Hellenistic age had this feature in common, that they limited their field of study to recent events. For the earlier history of Greece the work of Ephorus (an elder contemporary of Alexander) was accepted as definitive; on the other hand the new world created by Alexander and his successors was eager to read about its own beginnings. Among the broader topics of Hellenistic history the Anabasis of Alexander was of course a favourite. Apart from its intrinsic interest, it was a comparatively easy subject to handle, because of the natural unity of the story and the wealth of authentic material available from the king's carefully compiled Journals. The best accounts of his campaigns

[1] A fragment of Satyrus' Life of Euripides has been recovered in a papyrus. See L. C. Lewis, in J. U. Powell and E. A. Barber, *New Chapters in Greek Literature*, p. 144 ff.

[2] The so-called Memoirs of Demetrius I and Pyrrhus were probably nothing more than their administrative " acta diurna," which all Hellenistic kings compiled, in imitation of Alexander's gazettes.

were given by two officers who had accompanied him on his Grand Tour, Aristobulus and Ptolemy (the future king of Egypt). Each of these wrote a straightforward and generally truthful tale, and it is due to the good judgment of the later historian Arrian in selecting these as his chief authorities that his is the best surviving narrative of Alexander's campaigns. But the works of Ptolemy and Aristobulus met with less success than they deserved. Their market was eventually spoilt by a writer named Clitarchus [1] (probably *c.* 275 B.C.), who divined that the Hellenistic reading public would not be content with the bare truth about Alexander and boldly added fresh hues to the king's rainbow. His "romantic" history therefore gained a wider vogue than Arrian's in Roman days, and went a long way to shape the Alexander tradition of the Middle Ages.

The history of the fifty or sixty years after Alexander's death was composed by an ex-officer named Hieronymus, who had served on the staffs of Eumenes, Antigonus I, and Antigonus Gonatas. His work for the period 323–302 is partly preserved in the compilation of Diodorus. This writer's abridged narrative suffices to show that Hieronymus equalled Ptolemy or Aristobulus in accuracy, and possessed a peculiar skill in reducing an unusually complex episode of military history to a comprehensible narrative. The period between the battle of Leuctra and the death of Seleucus was covered by a writer of the early third century named Duris. This author, who also wrote monographs on Greek art and literature, clearly had a wider range of interest than constitutions and campaigns; but for him history was a kind of peep-show, and his object in composing it was to feast his readers' eyes with gaudy scenery. Needless to say, he achieved popularity, and it is strange, though not lamentable, that he has left few traces of himself. A more serious loss is that of a writer named Phylarchus (*c.* 200), who continued the history of Hieronymus to the death of Cleomenes, with special reference to the events of European Greece. As a partisan of Sparta in her struggle against Achæans and Macedonians, Phylarchus wrote more like an advocate than a judge and imitated the pleaders in Greek law-courts with a

[1] On Aristobulus, Ptolemy and Clitarchus, see esp. Tarn, *Alexander the Great*, II, pp. 16–55.

lachrymose style of argument. But at least he was a serious person who wrote to convince rather than to entertain.

Another writer whose loss is both strange and regrettable is Timæus of Tauromenium (early and middle third century), who wrote a comprehensive work on Sicily and the western Mediterranean from the earliest times to 264. Timæus is chiefly known to us through Polybius, who branded him as a pedant without any standards of judgment, standing helpless before the mass of his materials. Yet he became the standard historian for the western Greeks ; if his critical powers were defective, his zeal in collecting information was invaluable, and he appreciated the importance of documentary evidence.

A bridge between the histories of East and West was built *c.* 150 B.C. by Polybius of Megalopolis, who by general consent ranks as second only to Thucydides among Greek historians.[1] In a work of forty volumes he covered the period 264–146, in which the two halves of the Mediterranean became merged into one political system. Of this treatise we possess several books intact, others in excerpts, others again in the paraphrase of Livy. Great as was Polybius' task, he was excellently qualified for it, for he gained first-hand knowledge of Greek politics as a leader of the Achæan League, and subsequently obtained insight into the Roman world as the friend and travelling-companion of Scipio Æmilianus. On first acquaintance, it is true, Polybius gives an impression of fussiness rather than of power. In style he is as verbose as Thucydides was compact—the literary counterpart of the interminable public documents of the Hellenistic cities. It was perhaps a venial error in him that he oscillated between two inconsistent philosophies of history, now ascribing the march of events to Providence, and now to Chance, and that he gave a disporportionate amount of space to the petty doings of his own Achæan League. A worse defect was his narrowly intellectual outlook and his tendency to reduce statesmanship to a mere knack of managing people : compared with Livy, one might say that Polybius was all head and no heart. But if Polybius did not quite rise to his theme, he produced one of the few ancient histories which may reasonably claim to be called scientific. In amassing materials for his vast

[1] For an appreciation of Polybius, see especially T. R. Glover in *Cambr. Anc. Hist.*, VIII, ch. 1.

subject he displayed unwearied industry, often conducting an independent research on a point of detail, sometimes undertaking a journey in order to understand a campaign. His critical acumen and impartiality have generally stood the test of attacks by modern critics.[1] Above all, he was on the whole successful in grasping the reason and the significance of the Roman conquests—no mean achievement for a contemporary,—and he has been the chief means by which modern readers have been able to envisage them in their proper light.

The tale of notable Hellenistic historians ends with Posidonius of Apamea-on-Orontes (early first century), who continued the narrative of Polybius to the time of Sulla. Like his predecessor, Posidonius was a well-travelled man and had acquaintance with the leading Roman politicians of his day. Since history was but one of his fields of study, it may be assumed that his work was more superficial; on the other hand he was accounted far superior to Polybius as a stylist. His disappearance is as strange as that of Duris, and more to be deplored.

An important accessory to the historical works of the Hellenistic period was the *Chronographiæ* of Eratosthenes of Cyrene (*c.* 225), who fixed the dates of Greek history from 1184/3 (the estimated year of the fall of Troy) in reference to years of Spartan kings, of city-magistrates and of Olympian festivals, and thus created the first comparative time-table with any pretension to accuracy. His work is a fine example of the scientific vein which runs through the writings of the best Hellenistic historians.

In the Hellenistic age prose fiction, which had hitherto lived as a parasite on history, was established as an independent branch of literature. In Alexander's time the art of the story-teller was of course nothing new in Greece, yet its products had not found their way into books, save as parentheses in historical texts. But Alexander's conquests stimulated the naturally healthy appetite of the Greeks for tales of adventure to such an extent, that alongside of the more imaginative histories like that of Clitarchus a literature

[1] The most notable exception to this rule is in his discussion of the causes of the Second Punic War (III, 15), which is a confused and ineffective piece of special pleading in the interests of Rome.

of avowed fiction came into existence. Most of the Hellenistic writers of fiction were merely concerned to satisfy the general public's craving for the marvellous; the most audacious of them, Antiphanes of Berge in Macedonia, gave his readers such monstrous morsels to swallow that he earned fame as an ancient Baron Münchhausen. Less imaginative writers contented themselves with compiling collections of *mirabilia*, a prolific minor branch of Hellenistic literature. Others again used the tale of travel as a vehicle of propaganda, in the manner of Swift or Montesquieu. A writer named Euemerus (*c.* 300) described a journey to "Panchæa" in the Indian Ocean (for which Socotra perhaps served as a rough model), and pretended to have discovered there documentary evidence about the origin of the gods, in whom he saw nothing but departed heroes. Another Erewhon of the Indian Ocean (which may have embodied hazy memories of Ceylon) was invented by an author named Iambulus;[1] in this "Land of the Sun" communism had been established and class-war abolished. It is not unlikely that the love-romance was also a creation of the Hellenistic period. In Roman times it was well-established genre, and the similarity of its plots to those of the New Comedy suggests that it dated back to the third or second century. But no books, or names of books, in this branch of fiction have survived from Hellenistic times.

§ 6. PHILOLOGY AND SCHOLARSHIP

The contribution of the Hellenistic Greeks to the world's literature is to be measured not only by their own production, but also by the services which they rendered towards the preservation and better appreciation of the classical authors. By the formation of libraries and the multiplication of copies in the book-market they averted the risk—which in days of MS. reproduction was never negligible—of classical works disappearing altogether. They coped with another danger resulting from the lack of authenticated originals, the progressive metamorphosis of texts by copyists' errors.[2] The

[1] To judge by his name, Iambulus was a Semite. But the vein of socialistic propaganda in which he wrote was thoroughly Greek. Presumably he used a *nom de plume*.

[2] Official texts of Æschylus, Sophocles and Euripides were kept at Athens. But this method of safeguarding texts was unusual.

fixing of standard texts of the classical authors was undertaken at the two great libraries of Alexandria and Pergamum, but more especially at Alexandria, where more than one copy of any classic was generally available for comparison. The Alexandrian librarians prepared more or less accurate texts of the classical Greek poets, but they gave particular attention to the Iliad and Odyssey, and their recensions of these works represent their editorial methods at their best. The first recension of Homer was made *c.* 275 by Zenodotus, who relied mainly on a collation of the numerous available MSS. to establish a trustworthy text ; a final and authoritative edition was prepared by Aristarchus of Samothrace (*c.* 175),[1] who based his text on a careful study of Homer's language and point of view. A third service of the Hellenistic scholars to the classics was the provision of explanatory notes on authors whose language or thought offered difficulties to the reading public of their day. The author who needed and received most elucidation was Homer ; but the difficulties of interpreting him were enhanced by a tendency to canonize him not only as a literary artist but as an infallible source of correct information. This fundamentalism culminated in the vagaries of a Pergamene scholar named Crates (*c.* 170), who explained away all awkward passages in Homer as having an allegorical meaning. But the Alexandrian scholars, and particularly Aristarchus, showed better historical sense and composed their commentaries on substantially the same methods as those of modern annotators. The work of the Hellenistic commentators is partly preserved in the " scholia " of Roman and Byzantine times, which drew largely upon Hellenistic sources. The longest surviving commentary is a considerable fragment from the notes of the first-century scholar, Didymus, on Demosthenes.[2] Though Didymus lacked Aristarchus' acumen he preserved the Hellenistic tradition of learning and did his work very thoroughly according to his lights.

The analytical work performed on the classical texts by the Alexandrian scholars led them on to the systematic study of

[1] Not to be confused with the mathematician Aristarchus of Samos (p. 347), who lived a century earlier.

[2] H. Diels and W. Schubart, *Didymos' Kommentar zu Demosthenes.* (Berliner Klassiker texte, vol. I.)

language and grammar; and a group of Pergamene savants, whose starting-point was the Stoic curriculum in formal logic, was drawn into the same field of research. Alexandrians and Pergamenes came into conflict over the principles of classification in grammar, and Aristarchus polemized with Crates on this question as on Homeric interpretation. The work of the two schools is summed up in an extant grammatical primer by Aristarchus' pupil Dionysius the Thracian (*c.* **130**), from which our present-day grammatical terminology is derived. To another Alexandrian, Aristophanes of Byzantium (early second century) we owe the doubtful blessing of Greek accents, which he invented as an aid to foreigners in acquiring correct Greek intonation.

§ 7. CONCLUSION

A general verdict on Hellenistic literature can only be passed with diffidence, because so little of it can be read at first hand. In favour of the Hellenistic writers (of non-technical literature) it may be said that as a class they were highly industrious, both in collecting materials and in presenting them in an elegant form; they used their powers of observation well; they commanded the range of the gentler emotions—quiet humour, restrained pity, the mild exhilaration of the bon-vivant. But to say nothing of lesser defects, such as occasional excesses of erudition or over-refinement of style, they could not or would not let themselves go. Their feelings rarely rose to a passion, and their imagination fluttered rather than soared. Their lack of enthusiasm definitely relegates them to a level below the writers of the classical age.

What was the cause of this decline from classical standards? According to a common opinion it lay in the loss of political liberty. This reason may help to explain the far more profound deterioration which Greek literature underwent after the Roman invasions. But the Macedonian overlordship soon ceased to be felt as a foreign domination; and the humiliation, if such it was, of a restricted municipal sovereignty was more than compensated by the commanding position which the Greek nation had won for itself in all the countries of the Near East. In giving the Greeks a new sense of power and widening their range of experience, the campaigns of Alexander were calculated to stimulate rather than to damp down the play of the Greek mind.

Was Hellenistic literature emasculated by the patronage which it enjoyed? It would be possible to name one or two minor bards who served no purpose but to glorify their employers, and to pick out occasional passages in the major poets which are studiously devotional in tone. But there is even less evidence of illegitimate pressure exercised by the Hellenistic kings upon their clients than appears among the Augustan poets. There is no ground for believing that the Greek monarchs dictated to the Hellenistic writers what they should say, or how they should say it. Still less need we suppose that the ladies of the Hellenistic courts were responsible for the lack of robustness which is noticeable, for instance, in the Alexandrian poets. These full-blooded princesses were not the sort to deal by half-measures, or to prefer a canary to a nightingale.

A more cogent reason for the comparative tameness of the Alexandrian poets may be found in their secluded existence in the Museum, which one of their critics not unjustly called a "literary hen-coop." Life in such institutions might be congenial to workers in the exact sciences; among literary men it would no doubt make for good taste and high polish, but it would tend to discourage free play of imagination or sentiment. The hypercritical attitude of the coterie at Alexandria is illustrated by the quarrel, truly infantile in its ferocity, which broke out between Callimachus and Apollonius over the correct length of an epic poem, and by a confession of Callimachus, the prototype of Horace's "odi profanum vulgus," in which he wrote himself down more than the vulgar.[1]

Another explanation, which carries further afield than the Alexandrian fowl-run, is that the settlers in the Near East were at first too much preoccupied with their material interests and had too little leisure to give much thought to literary composition. It is significant that among the Hellenistic men of letters only a mere handful were natives of Alexandria or of other new foundations; the great majority of them came from the older towns in the Aegean and Hellespontine areas, from Cyrene or Sicily.

[1] *σικχαίνω πάντα τὰ δημόσια* (*Epigrs.*, 29, 4).

Lastly, in the second century the Roman conquest cast its shadow before, and bred disillusionment in intellectual as well as in political circles. After 200 the Greek world still produced excellent scholars and men of science, but no great literary figure save that of Polybius, and this author's message, significantly enough, was one of resignation rather than of hope. In this loss of nerve we may see the forerunner of the intellectual quietism which spread across the Greek world under Roman sway.

But a full explanation for the abundance of talent and lack of genius in the literature of the Hellenistic age will probably never be given. Besides, if Hellenistic literature marks a decline compared with that of the classical period, we must remember at what a level the classical authors wrote. It has been well said that Hellenistic literature was "merely first-rate."[1] But it was no less than that.

[1] Gilbert Murray, *Greek Literature*, p. 371.

CHAPTER XIX

HELLENISTIC SCIENCE

§ 1. GEOGRAPHY

WHEN Alexander set forth to invade the Persian Empire, it was his deliberate intention to make scientific as well as political conquests. He explored as well as overran the Persian dominions, and he made provision for collecting strange specimens of the fauna and flora of the countries occupied by him. Moreover, while the Macedonian king was accumulating fresh materials for study, a new impulse to scientific research was being given by Aristotle and the Peripatetic school. While the Peripatetics in theory retained Aristotle's ideal of encyclopædic knowledge, in practice they specialized in the study of nature, leaving philosophy in the narrower sense to the Academy and other schools. In their special field of research they were the first to apply consistently the practice of systematic observation, which Hippocrates had introduced into medical science in the fifth century, but Aristotle had been the earliest to recognize as of fundamental importance in all branches of natural science. But in acquiring the habit of methodical observation the Hellenistic men of science did not neglect the use of abstract reasoning which the Greeks of the classical age had applied with excellent results in the field of mathematical studies. It would be hard to say whether the achievements of Hellenistic science were mainly due to the newer or the older method of research.

A special feature of scientific study in the Hellenistic period was its concentration at Alexandria. While Athens remained the headquarters of the humanistic faculty, the atmosphere of that city was not congenial to the pursuit of natural science. Accordingly those members of the Peripatetic school who remained at Athens devoted themselves to other subjects—notably to historical research; those who followed Demetrius of Phalerum to Alexandria mostly turned to natural science. In the Museum at Alexandria the Fellows found ideal conditions for scientific study. They had the necessary material equipment ready to hand; they were absolutely untrammelled in their freedom of research; in the early days of the dynasty they received personal encouragement from the kings, whose interests were directed no less to science than to literature.

Geographical studies received a great impetus from the campaigns of Alexander, which doubled the width of the Greek horizon, and interest in them was kept up by the explorations of Alexander's successors in Asia and the Red Sea, by Pytheas' voyage in the Atlantic, and by Timosthenes' survey of the Mediterranean coastlands (p. 297). But the really distinctive contribution of the Hellenistic Greeks to geography lay in the use of mathematics to determine the size of the earth and the outline of its continents. By the time of Aristotle the fundamental discovery that the earth is spherical in shape had already been made, but estimates of its size were still mere guesswork. Its magnitude was ascertained by Eratosthenes (*c.* 225) by a method of measurement which gave a result of 252,000 stadia (*c.* 24,675 miles) for the globe's circumference, i.e. barely two hundred miles short of the true perimeter.[1] The first step towards creating a network of latitudes and longitudes was taken by the traveller Pytheas, who ascertained the latitude of his native Massilia, and of other places visited by him, by measuring the sun's shadow. The use of two perpendicular axes as reference lines in plotting the world's map was suggested by Aristotle's pupil Dicæarchus, who selected a west-to-east line from the Straits of Gibraltar to Mount Taurus, and a north-to-south transverse from Lysimachia to Syene (Aswan). Eratosthenes went on to mark out the "inhabited earth" (from Thule to Meroë in Nubia) in seven parallel zones, which he determined as far as possible by comparing the known data of latitude. In default of accurate meridian lines, which ancient geographers could not trace for lack of efficient chronometers,

[1] The stadium employed by Eratosthenes was probably the short one of 157·6 metres or 517 feet. (See Jüthner in Pauly-Wissowa-Kroll, s.v. Stadion.) On the method of demonstration, see Appendix 15.

he drew a number of north-to-south cross-lines on the basis of surface mensurations, and thus completed the first grid of latitudes and longitudes. By combining the observations of Pytheas and of Alexander's admiral Nearchus, who had reported a strong flow of ebb and tide in the Atlantic and Indian Oceans respectively, Eratosthenes further discovered that the seas are all one and that Europe, Asia and Africa constitute one huge island. Combining the new data from explorers with his own calculations, he wrote a standard geographical handbook which naturally erred in many details but was none the less the first scientific description of the world. Indeed it is not too much to say that Eratosthenes has contributed more than any other individual to a correct delineation of the earth's map.

Eratosthenes' work was refined on by another Alexandrian scientist named Hipparchus (*c.* 140), who proposed a narrower and more carefully drawn mesh of latitudes and longitudes. For the determination of latitudes he suggested a systematic measurement of the sun's shadow by observers in all countries. But this promising plan was never carried into effect. In Hipparchus' own lifetime a new turn was being given to geographical studies by the historian Polybius, who could not understand the value of mathematical observation and laid a one-sided stress on mere description and surface mensuration. After the second century the only important new contribution to geography was a treatise *On the Ocean* by Polybius' successor Posidonius, who travelled in Spain under the protection of the Roman legions and made the last serious attempt by an ancient writer to study the Atlantic. Fortunately, the work of the Hellenistic geographers is preserved for us in large measure in the descriptive manual of Strabo (of the Augustan era), and in the Γεωγραφικὴ Σύνταξις of Claudius Ptolemæus (*c.* A.D. 150), who realized, in however imperfect a way, Hipparchus' ideal of a close network of latitudes and longitudes.

§ 2. PURE AND APPLIED MATHEMATICS

The study of pure mathematics had reached a comparatively advanced stage before the time of Alexander, and geometry in particular had been systematically attacked by the school of Pythagoras in Italy and by Eudoxus of Cnidus (early fourth century). At the outset of the Hellenistic age it received a fresh impetus from a scholar named Eucleides, who was one of the first men of learning to take up his residence at Alexandria. (*c.* 300) Eucleides pursued several branches of mathematical research (Conic Sections, Optics, etc.), but his fame rests on his *Elements* (Plane and Solid Geometry, and Theory of Numbers), and especially on the first six books thereof, in which he summed up and rounded off existing knowledge of plane geometry. The structural coherence of the *Elements*, and the elegance and compactness of his proofs of individual propositions, at once raised his work to the position of a standard textbook, from which it was not deposed until a generation ago. The geometry of plane curves was further advanced by Archimedes of Syracuse (*c.* 287–212), and by Apollonius of Perga (*c.* 230), who composed a standard work on Conic Sections and fixed its terminology. Solid geometry was carried several stages further by Archimedes, who considered that his life's work was crowned by his discovery of the ratio of volume between a cylinder and an inscribed sphere. The age-old problem of the value of *pi* also received its best solution until modern times from the Syracusan mathematician. In the second century trigonometry was raised into an independent branch of study by Hipparchus.

With this last scholar the heroic age of discovery in pure mathematics came to an end : indeed, the Greeks were already bordering upon the limits of what was attainable by purely geometric methods of reasoning. In the sphere of pure numbers Archimedes invented the "Sand-Reckoner," a method of denoting inconceivably great magnitudes ;[1] but this was a poor substitute for an algebraic notation, which was the chief deficiency in Greek mathematics. In the third century A.D. a belated Alexandrian genius named Diophantus invented a rudimentary system of algebraic symbols ;[2] but this discovery, which might have revolutionized Greek

[1] According to Sir T. L. Heath (*Cambr. Anc. Hist.*, VII, p. 306), the Sand-Reckoner could express any number up to the 80,000th millionth-millionth power of ten.

[2] Some isolated algebraic symbols have been found in a papyrus of the second or late first century A.D. See F. E. Robbins, *Classical Philology*, 1929, p. 321 ff.

mathematics if it had been made in the third century B.C., came too late to stimulate fresh research.

In the field of applied mathematics the interest of the Hellenistic men of science was mainly confined to astronomy. In this branch of studies the problem which invited most discussion concerned the relative motions of the solar system. Previous to the time of Alexander the prevalent theory (formulated by Eudoxus of Cnidus) was that the sun, moon and planets revolved round the earth on paths produced by the motions of a complicated system of concentric spheres. On the other hand, observations by a scholar named Heraclides Ponticus (a contemporary of Aristotle) had suggested to him that Venus and Mercury were satellites of the sun, and that the earth rotated daily round its own axis. Heraclides' theories gave birth to a yet more momentous hypothesis, which was first put forward by Aristarchus of Samos[1] (early third century), that the sun was the centre of the entire planetary system. This opinion was denounced by the Stoic philosopher, Cleanthes, on the score of impiety (p. 362), but no secular arm offered to avenge the injury to Heaven, and discussion of the heliocentric view remained on a scientific plane. In the second century Aristarchus won a notable adherent in a Hellenized native of Seleucia-on-Tigris named Seleucus (*c.* 150);[2] but the general consensus of ancient astronomers pronounced against him. Their opinion was summed up by Hipparchus, who declared that "we must abide by the facts of observation." In truth the data available in the Hellenistic era were insufficient to decide the question one way or another: it required a prolonged use of the telescope in modern times before it could be finally solved. But Aristarchus' hypothesis bore fruit in due time, for it was the starting-point of the researches of Copernicus.[3] Another legacy of Hellenistic astronomers to modern science was the epicyclic theory of planetary motion (probably invented by Apollonius of Perga), which was not definitely

[1] This Aristarchus lived a century before the Homeric editor, Aristarchus of Samothrace. It is not known whether he was one of the Alexandrian men of science.

[2] According to Plutarch (*Platonicæ Quæstiones*, VII, ch. 1), Seleucus actually proved the heliocentric hypothesis. This is out of the question, because he lacked the necessary data.

[3] Sir T. L. Heath, *Aristarchus of Samos*, p. 301.

driven from the field until the time of Newton and Kepler. This hypothesis sought to explain the apparent retrograde motion of the outer planets by assuming that they moved on a circular orbit which itself was carried round on the circumference of a larger circle.

A vague anticipation of the greatest of modern astronomical discoveries may be detected in an explanation offered by the Babylonian scholar Seleucus for the fluctuations of the ocean tides. From the synchronism of the tidal variations with the phases of the moon he inferred a causal relation between the two phenomena, and went so far as to suggest that the interaction of moon and earth was the prime cause of tidal motion.[1] But this dim recognition of the force of gravitation was bound at best to remain an unconfirmed hypothesis; in point of fact, it did not even succeed in creating a stir, like the heliocentric theory of Aristarchus. A topic to which the Hellenistic astronomers gave more general attention was the size and distance of the sun and moon from the earth. Their solutions of these problems were mostly wide of the mark, but with the help of trigonometrical methods Hipparchus estimated the distance of the moon from the earth at about thirty-three earth-diameters, which was a close approximation to the true ratio.

To Hipparchus credit is also due for some notable discoveries which were obtained by systematic observation rather than by acute theorizing or skilful calculation. This patient researcher constructed a chart of some 850 stars which he located accurately by measuring their angular distance from the ecliptic, and he went on to compare his results with data from earlier Greek astronomers and from Babylonian men of science. In the light of these observations he deduced the length of the solar year with an error of six minutes and fourteen seconds, and the length of the lunar month within one second of the true figure. In making this second calculation Hipparchus almost certainly made use of some very accurate Babylonian observations. It is a matter of dispute whether he also drew upon a Babylonian astronomer, Kidenas, in proving the precession of the equinoxes; but in computing the rate of abbreviation of the solar year he certainly applied the results of personal observations which he compared with

[1] Tarn, *Hellenistic Civilisation*, p. 270.

those of a Greek named Timocharis, who had lived some 150 years before his own time.[1]

Hipparchus closes the list of great astronomers, as of geographers, in ancient times. The example of methodical observation which he had set was lost upon his successors, and with it the habit of independent research. A special reason for the decline of astronomical studies may be found in their progressive infection with astrology. This parasite upon astronomy, which had long flourished in Babylon alongside the genuine science, had little effect upon Greek thought until the second century; but from that time it permeated the Greek world and deflected men of science into an apparent short cut which was in reality a blind alley. But the ground won by the Hellenistic astronomers was mostly held by their successors. One of the last Alexandrian men of science, Claudius Ptolemæus (A.D. 150), embodied much of the work of the Hellenistic pioneers in his treatise, the Μεγάλη Σύνταξις, which was used as a standard textbook by the Arabian scholars (under the name of "Almagest"), and after its translation into Latin in 1496 became the starting-point of modern astronomical research.

As a diversion from his studies in pure mathematics the Syracusan scholar Archimedes made fruitful excursions into mechanics and hydrostatics. In the former branch of studies he worked out the rules of action of the lever, the pulley and the screw; in the latter he determined the effects of immersion in a fluid upon the weight of solid objects. The practical value of his mechanical researches is shown in his inventions, the compound pulley, the "Archimedean screw" (a predecessor of the modern turbine, which was used for hoisting irrigation water, and for draining sumps out of mines), and various engines of war with which he kept at bay the Roman besiegers of Syracuse in 213–2. We may dismiss the story that he once ran undressed out of his bath into the streets of Syracuse, crying "I've got it!" (the solution of a hydrostatic problem). But we would fain cherish as historical his proud boast, "Give me a fulcrum, and I'll shift the earth," as his formulation of faith in the unlimited powers of science.

As a practical inventor, Archimedes was rivalled by an Alexandrian contemporary named Ctesibius. His discoveries

[1] Heath, *op. cit.*, p. 310.

are in some cases difficult to distinguish from those of his successors Philo (second century) and Hero (probably of the first century A.D.). But it is fairly certain that he devised a taximeter, an air-gun and a water-organ ; and we may probably assign to him the first penny-in-the-slot machine and the first steam-engine.[1] But Ctesibius and his school lived in a society which enjoyed the doubtful blessings of cheap labour and so did not appreciate machinery of the useful order. Therefore they mostly wasted their energy in the contrivance of mere playthings.

§ 3. THE ORGANIC SCIENCES

In the field of organic science the achievement of the Hellenistic Greeks was comparatively slender. The relative lack of interest in this branch of research is all the more surprising, as Alexander had provided plenty of fresh material for investigation, and Ptolemy II laid out a zoological garden at Alexandria, which he filled with novel specimens captured by his hunting parties in the interior of Africa. Nay more, some brilliant examples of methodical observation and classification of organic species had been given by Aristotle in his biological treatises. But the science of zoology which he had created was carried no further by his school. On the other hand, Aristotle's chief pupil, Theophrastus, applied his master's methods to the study of plants. In his surviving treatises, the *History of Plants* and the *Causes of Plants,* he furnished a description of some five hundred species (inclusive of various exotics which had first been brought to the notice of the Greeks during Alexander's campaigns), and gave a rudimentary account of the essentials of plant life. Theophrastus knew little of plant nourishment and reproduction, so that he remained at a loss for a scientific basis of classification. But his accurate descriptions laid a good foundation for a science of botany, and it is strange that after his death the study of plants again shrank into an empiric pursuit for agricultural or medicinal purposes.

[1] See Appendix 16. Like all engines previous to James Watt's, Ctesibius' machine was propelled by the suction of escaping steam ; unlike these others, it produced a rotary, not a reciprocating motion. The penny-in-the-slot machine, the steam-engine and the water-organ are described in Hero's *Pneumatica,* chs. 21, 50, 76. Cf. also H. Diels, *Die Antike Technik,* pp. 57–69.

Of the organic sciences medicine had already made considerable progress before the days of Alexander. An extensive empirical knowledge of the healing art had long been in existence among the Egyptians and Babylonians, and it was perhaps from Babylon that the Hellenistic Greeks adopted the custom of appointing public officers of health, who gave free treatment to all-comers in return for a fixed salary.[1] But medicine as a science was the creation of Hippocrates and his school in the fifth century ; and the Hellenistic physicians were in a direct line of descent from the Hippocratics. They improved upon the Hippocratic method of research, which consisted in careful observation of patients, by dissecting the dead bodies of animals and of men.[2] Anatomical research was particularly in favour at Alexandria, which in consequence became the principal school of Hellenistic medicine. The value of dissection was demonstrated by two of its first practitioners, Herophilus and Erasistratus (the latter of whom subsequently became court doctor to Seleucus I). The work of these pioneers is not easy to distinguish, though it appears that Erasistratus did little more than refine upon his predecessor in matters of detail. Their most momentous achievement was to explain the functions of the brain and of the nervous system. They made these discoveries by tracing the nerves (which they were the first to distinguish from the sinews) to the brain, and by discriminating between the sensory and the motor nerves. Thus they solved once for all the puzzle of the grey matter in the skull, which had completely baffled Aristotle and his predecessors, and they created the new science of physiology. Herophilus also came within short distance of another fundamental discovery by his investigation of the blood-system and the lungs. He traced back the motions of the pulse through the arteries to the heart, which he recognized as the cause of the pulsations. He did not follow out the circuit of arteries and veins, and he failed

[1] This practice is illustrated by an Athenian inscription of *c.* 250 B.C. (*Inscr. Græc.*, 2nd ed., II, 1, 772) : *ἐπειδὴ πάτριόν ἐστι τοῖς ἰατροῖς ὅσοι δημοσιεύουσιν θύειν τῷ 'Ασκληπίῳ.* A special tax for medical services was levied at Delphi (Ditt., *Syll.*, 437), at Halicarnassus (*P. Zeno Cairo*, 59035), and in Egypt (*P.S.I.*, III, 371).

[2] The story that the Hellenistic physicians practised vivisection on human subjects is probably to be dismissed as a malicious invention. (W. H. S. Jones in *Cambr. Anc. Hist.*, VII, p. 286.) There is certainly no evidence of their having learnt anything by experiments on the living subject.

to explain the connection between the blood-system and the lungs. But his study of pulse and lung rhythms was a big step towards discovering the circulation of the blood.

The work of the Alexandrian pioneers did not lead to those further discoveries to which it pointed. But it made possible a great development of surgery, for with the increase of anatomical knowledge major operations ceased to be mere gambles against desperate odds. Surgical art also benefited from research on anæsthetics, though nothing stronger than opium was discovered in antiquity. The researches of Herophilus and Erasistratus were recorded in the medical encyclopædia of Galen (*c.* A.D. 130), and thus became known to the second founders of medical science in the sixteenth and seventeenth centuries.

The status of Hellenistic physicians is revealed by their not infrequent appointment (by kings or cities) as official doctors, and their professional spirit by their readiness to visit areas of epidemics at great personal risk, or to render service unpaid.[1]

§ 4. CONCLUSION

The record of Hellenistic science shows a few notable gaps, such as the lack of systematic work in geology, which might have been expected to grow out of geography, and of the study of chemistry, whose fundamental problems had already been raised by the " physicists " of the classical period. But the most remarkable feature in its history was its failure to lead on from its first successes to a continuous growth like that which the modern pioneers of science inaugurated. This general falling off from an earlier promise can hardly be attributed to ignorance of scientific method. The best specimens of Hellenistic research reveal precisely that blend of observation and reasoning which usually yields the most solid results in scientific discovery. A more valid if partial explanation is that Hellenistic science lacked instruments of precision, such as the telescope and microscope, and this

[1] Public votes of thanks to self-sacrificing physicians are preserved from Tenos (Ditt., *Syll.*, 620), Rhodes (*ibid.*, 335), Cos (*ibid.*, 943), Carpathus (Michel, 436), and Lamia (*ibid.*, 297). On appointments of official doctors, see Rostovtzeff, *op. cit.*, II, pp. 1290–4.

at a stage when observation by the unaided eye could not carry them much further. This deficiency would help to explain the eventual stagnation of astronomy, botany and medicine. But the chief reason is, no doubt, to be found in that general loss of the spirit of hope and adventure which befell the Greek nation in the second century. It is significant that in the second century the Greek world became addicted to the practices of astrology and magic. In pursuing these delusive short cuts to success it proved that it had lost the faculty of patient research which distinguished the earlier Hellenistic pioneers.

Yet in the two centuries that followed the death of Alexander the Greeks achieved greater progress in natural science than was attained in any previous period of like duration, or in any subsequent two hundred years until the birth of the modern age of science. Moreover, Hellenistic discovery played a notable part in directing the efforts of early modern research. If the Greeks of the Roman and Byzantine periods added little to the Hellenistic heritage, at any rate they preserved a substantial portion of it for the benefit of the modern student. Whether the modern pioneers strove to supplement the information of the surviving ancient text-books, as the geographers did with Ptolemy's standard work on that subject, or revolted against their teachers, as did the astronomers against Ptolemy's *Almagest*, and the physicians against Galen's *Encyclopœdia*, their starting-point in discovery was usually not far from the position where some Hellenistic pioneer had left off. On the ground of its scientific achievement alone the Hellenistic age is entitled to a substantial space in world history.

CHAPTER XX

HELLENISTIC PHILOSOPHY

§ 1. THE OLDER SCHOOLS

IN the classical period Greek society derived its standards of behaviour from the teachings of the epic and gnomic poets and from the "custom of the city." But these traditional codes eventually ceased to satisfy the more reflective minds. In the fifth century they were attacked by the tragedians, and in the fourth century by the philosophers, who now definitely replaced the poets as the prophets of a more advanced morality. In the Hellenistic age the philosophers came into such wide request for ethical advice as they had never before experienced. The reason for their increased authority has often been sought in a general feeling of despair which is supposed to have overtaken the Greek people from the time of the Macedonian conquests, and to have turned them to philosophy as a solace and an anodyne. But, while we can undoubtedly detect a "loss of nerve" among the Greeks after the Roman conquest, there is no good evidence of similar symptoms of distress in the Hellenistic period. Such proof of discouragement as is usually offered is taken from the plays of Menander, whose ethics indeed might be summed up as a rule of resignation to capricious fortune. But Menander dealt in stock types rather than in the living representatives of his own age (p. 330), and his yielding temper did not reflect the mood of his Athenian fellow-citizens, whose pride and obstinacy survived more defeats than the poet lived to witness (chs. 8 and 9). Besides, Athens never was Greece, and in the early Hellenistic age its declining fortunes stood in sharp contrast with those of the Greek world in general. About 300 B.C., when Menander wrote his plays and the chief philosophic systems of the Hellenistic period were being formulated, the Greeks were still being carried on the wave of

Alexander's conquests and were not yet within sight of national decadence.[1] The demand made by the Hellenistic public upon its philosophers was not for an intellectual chloroform to stupefy it out of a sense of its misery, but for new standards of conduct to replace the old rules which had now definitely broken down. If the early Hellenistic period was one of hope rather than of despair, it was nevertheless one of difficulty and confusion. In the wholesale movement of population which followed upon Alexander's conquests the custom of the cities had plainly become inadequate as a guide of life, and the formulation of a new code was becoming a matter of practical urgency. In this respect we may compare the Hellenistic age with the present-day world, with its fundamental optimism and its transient bewilderment over the loss of its traditional standards.[2]

The demand for absolute moral guidance was eagerly met by the philosophers. Not only did they multiply the number of schools for regular students, but they conveyed their message to all that had ears to hear. They wrote systematic treatises for those taking the full course and tracts for those not yet initiated. Some laboured to convert kings,[3] others harangued the multitude at street corners.

Among the older schools the Academy had been securely endowed by Plato, and Aristotle's pupil Theophrastus made similar provision for the Lyceum. These two colleges carried with them a reputation that outlasted the Hellenistic period and seemed to mark them out as advisers-in-chief to the Hellenistic public. Yet neither school made use of its opportunity to become the keeper of the Greek conscience. At the Lyceum Theophrastus in person kept up the study of moral and political science and broke fresh ground in a treatise on jurisprudence (a field into which more Romans than Greeks followed him). But his successor Strato turned from

[1] Cf. Rostovtzeff, *op. cit.*, II, p. 1095 (" buoyant optimism ").

[2] A sign of the times was the elevation of Chance to a capricious ruler of the world. (See U. v. Wilamowitz-Moellendorff, *Der Glaube der Hellenen*, II, pp. 298–310.)

[3] On the Hellenistic kings, envisaged as *νόμος ἔμψυχος*, see E. R. Goodenough, *Yale Classical Studies*, II, pp. 55–102. Philonides the Epicurean, it is said, plied Antiochus IV with 150 tracts, and by this mass-attack secured him as a nominal adherent.

ethics to natural science, and although he failed to establish this branch of studies at Athens, he definitely altered the school's tradition in its choice of studies. Henceforth the Athenian Peripatetics became mainly concerned with historiography and paid no more than passing attention to philosophical subjects.

The Academics in so far remained true to the tradition of Socrates and Plato, as to give logic and theory of knowledge an important place in their curriculum, and of all Hellenistic schools they paid most regard to intellectual consistency. But their scrupulousness in avoiding unproved assertions played over into a merely destructive scepticism. The leading spirits of the "Middle Academy," Arcesilaus (315–240) and Carneades (213–128), used their dialectic ability with devastating effect in showing up the gaps in the more loosely compacted systems of other schools. But their advice to suspend judgment until the far-off day of certain knowledge should dawn must have seemed almost a mockery to a generation that could not wait, but demanded a positive moral doctrine as a matter of urgency. Arcesilaus, indeed, did allow for the need of a practical system of ethics based on mere probability, and Carneades made the same concession. But the Academics left it to the practical man to construct his code of working morals for himself.

§ 2. SCEPTICS, CYNICS, EPICUREANS

If the older schools lost by default their guardianship of the Greek conscience, several new schools offered to take up the trust. Among these the so-called Sceptics require no more than passing attention, for they held in themselves the least promise. The founder of this sect, Pyrrhon (365–275), not only shared the doubts of the Middle Academy as to the possibility of sure knowledge, but made a virtue of this disability. Asserting stoutly that nothing was known or could be known for certain, he welcomed this predicament, because if only we would be consistent in doubting everybody and everything, we should thereby attain a mood of complete indifference, and to achieve this attitude of utter unconcern was the goal of human conduct. But Pyrrhon, no less than the Academics, was taken aback by his own nihilism. Admitting the need to live and to act, he conceded the use of an empiric code of rules and in so doing stultified his entire doctrine. Like the Middle Academy, the Sceptical school did its best work in criticizing its neighbours. Pyrrhon's pupil Timon (320–230) made clever play in mock-epic poems (like Dryden's *Absalom and Achitophel*) at the expense of credulity and dogmatism, whether in the market-place or in the schoolroom. But throwing stones was a poor substitute for giving bread.

If the Sceptics carried indecision to the point of perversity, the rival philosophers of the Cynic sect, which was founded by Diogenes in the days of Alexander,[1] went to the other extreme of casting out doubt in too cavalier a fashion. In their opinion the path to virtue was perfectly straightforward. Accepted conventions had broken down, but what need to find others? Discard *all* conventions and return to nature—herein lay the sum of human wisdom. This doctrine had at least a negative value. Regarded as a protest against the over-refinements of civilization and the infatuations of the vulgar with their delusive quest for wealth, publicity and amusement, it was appropriate enough to its age, which certainly made a brave show of these substitutes for happiness. The Cynics, moreover, had the full courage of their convictions. They were not content, like some of their competitors, to found a college for those eager to learn, but set themselves to capture the incurious multitude. They went forth like mendicant friars to the market-places and delivered their message to any audience that might offer. In their speeches and tracts they were at pains to cultivate a catching style, and to this end they developed new forms of didactic literature, the satire and the "diatribe" or popular sermon. Among the Cynic propagandists the most notable figure was that of Bion of Olbia (*c.* 240), a manumitted slave who was perfectly at home with popular audiences and did not fear to give them unpalatable counsel. The surviving remnants of Cynical literature show that it possessed far more tang than the methodical treatises of other schools, whose members were usually too proud to express themselves forcibly.

[1] The name of "Cynic" was first applied to a pupil of Socrates named Antisthenes; but the real founder of the school of that name was Diogenes.

But the missionary zeal of the Cynics was worthy of a better cause. A "return to nature," strictly interpreted, meant a denial of all civilized custom, good as well as bad: as Voltaire wrote in reply to Rousseau, the modern advocate of "natural" simplicity, "cela nous donne le désir de marcher à quatre pattes." Some of the Cynics acted so far on their principles as to go unkempt and unlaundered, and even to neglect the ordinary decencies of life. In their anxiety to make a hit with its audiences this sect was tempted to throw dignity clean overboard. Bion, no doubt, was careful not to pass the line between the humorist and the clown, but his chief contemporary, Menippus of Gadara in Syria, ended by making caricature an object in itself. His satires, a medley of prose and verse, sank to the level of mere entertainment literature, like the Roman "saturæ," for which they served as a model. But the most serious deficiency in the Cynic philosophy was that it merely touched upon the individual's duty to himself and did not grapple with the more difficult and essential problem of his social obligations. True, it advocated "philanthropy" and held up Heracles as an example of manly worth; but the ideal of a self-contained life robbed Cynical philanthropy of its motive and object. In sum, the lack of intellectual application in the Cynical school condemned it to be either eccentric or commonplace in its teachings.

A more serious attempt to work out a new rule of life was made by the sect of the Epicureans. This school took its name from the founder Epicurus (341–270), who established the third of the Athenian colleges (commonly known as "the Garden"), and expounded a complete system of philosophy which underwent no modification after his death. Epicurus recognized the need of a logical basis to his ethical precepts, and in deference to the renewed interest in natural science which characterized his age he also provided them with a physical foundation. Reverting to the problem of the nature and origin of matter, he revived the doctrine of Leucippus and Democritus, that the world was created by the fortuitous concourse of atoms. In answer to the question, what is truth? he ruled that the evidence of the senses might be accepted, on condition that their impressions should be verified by repeated observation. It is true that the atomic theory as formulated by him was mere guesswork and would have been turned down at once by the men of science at Alexandria, and that his theory of knowledge left out of account the part played by the mind in analysing and re-combining sense-impressions. Though Epicurus professed a purely mechanical explanation of the universe and relegated the gods (whom in deference to popular opinion he would not deny altogether) to a remote heaven from which they could not or would not interfere in human affairs, yet he admitted the freedom of the will, and he slipped back here and there into a belief in a kindly providence.[1] But he had no interest in physics and logic save as a substratum to his ethical system, and so made shift with theories that appeared plausible and appropriate to his moral doctrine ; it is by this latter that his philosophy stands or falls. To the all-important question, what is the object of life ? Epicurus gave a reply that seemed overwhelmingly justified by the evidence of the senses—the pleasures thereof. But instead of making blind impulse the arbiter of pleasure, he allotted this function to reason, whose duty it was to discriminate between better and worse pleasures (i.e. between more or less pleasurable ones). Applying this rational test, he deprecated physical pleasures on the convincing ground that they were poor of their sort, and gave the preference to those that are born of reflection.

Needless to say, some mere voluptuaries took the name of Epicurus in vain, and supplied welcome ammunition to the traducers of that school, who with eager disgust compared it to a pigsty. But the genuine disciples of Epicurus gained a reputation among fair-minded observers for their abstemiousness and their refinement of taste. Yet for the serenity of life (*ἀταραξία*) which distinguished them the true Epicureans paid a high price. Accepting the Platonic equation of pleasure with mere absence of pain, they gave an almost passive content to the idea of enjoyment, and neglected the pursuit of those more exhilarating pleasures (well-known to Aristotle) that go with successful effort and a sense of difficulties overcome. While in theory they admitted that a greater pleasure was worth buying with a lesser pain, in practice they were too intent on excluding minus quantities

[1] These inconsistencies appear plainly in the poem of Lucretius, which may be accepted as a faithful exposition of the views of Epicurus himself.

from their hedonistic calculus, and in so doing also lost some of the largest positive amounts. But granted that even so they could realize the greatest net overplus of pleasurable feeling, their system cut them off imperatively from that participation in social life which the Hellenistic, no less than the classical Greeks, considered as their birthright. An Epicurean sage might, in strict moderation, cultivate art, literature or science, and he might tie himself by the simple social bonds of family and of friendship—indeed the friendships of the Epicureans were exemplary; but he lived under express orders to avoid entanglement in politics, as being too strenuous for his peace of mind, and to retreat from the public gaze.[1] This obligation prejudiced the Epicureans in the eyes of all those who regarded citizenship and general social intercourse as a privilege and as a duty. In the robust days of the founder's own lifetime his sect came under suspicion of being shirkers from the battle of life, and even in the age of helpless resignation which followed the Roman conquests the Garden was less in request as a haven of repose than might have been expected.

§ 3. THE STOIC SCHOOL

Of the Hellenistic philosophies the only one that achieved any notable practical success was that of the Stoics. This sect owed its origin to a half-breed named Zeno (*c.* 330–260) from the Phœnician town of Citium in Cyprus, who came to Athens in pursuit of trade and stayed on as a student and teacher. When he first set up his own school Zeno was content to use one of the public porticos, the Stoa Pœcile, as his lecture hall, and thus affixed the name of Stoa or porch to his sect; but at some later date he established a college like that of the other philosophers. The founder and his successor Cleanthes (*c.* 305–230) mostly confined themselves to oral instruction; but the "second founder" Chrysippus (*c.* 280–207) made the Stoic tenets familiar to the general public by a never-ending flow of tracts. Following the

[1] Epicurean quietism was characteristically expressed by the founder's pupil Metrodorus, who regarded the state as a mere policeman—an agency for dealing with noise and disorder—and advised his students "not to trouble to save Greece."

example of the Epicureans, the Stoics made a perfunctory study of physics and of the theory of knowledge. But for their physical doctrine they harked back to the crude notions of Heraclitus, who vaguely derived all material substance from fire. As the test of truth they selected mere vividness of experience, a more subjective criterion than the continuity of experience postulated by the Epicureans. This weak joint in their armour did not escape the attention of their Academic critics, and Carneades in particular sped many a shaft through it. Yet the Stoics, like the Epicureans, should be mainly judged by their ethical teaching, to which their other studies merely served as an introduction. In the formulation of their moral precepts the Stoics were less definite than the Epicureans. They bade their followers live "according to nature" (a formula borrowed from the Cynics) or "according to reason," without offering a clear test of natural or reasonable action. Perhaps their point of view is rendered most accurately by a favourite metaphor of theirs, "play your allotted part like a good actor." Having thus reduced virtue to a kind of technical proficiency, they laid down the most exacting conditions for a complete Stoic sage. They not only expected him to perform every duty of life according to the strictest letter of the rules, but they required him to do so for no other end than the perfectness of his action, and allowed him no satisfaction therefrom, save as a detached spectator of his own virtuosity.

It is true that in this extreme form the Stoic doctrine soon proved itself untenable. It was perhaps a minor matter that the picture of the Stoic sage, enshrouded in the cerecloth of his own highly starched virtue, was a heaven-sent theme for the wits of rival schools. A more serious defect was that the pedestal on which the Sage stood exalted cut him off alike from infection by human weakness and from the power to relieve it. Thus the Stoics were obliged to follow the Sceptics and Cynics in making allowance for the undeniable needs of daily life. The founder himself allowed that the affairs of the world should be not absolutely but relatively indifferent to the Sage, and the chief exponent of Stoicism in the second century, Panætius (184–110), went so far as to admit that the philosopher's life was a progress towards perfection rather than a rigid pose on that frozen pinnacle.

The Stoics also went a remarkable distance in offering concessions to religious belief. They made vain efforts to salvage the popular myths about the gods by allegorical interpretations which sometimes were sillier than the myths themselves. Cleanthes explained away the triple-headed Cerberus as a symbol of the triple division of philosophy into logic, physics and ethics—surely the most insipid of all sops to that monster. The same teacher left his own orbit in order to denounce the heliocentric theory of Aristarchus (p. 347). On the question of seercraft the school was divided. Addressing himself to educated Romans, who had ere this reduced their native augural lore to a bad joke, Panætius pronounced against the practice of prophecy. But his successor Posidonius contrived to unite a wide knowledge of natural science with an impartial belief in all manner of divination, from astrology to the observation of muscular twitchings. Yet these were mere excrescences upon the Stoic system, and did not enter into its blood. The real essence of Stoic theology lay in its postulate of an ubiquitous deity which was immanent in all matter and guided the universe with a kindly providence, yet free from anthropomorphic vagaries.

In its amended form Stoicism proved the most inspiring of Hellenistic philosophies. It allowed and even encouraged active citizenship as a worthy moral discipline.[1] Its worst failure in the field of practical politics was that though it proclaimed without reserve the universal brotherhood of man it compromised too readily with slavery and other social iniquities. But if it did not exercise a sufficiently strong drive towards practical benevolence, it had the peculiar merit of playing frankly upon man's pride and self-respect, and it drew out the moral reserves of persons with innate strength of character as no other philosophy and few religions have done.

[1] The Stoic school as such took no side in the issue of republicanism *v.* monarchism. Its founder Zeno was a lifelong friend of Antigonus Gonatas.

Addendum.—The influence of Stoicism is apparent in the wide vogue attained by the *Phænomena* of Aratus of Soli, which made up for its mediocre poetry by revealing the hand of Providence behind the movement of the stars.

CHAPTER XXI

HELLENISTIC RELIGION

§ 1. GREEK RELIGION ON ITS TRIAL

THE campaigns of Alexander introduced into the East a new ruling race who possessed both the power of the sword and the pride of higher culture. But in one respect the Greeks could not and indeed did not claim an inherent superiority, in matters of religion. On this ground their Oriental subjects met them at least on equal terms. In all the Near East the national religions were firmly established and received an undivided allegiance, against which no secular philosophies competed. Under the Hellenistic rulers, moreover, the eastern cults, with one notable but short-lived exception (p. 228), enjoyed complete toleration. However much the kings might limit the secular power of the native priesthoods, they allowed perfect freedom of worship to their subjects of whatever race. Thus assured of a free field, several Oriental religions gave signs of renewed vitality. In Babylon the restoration of the temple of Esagila, which the Persians had destroyed but the Seleucids allowed to be rebuilt, stirred up the priesthood to new literary activity, and its temple chronicles (in cuneiform) were carried on to the end of the pre-Christian era. From Egypt the cults of Sarapis and Isis were spread far and wide by missionary enterprise (p. 372). In Judæa the period of quiescence which followed upon the return from the Captivity made way in the second century for a new age of religious ferment. Greek religion, which until the time of Alexander had lived in comparative seclusion, was now called upon to share the world with other forms of worship, all of which were well entrenched, while some prepared for a new advance.

The Greek cults could well bear comparison with most of the Eastern worships. Their ritual was singularly attractive and gave peculiar scope for the display of human skill and prowess. A Greek " panegyris," at which musicians and dancers, athletes and actors and literary men made show of their rival talents in a precinct adorned with the world's best architecture, had no rival among eastern ceremonies. Within the Greek pantheon many deities enjoyed a special prestige as patron gods of their city or (as in the case of Zeus Olympius) as protectors of the whole nation, and their service was upheld by a long tradition of local or pan-Hellenic patriotism. Lastly, Greek religion was not wholly without means of satisfying those more deeply religious souls who craved for relief from a sense of sin or for a promise of future immortality. If the state cults and the worship of the " Olympian " gods took little account of these profounder stirrings of the heart, other forms of ritual offered to supply the deficiency. At Eleusis the mysteries of Demeter and Persephone drew pilgrims from all parts of Hellenedom. Similar cults, which gave expression to " Orphic " doctrines of a new life after death, were practised in numerous " thiasi " or private religious associations.

The Greeks accordingly did not forsake their gods on first introduction to the Oriental deities. It is true that in the Hellenistic period less zeal was displayed in the construction of temples than might have been expected (p. 310). On the other hand the public festivals were increased in number and celebrated with greater splendour. The priesthoods attached to the state-cults, far from falling into disrepute, were objects of competition among the leading citizens, despite the heavy expenditure which they sometimes imposed upon their holders. In the border-cities of Asia Minor the most coveted offices were regularly put up for sale, and substantial purchase-prices were offered.[1] Seer-craft was still held in common esteem, and the oracles of Delphi and Dodona, besides receiving dedications *pro forma* from kings and cities, were consulted in real earnest by ordinary folk. Even the incubation-sanctuaries, despite all progress of medical science, received fresh streams of pilgrims, and the usual miracles of healing were reported from time to time.[2] Mystery religions

[1] At Priene 12,000 drachmas were offered for the priesthood of Poseidon (*Priene*, 174), and 4610 drachmas for that of Hermes Agoræus at Erythræ. (Ditt., *Syll.*, 1014.)

[2] Specimens in Ditt., *Syll.*, 1168–73.

like those of the "Great Gods" on the island of Samothrace attained a vogue scarcely inferior to that of Eleusis.[1] Private religious societies experienced a mushroom growth and supplied a new focus of interest for worshippers cut off from the old city-cults.[2]

The Greek Gods established themselves in Macedon, where the process of Hellenization introduced the Olympian deities alongside of the native nature-spirits, and they followed the Greek soldiers and colonists into the newly conquered lands. In the new capitals the Hellenistic kings set up the cult of their special patrons. The Seleucids fostered the worship of Apollo, the Attalids of Athena; of the fourth Ptolemy it might be said that his only serious pursuit was the propagation and organization of the Dionysus-cult in his dominions. The Greek cities in the Near East ordinarily made choice of their protecting deities among the members of the old Hellenic pantheon. At Alexandria the trinity of Zeus, Hera and Poseidon were made the tutelary gods of the Greek community, whose citizens took oath by them. Though details are lacking about these municipal cults, it may be taken for granted that wherever Greeks settled down, they brought with them a selection of the gods of the old country. Finally, the Greek clubs played their part in New Greece as well as in the Homeland towards maintaining the worship of the traditional deities.

On the other hand, Greek religion suffered at all times from inherent defects which it never succeeded in shaking off. Though it gave an excellent display of ritual, it offered little else. Even the mysteries and the Orphic cults were mostly taken up with ceremonial and made no serious attempt to teach a rule of life: while Greek religion and ethics met at points, they were pinned rather than welded together. Again, if the Macedonian conquests shed a new lustre upon the Greek gods, the migrations that followed them weakened local patriotism and thereby cheapened the function of the tutelary deities of cities. This depreciation naturally went furthest among the Greek colonies in the conquered lands, for

[1] For the mysteries of Artemis at Andania in Messenia see the elaborate code of ceremonial in Ditt., *Syll.*, 735.

[2] Examples in Ditt., *Syll.*, 1095–1120; Michel, 961–1016. Some of these clubs had a mainly social object, but in many of them the religious service was more than a formality.

the transplanting of city-gods to the East was a more delicate undertaking than Apollonius' experiments in the acclimatization of fruit trees. The delocalized city-patrons tended to sink back into the mere nature-forces from which they had sprung, and thus lost the benefit of the strong municipal loyalty which had once supported them.

The general attitude of the Hellenistic Greeks towards traditional religion may be compared with that of the Italians under the early Roman principate or of Western Europe in the eighteenth century. Unsophisticated folk still adhered in all sincerity to the established practices; the emancipated classes made obeisances to customary deities and maintained a show of observance as a matter of good form. But thinking people mostly looked elsewhere for guidance. The more robust intellects took to philosophy. The more shallow hovered in the borderland between religious faith and mere negation by paying homage to Chance, a vaguely conceived force, but not wholly impersonal, and more capricious than blind. Others had recourse to the frankly non-religious expedients of astrology and magic. Both of these practices were of ancient origin in the Near East, but in the second century they attained a vogue which endured to the modern age of science. Astrology, which revived in Babylon with the resumption of astronomical studies under the Seleucids, imposed with its illusion of mathematical precision upon those who were impressed by science but did not understand it. Though we need not accept a doubtful tradition that a school of astrology was established at Cos by the Babylonian chronicler Berossus (early third century), we have plentiful evidence of the intrusion of the New Thought into the Greek world a hundred years later.[1] Even Hipparchus is said to have dabbled in it, and Posidonius accommodated the Stoic doctrine to it as to other forms of seer-craft. For those who had lost religion and were repelled by the rigour of astrological systems, magic promised sure and quick results. This practice had since time immemorial been observed in Egypt, which remained its chosen home to the end of antiquity, and it was prevalent in other religions of the Near East. Yet in

[1] It has been suggested that if Aristarchus' heliocentric theory had gained acceptance it would have sent astrology into bankruptcy. More probably it would have entailed a reconstruction. Such concerns die hard.

Egypt at least the mass of magical literature in the Greek tongue shows that native superstitions were eating their way into the weaker intellects among the ruling race.[1]

§ 2. KING-WORSHIP

The weakening of belief in traditional religion among the educated and politically-minded Greeks is illustrated by the spread of king-worship. The germs of this institution may be found in the hero-cults which the Greeks from early times had accorded to men of outstanding merit after death. This practice is evidence of a conviction that the gap between the human and the superhuman could be bridged. But it also shows that in Greek opinion the bridges were made after death in the next world. An isolated and short-lived experiment in the deification of living men was made *c.* 400 B.C., when the Spartan admiral Lysander received divine worship from his political partisans at Samos. In 324 the cities of the Greek Homeland of one accord complied with the demand of Alexander that he should be recognized as a god ; but there is no evidence of their having instituted state-cults in his honour, and their acceptance of the king's claim had a strongly ironical tinge.[2]

The precedent set by Alexander led in due course to the establishment of state-cults of living Hellenistic kings. But in taking this next step the Successors were remarkably slow and tentative. In 323 the Macedonian marshals of Alexander, in whose native land men were worshipped neither alive nor dead, never raised the question of his deification. Had Alexander been buried at Ægæ according to the original plan, it is quite possible that he would never have received worship as a " divus " deified after death. But when Ptolemy stole the dead king's remains, he was virtually compelled to raise

[1] On the state of traditional religion in the Hellenistic age see esp. K. Latte in *Die Antike*, I, p. 146 ff. ; E. R. Bevan, *Later Greek Religion*.

[2] On these first experiments in man-worship see A. D. Nock in *Journ. Hell. Stud.*, 1928, p. 21 ff. ; *Harvard Studies in Classical Philology*, vol. 41, p. 59 ff.

Evidence of a change of mind among the fourth-century Greeks has been found in the remarks of Plato and Aristotle that rulers of outstanding merit should be treated as gods. (Ed. Meyer, *Kleine Schriften*, I, p. 288.) But this was plainly no more than a figure of speech and will not bear pressing.

him to the rank of a god, for only on these terms could he reap the full benefit of his larceny. By 285/4 at the latest, a cult of Alexander was established at Alexandria ;[1] whose annual high priest received the honour of giving his name to the year in official documents. The example of deifying dead rulers which Ptolemy I thus set was followed by Ptolemy II, who instituted a joint cult of his deceased father, together with his mother Berenice, under the name of θεοὶ Σωτῆρες, and founded the festival of the Ptolemaieia in connection with this rite (probably in 280). Henceforth it became the regular practice of the Ptolemies to raise their predecessors to the status of "divi." The precedent set by the Ptolemies was adopted by the Seleucids, who deified the founder of the dynasty as Σελευκὸς Ζεὺς Νικάτωρ and Antiochus I as 'Απόλλων Σωτήρ, and by the Attalids, who gave similar honours to all rulers of their line from Attalus I. In Macedon alone the worship of "divi" was never introduced ; here native tradition seems to have been strong enough to prevent the worship of rulers in any form.

The first step towards the deification of living rulers was also taken in Egypt. Here Ptolemy I imitated Alexander in assuming the divine honours which the native Pharaohs had received as incarnations of the sun-god. From the time of Ptolemy IV or V every king on his accession required the native priesthood at Memphis to perform the ritual of deification at the same time as they conferred upon him the twin crowns of Lower and Upper Egypt. But this ceremonial was intended solely to impress the native subjects of the Ptolemies, and it had no meaning for the Greek population ; when a collateral form of king-worship came to be instituted for the Greeks, the Pharaonic service kept its own temple and its separate staff of priests. A Greek cult of a living Ptolemy was not established until 273–1 B.C., when Ptolemy II deified himself and his queen, Arsinoë II, and caused temples or altars of the θεοὶ 'Αδελφοί to be set up at Alexandria and in the capitals of his overseas possessions. Presumably the initiative in this measure, as in his sister-marriage, came from Arsinoë, and the motive for it was probably personal ambition on her part rather than Ptolemy's desire to strengthen his

[1] An eponymous priest of Alexander of that date is mentioned in *P. Elephantine*, 2.

authority over his Greek subjects.[1] Under the fourth Ptolemy the cult of the reigning monarch and of his predecessors was consolidated in a permanent fashion; the priests who had charge of the service were partly assigned to the worship of the entire dynasty, partly to that of individual kings or queens. At Alexandria they were often taken from the royal family, and in the foreign possessions the governor sometimes doubled his part with that of high-priest.

The lead given by Ptolemy II was followed by his neighbour Antiochus II, who instituted a cult of himself and his queen, Laodice I, not long after. This worship was established in every province of the realm,[2] but it concerned the Greek settlers only. Adoration of kings was known to the Asiatic peoples in the form of "proskynesis" only, which the Hellenistic kings made a point of not receiving; the Greek form of king-worship was not imposed by the Seleucids upon their native subjects. The Attalid kings organized no state cult of their living selves, but remained content with apotheosis after death. In Macedonia, where no dead kings received worship, *a fortiori* no state cult of living monarchs was introduced.

From this survey it appears that king-worship never became universal in the Hellenistic monarchies, and that it was introduced in the first instance by an afterthought. Nay more, Hellenistic rulers did no more than follow a precedent which their Greek subjects had set them of their own accord. The most significant fact about the deification of living monarchs is that the initiative in this practice came from their Greek subjects. Within a few years after Alexander's death one Greek city after another had set up a municipal cult to one or other of the Successors.[3]

The towns which came under Attalid rule presently followed suit, and as a matter of course the new settlements in the Near

[1] From the reign of Ptolemy II the names of the reigning couple were taken in official oaths; but previous to Ptolemy VII none of the kings styled himself a god in his proclamations.

[2] On Seleucid king-worship see esp. Ditt., *O.G.I.*, 224 (an order by Antiochus II to a governor of Phrygia).

[3] Antigonus I was receiving worship at Scepsis by 311 (Ditt., *O.G.I.*. 5); Antigonus and Demetrius at Athens in 307 (Plutarch, *Demetrius*, ch. 11); the same pair in the Cyclades by 306 (Dürrbach, *Choix*, 13); Ptolemy at Rhodes in 304 (Diodorus, XX, 100); Cassander at Cassandreia by 286 (Ditt., *Syll.*, 380).

East instituted a cult of the monarch to whom they owed their existence.[1] In the second century the Greek cities made similar overtures to the Roman Republic and its officials. In 195 Smyrna established a cult of the city of Rome, and soon afterwards Chalcis deified Flamininus. In addition, private groups of worshippers set up chapels and made dedications to their sovereigns. The spontaneous character of Hellenistic king-worship in most of its manifestations is the most notable feature of it.[2]

The adoration of living kings has been taken as evidence of the extreme self-abasement of Hellenistic cities before their superiors in power or wealth. At first, indeed, it comes as a shock to read the hymn addressed by the Athenians to Demetrius: "thou alone art a true god; the others are asleep or away, or are not."[3] Still worse, apparently, was the assignation of the Parthenon as a residence to Demetrius on his visit to Athens in 304–3. Yet Athenian history in particular proves how far the Greeks of that age were from having abandoned their self-respect. In 295–4 Demetrius' flatterers endured the extremes of famine before they would surrender to their "very present god." The offer of divine honours to a Hellenistic king was not an act of prostration, but a mere obeisance that did not differ in essence from the conferment of proxenia upon a private benefactor. But if it was not a mark of depravity, it showed at all events that in the Hellenistic period the Greeks, or at any rate those among them who took an active share in politics, had rapidly reduced religion to a pure matter of form.

§ 3. RELIGIOUS CONTACTS BETWEEN GREEKS AND ORIENTALS

The lack of conviction among the later Greeks in regard to their religion was enough to ensure that none of the Oriental

[1] At Ptolemais in Upper Egypt a separate priest was eventually provided for every deified member of the dynasty. At Seleucia-ad-Orontem one priest was assigned to the living king, another to all the "divi." (Ditt., *O.G.I.*, 245.)

[2] The attitude of educated Greeks in the Hellenistic age to king-worship is also reflected in the view set forth by the romance writer Euemerus (p. 338), who professed to have found documentary evidence on his island of Panchæa proving that the gods in general were nothing but departed men.

[3] Demochares ap. Athenæum, VI, 250c.

peoples should adopt it in place of their old but hale faiths. The Hellenizers among them (outside of Judæa) no doubt conformed outwardly to the rites of the ruling race, and joined in such Greek ceremonies as their political duties or social ambitions might impose upon them. But there is no evidence of any Oriental worship, Iranian or Babylonian, Asianic or Egyptian, being dispossessed by an invading Greek cult. On the other hand, pride of race and culture restrained the Greeks from an abandonment of their worships in favour of those of the conquered races. Disdaining to study the copious religious literature of the Jews, they acquired but a vague idea of the Israelitic faith. Though they became addicted to Babylonian astrology, they gave scant attention to the Babylonian gods. To the Asianic deities, Attis and Cybele, which had already gained a foothold in the Greek world before Alexander's time, they paid more deference, yet not in such measure as the proximity of Phrygia to the Aegean lands might have suggested. It may further be laid down as a rule that no Oriental religion made much headway among the Greeks before the second century; and it may be surmised that Oriental cults were first introduced into those families where Greek settlers had intermarried with native women, so that their acceptance was as much evidence of racial dilution as of religious conversion. In any case, the Oriental cults made comparatively little impression upon the educated Greeks. If these were the readiest to abandon their traditional religion, they were also the most likely to find a satisfactory substitute in a philosophic creed.

Among Oriental worships the two which made the widest appeal to the Hellenistic Greeks were the cults of the Egyptian deities Sarapis and Isis. The attraction exerted by Sarapis is difficult to explain at first sight. In his original form this god was the mummified bull-calf Apis, whom the Egyptians deemed to have become merged in the god Osiris after death, and worshipped at one of their chief temples in the neighbourhood of Memphis.[1] But Sarapis underwent transformation at the hands of Ptolemy I, who made a unique experiment in the reconstruction of an established cult, with a view to rendering it equally acceptable to natives and to Greeks.

[1] On the Egyptian Sarapis see esp. Wilcken, *Urkunden der Ptolemäerzeit*, I, p. 17 ff.

A second temple was built for him at Alexandria, and a cult-statue was here set up, whose features recalled those of Pluto (the nearest equivalent to Osiris in the Greek pantheon). This attempt to provide by official action a link between the Egyptian and the Greek religion appears to have been no more than a passing fancy of the first Ptolemy, and it never fulfilled its original intention, for the Egyptians soon reverted from the new hybrid cult to the native ritual as observed at Memphis.[1] But to the Greeks the metamorphosed Sarapis made a curiously strong appeal. Once deprived of his original attributes, this Protean deity passed through further transformations, so that in the popular Greek idea he became a god of healing and a kind of pagan St. Nicholas, the protector of seamen. Sarapis also had the faculty of turning his votaries into active missionaries. Under Ptolemy II we find a person with a Greek name bearding the minister Apollonius and pestering him to build yet another Sarapeum in some over-sea town (probably Cnidus).[2] But the most efficient propagators of his worship were the sailor-folk, who carried the cult to the Aegean lands and the western Mediterranean. By 200 B.C. shrines had been built for his service at the Bosporus entrance and at Syracuse; about 180 his votaries, aided by a timely epiphany of the god, broke down official resistance to the building of a temple at Delos.[3]

The popularity of Sarapis was matched by that of Isis. Originally, as it would seem, a goddess of fertility, Isis had in Egyptian theology been mated with Osiris and had thus become a power of the underworld. Her ritual was an initiation into a new life on earth, which carried with it the promise of future happiness after death. To reflective Greeks who could not find consolation in philosophy Isis made an even more potent appeal than Sarapis. Though she did not receive royal patronage in the same degree as Sarapis, her private missionaries were no less active in her cause. Of all Oriental deities Isis made the most extensive conquests in the Hellenistic world. Already established at Athens during the reign of Alexander, she took possession of the Aegean area

[1] J. G. Milne, *Journ. Egypt. Archæology*, 1928, p. 226 ff.

[2] *P. Zeno Cairo*, 59034; *P.S.I.*, IV, 435. In the latter papyrus the writer half pleads, half commands, "you must obey the god—it won't cost you much—he will give you health and influence at court."

[3] Ditt., *Syll.*, 663–4. See also P. Roussel, *Les cultes égyptiens à Délos.*

pari passu with Sarapis, and preceded him in the capture of Italy and the western Mediterranean. Like Sarapis, Isis owed the propagation of her cult to the mercantile population, which often associated the Egyptian couple in its worship.

Yet despite the vogue of Sarapis and Isis, the rule holds good that the Greeks showed no general willingness to incorporate Oriental deities into their pantheon.[1] In fine, neither they nor their subjects could achieve or would submit to complete spiritual conquest. On the other hand, both parties were ready for a compromise, by which their deities instead of displacing each other were fused into a composite godhead. It became, therefore, a common practice of Hellenistic religion to associate and eventually to blend in prayer and ritual the cognate deities of East and West. Of the many instances of this kind of coalescence it will suffice to mention the statues of "Zeus Oromasdes," "Hermes Mithras," and other equated couples of the Greek and Iranian pantheon, which king Antiochus I of Commagene set up on his mausoleum (*c.* 98–35 B.C.).[2] The syncretism here illustrated was but a natural result of a religious tendency which affected Orientals no less than Greeks. The delocalization of worships, which was a comparatively new feature of Greek religion in the Hellenistic age, had set in among the Orientals many centuries before, and under the Persian dominion it had made considerable progress. In a world where the patron deities of cities or tribes were developing or reverting into powers of nature, their eventual amalgamation was almost an inevitable consequence. Thus syncretism paved the way for the diffusion of strictly monotheistic religions.

But the breakdown of religious barriers in the Hellenistic age did something more than lead up to formal monotheism. It helped to familiarize Greece and the Near East with the idea of a deity that is not only worshipped by all men, but wishes all men well. At the same time this conception was being introduced into the thought of educated men by the Stoic philosophers, and Cleanthes gave it clear and strong

[1] The worship of the Iranian light-god Mithra, which eventually gained such a vogue in the Roman empire, does not appear to have made any special appeal to the Greek population. In any case, this cult did not spread far beyond the Iranian lands before the first century B.C.

[2] Ditt., *O.G.I.*, 382, l. 53 ff.

expression in his Hymn to Zeus (i.e. the universal deity, of whom the many traditional gods were but manifestations):

> *ἀλλὰ σὺ καὶ τὰ περισσὰ ἐπίστασαι ἄρτια θεῖναι*
> *καὶ κοσμεῖν τὰ ἄκοσμα, καὶ οὐ φίλα σοὶ φίλα ἐστίν.*
>
> (Ls. 18–9.)

The full consequences of this confession were not drawn in the Hellenistic age. But it was a sign that a revolution was being prepared in the world's religious thought.

CONCLUSION

IT will suffice here to sum up in a few words the main results of Hellenistic History.

In the two centuries following upon the death of Alexander the Greeks missed their chance of establishing a durable world-empire, and passed from the status of a ruling to that of a subject people. Within the same period their culture ceased to be creative and became merely traditional.

Yet though the Hellenistic age ended in failure, it was by no means barren of achievement. The Hellenistic Greeks carried out the greatest colonial movement of ancient history, and established themselves for almost a thousand years as the predominant nation of the Near East. They made notable and by no means unfruitful experiments in imperial and in federal statecraft. They took a distinct step in advance towards the creation of a world-economy. They broke new ground in many departments of art and literature, of science, philosophy and religion. In fine, they were still in essentials the same people as made the glorious and dismal record of classical Greek history. They displayed the same many-sided energy, and their failures, like those of the classical Greeks, were due to misdirection rather than to lack of vigour.

Hellenistic history is therefore not like a fringe of different material pinned on to the fabric of earlier Greek history, but forms part of its texture. Without the study of Hellenistic history the general pattern of Greek history cannot be fully perceived and appreciated.

But a knowledge of Hellenistic history is also needed by those who would gain insight into the process by which the Roman Republic became an empire-state and a culture-state. It is a commonplace to observe that Rome was the pupil of Greece; but it is often forgotten that Hellenistic, not Classical Greece, was her teacher.

Lastly, the Hellenistic Greeks have helped to fashion the course of the modern world. Their science was the starting-point of modern science. The Stoic ethics are a living force to this day. And in the Hellenistic period the contact and occasional clash of religions prepared the way for a new religious era in which we still live.

APPENDICES

1

SOURCES AND AUTHORITIES FOR THE HELLENISTIC PERIOD

(a) *Literary texts.*—The literary sources for Hellenistic history are even more exiguous than those for the classical period. This deficiency is not due to any lack of historical writers in the Hellenistic age itself, but to the almost complete disappearance of their work in later antiquity (p. 326).

Among the Hellenistic historians the only one whose work has survived in more than small fragments is Polybius (p. 336). Of the forty books composed by this author we possess the first five in their entirety, and more or less copious extracts (by Byzantine scholars) from the remainder. The chief contribution of Polybius to our knowledge of Greek history relates to the affairs of Greece and Macedon from 228 to 196 B.C., and to the subsequent history of the Achæan League. But we also owe to him an almost continuous account of the early campaigns of Antiochus III, and a detailed description of the revolutions at Alexandria in the opening years of Ptolemy V.

Of our secondary Greek authors the earliest is Diodorus, a writer of Cicero's time, who composed a History of the World to his own day in some forty volumes. Of this work, books 18–20, covering the years 323–302 B.C., have been preserved in full. Diodorus was a mere compiler, who mutilated his sources in condensing them, and in combining them created occasional confusion. Yet he had at least the merit of going to approved authorities for his materials. In books 18–20 he drew mainly upon Hieronymus of Cardia (p. 335); for events connected with European Greece he probably used a contemporary Athenian author named Diyllus.[1] We are mainly indebted to Diodorus for our relatively good understanding of the age of Alexander's first successors.

[1] On Diyllus as a source for Diodorus see W. Schwahn in *Philologus*, vol. 86, p. 145 ff.

From the pen of Plutarch (*floruit* A.D. 100) we have no less than twelve Lives which provide material for Hellenistic history (Demosthenes; Phocion; Eumenes of Cardia; Demetrius I; Pyrrhus; Agis; Cleomenes; Aratus; Philopœmen; Flamininus; Cato the Elder; Æmilius Paullus). These Lives are mere sketches, based on haphazard information. But, while much doubt exists as to the exact nature of Plutarch's ultimate sources, it is fairly certain that he derived much of his information from standard authorities like Hieronymus and Phylarchus, or from the Memoirs of Aratus (p. 334), and that if he did not always use these at first hand he employed some well-read Alexandrian scholar as his channel of transmission. Apart from their high literary merit—and the Lives of Eumenes and Demetrius, of Agis, Cleomenes and Aratus, are among the most entertaining pieces of Greek literature—Plutarch's biographies constitute a valuable supplement to Diodorus for the end of the fourth century, and for the early and middle parts of the third century they are our principal quarry for materials.

Our knowledge of the Jewish Wars of Independence and of the rise of the Maccabee dynasty is almost wholly derived from the first two books of Maccabees. On the authorship, the date and the merit of these books scholars are much divided. But it is probable that they were written not long after the events described in them, or drew directly upon writers not far removed from the events, and that they are generally trustworthy in their facts; and the nationalist or theocratic bias in them is less than might have been expected.[1] Other quasi-historical works by Jewish writers, such as Third Maccabees and the Letter of Aristeas, are generally regarded as being mere propagandist fiction.

Of our Latin sources the earliest and best is Livy, who covered the period 220–167 B.C. in the surviving books 21 to 45, and from book 31 onwards devoted a good deal of space to Greek affairs. For the history of the First Macedonian War, Livy was mainly content to excerpt some Roman annalist, but for the subsequent relations between Greece and Rome he used Polybius as his chief informant, and in some passages reproduced him almost verbally. Our relatively full and accurate knowledge of these relations is ultimately due to Polybius, but in the first instance it has reached us through Livy.

The only other Latin writer to require mention here is Justin, a writer of the second or third century A.D., who arranged for the public of his day the *Historiæ Philippicæ* of Pompeius Trogus, a Gaulish scholar of the time of Augustus. The work of Trogus was

[1] See the judicious remarks by E. R. Bevan in *Cambr. Anc. Hist.*, VIII, pp. 710–13.

a history of the ancient world without the Romans, in 44 books, of which no less than 30 (bks. 13–42) were devoted to the Hellenistic period. It was probably a well-informed, as it certainly was a skilfully arranged treatise. But Justin's epitome of Trogus is a mere skeleton (occasionally padded with the arranger's own flabby rhetoric); though it is our only continuous record of the Hellenistic world, it is too tenuous and episodic to serve as a framework for a modern narrative.

(b) *Inscriptions.*—Apart from a few stray texts discovered by earlier travellers, the epigraphic material for Hellenistic history has been the product of systematic search in the last fifty years. The principal hauls of inscriptions have been made on excavated sites such as Delphi and Epidaurus, Delos, Magnesia-on-Mæander, Miletus, Pergamum and Priene. Epigraphic finds in Egypt, if important, have been few in number, and other promising regions of the Near East, such as Macedon, Asia Minor and Syria, await more thorough exploration. But the total of inscriptions relating to the Hellenistic world is already far greater than that pertaining to Classical Greece; and if most of them (e.g. the large surviving quantity of honorary decrees) are of small value taken singly, in the aggregate they have placed the study of Hellenistic Greece on an altogether new basis.

(c) *Papyri.*—Although a few valuable texts had previously been unearthed by clandestine native diggers (e.g. the London documents on the "Twins" case, the Turin dossier on the "Hermias" case, and a Paris papyrus of 167 B.C., containing a severe edict by Ptolemy VI against administrative misfeasances),[1] scientific search for papyri was not begun until forty years ago. The most important single document discovered since then is the *Revenue Law of Ptolemy Philadelphus;* the chief collection of texts is that of the Zeno papyri. The Zeno documents, strangely enough, were discovered by illicit native diggers; fortunately the great majority of them have been acquired by responsible institutions such as the Cairo Museum of Antiquities and the *Societa Italiana per la Ricerca dei Papiri Greci e Latini.* For the historical value of the Ptolemaic papyri, see my remarks at the beginning of section 8 in chapter 14.

(d) *Coins.*—The historical value of these is somewhat less than for the classical period. Because of the closing down of many city mints in the Hellenistic period, the variety of coin-types of that age falls below that of the city-state era. Intensive study of mint-marks by present-day numismatists has shed some fresh

[1] The London and Turin papyri have been republished by U. Wilcken, *Urkunden der Ptolemäerzeit,* vol. I; the text of the Paris papyrus is reproduced in the *Petrie Papyri,* vol. III, p. 18 ff.

light on the relations of the monarchs to the dependent cities; but on the whole the evidence of Hellenistic coins is of greater concern to the advanced than to the general student.

The chief modern collections of historical inscriptions and papyri are set forth in the list of abbreviations on pp. xiii, xiv.

2

THE NAVAL OPERATIONS OF THE LAMIAN WAR

ALTHOUGH the decision of the Lamian War was obtained on sea, no continuous account of the naval operations survives. The following points require further discussion :—

(a) *The Athenian fleet.*—Diodorus (XVIII, 10, 2) states that at the outset the Athenians resolved to mobilize 200 quadriremes and 40 triremes. He adds (XVIII, 10, 8) that in the decisive campaign of 322, after further preparations, they had 170 ships all told. There is no reason to doubt the former of these statements, for the surviving naval inventories of the period show that the Athenians had fully 240 seaworthy ships. But it is unlikely that they lost over 70 ships in the early stages of the war, so that they would need to make a fresh effort to bring their strength up to 170. Diodorus' second figure should therefore be regarded as a battle total, not as a campaign total. Probably the Athenians held back part of their fleet for service nearer home. In view of the hostility of the Bœotians, they needed a detachment to keep open the sea route to Lamia ; and they may have deputed a squadron to protect their corn supply. In Justin (XIII, 5, 8) the original Athenian strength is estimated at 200. This figure suggests that he left out of account the 40 triremes mentioned by Diodorus. We need not doubt that these were commissioned, but we may surmise that they were held back for cruiser service, and that the actual battle-strength of the Athenians was not above 200 at the outset. In that case, if allowance is made for the casualties incurred in 323 against Antipater's fleet, it is not unlikely that the battle-fleet was reduced to a strength below 170, and that fresh construction was needed to bring it to that figure in 322.

It is suggested by T. Walek (*Revue de Philologie*, 1924, p. 23 ff.) that in 322 an Athenian squadron was kept back to watch the fleet of Antipater, which in his opinion was not absorbed in that of Clitus. But it seems more likely that Antipater's contingent was incorporated in Clitus' fleet (see next paragraph).

(b) *The Macedonian forces.*—At the beginning of the war

Antipater had 110 ships, which had been told off from Alexander's Grand Fleet in the Levant to escort a treasure convoy to Macedonia (Diodorus, XVIII, 12, 2). In 322 Clitus had 240 galleys at his disposal (Diod., XVIII, 15, 8). Did these 240 include Antipater's 110, or rather the survivors of his fleet after the campaign of 323 ? According to Walek the entire 240 were a reinforcement from the Levant. In this case Alexander's fleet at the time of his death must have been at least 350 strong. But this total seems excessive. In 332, when Alexander was straining every nerve to capture Tyre, he collected no more than 225 men-of-war (Arrian, II, 20). In 318 Antigonus had only a little over 100 ships to put into line against Clitus (Diod., XVIII, 72, 3) ; in 314 it required a very special effort on his part to raise 240 (Diod., XIX, 58, 62). In 306 the rival fleets of Demetrius and Ptolemy, which between them included the entire naval force of the Levant and the Aegean, mustered some 360 to 370 men-of-war all told (see Appendix 4). Even when allowance is made for losses sustained and not replaced since 323, these figures indicate that in the Lamian War the combined fleets of Antipater and Clitus could hardly have amounted to 350 ships. It is therefore preferable to suppose that the 240 ships of Clitus included the remnants of Antipater's 110, and that his reinforcements from the Levant numbered some 150 or possibly 175 ships.

(c) *The campaign of* 322.—The operations of this year are summed up by Diodorus (XVIII, 15, 9) as follows : οὗτος δὲ (Κλεῖτος) *ναυμαχήσας πρὸς Ἠετιῶνα τὸν Ἀθηναίων ναύαρχον ἐνίκησε δύσι ναυμαχίαις, καὶ συχνὰς τῶν πολεμίων νεῶν διέφθειρε περὶ τὰς καλουμένας Ἐχινάδας νήσους.*

Does this mean that the Athenian losses off the Echinades were additional to those in the two battles (as Walek contends), or that the Echinades were the scene of the more disastrous of the two battles ? Diodorus' words can be taken in either sense. But our other sources only know of two actions in all, at Abydus and Amorgos, and it is hardly credible that they should have failed to mention the third and really disastrous encounter at the Echinades, if this had been a separate engagement. It therefore seems preferable to identify the battle of the Echinades with one or other of the previous actions. The site of the Echinades is not certain (the only known group of that name being in the Ionian Sea, which was certainly not the scene of any engagement in the Lamian War). But there are no islands near Abydus, therefore the Echinades must be located near Amorgos (perhaps between this island and Naxos). In this case Diodorus reckoned the battle usually called after Amorgos as the decisive one. This fits in well with our other sources (Plut., *Demetrius*, ch. 11 ;

Marmor Parium, 323–2 B.C.), both of which imply that the chief naval action was fought there.

(d) *The relation between the campaigns on sea and on land.*— The battle of Amorgos fell in the archon-year 323–2 (Marmor Parium), i.e. before July 322. On the other hand Clitus could hardly have left the Levantine ports before April, the earliest month in which it was considered safe to put out with a fleet, and he could not have reached the scene of war before the end of that month, or in May. In this case we must conclude that Leonnatus crossed the Dardanelles before the battle of Abydus. Since he stopped in Macedonia to enrol fresh troops (Diod., XVIII, 14, 5), his march from the Dardanelles to Thessaly could not have lasted less than a month. But if he did not cross the Dardanelles until end of April or May, he could not have reached Lamia before June, and it is incredible that this town, which was not prepared for a blockade, could have held out until then. Presumably Leonnatus slipped across the straits in early spring, before the Athenian fleet had put out from its winter-quarters. In that case the Athenian fleet which suffered defeat at Abydus was sent to prevent the subsequent passage by Craterus' army.

For recent discussions, see Beloch, *Griech. Gesch.*, IV, pt. 1, p. 78, n. 1, and esp. T. Walek, *Revue de Philologie*, 1924, p. 23 ff.

3

SELEUCUS AND THE PEACE OF 311 B.C.

ATTEMPTS have been made from time to time (most recently by Beloch, *Griech. Gesch.*, IV, pt. 1, p. 133 n., and by Corradi, *Studi Ellenistici*, p. 16 ff.) to prove that Seleucus was included in the treaty of 311. Antigonus' reticence about him in the letter of Scepsis (Ditt., *O.G.I.*, 5) is not sufficient proof to the contrary. But the entire absence of references to Seleucus in Diodorus' comparatively full statement of the peace terms (XIX, 105) is strong presumptive evidence for his exclusion. Moreover Antigonus' recognition in the peace terms as " general of *all* Asia," (an expression which Corradi hardly succeeds in explaining away as due to a misinterpretation of the treaty by Diodorus), plainly implies that Antigonus claimed back Seleucus' recent conquests, and that the other signatories of the peace gave him a free hand to recover them.

Further light on the problem has been thrown by a recently discovered Babylonian tablet (S. Smith, *Babylonian Historical Texts Relating to the Capture and Downfall of Babylon*, ch. 5). This document mentions continuous fighting between Seleucus and Antigonus in the seventh and ninth years of Alexander IV. The starting-point of Alexander's reign on this system of reckoning cannot have been 323/2, for in the seventh year from 323/2, i.e. 316/5, Seleucus escaped from Babylon without fighting, and in the ninth year he was still a fugitive. The *terminus a quo* must therefore be 317/6, the year in which Alexander, technically, became sole king, and the " seventh " and " ninth " years must be 310/9 and 308/7. (On this point see J. Kaerst, *Gesch. des Hellenismus*, 2nd ed., II, p. 57, n. 4.) But if Antigonus was heavily engaged with Seleucus in 310/9, it is scarcely credible that he should have admitted him to the peace of 311.

4

THE STRENGTHS OF THE FLEETS AT SALAMIS

ACCORDING to Diodorus (XX, 49, 2), Ptolemy had 140 ships actually engaged. Plutarch (*Demetrius*, ch. 16) assigns 150 ships to Ptolemy and 60 to his brother Menelaus. Since Menelaus' squadron did not take part in the fight, our two authorities are in substantial agreement about the Egyptian fleet.

The numbers of Demetrius' fleet are more problematical. Plutarch (*loc. cit.*) states that Demetrius left 10 vessels to contain Menelaus in the harbour of Salamis, and put out to fight Ptolemy with 180. Polyænus (IV, 7, 7) gives Demetrius 170 all told, Diodorus (XX, 47, 1) enumerates Demetrius' ships as follows : ναῦς ταχυναυτούσας μὲν τριήρεις πλείους τῶν ἑκατὸν δέκα, τῶν δὲ βαρυτέρων στρατιωτίδων πεντήκοντα καὶ τρεῖς, καὶ πορεῖα τῶν παντοδάπων ἱκανὰ τῷ πλήθει τῶν ἱππέων τε καὶ πεζῶν. He goes on to say (XX, 50, 1–2) that after detaching 10 ships to contain Menelaus, Demetrius took into battle τὰς ἁπάσας ὀκτὼ πλείους τῶν ἑκατὸν σὺν ταῖς πληρωθείσαις ἐκ τῶν χωρίων τῶν ληφθέντων · τούτων δ' ἦσαν αἱ μέγισται μὲν ἑπτήρεις, αἱ πλεῖσται δὲ πεντήρεις. No certain conclusions can be drawn from the second of these passages, for the preposition σὺν may equally well have inclusive or exclusive force here. The crux of the problem therefore lies in the meaning of βαρυτέρων στρατιωτίδων in the first passage : were these battleships of heavier tonnage or transports ? In the one case Demetrius had about 110 warships all told, and 100 engaged in battle ; in the other his figures were 163 and 153 respectively.

On the former hypothesis the discrepancy between Diodorus' figures and those of Plutarch and Polyænus could perhaps be explained away by supposing that these two authors counted in non-combatant ships with men-of-war, a not unusual error among ancient writers. But on several grounds this theory must be rejected. (i) The transport was provided by the πορεῖα τῶν ἱππέων καὶ πεζῶν. The στρατιωτίδες, being distinct from these, must therefore be warships, presumably with a large complement of marines. (ii) The 110 triremes of Demetrius cannot have constituted his entire battle-fleet, for he took ships of higher displacement into action (Diod., XX, 50, 2–3). (iii) An annihilating victory by 100 triremes over 140 or 150 ships of heavier type (quinqueremes and quadriremes according to Diod., XX, 49, 2) would have been a miracle; if the 100 were reinforced by 53 heavier vessels (quinqueremes and hepteres—Diod., XX, 50, 2), Demetrius' triumph was brilliant but not superhuman. We may therefore conclude that Demetrius had some 150 battleships in action at Salamis.

Diodorus relates that Ptolemy lost some 120 ships in action, so that about 20 escaped from the disaster. This estimate seems more credible than that of Plutarch, according to whom only eight of Ptolemy's ships survived.—See esp. Beloch, *Griech. Gesch.*, IV, pt. 1, p. 154 and n.

5

THE FIRST SYRIAN WAR

THE third-century wars between Ptolemies and Seleucids are usually named in accordance with the scheme set up by Droysen a hundred years ago :—

First Syrian War	..	*c.* 280–272 B.C.
Second ,, ,,	..	*c.* 260–255 ,,
Third ,, ,,	..	246–241 ,,
Fourth ,, ,,	..	219–217 ,,

Since all these wars involved the transfer of Syrian territory, the above names are accurate as well as convenient. But it is now fairly certain that the so-called First War really consisted of two sets of campaigns with an intervening peace, viz. 280–279 and 276 (or 274)–272. (W. Otto, *Beiträge zur Seleukidengeschichte des dritten Jahrhunderts v. Chr.*, p. 20 ; Tarn, *Hermes*, 1930, p. 446.) The re-numbering of the series would however cause great confusion. The best way of distinguishing the two wars will be to reserve the name of " First Syrian " for the campaigns of 276 (or 274)–272, and to call the previous operations the " Carian War " from Ptolemy's capture of Miletus (the name suggested by Tarn), or the " Damascus War."

The chronology of the war that ended in 272 is a peculiarly difficult problem. No continuous account of it survives, and the various episodes of it to which reference is made in authors and inscriptions can hardly ever be dated with certainty.

A new turn has been given to the problem by the recent discovery of a Babylonian tablet.[1] This document furnishes one certain new date. Under S(eleucid) A(era) 37 (i.e. 275 B.C.) it records that the governor of Babylonia returned to Seleucia-on-Tigris from a journey to the king's head-quarters at Sardes, on which he had entered in the previous year. In 276, therefore, Antiochus I was stationed at Sardes.

[1] S. Smith, *Babylonian Historical Texts relating to the Capture and Downfall of Babylon*, ch. 6.

The document also provides one valuable piece of information about the war-operations. It states that Antiochus, having left Sardes for Syria, defeated an Egyptian army there. Unfortunately the portion of the tablet containing the date of this campaign has been lost.

Since the entry relating to the king's campaign in Syria immediately precedes the paragraph date S.A. 37, it might be supposed that the victory which he won in Syria belongs to S.A. 36, i.e. 276 B.C. On the other hand, the obverse side of the tablet (which was presumably inscribed before the reverse, from which the above notices are drawn) contains the date-mark S.A. 38, i.e. 274. From this it might appear that the Syrian campaign took place not before 274.

As a matter of fact, both of these opposite conclusions are unwarranted, for the scribe of the tablet did not make his entries in chronological order, but jumped forward and backward on no intelligible system.[1] On the date of the Syrian campaign, therefore, the tablet throws no light.

The time-table of the war must rest mainly on the Greek evidence. The crucial question here is the date of an inscription from Miletus (A. Rehm, Das Delphinion in Milet, in *Milet*, I, pt. 3, no. 139). This text contains a *communiqué* from Ptolemy II to Miletus and a decree of the Milesian assembly in reply, which indicate that at the time Miletus was being beset by land and sea, and that the king could bring no immediate relief. Most scholars, following the editor, have assigned the inscription to the period of the Second Syrian War (so recently E. R. Bevan, *Egypt under the Ptolemaic Dynasty*, p. 386–7). But strong reasons have been given by Tarn for dating it to the First Syrian War (*Hermes*, 1930, p. 447–450). If this view of the case is correct, the siege of Miletus by Antiochus I may be placed with approximate certainty at 276/5 or 275/4. Another Milesian document (*Milet*, I, 3, 123) shows that in these years the Stephanephoria, a costly honorary office, was held by the god Apollo. A study of all the known cases in which Apollo held this office shows that these were years of peril or distress, in which no ordinary citizen would shoulder the burden and the god was left, so to speak, to pay himself out of his own pocket. In 276/5 and 275/4, then, Miletus was in difficulties ; and in all probability 275 was the year of the investment by Antiochus. But it is in the last degree unlikely that Antiochus should have begun this siege before dealing with the Egyptian invasion of Syria, which was a far more urgent operation. The most likely year for the Syrian campaign therefore is 276.

The important text from Ilium (Hicks, 165 ; Ditt., *O.G.I.*,

[1] I am indebted to Mr. Sidney Smith for this piece of information.

219), in which this city thanks Antiochus I for pulling the Seleucid empire together and recounts his exploits in Seleucis and in Asia Minor, cannot be made a basis for the chronology of the First Syrian War, for its interpretation is by no means certain. But it can at any rate be made to fit without difficulty into a time-table which makes the Syrian War begin in 276. (Tarn, *Journ. Hell. Stud.*, 1928, p. 155 ff.)

6

PTOLEMY "THE SON"

In a series of papyri dating from 267 to 259 B.C. a "Ptolemy son of Ptolemy" appears as co-regent of Ptolemy II. In the Revenue Law of Ptolemy Philadelphus (259 B.C.) there is evidence of the Son's name having been inscribed and subsequently erased. The disappearance of the Son from documents of later date, and especially the erasure of his name in the Revenue Law, suggest that in 259 he fell into disfavour.

In Trogus, *Prologue* 26, we read of a "son of king Ptolemy" who combined with one Timarchus in a rebellion against his father. This Timarchus is plainly none other than the governor of Miletus in the Second Syrian War, who was suppressed by Antiochus II in 258 (pp. 104–5). It appears, therefore, that Trogus' "Son" disgraced himself at the same time as the "Son" of the papyri; presumably they were one and the same person. The "Son" of these two sources may also be identified with the "Son" of a Milesian inscription (*Milet*, I, 3, 138, on the date of which see Appendix 5), in which he appears as the bearer of a message from Ptolemy II to Miletus.

Was the Son a real or only an adoptive child of Ptolemy II? And who was his mother? On these questions modern scholars are sharply divided.

We may rule out the supposition that the Son was the future Ptolemy III. There is no evidence of this prince having fallen into disfavour in 259; but if he had done so, it is almost certain that this fact would have been recorded in one or other of our surviving sources.[1]

Ptolemy the Son has been identified with several hypothetic personalities. But none of these meets the conditions of the case.

(1) A child of Ptolemy II and Arsinoë II.—But Ptolemy II had no children by this queen (Pausanias, I, 7, 3: οἱ δὲ οἱ παῖδες

[1] It is possible, though not certain, that the future Ptolemy III left Alexandria about 258 to become viceroy of Cyrene. But this would not explain the disappearance, much less the erasure of his name, from Egyptian documents.

(i.e. Ptolemy II's) ἐγένοντο ἐξ Ἀρσινόης, οὐ τῆς ἀδελφῆς (Arsinoë II), Λυσιμάχου δὲ θυγατρός (Arsinoë I). τὴν δέ οἱ συνοικήσασαν ἀδελφὴν κατέλαβεν ἔτι πρότερον ἀποθανεῖν ἄπαιδα. Schol. Theocr., XVII, 128: καὶ (Ptolemy II) εἰσεποιήσατο αὐτῇ (Arsinoë II) τοὺς ἐκ τῆς προτέρας Ἀρσινόης γεννηθέντας παῖδας.

(2) An elder brother of Ptolemy III.—On this theory it is easy to explain why Ptolemy III was passed over as co-regent in 267–259. But the existence of such an elder brother is implicitly denied by the scholium to Theocritus, which goes on to say that Ptolemy III was the eldest of his family (himself, Lysimachus and Berenice).

(3) An illegitimate offspring by one or other of Ptolemy II's mistresses. We are not in a position to deny that there may have been such illegitimate issue to Ptolemy II, or that he employed one of them as his representative at Miletus. But it is scarcely credible that, having lawful issue, he should have nominated a bastard as co-regent. This would have been in plain defiance of his dynasty's law of succession, which followed the ordinary rules of Greek family right and therefore gave bastards no legal standing at all. (M. Strack, *Die Dynastie der Ptolemäer*, p. 94; E. Breccia, *Il diritto dinastico nelle monarchie dei successori d'Alessandro Magno*, p. 8.)

There remains one known personage with whom Ptolemy the Son may be equated, the eldest child of Arsinoë II by her first husband, king Lysimachus. This youth, after escaping death at the hands of Arsinoë's second husband Ptolemy Ceraunus (p. 58), became a minor pretender to the crown of Macedon and was finally expelled by Antigonus Gonatas. After this all certain trace of him is lost, and it cannot be said definitely that he rejoined his mother in Egypt. But granted that he did find his way to Ptolemy II's court, it would not be surprising to find that he was adopted by the king and supplanted the future Ptolemy III as heir apparent. His mother, who supplanted Arsinoë I as Ptolemy II's queen, assuredly had enough influence over Ptolemy II to supplant Arsinoë I's son (Ptolemy III) by her own child.

It may be objected that according to Pausanias and the Theocritus scholium (quoted above), Arsinoë II died childless. But in these passages it is plain that " childless " means " without any children by Ptolemy II "; they do not preclude the survival of a son by an earlier marriage. It has also been urged that Ptolemy III on his eventual accession would never have styled himself " son of the divine brother and sister " (i.e. of Ptolemy II and Arsinoë II), if his claims to the throne had been postponed by Arsinoë II's influence to those of her own son. But, whether he liked it or not, Ptolemy III had in fact been adopted by Arsinoë II, and his legal title to the throne was derived from Arsinoë II rather than from Arsinoë I.[1] Ptolemy III would have been strangely unlike the rest of his dynasty if he had allowed feelings of love or anger to interfere with his claims to power and position.

The identification of Ptolemy, the child of king Lysimachus and Arsinoë II, with "Ptolemy the Son" is contingent upon Lysimachus' and Arsinoë's child having survived his early trials and rejoined his mother at Alexandria. But it is free from positive objections, and pending fresh light from papyri or inscriptions it deserves to hold the field.

The most instructive treatment of this problem is by E. v. Stern, *Hermes*, 1915, p. 427–444. For other recent discussions, see Tarn, *Antigonos Gonatas*, p. 445–7 ; A. W. de Groot, *Rheinisches Museum*, 1917–8, p. 446–63 ; Beloch, *Griech. Gesch.*, IV, pt. 1, p. 186–9 ; Bevan, *Egypt under the Ptolemies*, p. 65–7.

[1] Schol. Theocr., XVII, 128 (quoted above). Presumably Ptolemy II on adopting the son of Lysimachus made it a condition that Arsinoë II should adopt his children by Arsinoë I. There is no need to assume that the adoption took place in 267, after the death of Arsinoë II (as is done by C. C. Edgar, *Journ. Egypt. Archæol.*, 1928, pp. 198–9). It might have happened immediately after Arsinoë II's marriage with Ptolemy II, *c.* 275 B.C.

Addendum.—The Ptolemy discussed above is to be held distinct from " Ptolemy, son of Lysimachus " (see p. 411, no. (*c*) (4), who entered the service of Ptolemy II and was governor of the Lycian town of Telmessus on his behalf (*c.* 265–257).—See M. Segre, *Clara Rhodos*, 1938, p. 179 ff.

7

THE REIGN OF MAGAS OF CYRENE

THE civil war which commenced at Cyrene after the death of Magas has usually been dated near 258 B.C. (So recently by Tarn, *Antigonos Gonatas*, p. 450–1 ; J. W. H. Tillyard and A. J. B. Wace, *Annual Brit. School Athens*, XI, p. 112 ff.) On the other hand Beloch (*Griech. Gesch.*, IV, pt. 2, p. 186–9) brings the date down to 250. Several of the texts invoked for or against these theories are inconclusive. On this ground we shall omit discussion of (1) Justin, XXVI, chs. 2 and 3 ; (2) Eusebius, *Chronicon*, I, 237 ; (3) Catullus, *Coma Berenices*, l. 25 ff.

The real crux of the problem lies in the interpretation of Pausanias, I, 6, 8 : *ἀποθανόντος δὲ Ἀντιγόνου* (i.e. Antigonus I) *Πτολεμαῖος Σύρους τε αὖθις καὶ Κύπρον εἷλε, κατήγαγε δὲ καὶ Πύρρον ἐς τὴν Θεσπρωτίδα ἤπειρον, Κυρήνης δὲ ἀποστάσης Μάγας Βερενίκης υἱὸς Πτολεμαίῳ τότε συνοικούσης ἔτει πεμπτῷ μετὰ τὴν ἀπόστασιν εἷλε Κυρήνην.*

It is usually supposed that the revolt of Cyrene here referred to is that of 313 (Diodorus, XIX, 29, 1), and that the reconquest by Magas on Ptolemy's behalf occurred in 308. These dates tally with a notice in Suidas (s.v. Δημήτριος) that Ptolemy regained Cyrene after the death of Ophellas (in 309). As Magas is stated to have reigned 50 years (Agatharchides ap. Athenæum XII, 550 b), his death on this reckoning befell in or about 258.

Beloch, assuming that the recovery of Cyrene by Ptolemy, like his reconquest of Syria and Cyprus, happened *ἀποθανόντος Ἀντιγόνου*, dates it to 301, and its loss to 306. In favour of this chronology it may be said that 306 (after Salamis) was a likely date for the revolt of Cyrene, and 301 (after Ipsus) for its recapture. But no ancient author records a defection in 306, though one would have expected Diodorus, who writes at length on the events of that year, to have mentioned it. Besides, Pausanias' list of events is plainly not in chronological order, for the restoration of Pyrrhus did not occur until 297 B.C. (i.e. after the latest possible date for the recapture of Cyrene). Therefore no conclusions can be drawn as to the time-relation between the reconquest of Cyrene and the death of Antigonus.

Beloch further contends that Magas can hardly have been more than twenty-five years older than his half-brother Ptolemy II, who was born in 309. Therefore he must have been too young to assume control at Cyrene in 308. This argument would carry much weight if Magas had been a man of common family promoted to a governorship. But as a stepson of Ptolemy I he might perfectly well have been made a viceroy at the age of 25 : Demetrius the son of Antigonus Gonatas was put in command of an army at age 13 (p. 135).

A positive argument against Beloch's chronology is that the intervention of the Antigonid prince Demetrius the Fair, which followed upon the death of Magas, can hardly have happened at a time when the Antigonid power had been crippled by the rebellion of Alexander, which happened *c.* 252 (see Appendix 10). It falls most naturally in the period of the Macedonian thalassocracy after the battle of Cos, i.e. about 256. As Magas' " fifty years " of reign may be a round number, there is no difficulty in post-dating his death from 258 to 256 or 255 ; but 250 is too late.

8

THE THIRD SYRIAN WAR

No series of events in Hellenistic history is more open to controversy than the Third Syrian War or "War of Laodice." The story of the war has to be made up out of a random collection of brief allusions, which frequently contradict each other.

The chief problems for discussion are as follows:—(1) *Did Antiochus II restore the succession to Laodice's son Seleucus?* No statement to this effect is made by any ancient author. On the other hand Valerius Maximus (IX, 14) and Pliny (VII, 53) assert that after Antiochus' death Laodice procured a double of the deceased king, who assumed the part of a dying but not dead Antiochus and commended his children to the loyalty of his lieges (who had been freely admitted into the sick room). Nevertheless, we need not hesitate to assume that Antiochus really bequeathed his crown to Seleucus. It is perhaps a minor point that the details of Valerius' and Pliny's stories are in conflict, that in Valerius' account the mock-Antiochus is of the blood-royal, but in Pliny's version he is a plebeian. The decisive consideration is the undisputed fact that before his death Antiochus summoned Laodice to Ephesus from her quasi-exile. This is clear evidence of a change of heart on Antiochus' part, and it may safely be assumed that a masterful queen like Laodice at once took advantage of her return to favour in order to secure the succession for her son. Indeed, it is not unlikely that Antiochus called back Laodice with the intention of restoring the right of succession to her line: feeling that his hour had come, and realising the dangers of a long minority reign, if his crown were to pass to Berenice's infant child, he re-appointed the adolescent Seleucus as his heir.

(2) *Did Laodice poison Antiochus?*—So say Valerius and Pliny, and Appian (*Syriaca*, ch. 65) into the bargain. If we accept the story of a supposititious Antiochus, it follows that the real Antiochus died at a pre-arranged hour, for the scene in the king's bedchamber could hardly have been improvised after his natural death. If the succession was devised *bona fide* upon Seleucus by his real father, it still remains possible that Laodice should have

murdered Antiochus lest having changed his mind once he should alter it again. A parallel case might be found in the death of the Roman emperor Claudius, whom Agrippina was believed to have poisoned lest he should transfer the succession back from Nero to Britannicus. But this analogy cuts both ways. The sudden collapse of an elderly glutton like Claudius needs no foul play to explain it, and the death of Antiochus, who was past his prime and had the reputation of being a toper, may equally well be attributed to natural causes. In both of these cases the wisest course is to enter an open verdict. It is enough to know that legally, as well as on grounds of equity and expediency, Seleucus was entitled to the succession.

(3) *What was the state of parties at Antioch?*—The existence of a strong sentiment in favour of Berenice and her son is implied by Polyænus (VIII, 50), who relates that after the death of Berenice's son the partisans of Laodice found it necessary to pretend that he was still alive, and accordingly presented to the Antiochenes another little boy of similar appearance. This tale may not be true in itself—in our sources for the Third Syrian War vicarious resuscitations of dead personages form a veritable *Leitmotif*—but it is good evidence of popular indignation against the murderers. Speculation on this point, however, is hardly necessary, for the question is settled by a surviving papyrus (the so-called "Gurob" text),[1] which describes the reception given by the Antiochenes to the Egyptian relief expedition :—

"We were met outside the gate by the satraps, the military chiefs and their troops, the priests, the boards of magistrates, the young men from the gymnasia, and a crowd of other folk bearing wreaths."[2]

However much we allow here for propagandist exaggeration, we must admit that feeling in Antioch ran high in favour of Berenice, and that part at least of the army in Syria took sides with her.

Yet Laodice's supporters at Antioch were more than a handful. Valerius, describing an attempt by Berenice to rescue her kidnapped child, states that she mounted a chariot and charged *infesta contrariæ partis agmina*. Polyænus relates that the murderers of the child surrounded the boy whom they passed off in his stead with the βασιλικὴ δορυφορία, and that when they got Berenice herself into their power φυλακὴν (αὐτῇ) μισθοφόρων

[1] *P. Petrie*, II, 45; improved texts in III, 144, and in Mitteis–Wilcken, *Chrestomathie*, no. 1. English translation in Bevan, *Egypt under the Ptolemies*, pp. 198–200.

[2] Col. III, l. 21 ff. The text contains a few lacunæ, but there is no serious doubt as to the missing words.

Γαλατικῶν ἐπέστησαν. The issue probably lay between (i) the civilians at Antioch and the line troops from the surrounding districts (e.g. from Apamea), (ii) the household troops and the Galatians (who naturally took orders from the queen at Ephesus in preference to the one in Syria). The murder of Berenice and her child must have happened before the line troops came in, for these plainly were in possession of Antioch when the Egyptian expedition arrived.

(4) *How was Berenice put to death?*—According to Justin, Berenice escaped to Daphne and entrenched herself there. But the more detailed account of Polyænus indicates that she was taken prisoner by Laodice's partisans : presumably the " infesta agmina " into which she charged held her fast. The τόπος τῶν βασιλείων ὀχυρώτατος where she was lodged may well have been in the suburb of Daphne, where a rescue by the Antiochenes was less to be feared.[1]

Polyænus further states that Laodice's party agreed to do her no violence, but subsequently broke their promise. Similarly Justin says that she was " circumvented by guile." If her captors intended to kill her, why did they not do so at once, while they still had control of affairs ? The simplest explanation is that they intended to hold her to ransom, but that the Galatians who were set to keep watch over her took matters into their own hands.

(5) *Who led the Egyptian naval expedition?*—The sole authority for this expedition is the Gurob papyrus mentioned above. This text was a communiqué (published presumably for the benefit of the Alexandrians) by the commander of the expedition. We have only two clues as to the identity of his commander, (i) his description of the reception at Antioch, quoted above, (ii) the statement that after the reception εἰσήλθομεν πρὸς τὴν ἀδελφήν.

In spite of attempts to prove that ἡ ἀδελφή was an official expression for " the queen," and that the commander was therefore not a relative of Berenice, it may be safely assumed that ἀδελφή here has its ordinary sense of " sister."[2] The author of the papyrus

[1] Beloch (*Griech. Gesch.*, IV, pt. 1, p. 675 and n. 2) suggests that Berenice took sanctuary in the temple of Apollo at Daphne, and not in a royal villa. But if her death had involved a violation of sanctuary, our sources, which have a marked bias against Laodice, would not have failed to inform us.

[2] In *P. Zeno Cairo*, 59251, the term with which Berenice is designated by her court doctor is not ἡ ἀδελφή, but ἡ βασίλισσα.

It is suggested by Bevan (*Egypt under the Ptolemies*, pp. 201–2) that ἡ ἀδελφή was not Ptolemy's sister but his queen, Berenice III. Possibly his queen might have accompanied Ptolemy, but she would hardly have preceded him and have taken control of military operations previously to his arrival (as ἡ ἀδελφή does in the papyrus).

was therefore either Ptolemy III or his younger brother Lysimachus.

Since it is certain that Ptolemy conducted an expedition to Antioch, but no independent evidence exists of Lysimachus' participation in it, there is a strong *a priori* probability in favour of the view that the papyrus is from the pen of the king himself. Against this conclusion it may be urged that Ptolemy did not reach Antioch until after the murder of Berenice (a point on which Justin and Polyænus are agreed), but that the words of the papyrus εἰσήλθομεν πρὸς τὴν ἀδελφήν, imply that Ptolemy's sister was alive at the time of her rescuer's arrival. Thus it may seem preferable to suppose that Lysimachus led an advance force to Antioch, previous to the arrival of the king, and that the papyrus relates to this earlier expedition. In this case presumably Lysimachus held a naval command in Cyprus or Phœnicia, in the same way as Menelaus, the younger brother of Ptolemy I, in the campaign of 306 B.C.

But granted that Lysimachus arrived in Antioch before any harm had happened to Berenice, how came it that she was subsequently overpowered and killed by Laodice's party? The papyrus shows that even before the arrival of the first Egyptian contingent the Seleucid troops that were friendly to Berenice had obtained control of Antioch, and the Egyptian reinforcements ought to have made assurance doubly sure for her. If Berenice nevertheless was captured by her opponents, there must have been some perfectly incredible negligence on the part of her supporters. It is therefore difficult to avoid the conclusion that Berenice's death took place before any Egyptian reinforcements arrived,[1] and that the statement in the papyrus about the visit to the sister was deliberately misleading.[2]

Such a misstatement in an official communiqué is in itself no matter for surprise. Moreover, there is evidence that Ptolemy did actually keep dark the death of his sister. According to Polyænus Berenice's attendants concealed the body of the murdered queen and found a woman of similar appearance who was suborned to go through the motions of nursing a wound and recovering from it. Thereupon, Ptolemy sent dispatches all over the Seleucid dominions in the name of Berenice and her child, pretending that the pair were still alive. No doubt the first half

[1] It is clear from col. I of the papyrus that an advance Egyptian squadron (from Cyprus or Phœnicia ?) got into touch with Berenice before her death but was diverted by her to Cilicia, presumably because she felt in no immediate danger at Antioch. If that was the case Berenice made a fatal blunder.

[2] This is the suggestion of M. Holleaux (*Revue des Études Anciennes*, 1916, p. 153 ff.).

of this story is merely another variant of the familiar substitution-theme ; but the second part deserves credence.[1] The oddest of all the strange happenings in the Third Syrian War, the triumphal march of Ptolemy III through the Seleucid dominions, requires some such explanation as Polyænus supplies. It is clear in itself, and stated expressly by Justin, that Ptolemy was not regarded as a foreign invader, but as the champion of Berenice against Laodice ; but he could not have assumed this part unless the news of Berenice's death had been kept secret. Lastly, if Ptolemy could tell a lie to the subjects of Berenice, he was surely not incapable of deceiving his lieges in Alexandria. Moreover, granted that the phrase εἰσήλθομεν πρὸς τὴν ἀδελφήν was a trap, it is far more likely that Ptolemy than that Lysimachus laid it. We may therefore recognize Ptolemy III as the author of the Gurob papyrus.

(6) *How far did Ptolemy III carry his invasion into the Seleucid dominions ?*—(i) Polyænus asserts that Ptolemy μέχρι τῆς Ἰνδικῆς χώρας πολέμου καὶ μάχης ἐκράτησε. (ii) St. Jerome (Commentary on Daniel 11, 6, in Migne, *Patrologia Latina*, vol. 25, p. 560) makes him master of " the upper regions beyond the Euphrates, and *almost all Asia*." (iii) A memorial set up by some Ptolemaic official at the Red Sea port of Adule (near Massowa)—probably the copy of an official bulletin in the style of the nineteenth-dynasty Pharaohs—claims " Mesopotamia, Babylonia, Susiana, Persis, Media, and all the lands as far as Bactria " for Ptolemy. (Ditt., *O.G.I.*, 54.) On the other hand (iv) Appian (*Syriaca*, ch. 65) takes Ptolemy no farther than Babylonia. (v.) A cuneiform tablet proves that by midsummer 245 Babylon had restored its allegiance to Seleucus II. Since Ptolemy can hardly have set out from Antioch before summer 246, it is obvious that he cannot have been anywhere near India. Presumably his conquest of the upper provinces amounts to this, that he took possession of Seleucia-on-Tigris, and there received the submission (in person or by letter) of the governors of the eastern districts.[2]

For recent discussions of this problem, see Bevan, *The House of Seleucus*, I, p. 181 ff. ; *Egypt under the Ptolemaic Dynasty*, p. 189 ff. ; Beloch, *Griech. Gesch.*, IV, pt. 1, pp. 673–6 ; W. Otto, *Beiträge zur Seleukidengeschichte*, p. 56 ff. ; A. G. Roos, *Mnemosyne*, 1923, pp. 262–78 ; A. Bouché-Leclercq, *Histoire des Lagides*, I, pp. 246–55 ; *Histoire des Séleucides*, II, pp. 555–8 ; G. De Sanctis, *Atti Accademia Torino*, vol. 47, p. 957 ff. ; M. Holleaux, *Revue des Études Anciennes*, 1916, p. 153 ff.

[1] It may be suggested that Ptolemy's false dispatches were the historical basis of all the substitution legends of the Third Syrian War. Such clouds of smoke can only arise from a fire.

[2] Beloch, *Griech. Gesch.*, IV, pt. 2, p. 518.

9

ANTIGONEIA-ON-THE-AOUS

In describing the attack of the Illyrians upon the Epirote town of Phœnice in 230, Polybius (II, 5, 6) mentions that the Epirote defenders sent troops to the Aous gorges παραφυλάξοντας τὴν Αντιγόνειαν. The term παραφυλάσσειν, as Beloch (*Griech. Gesch.*, IV, pt. 2, p. 380 n.) has pointed out, means to guard, rather than to put under hostile observation. In 230, therefore, Antigoneia was in Epirote hands. But it is difficult to believe with Beloch that this fortress was built by Pyrrhus and named from one of his wives, the Ptolemaic princess Antigone. As the other towns carrying that name were indubitably foundations of Antigonus Gonatas, we may with greater reason attribute Antigoneia-on-the-Aous to him. In that case Gonatas took the district of Atintania, in which Antigoneia lies, off Pyrrhus' son Alexander II (either in 272, after Pyrrhus' death, or more probably after Alexander's disastrous interference in the Chremonidean War[1]). Its retrocession to Epirus may have taken place about 233 B.C., when Demetrius II of Macedon was crippled by the Dardanians and had to concentrate upon the defence of Macedonia proper. He may have surrendered it to the Epirote royal house as compensation for the divorce of the Epirote princess Phthia.

[1] Tarn, *Antigonos Gonatas*, p. 312.

10

ALEXANDER, SON OF CRATERUS

THE reign of Alexander, son of Craterus, at Corinth has recently been dated by W. H. Porter (*Hermathena*, XLV, p. 293–311) to 250–245 or 249–244 B.C. His main support for this chronology is derived from a speech made by Antigonus Gonatas at a festival in Corinth, in which he used the following *ad captandum* words about Aratus: πρότερον γὰρ ἡμᾶς ὑπερεώρα . . . . καὶ τὸν Αἰγύπτιον ἐθαύμαζε πλοῦτον . . . . νυνὶ δε ὑπὸ σκηνὴν ἑωρακὼς πάντα τὰ ἐκεῖ πράγματα τραγῳδίαν ὄντα καὶ σκηνογραφίαν ὅλος ἡμῖν προσκεχώρηκεν. (Plutarch, *Aratus*, ch. 15.) He assumes that this speech must have been delivered soon after Aratus' return from the court of Ptolemy II (spring 250). On the other hand it could not have been made after 249, for in that year Ptolemy recovered the thalassocracy of the Aegean (p. 140), and Gonatas would merely have stultified himself after this by describing the power of Egypt as mere pasteboard and tinsel. Therefore Gonatas was still in possession of Corinth in 250, and possibly in the early part of 249.

This attractive piece of reasoning rests on the supposition that Gonatas did not wait long after Aratus' return from Egypt before he made his speech.

But this conclusion does not follow imperatively from Plutarch's order of narrative, which is as follows:—

Chapter 13: Aratus returns from Egypt (250).
,, 14: Aratus composes party-quarrels at Sicyon.
,, 15: Gonatas makes his speech.
,, 16: Aratus is elected and re-elected general of the Achæan League (245 and 243).

According to this sequence, Gonatas' speech may have been delivered in any year from 250 to 245 inclusive. Furthermore, a liberal allowance of time must be made for the composure of the disputes at Sicyon, which Plutarch declares to have been a very tedious business. On the whole, therefore, Plutarch's narrative tells in favour of a later date than 250 or 249.

Again, it is almost necessary to assume that Gonatas had

recovered possession of his naval arsenals at Chalcis and Corinth before he engaged and defeated Ptolemy's fleet at Andros (246). But he did not recover Corinth until some time after the death of Alexander (Plutarch, *Aratus*, ch. 17); therefore the end of Alexander's reign cannot be placed later than 246, and the beginning not after 251.

The most likely occasion for Gonatas to celebrate a festival at Corinth and to make disparaging remarks about the hollowness of Ptolemy's might was immediately after the battle of Andros. In this case his speech was made after the recovery of Corinth, not before its loss.

Addendum.—Porter's system of dating has been restated in his edition of Plutarch's *Life of Aratus* (Introduction, p. xxxvii ff.), and has been confirmed by Walbank (*Aratos of Sicyon*, pp. 179–81).

Against the view set forth above, that Gonatas must have recovered Corinth before he could venture on the naval campaign of 246, Porter contends that he could have built up his battle-fleet at Thessalonica or Demetrius. True; but would he have had any chance of a victory against the *combined* navies of Ptolemy and of Alexander, so long as Alexander retained Corinth and Chalcis?

Porter and Walbank further argue that an expedition which Aratus undertook during his first term of office as Achæan strategus (i.e. in 246) to assist the Bœotians in repelling an Ætolian raid (Plutarch, *Aratus*, 16, 1), would not have been feasible while Antigonus, who was a potential enemy of the Achæan League, was in possession of Corinth, for Aratus could not have taken any considerable force to Bœotia except by the Isthmus route. But in 457 B.C. the Spartans succeeded in conveying a large force across the Corinthian Gulf, despite Athenian patrols (Thucydides, I, 107, 3); could Aratus not have done likewise? In any case, he arrived in Bœotia too late for the decisive battle: perhaps Gonatas *did* undertake a delaying action.

11

THE PTOLEMAIC THALASSOCRACY IN THE AEGEAN

According to W. Kolbe (*Göttingen Gelehrte Anzeigen*, 1916, p. 473 ff.), the Egyptian thalassocracy in the Aegean was not seriously curtailed by the battle of Andros, but lasted to the end of the reign of Ptolemy III. This view, which has recently received support from A. Fellmann (*Antigonos Gonatas*, p. 63 ff.) and E. Bikerman (*Rev. Ét. Anc.*, 1938, p. 369 ff.), is based on inscriptions from various islands which prove that these were subject to some Ptolemy or other. But in most of these documents (as set forth in the table appended by Kolbe) the Ptolemy in question cannot be identified with any particular king of that line, and the texts themselves may be anterior to Andros and even to Cos. Of the datable texts, Ditt., *O.G.I.*, 54 (the Adule inscription) refers to the *beginning* of the reign of Ptolemy III, i.e. just before the battle of Andros.

The evidence for a Macedonian thalassocracy after Andros is based partly on some further inscriptions (also tabulated by Kolbe), which refer to a king Antigonus as overlord. Conceivably all these fall into the short period between Cos and Andros, but their number (seven in all) makes it more likely that they should be spread over a wider range of time, and that some at least belong to the reign of Antigonus Doson. Support for this view may be derived from dedications at Delos made *nominatim* by Gonatas, Demetrius II and Doson. Kolbe, it is true, denies that royal dedications at Delos imply political overlordship, for he regards Delos as a "neutral" island and always open to all comers. Against this Tarn has pointed out that Delos was indeed inviolable by belligerents, but not neutral (*Journ. Hell. Stud.*, 1924, p. 141 ff.); and Kolbe's rejoinder (*ibid.*, 1930, p. 20 ff.) only meets part of Tarn's argument.

The balance of evidence, therefore, is in favour of a resumption of the Macedonian thalassocracy, at any rate in the group of the Cyclades. It is admitted on all hands that Thera remained Ptolemaic.

12

CLEOMENES III AND ARCHIDAMUS

POLYBIUS (V, 37, 3–5) asserts that Cleomenes killed his fellow-king Archidamus ; Plutarch (*Cleomenes*, ch. 5) states that the murder was committed by the former enemies of king Agis IV for fear of reprisals from the dead king's brother. Both authors agree that Cleomenes in the first instance procured the recall of Archidamus from exile.

It is difficult to understand why Cleomenes should have feared Archidamus' presence in Sparta ; still more so to explain why in that case he did not leave him in banishment.

By way of compromise, E. v. Stern (*Hermes*, 1915, p. 554 ff.) has suggested that Cleomenes after recalling Archidamus connived at his assassination by Agis' foes in order to lull their suspicions and throw them off their guard against his impending attempt at revolution. But this theory does not save the credit of either ancient author, and it represents Cleomenes as not only a crafty but also a weak personality—a view which squares ill with the known facts of his career.

In this case it seems preferable to accept Plutarch (i.e. Phylarchus) and to reject Polybius (*sive* Aratus) *in toto*.

13

THE NUMBERS OF THE PTOLEMAIC ARMY AT RAPHIA

In his enumeration of the contingents which Sosibius recruited and trained for the campaign of Raphia Polybius mentions (1) a phalanx of 25 000 men, of unspecified nationality, (2) an Egyptian corps of 20,000, serving in a phalanx (V, 65, 4 and 9). This may mean (1) that there were two phalanxes, a corps of 20,000 Egyptians, and another of 25,000 Greeks, or (2) that there was one phalanx, composed of 20,000 Egyptians, and of 5000 Greeks to stiffen them. In the former case the Ptolemaic army totalled some 75,000 men, in the latter only 55,000.

The actual course of the battle makes it seem more likely that there was only one phalanx. Had there been two such corps, with an aggregate strength of 45,000, it would be difficult to understand why this force failed to overthrow at the first shock the phalanx of Antiochus, which numbered only 20,000 (V, 79, 5). Though the Ptolemaic heavy infantry eventually decided the battle, it did so only at the eleventh hour, and by a special effort under the personal direction of the king. From this fact it may be inferred that it had only a slight preponderance of numbers.

14

THE ANTIGONIDS AND THE ADRIATIC

In *Cambr. Anc. Hist.*, VII, p. 837 ff., M. Holleaux expresses the view that the kings of Macedon had a long-standing interest in the Adriatic Sea, and that the establishment of a Roman zone in Illyria created a serious conflict of interests between the Antigonids and the Roman Republic. This view runs counter to his general thesis, that the clash between Rome and Greece was not the inevitable effect of deep-seated causes, but resulted from a chapter of accidents. Accepting this thesis in full, I acknowledge myself "plus Holleauxiste que M. Holleaux" on the question of the Adriatic. Though Cassander pursued an Adriatic policy for a few years, he did not persist in it (p. 124). Gonatas appears to have lived at peace with his Illyrian neighbours; he probably took Atintania from the kings of Epirus (App. 9), but there is no evidence of his having acquired or desired an Adriatic sea-front. Doson employed Demetrius of Pharos as an auxiliary in the campaign of Sellasia, but there is nothing to show that he fell in any way under the influence of his ally in matters of politics, as Philip unquestionably did after 217. On the other hand, Doson's neglect of the Macedonian fleet points to a lack of interest on his part in Adriatic affairs.

From the standpoint of frontier security the Antigonids were naturally concerned to hold the Pindus range to its watershed, and the occupation of Atintania on its western slope gave them added security against invasion; but they had little or nothing to gain by descending to the Adriatic.

From the economic point of view Macedon had little need of an Adriatic outlet. Not even the construction of the Via Egnatia by the Romans could create any considerable volume of traffic between Aegean and Adriatic.

Addendum.—The view set forth above has been developed by J. V. A. Fine (*Journ. Rom. Stud.*, 1936, p. 24 ff.). His argument has received support from P. Treves (*Athenæum*, 1934, p. 396 n. 3).

15

ERATOSTHENES' MEASUREMENT OF THE EARTH'S CIRCUMFERENCE

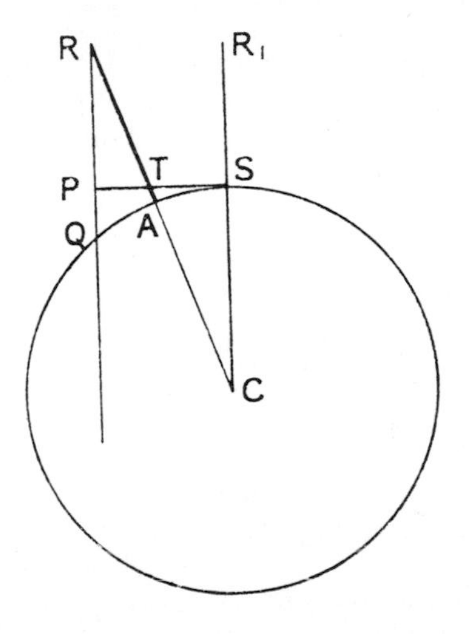

Eratosthenes' data.

(1) The angle of the sun's shadow at Alexandria at noon on a midsummer day. By setting up a perpendicular measuring-stick Eratosthenes was able to read off the shadow of the angle as $=7° 12'$. (For the sake of clearness in the diagram the angle /PRA has been considerably, and the measuring-rod AR has been enormously, exaggerated.)

(2) The information that at Syene (Assuan, a little N. of the tropic of Cancer) the rays of the sun fell vertically at noon on a midsummer day, so as to illuminate the bottom of a deep well. (R_1S in the diagram.)

(3) The distance from Alexandria to Syene, as measured on the earth's surface.

(4) The *Elements* of Euclid.

Eratosthenes' constructions.

(1) Prolongation of RA and R_1S to their meeting-point C. Since RA and R_1S were vertical, their meeting-point must be at the earth's centre.
(2) Extension of RPQ, a parallel to R_1SC, from the point R.
(3) Projection of a perpendicular STP from S to T (the intersection-point of RAC) and P (the intersection-point of RPQ).
(4) Description of a circle with centre C and radius CA or CS. This circle, *ex hypothesi*, must represent the earth's circumference.

Eratosthenes' demonstration.

In the $\triangle$s CST, RPT :—

the intersecting angles $\angle CTS$ and $\angle RTP$ are equal;
the right angles $\angle CST$ and $\angle RPT$ are equal;
therefore the remaining angles $\angle SCT$ and $\angle PRT$ are equal.

But $\angle PRT = 7° 12'$;
$\therefore \angle SCT = 7° 12'$
$= \frac{1}{50}$th of four right angles.

$\therefore$ the arc AS subtending $\angle SCT$ = one-fiftieth of the perimeter of which it forms part.
$\therefore$ the earth's circumference = 50 times the length of AS (a known magnitude).

(Eratosthenes' data of distances and angles were not strictly accurate, but his errors happened to cancel out rather than to accumulate. In any case, his method was perfectly sound in principle, and has been used for the same purpose by modern men of science.)

LISTS AND STEMMATA OF THE HELLENISTIC DYNASTIES

(For fuller details, see the *Cambridge Ancient History*, vol. VII, and Beloch, *Griechische Geschichte*, vol. IV, pt. 2.)

(A) *Rulers of Macedon* before the foundation of the Antigonid dynasty.

(1) PHILIP III ARRIDÆUS	323–317
(2) OLYMPIAS (D. 5)	317–316
(3) CASSANDER	316–297 (king since 305)
(4) PHILIP IV	297
(5) ANTIPATER	297–294
(6) ALEXANDER IV	297–294
(7) DEMETRIUS I (B. 2)	294–288
(8) LYSIMACHUS (C. 1)	288–281
(9) PTOLEMY CERAUNUS (F. 4)	281–279

(B) *The Antigonids.*

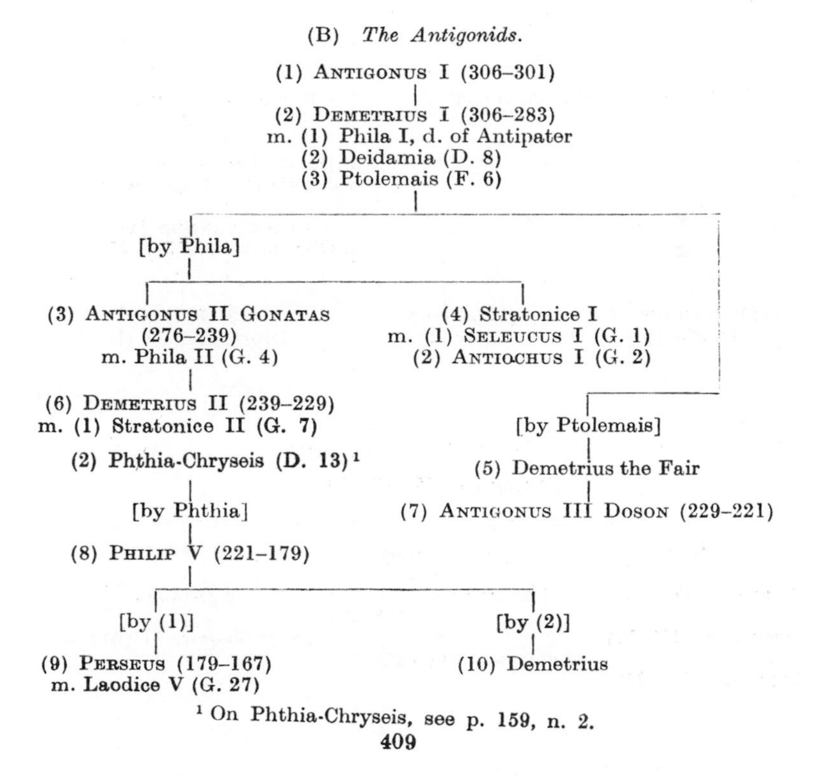

[1] On Phthia-Chryseis, see p. 159, n. 2.

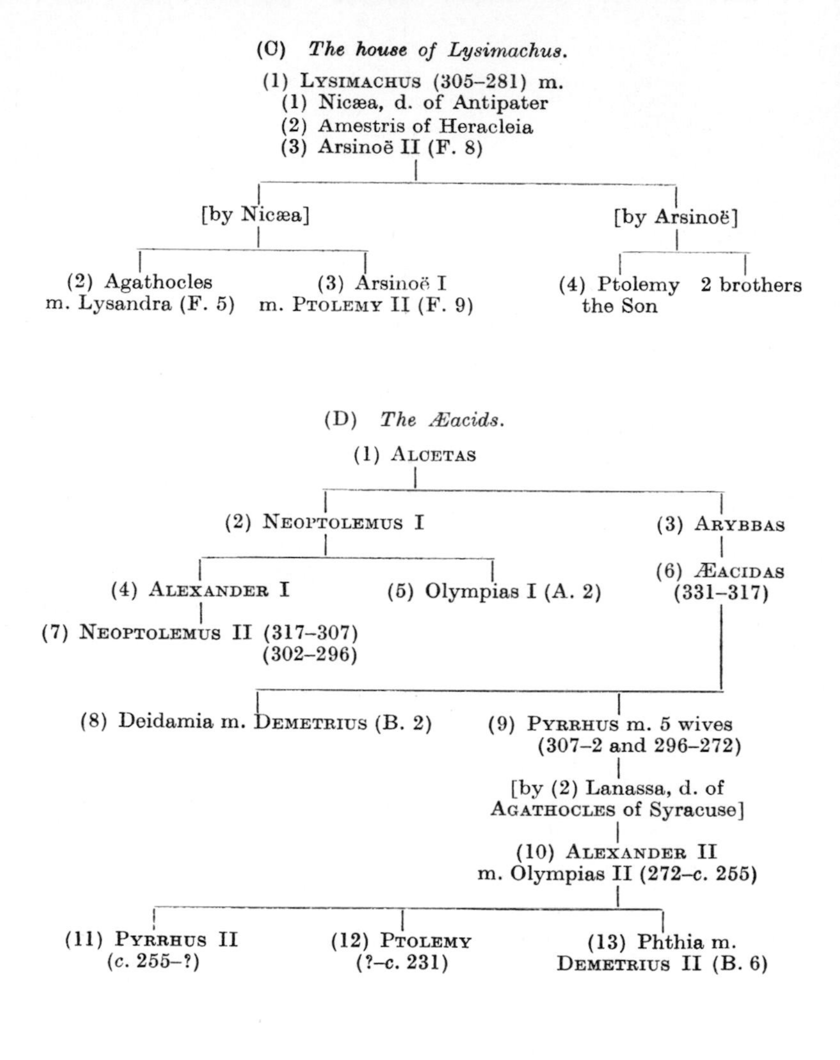
(C) The house of Lysimachus.
(1) Lysimachus (305–281) m.
(1) Nicæa, d. of Antipater
(2) Amestris of Heracleia
(3) Arsinoë II (F. 8)
[by Nicæa]
[by Arsinoë]
(2) Agathocles
m. Lysandra (F. 5)
(3) Arsinoë I
m. Ptolemy II (F. 9)
(4) Ptolemy
the Son
2 brothers
(D) The Æacids.
(1) Alcetas
(2) Neoptolemus I
(3) Arybbas
(4) Alexander I
(5) Olympias I (A. 2)
(6) Æacidas
(331–317)
(7) Neoptolemus II (317–307)
(302–296)
(8) Deidamia m. Demetrius (B. 2)
(9) Pyrrhus m. 5 wives
(307–2 and 296–272)
[by (2) Lanassa, d. of
Agathocles of Syracuse]
(10) Alexander II
m. Olympias II (272–c. 255)
(11) Pyrrhus II
(c. 255–?)
(12) Ptolemy
(?–c. 231)
(13) Phthia m.
Demetrius II (B. 6)
(E) The Agid kings of Sparta.

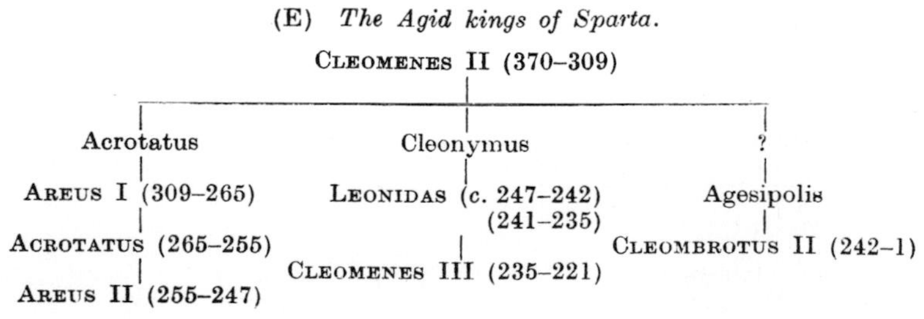
Cleomenes II (370–309)
Acrotatus
Cleonymus
?
Areus I (309–265)
Leonidas (c. 247–242)
(241–235)
Agesipolis
Acrotatus (265–255)
Cleombrotus II (242–1)
Cleomenes III (235–221)
Areus II (255–247)

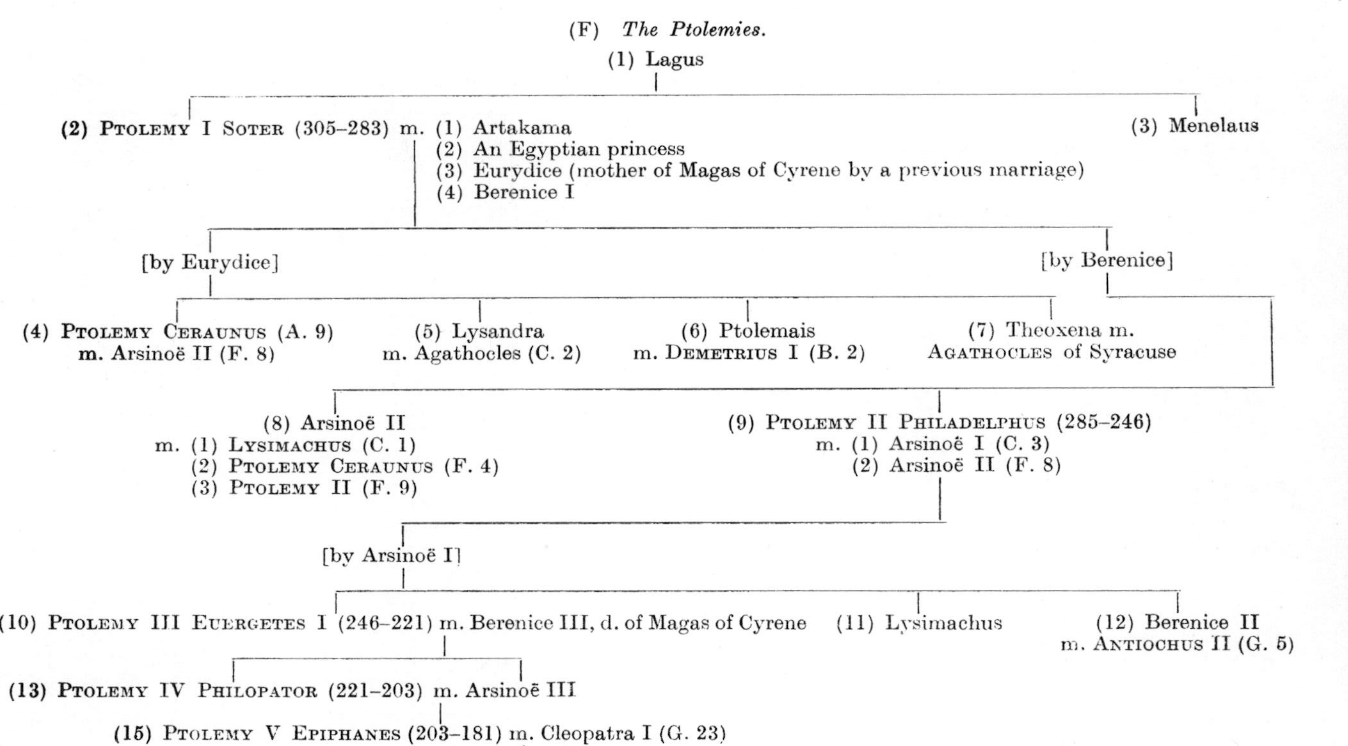
(F) *The Ptolemies.*
(1) Lagus
(2) Ptolemy I Soter (305–283) m. (1) Artakama
(2) An Egyptian princess
(3) Eurydice (mother of Magas of Cyrene by a previous marriage)
(4) Berenice I
(3) Menelaus
[by Eurydice]
[by Berenice]
(4) Ptolemy Ceraunus (A. 9)
m. Arsinoë II (F. 8)
(5) Lysandra
m. Agathocles (C. 2)
(6) Ptolemais
m. Demetrius I (B. 2)
(7) Theoxena m.
Agathocles of Syracuse
(8) Arsinoë II
m. (1) Lysimachus (C. 1)
(2) Ptolemy Ceraunus (F. 4)
(3) Ptolemy II (F. 9)
(9) Ptolemy II Philadelphus (285–246)
m. (1) Arsinoë I (C. 3)
(2) Arsinoë II (F. 8)
[by Arsinoë I]
(10) Ptolemy III Euergetes I (246–221) m. Berenice III, d. of Magas of Cyrene
(11) Lysimachus
(12) Berenice II
m. Antiochus II (G. 5)
(13) Ptolemy IV Philopator (221–203) m. Arsinoë III
(15) Ptolemy V Epiphanes (203–181) m. Cleopatra I (G. 23)

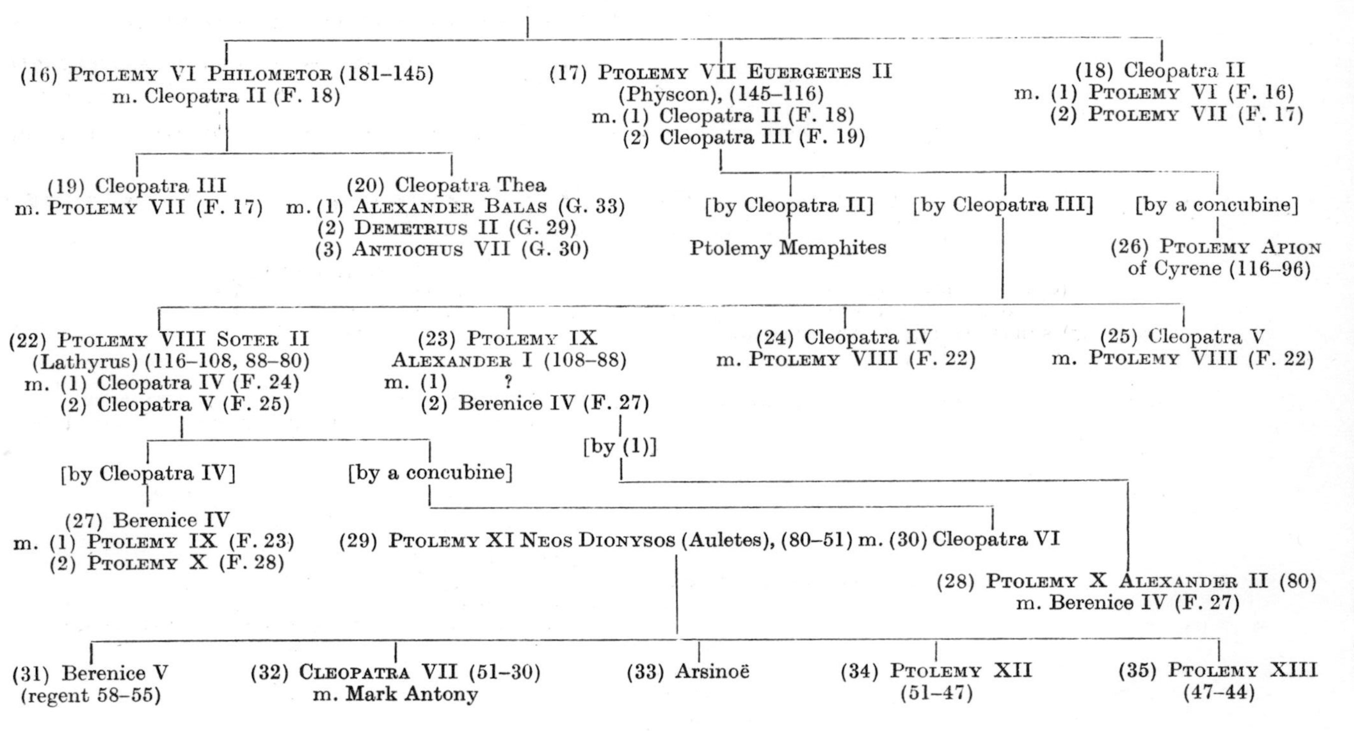
(16) Ptolemy VI Philometor (181–145)
m. Cleopatra II (F. 18)
(17) Ptolemy VII Euergetes II
(Physcon), (145–116)
m. (1) Cleopatra II (F. 18)
(2) Cleopatra III (F. 19)
(18) Cleopatra II
m. (1) Ptolemy VI (F. 16)
(2) Ptolemy VII (F. 17)
(19) Cleopatra III
m. Ptolemy VII (F. 17)
(20) Cleopatra Thea
m. (1) Alexander Balas (G. 33)
(2) Demetrius II (G. 29)
(3) Antiochus VII (G. 30)
[by Cleopatra II]
Ptolemy Memphites
[by Cleopatra III]
[by a concubine]
(26) Ptolemy Apion
of Cyrene (116–96)
(22) Ptolemy VIII Soter II
(Lathyrus) (116–108, 88–80)
m. (1) Cleopatra IV (F. 24)
(2) Cleopatra V (F. 25)
(23) Ptolemy IX
Alexander I (108–88)
m. (1) ?
(2) Berenice IV (F. 27)
(24) Cleopatra IV
m. Ptolemy VIII (F. 22)
(25) Cleopatra V
m. Ptolemy VIII (F. 22)
[by Cleopatra IV]
[by a concubine]
[by (1)]
(27) Berenice IV
m. (1) Ptolemy IX (F. 23)
(2) Ptolemy X (F. 28)
(29) Ptolemy XI Neos Dionysos (Auletes), (80–51) m. (30) Cleopatra VI
(28) Ptolemy X Alexander II (80)
m. Berenice IV (F. 27)
(31) Berenice V
(regent 58–55)
(32) Cleopatra VII (51–30)
m. Mark Antony
(33) Arsinoë
(34) Ptolemy XII
(51–47)
(35) Ptolemy XIII
(47–44)

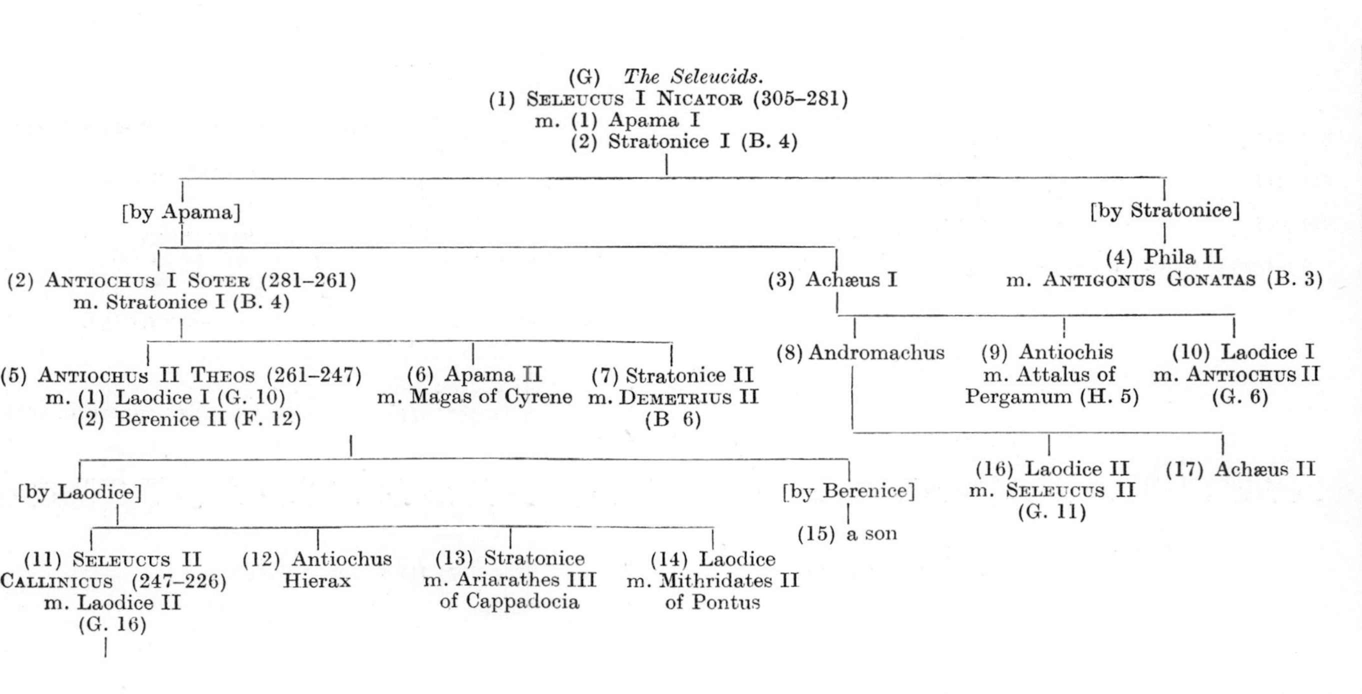
(G) The Seleucids.
(1) SELEUCUS I NICATOR (305–281)
m. (1) Apama I
(2) Stratonice I (B. 4)
[by Apama]
[by Stratonice]
(2) ANTIOCHUS I SOTER (281–261)
m. Stratonice I (B. 4)
(3) Achæus I
(4) Phila II
m. ANTIGONUS GONATAS (B. 3)
(5) ANTIOCHUS II THEOS (261–247)
m. (1) Laodice I (G. 10)
(2) Berenice II (F. 12)
(6) Apama II
m. Magas of Cyrene
(7) Stratonice II
m. DEMETRIUS II
(B 6)
(8) Andromachus
(9) Antiochis
m. Attalus of
Pergamum (H. 5)
(10) Laodice I
m. ANTIOCHUS II
(G. 6)
[by Laodice]
[by Berenice]
(16) Laodice II
m. SELEUCUS II
(G. 11)
(17) Achæus II
(15) a son
(11) SELEUCUS II
CALLINICUS (247–226)
m. Laodice II
(G. 16)
(12) Antiochus
Hierax
(13) Stratonice
m. Ariarathes III
of Cappadocia
(14) Laodice
m. Mithridates II
of Pontus

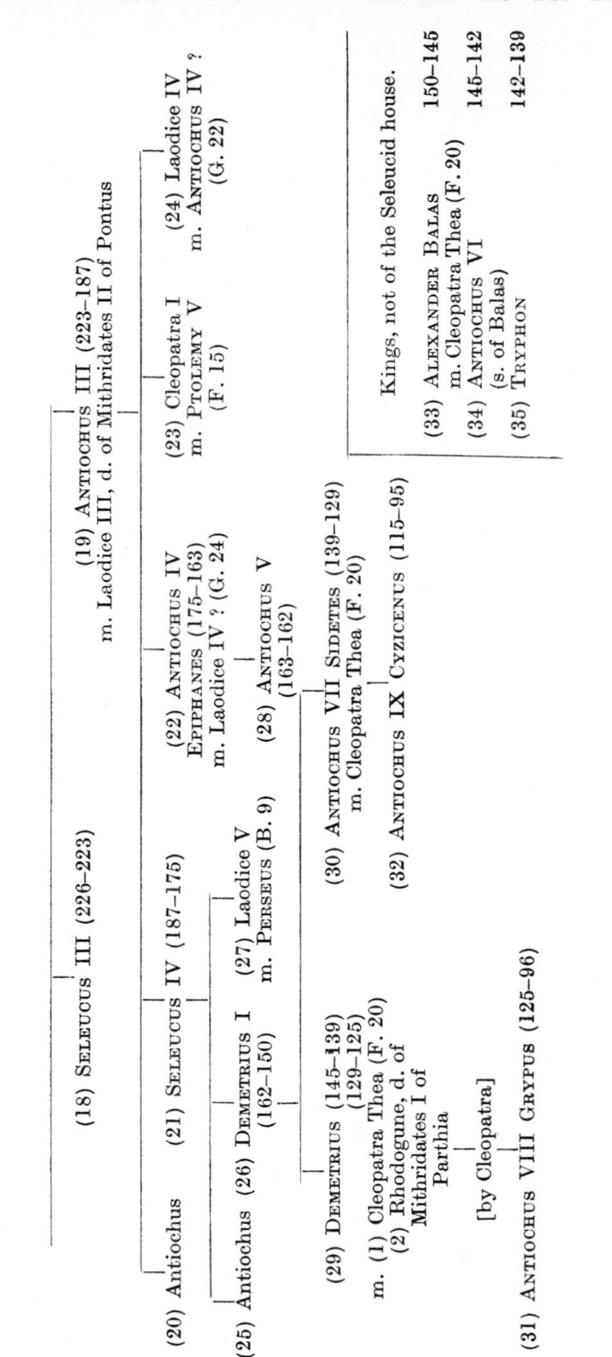
(18) Seleucus III (226–223)
(19) Antiochus III (223–187)
m. Laodice III, d. of Mithridates II of Pontus
(20) Antiochus
(21) Seleucus IV (187–175)
(22) Antiochus IV
Epiphanes (175–163)
m. Laodice IV ? (G. 24)
(23) Cleopatra I
m. Ptolemy V
(F. 15)
(24) Laodice IV
m. Antiochus IV ?
(G. 22)
(25) Antiochus
(26) Demetrius I
(162–150)
(27) Laodice V
m. Perseus (B. 9)
(28) Antiochus V
(163–162)
(29) Demetrius (145–139)
(129–125)
m. (1) Cleopatra Thea (F. 20)
(2) Rhodogune, d. of
Mithridates I of
Parthia
(30) Antiochus VII Sidetes (139–129)
m. Cleopatra Thea (F. 20)
(32) Antiochus IX Cyzicenus (115–95)
[by Cleopatra]
(31) Antiochus VIII Grypus (125–96)
Kings, not of the Seleucid house.
(33) Alexander Balas
m. Cleopatra Thea (F. 20)
150–145
(34) Antiochus VI
(s. of Balas)
145–142
(35) Tryphon
142–139

(H) *The Attalids.*

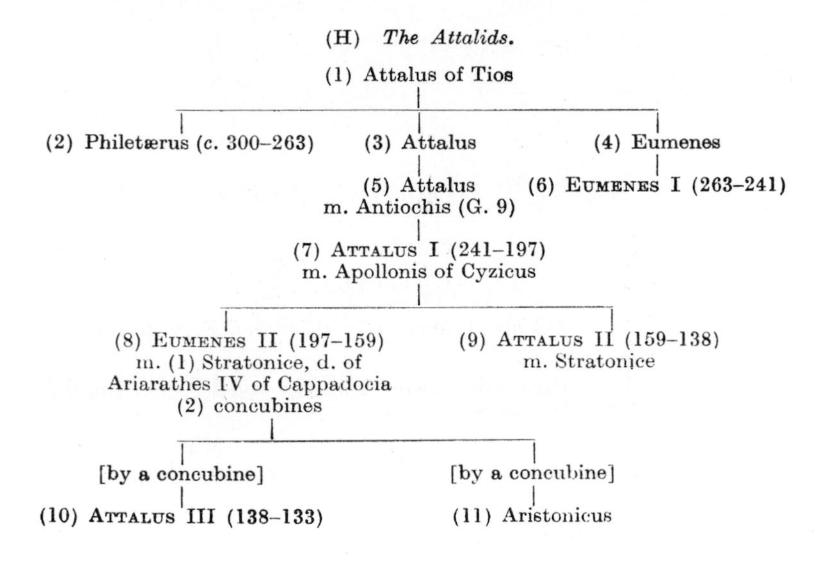

SELECT BIBLIOGRAPHY

A. GENERAL

F. ALTHEIM, *Weltgeschichte Asiens im griechischen Zeitalter*, 2 vols. (Halle, 1947–8.)

K. J. BELOCH, *Griechische Geschichte*, 2nd ed., vol. IV, pts. 1 and 2. (Berlin–Leipzig, 1925–7.)

H. BENGTSON, *Griechische Geschichte*, 2nd ed. (Munich, 1960.)

J. B. BURY and others, *The Hellenistic Age*, 2nd ed. (Cambridge, 1925.)

The Cambridge Ancient History, vol. VI, chs. 14–15 ; vol. VII, chs. 1, 3–9, 19–20, 22–23, 26 ; vol. VIII, chs. 1, 5–9, 16, 18–21. (Cambridge, 1927–30.)

R. COHEN, *La Grèce et l'hellénisation du monde antique*, bk. III, 2nd ed. (Paris, 1939).—(Good bibliographies.)

G. CORRADI, *Studi Ellenistici.* (Turin, 1930.)

J. G. DROYSEN, *Geschichte des Hellenismus*, 3 vols., 3rd ed. (Gotha, 1871–8.)

V. EHRENBERG, *The Hellenistic Age. Encyclopaedia Britannica.* (London, 1964.)

M. HADAS, *Hellenistic Culture.* (New York, 1959.)

M. HOLLEAUX, *Rome, la Grèce, et les monarchies hellénistiques au 3ème siècle av. J.-C.* (Paris, 1921.)

P. JOUGUET, *L'impérialisme macédonien et l'hellénisation de l'Orient.* (Paris, 1926.)

J. KAERST, *Geschichte des Hellenismus*, 2nd ed., vol. II. (Leipzig, 1926.)

H.-J. MARROU, *Histoire de l'éducation dans l'antiquité.* (Paris, 1950.)

B. NIESE, *Geschichte der griechischen und makedonischen Staaten.* (Gotha, 1893–1903.)

M. ROSTOVTZEFF, *Social and Economic History of the Hellenistic World*, 3 vols. (Oxford, 1941.)

P. ROUSSEL, in GLOTZ-ROUSSEL-COHEN, *Histoire grecque*, vol. IV, pt. 1. 2nd ed. (Paris, 1945.)

W. W. TARN and G. T. GRIFFITH, *Hellenistic Civilization.* 3rd ed. (London, 1952.)

B. PARTICULAR COUNTRIES AND CITIES

(1) *Athens*

E. BAYER, *Demetrios Phalereus der Athener.* (Tübingen, 1942.)
W. S. FERGUSON, *Hellenistic Athens.* (London, 1911.)

(2) *Sparta*

V. Ehrenberg, *Sparta* (Geschichte). Pauly-Wissowa-Kroll, *Realencyclopädie der klassischen Altertumswissenschaft* (= *RE.*) III A (1929.)
V. EHRENBERG, *Nabis. RE.* XVI (1935.)
E. GABBA, *Studi su Filarco.* (Pavia, 1957.)

(3) *Boeotia*

M. FEYEL, *Polybe et l'histoire de Béotie au IIIème siècle.* (Paris, 1942.)

(4) *The Achæan and Aetolian Leagues*

A. AYMARD, *Les assemblées de la confédération achéenne.* (Bordeaux, 1938.)
R. FLACELIÈRE, *Les Aitoliens à Delphes.* (Paris, 1937.)
E. A. FREEMAN, *History of Federal Government in Greece and Italy*, 2nd ed., by J. B. Bury. (London, 1893.)
J. A. O. LARSEN, *Representative Government in Greek and Roman History.* (Berkeley, 1955.)
W. H. PORTER, *Plutarch's Life of Aratus*, Introduction. (Cork, 1937.)
W. SCHWANN, *Sympoliteia. RE.* IV A. (1931.)
F. W. WALBANK, *Aratos of Sicyon.* (Cambridge, 1933.)

(5) *Delphi*

G. DAUX, *Delphes au IIème et Ier siècle.* (Paris, 1936.)

(6) *Sicily*

H. BERVE, *Die Herrschaft des Agathokles.* (Abh. Bayr, Akad., Munich, 1952.)
H. BERVE, *König Hieron II.* (Abh. Bayr. Akad., Munich, 1959.)
J. CARCOPINO, *La loi de Hiéron et les Romains.* (Paris, 1919.)
A. SCHENK VON STAUFFENBERG, *König Hieron II.* (Stuttgart, 1933.)
H. J. W. TILLYARD, *Agathocles.* (Cambridge, 1908.)

(7) *Epirus*

G. N. CROSS, *Epirus.* (Cambridge, 1932.)
P. R. FRANKE, *Alt-Epirus und das Königtum der Molosser* (Diss. Erlangen 1935).
P. LEVÈQUE, *Pyrrhos.* (Paris, 1957.)

27

(8) *Macedonia*

P. MELONI, *Perseo e la fine della monarchia macedone.* (Rome, 1953.)
W. W. TARN, *Antigonos Gonatas.* (Oxford, 1913.)
F. W. WALBANK, *Philip V of Macedon.* (Cambridge, 1940.)

(9) *Asia Minor*

ERNST MEYER, *Die Grenzen der hellenistischen Staaten in Kleinasien.* (Zürich–Leipzig, 1925.)

(10) *Pergamum*

G. CARDINALI, *Il regno di Pergamo.* (Turin, 1906.)
ESTHER V. HANSEN, *The Attalids of Pergamon.* (Ithaca, N.Y., 1947.)

(11) *Pontus and Cappadocia*

TH. REINACH, *Mithridate Eupator, Roi de Pont*, ch. 1. (Paris, 1890.)

(12) *Galatia*

F. STÄHELIN, *Geschichte der kleinasiatischen Galater.* (Leipzig, 1907.)

(13) *The Seleucid Empire*

E. R. BEVAN, *The House of Seleucus*, 2 vols. (London, 1902.)
E. BIKERMAN, *Institutions des Séleucides.* (Paris, 1938.)
A. BOUCHÉ-LECLERCQ, *Histoire des Séleucides*, 2 vols. (Paris, 1913.)
N. C. DEBEVOISE, *A Political History of Parthia.* (Chicago, 1938.)
EDUARD MEYER, *Blüte und Niedergang des Hellenismus in Asien.* (Berlin, 1925.)
W. OTTO, *Beiträge zur Seleukidengeschichte des 3. Jahrhunderts v. Chr.* (Abh. Bayr. Akad., Munich, 1928.)

(14) *Bactria and India*

The Cambridge History of India, vol. I, chs. 17–23. (London, 1922.)
A. K. NARAIN, The Indo-Greeks. (Oxford, 1959.)
W. W. TARN, *The Greeks in Bactria and India.* 2nd ed. (Cambridge, 1951.)

(15) *Syria and Palestine*

E. R. BEVAN, *Jerusalem under the High Priests.* (London, 1912.)
W. KOLBE, *Beiträge zur syrischen und jüdischen Geschichte.* (Stuttgart, 1926.)
V. TCHERIKOVER, *Hellenistic Civilization and the Jews.* (Philadelphia, 1959.)

(16) *Egypt*

H. I. BELL, *Egypt from Alexander the Great to the Arab conquest*, chs. 1 and 2. (Oxford, 1948.)

E. R. BEVAN, *A History of Egypt under the Ptolemaic Dynasty*. (London, 1927.)

A. BOUCHÉ-LECLERCQ, *Histoire des Lagides*, 4 vols. (Paris, 1903–7.)

C. C. EDGAR, *Zeno Papyri in the University of Michigan*, Introduction. (Ann Arbor, 1931.)

P. JOUGUET, *L'Égypte gréco-romaine de la conquête d'Alexandrie à Dioclétien*. (Cairo, 1932.)

L. MITTEIS and U. WILCKEN, *Grundzüge und Chrestomathie der Papyruskunde*, 2 vols. (Leipzig, 1912.)

W. PEREMANS and E. VAN'T DACK, *Prosopographia Ptolemaica*, 4 vols. (Louvain, 1950–4.)

CLAIRE PRÉAUX, *L'économie royale des Lagides*. (Brussels, 1939.)

M. ROSTOVTZEFF, *A Large Estate in Egypt*. (Madison, 1922.)

M. STRACK, *Die Dynastie der Ptolemäer*. (Berlin, 1897.)

(17) *Individual Towns*

(i) *Alexandria*—H. I. BELL, *Alexandria*. (Journ. Egypt. Archæol., 1927, p. 171 ff.)

E. BRECCIA, *Alexandrea ad Ægyptum*. (Bergamo, 1922.)

(ii) *Antioch*.—E. S. BOUCHIER, *A short history of Antioch*. (Oxford, 1921.)

G. DOWNEY, *A history of Antioch in Syria from Seleucus to the Arab Conquest*. (Princeton, 1961.)

(iii) *Delos*.—P. ROUSSEL, *Délos*. (Paris, 1925.)

(iv) *Dura-Europos*.—*Excavations at Dura-Europos*. Final Reports. (New Haven, Conn., 1943 ff.)

M. ROSTOVTZEFF, *Dura-Europos and its Art*. (Oxford, 1938.)

(v) *Miletus*.—F. HILLER VON GAERTRINGEN, *RE*. XV (1932).

(vi) *Ptolemais*.—G. PLAUMANN *Ptolemais in Oberägypten*. (Leipzig, 1910.)

(vii) *Rhodes*.—HILLER VON GAERTRINGEN, *RE*. Supplement V (1931).

(viii) *Seleucia-on-Tigris*.—M. STRECK, *Seleukeia und Ktesiphon*. (Der alte Orient, vol. XVI, pts. 3 and 4.)

C. SPECIAL SUBJECTS

(1) *Constitutions*

S. ACCAME, *Il dominio romano in Grecia dalla guerra acaica ad Augusto*. (Rome, 1946.)

H. Bengtson, *Die Strategie in hellenistischer Zeit*, 3 vols. (Munich, 1937–52.)
G. Busolt and H. Swoboda, *Griechische Staatskunde*, vol. II. (Munich, 1926.)
E. Breccia, *Il diritto dinastico nelle monarchie dei successori d'Alessandro Magno.* (Rome, 1903.)
V. Ehrenberg, *The Greek State.* Part 2 : *The Hellenistic State.* (Oxford, 1960.)
W. S. Ferguson, *Greek Imperialism.* (London and New York, 1913.)
A. Heuss, *Stadt und Herrscher des Hellenismus.* (*Klio, Beiheft* 39. Leipzig, 1937.)
A. H. M. Jones, *The Greek City.* (Oxford, 1940.)
P. Jouguet, *La vie municipale dans l'Égypte romaine*, ch. 1. (Paris, 1911.)
C. B. Welles, *Royal Correspondence in the Hellenistic Period.* (New Haven, 1934.)
Paola Zancan, *Il monarcato ellenistico nei suoi elementi federativi.* (Padua, 1934.)

(2) *Colonization*

F. Heichelheim, *Die auswärtige Bevölkerung im Ptolemäerreich.* (Klio Beiheft 18.)
V. Tscherikower, *Die hellenistischen Städtegründungen von Alexander dem Grossen bis auf die Römerzeit.* (Philologus, Suppl., vol XIX, 1927.)

(3) *Military affairs*

G. T. Griffith, *Mercenaries of the Hellenistic World.* (Cambridge, 1935.)
J. Kromayer, G. Veith and others, *Heerwesen und Kriegführung der Griechen und Römer*, p. 120 ff. (Munich, 1928.)
M. Launey, *Recherches sur les armées hellénistiques.* (Paris, 1949–50.)
J. Lesquier, *Les institutions militaires de l'Égypte sous les Lagides.* (Paris, 1911.)
H. A. Ormerod, *Piracy in the Ancient World.* (Liverpool, 1924.)
H. W. Parke, *Greek Mercenary Soldiers*, pt. VI. (Oxford, 1933.)
W. W. Tarn, *Hellenistic Military and Naval Developments.* (Cambridge, 1930.)

(4) *Economics*

M. Cary and E. H. Warmington, *The Ancient Explorers.* (London, 1929.)
M. I. Finley, *Studies in Land and Credit in Ancient Athens.* (New Brunswick, 1951.)

F. Heichelheim, *Wirtschaftliche Schwankungen der Zeit von Alexander bis Augustus.* (Jena, 1930.)

F. M. Heichelheim, *Wirtschaftsgeschichte des Altertums,* 2 vols. (Leiden, 1938.)

F. M. Heichelheim, *An Ancient Economic History II* (Leiden, forthcoming.)

F. Poland, *Geschichte des griechischen Vereinswesens.* (Leipzig, 1909.)

Claire Préaux, *L'économie royale des Lagides.* (Brussels, 1939.)

F. Preisigke, *Girowesen im griechischen Ägypten.* (Strassburg, 1910.)

M. Schnebel, *Die Landwirtschaft im hellenistischen Ägypten.* (Munich, 1925.)

W. L. Westermann, in Pauly-Wissowa-Kroll, *Realencyclopädie,* Supplement VI, s.v. Sklaverei, cols. 927–42.

U. Wilcken, *Alexander der Grosse und die hellenistische Wirtschaft.* (Schmoller's Jahrbuch, vol. 45, 1921.)

E. Ziebarth, *Beiträge zur Geschichte des Seeraubes und Seehandels im alten Griechenland.* (Hamburg, 1929.)

(5) *Art and Architecture*

A. Adriani, *Una coppa paësistica del Museo di Alessandria.* (Rome, 1959.)

M. Bieber, *The Sculpture of the Hellenistic Age.* (New York, 1955.)

B. R. Brown, *Ptolemaic Paintings and Mosaics and the Alexandrinian Style.* (Cambridge, Mass., 1957.)

T. Fyfe, *Hellenistic Architecture.* (Cambridge, 1936.)

A. v. Gerkan, *Griechische Städteanlagen.* (Berlin–Leipzig, 1924.)

A. W. Lawrence, *Later Greek Sculpture.* (London, 1927.)

E. Pfuhl, *Malerei und Zeichnung der Griechen.* (Munich, 1923.)

D. S. Robertson, *Greek and Roman Architecture,* 2nd ed. (Cambridge, 1943.)

M. Rostovtzeff, *Iranians and Greeks in South Russia.* (Oxford, 1922.)

R. E. Wycherley, *How the Greeks Built Cities.* (London, 1949.)

(6) *Literature*

J. B. Bury, *The Ancient Greek Historians,* ch. on Polybius. (London, 1909.)

A. Körte, *Hellenistische Dichtung.* (Leipzig, 1925.)

R. Pfeiffer, *Callimachus,* 2 vols. (Oxford, 1949–53.)

J. U. Powell and E. A. Barber, *New Chapters in the History of Greek Literature,* First, Second and Third Series. (Oxford, 1921–33.)

E. ROHDE, *Der griechische Roman und seine Vorläufer*, 3rd ed. (Leipzig, 1914.)

SIR J. E. SANDYS, *A History of Classical Scholarship*, 2nd ed., vol. I. (*Cambridge*, 1906.)

W. SCHMID and O. STAHLIN, *Geschichte der griechischen Literatur*, 6th ed., vol. II, pt. 1. (Munich, 1920.)

F. SUSEMIHL, *Geschichte der griechischen Litteratur in der Alexandrinerzeit*. (Leipzig, 1891–2.)

F. W. WALBANK, *A Historical Commentary on Polybius*, Vol. I. (Oxford, 1957.)

P. WENDLAND, *Die hellenistisch-römische Kultur*, 3rd ed. (Leipzig and Berlin, 1914.)

U. v. WILAMOWITZ-MOELLENDORFF, *Hellenistische Dichtung in der Zeit des Kallimachos*. (Berlin, 1924.)

F. A. WRIGHT, *A History of Later Greek Literature*. (London, 1932.)

(7) *Science*

H. BERGER, *Geschichte der wissenschaftlichen Erdkunde der Griechen*, 2nd ed. (Leipzig, 1903.)

B. FARRINGTON, *Greek Science*, ch. VIII. (London, 1936.)

SIR T. L. HEATH, *Aristarchus of Samos*. (Oxford, 1913.)

SIR T. L. HEATH, *A History of Greek Mathematics*. (Oxford, 1921.)

SIR T. L. HEATH, *Archimedes*. (London, 1920.)

J. L. HEIBERG, *Mathematics and Physical Science in Classical Antiquity*. (Trans. D. C. Macgregor; Oxford, 1922.)

O. NEUGEBAUER, *The Exact Sciences of Antiquity*. (Copenhagen, 1951.)

A. REHM and K. VOGEL, *Exacte Wissenschaften*. *Gercke u. Norden, Einleitung in die Altertumswissenschaft, II*, 3rd ed. (Leipzig, 1933.)

C. SINGER, *Greek Biology and Greek Medicine*. (Oxford, 1922.)

J. O. THOMSON, *History of Ancient Geography*. (Cambridge, 1948.)

H. F. TOZER, *A History of Ancient Geography*. (2nd ed., by M. Cary. Cambridge, 1935.)

(8) *Philosophy*

C. R. BAILEY, *The Greek Atomists and Epicurus*, pt. II. (Oxford, 1928.)

E. R. BEVAN, *Stoics and Sceptics*. (Oxford, 1913.)

P. E. MORE, *Hellenistic Philosophies*. (Princeton, 1923.)

M. POHLENZ, *Die Stoa*. (Göttingen, 1948.)

A. E. TAYLOR, *Epicurus*. (London, 1911.)

H. W. DE WITT, *Epicurus and his Philosophy*. (Minneapolis, 1954.)

(9) *Religion*

L. Cerfaux and J. Tondriau, *Le culte des souverains dans la civilisation gréco-romaine.* (Paris, 1957.)

E. R. Dodds, *The Greeks and the Irrational.* (Oxford, 1951.)

C. Habicht, *Gottmenschentum und griechische Städte.* (Munich, 1956.)

J. Ijsewijn, *De sacerdotibus sacerdotiisque Alexandri Magni et Lagidarum eponymis.* (Brussels, 1961.)

O. Kern, *Die Religion der Griechen*, vol. III, chs. 4–12. (Berlin, 1938.)

Ed. Meyer, *Ursprung und Anfänge des Christentums*, vol. II. (Stuttgart and Berlin, 1921.)

G. G. A. Murray, *Five Stages of Greek Religion*, p. 103 ff. (Oxford, 1925.)

M. P. Nilsson, *Geschichte der griechischen Religion II*, 2nd ed. (Munich, 1962.)

A. D. Nock, *Conversion.* (Oxford, 1933.)

A. D. Nock, *Σύνναοζ θεόζ.* (Harvard Studies in Classical Philology, vol. XLI, p. 1 ff.)

W. Otto, *Priester und Tempel im hellenistischen Ägypten.* (Leipzig, 1905–8.)

F. Taeger, *Charisma I.* (Stuttgart, 1957.)

U. v. Wilamowitz-Moellendorff, *Der Glaube der Hellenen*, vol. II. (Berlin, 1932.)

U. Wilcken, *Zur Entstehung des hellenistischen Herrscherkults.* (Sitzungsber. Akad. Berlin, 1938.)

INDEX

Abantidas, 140
Abdera, 120, 325
Abydus, battle in Lamian War, 7, 240, 382–3; siege by Philip V, 188
Academy (Athens), 320, 343, 361; doctrine and influence, 355–7
Acarnania, acquired by Pyrrhus, 47; by Lysimachus, 54; relations with Epirus, 135, 145–7; with Ætolia, 145–7; with Illyria, 150–2; with Antigonus Doson, 162–3; with Philip V, 189–90
Achæa, secedes from Antigonus Gonatas, 127; gives aid to Pyrrhus, 129; annexes Sicyon, 140; expansion in Peloponnesus, 141–4, 148, 194; at war with Cleomenes III, 155–9; in Doson's Hellenic League, 163; at war with Ætolia, 165; relations with Sparta, 192, 194, 197–8; declares war on Antiochus III, 195; relations with Rome, 190, 203–5; military strength, 231, 234; federal constitution, 285–6
Achæa Phthiotis, 152
Achæmenids, 244, 250, 257–8
Achæus, 111–14
Acilius Glabrio, 195–6
Acragas, 168, 171–2, 174,
Acra Leuce, 181
Acrocorinth, captured by Aratus, 142–3; ceded to Doson, 158–9
Acrotatus, 129, 135, 139
Actium, 225
Adramyttium, 108
Adriatic Sea, 53, 124; patrolled by Athenians, 151 n.; attempted control by Agathocles, 171; Roman intervention, 183–4; acquisitions of Philip V, 186, 406
Adule, 399, 403
Æacidas, 20, 46
Ægæ, 13, 128, 367
Aegean Sea, battles in Lamian War, 7–8; ascendancy of Antigonus I, 18–19; importance to new monarchies, 21; Ptolemaic interests, 30–2, 50, 53, 89, 101, 105–6, 121, 125, 137, 139, 141, 146, 160, 401, 403; Seleucid interests, 95, 125, 209–10, 212, 216; Antigonid interests, 105, 137, 141, 160, 185–6, 188, 403; trade, 275, 293, 298–9, 301
Ægina, 64 n., 288
Ægium, 163
Ægospotami, 45
Ægosthena, 64 n.
Ænus, 121, 199
Æolis, 108
Æschylus, 338 n.
Ætolia, in Lamian War, 6, 8; relations with Demetrius and Pyrrhus, 48–50, 54; allied with Lysimachus, 54; in the Galatian raid, 60–1, 239; attacked by Areus, 127, 129; agreement with Gonatas, 131–2, 141, 143; interests in Peloponnesus, 144, 149, 154–5, 185; expansion in Central Greece, 145–6, 148; relations with Acarnania and Epirus, 146–7, 150–1; policy of plunder, 152, 242; hostility to Doson and Philip V, 163–6; alliance with Rome, 185–6, 190–4; treaties with Dardanelles towns, 187; with Chios, 280 n.; alliance with Antiochus III, 194–6, 198, 209, 213; domestic faction in, 203; federal constitution, 284–6; debt question, 305 n.; dialect, 323
Afghanistan, 73–4
Agathocles (of Syracuse), 167–73, 176, 247, 317 n.
Agathocles (son of Lysimachus), 51, 56–7, 85, 107
Agathocles (minister of Ptolemy V), 91, 93
Agathostratus, 105
Agelaus, 166 n.
Agesilaus I, 130
Agesilaus (uncle of Agis IV), 154
Agis IV, 144, 153–7, 404
Agron, 151, 183
Akaba (Gulf), 81
Albania, 124, 151
Alcimus (Eliakim), 229
Alexander III (the Great), death at

Babylon, 1; heirs, 1, 2, 20–21; state papers, 3; prestige after death, 4; dealings with the Greek Homeland, 5, 6, 9, 18, 38, 163; effects of his Anabasis on the Greek nation, 10; rivalry among his marshals, 11; princesses of his house, 12, 19, 20; burial, 13; effects of his conquests upon Macedon, 22; attempts to revive his monarchy, 22 ff., 42; in Eumenes' war-council, 23; destruction of Thebes, 7, 27; supposititious offspring, 30; comparison with Demetrius I, 52; comparison with Seleucus I, 57; campaign in Illyria, 59; break-up of his empire, 63–4; influence on Chandragupta, 66; comparison with Antiochus, 72–3; policy in Asia Minor, 95, 97, 100; plans for conquests in Russia, 115–16; conquests in the Balkans, 117, 122; comparison with Pyrrhus, 130; influence on Agathocles of Syracuse, 169; on Alexander I of Epirus, 177; alleged plan for conquests in the West, 182; policy in Judæa, 228; strategy and tactics, 24, 34, 179, 236–9; siegecraft, 166, 240; colonizing policy, 244, 258; policy of racial fusion, 245; effects of conquests on Macedonian nobility, 248; orientalizing habits, 249; precautionary murders, 250; use of Persian postal system, 256; haul of Persian treasure, 287, 315; imperial coinage, 287–8; plans to circumnavigate Arabia, 115, 289; explorations, 290; consequent stimulus to agriculture, 291; effects of conquests upon Greek culture, 307; scenes from his life on the "Alexander Sarcophagus," 313; coin types, 315; effects of conquests on the Greek language, 322–3; histories of his conquests, 334–5; scientific interests, 343; influence on geography, 344; on botany, 350; effects on Greek religion, 363; Alexander-worship, 367–8; strength of his fleet, 382
Alexander IV (son of above), 2, 20–1, 29, 384
Alexander V (son of Cassander), 43, 46–7, 50
Alexander I of Epirus, 177–8, 180
Alexander II of Epirus, receives envoys from Asoka, 67, 131; invades Macedon, and loses Epirus, 135; makes treaty with Ætolia, 145–6; loses Atintania, 400
Alexander, son of Craterus, 139–40, 143, 394, 401–2
Alexander Balas, 221, 225–6, 229, 252
Alexander Jannæus, 230
Alexander the Ætolian, 302
Alexandria (ad Ægyptum), capital of the Ptolemies, 13; attacked by Magas, 85; palace crises, 90, 93, 219, 222–4; riot of Cleomenes III, 163; commerce, 183, 297–8; attacked by Antiochus IV, 218; law of intermarriage with Egyptians, 245 n.; court aristocracy, 248; approval of new kings, 251; pomp of court, 260; liturgies, 264; centre of administration, 265; Jewish residents, 268, 323–5; status of Greeks, 274; manufactures, 295; banks, 301; plan of town, 309; pleasure gardens, 311; musical festivals, 317; the Museum, 318–19; the Library, 321–2; literature, 327–332, 340–1; scholarship, 339–40; science, 343–7, 349–52, 359; cults, 365; king-worship, 368–9; temple of Sarapis, 372; latitude taken by Eratosthenes, 407
Alps, 71, 331
Altai, Mt., 73, 298 n.
Ambracia, 47, 150, 166
Amestris, 55, 98
Amitraghata, 67
Ammonitis, 81, 91, 265
Amon, 13, 270
Amorgos, 7, 8, 382–3
Ampelone, 81
Amphictionic League, 131, 145–6, 283; Athenian deputies, 133; court of arbitration, 320 n.
Amphipolis, 253
Anaitis, 76
Ancyra, 110
Andania, 365 n.
Andragoras, 68
Andriscus, 203
Andromachus, 111–12
Andros, 106, 141, 402
Antander, 170
Antigenes, 15, 25
Antigone, 400
Antigoneia (Atintania), 135, 400
Antigoneia (Syria), 35, 40
Antigoneia (Troad), 270 n.
Antigonis, 34
Antigonus I, disobeys Perdiccas, 11–12; campaigns in Asia Minor, 16, 17, 100; passed over for the

regency, 17 ; gains control of the Aegean, 18–19 ; abilities, 22 ; bid for empire, 22–32, 34–41 ; founds League of Islanders, 27 ; proclaims Greek liberty, 26, 126 ; contrast with Demetrius I, 51 ; political talent, 57 ; rescript to Lebedus and Teos, 64 n. ; attack upon Petra, 81 ; executes the elder Mithridates, 96 ; allies with Heraclea-ad-Pontum, 98 ; popularity in Phrygia, 99 n. ; campaign in the Balkans, 118 ; intrigues in Illyria, 124 ; size of his army, 35, 231 ; strategy, 237 ; constitutional observances, 251 ; phil-Hellenism, 256, 270 ; land-grants, 302 ; object of worship, 369 n. ; size of fleet, 382 ; excludes Seleucus I from the peace of 311 B.C., 384

Antigonus II (Gonatas) : loses his father's possessions in Greece, 53, 126–7 ; bids for Macedon, 58, 62–3 ; defeated by Ptolemy Ceraunus, 58, 99 ; sends troops to defend Delphi, 60 ; receives envoys from Asoka, 67 ; comes to terms with Antiochus I, 83, 120 ; warfare with Ptolemy II, 89 ; wins a naval battle at Cos, 105, 137 ; rounds up Galatian bands, 62–3, 118 ; establishes his authority in Macedon, 121–2 ; defends its northern frontiers, 123 ; war with Pyrrhus, 127–131 ; extent of his power in Greece, 131–2 ; supports despots in Greece, 131, 134, 144–5, 247, 272 ; wins the Chremonidean War, 133–6 ; intervenes at Cyrene, 138 ; loses Corinth to Alexander, son of Craterus, 139–40 ; recovers Corinth, 140–1 ; wins a naval battle at Andros, 141 ; loses Corinth to Aratus, 106, 142–3 ; relations with Ætolia, 131, 143 ; character of his rule, 144–5 ; enlists Galatians, 233, 235 ; strength of his fleet, 240 ; his flagship, 241 ; his court, 253 ; constitutional observances, 254 ; studies Stoicism, 318 ; friend of Zeno, 362 n. ; captures Atintania, 400, 406 ; makes a speech at Corinth, 401 ; dedications to Delos, 403

Antigonus III (Doson), raid on Caria, 106, 160 ; wars against the Dardanians, 123, 160 ; against the Illyrians, 124, 164 ; bargains with Aratus, 158–9 ; assumes the crown of Macedon, 160 ; campaigns against Cleomenes III, 161–2 ; wins the battle of Sellasia, 162, 233–4, 239 ; his Greek confederacy, 163–4, 185–6, 189, 193, 247 ; constitutional observances, 254 ; dedications at Delos, 403 ; relations with Demetrius of Pharos, 406

Antigonus of Carystus, 334

Anti-Lebanon, 90

Antioch-ad-Orontem, vicissitudes in the Third Syrian War, 76, 87–9, 396–9 ; revolution by Stratonice II, 111–12 ; attacked by Achæus, 113 ; under mock ædiles, 216 ; visit of Cn. Octavius, 220–1 ; civil wars, 221–2, 225–6, 229 ; court aristocracy, 248 ; pomp at court, 260 ; municipal self-government, 273 ; trade, 299 ; pleasure gardens, 311 ; men of letters at court, 318 ; library, 321

Antioch-in-Persis, 273, 279

Antioch-in-Scythia, 68

Antioch (Jerusalem), 228

Antiochis, 108 n.

Antiochus I, joint-king with Seleucus I, 54 ; defeats the Galatians, 62 ; relations with Hindu rulers, 67 ; colonies in Merv oasis, 68, 258 ; wages in the First Syrian War, 83–5, 387–9 ; relations with Bithynia, 98 ; with Heraclea-ad-Pontum, 99 ; defeated by Eumenes I, 108 ; relations with Gonatas, 83, 120 ; subsidizes Areus, 126 ; subsidizes Pyrrhus, 179 ; patron of Berossus, 324 ; worshipped as Apollo Soter, 368

Antiochus II, receives envoys from Asoka, 67 ; relations with Ptolemy II, 86–102, 108–9 ; devises the succession to Seleucus II, 87, 395–6 ; receives allegiance of Ionian cities, 105, 137 ; marries his cousin, 250 n. ; character of rule, 252 ; founds colonies in Asia Minor, 258 ; frees towns from tribute, 272 ; institutes king-worship, 369

Antiochus III, restores Seleucid authority in the East, 69–73, 237 ; policy in Armenia and Susiana, 76 ; wages the Fourth Syrian War, 90–3 ; is defeated at Raphia, 92, 239 ; wins the Fifth Syrian War, 93–4 ; makes conquest in S. Asia Minor, 102–3 ; in W. Asia Minor, 106–7 ; subdues the rebellion of Achæus, 111–14 ; makes terms with Attalus I, 113–14 ; makes a compact with Philip V, 93, 121, 186–7, 189 ; makes a treaty with

Ætolia, 194 ; invades Greece, 195 ; is expelled by the Romans, 195–6 ; wages a diplomatic war with the Romans, 206–9 ; naval campaign against the Romans, 209–10 ; is defeated at Magnesia, 211–12, 239 ; cedes Asia Minor, 212–13 ; numbers and composition of his army, 231, 233 ; creates a court hierarchy, 259
Antiochus IV, sends Eucratides to Bactria, 74 ; invades Susiana, 76 ; character of his rule, 216–17 ; invades Egypt, 218–19 ; dies prematurely, 220 ; robs the temple of Jerusalem, 227 ; institutes worship of Zeus at Jerusalem, 228 ; supposed marriage with his sister, 250 n. ; reconstitutes colonies, 258 ; showmanship, 259 ; his pageant at Daphne, 219, 260 ; allows municipal coinage, 273 ; explores the Persian Gulf, 289 ; carries on the construction of the Olympieum at Athens, 308 ; converted to Epicureanism, 355 n.
Antiochus V, 220, 229
Antiochus VII, 77–8, 226–7, 230
Antiochus Hierax, 89, 109–12
Antiochus (son of Seleucus IV), 220
Antiochus I of Commagene, 373
Antipater (marshal of Alexander), confirmed in viceregency of Macedon, 2 ; in the Lamian War, 6–8, 381–2 ; settlement of Athens and Greece, 9–10, 32 n., 125, 270 ; at war with Perdiccas, 11–14 ; makes matrimonial alliances, 13, 55 ; appointed regent, 15–16 ; appoints Polyperchon to succeed him, 16–17
Antipater (son of Cassander), 46–7
Antipater (nephew of Cassander), 60, 63
Antipatreia, 124
Antiphanes of Berge, 338
Antisthenes, 357 n.
Aous, r., 128, 151, 184, 186, 190, 400
Apama (wife of Seleucus), 54, 250
Apama (daughter of Antiochus I), 84, 138
Apamea-ad-Orontem, 83, 225, 337, 397
Apamea Cibotus, 100, 213, 216, 220
Apollo, at Delos, 27, 31, 138, 303 ; at Delphi, 61 ; at Didyma, 62 ; at Daphne, 397 n. ; patron of Seleucids, 365 ; identified with Antiochus I, 368 ; stephanephorus of Miletus, 388
Apollodorus, 121, 329
Apollodotus, 74
Apollonia (in Babylonia), 70
Apollonia (in Illyria), 124
Apollonis, 255
Apollonius (minister of Ptolemy II), his power as minister of finance, 265–7 ; his private enterprises, 288 ; land-improvements, 292–3 ; textile factory, 295 ; merchant fleet, 293 ; exhorted to build a Sarapeum, 372
Apollonius (of Perga), 346–7
Apollonius (of Rhodes), 327–8, 341
Appius (the Censor), 179
Apsus, r., 124, 186
Apulia, 177–8
Arabia, penetration by Ptolemy II, 80–2 ; plans for circumnavigation, 115, 289 ; trade, 82, 298–9, 301
Aradus, 83, 268
Aral Sea, 289 n.
Aratus, recaptures Sicyon, and annexes it to the Achæan League, 140 ; captures Corinth, 142 ; extends the Achæan League, 142–3 ; attacks Piræus, 144 ; invades Attica, 148 ; subsidizes Athens, 149 ; defeated by Cleomenes III, 156–8 ; comes to terms with Doson, 158–9 ; exercises reprisals upon Mantinea, 161, 187, 243 ; advises Philip V, 165 ; estranged from Philip, 185 ; statesmanship, 197 ; sends old paintings to Ptolemy II, 307 ; writes memoirs, 334 ; at Ptolemy's court, 401
Aratus (son of the above), 185
Aratus of Soli, 362 n. 1
Arbela, 239
Arcadia, 7, 126, 134, 144, 146, 148–9, 156–7, 161, 165
Arcesilaus, 356
Arcesine, 277 n.
Archagathus, 170–2
Archidamus, 157, 404
Archimedes, 323, 346, 349
Areopagus, 9, 32, 136
Areus, 126–7, 129–30, 132–5
Argead dynasty, 122, 248, 250–1, 253–4
Argolis, 10, 127, 143, 148–9, 161, 165
Argos, expels Gonatas' garrison, 126–7 ; attacked by Pyrrhus, 130 ; despotism of Aristomachus, 139 ; attacked by Aratus, 143–4, 148 ; joins the Achæan League, 149, 155 ; surrendered to Cleomenes III, 158 ; rejoins the Achæan League, 161 ; surrendered to Nabis, 192 ; detached from the Achæan League by the Romans, 204
Ariaramnes, 96
Ariarathes I, 11, 95–6

Ariarathes II, 96
Ariarathes IV, 214
Aristarchus of Samos, 339 n., 347–8, 362, 366 n.
Aristarchus of Samothrace, 339–40, 347 n.
Aristippus, 144, 148
Aristo (admiral of Ptolemy II), 80
Aristo (king of Pæonia), 122
Aristobulus (king of Judæa), 230
Aristobulus (historian), 335
Aristodamus, 135, 139
Aristomachus I, 139, 143–4
Aristomachus II, 148–9, 155, 158
Aristomenes, 93, 217
Aristophanes (poet), 330
Aristophanes (grammarian), 340
Aristotimus, 134
Aristotle, friend and teacher of Demetrius of Phalerum, 19, 33; teacher of Theophrastus, 320, 350, 355; writes a treatise on rhetoric, 332; writes local history, 333; teacher of Aristoxenus, 334; influence on Hellenistic science, 343; limitations in medical knowledge, 351; views on king-worship, 367 n.
Aristoxenus, 326, 334
Arius, r., 71
Armenia, projected invasion by Demetrius I, 51; becomes independent of the Seleucids, 69; submits to Antiochus III, 70; is formed into two independent principalities, 76; temporarily subdued by Antiochus IV, 76, 228; Greek plays at court of kings, 323
Arsaces, 68
Arsames, 69, 70, 111
Arsamosata, 69, 70
Arsinoë I, 57, 84, 86–7, 391–2
Arsinoë II, marries Lysimachus, 43, 98; procures the death of Agathocles, 55–7; marries Ptolemy Ceraunus, 58; marries Ptolemy II, 84, 250; her part in the First Syrian War, 85; attitude to Gonatas, 133 n.; deification, 269 n., 368; relation to Ptolemy the Son, 390–2
Arsinoë III, 92–3
Arsinoë (Suez), 81
Arsinoë-Methana, 134, 149
Artabazanes, 69, 70
Artavasdes, 324
Artaxata, 76
Artaxias, 70, 76
Artemis, 76, 365 n.
Asculum, 179
Asia Minor, campaigns of Antigonus I, 16–18, 22, 32, 237; Ptolemy I's conquests on the S. coast, 30; the campaigns of, 302–1 B.C., 39–40; acquisitions by Lysimachus, 42, 54, 56; the principality of Pleistarchus, 42–3; Demetrius' last campaign, 51–2; conquest by Seleucus I, 56; Galatian invasion, 61–2, 83–4; holds with Laodice I, 88; policy of Alexander, 95; native monarchies, 95–9; the Galatian confederacy, 99–100; campaigns between Ptolomies and Seleucids on the southern border, 100–3, 206; on the western border, 103–7, 141; campaigns of the Pergamene rulers, 107–13; campaigns of Antiochus Hierax, 109–11; campaigns of Achæus, 112–13; warfare of Antiochus III against the Romans, 209–12; cessions by Antiochus III to Pergamum and Rhodes, 212; minor wars in the second century, 213–16; Hellenistic colonies, 245; weakness of the native nobility, 248; mines, 257; temple-states, 258; status of older Greek cities, 272; agriculture, 275, 293; neighbourly feuds, 279; industry, 294–5; slave risings, 305; new cities, 308–9; spread of the Greek tongue, 323; study of rhetoric, 333; sale of priesthoods, 364
Aspendus, 235
Astavene, 68
Atbara, r., 80
Athens, grievances against Alexander, 6; leads the revolt against Macedon, 6–9; loses its thalassocracy, 8, 381–3; political settlement of Antipater, 9; makes terms with Cassander, 18–19; rules of Demetrius of Phalerum, 19, 32–3; allied with Antigonus I, 33–4; the Four Years' War against Cassander, 37–8; relations with Demetrius I, 43–5, 48, 50; revolt against Gonatas, 53; sends force to defend Delphi, 60; dedications by Attalus I, 111; relations with Spartocids, 116 n.; receives corn from the Balkans, 122; overawed by Gonatas' garrison in 280 B.C., 127; in the Chremonidean War, 133–6; abandons hopes of political leadership, 136; resists Alexander, son of Craterus, 139; attacked by Aratus, 143–4, 148; recovers the Piræus, 149; political neutrality, 150; stands out of Doson's League, 163; attacked by Philip V, 189;

allies with Rome, 189–90 ; recovers Delos, 214 ; supposed mint of Gonatas, 272 n. ; financial administration, 277 ; confers franchise on the Rhodians, 280 ; the strategi, 284 n. ; economic decay, 294, 298 ; banking, 300 ; a show-site, 307 ; crooked streets, 308 n. ; architectural features, 309–10 ; statues of Demetrius of Phalerum, 311 ; philosophical schools, 319, 324, 343, 355–6 ; drama, 329–30 ; oratory, 333 ; archives, 334 ; texts of plays, 338 n. ; not typical of Hellenistic Greece, 354 ; king-worship, 369 n., 370 ; cult of Isis, 372
Atintania, 124, 128 n., 135, 151, 400, 406
Atlantic, 290, 344–5
Atropatene, 69, 70
Attalus (father of Attalus I), 108 n.
Attalus I, victories over the Galatians, 110–11 ; over Antiochus Hierax, III ; campaigns against Achæus, 112–13 ; treaty with Antiochus III, 113–14 ; sustains defeat in the First Macedonian War, 185 ; builds a fleet, 186 ; embroiled with Philip V, 187–8 ; calls in the Romans, 188–9 ; court life, 255 ; commemorative sculpture, 313 ; patronizes actors, 320
Attalus II, 215–16, 221, 307–8, 321
Attalus III, 216
Attica, invaded by Cassander, 38 ; picketed by Gonatas, 134 ; garrisoned by Gonatas, 139–40 ; invaded by Aratus, 143 ; raided by Philip V, 190 ; dialect, 322
Attis, 371
Audoleon, 122
Aufidus, r., 178 n.
Autariatæ, 122
Axiopolis, 119
Axius, r., 46, 53, 60, 122–3, 166

Bab-el-Mandeb, 80
Babylon, conference at Alexander's death, 1, 3, 11–14 ; head-quarters of Seleucus, 25, 28, 41 ; in Parthian hands, 76–7 ; restoration of temples, 258, 363 ; Alexander's proposed harbour, 298 ; supplanted by Seleucia, 299, 309 ; astrological studies, 349, 366 ; public officers of health, 351 ; cults, 371 ; recovered by Seleucus II, 399
Babylonia, invaded by Eumenes, 23 ; recovered by Seleucus I, 28 ; invaded by Ptolemy III, 68, 399 ; captured by Molon, 69–70 ; trade, 72, 82 ; value to Greeks, 78 ; regained by Seleucus II, 89 ; campaigns of Antiochus III, 112–13 ; colonization, 216, 258 ; governorship of Timarchus, 220 ; invaded by Parthians, 226 ; disappearance of native nobility, 248 ; condition of native towns, 269 ; vine-planting, 293 n. ; absence of art-revival, 315 ; use of the Greek tongue, 323
Bacchides, 229
Bactra, 71, 74
Bactria, campaign against Greek deserters, 4 ; secession from Seleucid monarchy, 68–9 ; invasion by Antiochus III, 71 ; later Greek rulers, 74–5, 77, 316 ; expulsion of the Greeks, 75, 78 ; colonization, 245 ; alleged capture by Ptolemy III, 399
Bætocæce, 258 n.
Balkan lands, under Lysimachus, 54 ; anarchy during Galatian invasion, 62 ; adventures of Ptolemy the Son, 105 ; conquests by Alexander, 117 ; by Lysimachus, 118 ; by the Galatians, 118 ; relations with Macedon, 122–3 ; unrecorded wars, 140 ; pressure of invaders, 145 ; Dardanian wars, 203 ; send contingents to Alexander's army, 231 ; sale of wine, 293
Bargylia, 188
Barsine, 1 n., 30
Barygaza, 75
Berenice I, 43, 55, 84, 368
Berenice II, 86–9, 102, 109, 391, 396–9
Berenice III, 87 n., 90, 138, 397 n.
Berenice V, 224
Berenice (port), 81
Berge, 338
Berœa, 50
Berossus, 324, 366
Bessarabia, 116
Bion, 357–8
Bithynia, 61, 97–8, 114, 213–14, 238
Bithys, 148
Bœotia, sides with Antipater, 7, 381 ; rebels against Demetrius I, 48–9 ; retained by Gonatas, 53 ; sends force to defend Delphi, 60 ; secedes from Gonatas, 127 ; abandoned by him, 131 ; remains neutral in Chremonidean War, 133 ; dependent upon Ætolia, 145 ; recovered by Demetrius II, 147, 152 ; allied with Doson, 160, 163 ; sides with Philip V, 190 ; with Perseus, 201 ;

ephebic records, 275 n.; survival of League, 282–3; debt-moratorium, 304; ceramic industry, 314–15; dialect, 323
Bolgius, 59, 60
Borysthenes, r., 115
Bosporus (Thracian), 18, 61–2, 97, 118–19, 277, 372
Bosporus (Tauric), 116
Brennus, 60, 61
Britain, 290
Brittany, 290
Brundisium, 178 n.
Bruttians, 171, 176
Buddha, 316
Byblus, 268
Bylazora, 166
Byzantium, relations with Antigonus I, 19, 27; with Lysimachus, 39, 118; allied with Heraclea, 99; relations with the Crimea, 116; blackmailed by Galatians, 119; at war with Rhodes, 119; military obligations, 275; levies tolls at Bosporus, 119, 277

Caicus, 108, 110, 114
Calauria, 10
Callatis, 118–19
Callias, 303
Callicrates (admiral of Ptolemy II), 104
Callicrates (Achæan politician), 198, 203–4
Callidromus, Mt., 61, 196
Callimachus, 322, 326, 328–9, 331–2, 341
Callippus, 60
Callium, 61
Calycadnus, r., 102
Calymna, 281
Cambay, Gulf, 73, 75
Campania, 172
Cannæ, 184, 212
Canopus, 263 n., 270 n., 311
Canusium, 314
Cappadocia, conquered by Perdiccas, II; provides horsemen to Hellenistic armies, 14, 233; held by Eumenes of Cardia, 16; becomes independent, 95–6; curtailed by the Galatians, 99; relations with Antiochus III, 114; disputed succession, 221; intermarriage of royal house with Seleucids, 250
Cappadocia-ad-Pontum, see Pontus
Capua, 169
Cardia, 13, 377
Caria, occupied by Ptolemy I, 31; under Pleistarchus, 42; under the Seleucids, 100–1, 104; raided by Doson, 106, 160; regained by Antiochus III, 107; lost by Antiochus Hierax, III; raided by Philip V, 188; acquired by Rhodes, 206; detached from Rhodes, 214
Carmel, Mt., 227, 230
Carneades, 356, 361
Carpathus, 352 n.
Carrhæ, 78
Cartagena, 181
Carthage, at war with Syracuse, 168–76; allied with Rome, 179; relations with Massilia, 181; supposed plan of conquest by Alexander, 182; allied with Philip V, 184; at Straits of Gibraltar, 290; trade monopoly, 298; trade in Red Sea, 301; art, 316; coin-types, 317; use of the Greek tongue, 324
Carystus, 334
Caspian Sea, 71, 289
Cassander, at war with Polyperchon, 17; wins Athens, 18–19; captures and kills Olympias and Alexander IV, 20; limited ambitions, 21–2; at war with Antigonus I, 25–32; loses Athens, 34; assumes the title of king, 36; sends supplies to Rhodes, 37; at war with Athens and Demetrius I, 38; negotiates with Antigonus I, 39; sends troops to Lysimachus, 40; renounces possessions in Greece, 44; dies prematurely, 45; character of rule, 45; foments revolution in Epirus, 46; fixes his capital at Cassandreia, 58, 121, 253; advances to the Adriatic, 124, 183, 406; garrisons Greek towns, 125, 270; defeated by Cassander, 171; holds Corcyra, 171, 178 n.; strategy, 237; does not annex Thessaly, 247; studies Homer, 318; receives worship, 369 n.
Cassandreia, 58, 63, 121, 253, 270 n., 272, 329, 369 n.
Cato, 195, 325
Cattaro, 151
Caucasus, 72, 116
Celænæ, 22, 35, 100
Celts, 59
Ceos, 134, 146
Ceylon, 338
Chæroneia, 45, 133–4, 143
Chalcedon, 99, 187
Chalcis (in Eubœa), link between Macedon and Peloponnesus, 49; garrisoned by Gonatas, 131; seized by Alexander, son of Craterus, 139; recovered by Gonatas, 143,

402; base of Doson, 160; of Philip V, 191; taken from Philip V by Flamininus, 192; repels the Ætolians, 194–5; worships Flamininus, 370
Chalcis (in Syria), 258
Chandragupta, 40, 41, 66–7, 316, 325
Chaones, 46, 150
Chersonese, see Thracian Chersonese.
China, 74, 75, 298–9, 316
Chios, 104, 107, 146, 188, 209, 280 n.
Chremonides, 105, 133–4, 136–7, 144, 400
Chryseis, 159 n.
Chrysippus, 326, 361
Cilicia, occupied by Eumenes of Cardia, 18; under Pleistarchus, 42; partly occupied by Seleucus I, 48; invaded by Demetrius I, 51; garrisoned by Ptolemy III, 88; colonization, 95, 216; changes hands between Ptolemies and Seleucids, 100–2, 398 n.; occupied by Demetrius II, 221; ceded to Cleopatra VII, 225; reunited to Syria, 226; annexed by Pompey, 227
Cimon, 133
Cincius Alimentus, 325
Cinnamon Country, 80
Citium, 324, 360
Cius, 187
Cleanthes, 347, 360, 362, 373
Cleomenes (minister of Alexander), 14, 262
Cleomenes III (king of Sparta), 155–63, 192, 239, 335, 404
Cleonæ, 148
Cleonymus, 129, 178
Cleopatra (sister of Alexander), 12
Cleopatra I, 94, 217
Cleopatra II, 222
Cleopatra III, 222–3, 289
Cleopatra VII, 85, 223–5, 260, 325
Clitarchus, 335, 337
Clitus, 7, 8, 17, 18, 381–3
Cnidus, 293, 296, 346–7, 372
Cœle-Syria, rival claims of Ptolemies and Seleucids, 42; warfare for its possession, 82–94, 102, 217–18, 221–2; governorship of Simon, 229
Corcyra, 150, 152, 171, 178 and n. 184
Corinth, in Macedonian hands, 7; occupied by Ptolemy I, 31; held by Demetrius I, 38, 43–4, 49; by Gonatas, 60, 127, 130–2, 134; under Alexander, son of Craterus, 139, 401–2; regained by Gonatas, 140, 240; captured by Aratus, 142–4, 152, 240; besieged by Cleomenes, 158; ceded to Doson, 159–61; congress convened by Philip V, 165; receives Roman embassy, 183; controlled by Philip V, 190–1; ceded to Flamininus, 192; heads resistance to Rome, 204; destroyed, 205, 299; coinage, 272; industry, 294; headquarters of dramatic troupe, 320
Cornwall, 290
Corupedium, 56–7, 96–7, 99, 104, 108, 120
Corycus, 209
Cos, occupied by Ptolemy I, 30–1; part of the Ptolemaic dominions, 102; Gonatas' naval victory, 105, 137–8, 240–1, 394, 403; silk industry, 294; viticulture, 293; school of astrology, 366
Crannon, 8, 12
Craterus (marshal of Alexander), 3, 7, 8 n., 10–14, 98 n., 139, 383
Craterus (son of the above), 139, 334
Crates, 339–40
Crete, furnishes a naval base to the Ptolemies, 53, 139, 141; provides mercenaries, 71, 113, 225–6, 229; campaign of Areus, 129–30; conventions for ransom, 242 n.; feuds between cities, 279; arbitration, 280
Crimea, 116
Critolaus, 204
Crœsus, 113
Croton, 176–7
Ctesibius, 349–50
Cumæ, 314
Cybele, 371
Cyclades, acquired by Antigonus I, 27; taken by Polemæus, 30; held by Demetrius I, 43; fall to Ptolemy I, 52–3 n.; ceded to Gonatas, 137; recovered by Ptolemy II, 140; recaptured by Gonatas, 141, 403; held by Demetrius II, 152; king-worship, 369 n.; confederacy, 27, 38, 265
Cyme, 108
Cynics, 357–8, 361
Cynoscephalæ, 191, 201–2
Cyprus, conquered by Ptolemy I, 26–7; annexed to Egypt, 30; taken by Demetrius I, 34–5, 43; recovered by Ptolemy I, 48; naval station, 88, 398; retained by Ptolemy V, 103; occupied by Antiochus IV, 218; disputed between Ptolemy VI and VII, 219–20; coveted by Demetrius I of Syria, 221; in later civil wars

of the Ptolemies, 222–3 ; ceded to Cleopatra VII, 225
Cyrenaica, 84, 138
Cyrene, acquired by Ptolemy I, 12, 13 n. ; secession of Ophellas, 27, 169 ; recovered by Ptolemy I, 31 ; held by Magas, 85, 393–4 ; seized by Demetrius the Fair, 138 ; recovered by Ptolemy III, 138 ; claimed by Philip V, 187 ; awarded to Ptolemy VII, 219, 221–2 ; bequeathed to Apion, 223 ; annexed by Rome, 223 ; method of government, 265 ; ceramic industry, 314 ; Jewish residents, 324 ; home of literary men, 341
Cyrus (Persian king), 113
Cyrus (Persian prince), 51
Cyzicus, 255, 272, 275, 280 n.

Damascus, 13, 82–5, 89, 227, 230
Damophon, 313
Danube, r., 54, 59, 115–19
Daphne, 219, 311, 397
Dardanelles, 7, 14, 27, 40, 57, 61, 106, 111, 120, 210, 383
Dardanians, 123, 148, 152, 160 n., 165–6, 190, 198, 203
Darius, 115
Dead Sea, 81–2
Deidamia, 150
Deinocrates, 171
Delhi, 73, 75
Delos, the sanctuary under patronage of Antigonus I, 27 ; visit of Ptolemy I, 31 ; festival of Ptolemaieia, 140 n. ; passes under Macedonian control, 141, 403 ; made a free port, 214 ; free corn, 276 ; temple loans, 277 ; Aegean entrepôt, 298–9 ; wage-levels, 303–4 ; royal dedications, 308 ; surviving houses, 311 n. ; paintings, 313 ; festivals, 319 ; temple of Sarapis, 372 ; inscriptions, 379
Delphi, occupied by Ætolians, 49, 145 ; raided by Galatians, 61–2 ; remains in Ætolian control, 131, 146, 165, 283 ; relations with Athens, 133 ; freed from Ætolian control, 196 ; visit of Eumenes II, 200 ; proxenia list, 279 n. ; visiting justices, 281 ; old paintings, 307 ; royal dedications, 308 ; musical displays, 317 ; the Soteria, 319 ; educational endowments, 321 ; dialect, 323 ; oracle still in esteem, 364 ; inscriptions, 379
Delta (Egypt), 93, 217
Demades, 6
Demeter, 364
Demetrias (in Magnesia), founded by Demetrius I, 49 ; retained by Gonatas, 53, 60, 126–7, 131 ; military base of Demetrius II, 147 ; held by Philip V, 191 ; taken from Philip V by Flamininus, 192 ; seized by the Ætolians, 195 ; restored to Philip V, 198–9
Demetrias (in India), 73
Demetrias (Attic tribe), 34
Demetrius I (of Macedon), marries Phila, d. of Antipater, 16 ; defeated at Gaza, 27–8 ; captures Athens, 32–3 ; defeats Ptolemy I at Salamis, 34–5, 382, 385–6 ; proclaimed king, 35 ; fails to land in Egypt, 35 ; besieges Rhodes, 36–7, 242 n., 282 ; forms Greek League, 38 ; campaign against Cassander, 38–40 ; at battle of Ipsus, 41 ; relations with Seleucus, 43, 82 ; further relations with Athens, 43–5 ; becomes king of Macedon, 47 ; loses his eastern possessions, 48 ; at war with Pyrrhus, 48–9, 128 ; loses Macedon, 50 ; invades Asia Minor, 51 ; capture and death, 52 ; retains Caria after Ipsus, 102 ; duel with Lysimachus, 103 ; establishes garrisons, in Greece, 125 ; repairs Long Walls at Athens, 136 n. ; captures Corcyra, 178 n. ; comparison with Philip V, 199, 200 ; military ability, 240–1 ; marriages, 250 ; autocracy, 50, 252–3, 270 ; official gazette, 334 n. ; receives worship, 369 n., 370
Demetrius II (of Macedon), marriages, 111 n., 159 n., defeats Alexander II of Epirus, 135 ; pretended wedding at Corinth, 140; alliance with Epirus, 147 ; at war in Greece, 147–8 ; defeated by Dardanians, 148, 400 ; pact with Illyrians, 151 ; dedications at Delos, 403
Demetrius the Fair, 138–9
Demetrius (son of Philip V), 199
Demetrius I (of Syria), 74, 220–1, 229
Demetrius II (of Syria), 74, 76–8, 221, 225–7, 229–30, 249 n.
Demetrius (of Bactria), 72–5
Demetrius of Phalerum, in power at Athens, 19, 32 ; his administration, 33, 321 n. ; images at Athens, 311 ; invited to Egypt, 318, 344 ; befriends Theophrastus, 320 n.
Demetrius of Pharos, 183–5, 406
Demochares, 38, 44, 50, 127 n., 333
Democritus, 358

Demodamas, 68, 289
Demophanes, 138–41
Demosthenes, holds his hand during Alexander's reign, 5; banishment from Athens, 10; death, 10; administrative talent, 38; statue at Athens, 127 n.; becomes a classic, 332; commentary of Didymus, 339
Didymus, 326, 339
Diodotus I, 68
Diodotus II, 68 n. 1, 69, 74
Dionysiac artists, 320
Dionysius (of Heraclea), 98
Dionysius (of Syracuse), 168–9, 171, 310
Dionysius (grammarian), 340
Dionysus, 365
Diophantus, 346
Diphilus, 326, 330
Dium, 165
Dodona, 165, 364
Domitius, Ahenobarbus, 211 n.
Dorimachus, 164
Dorylachum, 40
Doson, see Antigonus III
Drerus, 279
Dromichætes, 116
Druids, 324
Dura-Europus, 273, 311 n., 313
Duris, 335, 337

Ebro, r., 181
Ecbatana, 70, 76–7
Ecdemus, 138–41
Echinades, 382
Edessa, 258
Egypt, awarded to Ptolemy I, 12; invaded by Perdiccas, 14–15; a source of large revenue, 21; invaded by Antigonus I, 35; relations with Ethiopia, 79–80; Red Sea trade, 80–1; relations with Arabia, 81–2; invaded by Magas, 85; attacked by Antiochus III, 90–3; native risings, 93, 217, 305; early relations with Pergamum, 108–9, 112; relations with Macedon in mid-third century 132–44; relations with Athens, 50, 133–5, 150; at war with Doson, 160; early alliance with Rome, 182–3; at war with Philip V, 187–9; attacked by Antiochus IV, 216–19; civil strife, 93, 218–20, 222–5; later relations with Rome, 218–19, 223–5; military forces, 231; organization of army, 233–6; fleet, 240; calendar, 246; status of natives, 246; disappearance of native nobility, 248; administration, 251–2, 259–67; native self-government, 268; position of native priests, 269–70; status of Greek cities, 274–5; trade, 288, 296–8, 300–1; agriculture, 291–3; industry, 295–6; gilds, 302; economic policy, 304; native sculpture, 315; local Greek festivals, 319; use of Greek among natives, 323; history of Hecatacus, 325; influence of native religion upon the Greeks, 363, 371–3; vogue of magic, 366–7; deification of rulers, 368; lack of epigraphic finds, 379; papyri, 379
Elatea, 38
Elburz, Mt., 71
Eleusis, 365
Eleutherus, r., 43, 82
Elis, rebels against Gonatas in 280 B.C., 126; gives aid to Pyrrhus, 129; despotism of Aristotimus, 134; client of Ætolia, 146; stands out of Doson's League, 163; allies with Ætolia against Philip V, 165, 185; ravaged by Philip, 166; annexed to Achæan League, 194; an economic backwater, 288
Elymais, 76–7
Ennius, 238, 325
Epaminondas, 34, 130, 153, 238, 310
Ephesus, 32, 87, 104–7, 209, 270 n., 273, 298, 310, 395–7
Epicureans, 320, 355 n., 358–61
Epicurus, 358–9
Epidamnus, 124
Epidaurus, 39 n., 379
Epirus, residence of Olympias, 20; constitution, 46; accession of Pyrrhus, 46–7; submission to Philip II and Alexander, 122; extent of territory, c. 300 B.C., 124; at war with Gonatas, 127–31, 135; dispute with Ætolia, and alliance with Macedon, 147; becomes a republic, 150; overrun by Illyrians, 151–2; enrolled in Doson's League, 163; invaded by Ætolians, 165; campaigns of kings in Sicily, 173–4; in Italy, 177–80; joins Philip V against the Romans, 190; allied with Perseus, 201; dragonaded by the Romans, 203; relations with Magnesia-on-Mæander, 279; relations with Atintania, 400
Erasistratus, 351–2
Eratosthenes, 337, 344–5, 407–8
Ergamenes, 80
Erythræ, 106, 364 n.
Eryx, Mt., 173

Esagila, 258, 363
Ethiopia, 80, 326
Etruscans, 316
Euas, Mt., 162
Eubœa, retained by Gonatas, 53; secedes from him, 127 and n.; regained by him, 131, 133; temporary defection under Alexander, son of Craterus, 140; retained by Demetrius II, 152; enrolled in Doson's League, 163; made into a separate federation by Flamininus, 192; captured by Antiochus III, 195
Eucleidas, 162
Eucleides, 346, 407
Eucratides, 74–5
Eudamus (Macedonian satrap), 66
Eudamus (Rhodian admiral), 210
Eudoxus (of Cnidus), 346–7
Eudoxus (of Cyzicus), 289–91
Euemerus, 338, 370 n.
Eulæmus, 217–18
Eumelus, 116, 118
Eumenes of Cardia, chancellor of Alexander, 13; defeats Craterus, 14, 233; penned up in Macedonia, 16; negotiates with Antigonus I, 17; invested with new authority by Polyperchon, 17–18; last campaigns with Antigonus, 22–6; relations with Mithridates I, 96
Eumenes I of Pergamum, 104, 106, 108–9, 112, 235 n.
Eumenes II, claims Ænus and Maroneia, 199; informs at Rome against Perseus, 200; appeals to Rome against Antiochus III, 206–7; ally of Rome against Antiochus, 209–13; at Magnesia, 211–12, 237; receives new territory in Asia Minor, 212–13; at war with Pharnaces, 96 n., 214; equivocal behaviour in Third Macedonian War, 214–15; administration, 255; builds colonnade at Athens, 308, 310; erects a great altar at Pergamum, 312; patron of literature, 318; endows education at Delphi, 321; collects a library, 322
Euphrates, r., 78, 245, 257–8, 298, 399
Euripides, 329, 338 n.
Europus, see Doura
Eurotas, r., 154, 166
Eurycleides, 148
Eurydice (granddaughter of Philip II), 15, 16, 19, 20, 251
Eurydice (daughter of Antipater), 13, 43, 55, 58
Euthydemus, 71–3

Fabius Pictor, 325
Fayum, 259, 291–2, 295
Flamininus, 123, 190–4, 207–8, 370
Fulvius Nobilior, 196–7

Gabiene, 24–5, 239
Gabinius, 224
Gadara, 332 n., 358
Gades, 290
Galatians, invasions of Macedonia, 59–60, 253; of Greece, 60–1, 145, 239; of Thrace, 61, 117–19; of Asia Minor, 62, 97, 120, 271 n.; defeat by Antiochus I, 62, 84, 104; mercenaries, 85, 109, 112–13, 128, 233, 237, 242, 397; settlement in Asia Minor, 99; constitution, 100; allied with Antiochus Hierax, 109–11; defeated by Attalus I, 110–11; plundered by Manlius Vulso, 213
Galen, 353
Galilee, 91, 230
Gallia Cisalpina, 188
Gallia Narbonensis, 181
Gallipoli, 62, 120, 207
Gandhara, 316 n.
Ganges, r., 75
Garganus, Mt., 177
Gaul, 59, 61 n., 77, 324
Gaza, 26–7, 93, 229
Gaziura, 96
Gela, 168
Gerra, 72
Getæ, 116–17, 119
Gibraltar, 290, 344
Glaucias, 46, 124
Gonatas, see Antigonus II
Gracchus, C., 155
Gracchus, sen., Tib., 221
Gracchus, jun., Tib., 155

Halicarnassus, 103, 264 n.
Halycus, r., 170
Halys, r., 96, 99
Hamilcar, 168, 170
Hannibal, 71, 76, 169, 180, 182, 184, 189, 208, 210, 213, 239
Harpalus, 6, 10
Hecatæus of Abdera, 325
Hecatombœum, 157
Hecatompylus, 70
Hegesias, 333
Heligoland, 290
Heliocles, 74–5
Heliodorus, 227
Helots, 155, 161, 197
Hera, 365
Heraclea-ad-Latmum, 43, 240 n., 279
Heraclea-ad-Œtam, 196, 204–5
Heraclea-ad-Pontum, 54–5, 58, 98–9, 115, 247, 275

Heraclea (in S. Italy), 179
Heracleides Criticus, 308 n.
Heracleides Ponticus, 347
Heracleides (of Syracuse), 167–8, 176
Heracles, son of Barsine, 1 n., 30
Heraclitus, 139
Hermæus, 75
Hermias (minister of Autiochus III), 90 n., 302
Hermias (litigant in Egypt), 266
Hermippus, 334
Hermon, Mt., 82 n.
Hermus, r., 100
Hero, 350
Herodotus, 325, 333
Herondas, 323, 326, 331
Herophilus, 351–2
Hicetas, 172
Hierax, see Antiochus Hierax
Hiero, 174–5
Hieronymus, 335, 377–8
Himalayas, 331
Hindus, 289, 316, 325
Hindu-Kush, Mt., 65, 69, 72, 75
Hippalus, 290 n.
Hipparchus, 345–9, 366
Hippocrates, 343, 351–2
Homer, 339
Huns, 73, 75
Hydarnes, 196
Hydaspes, r., 65–6
Hyperides, 6
Hyphasis, r., 65–6, 74
Hyrcania, 68, 71

Iambulus, 338
Iasus, 281
Iaxartes, r., 68, 289
Idumæa, 81
Ilium, 207, n., 272, 307 n., 334, 388
Illyria, invasion by Alexander, 59; settlement of Galatians, 60; general history in third century, 123–4; acts of plunder and piracy, 151–2; supplies mercenaries, 162, 233, 239; invasion of Macedon, 124, 164; chastised by Romans, 152, 183; Roman zone of observation, 183–4; relations with Gonatas, 406
India, Alexander's campaigns, 16, 24; condition after Alexander's death, 65–6; rise of native kingdoms, 66–7; campaign of Antiochus III, 72; conquests by Greco-Bactrian chiefs, 74–5; trade with Egypt, 80–1; trans-continental communications, 115, 289, 298–9; influence of Greek art, 316; use of Greek tongue, 323; alleged conquests by Ptolemy III, 399
Indus, r., 65, 72–4, 75
Ionia, 103–7, 120
Ionian Sea, 146, 184, 382
Ipsus, 41–4, 46, 66, 92, 231, 237, 256
Iran, 67–8, 73, 75, 211, 233, 246, 323–4, 371, 373
Iris, r., 96
Iron Gates, 122–3
Isis, 363, 371–3
Isocrates, 246, 333
Isthmian Games, 183, 193
Isthmus, 132, 135, 144, 160, 205
Istria, 118–19
Italy, troubled by Illyrian pirates, 152, 183; raided by Agathocles, 171; sends mercenaries to Sicily, 172, 175; invaded by Alexander of Epirus, 177; by Cleonymus, 178; by Pyrrhus, 174, 179–80; projected invasion by Alexander, 182; deportation of Achæans, 203; projected second invasion by Hannibal, 208; forbidden to Eumenes II, 215; united against a divided Greece, 236; industry, 294; trade, 298–9; ceramic art, 314; imports Greek works of art, 317; use of the Greek tongue, 325; receives cults of Sarapis and Isis, 373
Itanus, 53

Japan, 316
Jason, 328
Java, 316
Jerusalem, 227–30
Jews in conflict with the Seleucids, 227–30; establish the Maccabee dynasty, 229; make conquests, 230; mercenaries in Egypt, 233, 236; status at Alexandria, 268, 274; tax-farmers, 301 and n.; use of the Greek tongue, 323–4; discussed in Hecatæus' history, 325; religion, 371; sources of history, 378
John Hyrcanus, 230
Jonathan, 229–30
Jordan, r., 82 n., 91, 93
Judæa, 227–30, 238, 363, 371
Judas, 228–9
Justin, 379

Kabul, 75
Kandahar, 72
Kertch, 116
Khartum, 80
Khiva Bay, 289 n.
Kidenas, 348

Koptos, 81
Korea, 316

Lachares, 44–5
Lacinian Cape, 177–8
Laconia, 153–5, 192, 194, 197, 333
Ladoceia, 156
Lævinus, 184–5
Lamia, 6–8, 10, 16, 138 n., 352 n., 381–3
Lampsacus, 40 n., 111, 114, 207, 209
Laodice (queen of Antiochus II), 86–8, 109, 369, 395–9
Laodice (sister of Antiochus IV ?), 250 n.
Laodicea-ad-Lycum, 100, 294
Laomedon, 17
Larissa, 195, 201, 272 n.
Laurium, 305
Lebanon, 90
Lebedus, 64 n., 270 n.
Lemnos, 315
Lenæus, 217–8
Leonidas I, 61, 91, 196
Leonidas II, 154–5
Leonnatus, 7, 11, 383
Leontes, r., 83, 90
Leosthenes, 6
Lesbos, 107
Leucippus, 358
Leuctra, 153
Libyans, 169
Lihyanites, 81
Lilybæum, 173
Lissus, 152, 184
Livy, 182, 336, 378
Locri (in S. Italy), 176
Locris, 196
Lucanians, 176–8, 180
Luceria, 178
Lucretius, 359 n.
Lucullus, 211
Lycæus, Mt., 156
Lyceum, 320, 355
Lychnis, Lake, 124
Lycia, 100–2, 213 n., 264 n.
Lycophron of Chalcis, 329
Lycophron of Rhegium, 329
Lycortas, 203
Lycurgus (of Athens), 5, 45
Lycurgus (of Sparta), 126, 153, 157, 197–8
Lydia, 17, 109, 111, 323
Lydiadas, 141, 148, 155–6
Lysander (admiral), 8, 367
Lysander (ephor), 153–4
Lysandra, 43
Lysias, 220, 228–9
Lysimachia, 57, 120–1, 187, 207, 344
Lysimachus (king of Thrace), marries Nicæa, d. of Antipater, 13 ; campaigns against Antigonus I, 25–8, 36–41 ; proclaims himself king, 36 ; subdues Thrace, 39, 117–18, 122 ; receives part of Asia Minor, 42 ; marries Arsinoë I, 43 ; campaigns against Demetrius I, 48–51 ; seizes Macedon, 50, 53–4 ; conquests in Greece, 54 ; family quarrels, 55–6 ; defeated and killed by Seleucus I, 56–7 ; defeated by Bithynians, 97 ; relations with Heraclea, 98 ; acquires Ionia, 48, 103–4 ; relations with Philetærus, 107 ; schemes of Russian conquests, 115–16 ; resides at Lysimachia, 121 ; annexes Pæonia, 122–3 ; enrols Thracian troops, 233 ; containing strategy, 40, 238 ; character of rule, 270 ; arbitrates a dispute, 281 n. ; coinage, 315
Lysimachus (brother of Ptolemy III), 391, 398–9
Lyttus, 279

Macedon, viceroyalty of Antipater, 2, 12 ; supremacy over Greece contested, 4–9 ; fusion with Greece, 10, 340 ; return of the royal family, 16 ; recognizes Polyperchon, 16–17 ; accepts Cassander, 19 ; invaded by Olympias, 20 ; impoverishment, 22 ; attempted invasion by Antigonus I, 26–7 ; Cassander's rule acknowledged by Antigonus, 28 ; renewed alliance with Greek confederacy, 38 ; recovers under rule of Cassander, 45–6 ; confusion after Cassander's death, 46–7 ; receives Demetrius I as king, 47 ; raided by Pyrrhus, 49 ; partitioned between Pyrrhus and Lysimachus, 50 ; reunited under Lysimachus, 54 ; coveted by Seleucus I, 57 ; accepts Ptolemy Ceraunus, 57–8 ; overrun by Galatians, 59–63 ; accepts Gonatas, 63 ; dynastic law, 84 ; claims of Antiochus I abandoned, 120 ; authority of Gonatas confirmed, 121–2 ; northern frontiers protected, 122–3 ; relations with Illyria, 124 ; relations with Greece under Gonatas, 125–7, 131–6, 139–46 ; relations with Ptolemy II, 127–8, 132–9, 141, 145 ; again invaded by Pyrrhus, 128–9 ; invaded by Alexander II of Epirus, 135 ; relations with Greece under Demetrius II, 147–50 ; relations with Illyria, 151 ; relations with Greece under Doson, 158–64 ; renewed alliance with a

Greek confederacy, 163 ; relations with Greece in the early years of Philip V, 164–5 ; the First Macedonian War with Rome, 183–6 ; relations with Syria and Egypt, 186–8, 195 ; the second Macedonian War, 188–93 ; loss of hegemony in Greece, 193 ; reorganization by Philip, 198 ; the Third Macedonian War, 200–2 ; partition into four republics, 202 ; invasion by Andriscus, 203 ; annexation by Rome, 204 ; passage of Roman troops to Asia, 210 ; military strength, 231–3, 239 ; naval strength, 240 ; calendar, 246 ; personal union with Thessaly, 247 ; disappearance of nobility, 248 ; court institutions, 249 ; organization under the Antigonids, 253–5 ; conscription, 271 ; residence of Demetrius of Phalerum, 318 n. ; use of the common Greek tongue, 323 ; adoption of Greek gods, 365 ; attitude to king-worship, 367–9 ; thalassocracy, 403 ; interest in the Adriatic, 406
Machanidas, 185, 192
Mæander, 62, 100, 212
Magas, 67, 84–5, 87 n., 138, 393–4
Magnesia-ad-Mæandrum, 71 n., 279, 281, 308 n., 310, 319, 379
Magnesia-ad-Sipylum, 56, 71 n., 76, 211, 231, 237, 239, 312 n., 333
Malacca, 316
Malian Gulf, 48
Mallus, 102
Mamertines, 172, 174–5
Manetho, 324
Manlius Vulso, 213
Mantinea, 144, 146, 149, 161, 185, 187, 243
Maronea, 121, 199
Massilia, 181, 290, 301, 324, 344
Mattathias, 228
Media, 23, 66, 69, 70, 76–7, 110, 216, 399
Media Atropatene, see Atropatene
Megalopolis, rebels against Gonatas, 127 ; hostile to Sparta, 126, 129, 155, 279 ; recovered by Gonatas, 131 ; holds aloof from the Chremonidean War, 134 ; beats off a Spartan attack, 135 ; under tyranny of Aristodamus, 139 ; annexed to the Achæan League, 148, 155–6, 158 ; attacked by Cleomenes, 156 ; raided by Cleomenes, 161 ; native town of Polybius, 336
Megara, 64 n., 143, 242 n., 314
Megasthenes, 66–7, 325–6
Meleager (Macedonian officer), 11
Meleager (son of Ptolemy I), 60
Meleager of Gadara, 332 n.
Memnon, 98 n.
Memphis, 13, 218, 268–70, 274, 288, 291, 293, 295, 368, 371–2
Menander (of Athens), 326, 330–1, 354
Menander (of Ephesus), 326
Menander (Greco-Bactrian ruler), 74–5
Menelaus (brother of Ptolemy I), 34–5, 385, 398
Menelaus (Jewish High Priest), 229
Menippus, 358
Meroë, 80, 326, 344
Merv, 68, 258
Mesopotamia, 77, 111, 297–9, 309, 399
Messana, 168, 172, 174
Messapia, 177
Messene, excluded from Demetrius' Hellenic League, 38 ; fortifications, 43, 310 ; independent of Gonatas, 126 ; hostile to Sparta, 129 ; accepts an Ætolian protectorate, 146 ; stands out of Doson's League, 163 ; subsequently becomes a member, 165 ; allied with Rome against Philip V, 185 ; annexed to the Achæan League, 194 ; rebels, 197–8 ; treaty with Phigaleia, 280 n.
Metellus, 203–5
Miletus, passes from Lysimachus to Demetrius, 51, 103 ; temple of Apollo, 62 ; passes successively to Lysimachus, to Seleucus, to Ptolemy II, 104 ; in the First Syrian War, 104, 387–8 ; in the Second Syrian War, 105, 390 ; independent in 197 B.C., 107 ; raided by Doson, 160 ; treaties with Cretan towns, 242 n. ; state-loans, 277 n. ; wars with neighbours, 279 ; grants of franchise, 280 n. ; pedigree rams, 293 ; textile workshops, 296 ; school endowment, 321 n.
Miran, 316
Mithra, 373 n.
Mithridates I of Parthia, 75–6, 226
Mithridates II, 75, 78
Mithridates I of Pontus, 96
Mithridates II, 109
Mithridates VI, 97, 117
Mnesimachus, 258 n., 302
Modein, 228
Molon, 69, 70, 77, 90, 113
Molossi, 46, 150

Mongolia, 299 n.
Morava, r., 122
Moschus, 329
Mummius, 205
Munychia, see Piræus.
Museum (at Alexandria), the, 318–19, 321–2, 341, 344
Museum Hill (at Athens), 45, 50, 136
Myonnesus, 210
Myrina, 315
Mysia, 233
Mytilene, 5 n., 146 n.

Nabatæans, 81, 227, 230
Nabis, 192, 194, 197, 296
Naucratis, 245 n., 274
Naupactus, 166 n.
Naxos, 382
Neapolis, 176
Nearchus, 289, 345
Nectanebo, 55
Nestus, r., 120, 202
Nicæa (d. of Antipater), 12–13, 55–7
Nicæa (widow of Alexander, son of Craterus), 140
Nicæa (near Thermopylæ), 191
Nicanor, 28
Nicias, 170
Nicocles, 139–40
Nicomedes I, 97–8
Nicomedes II, 216
Nicomedia, 98
Nile, r., 14–15, 35, 80–1, 260, 262, 288, 291, 296–7, 309
Nomophylakes, 32–3
Nubia, 79–80, 296, 344
Numenius, 289
Nymphis, 98 n.

Octavius, Cn., 220
Odessus, 118
Œnus, r., 162
Œta, Mt., 61, 145
Olbia, 115, 117, 278 n., 280 n., 357
Olympia, 307–8
Olympias (mother of Alexander), 12, 20, 46, 251
Olympias (queen of Epirus), 147, 150
Olympiodorus, 38, 50, 53
Olympus, Mt. (Laconis), 162
Olympus, Mt. (Thessaly), 191, 201
Olynthus, 253
Ophellas, 27, 31, 169–70, 393
Orchomenus, 277 n.
Ormuz, 72
Orontes, r., 15, 35, 226, 311
Oropus, 279 n.
Osiris, 371–2
Ostia, 297
Otranto, Gulf, 177
Ovid, 328
Oxus, r., 115, 289
Oxyartes, 65

Pæonia, 122–3
Pæstum, 180 n., 314
Pagasæ, Gulf, 49, 53, 152, 164, 166
Palestine, trade with Arabia, 72; Ptolemaic frontier, 81; scene of Syrian Wars, 91–3; reunited by Antiochus VII to the Seleucid dominions, 226; Hellenizing party, 228; the Maccabæan revolt and conquests, 229–30; colonization, 245; trade with Delos, 299; continued use of Aramaic tongue, 323
Palibothra, 66
Pallantium, 156
Palos, Cape, 181
Pamirs, 73
Pamphylia, 100, 102, 210, 213 n.
Panætius, 361–2
Panchæa, 338
Pangæum, Mt., 254
Panium, 93
Panticapæum, 116, 118, 298 n.
Paphlagonia, 96, 214
Parætacene, 24, 239
Parnassus, Mt., 61, 200
Parni, 68
Parthenon, 45, 370
Parthia, occupied by the Parni, 68, 110; conquered by Tiridates, 69, 111–12; invaded by Antiochus III, 70–1; under Mithridates I, 74; invaded by Sacæ, 75; at war with the Seleucids for the possession of Babylonia, 76–8, 226–7, 230; Greek plays at Court, 323
Pataliputra (Patna), 73
Patavium, 178
Patræ, 60, 126
Patrocles, 120, 289
Patroclus, 134–5
Patronomi, 157
Paullus, Æmilius, 201–3, 219
Peisistratus, 308
Peithon, 4, 15, 23, 25
Pella, 253, 318, 321
Pellene, 144
Peloponnesus, joins the rebellion against Macedon, 7; conquests of Cassander, 19, 28, 38; relations with Ptolemy I, 31; campaign of Demetrius I, 47; Macedonian line of communications, 49; retained by Gonatas, 53; secedes from Gonatas, 60; abstains from defence of Delphi, 60; losses and gains of Gonatas in his early reign, 129; régime of Gonatas, 131–2,

134, 136, 247, 272 ; Sparta's hopes of new hegemony, 126, 133–5, 155–9, 192 ; renewed loss of Gonatas' dependencies, 139–40, 142 ; annexations by Achæan League, 143, 148, 194, 286 ; Ætolian invasions, 144, 165 ; invasions by Doson, 159–63 ; raids of Philip V, 166 ; unrest due to enmity of Achæa and Sparta, 197–8; hostility to Rome *c.* 150 B.C., 204 ; coinage, 288 ; companies of actors, 320 ; dialect, 323
Pelusium, 14, 91, 103, 218
Peræa (of Rhodes), 188
Perdiccas, 2–4, 10–16, 28, 35, 57, 96, 100
Perga, 346–7
Pergamum, rise of the kingdom, 107–14 ; at war with Philip V, 185, 187–8, 190 ; claim on Ænus and Maroneia, 199 ; hostility to Perseus, 200–1 ; at war with Antiochus, 207–12 ; aggrandizement, 212 ; subsequent wars in Asia Minor, 213–16 ; government, 255 ; coinage, 273 ; treaty with Temnos, 280 n. ; husbandry, 291 ; textile industry, 294, 296 ; treasures, 302 ; rising of serfs and slaves, 305 ; architecture, 309–10 ; sculpture, 312–13 ; literary centre, 318, 339–40 ; pan-Hellenic festivals, 319 ; educational endowment, 321 ; library, 322
Pericles, 33, 307
Perinthus, 120
Periocci, 154–5, 157
Peripatetics, 343
Persephone, 364
Perseus, 199–203, 215, 231, 249 n.
Persia, quiet after death of Alexander, 4 ; warfare between Alexander's officers, 23–5 ; invasion by Parni, 68 ; relations with Seleucids, 69–71, 73, 76 ; invasion by Sacæ, 75 ; provides soldiers for the Hellenistic armies, 231, 233 ; colonization, 245 ; monarchical disposition, 248 ; organization under Seleucids, 256–9 ; treasure hauled by Alexander, 287, 294 ; viticulture, 293 ; trunk roads, 296 ; influence of Greek art, 315 ; influence upon Hindu art, 316
Persian Gulf, 289, 299
Persis, 24, 69, 399
Peshawar, 316 n.
Petra, 72, 81–2, 227, 230
Peucestas, 24–5
Phædrus, 50
Pharnaces, 96 n., 214
Pharos (Egypt), 297
Pharos (Illyria), 183–5, 406
Pharsalus, 224
Pheidias, 45
Phigaleia, 280 n.
Phila (d. of Antipater), 13, 16, 43, 139
Phila (queen of Gonatas), 120 n.
Philadelphia (Egypt), 311 n.
Philadelphia (Palestine), 81, 91
Philæ, 80
Philemon, 326, 330
Philetærus, 108
Philinus, 324–5
Philip II, father of Arridæus, 1 ; Hellenic League, 4, 9, 18, 38, 163, 247, 282 ; Balkan campaigns, 122 ; organization of Macedon, 145, 253 ; relation to Amphictionic League, 283
Philip III, Arridæus, 1–3, 11, 17, 19–21
Philip, IV, 46
Philip V, pact with Antiochus III, 93, 106, 186, 195 ; occupies the coast of Thrace, 121, 199 ; defence of northern frontier of Macedon, 123, 165–6, 190, 198 ; campaign in Illyria, 124 ; temporarily supplanted by Doson, 159–60 ; warfare in Peloponnesus and Ætolia, 164–6, 237 ; designs on the Adriatic, 183–4 ; alliance with Hannibal, 184 ; the First Macedonian War, 183–6 ; raids in the Aegean, 186–8 ; the Second Macedonian War, 189–93 ; loss of hegemony in Greece, 193 ; co-operates with Rome against Antiochus III, 195, 198 ; new disputes with Rome, 198–9 ; domestic conflicts, 199 ; character, 199–200 ; suggested alliance with Antiochus, 210 n. ; strength of his army, 231 ; siegecraft, 240 ; wears a beard, 249 n. ; coinage, 254 ; letters to Larissa, 272 n. ; under influence of Demetrius of Pharos, 185, 406
Philippi, 22
Philippides, 43 n.
Philippus, Marcius, 201
Philo, 350
Philochorus, 137, 333
Philocles, 52
Philonides, 355 n.
Philopœmen, 162, 185, 194, 197–8
Phintias, 172
Phocæa, 108
Phocion, 6, 18
Phocis, 145, 148, 163, 192
Phœnice, 150–1, 186

Phœnicia, occupied by Ptolemy I, 17; by Eumenes, 18, 22; by Antigonus I, 21, 23, 26; reoccupied by Ptolemy I, 42; object of conflict between Ptolemies and Seleucids, 82, 85–6, 102; provides fleets for Antigonus I, 26; for Antiochus III, 102, 210; local autonomy, 258, 268; coin-standard, 288; influence of Greek art, 315–16; histories, 326
Phraates I, 77–8
Phrygia, under Leonnatus, 7, 11; under Arridæus, 17; province of Antigonus I under Alexander, 22, 26; under Polemæus, 29; scene of campaign of 302–1 B.C., 40–1; occupied by Galatians, 62, 99 n.; raided by Manlius Vulso, 213; supplies wool, 294; use of the Greek tongue, 323; worship of Attis and Cybele, 371
Phrygius, r., 97 n.
Phthia, 147, 159, 400
Phthiotis, 166
Phylacia, 148
Phylarchus, 335, 378
Physcon, 222 n.
Pindus, Mt., 124, 131, 406
Piræus, garrisoned by Antipater, 9; by Cassander, 18–19; by Demetrius, 45, 50; by Gonatas, 53, 60, 126–8, 133, 136, 139, 144; recovered by the Athenians, 149
Pisidia, 16, 100, 113
Plato, 320, 355–6, 359, 367 n.
Plautus, 300, 325
Pleiad, the, 329
Pleistarchus, 42–4
Plutarch, 378
Pluto, 372
Polemæus, 29, 30
Polemo, 307 n., 334
Polybius, advocates neutrality between Rome and Macedon, 203; hatred of tyrants, 247; judgment on Achæan constitution, 286; historical writings, 336–7, 377–8; last great literary figure, 342
Polycrates, 186
Polyperchon, appointed regent, 16; conflict with Cassander, 17–20; proclaims liberty of Greek cities, 18, 26, 126; alliance with Eumenes, 18, 23; in the service of Antigonus and Cassander, 30, 38
Polyxenidas, 209–10
Pompeii, 255, 311, 313–14
Pompeius Trogus, 378
Pontus, 96, 109, 117, 214, 250
Popilius Lænas, 218–19
Porus, 66, 72
Poseidon, 10, 364–5
Posidonius, 337, 345, 362, 366
Priapatius, 70, 71, 77
Priene, defence against Galatians, 62 n.; sends out visiting justices, 281; architecture, 309; houses, 311 n.; sale of priesthoods, 364 n.; excavations, 379
Protogenes, 117, 278 n.
Prusias I, 213–14
Prusias II, 215
Ptolemæus, Claudius, 345, 349, 353
Ptolemaieia (Alexandria), 319, 329, 368
Ptolemaieia (Delos), 140 n.
Ptolemais (mod. Acre), 91
Ptolemais (Upper Egypt), 275, 319, 320 n., 370 n.
Ptolemais-of-the-Hunts, 81
Ptolemais (Attic tribe) 150 n.
Ptolemy I, steals the body of Alexander, 12–13; defies Perdiccas, 13–15; refuses regency, 15; seizes Syria, 17; general policy, 21; evacuates Syria, 22; campaigns against Antigonus, 25–40; annexes Cyprus, 30; schemes in the Aegean and Peloponnesus, 31, 104; defeats Demetrius at Gaza, 27–8; defeated by him at Salamis, 34–5; proclaims himself king, 36; gives aid to Rhodes, 37; not present at Ipsus, 40, 42; occupies Cœle-Syria, 42; matrimonial alliances, 43; dispute with Seleucus, 82; understanding with Seleucus, 44; aids Athens against Demetrius, 45, 50; gives support to Pyrrhus, 47, 128; restores his fleet, 48; wins Demetrius' fleet and Phœnicia, 52; thalassocracy, 52, 54; marriages, 55; regulates the succession, 55; explores the Red Sea, 80; acquisitions in S. Asia Minor, 102; homely habits, 260; founds a colony at Ptolemais, 275; founds the Museum at Alexandria, 318–19; historical writings, 335; establishes cult of Alexander, 367–8; receives worship, 368, 369 n.; institutes cult of Sarapis, 371–2; strength of fleet at Salamis, 385–6; relations with Magas, 393–4
Ptolemy Ceraunus, displaced as heir-apparent by Ptolemy II, 55; at court of Lysimachus, 57; murders Seleucus, 57; king of Macedon, 58; defeats Gonatas, 8, 126; killed by Galatians, 59, 123; alliance with Heraclea, 99; assists Pyrrhus against the Romans, 179

Ptolemy II (Philadelphus), joint-king with Ptolemy I, 55; receives Buddhist mission, 67; general policy, 79; enterprise in Upper Egypt, 79–80; in Red Sea, 80–1; in Arabia, 81; in Palestine, 81–2; conflicts with Seleucids for the possession of Syria, 82–6; acquisitions in S. Asia Minor, 102; in W. Asia Minor, 104; assists Eumenes I of Pergamum, 104, 108; losses on W. coast of Asia Minor, 105; rivalry with Gonatas in Greece and the Aegean, 126–41; abets Pyrrhus, 128; prepares the Chremonidean War, 133; leaves Athens in the lurch, 134; defeated at Cos, 137; foments rebellion of Alexander, son of Craterus, 139; recovers the Cyclades, 140, 401; alliance with Rome, 182; strength of army, 231; strength of fleet, 240; marries his sister, 250; works out his dynasty's system of government, 260, 304; financial policy, 263; amount of his income, 264; government of outlying dependencies, 265; makes Egypt prosperous, 267; interest in husbandry, 292; connoisseur of art, 307; founds the Ptolemaieia, 319; patronizes Theocritus, 331; lays out a zoological garden, 350; deification, 368–9; family relations, 390–1

Ptolemy "the Son," 58, 63, 87 n., 104–5, 390–2

Ptolemy III, character, 87; conquests in Third Syrian War, 88–9, 397–9; retreat, 89; conquests in S. Asia Minor, 102; in W. Asia Minor, 105–6, 109; supports Attalus I, 112; abets Achæus, 113; attacked by Doson, 160; relations with Cleomenes, 160–2; receives thanks from Egyptian priests in the "Canopus Decree," 263 n.; endows Athens, 308; relations with "Ptolemy the Son," 391–2; Aegean thalassocracy, 403

Ptolemy IV, relations with Ethiopia, 80; character, 90, 267; wins the day at Raphia, 92, 233, 237; relations with Cleomenes of Sparta, 162–3; liberality to mercenary officers, 235; cult of Dionysus, 365; deification, 368–9

Ptolemy V, minority reign, 93; surrenders Cœle-Syria to Antiochus III, 94; victim of partition-pact between Antiochus III and Philip V, 186; matrimonial alliance with Antiochus III, 94, 206; subdues native rebellions, 217; receives thanks of Egyptian priests in the "Rosetta decree," 234 n.; deification, 368

Ptolemy VI, 80, 217–23, 379

Ptolemy VII ("Physcon"), 218–19, 222–3, 250, 289, 369 n.

Ptolemy Memphites, 222

Ptolemy VIII, 223–4

Ptolemy IX, 223–4

Ptolemy X, 224

Ptolemy XI (Auletes), 224

Ptolemy XII, 224

Ptolemy XIII, 224

Ptolemy Apion, 223

Ptolemy (King of Epirus), 150

Punjab, 75

Puteoli, 290, 298

Pydna, 20, 202, 218–19, 237

Pyrrhon, 356–7

Pyrrhus I, accession, 46–7; wins Ambracia, 47; campaigns against Demetrius, 49–50; part king of Macedon, 50; wins Thessaly, 53; expelled from Macedon and Thessaly by Lysimachus, 54; makes pact with Ceraunus, 58; alliance with Glaucias of Illyria, 46, 124; invades Macedon, 127–9; besieges Sparta, 129–30; killed at Argos, 130; character, 130–1; creates an autocracy in Epirus, 150; campaigns in Sicily, 173–4; in Italy, 178–80, 182; personal valour, 237; bigamy, 250

Pyrrhus II, 147, 150

Pythagoras, 346

Pytheas, 290, 344–5

Pythian Games, 319

Ragusa, 151

Raphia, 92–3, 211, 231, 233, 236, 239, 405

Red Sea, 80–1, 289, 296, 298, 301, 344, 399

Rhegium, 176

Rhodes, besieged by Demetrius, 36–7, 240; acquires possessions in Caria, 103; allies with Antiochus II in the Second Syrian War, 105, 137; makes war on Byzantium, 119; offers mediation in wars of Greek Homeland, 186; alleged early treaty with Rome, 183 n.; opposition to Philip V, 186–8; invokes help of Rome, 188, 206; naval operations in Second Macedonian War, 90; supplies contingent for the Third Macedonian War, 201;

naval operations in the Roman war against Antiochus III, 209–10; acquires S.W. Asia Minor, 212–13; offers mediation in Third Macedonian War, 214; loses mainland territory, 214–15; offers mediation between Antiochus III and Ptolemy VI and VII, 218; thalassocracy in the second century, 242, 283; war-organization, 275; revenue from tolls, 277; earthquake, 280; gift of Athenian franchise, 280; viticulture, 293; ceramic industry, 296; commerce, 298–9; banking, 301; dialect, 323; study of rhetoric, 333; king-worship, 369 n.

Rome, enlists Dardanians against Macedon, 123; campaigns against Illyrian piracy, 151–2; conquest of Sicily, 174–5; protectorate in S. Italy, 176–7; friction with Tarentum, 177–8; war with Pyrrhus, 179–80; alliance with Massilia, 181; early contacts with Greece, 182–3; challenged by Philip V, 184; First Macedonian War, 184–6; Second Macedonian War, 188–94; campaign against Antiochus III in Greece, 194–6; Ætolians subdued, 196; difficulties of protectorate in Greece, 196–8; later relations with Philip V, 198–9; the Third Macedonian War, 200–3; final settlement of Macedon and Greece, 203–5; negotiations with Antiochus III, 207–9; naval campaign against Antiochus III, 209–10; victory of Magnesia, 211–12; terms imposed upon Antiochus III, 212–13; later relations with states of Asia Minor, 213–16; relations with the later Ptolemies, 218–19, 223–5; with the later Seleucids, 220–1, 227; treaty with Judæa, 229 and n.; reason for victories over Greeks, 236, 240; influence of Greek Architecture, 309, 311; importation of Greek works of art, 317; use of the Greek tongue, 324–5; appreciation by Polybius, 336–7; effects of the Roman conquest upon Greek literature, 342, 354; attitude to Stoicism, 362; worship by Greek cities, 370; pupil of Hellenistic Greece, 375; causes of clash with Greece, 406

Rosetta Stone, 234 n., 270 n.

Roxane, 2, 20, 29, 65

Russia, 115–17, 298, 314–15

Sacæ, 75, 78

Salamis, 34–5, 48, 240, 385–6, 393

Sallentines, 178 n.

Samaria, 44 n., 91, 228 n.

Samnites, 177–8, 182

Samos, claimed by Athens, 6; naval base of Ptolemies, 104, 137, 186, 188; capture by Antiochus II, 105; attacked by Philip V, 107, 188; scene of naval action in 190 B.C., 210; free corn distributions, 276; viticulture, 293; offers worship to Lysander, 367

Samothrace, 138, 339, 347 n., 365

Sandrakottos, see Chandragupta.

Sangarius, r., 97–8

Sarapis, 363, 371–3

Sardes, 40, 51, 62, 83, 87, 108–11, 113, 387–8

Sarmatians, 117, 119

Satyrus, 334

Scepsis, 29, 369 n., 384

Sceptics, 356–7, 361

Scerdilaidas, 151, 183–4

Scipio Æmilianus, 223, 336

Scipio Africanus, 170, 210–11, 239

Scipio, L., 196, 210

Scopas, 93, 164

Scythia, 75, 115, 117

Seistan, 72–5

Seleucia-ad-Orontem, 88–9, 91–2, 112, 240, 273, 299, 309, 370 n.

Seleucia-ad-Tigrim, 70, 72, 88, 257, 273 n., 298–9, 309, 347, 387, 399

Seleucis, 82, 83–4, 89, 389

Seleucus I, murders Perdiccas, 15; opposes Eumenes, 23; flees from Antigonus I, 25; secures Babylonia, 28; excluded from peace of 311 B.C., 29, 384; warfare with Antigonus, 29–30, 32; proclaims himself king, 36; wins the eastern provinces, 40; defeats Antigonus at Ipsus, 41; dispute with Ptolemy I about Syria, 42, 82; relations with Demetrius, 43–4; acquires Cilicia, 48; captures Demetrius, 51–2; defeats Lysimachus at Corupedium, 56; claims Macedon, 56–7; murdered by Ptolemy Ceraunus, 57; character, 57; relations with Chandragupta, 66–7; makes a raid across the Iaxartes, 68; temporary acquisitions on Black Sea border, 96–7; in W. Asia Minor, 104; assisted by Philetærus, 107–8; marriage with a Persian princess, 250; preoccupation with state affairs, 253 n.; administrative policy,

256; explores Central Asia, 289; deification, 368
Seleucus II, warfare against the Parthians, 68–9; succeeds Antiochus II, 87; at war with Ptolemy III, 89, 102, 120–1, 141, 395–6, 399; comes to terms with Cappadocia, 96; with Pontus, 97; friendship with Smyrna, 106 n.; at war with Antiochus Hierax, 109–12; married his cousin, 250 n.
Seleucus III, 112, 207 n.
Seleucus IV, 216, 220, 227
Seleucus (astronomer), 347–8
Sellasia, 161–3, 185, 233–4, 239, 254, 406
Seres, 73
Seuthes, 118
Sibyrtius, 65
Sicily, condition at Alexander's death, 167; domestic warfare, 168–9, 170–1, 172–3; warfare with Carthage, 168–74; becomes a Roman dependency, 174–5; trade with Rhodes, 293 n.; slave revolt, 305; dialect, 323; pastoral poetry, 331; history by Timæus, 336; home of men of letters, 341
Sicyon, 31, 127, 139–43, 158, 307, 334, 401
Side, 210
Sidon, held by Demetrius, 44, 48; acquired by Ptolemy I, 52; coveted by Ptolemies and Seleucids, 82–3; autonomy, 268; commerce, 82, 298–9; coinage, 299; the "Alexander Sarcophagus," 313
Silenus, 324–5
Simon, 229–30
Simonides, 326
Sinai, 35
Sinope, 11, 54, 96–7, 214
Smyrna, loyalty to Seleucus II, 106 n., 109; secedes to Attalus I, 111; appeals to Rome against Antiochus III, 207, 209; favoured by Seleucids, 272; town plan, 309; worship of Rome, 370
Socotra, 338
Socrates, 356–7
Soli, 88, 102
Solon, 9
Somaliland, 80–1, 245, 301
Sophagasenus, 72
Sophene, 76 n.
Sophocles, 338 n.
Sophron (Seleucid officer), 106
Sophron (admiral of Ptolemy III), 141
Sosibius (minister of Ptolemy IV), 90–1, 93, 206, 405
Sosibius (historian), 333
Sosistratus (the Elder), 167–8, 176
Sosistratus (the Younger), 172–3
Sosthenes, 60, 62
Sostratus, 297
Soteria, 146, 319
Spain, 188, 345
Sparta, holds aloof from Lamian War, 7; excluded from Demetrius' Greek League, 38; escapes capture by Demetrius I, 47–8; heads a war against Gonatas, 126–7; besieged by Pyrrhus, 129–30; participates in the Chremonidean War, 133–5; defeated by Megalopolis, 135; habitual hostility to Gonatas, 143; holds the Isthmus against the Ætolians, 144; threatens the Messenians, 146; social revolution, 152–7, 304; gains and losses under Cleomenes III, 155–61; captured by Doson, 163; allies with Ætolia, 165; supplies Tarentum with generals, 177–8; at war with Achæa, 185, 190; tyranny of Nabis, 192; incorporation into Achæan League, 194; institutions recast by Philopœmen, 197; Lycurgus' institutions resumed, 198; appeals to Rome against Achæa, 204; feud with Megalopolis, 155, 279; municipal industry, 296
Spartocids, 116–17
Spercheus, r., 145
Sphærus, 156
Stoics, 56, 320, 347, 360–2, 366, 373, 376
Strabo, 345
Strato, 355
Stratocles, 34, 44
Stratonice (queen of Seleucus I and Antiochus I), 43, 54
Stratonice (queen of Demetrius II of Macedon), 111–12, 147
Strymon, r., 203
Sudan, 79–80
Suez, 80–1
Susa, 23–4, 76, 273
Susiana, 293 n., 399
Syene, 344, 407
Syracuse, patrol-fleets in Adriatic, 151; domestic strife, 167–8, 172–3; relations with Carthage, 168–75; with Pyrrhus, 173–4; with Rome, 174–5; with S. Italian Greeks, 176; commerce, 298; architecture, 309–10; influence of coin-types upon Carthaginian money, 317; home of Theocritus, 331; of Archimedes, 346; worship of Sarapis, 372

Syria, meeting-place of rival Macedonian armies, 15 ; acquired by Ptolemy I, 17, 42–3 ; disputed between Ptolemy I and Antigonus I, 26–8 ; between Ptolemies and Seleucids, 42–3, 83–6, 88–94, 387–9 ; colonization, 216, 245, 258 ; civil war between Seleucids, 220–2, 225–7 ; temple-states, 257, 258 n. ; coinage of towns, 273 ; Apollonius' estates, 288 ; slave exports to Egypt, 295

Tænarum, C., 6, 135
Tanagra, 314
Tanais, r., 115, 289
Tarentum, 151, 176–80, 294, 298, 314
Tarim, 73, 75
Tauromenium, 300 n., 336
Taurus, Mt., 16, 51, 88–9, 95, 101, 212, 257, 344
Taxilas, 66, 72
Tectosages, 111
Tegea, 5 n., 146, 148–9
Telmessus, 264 n
Temnos, 280 n.
Tenos, 352 n.
Teos, 64 n., 111, 114, 210, 270 n., 280 n., 320–1
Teuta, 151, 183
Thasos, 187, 293
Thebais, 80
Thebes (in Bœotia), destroyed by Alexander, 7 ; restored by Cassander, 27, 280 ; revolts against Demetrius, 48, 126 ; makes a loan to Athens, 149 ; assists the Achæan League against Rome, 205 ; decline, 282
Thebes (in Egypt), 80, 217, 270
Thebes (in Phthiotes), 166
Theocritus, 323, 329, 331
Theodorus, 91
Theophrastus, 33, 291, 320, 333, 350, 355
Thera, 141, 187
Thermæ, 167
Thermophylæ, circumvented by Cassander, 20 ; by Demetrius, 39 ; by Pyrrhus, 50 n. ; by Brennus, 60 ; by Cato, 195–6 ; controlled by Ætolia, 131
Thermum, 166, 284, 311
Thespiæ, 149, 300
Thesproti, 46, 150
Thessalonice (queen of Cassander), 22, 46, 109 n.
Thessalonice (town in Macedon), 253, 270 n.
Thessaly, rebels against Macedon, 6–8 ; under Cassander, 28 ; home of Lysimachus, 39 ; under Alexander V, 46 ; under Demetrius, 48, 50 ; seized by Pyrrhus, 53 ; by Lysimachus, 54 ; by Gonatas, 63, 126 ; recovered by Pyrrhus, 128 ; by Gonatas, 131 ; partly annexed by Ætolians, 152 ; enrolled in Doson's League, 163 ; regained by Philip V, 185–6 ; invaded by Flamininus, 190–1 ; partly freed by him, 192 ; overrun by Antiochus III, 195 ; claimed by Philip V, 198–9 ; retains autonomy after 146 B.C., 205 ; personal union with Macedon, 247 ; status of cities, 272 ; self-contained, 288 ; dialect, 323
Thœnon, 172–3
Thrace, settlement of Athenians, 9 n. ; under Lysimachus, 39, 117–18 ; seized by Ceraunus, 58 ; invaded by Galatians, 59, 61–2, 118–19 ; Ptolemaic outposts, on coast, 106 ; natives destroy Lysimachia, 121 ; evacuated by Antiochus III, 210–11 ; provides mercenaries, 233
Thracian Chersones, 120–1
Thucydides, 336
Thule, 344
Thurii, 176–8
Tiber, r., 196 n.
Tibet, 316
Tien-Shan, Mt., 298 n.
Tigranes, 227
Tigranocerta, 211
Tigris, r., 23, 70, 77
Timæus, 336
Timarchus (tyrant of Miletus), 105, 390
Timarchus (governor of Babylonia), 220
Timocharis, 349
Timoleon, 167, 173
Timon, 357
Timosthenes, 297, 344
Tiridates, 68–70
Tochari, 75, 78
Tolistoagii, 110
Transjordania, 230
Trapezus, 11, 96–7
Triparadisus, 15, 17
Troad, 29, 109, 112, 114, 212
Tryphon, 226, 229–30
Tubias, 265
Turkestan, 289
Tylis, 118–19, 122
Tyre, besieged by Antigonus, 26 ; held by Demetrius, 44, 48 ; acquired by Ptolemy I, 52 ; coveted

by Ptolemies and Seleucids, 82–3 ; captured by Antiochus III, 91 ; autonomy, 268 ; commerce, 298 ; coinage, 299

Utica, 170

Venusia, 178

Xenodicus, 171
Xerxes (king of Persia), 7, 35, 60–1, 190
Xerxes (king of Armenia), 70

Yemen, 80
Yueh-Chi, 75

Zagrus, Mt., 70
Zama, 189 n., 239
Zariadris, 70, 75–6
Zebirget, isle, 80
Zeno (bailiff of Apollonius), 86 n., 379
Zeno (philosopher), 324, 360, 362 n.
Zenodotus, 339
Zeus, 43, 76, 228, 308, 364–5, 368, 373–4
Zeuxis, 70
Zibœtes, 97
Zopyrion, 115, 117